TO
THE END
OF REVOLUTION

TO THE END OF REVOLUTION

The Chinese Communist Party and Tibet, 1949–1959

XIAOYUAN LIU

Columbia University Press
New York

Columbia University Press
Publishers Since 1893
New York   Chichester, West Sussex
cup.columbia.edu

Copyright © 2020 Columbia University Press
All rights reserved

Library of Congress Cataloging-in-Publication Data
Names: Liu, Xiaoyuan, 1952– author.
Title: To the end of revolution : the Chinese Communist Party and Tibet, 1949–1959 / Xiaoyuan Liu.
Description: New York : Columbia University Press, [2020] | Includes bibliographical references and index.
Identifiers: LCCN 2019046848 (print) | LCCN 2019046849 (ebook) | ISBN 9780231195263 (cloth) | ISBN 9780231195270 (paperback) | ISBN 9780231551274 (ebook)
Subjects: LCSH: Tibet Autonomous Region (China)—Relations—China. | China—Relations—China—Tibet Autonomous Region. | Communism—China—Tibet Autonomous Region. | Tibet Autonomous Region (China)—Politics and government—1951–
Classification: LCC DS786 .L5923 2020 (print) | LCC DS786 (ebook) | DDC 951/.5055—dc23
LC record available at https://lccn.loc.gov/2019046848
LC ebook record available at https://lccn.loc.gov/2019046849

Columbia University Press books are printed on permanent and durable acid-free paper.
Printed in the United States of America

Cover image: Nationaal Archief/Collectie Spaarnestad/Anefo/ Fotograaf onbekend/Bridgeman Images
Cover design: Lisa Hamm

CONTENTS

Preface vii
Nomenclature and Transliteration xi

Introduction 1

1. A Protracted Agenda 13
2. The "Dalai Line" 44
3. A Time to Change 90
4. A New Phase 148
5. A Waiting Game 190
6. The Showdown 246

   Epilogue: Tibet and the World, According to Beijing 295

Notes 311
Bibliography 373
Index 385

PREFACE

For my generation, who grew up in Mao Zedong's China, two pieces of our collective memory of childhood are connected to Tibet. One is a movie made in the early 1960s, *Nongnu* (The Serf), about how the Chinese Communist Party (CCP) liberated Tibetan serfs from the cruel, oppressive system of the old Tibet. The other is a female Tibetan singer named Caidan Zhuoma (Tseten Dolma), who gained national fame in the 1960s and 1970s by singing songs like "The Golden Mountain of Beijing" and "Song of Liberated Serfs." Personally, my earliest memory about Tibet dates from when I was six or seven years old. It was a horrific story related by adults about a certain means used by "Tibetan feudal masters" to punish their serfs. Many years later, I realized that the story was just part of the official narrative at the time. Aside from this vivid memory and its reinforcement by *Nongnu*, I would not encounter anything Tibetan again until I went to Inner Mongolia in the late 1960s as a *zhishi qingnian* (literally, "intellectual youth," but historically, "sent-down student"). In my "people's commune" in East Uzhumuqin Banner, I saw a Tibetan Buddhist temple destroyed during the Cultural Revolution. In my "production brigade," I came to know a few "secularized" lamas, one of whom was famous for having made an arduous pilgrimage to Lhasa.

Today, Chinese youths' knowledge and imagination about Tibet are neither as dark nor as sporadic as my generation's. Today's young people do not sense the kind of alienness or physical and mental distance between Tibet and *neidi*, or the Chinese heartland, that my generation did. Though still mysterious, Tibet is now one of their favorite tourist attractions inside China, easily reachable via airlines, the famed Qinghai-Tibetan Railway, and several highways. Among young Chinese nowadays, even a bicycle ride to Lhasa from Qinghai or Sichuan or any other Chinese province does not seem such an unusual adventure. Folksongs in the Tibetan and Mongolian styles are popular in China, though many of the songs currently in circulation are not necessarily Tibetan or Mongolian by origin. For instance, an enduring contest among China's karaoke-goers and in talent shows on Chinese television is to see who can sing the well-nigh impossible high note of a song named "Qingzang Gaoyuan" (Qinghai-Tibetan Plateau). In Baidu, the Chinese alternative to Google, the song is listed as one of the best "Tibetan folksongs." The song was written, however, by a People's Liberation Army songwriter named Zhang Qianyi, an ethnic Korean, and it was first sung by the famed female singer Li Na, an ethnic Han. Nevertheless, from Tseten Dolma's ode about Beijing as a "gold mountain" to Li Na's pastorale about the Tibetan Plateau, Chinese society has gone through a mental reversal about Tibet as tremendous as that of Tibetan society itself through its physical integration with the People's Republic of China (PRC).

These easily observable and seemingly superficial changes are actually complicated and profound. The question of what happened to cause these changes does not have simple answers. Today, a visitor in Lhasa cannot help but carry away an eerie feeling. In Lhasa's streets and around monasteries, the presence of the Chinese Communist authorities is highly visible in the black or camouflage uniforms of the *Tejing* (special police) and the *Wujing* (military police). It is not unusual for a local resident to be stopped by the police several times a day for an identification check. Meanwhile, residents of Lhasa and pilgrims from other places calmly carry out their daily activities, seemingly oblivious to this heavy presence of security forces. Local tour guides may talk about the fourteenth Dalai Lama as if he had never departed from the Norbulingka in the fateful month of March 1959. One does not have to witness a self-immolation or remember the riots of 2008 to sense the tensions of the place. "Globalization" has indeed reached Tibet since China's "opening" to the world in the 1980s, but the CCP authorities' on-again, off-again restrictions on foreign visitors have kept Tibet a "frontier region" that remains largely sealed, with international borders from the outside and provincial boundaries from the inside. Why has Tibet become so much closer to the rest of China but remained, like Xinjiang, a jarring problem in the eyes of the PRC authorities? This book is about how, sixty years ago, Chinese Communist leaders made a "Tibetan question" that they inherited from history into a "Tibetan problem" of their own.

***

More than any previous occasion, the publication of this book affords me an opportunity to acknowledge, with heartfelt gratitude, the assistance and encouragement I have received during the many years spent researching and writing it. From the outset, I knew that a book project about Beijing's Tibet policy of the Mao years would be an undertaking much more challenging than any of my previous projects. However, I did not expect a long interruption of my work by circumstances beyond my control. A special group of people must therefore be acknowledged for helping me overcome a tremendous hurdle in my personal as well as professional life. Their care, support, and counsel were physically healing, spiritually uplifting, and intellectually stimulating, and without them I would not have been able to present this book to its readers. These people include my mentors, friends, colleagues, and physicians who, each in her/his own way, enabled the completion of this study. I am blessed to have them in my life: Warren Cohen, Larry and Mariam Gelfand, Akira Iriye, William Kirby, Steven Levine, Rod MacFarquhar, Peter Perdue, Qi Shirong, and Ezra Vogel; Uradyn E. Bulag, Bi Aonan, Chen Jian, Hamilton Cravens, Dai Chaowu, Charles Dobbs, Fan Xin, He Yan, Gan Qi, Ge Hao, Guo Jianping, Han Gang, Hao Rui, Bob Hathaway, Carma Hinton, Huang Haoru and Zhu Rongjun, Jiang Huajie, Angela Kao, Sulmaan Khan, Li Danhui, Li Suwu, Li Xiaobing, Hsiao-ting Lin, Liu Yuan, Mao Sheng, James Millward, Aili Mu and Ren Yue, Niu Jun, Christian Ostermann, Qian Xiaohua, Sergey Radchenko, Pamela Rinay-Kehrberg, Patrick F. Shan, Shao Fangchen, Shen Zhihua, Richard J. Smith, Sun Baowen, Tian Xiansheng, Alan M. Wachman, Wang Haiguang, Wang Jinping, Wang Xi, Wang Zheng, George C. X. Wei, David Wilson, Xiao Xiaohong, Xie Jun, Xu Guoqi, Xu Lan, Yang Kuisong, Yang Zhiguo, Yao Baihui, Yao Ping, Yao Yu and Guo Youxin, Min-lei Ye, Ye Xiangdong and Li Shuxian, Yu Jiandong, Yu Kwok-leung, Yu Qun, Zhang Baijia, Ellen Zhang, Zhang Xiaojun, Zhang Yang, Zhang Yijun, and Zhou Na; and Dr. Peter Enzinger, Dr. Ahmad Fotovat, Dr. Larry Otteman, and Dr. Lansheng Wang.

During the taxing period, my former classmates and fellow "sent-down students" in several WeChat groups were always there to cheer me up; their names are too many to list here.

Finally, the most powerful support came from a very tight family circle: Hongxing, Ying Ying, Tanya, Xiaohong, John, Xiaoxi, Karen, Mutian, Xiaolin, and Lao Qiao.

The unplanned interlude in my work was nevertheless a blessing, enabling me to amass information that became available to me only gradually. My archival research was accomplished with indispensable assistance from numerous people whom I had the privilege to know over a decade. As my drafting of the book dragged on, a number of institutions provided opportunities for me to present segments of my work, including the Fairbank Center for Chinese Studies at Harvard University, the Cold War International History Project of the Woodrow Wilson International Center for Scholars, the Hoover Institute of Stanford University, the Paul H. Nitze School of Advanced International

Studies (SAIS) of Johns Hopkins University, the Institute for Global History and the Mortara Center for International Studies of Georgetown University, the National Institute of Eastern Languages and Civilizations in Paris, the Center for Cultural Studies of the Chinese University in Hong Kong, the Center for Cold War International History Studies of the East China Normal University in Shanghai, the University of Wisconsin–River Falls, Göttingen University, Northeastern Normal University in Changchun, Central Minzu University in Beijing, Capital Normal University in Beijing, Inner Mongolia Normal University in Hohhot, South China Normal University in Guangzhou, and Shihezi University in Shihezi, Xinjiang. The research and publication of this study have received generous support from the Department of History at the State University of New York at Potsdam, the Department of History at Iowa State University, the Department of History at Harvard University, the Asia Program at the Woodrow Wilson International Center for Scholars, the Corcoran Department of History at the University of Virginia, the David Dean Endowment for East Asian Studies, the Buckner W. Clay Dean of Arts and Sciences and the Vice President for Research at the University of Virginia, and the East Asia Center at the University of Virginia.

During the process of publishers' manuscript review, several anonymous readers offered valuable critiques and suggestions for improving the manuscript. Zhao Yuchen helped me in diligently checking the Tibetan terms that appear in the book. Caelyn Cobb and Kathryn Jorge, my editors at Columbia University Press, patiently and adroitly guided the process of bringing the book to fruition, and their associates worked hard and efficiently in improving the manuscript. I am, of course, alone responsible for any remaining defects in the book.

NOMENCLATURE AND TRANSLITERATION

All Chinese names in this study are transliterated with pinyin, with some exceptions. Chinese names and terms familiar to Western readers, such as Chiang Kai-shek, Sun Yat-sen, and Kuomintang, are not converted into their pinyin forms (Jiang Jieshi, Sun Yixian, and Guomindang).

Most of the Tibetan personal names in this study are from Chinese texts. Their transliterations, if known, are done with the THL Extended Wylie Transliteration Scheme (EWTS). If the romanized form of a Tibetan personal name cannot be ascertained, italicized pinyin is used to indicate its Chinese pronunciation, followed by Chinese characters in parentheses.

Most geographic names in the Tibetan areas, if ascertainable, appear in their transliterated Tibetan forms followed by Chinese forms in parentheses. If a location's Tibetan name cannot be ascertained, its Chinese name, italicized, is used. The most difficult cases involve geographic names, which, depending on their users, mean rather different areas. For instance, in any discussion pertinent to Tibet, the name of the region itself is a disputed subject. "Tibet" and its corresponding Chinese term *Xizang* (西藏) mean rather different areas when used by the PRC authorities and the Tibetan government in exile. The PRC authorities use Tibet/Xizang to refer to the area of the current Tibetan Autonomous Region (TAR), which is largely congruent with the political domain of the traditional Tibetan government, or Kashag, before 1959. In contrast, the Tibetan authorities in Dharamshala use "Tibet" to mean a much larger area populated by ethnic Tibetans, including not only Ü-Tsang and Ngari of the TAR but also Kham (Kang) and Amdo (Anduo) in today's Qinghai, Gansu, Sichuan, and Yunnan provinces of the PRC. Because this study is a focused analysis and narrative of the Chinese Communist Party's policy conceptions and practices with respect to Tibet, to avoid confusion, this study follows the usage of "Tibet" in the Chinese primary sources. In the 1950s, in Beijing's policy directives and the CCP's internal discussions, Xizang, or Tibet, was used as a noun to refer unmistakably to the political and territorial domain under the fourteenth Dalai Lama.

Meanwhile, the adjective "Tibetan"—as in "Tibetan areas" (*Zangqu*), "Tibetan population" (*Zangmin*), and "Tibetan nationality" (*Zangzu*)—carries a broader ethnographic meaning beyond the limits of Lhasa's political power. Confusion, however, cannot be avoided completely, and specific explanations are provided wherever necessary.

Finally, all Chinese titles of documents and scholarly articles in the notes are translated but not transliterated. This practice is open to criticism in the field but is used solely for reducing the bulkiness of the citations.

TO THE
END OF
REVOLUTION

INTRODUCTION

How did Tibet become part of the People's Republic of China (PRC) but remain a problem for Beijing? To help answer this question, this study examines aspects of the past that have been overlooked, misunderstood, distorted, or concealed by the narratives that have been constructed to produce different versions of the Tibetan story. This study is not a complete historical narrative about Tibet. Rather, it continues my own effort to understand the Chinese Communist Party's (CCP) historical relationship with China's ethnic minorities in particular, and China's modern transformation in general. This effort began more than two decades ago and has resulted in two books, one on the CCP's evolving ethnopolitics from 1921 to 1945 and the other on China's "Mongolian question" from 1911 to 1950.[1] This third installment focuses on Beijing's policymaking about Tibet from 1949 to 1959.

The narrow focus of this study reflects a conscious choice on my part. A "complete" account of modern Tibetan history requires multilinguistic and multicultural facility as well as multinational archival access. As I am not a Tibetologist, I cannot do an original study of the developments in Tibet in the 1950s; nor can I critically use secondary works of Tibetan studies that are subject to heated debates about modern Tibet. The subject of modern Tibet involves two distinct scholarly disciplines, China studies and Tibet studies, causing a chaotic academic/political battle involving many sides. As illuminated by John Powers's analysis of the historiography on modern Tibet, official propagandas of Beijing and Dharamshala have reached a "stalemate" in their contest for "historical truth." Affected by this prolonged political struggle, relevant scholarly communities have become polarized as well.[2] Intentionally staying away from the ongoing academic/political battle, this study does not pursue holistic "historical truth" but provides empirical evidence about a historical process in which Beijing endeavored to solve the modern Tibetan question but created its own Tibetan problem. It is a political history of the People's Republic of China based on a close reading of the CCP's internal discussions, public statements, and operative directives and reports pertinent to Tibetan affairs. What I discuss in this study is limited by the primary sources I have been able to collect. The bibliography at the end of the book lists the primary sources used in this study but does not include all the secondary sources cited in the notes.[3]

How useful is such a narrowly focused, Sinocentric, and elitist approach for an understanding of the multifaceted Tibetan question? The historian Tsering Shakya once vented his frustration with "some Chinese intellectuals" in these words:

> It seems that asking some Chinese intellectuals—be they Communist Party officials, liberal democrats or dissident writers—to think about Tibet in an objective and reasonable manner is like asking an ant to lift an elephant; it is beyond their capabilities and vision.[4]

As an historian of Han Chinese background, albeit the overseas type, I am very conscious of my own limitations in terms of both capabilities and vision. But Shakya's "ant versus elephant" parable may similarly be applied to some Tibetan and Western intellectuals who are trying to think about China's or each other's cultural/national affairs. While Shakya's allegory is instructive, I think it also useful to consider the moral of another famous parable, "the blind men and the elephant," in which each man felt a different part of the animal. The nineteenth-century American poet John Godfrey Saxe aptly summarized the story's conclusion:

> And so these men of Indostan
> Disputed loud and long,
> Each in his own opinion
> Exceeding stiff and strong,
> Though each was partly in the right
> And all were in the wrong.[5]

This ancient parable teaches us not to draw sweeping conclusions from one person's limited capability and vision. However, by putting their partial and distorted images together, the "blind men" may collectively see the "elephant" more accurately.

Such collective effort is especially necessary for historians working on the modern Tibetan question, helping scholars balance out one another's interpretive biases and piece together reliable factual evidence that they have unearthed individually. Unlike social scientists, who collect information through fieldwork and explain their data with theoretical models, historians rely on unfiltered primary sources in constructing historical narratives. The late anthropologist Michel-Rolph Trouillot made an incisive comment about historical writing: "Archival power determines the difference between a historian, amateur or professional, and a charlatan."[6] Yet empowerment with archival information is not always a decision up to the historian. As with many other subjects concerning twentieth-century China, studies of the modern Tibetan question in Chinese history have suffered from "archival impotence." Hsiao-ting Lin and Gray Tuttle have used archival information to enhance our understanding of China's Tibetan question during the Republic of China (ROC) period.[7] They have been able to achieve "archival power" to a certain degree because the Chinese Nationalist government's relocation in 1949 and the political democratization of Taiwan a few decades later made Taipei a rich source of archival information. The archival collections in Taipei are, however, incomplete. When the Kuomintang (KMT) regime was retreating in 1949, it was unable to take the entire official records of the ROC period to Taiwan. Researchers interested in the KMT's Tibetan policy in the ROC period, therefore, must also knock on the doors of the Second Historical Archives of China in Nanjing and relevant provincial archives of the PRC.

The situation for researchers interested in the PRC period is different. So far, archive-based historical studies do not exist. In view of the Dalai Lama's hurried departure from Lhasa in March 1959, relocation of Tibetan archives to India on any scale would be a surprise. Inside the PRC, aside from the forbidden Central Archives in Beijing, the provincial archives of Qinghai, Sichuan, and the Tibetan Autonomous Region are logical places for researching Tibet-related information. But all of these are tightly guarded and largely inaccessible—despite the modernization of Chinese archives in recent decades and adoption by the Chinese government of some rather liberal laws and regulations about archival declassification. Trouillot's distinction between a historian and a charlatan, therefore, cannot be applied to the production of Tibet-related histories without misrepresenting serious scholars who have been striving, often abortively, to attain archival power. While historical research is understood as an ongoing undertaking of detecting, presenting, and interpreting sources, individual practitioners have had drastically different experiences. Under current circumstances in the PRC, archival access is rare, contingent, and by no means commonplace. Therefore, independent scholarly works on ethnic minority–related subjects, especially Tibet and Xinjiang, tend to be idiosyncratic in their sources as well as their interpretations. One scholar's research venture can hardly be replicated by another, and certainly there are no "standard bodies" of sources for all researchers to explore. Whenever an original new work appears in the field, it usually brings new sources to the fore. Unsurprisingly, as far as the history of Beijing's Tibetan policy is concerned, none of the previous works is based on archival research.[8]

Having also hit stone walls during my research for this book, I claim neither full-fledged "archival power" nor "evidentiary satisfaction."[9] As far as sources are concerned, the study is a patchwork of archives, classified periodicals, "internal publications," unpublished reminiscences, and published documents. As such, "archival power" appears unevenly in the chapters. The study takes advantage of the centralized political system of the PRC in Mao's time and uses archival sources from areas outside Tibet. Under that highly centralized system, any local development deemed of national significance by Beijing would generate "directives" and "circulars" from the "Center" (*Zhongyang*), a code name for the CCP central leadership, to CCP officials at the provincial or even the country level.[10] During the past decade or so, working through professional contacts, visiting at the right time, and even helped by pure luck, I was able to enter the revolving doors of some archives in China and collect information about the CCP's Tibet policy. As such, this is the first archive-based study of Beijing's policymaking about Tibet. To share information with interested scholars, the study includes lengthy translations of CCP documents. Readers who want to follow closely the main story line may skip these documents to avoid distraction.

As the side pushing for changing the status quo of Sino-Tibetan relations after 1949, Beijing's or the CCP's policies and practices in Tibet assumed the principal responsibility for shaping the course of Tibetan affairs. But two types of previous scholarship have often misunderstood these policies and practices. The first category includes independent studies that are insightful and informative about various aspects of Beijing's Tibetan policies but have no, or only limited, access to information about the core process of Beijing's policymaking and CCP leaders' thinking.[11] The second category includes works by just one scholar, the sociocultural anthropologist Melvyn C. Goldstein. Goldstein's multivolume study of modern Tibet has stood as the most informative and authoritative account of Tibet's political development and Lhasa's relationship with the Chinese authorities in the twentieth century. Three published volumes cover the period from 1913 to 1957; a fourth volume, released in 2019, covers the years from 1957 to 1959.[12] Chronologically, my study overlaps Goldstein's volumes two through four. Yet my approach to and conclusions about Beijing's Tibet policy differ markedly from Goldstein's.

As a social anthropologist specializing in Tibetan studies, Goldstein's central concerns are the arduous experience of Tibetan society and the dire situation of Tibetan culture in the modern age. I would defer to Goldstein and other Tibetologists such as Tsering Shakya for insights about the Tibetan experience.

The point of departure of my inquiries about frontier histories, by contrast, is China's modern experiences in which its non-Chinese frontiers have assumed a central significance. I propose to study Beijing's Tibet policy within a multilayered and temporally cumulative frame that makes sense of China's modern developments. This frame includes four overlapping "timescapes," each accentuated by a distinct thread of China's sociopolitical development.[13] The study therefore differs from Goldstein's Tibetocentric anthropology in being a Sinocentric history. In explaining Beijing's policymaking, this study also deviates somewhat from the historian John Gaddis's wise advice that a historical investigator follow a "principle of diminishing relevance" in deciding the relationship between "causes" and "consequences."[14] In this study of factors affecting Beijing's policymaking about Tibet in the 1950s, Manchu emperors' actions for incorporating Tibet into the Qing dynasty during the eighteenth century are as relevant as Washington's secret operations for undermining the CCP's position in Tibet during the Cold War. Following is an explanation of the large frame of interpretation used in this study.

A Geo-Ethno-Security Landscape

The first timescape is simultaneously a *geo-ethno-security landscape*. In his insightful study of the Taiwan question, Alan M. Wachman poses, in his words, a "deceptively difficult question": Why Taiwan? Wachman finds a "territorial salience" of Taiwan that was sometimes registered in and sometimes expunged from Chinese elites' "mental map" about China.[15] A "Why Tibet?" question in relation to Beijing's statecraft is deceptively simple but entails a rather complex answer. Tibet—and Taiwan as well, in my opinion—has not been a mirage in modern Chinese elites' imaginations but a physical fixation in the most recent realm of China's geopolitical operations. This realm, or geo-ethno-security landscape, was created by the Qing dynasty. In Chinese history, every ruling dynasty prior to the CCP carried out political landscaping—a behavior of consciously reshaping and rearranging China's geographic and human surroundings to create and maintain a geopolitically secure and ethnographically stable environment. In several cycles of such landscaping in China's long history, the areas and peoples affected thereby were hugely different.[16] The Manchu emperors were the latest shapers of a relatively stable geo-ethno-security environment for China before the modern era. Prior to the arrival of the "Western impact," China's ruling elites imagined their physical environment in terms of *tianxia*, or "all under heaven," but actually managed their dynastic state affairs in a dependency/tribute system around the Manchu court. In the twentieth century, the Qing rulers' achievements and failures in maintaining such a *tianxia* system were bequeathed to the ROC and the PRC. Miraculously, despite their empire-breaking and state-forming effects, World Wars I and II did not lead to a new cycle of geo-ethno-security landscaping. On the contrary, these wars actually rolled back Western and Japanese empires that had surrounded China since the mid-nineteenth century and, to a degree and in most directions, restored the geo-ethno-security environment bequeathed by the Qing dynasty.

Mindful of current scholarly debates about modern China's being an "empire," a "nation-state," or a "civilizational state," this study treats the inherited landscape of the PRC neither as a traditional, amorphous Qing "empire" nor as a modern, bordered Chinese "nation." Rather, the landscape has been a multiplicity of processes and relationships that involve locales and peoples both internal and external to the PRC and are directly relevant to the Qing. In continental and maritime Asia, Manchu rulers arranged several layers of relationships around their ruling center, managing differentially the Han society, inner and outer non-Han and non-Chinese dependencies, and tributary and "guest" states. In the 1950s, the CCP leadership operated in an area largely congruent with the geopolitical arena of the Qing. But the layered relationships around the CCP's Beijing assumed different connotations. As perceived by the CCP leadership, these layers included the "socialized and collectivized" Chinese society, "democratically" reformed and yet-to-be-reformed non-Han frontiers, socialist and "nationalist" neighbors, and "imperialist" and "reactionary" forces nearby. It was in these layers that CCP leaders considered the meaning of their inherited Tibetan question. Accordingly, during the first decade of the PRC, Tibet's dependency status in the Qing dynasty was converted into a yet-to-be-reformed "minority region" in Beijing's geo-ethno-security landscaping, sandwiched between revolutionary Chinese provinces on the inner side and a group of "nationalist countries" along the Himalayas on the outer side. In envisioning the scope and extent of their new state power, CCP leaders paid close attention to the geostrategic location and ethnopolitical complexity of the Tibetan frontier. South Asia used to be a stronghold of British influence before the British Empire bowed out of the region in the late 1940s. Guarding the Himalayan gateway to a world alien to the CCP, both ideologically and socioeconomically, Tibet assumed a special geostrategic significance for the PRC. Furthermore, Tibet was the cultural and religious homeland of the Tibetan populace, who resided in several provinces of the PRC. To CCP leaders, therefore, their landscaping in the Tibetan frontiers was a crucial step for maintaining the security and stability of their newly founded communist state.

Modern Transformation of Chinese Territoriality

Whereas both Chinese Nationalists and Chinese Communists were conscious builders of a modern Chinese state, the Qing dynasty did not bequeath to them a clearly and definitively demarcated territorial entity. What the late Qing left to its twentieth-century successors was a historical process of transforming China into a modern territorial entity, or the second timescape: *modern transformation of Chinese territoriality*. During the first half of the twentieth century, "maps of national humiliation" became an important tool of national education in China. Such maps, which exist in digitized versions in our own time, usually carry a message about how the area of China was reduced and reshaped during a "century of national humiliation" between the 1840s and World War II. Holders of such cartographic ideas, Sun Yat-sen among them, tend to make some typical mistakes of presentism about the Qing state before the nineteenth century.[17] They take the large area of the Qing landscaping for territorial possessions; treat the Qing's occasional border arrangements as a general, standard, and even legal practice; and conceptualize divides between directly administered areas of the Qing and its "inner" or "outer" dependencies as international boundaries. In actuality, despite sporadic practices of border demarcation during its first two centuries, the Qing dynasty did not achieve a bordered "geo-body" until Western powers included East Asia in their own overseas landscaping, cajoling or forcing the Qing court to give up dependencies and even lands under its direct control during the second half of the nineteenth century.[18] In these contests, borderlines emerged around the Qing and began to give China a legally defined cartographic shape.[19] Such territoriality transformation occurred not only in China but in all the Asian states that used to be part of the Sinocentric *tianxia* system. Gradually, the Sinocentric tribute/dependency system gave way to a West-dominated imperial/colonial system. In the process, the Qing's former dependencies became either internalized or externalized to the Qing state. As those externalized states and areas either achieved independence or fell prey to Western or Japanese colonization, the Qing state became surrounded by newly configured "national" or "imperial" neighbors. Inevitably, the Qing state had to assume a territorial contour and adopt behavioral norms of a "national state" on the international scene. The original geo-ethno-security landscape of the Qing dynasty that used to include ambiguous frontier zones and fluctuating relations now gradually became lineated and ossified.

For China, the process produced two problems that would follow a newly minted "Chinese nation" into our own times. One is psychological. To China's "national consciousness," most of the modern boundaries of China were products of foreign imperialist encroachment or bullying and, therefore, marks of "national humiliation." Although Chinese foreign policy was not necessarily aimed at erasing these blemishes, the Chinese psyche would not be satisfied until those wrongdoers and their successors admitted historical injustice about China's "lost territories." The other is at once ethnopolitical and international. Having transformed into a "national" dynastic state before its demise, the Qing bequeathed to its twentieth-century successors a polyethnic domain that was contested from several sides along China's frontiers.

Since the end of the Qing dynasty, successive Chinese authorities have engaged a number of foreign powers and frontier regimes and peoples in contests over the status and identity of frontier regions. As Matthew W. Mosca contends, encounters with the West during the eighteenth and nineteenth centuries ended the Qing government's premodern management of frontiers, which used to bestow differentiated and mutually isolated treatments on China's ethnically diverse and geographically scattered frontiers.[20] Between the mid-nineteenth and mid-twentieth centuries, a weakened and divided China was hard put to come up with a centralized and coordinated policy in dealing with frontier affairs and related foreign relations. In seizing power in China, CCP leaders inherited from their Qing and Nationalist predecessors not only a geostrategic outlook but also an onerous task of unifying China's "national territories." After 1949, although the independence of Mongolia could not be reversed, the CCP leadership was committed to "liberating" Tibet and Taiwan. A rudimentary requirement of modern Chinese territoriality was to round out the geo-body of the PRC both cartographically and practically, which entailed incorporation of frontier regions like Tibet and Taiwan into the PRC and settlement of all disputed borderlines between China and its neighbors.

In pursuing this historical agenda, the PRC could not evade the issue of legitimacy with respect to its territorial behavior. Max Weber's three types of legitimate authority, based separately on tradition, charisma, and legality, can be usefully contemplated here.[21] Weber identified "legality" as the prevalent type of legitimacy in modern times, and the long modern transformation of Chinese territoriality can be understood as a process of creating "legal" territorial authority. In the process, the Qing imperial authority, based on both Chinese tradition of heaven's mandate and Manchu charisma of dynasty building, was converted into a Chinese national authority legitimized partially by international-cum-Western legal norms and partially by a peculiar Chinese revolutionary ethos. This statement, of course, simplifies a rather complex historical journey between its Qing and CCP stations. The authority of the Qing dynasty over its imperial peripheries, far from being a uniform Weberian "imperative control," consisted of influences of various forms and intensities.[22] Entering the twentieth century, the authority of the Chinese "national state" over China's continental frontiers was no less flimsy. During the ROC period, the Nationalist government made strides in claiming diplomatic sovereignty over estranged or detached frontier regions such as Manchuria, Mongolia, Tibet, and Xinjiang. But none of these regions was actually under the KMT's control. After seizing power in1949, the CCP put all these regions, except Outer Mongolia, under the sovereignty of the central government. Yet during the following decades, while the legality of the PRC remained a question to an international society ruptured by the Cold War, the legitimacy of CCP power was contested in a number of borderlands. Thus, the issue of modern Chinese territoriality involved a process of attaining legality and legitimacy shot through with national revolutions, interethnic contentions, and international clashes.

The Chinese Revolution

Clearly, in political landscaping and territoriality transformation, the Qing, the ROC, and the PRC shared a common agenda. But in our third timescape, the *Chinese Revolution*, the three political entities negated one another completely. A view in the field holds that China's "Great Revolution" has been an ongoing process of modern transformation since the mid-nineteenth century.[23] This allegedly continual transformation has been punctuated by recurring destruction of established sociopolitical systems and repeated inauguration of a "new China." China's "modern transformation" would have been historically meaningless without constructive accomplishments, but the Chinese Revolution always, in Mao Zedong's words, "put destruction first."[24] The first three decades of the PRC, or the "Mao era," saw the most tumultuous, destructive, yet self-righteous phase of the Chinese Revolution. Mao Zedong's "continuous revolution" executed one of the most drastic experiments in social engineering in human history, whose evaluations have ranged from a senseless "catastrophe" to "a forest fire that clears the way for new growth."[25]

While historians will continue debating the destructive, constructive, or destructively constructive meanings of the Mao era within different interpretative frames, one aspect of Chinese Communist behavior in the Mao years has been explored only recently. A small number of new studies have examined a discernible outward projection of Mao's China into Third World regions during the Cold War.[26] Although the Chinese sense of cultural and moral superiority to the West was notorious long before the nineteenth century, Confucianism was mainly about self-cultivation, not missionary indoctrination. Ancient Chinese dynasties tended to be on the receiving end of their external relations and rarely threw cultural influence outward. Brewed in one of China's most downtrodden eras, the Chinese Revolution nevertheless introduced into China's political discourse and behavior a "missionary" zeal that was new to Chinese cultural-political norms, reflecting China's entry into the global age in both material and ideational senses. A notion that China would again surpass the West materially and spiritually began with Sun Yat-sen, if not earlier. In his lectures on the "Three People's Principles," Sun famously extolled China's allegedly inherent "kingly way," or "way of right," as a means to displace the Western hegemonic way, or "way of might."[27] Although taking a stance opposing Sun's exaltation of China's "old virtues," the Chinese Communists acted with the same kind of conviction about their mission of "liberation" in an unjust world. Necessarily, the mission, construed as class warfare with Marxist connotations, had to begin at home with liberating both the Han and non-Han peoples. In the PRC, the CCP's revolutionary goal in ethnic minority regions was to integrate these peoples and lands into the country's socialist system.

As far as Tibet was concerned, a fundamental difference between the CCP and its Manchu and Nationalist predecessors was its drive for fundamental sociopolitical changes. Shortly after the Boxer Uprising, the Manchu court initiated a reform effort, the New Policy. At the time, a Western observer characterized the development as "the greatest movement . . . on the face of the globe," even dwarfing the contemporaneous Russian Revolution.[28] This Manchu "revolution" failed to resuscitate the Qing dynasty from its last breath. A program of the New Policy for "taking back administrative power" (*shouhui shiquan*) in Tibet was similarly abortive.[29] Next, the Chinese Nationalist government pledged rhetorically to spread Sun Yat-sen's "Three People's Principles" to remote frontier regions within China's international boundaries. Yet the regime was never able to go beyond making plans on paper for "liberating" the Tibetan people from their "inhumane" conditions.[30] Not until the time of the PRC could China's central authorities put words into deeds as far as Tibet was concerned. At first, the CCP sent troops to occupy Tibet. Then, Beijing's drive to socialism turned Tibetan society upside down.

On the Asian continent, Tibet was the last region the Chinese Communist Revolution reached. A Han-centric sociopolitical movement that turned into state power, the Communist Revolution, in spite of its supraethnic claim and emphasis on class struggle, was ethnopolitically alien to many of China's non-Han peoples, or *shaoshu minzu* (minority nationalities) in CCP terminology. While assessing the incompatibility between their revolution and non-Han communities, CCP leaders were keenly aware of the wide gaps between the Tibetan and Chinese cultures and systems. Yet CCP leaders would not deem their geopolitical and national sovereign goals fulfilled in Tibet unless and until their revolutionary mission was accomplished there as well. A missionary drive would not be such without its devoted grassroots "missionaries," the rank and file of the People's Liberation Army and CCP cadres. Those who participated in "liberating" and "constructing" Tibet believed they were making a tremendous personal sacrifice for a great cause. One of them wrote this in his diary before setting foot in Tibet:

> Tomorrow will be the birthday of the [Chinese Communist] Party. Beginning today, in this diary I will record miracles of the human struggle with the natural environment of the Tibetan Plateau; the efforts and sacrifice made by the Red Army's successors for liberating various nationalities of the country and realizing the ideal of the humanity; the battles and hard work waged by the Han and the Tibetan people for achieving liberation and creating a new life under the leadership of the Communist Party and Chairman Mao.[31]

In the 1950s, such words were recorded or voiced often with sincere conviction. With this sense of mission, Chinese Communists forged ahead ruthlessly into Tibet. Years later, many of these *Lao Xizang* (literally "old Tibetans," but actually "[Han] pioneers in Tibet"), believing they had devoted the best years of their lives to the Tibetan people, would be vexed and perplexed by Tibetans' misgivings against CCP policies.

The Cold War

Finally, the evolution of the Tibetan situation in the 1950s has to be understood in international circumstances. More than any other element in the ideological repertoire of the CCP, notions of the "national liberation" of China and class liberation of the Chinese people and the peoples of the world determined Beijing's taking sides in the Cold War. In this study, the *Cold War* is the fourth and the most recent timescape.[32] The question of when and how the PRC actually became a belligerent in the Cold War does not have a generally accepted answer among historians. It is clear, however, that even before the CCP explicated its affiliation in the "cold" confrontation between the two superpowers, Washington and Moscow had already picked sides in the hot Chinese Civil War. In retrospect, although Beijing's diplomatic maneuvering and war making in the 1950s and 1960s can be understood in the ideological and geopolitical frames of the Cold War, an astonishing fact remains: the PRC was alone among the Cold War principals in changing its international alignment more than once. Most strikingly, the changes on Beijing's part involved not only expedient readjustments of diplomatic and geopolitical stances but also profound reorientations of socioeconomic practices at home. Call it Maoist guerrillaism or pragmatism of the Deng Xiaoping style, such behavior made the struggle between capitalism and communism, which was fundamental in the USA–USSR confrontation, appear instrumental, or just a means, for Beijing. If, as the historian Odd Arne Westad suggests, the global significance of the Cold War was to provide two models of development to non-Western countries, this originally intra-West contest presented a developmental question to China, a quintessentially "East" country.[33] In the Cold War years, when Beijing selectively adopted and rejected elements from both the communist and capitalist models, the PRC did not operate in a developmental straightjacket at home and was not a fixture in any ideological-geopolitical monolith abroad. This fluidity of Beijing's domestic and international orientations had some devastating effects, specifically for the ethnic frontiers of the PRC. Whenever Beijing made readjustments in its development strategy, these frontiers usually lagged a few steps behind the rest of China and were pressured to catch up. Conversely, whenever Beijing changed its international orientation or shifted its geostrategic focus in the Cold War, the frontier societies always bore the brunt of the impact.

In the mid-twentieth century, both communism and capitalism were alien to a Tibetan society that, if left alone, would probably have stayed in its own conditions for a considerable length of time. Nevertheless, at least initially, the confrontational international atmosphere of the Cold War appeared useful for Lhasa, which hoped to keep the Chinese Communists at arm's length with foreign support. Yet for CCP leaders who did not accept aloofness in an all-inclusive "international class struggle," Tibet could become either a virgin land for socialist cultivation or a hotbed of imperialist conspiracies. For Beijing, therefore, Tibet constituted a third, Himalayan front in its international struggles, along with the eastern, maritime front fending off American imperialism and the northern, steppe-forest front facing the dubious Soviet ally. Insulated from the travesties of contested modernity and bordering a nonaligned India and some other "nationalist states," Tibet nevertheless followed a sinuous path into the Cold War by way of gradual integration with the PRC. During the first decade of the PRC, CCP policymakers viewed Tibet alternately as a buffer zone against the capitalist world, a "capitalist" loophole in their socialist construction, a battleground for implementing "democratic reforms" and purging imperialist agents, and a frontline of national defense. Thus, in spite of the great physical and sociotemporal distances between Beijing and Tibet, Tibet was always a dynamic factor in the PRC's tortuous international socialization during the Cold War years.

In summary, this study uses the four timescapes delineated here to reveal the complex meaning of Beijing's international and domestic behaviors in general and Tibet's evolving position in the PRC in particular. This quadruple frame of interpretation calls the reader's attention to the multifaceted policy behavior of CCP leaders and cautions against explanations of Beijing's policies and practices in Tibet as based on any single-plank agenda. The title of this study is derived from Mao Zedong's New Year's message for 1949, "Carry the Revolution Through to the End," in which he projected the Chinese Communists' military victory and ensuing sociopolitical revolution in China.[34] As this study shows in six chapters, during the first decade of the PRC, step by step, the Chinese Communist Party extended the Revolution to Tibet, reaching the continental terminus while creating a perpetual conundrum of the Revolution.

CHAPTER 1

A PROTRACTED AGENDA

In the early months of 1949, Chinese Communist leaders were entertaining an important guest from Moscow in their makeshift headquarters in Xibaipo, Hebei. With the CCP close to winning the Chinese Civil War and ascending to power in China, Joseph Stalin, who had never really trusted Mao Zedong, became increasingly uneasy about this long-term ideological ally. Not yet ready to sound out Mao face to face, in January Stalin sent Anastas Mikoyan, a member of the Politburo of the Soviet Communist Party, to Mao as his surrogate.[1] Until then, Mao had been on the receiving end in all of his foreign encounters, starting with Edgar Snow, who came to the CCP base in northern Shaanxi in 1936 and afterwards turned his lengthy interviews with Mao and other CCP leaders into a would-be classic, *Red Star Over China*. When Mikoyan came to the CCP in early 1949, China's domestic and international circumstances differed drastically from earlier occasions. Mikoyan did not come just to listen to Mao's monologues about the CCP's past. With world politics becoming increasingly polarized by a confrontation dubbed the Cold War, Stalin's envoy wanted to find out what Moscow would face along its southern flank when a Chinese brand of communism took hold in China. The sounding-out was mutual. Although he had maintained telegraphic communication with Stalin, Mao was anxious to consult the Soviets in person and wanted to try his blueprints for a new China on the founders of the world's first communist state. Mao had previously proposed coming to Moscow, but Stalin demurred. The Mikoyan mission, therefore, became the next best option for the two sides, both realizing that their long interparty relationship had changed gears and was entering an interstate phase.[2]

In contemplating, exploring, and even occasionally contesting important steps for launching the largest communist state in Asia, neither Mao nor Mikoyan seemed to realize that together they were observing one of the oldest rituals in Chinese history. Mao, as all dynastic founders before him, had to reenvision a geographic realm over which his communist state would claim to exercise full authority and power. In the past, when China was still a dynastic state without rigid "national" boundaries, each new dynastic founder had to round up peoples and territories in various ways that were appropriate to the power relations of the time, as well as to the interethnic and intercultural configurations along the mostly mercurial margins of "China." In this regard, the CCP leaders' task in 1949 was at once simpler and more difficult than that of their predecessors because China had already had its "modern" experience for a century. On the one hand, "modern China" had achieved a relatively stable geo-body that, in a legal sense, was accepted by the international community. On the other hand, in places, the contour of this geo-body had been severely contested ever since the nineteenth century. Tibet was one of the most complicated cases in this regard. When talking to Mikoyan, Mao inevitably brought up issues pertinent to the territorial realm and multiethnic configuration of the incoming communist state.

This chapter addresses the question "What was the essence of the Tibetan question at the beginning of the PRC?" Previous studies have provided single-dimensional analyses of "communist aggression" or "Han Chinese expansion." Although communist ideology and Han-centrism were significant elements in Beijing's policymaking, such analyses are far too narrow and lack historical context. Notably, certain items brought up by Mao in his meetings with the Soviets had also been prominent in official agendas of the late Qing court and the outgoing Nationalist government. In the context of Chinese history, the modern Tibetan question has spanned several political periods and been part of a protracted agenda shared by all the "central" regimes of China since the mid-nineteenth century. Taking on the Tibetan question in the mid-twentieth century, CCP leaders were poised to continue the geopolitical landscaping initiated by the Manchus a few centuries before; resume the modern transformation of territoriality imposed on China by Western powers in the mid-nineteenth century; push their brand of communist revolution to all territories they claimed, including Tibet; and join the international struggle for human destiny dubbed the Cold War. The impact on Tibet was brutal, combining momentum accumulated from the recent past with anxieties stimulated by the perilous present.

In seeking to understand the Tibetan question in the mid-twentieth century, our narrative necessarily begins with an overview of the Manchu prelude before proceeding to an investigation of the CCP's entry onto the scene of the Himalayan frontiers.

A Geopolitical Legacy

Strategic thinking on a global scale is a modern phenomenon, a cumulative achievement of globalization in strategic scheming for physical security, ideological/cultural influence, and material gains. Mao Zedong was probably the first Chinese strategist in history to conceive Chinese schemes on a global scale, as in his ideas about "intermediate zones," "a horizontal line and a big terrain," and "the three-world theory." In the 1970s, interacting with Mao as a rival and a partner, Henry Kissinger was impressed by these ideas "less as a national concern than as a broader view of global conditions."[3] Yet Mao conceived these ideas from a massive home base, stretching from the Gobi Desert in the north to tropical rainforests in the south and from the western Pacific coast in the east to the Tarim Basin in the west. Without "China marching west" under the Manchus in the previous few centuries, Communist China would have occupied only China's eastern provinces without a Central Asian position.[4]

It will be shown later that the inheritance relationship between the Qing dynasty and the PRC is neither direct nor simple. This relationship is nevertheless an undeniable historical fact. History is indeed fabric-like, with threads stretching from one point to another.[5] Yet in the process, certain threads are broken, and the so-called continuity of history involves only those that remain unbroken. As far as the Himalayan frontier is concerned, a certain number of such threads connect the Qing state and the PRC.

When Mao talked to Mikoyan in 1949 about the Tibetan question, he was preceded by a string of political leaders based in eastern China who were vexed by the situation in Tibet. In the early eighteenth century, Emperor Kangxi of the Qing dynasty set a precedent of using military force to facilitate the management of Tibet. Unlike his Han Chinese predecessors of the Ming dynasty, who had extolled the ancient imperial ideology about *Tianxia* (all under heaven) but never actually projected power into Tibet, Emperor Kangxi saw a security threat to his empire and dispatched military expeditions to Tibet between 1718 and 1720. Kangxi waged a "war for pacifying Zunghar and securing Tibet," despite strong objections from some court officials that Tibet was too remote and its terrain too hazardous. Afterwards, Kangxi decreed:

> Since my minor years I have paid close attention to geography. . . . Now that Tibet was obtained with a mighty force and all the frontier tribes become submissive in their hearts, the three Tibetan areas plus Ngari [*Ali* in Chinese] should be entered into our political map [*bantu*], and the Chinese and Tibetan names for mountains and locations in these areas be checked and investigated in order to pass a reliable record to future generations.[6]

Once the Qing court had incorporated Tibet into its political realm and assumed military responsibility for the territory, military force had to be used repeatedly in this remote land to prevent external intrusions and internal mischiefs from disturbing the tranquility of the imperial frontier. During the process, a political region of Tibet emerged in Qing governance. Buttressed by military force, the Qing government shaped Tibet's eastern peripheries without much resistance from Lhasa. As the meaning of the Tibetan frontier to the Qing dynasty continually changed, Tibet's western margins followed suit. Under Emperors Kangxi and Yongzheng, the Qing's security concern in the southwest was mainly to maintain a proper inner buffer between Tibet and its surrounding *neidi*, or heartland provinces. In the late eighteenth century, Emperor Qianlong oversaw a change in the dynasty's security policy in the southwest, reconceptualizing Tibet from a frontier to be guarded against, or *fangbian*, to a frontier to be defended, or *bianfang*.

Triggering the change were continuous interstate crises in the Himalayas between 1788 and 1792. In 1788 and again in 1791, Nepal, known to the Qing as *Kuo'erka* (Gurkha), invaded Tibet. The Qing campaigns against the Gurkhas constituted the first effort ever launched by a central government of China to defend the outer Himalayan frontier. Protagonists involved in the conflicts were hardly "national," and the Qing campaigns ended in upholding the old tributary norms of China's external relations. Nevertheless, these events changed the dynamics of Himalayan politics and created opportunities for British India, known to the Qing as Pileng, to project its influence into Himalayan affairs. Eventually this high-altitude frontier became part of the great game of modern imperialism.[7] Not understanding the long-term impact of his triumph over the Gurkhas, Emperor Qianlong glorified the two campaigns against the Gurkhas as events capping his "ten perfect martial feats," wishing that, once demarcated, the Tibetan boundaries would be settled for good.[8] Investigation and demarcation of the borders began right away in 1792. Two years later, He Lin, the *amban* (residential imperial commissioner in Tibet) reported to the emperor that, with assistance from Tibetan officials and senior residents of the borderland, the borders of Tibet had been clarified. The southwestern and western boundaries of Tibet with several Himalayan states were all clearly demarcated with *Mani* or *Ebo* stone piles.[9] Of course, these Qianlong borders differed from modern international boundaries. They were premodern not so much because they were dictated by the Manchu court to the Himalayan regimes as because they carried only a hazy meaning of sovereignty. For instance, Gurkha was now "upgraded" to tributary status in its relationship with the Qing court. It, as He Lin memorialized to Qianlong, "has entered the *bantu* [meaning the Qing domain] and become the same as Tibet," which Qianlong was pleased to endorse.[10]

For Emperor Qianlong, boundary demarcation in the Himalayas was to achieve a buffer layer for Tibet. During the nineteenth century, under the pressure of Western imperialism, the layered continental frontier of the Qing state collapsed along with its maritime frontiers. But Qing emperors did leave their permanent marks on Tibet. For the first time in history, the geographic shape of Tibet and its relation with neighboring areas had been mapped in the Chinese cartographic tradition. From his tours within Tibet, Songyun, the twenty-seventh *amban* (1794–99), created *Xizang Tushuo* (Illustrated survey of Tibet), which included sixteen detailed maps showing topographic features, roads, posthouses, and neighboring states. The practice of mapping Tibet continued. In 1897, a book by Huang Peiqiao, *Xizang Tukao* (Illustrated examination of Tibet), presented a Chinese cartographic conception of Tibet in a map with grid lines.[11] These would become part of the Qing's cartographic legacy to modern China.

One more thread worth mentioning in the Tibetan story links the Manchus and the Chinese Communists in a historical continuum. The Qing governance of Tibet established an "ordained patronage" between the ruling regime of China and the Tibetan government. "Ordained" is the key, a feature that had existed neither in the mutually supplemental relationship between Mongolian military power and Tibetan religious clout during the Yuan dynasty nor in the largely ceremonial relationship between Tibetan ruling elites and the Ming dynasty. Between 1724 and 1907, the Qing government drafted five sets of *zhangcheng* (ordinances) for Tibet. All but the last one took effect to some degree.[12] For all practical purposes, these were imperial decrees bestowed on the Tibetan theocracy by the throne in Beijing. In the Manchu court's management of its imperial domains of various ethnic and geographic composition, this ongoing approach of controlling with written "constitutions" was unique, reflecting the peculiar geo-ethnic character of Tibet.

The crux of the Qing patronage was Tibet's geo-ethno-security position in recurring struggles over the East Asian landmass. The geo-ethnic configuration of the Qing dynasty set a precedent for the People's Republic of China. Unlike the Mongols, who devised a southwest strategy of conquering the Southern Song while maintaining their home base in the steppes, the Manchus left their homeland in Manchuria and assumed the ruling position in China by taking root in Chinese provinces. Geostrategically speaking, Tibet was in a remote corner of Asian politics that initially had little relevance to the Manchus. The Qing, however, was a multiethnic entity from the very beginning. After consolidating their hold on Chinese provinces, the Manchu rulers became increasingly conscious of Tibet's ideological significance for their management of the Buddhist Mongols, who were the Manchus' vital partners in ruling China. A security corollary of the Tibetan-Mongolian connection to the Qing rule was Tibet's importance to stability along the fault lines between Chinese society and the non-Chinese inner Asian frontiers. Tibet thus became an indispensable link in the interethnic chains that bound the Manchus' dynastic state together.

For this reason, Tibet was, in the words of the historian Pamela Crossley, an "empty constituency" of the Qing dynasty: the people, land, and socioeconomic well-being of Tibet had little meaning to the Manchu emperors as long as Lhasa remained docile under their throne.[13]

The socioeconomic emptiness of Tibet to the Qing court was best shown in Qianlong's admonishment of an overzealous amban who proposed to prospect coalmines in Tibet: "Tibet is an extremely remote place incomparable to the inner provinces. Its livelihood and custom should be allowed to continue according to established practices, and we must not act as a ruling surrogate and try to run the place."[14]

Qianlong's disinterest in Tibet's socioeconomic conditions was in sharp contrast to his eagerness to assert political authority over the Tibetan theocracy. The distance, difficult terrain, high altitude, and peculiar religious-political system of Tibet, and especially its indirect role in the multiethnic structure of the Qing state, all dictated an economical approach to governance. In the times of Kangxi and Yongzheng, this consideration led to the appointment of amban to Lhasa who, on behalf of the emperor, watched over the operations of the Tibetan government. When this symbolic presence of imperial authority was found inadequate, imperial ordinances came into play. Most of these written rules were installed in the wake of internally or externally inflicted crises, which either required the Qing court to pacify Tibet with troops or became occasions for Beijing to censure the Tibetan authorities. Either way, a new set of rules would be imposed on Lhasa to rectify the supposed wrongs. Manchu emperors were not reformers. They did not anticipate a changed Tibet in the future as a result of accumulative policy measures. Rather, they constantly looked for a permanent solution. When a set of rules was established, they wanted these rules to, in Qianlong's words, "last long without causing any malpractice, and settle the problems once and for all."[15]

Yet the Qianlong years did see one significant change: transformation of the amban's function. This change came in the wake of the second Gurkha war. Beyond serving as the emperor's informant and representative, the amban would function as a political governor on behalf of the emperor. In the famous "Twenty-Nine-Article Ordinance" of 1793, the amban's new role was central. The ordinance gave the amban authority on a par with that of the Dalai Lama and the Panchen Erdeni in administering the internal affairs of Tibet. His power would be superior to that of the two Tibetan leaders in handling Tibet's foreign affairs. Among the twenty-nine articles, nineteen were about the amban's authority and responsibilities. The intended precedent for this fortified amban authority was the imperial residential commissioner in Xinjiang, who "could decide everything."[16] About the 1793 ordinance, the Qing chronologist Wei Yuan wrote:

> Now the [Tibetan] affairs and the power [of governing Tibet] became consistent with each other. Since the Tang Dynasty, Tibet has never been administered as

prefectures and counties as today.... Since the Yuan and the Ming Dynasties, the Tibetan clerics have never been ruled as ordinary subjects as today.¹⁷

Wei Yuan thus saw in the 1793 measures a political integration between the outer frontier of Tibet and the inner provinces of China. Wei probably exaggerated the intensity of Qianlong governance inside Tibet, which, far from direct rule, remained an ordained patronage. Yet Wei's assessment would later be embraced by Chinese nationalists in the twentieth century.

Retying the Knot

History has proceeded in twisted ways. When China entered its PRC phase in 1949, the Qing governance of Tibet was already a historical legacy to be salvaged. Before 1949, there were moments when the Qing's Tibetan enterprise could have been completely relegated to history. The Qing did not escape the fate of dynastic cycle and was in decline after the Qianlong reign. During the nineteenth century, this dynastic decline was compounded and expedited by a novel development, the arrival of the West. Contemporaries summarized what they were experiencing with four Chinese characters, *shi yi shi yi* (change of time and alteration of trends).¹⁸ The erosion of Qing power after the Opium War of 1840–42 was evident in the opening of China's eastern coasts as doorways for Western powers to make inroads into China. In time, as the Qing's inner Asian frontiers also collapsed, the very geographic meaning of China was redefined. Pounded by the transmuting force of West-dominated globalization, China the imperial was recast into China the national. The legacies of the Qing became problematic.

The change of time and trends also meant that the geostrategic position of Tibet shifted from the fringe of the Qing security system to the board of a "great game" between the British and Russian empires. Zhang Yintang, who went to Tibet in 1907 as imperial commissioner to rectify the situation in the wake of a recent British invasion led by Colonel Francis Younghusband, described the altered geostrategic significance of Tibet this way:

> The land of Tibet runs about five thousand *li* [2,500 kilometers] vertically and horizontally, and has millions of people. It is caught between the British-Russian pressures and presents a difficult situation. Since the British nipped away Zhemengxiong [Sikkim] in the sixteenth year [of Guangxu, or 1890], they have endeavored to develop the northwest and laid a string of blockhouses from Darjeeling to Xinla [?] to fend off Russia. The areas of Gyantse [Jiangzi] and Qunbi [?] of Tibet form a dustpan-like shape inserting between and interlocking with Zhemengxiong and Bulukeba [Bhutan].... The British intend to nip away the Jiangzi-Qunbi region and then engulf Houzang [Rear Tibet; Shigatse] in

order to open a passage through Ngari, Ladakh, Afghanistan, and Persian Gulf, counterbalancing the Siberian Railway of Russia. . . . If Tibet is lost, Mongolia, Xinjiang, Qinghai, Sichuan, and Yunnan will not be able to have peace even for one day.[19]

A Chinese security perception on such a geographic scale, unthinkable in Qianlong's time, was contemporaneous with a development in Western political thinking. In 1904, the same year Younghusband led the British expedition into Tibet, his compatriot H. J. Mackinder published an influential essay, "The Geographical Pivot of History," delineating an ongoing global power struggle and the world's principal states' respective geopolitical positions in it. Contending that Russia occupied the pivotal area of world power, Eurasia, Mackinder warned of a "yellow peril": the Chinese, organized by the Japanese, would overthrow the Russian Empire and take over its territory before threatening the world's freedom.[20]

Probably Zhang Yintang had never heard of Mackinder. He did however try to deal with the latter's beloved "world's freedom" that was wreaking havoc for the Qing dynasty. To keep the southwest corner of the Qing state intact, Zhang's solution was a new set of rules that went beyond the established ordained patronage of Tibet and headed toward direct control. Since Tibet was not yet ready to integrate with the inner provinces, Zhang proposed that it be administered in the same way as the British administered India. Going against previous Qing pursuit of stability and permanence in Tibet, Zhang's new rules were intended to achieve "development" and "progress" in every aspect of Tibetan life, anticipating a modernized Tibet in ten years.[21] In this sense, Zhang Yintang preceded Chinese Communist reformers in Tibet after 1949, who, by coincidence, were led by two officials also named Zhang.

Zhang's proposed rules broke new ground—but the old ground of the Qing-Tibetan relationship had already been broken by the British inroads into Tibet as well as by Western powers' encroachment on Qing China itself. In other words, Zhang's reform ideas were historically ironic: he pushed for drastic changes in Tibet exactly because of conditions that already deprived the Qing court of its ability to implement meaningful measures in Tibet. Zhang's abortive plan for Tibet was thus part of the Qing court's desperate effort to save itself through a series of reforms in China, known as the "New Policies." As far as the Qing borderlands were concerned, the New Policies opened the Manchurian and Mongolian frontiers for Han agricultural migration and cultural-economic integration with the rest of China. Along the ethnographic fault lines between Tibetan and Chinese society, *gaitu guiliu* (bureaucratization of native officials and systems) was forcefully implemented.[22] Inside Tibet, however, Zhang's lasting legacy would only be a flower that he brought with him to Lhasa, *cosmos bipinnatus*, known to the

Chinese as *qiuying* (autumn bloom) but to Tibetans simply as *drang ta rin*, or "His Excellency Zhang."[23]

As the Qing dynasty strived to become "national" in order to survive the chaotic world of nation-states, the future of China was no longer in monarchists' hands. During the last two decades of the Qing dynasty, a great polemic took place among China's political elites in response to the country's debilitating crises. Dividing into political camps labeled variously as "monarchist," "constitutionalist," and "revolutionary," participants in the polemic abused and attacked one another verbally. This was one of the few open and free political dialogues in the modern political history of China. The sword-crossing among the best and brightest minds that China afforded at the time ushered in the Revolution of 1911 and helped frame the political discourse of China in the twentieth century. In the debate, the question "Why Tibet?" was raised and answered; however, it would be asked again by founders of communist China in 1949.[24]

Given the Chinese revolutionaries' Han-centric disposition, had they had their way in the 1911 Revolution, the political map of the Republic of China would have differed drastically from that of the Qing. But the Revolution ended with a trilateral (revolutionaries, Yuan Shikai, and the Manchu court) and biethnic (Han and Manchu) compromise, embodied in a "five-race republic" formula. The "five races" reincarnated the five principal subject peoples of the Qing dynasty (Manchu, Mongol, Han, Hui, and Tibetan), "republic" was the political ideal of the revolutionaries, and the combination of the two was the handiwork of the manipulative Yuan Shikai. "Five-race republic" was one of the most notorious fantasies in twentieth-century Chinese history. First, by whatever political or social-scientific criterion, the number of ethnic groups in China is much larger than five. Second, the formula was based on a compromise between the political elites of two ethnic groups but not a consensus among all five ethnic groups concerned. Third, the formula, intended to keep the five ethnic territories of the Qing dynasty together, actually inaugurated an era of great interethnic and political division, starting with the secession of Tibet and Outer Mongolia.

As Yang Du, a ferocious and insightful opponent of the revolutionaries, had predicted, the question raised by the Qing crisis was not whether the territorial integrity of China should be maintained under Manchu or Han authority; rather, it was a matter of political fallout during power transition:

> At the juncture when the old regime has just demised and the new government is not yet strong enough, the latter does not have the necessary military prowess to subdue the other peoples and keep their lands as ours. Those Mongols, Hui, and Tibetans who harbor nationalistic aspirations and do not want to live with the Han under the same government and within the same state, will

take advantage of the opportunity to untie the knot [with China] and seek secession.²⁵

In Yang's opinion, converting the Manchu monarchy's multiethnic borderlands into the national territories of the Republic of China required both material strength and ideological gravity. These two conditions were even more imperative for the ROC than for its Qing predecessor because it was pursuing an integrated nationhood, not a loose imperium. The ROC soon proved that it possessed neither.

At the beginning of 1912, Sun Yat-sen, in the capacity of provisional president of the ROC, issued a proclamation expressing a strong aspiration for state integration, stressing uniformity of nation, territory, military, and domestic administration. Included in the statement were these words about the newly forged national state: "The essence of the state is the people. National unification is to combine the Han, Manchu, Mongolian, Hui, and Tibetan territories into one state, and the Han, Manchu, Mongolian, Hui, and Tibetan peoples into one people." A few months later, the new state issued a provisional constitution. The document was the first legal instrument in Chinese history that explicitly stipulated the territorial area of the Chinese state, which included the twenty-two provinces plus Qinghai, Mongolia, and Tibet.²⁶ Sun's statement and the provisional constitution articulated a twentieth-century version of the "grand unification" ideology that had run through China's dynastic history. But these documents merely recorded a grudging ideological shift of the 1911 revolutionaries, not an actual incarnation of the Qing dynasty into a Chinese national state.

Soon after relinquishing the presidency of the ROC to Yuan Shikai as part of the 1911 compromise, Sun was dismayed by Yuan's mischiefs ranging from dictatorship to imperial restoration. Revolution had to be reignited. As for the country's conditions, what baffled Sun most was not the secession of Mongolia and Tibet. Rather, he was exasperated at the Han people's lack of nationalistic spirit. Sun's new battle cry was therefore a Sinocentric, unitary conception, *Zhonghua Minzu* (Chinese Nation). In constructing this Chinese Nation, the Han majority would have to enhance their own sense of citizenry but also "sacrifice" their "Han" bloodline and ethnonym in the process of assimilating ethnic minorities. While eager to reinvigorate the Han as a "nation," Sun did not count out the other four "races." He just believed that they were too small in number to be count-worthy.²⁷ In 1924, to differentiate his reorganized Kuomintang from the counterrevolutionary regime in Beijing, Sun contended publicly that whereas any attempt at military conquest of the alienated borderlands would be foolhardy, all frontier peoples would be attracted to a new state based on revolutionary ideology.²⁸ Thus, Sun added one more thread to the historical fabric that would stretch into the PRC period: nation-building according to partisan ideology. Party-constructed state and party-construed nation would soon emerge as long-lasting twins in China's political life.

During the two decades from 1928 to 1949 when the KMT authorities endeavored to realign its party-state with estranged Tibet and Outer Mongolia, however, the Chinese Nationalist ideology offered little for the frontier peoples to gravitate toward. By the end of World War II, it became clear that the case of Outer Mongolia was a lost battle. In the summer of 1945, making the last effort of its wartime diplomacy, the KMT government negotiated with the Soviets and agreed to recognize Outer Mongolia's independence, which had actually been in effect even longer than the KMT government itself. The situation of Tibet still seemed hopeful, though. Unlike the case of Outer Mongolia, since the 1930s the KMT government had managed to maintain an office in Lhasa as a feeble symbol of Chinese presence in Tibet. Over the years, the question facing KMT leaders had been, positively, how to augment this meager liaison into a symbol of Chinese sovereignty and, negatively, how to prevent Tibet from hardening its alienation from China and seeking international support to its separate statehood.[29] Chiang Kai-shek, whose political acumen and military skill made him a paramount figure in the KMT regime, believed early on that "betrayal by Mongolia and Tibet" must be rectified by military means.[30] However, failing to stabilize its power even in Chinese provinces and continuously fighting warlords, the Chinese Communists, and the Japanese, the KMT government did more planning for the borderlands than taking effective steps.

The largely inconsequential KMT deliberation of the Tibetan question nevertheless has historical value in preserving Chinese official thought on paper. A number of features of the KMT planning for Tibet are notable. Though resembling those weak dynasties in Chinese history unable to control the whole country, the KMT government relentlessly upheld its goal of achieving "grand unification." Thus, the "highest goal" of Chinese frontier administration was to amalgamate frontier ethnic groups with the Han into a "new nation just like the nation of the United States." Manchuria, Outer Mongolia, Tibet, and Xinjiang were proclaimed the "first lines" of China's national defense.[31] The problem for the KMT government was that since the ethnopolitical knot between the Qing court and these frontier regions was untied in 1911, the KMT government had never been able to establish its authority in these places. The situation of Tibet, as made clear by a document of the Chinese Ministry of Foreign Affairs, was that until World War II, "the orders and laws of the central government have never been able to reach Tibet."[32]

However, Tibet was never omitted from KMT officials' geostrategic vision. Among numerous KMT documents contemplating military moves toward Tibet, the most interesting was a directive drafted by Chiang Kai-shek himself in October 1942. Chiang believed that although international circumstances, meaning British and American attitudes, and situations in warlord-controlled

Xikang (eastern Kham, then under Liu Wenhui) and Qinghai (Amdo, then under Ma Bufang) were important, they were not so overwhelming as to block the government's military move toward Lhasa. He outlined a two-phase stratagem for settling the Tibetan situation. In phase one, political measures should take the lead, with military measures used only as backup and a last resort. But Chamdo (Changdu) must be taken militarily as the first step to control Tibet. In phase two, political measures and propaganda would still be more important than military measures, but threat with airplanes should be used if necessary. As for military advance into Tibet, whereas the Qinghai direction had no problem, the central government's force must enter Tibet from Xikang, and therefore arrangements with the Xikang military authorities must be completed in advance.[33]

Chiang's plan took shape at a time when the KMT regime not only was cornered in Sichuan by the Japanese Army but also, as the plan indicated, had very shaky relations with local warlords entrenched in the so-called Tibetan-Yi corridor of the Qinghai-Sichuan-Yunnan area. The plan was therefore impractical and pretentious. Nevertheless, Chiang's plan revealed a hardened conviction among Chinese officials that China was inseparable from its inner Asian borderlands. By 1950, Chiang's presumptuousness became prescience: the newly installed Communist government was taking steps about Tibet, plagiarizing Chiang's plan.

During World War II, as the tide of China's geopolitical decline began to reverse, the KMT government was able to achieve some success in diplomatically retying its "knot" with lost and alienated territories. The KMT's "China" became a beneficiary of the legally oriented and ideologically agitated international politics of the time. Among a number of power centers in a fragmented China, the Western Allies not only recognized the KMT regime as the sole legitimate "national" government, but also, as America's wartime diplomacy indicated, treated China as a "great power." At an inter-Allied summit in Cairo in late 1943, U.S. president Franklin D. Roosevelt and British prime minister Winston Churchill gave their stamp of approval to Chiang Kai-shek's claim to China's "lost territories."[34] The allied endorsement, however, was incomplete. The Soviet Union, occupying the Mackinderian pivotal position of Eurasia, never loosened its grip on Outer Mongolia and, by the war's end, would press the KMT government to relinquish any claim of sovereignty over the landlocked country. The British Empire, like all other oceanic colonial empires in the Asia-Pacific region, was worn down by the war but was mounting a stubborn rearguard action. The war years did not see any change in the British stance on the Tibetan question. A stamina contest unfolded between the Chinese claim of sovereignty over Tibet and the British resolve on keeping a Tibetan buffer along the northern frontier of British India. President Roosevelt's eagerness to cheer up the Chinese did not help much in these regards.[35]

As World War II finally ended in Asia, the diplomatic glory and triumphal mood of the KMT government did not last long. Tibet was just one of many problems facing the KMT regime in the postwar years, and their solutions seemed even more remote than in the war years. A few months after Japan's surrender, the Ministry of Foreign Affairs commented somberly: "Our country has many internal problems and is in a terrible fix. Tibet's attitude [toward the KMT government] has therefore changed from one of awed watching to one of keeping an even greater distance."[36] Only briefly, postwar decolonization of India rekindled optimism in the KMT regime as far as Tibet was concerned. KMT officials hoped that the Tibetans would "lean inward" in a new atmosphere of Sino-Indian amity.[37] This sanguine prospect soon vanished. In 1947, a miscarried coup in Lhasa shattered any wishful thinking among KMT officials that they could manipulate the Tibetan situation from the inside. The incident involved a former regent named Reting who allegedly had "pro-center [Chinese] tendency" and tried to regain power. KMT secret agents were implicated in the plot.[38] The event convinced KMT officials that the central government's prestige in Tibet had hit bottom and had to be salvaged with direct military actions. Yet the KMT authorities were again tied up: they could not do anything on the Tibetan frontier while engaging the Chinese Communists in a life-or-death struggle in the rest of China.[39]

As the Chinese Civil War was winding down in the eastern provinces of China, the Himalayan frontier began to feel its impact. At the end of 1949, Luo Jialun, Nationalist Chinese ambassador to India, made two points to the foreign ministry: first, the newly independent India was actively seeking to control some disputed territories along the Tibetan border in order to deal with the incoming Chinese Communist power from a stronger position; second, the Communists had already infiltrated Lhasa, using Mongolian lamas and Tibetan women as agents, and the Tibetans would not be able to resist a full-scale Communist invasion.[40] Although Luo's intelligence about Chinese Communist infiltration was problematic, Tibetan affairs had unmistakably entered a new phase.

Means of "Liberation"

In 1949, the most important international discussion about Tibet did not take place between KMT and Indian officials but, as mentioned at the beginning of this chapter, between Mao Zedong and Stalin's envoy. As the Mao-Mikoyan talks took place in Xibaipo in early 1949, Mao Zedong and his associates were still novices at running a country as huge and complex as China. Nevertheless, the political outlook of the Chinese Communists, in spite of its Marxist-Leninist vein, grew out of the same geopolitical landscape that had fostered Emperor

Kangxi's empire and the same timescape that had given birth to Sun Yat-sen's revolution.[41]

Between January 30 and February 7, Mikoyan had twelve conversations with CCP leaders, devoting attention to the current military and political struggles in China as well as the CCP's domestic and foreign policies in the future. These talks envisioned social, economic, and governmental structures of a new China with novel conceptions like "new democracy," "worker-peasant alliance," "transition to socialism," and "people's dictatorship." As for new China's foreign affairs, Mao asserted that China would take the side of the Soviet Union, and that "there is no middle of the road for us," affirming which of the two superpowers would be China's model for domestic and international development.[42]

Yet underneath the excitement about creating a new China lurked a stubborn old element: geography. While the Chinese Communists and their Soviet ally cast the future sociopolitical systems of China in "red," they had to work with the "dark" past in maintaining China's geographic shape. Mikoyan told his hosts that Moscow would not support a CCP policy to let China's minority nationalities gain independence. Such a development, Mikoyan warned, would reduce China's territorial size once the CCP took power. The subject immediately brought to the minds of CCP leaders two shapes of China's political map, one bequeathed by the late Qing and another by the ROC. The former had a shape like a begonia leaf; the latter resembled a rooster, missing the area of Outer Mongolia. At the time of the Xibaipo meetings, Outer Mongolia was just one of the three territorial questions challenging the CCP leadership. The other two were Xinjiang and Tibet. Since Moscow's handiwork was clearly visible in Outer Mongolia's independence and Xinjiang's separatism, these regions were acute issues in the emerging relationship between Communist China and the Soviet Union. After awkward exchanges between CCP leaders and the Soviets, the two sides reached an understanding that Outer Mongolia would remain an independent state but Xinjiang would be part of China.[43]

In drawing a mental map for Communist China, Chinese and Soviet Communists probably vacillated between two perspectives. From a national geopolitical point of view, the sovereign identities of Mongolia and Xinjiang directly affected China's security concerns vis-à-vis possible threats from the north, and vice versa for Russia. But in terms of the inter-bloc fray of the Cold War that China was about to enter, Mongolia and Xinjiang changed from inner Asian buffers to part of the communist continuum in the Eurasian landmass, which would soon be perceived in the West as a Sino-Soviet monolith. In this sense, Tibet was the only frontier area among the three whose meanings to the new China's national and inter-bloc geostrategies were not overtly contradictory.

Because of the peculiar context of the Mao-Mikoyan meetings, Mao's remarks about Tibet differed from all previous CCP statements. This was the first time that Mao, or any CCP leader, talked about Tibet from the position of China's central authorities. Mao's Xibaipo remarks therefore constituted the very first sign of the Chinese Communist government's intention toward Tibet. In these words, Mao informed Mikoyan of a procedure for incorporating Tibet into the forthcoming Communist China:

> We are prepared to grant autonomy to the Tibetan people residing in southwestern China. The Tibetan question is extremely complicated. In practice Tibet used to be a British colony and belonged to China only in name. Lately the United States has spared no effort to ingratiate itself with the Tibetan people.... Once we end the civil war and begin to deal with political issues at home and when the Tibetan people can see that we do not threaten them with aggression and treat them equally, we can begin to decide the destiny of the region. We must be cautious and patient in dealing with Tibet, and we have to take into consideration the complex and troublesome religious affairs and the influence of Lamaism there.[44]

Mao's "autonomy" for Tibet had a CCP-supported precedent in the "regional autonomy" (*quyu zizhi*) of Inner Mongolia that began in 1947. A few months after the Mao-Mikoyan talks, in the 1949 Common Program, the CCP officially adopted "regional autonomy" as the standard way to rein in those alienated frontier territories and to peddle the idea of the Chinese nation to the frontier peoples. In categorizing Tibet erroneously as a British colony, Mao was just following standard CCP rhetoric since the 1930s. In referring to a nominal Chinese sovereignty over Tibet, Mao probably meant to imply the KMT regime's incompetence more than its perseverance in reclaiming Tibet diplomatically. In the CCP's scorecard, the historical credit for incorporating Tibet and other inner Asian territories into China always went to the Manchus, never to the Chinese Nationalists.[45] To Mao, the British and KMT pages of the Tibetan question could probably be turned. More pressing for the incoming CCP power, as Mao indicated, were, first, the United States as a newcomer to the troubled frontier and, second, the Tibetan society itself that remained totally unfamiliar to the CCP. Yet the most striking content of Mao's remark was his adherence to a "cautious and patient" political approach to the Tibetan situation and his explicit exclusion of Tibet from the CCP's ongoing "war of liberation." The CCP had always believed that the lama clergy was the most decadent and corrupting element in both the Tibetan and Mongolian societies, and that the Tibetan theocracy under the Dalai Lama was the principal pillar of foreign imperialism and Chinese counterrevolutionary influence in Tibet. Contextually, therefore, it was remarkable that Mao identified Tibetan Buddhism as the main reason for caution.[46]

Before 1949, the CCP had had only one substantive encounter with Tibetans. During the CCP's Long March in the mid-1930s, Red Army troops under

Zhang Guotao had lingered briefly in western Sichuan and Xikang and made contact with local Tibetan communities. Soon after, these operations were denounced inside the CCP as part of Zhang's "opportunist errors," which then caused Zhang to defect to the KMT. Consequently, the rare experience with the Tibetans became taboo in CCP discourse. The Long March, a "seeder" of revolution according to Mao, sowed very few seeds of Chinese Communism in the Tibetan areas. After the Red Army left, a small number of governmental and party organizations set up by the CCP disappeared altogether.[47] A small number of poverty-stricken Tibetans followed the Red Army northward and would not return until the People's Liberation Army (PLA) was poised to invade Tibet in 1950. The most famous among these was a Khampa named Sangye Yeshe from Ngawa (Aba), Sichuan. While a trainee in Yan'an, Sangye Yeshe came to the attention of Mao, who gave him a Chinese name Tianbao, meaning "heavenly treasure." KMT leaders had the same penchant to rechristen their trainees of non-Han ethnicity. For instance, Dai Chuanxian, president of the Examination Yuan of the KMT regime, gave Chinese names to nine young Khampas who studied in the KMT's Central Political School in the late 1920s and early 1930s. One of these had a nephew named Phüntso Wangye, shortened as Phünwang (aka Min Zhicheng in Chinese), from Bathang (Batang). In 1939, Phünwang started a communist group among Tibetan students in Chongqing and contacted the Soviet embassy and CCP representatives in Chongqing the next year. After 1942, he traveled to Tibet a few times and tried to persuade Tibetan officials to start reforms. While sojourning in Lhasa from 1947 to 1949, he organized a small Group of Plateau Communist Movement, which, after being expelled from Lhasa in July 1949, joined the CCP as the CCP Work Committee in the Xikang-Tibet Frontier in August 1949. Phünwang's group soon lost contact with the CCP again until January 1950. During most of 1949, therefore, these Tibetan connections did not feature in the CCP's policy deliberation about Tibet. Sangye Yeshe was given an underground assignment in Inner Mongolia, and Phünwang attempted to initiate radical changes in Tibet largely on his own.[48]

In spite of the enduring historical and religious connections between Tibetan and Mongolian affairs since the Qing dynasty, in the CCP perspective, Inner Mongolia and Tibet presented two rather different situations. During the Chinese Civil War of 1945–49, the CCP had an effective Inner Mongolian cadre that played a significant role in the military-political struggle for Manchuria and Inner Mongolia. Ulanhu (aka Yun Ze), the most prominent of the group and a member of the CCP Central Committee, was able not only to organize the first regional ethnic autonomy of the CCP brand in Inner Mongolia but also to advise the CCP leadership with respect to such high policy issues as minority nationalities' right to self-determination and a federated structure for the new Chinese state.[49] In contrast, as of 1949, a recognizable Tibetan element was still missing in the Chinese Communist movement.

Feeling remote from Tibet both physically and mentally, unsurprisingly Mao classified the Tibetan question as one of the "domestic political problems" to be handled in the future. In January 1949, the CCP Central Committee began to receive queries via its secret radio station in Xikang, or eastern Kham. General Liu Wenhui, KMT governor of Xikang, who had been in secret contact with the CCP for some time, wanted to know whether the CCP leadership had any instruction for him. Liu proved too anxious. The CCP did not instruct him to hold an "uprising" against the KMT regime until the very end of the year.[50] Naturally, Tibet would continue to stay off the CCP's operational agenda for an even longer time.

As for CCP leaders' geostrategic thinking and operational arrangements in 1949, several CCP and Soviet documents dated May and June of 1949 are especially illuminating. Given that the CCP conquest of China went from north to south and from east to west, when planning the PLA's two-pronged final march toward Xinjiang in the northwest and Tibet in the southwest, the CCP leadership was worried about a possible American intervention along China's eastern coasts, or from behind the PLA's westward advance. Stalin warned Mao that the Anglo-American-French powers, to protect their imperialist interests in Southeast Asia, might attack the PLA from its rear, or the eastern coasts. He suggested that the PLA postpone marching toward the borders of Indochina, Burma, and India, meaning in the general direction of Tibet. In the meantime, CCP and Soviet leaders agreed that Xinjiang, because of its rich oil deposits and strategic position between China and the Soviet Union, must be controlled by the PLA as soon as possible. Regarding the PLA's northwestward movement, Stalin even criticized the CCP leadership for overestimating the strength of the Ma brothers, the Muslim warlords in Gansu and Qinghai, and offered to provide aircraft to facilitate PLA operations.[51] The resultant plan was that after occupying China's eastern provinces, the PLA would secure the outer crescent of Chinese provinces from Qinghai to Guangdong before the end of 1949, and that Hainan Island, Taiwan, and Xinjiang would come under CCP control in 1950. As for Tibet, CCP leaders told Stalin that, because it was a "unique case" and "must be settled with political but not military means," the territory would not even be included in the CCP agenda for 1950. In July 1949, in preparing his speech at a national work conference, Zhou Enlai, would-be premier of the incoming People's Republic, clarified the meaning of "carrying the war and revolution through to the end," which was to march into Taiwan, Hainan Island, Kunming of Yunnan, and Xinjiang. Tibet was omitted from Zhou's speech and assumed no clear significance in the CCP's war and revolution.[52]

The CCP's insulation of Tibet conceptually from its "war of liberation" ended suddenly in September 1949. Between July 10 and 22, the Tibetan authorities drew the world's attention in expelling KMT personal from Lhasa. More than two hundred people were ousted in three groups, including the staff of the KMT office in Lhasa and their families, a number of Han merchants, and some

Khampas suspected as communist agents. Phünwang was included in the first group to leave. Lhasa's explanation was that the KMT presence in Tibet would likely cause a CCP invasion.⁵³ Chiang Kai-shek, who had already resigned from the ROC presidency and was preparing Taiwan as his new base, was not at all convinced of Lhasa's "anti-communist" sentiment. He condemned Lhasa for treason and suggested that the Chinese government coerce Lhasa to repent with a threat of "stern sanctions."⁵⁴ Yet, as the KMT regime itself was losing China, Chiang's proposed "stern sanctions" sounded more comical than menacing.

The CCP reacted to the frontier incident belatedly. Not until September 2 did an editorial in the *Xinhua News Agency Bulletin* name "British and American imperialism and their follower, the Nehru government of India" as coconspirators behind the July incident (known to the Chinese as the "Han expulsion incident"). For once, the KMT was not a target of the CCP propaganda. Accompanying the editorial were two news pieces by the Xinhua News Agency, one on the event and another on exposés by British and Indian "democratic newspapers" that implicated their own governments' involvement in the "Tibetan incident."⁵⁵ While censuring the "British and Indian aggressors" severely for this "extremely dangerous and foolish undertaking," the editorial also expressed a grave concern about American involvement:

> This plot falls into the same pattern as the recent conspiracy of American imperialism aimed at annexing Taiwan. . . . Since the end of World War II American imperialism actively planned for aggression against Tibet. American imperialism sent spies to Tibet and attempted to gain practical control of Tibet through certain upper-stratum Tibetans.

For the first time, the editorial included Tibet in the "war of liberation," stating that the PLA must liberate Tibet so that "not a single inch of land will remain outside the rule of the People's Republic of China."⁵⁶

After Lhasa's action and Beijing's reaction in the summer of 1949, the political attributes of China's Tibetan question transformed one more time. Since 1911, the question had been one of Sinocentric national reunification versus Tibetan independence and British intrigues, which was itself a modern embodiment of the late Qing's frustrated imperial management of the Tibetan constituency and dealing with British encroachment. Now the question was updated into the era of the Cold War, one of communism versus "American imperialism" and assorted accomplices. Inadvertently, Lhasa initiated the updating, even though the only "communist" group in Lhasa, Phünwang and his associates, became part of the CCP only after they were expelled. Whereas a British connection with the July incident probably cannot be denied, the Xinhua accusation of American involvement is groundless.⁵⁷ Many years later, historians still cannot agree whether the incident was incited by British influence or initiated by the Tibetan government itself.⁵⁸ As for Chinese fear of American involvement in Tibet, the KMT foreign ministry had already raised the issue years before: after the British influence left the Himalayan frontier, pragmatic Tibetan rulers would seek a new supporter in the United States. Such a turn of events, KMT officials feared, would gravely complicate China's Tibetan problem because the Americans sported an ostentatious mission of helping the world's weak peoples.⁵⁹ In 1949, this fear of American meddling was passed to the incoming CCP authorities as part of the Tibetan question.

At the time, the CCP leadership was in a bind to ascertain the nature of the delicate Tibetan situation. The editorial accusation of multiple foreign adversaries in September, though sound for CCP propaganda and useful for political maneuvering with Tibetan ruling elites, was probably based on sporadic reporting by the KMT and the Western press but not on any independent CCP intelligence about the makeup of Himalayan international politics.⁶⁰ In the Western press, the July incident was reported immediately but in a rather confused fashion. The KMT's *Zhongyang Ribao* (Central Daily) did not report the Lhasa incident until mid-August.⁶¹ Thus, the CCP's delayed reaction was understandable. Still, the long silence of the *Xinhua News Agency Bulletin* may have suggested difficulties that CCP leaders faced in deciding a proper stance about the July incident. Physical distance, unfamiliarity with Tibetan affairs, lack of reliable intelligence, and the war in hand may all have obstructed CCP leaders' comprehension of the Tibetan situation. Furthermore, the obvious ethnopolitical nature of the July incident was inconvenient to the main theme of the CCP's ongoing political-military struggle against the KMT regime, and this new trouble spot came from a direction that had not been carefully assessed in the CCP's strategic plan for victory.

Such awkwardness soon surfaced. A few days after the September editorial was published, Zhou Enlai told the participants of the People's Political Consultative Conference (PPCC) that to fend off imperialist plots against the reunification of China, the PRC would implement the principle of "nationality autonomy" but not that of "national self-determination" in handling the question of *shaoshu minzu*, or minority nationalities. As examples of such imperialist plots, Zhou mentioned British conspiracies in Xinjiang and Tibet but limited the American threat to Taiwan and Hainan Island.⁶² The geographic discrepancy between Zhou's and the September editorial's references to the danger of American imperialism was left unexplained. In this period, Mao simply stayed away from the Tibetan question in his public speeches. Late in September, at the opening session of the first PPCC meeting, Mao made a famous statement, informing the world that "the Chinese people stood up." In the same speech, Mao identified a series of territories yet to be liberated by the PLA but did not mention Tibet at all.⁶³ After Xinhua issued its spirited condemnation of foreign imperialists for plotting the July incident and a solemn promise to liberate Tibet, Mao's silence sounded louder than any words about Tibet voiced by the CCP at the time.

In the July incident, the Tibetan authorities appeared to reenact its severing of relations with China in 1911. The difference was that the symbolic presence of the KMT government in Lhasa was much easier to remove in 1949 than the Qing debris in 1911. But times had changed. In 1949, the situation that had informed Yang Du's "knot untied" metaphor was reversed: there was actually no knot to be untied between Lhasa and the outgoing KMT "central government" in China; the incoming CCP central government was very capable of applying military force to the Tibetan frontier. History does not tell us how much longer, without the July incident of 1949, CCP leaders would have continued their original idea of excluding Tibet from their "war of liberation." After the incident, the cushion of time was removed. Later, Tibetan officials must have had second thoughts about their use of anticommunism in July 1949. In late 1949 and early 1950, when asking the CCP leadership not to send PLA troops into Tibet, Lhasa protested that Tibet was a "land cultivated by Avalokiteshvara [*guanyin* in Chinese]" and had always maintained its independence without harboring a grudge against any people or country.[64] Lhasa embraced ideological neutrality several months too late.

In retrospect, in the context of China's domestic politics and foreign relations of the time, factual niceties about an event did not seem to matter as much as the color it was painted. Behind the July incident, Lhasa's stated anticommunism, committed or convenient, and foreign powers' plots, real or imagined, allowed or caused the CCP leadership to connect Tibet to its own ongoing war effort and international struggle. In mid-1949, Mao described China's international position this way: If imperialism was viewed as a lion, currently the lion's head and body were already pinned down by the powerful revolutionary force of the Soviet Union and the new democratic countries of East Europe; in the meantime, the CCP caught the lion's tail and was cutting it off so that the strength of the lion's head would be weakened.[65] Stalin agreed with Mao about the Euro-American significance of the Chinese Revolution. He reminded Mao that Great Britain, France, and the United States understood this significance as well because the PLA's march toward China's borders with Indochina, Burma, and India would stir up revolutionary crises in these countries and even in Indonesia and the Philippines. The imperialist powers would therefore spare no effort to block the PLA's way in order to keep southern China under their influence.[66] Informed by this general judgment, CCP leaders could derive enough reasons from the July incident to reconsider their original notion that the Tibetan question be resolved by political means and in an unhurried manner.

For CCP leaders, a change of plan was also opportune in military terms. In early August, the First Field Army under Peng Dehuai and the Second Field Army under Liu Bocheng and Deng Xiaoping were ready to advance northwestward and southwestward, respectively. In the next few months, the ancient Tibetan-Yi corridor would fall completely under the PLA. On August 1, the CCP Central Committee set up its Southwest Bureau under Deng Xiaoping, Liu Bocheng, and He Long; it would take charge of the entire "Southwest" including Yunnan, Guizhou, Sichuan, and Xikang. But it was in the Northwest that the PLA first met Tibetan affairs. In Qinghai, according to Peng's report to Mao, six hundred thousand Tibetans occupied more than three-fourths of the province's area. Soon after the First Field Army entered the province, Peng's headquarters devised the first set of CCP policies toward the Tibetans.[67] Having taken Gansu and Qinghai, the CCP not only made its first contact with the Tibetans since the Long March but also gained a trump card in dealing with Lhasa: the Panchen Lama.

The ninth Panchen Lama became estranged from Lhasa in the early 1920s and died outside Tibet in 1937. The tenth Panchen Lama was not enthroned until August 1949, twelve years after the ninth Panchen Lama's death. For the CCP's Tibetan enterprise in the years to come, the tenth Panchen Lama would prove a much more valuable legacy from the KMT regime than the feeble KMT office in Lhasa. On August 10, Guan Jiyu, chairman of the Mongolian and Tibetan Affairs Commission of the KMT government, presided over the ceremony to enthrone the tenth Panchen Lama, Choekyi Gyaltsen, in Xining, Qinghai, just in time to pass the Panchen Lama establishment to the CCP.[68]

Four days before the Panchen Lama's enthronement, Mao cabled Peng Dehuai that the Panchen Lama was in Lanzhou and that, when attacking Lanzhou, the PLA must protect the Panchen Lama and the Tibetans in Qinghai and Gansu for the sake of eventually solving the Tibetan question. Mao was obviously misinformed. Ever since 1943, Xining of Qinghai, not Lanzhou of Gansu, was the site of the Panchen Lama group. Twenty days after Mao sent his message, Peng's troops took Lanzhou. There was, of course, no Panchen Lama to be protected in the city.[69] But Mao's message did initiate the "Tibet work" in the CCP's northwestern military-political establishment. Peng assigned the work to Fan Ming, director of the Liaison Department of the Northwestern Field Army. Soon, Fan contacted the Panchen Lama's entourage and persuaded them to send to Beijing a telegram congratulating the establishment of the PRC. On October 1, the telegram was sent in the Panchen Lama's name; besides congratulating the PRC, it expressed the Panchen Lama's desire to return to a liberated Tibet. Beijing did not answer the Panchen Lama's message immediately but sent intelligence officers to Xining to investigate. Then, on November 23, Beijing communicated with the Panchen Lama, promising to "heed the Tibetan people's aspiration" and make Tibet a "member of the great family of new China." The message was published simultaneously in the *People's Daily*.[70] Thus began a long and tumultuous partnership between the tenth Panchen Lama and Beijing.

In the fall of 1949, the CCP contacted the Panchen Lama, not for implementing Mao's political solution of the Tibetan question but to seek his cooperation as political leverage or justification to facilitate the PLA's march into Tibet. Mao's military planning for Tibet preceded his response to the Panchen Lama's pledge of allegiance. On October 10, 1949, Mao cabled Wang Zhen, commander of the First Army Corps of the First Field Army: "The task of your military advance includes marching into Tibet and liberating northern Tibet."[71] This is the first known evidence that Mao included Tibet in the operational plan of the PLA.

"Dreams of a Long Night"

Actually, Mao changed his mind a few times about whether the northwestern or the southwestern branch of the PLA should spearhead the advance into Tibet, which had much to do with the newly achieved urgency of the Tibetan question in Beijing's agenda. In mid-November and early December, Zhou Enlai talked twice with Soviet ambassador Nikolai Roshchin. On these occasions, Zhou indicated that the PLA planned to eliminate KMT forces in Sichuan by January 1950. After Sichuan and Xikang were liberated, the PLA would immediately enter Tibet. In the meantime, the PLA's landing on Hainan Island was planned for March, and the offensive for liberating Taiwan was planned for the summer of 1950. Zhou remarked that the battles for Tibet and Hainan Island would be easy but the one for Taiwan could be very difficult.[72] The hitherto unhurriedness in CCP leaders' deliberation about the Tibetan question was thus replaced by a sense of urgency. Yet the reason CCP leaders switched their priorities between Taiwan and Tibet lay in the east. In late October, in trying to take a small offshore island named Jinmen (aka Quemoy), the PLA suffered its first serious setback in the Chinese Civil War. After the defeat, Mao warned PLA commanders sternly against impatience and underestimation of the enemy.[73] The battle of Jinmen exposed the PLA's lack of naval and air power and experience in amphibious operations. Clearly, Taiwan would be a much harder nut to crack than Tibet.

As to the CCP leaders' newly gained sense of urgency about Tibet, the July incident may have been one of the reasons for abandoning their initially unhurried political approach. On the other hand, the September editorial's accusation of "imperialist plots" may not have been convincing even to CCP leaders themselves. There is no evidence they were aware of any specific foreign plot about Tibet that required immediate action. For instance, in late October 1949, at the first meeting of the People's Revolutionary Commission of Military Affairs, Mao evaluated China's external security situation and identified eastern China as the anti-imperialist frontline. In outlining military preparations against imperialism, Mao mentioned a line in eastern China that connected Guangzhou, Shanghai, Qingdao, Tianjin, and the railroad between Beijing and Shenyang. Seeing Shanghai and Tianjin as "our two centers in dealing with imperialism," Mao assigned the task of taking these cities to the Third Field Army, which was also responsible for taking Taiwan. As for western China, Mao assigned the southwestern and northwestern frontiers separately to Deng Xiaoping's Second and Peng Dehuai's First Field Armies. Mao expected that "by this winter the entire Southwest will be liberated except Kunming [of Yunnan]." Notably, Mao's usage of the term *Xinan* (Southwest) still did not include Tibet, whereas he did include Xinjiang in *Xibei* (Northwest).[74]

Mao's eastward attention was corroborated by CCP intelligence at the time. In mid-November, Li Kenong, chief of the Intelligence Department of the People's Revolutionary Commission of Military Affairs, informed Soviet ambassador Roshchin that the Americans were waging espionage and subversive activities against the new China. Allegedly, the center of American espionage against China had now moved from the mainland to Hong Kong, and all the subversive activities focused on undermining Sino-Soviet friendship and China's new systems. American spies in China were mainly Chinese who had resided in the United States, the Philippines, and Japan, or had received education in the West. Some merchants from trading companies based in Hong Kong, Japan, and South Korea were actually American spies, and some missionaries and underworld organizations engaged in subversive activities under American direction.[75]

Yet suddenly, on December 9, when traveling by train to Moscow to hold his historic meeting with Stalin, Mao sent a letter to the CCP Central Committee and the Southwest Bureau, calling urgently for action on Tibet:

> Since both India and the United States were making plans about Tibet, determination on liberation of Tibet should now be made. An early military advance into Tibet is better than a late one lest a long night bring about many dreams [*ye chang meng duo*, or a long delay means trouble].[76]

Mao's letter is mysterious because, allegedly, the original letter and the CCP Central Committee's cable transmitting its content to the Southwest Bureau are both lost. Only a paraphrased version, cited above, was restored many years later from recollections of some senior PLA officers who, in mid-January 1950, learned about Mao's letter from Liu Bocheng and Deng Xiaoping.[77]

What "dream" or "dreams" did Mao want to avoid? In late 1949, the internal security significance of the Tibetan frontier was comparable to the KMT-CCP contest for the Tibetan-Yi corridor during the Long March, but with the two sides' positions switched. As Mao was traveling to Moscow, the Second Field Army, recently reinforced by the Eighteenth Army Corps from North China, was completing an encirclement of the KMT's last main force in the mainland, some three hundred thousand troops under Hu Zongnan in northern Sichuan.[78] At the time, the CCP leadership had intelligence about Chiang Kai-shek's instruction for Hu to retreat westward into Xikang and, if necessary, Tibet. Chiang's plan did not materialize. Before his force was annihilated in late December, Hu Zongnan escaped to Taiwan by air. In December, therefore, a scenario must have been close to Mao's mind that some KMT troops might flee into Tibet and complicate Beijing's Tibetan question.[79] Yet Mao's letter showed that his concern was mainly about external influence.

In late 1949, there were indeed obscure American activities in China's inner Asian frontiers. The question is when Beijing learned about these activities and how CCP leaders made sense of them. One such case was the Mackiernan episode. In early December, Zhou Enlai received a report from Wang Zhen that the British consul was still in Tihua (Urumqi) but the American vice-consul Douglas Mackiernan had left suddenly on September 26, and his whereabouts were unclear. Wang's headquarters of the First Army Corps arrived in Tihua on November 6. He did not seem to pay attention to the whereabouts of Western diplomats until Burhan, provisional chair of the Xinjiang People's Government, brought the matter to his attention a month later. Zhou instructed Wang to watch the British closely but did not seem able to comprehend the meaning of Mackiernan's departure.[80] Only in late January 1950 did the Chinese press begin to accuse Mackiernan as a spy because of his contacts with Osman Bator, an anticommunist Kazak warlord in Xinjiang. At the time, Mackiernan and his small party were making an arduous journey toward Lhasa. On April 29, shortly after entering Tibet, he was killed by the first group of Tibetan border guards that detected his party.[81] This chronology shows that the Mackiernan episode could not have been the cause of Mao's anxiety about "American plans" for Tibet.

The only development that might have alarmed Mao about possible American interference in Tibet was the visit by American journalist Lowell Thomas and his son in August and September 1949. The Thomases' activities in Tibet emerged through a series of reports in the *New York Times* between late September and early December. The first report, which appeared in the September 26 issue, indicated that Lowell Thomas had been carried out of Tibet on a litter after being injured "in a mishap while crossing a 17,000-foot-high pass in the Himalayas." The U.S. Air Force helped retrieve him by sending a rescue plane to the Tibetan border. In the ensuing reports, the *Times* revealed that the Thomases had met with the young Dalai Lama and a number of Tibetan officials. To the American visitors, the Tibetans asserted Tibetan independence and requested foreign support for Tibet's resistance against communist invasion. The Dalai Lama also asked Thomas to deliver written and oral messages to President Harry Truman and Secretary of State Dean Acheson. According to the *New York Times*, although the U.S. government had always regarded Tibet as part of China, the recent CCP victory became a new factor in diplomatic thinking. Reluctant to discuss the Tibetan issue in public, State Department officials nevertheless conceded that Tibet was in a "most strategic position." The last *New York Times* piece on the Thomas episode appeared on December 2. It paraphrased a Soviet press commentary that the Thomas trip to Tibet was part of an American-British "dirty adventure to detach Tibet from China and establish it as a colony and military base directed against the new Chinese Government."[82]

The *New York Times* reporting was surely noticed in Beijing. In those years, the Xinhua News Agency had a function of collecting information from foreign and KMT presses for CCP leaders' reference. After Germany attacked the Soviet Union in 1941, the agency added to its organization two branches responsible for translating news in English and Japanese, respectively. The *New York Times* was one of the major sources of information for the CCP, and it would continue to play a significant role in CCP policymaking in the years to come.[83] As CCP leaders were watching Tibet closely, relevant reporting by the *New York Times* could hardly have escaped Xinhua's screening. The Soviet commentary cited in the *New York Times* came from a Soviet weekly named *New Times*, which was frequently cited by the *New York Times* as an "authoritative foreign affairs journal" of the Soviet Union.[84] The gist of the commentary could either have been fed to the Soviets by Beijing or been conceived by Moscow pundits. Either way, given the emerging Beijing-Moscow alliance, the view was probably shared between the two communist capitals.

The commentary, however, reflected a communist perception more than Western intentions. Hugh E. Richardson, ex-officer in charge of the British mission in Lhasa who had stayed on after 1947 as head of the Indian mission, met with Lowell Thomas in Lhasa. Richardson believed that Thomas, having little background knowledge about Asian affairs and knowing nothing about the official U.S. policy of treating Tibet as part of China, was out of his league in encouraging the Tibetans to seek American aid for their independence cause. The Indian authorities, while disclaiming any active role in arranging the Thomas trip, believed that "Mr. Thomas had opened vistas of large scale American assistance and had probably led the Tibetans up the garden path."[85] The U.S. Department of State was able to get some valuable firsthand information about Tibet, such as the size of the Tibetan army and the unhindered reception in Lhasa of the Voice of America's English programs, by debriefing Thomas after his return to the United States. But in respect to Lhasa's request for arms and American diplomatic support, the department's view was that "it was now too late to get any arms to Tibet in time to be of any use and that to recognize Tibet's independence at this stage would merely be indecent as far as the Chinese Nationalist Government was concerned and provocative as far as the communists were concerned."[86] As the fourteenth Dalai Lama recalled many years later, in 1949 "the Tibetan government considered Lowell Thomas to be a very important person in the American government. But actually, he was just a broadcast journalist."[87] The Thomas visit, despite the official attention it aroused in several capitals, was therefore a private adventure, not a step in any American official scheme.[88]

The Thomas episode was nonetheless consequential as far as Beijing was concerned. Following closely on the July incident, the Thomas episode was alarming enough to cause Mao to reconsider his timetable for settling the Tibetan question. As the historian A. Tom Grunfeld points out, to Beijing, the Thomas visit and similar foreign interests in Tibet served as "sufficient circumstantial evidence to clearly demonstrate foreign involvement."[89] At the time, CCP leaders indeed could only have such circumstantial evidence as far as Tibet was concerned, and the CCP's intelligence apparatus was inconsistent about "imperialist" activities in the area. For instance, a report by the Intelligence Department of the CCP Central Military Commission, dated January 1950, stated: "In Tibet American imperialism does not have permanent personnel or organizations and has little connections with the Tibetans," and that, aside from some known American visitors in Tibet during World War II, "there has been no discovery of American imperialist activities in Tibet." Yet, shortly thereafter, the same agency used information collected from the Western press as evidence of "British and American special agents' aggressive ambition toward Tibet." Most of the information was about Western missionaries' attempts to enter Tibet reported in Western newspapers in late 1949. The information, however, did mention a British radio operator named Bob Ford in Chamdo and American writer Lowell Thomas as "the only foreigners who entered deeply into the barren land [of Tibet]."[90] At the time, in the CCP's understanding of international politics informed by class-struggle doctrine, which lumped together Western governments, businesses, missionaries, press and so on as hostile bourgeoisie, it did not really matter whether Thomas and his son went to Tibet on their own or as agents of the U.S. government. The fact was that a high-profile spokesman of American imperialism had entered and exited Tibet freely. It was enough to give Mao nightmares.[91]

As far as the relationship between Tibet and China's central authorities was concerned, 1949 marked the end of the latter's vacillations and ineffectual claim-making since 1911. In 1949, the CCP took power as a political-military movement whose speed, directions, and stops were set by brief and crisp communications among a small number of top CCP leaders. It is remarkable that a short letter from Mao in December 1949 set in motion grave policy steps toward Tibet. The process was typical of the time of the Chinese Civil War, however. Mao's decision was made in battleground fashion: one commander's instinct, anxiety, range of knowledge, and resolve would decide a vital step with all kinds of possible consequences.

In 1949 and 1950, Mao made another hasty decision that would have serious consequences for the CCP's handling of the Tibetan question. It concerned assigning responsibilities to regional CCP branches. Earlier in 1949, when still considering Tibet a "unique situation" to be handled patiently, Mao wanted to assign the Tibet task to the Second Field Army and the Southwest Bureau under Liu Bocheng and Deng Xiaoping. In a mid-June message to Stalin, Mao discussed this plan but estimated that the Tibetan question would probably not be settled until 1951. For PLA commanders in the field, Tibet entered their mental map only slowly. In a September message to Mao, Deng reported that after a recent political mobilization, troops of the Second Field Army had overcome some erroneous thoughts and were now quite enthusiastic about the prospect of advancing into and settling down in the Southwest. Previously, many troops had been reluctant to enter the remote, mountainous, and impoverished Southwest, believing that the Second Field Army had already endured extraordinary hardships in making special contributions to the "war of liberation." By "Southwest," however, Deng did not mean to include Tibet.[92] In late September, Deng came to Beijing to participate in the inauguration ceremony of the PRC. On October 10, he attended a CCP Central Committee meeting and discussed with Mao troop deployment in the Southwest. Three days later, Mao informed Peng Dehuai that the Second Field Army and the Eighteenth Army Corps under He Long, six hundred thousand troops in total, would operate in Yunnan, Guizhou, Sichuan, Xikang, *and* Tibet.[93] Mao's communication with Peng was logical because, aside from being the top official in charge of the Northwest and the First Field Army, Peng was also the second in command of the PLA. Curiously, Mao's communication with Peng was not a result of his consultation with Deng in Beijing. Later, Deng would assert categorically that the Second Field Army and the Southwest Bureau did not receive the Tibet assignment until early January 1950.[94]

Indeed, given that the Second Field Army was explicitly reluctant to enter the Southwest, not to mention Tibet, and that major battles with KMT forces were yet to be fought in that part of China, Mao quickly changed his mind and decided to assign Tibet to Peng Dehuai in the Northwest. By the end of October, the PLA wound up large-scale operations in the Northwest, which gave Mao confidence that it was time to take concrete steps on Tibet. On November 23, Mao sent out his long-delayed reply to the Panchen Lama's October 1 telegram. On the same day, Mao cabled Peng, enjoining the Northwest Bureau to assume the main responsibility for advancing militarily into Tibet while the Southwest Bureau would play an assistant role. Mao listed three reasons for this decision: the war had ended in the Northwest earlier than in the Southwest; the road from Qinghai to Tibet was supposedly easy to travel; and the Panchen Lama was in the Northwest. Mao wanted to take Tibet by the fall or winter of 1950, advancing the original timetable by at least a year. In the meantime, although replacing the Southwest Bureau with the Northwest Bureau as the main executioner of the Tibet operation, Mao gave Peng only a military role to play. In his telegram to Peng, Mao stressed: "The Tibetan question cannot be solved without using force. Of course, the military advance will not be made solely from the Northwest, and the Southwest will also send troops. After settling the situation of Sichuan and Xikang, the Southwest Bureau will begin to manage Tibet."[95] Thus, Mao's plan for a coordination between CCP's northwestern and southwestern branches was a division of labor between military and administrative responsibilities.

In the short run, Mao's idea about the division of labor made good sense. The different military paces in the Northwest and the Southwest meant that Peng's troops could make a move toward Tibet sooner than Deng's. And since the Northwest already shouldered the administrative responsibility for Xinjiang and Qinghai, and since geopolitically Tibet fell into the realm of the Southwest, the administrative task should logically go to Deng Xiaoping's rather than Peng Dehuai's quarters. The contrast between the personalities of Deng and Peng in their historical relations with Mao was between a tough and innovative executive and an outspoken and independent-minded general. Historically, the geostrategic difference between the Southwest and the Northwest was that the former had served as an inner frontier shielding Chinese provinces and the latter had been part of the "wild domains" either isolated from or posing challenges to China's central authorities. While it can only be speculated how these personnel and geopolitical factors weighed in Mao's decision, historical research can nevertheless reveal that the power structure of the CCP did not at all rid itself of the emperor-versus-provincial-governor type of tensions that had run through Chinese history.[96]

The official chronicle of Deng's life published in China indicates that Deng saw Mao's November 23 telegram. In early December, as Mao was aboard his train to Moscow, Deng and associates were in the thick of annihilating Hu Zongnan's forces around Chengdu, Sichuan, and probably not thinking much, if at all, of Tibet.[97] Then, suddenly, Mao's December 9 letter came via the CCP Central Committee. Apparently, Mao addressed the letter to his comrades both in Beijing and in the Southwest. On December 5, the day before Mao left Beijing for Moscow, in contradiction to Mao's November 23 telegram, Zhou Enlai informed the Soviet ambassador that the PLA would not advance into Tibet until the operations in the Southwest ended.[98] So, even after Mao instructed Peng to start preparations for entering Tibet from the Northwest, apparently neither adequate consultations nor consensus existed among leaders in Beijing about the timeline and task assignments. Mao's letter may therefore have been intended first to convince his comrades in Beijing that a move toward Tibet should no longer be delayed and that the Northwest Bureau was in position to act now. Meanwhile, since the Southwest Bureau had already been alerted about the Tibet task and since Mao was aware of the morale problems of the Second Field Army, he might have felt it necessary to explain his thought more clearly to Deng and associates. He wanted CCP officials in the Southwest to understand why part of the Second Field Army had to shoulder the Tibet task, which was definitely much tougher than any of their previous tasks. That was why Mao's letter took the form of suasion and conveyed emphatically Mao's own anxiety about the Tibetan situation. The letter proved contagious, and Mao's sense of urgency would soon become pandemic among CCP officials fighting for the Tibetan-Yi corridor.

Curiously, though assigning the military part of the Tibet task to Peng Dehuai, Mao did not include the Northwest Bureau among the recipients of his letter. Peng had his own ideas about Tibet. After investigating and studying the Tibetan question for more than a month, Peng came to Beijing and reported to the CCP Central Committee on December 30. In Peng's opinion, a military advance into Tibet from the Northwest could not be accomplished according to Mao's timetable.[99] In Moscow, Mao learned about Peng's protestation but would not change his timetable. On December 31, the CCP Central Committee issued a "Letter to All Compatriots and Troops in the Frontlines," publicly naming Taiwan, Hainan Island, *and* Tibet as Chinese territories to be liberated in 1950.[100]

However, the CCP leadership could not dismiss Peng's opinion lightly. Peng's report was originally authored by Fan Ming, an official responsible for the united-front work of the Northwest Bureau. In drafting the report, Fan was assisted by a "Tibetan seminar" including a number of Tibetan intellectuals from Gansu. In focusing on the terrain and conditions of the roads into Tibet, the report presented to Mao this conclusion: entering Tibet from Qinghai and Xinjiang would encounter insurmountable difficulties, but the two roads from Sichuan would be much easier. Allegedly, "if the task of entering Tibet is assigned to the Northwest, troops and supplies must be assembled in Hetian, Yutian [both in Xinjiang] and Yulshul [Yushu of Qinghai], roads must be built, and the preparations for entering Tibet will need two years to complete." Decades later, Fan Ming would reveal in his memoir a so-called historical reasoning behind the report: no one in history had succeeded in entering Tibet militarily from the northwestern direction, and therefore the direction was a military taboo.[101]

Fan Ming's arguments about the "insurmountable" difficulties of the Qinghai road were exaggerations, to say the least, and his fear of bad luck based on military history was simply misinformed. During the first century of the Qing dynasty, Qing officials did enter Tibet by an ancient route via Qinghai that had existed since the time of the Tang dynasty. Then, during the eighteenth century, the Qing government strengthened its connections with Tibet and maintained three routes into the region, from Qinghai, Sichuan, and Yunnan, respectively.

According to Wei Yuan, since the Qinghai route went through a vast stretch of grassland inhabited by Mongolian tribes, Qing officials preferred to enter Tibet from the direction of Sichuan. In 1941, Wu Zhongxin, chair of the Mongolian and Tibetan Affairs Commission of the KMT regime, traveled to Lhasa to attend the enthronement of the fourteenth Dalai Lama. He reported afterward that there were four routes to enter Tibet, two from Sichuan and Xikang, one from Qinghai, and one from Yunnan. All these were arduous passages and would need two and a half months to reach Lhasa, but merchants from Peiping (Beijing), Gansu, and Yunnan preferred respectively the routes from Qinghai and Yunnan. In January 1950, the Intelligence Department of the CCP Central Military Affairs Commission basically agreed with Wu's assessment, suggesting that the road from Yulshul of Qinghai to Nagqu (Heihe) of Tibet was an easier road to Lhasa and that, all things considered, a two-pronged advance from Qinghai and Xikang was militarily necessary and historically practiced.[102] Interestingly, in December 1949, when assessing the prospect of a communist invasion of Tibet, the British Foreign Office also got information suggesting that PLA troops might use the easier route through Jyekundo, the old name for the capital town of Yulshul, but not that through Chamdo.[103] As for military history, the Khoshot Mongols had invaded Tibet from Qinghai after the sixteenth century, and the Qing army also entered Tibet several times from Qinghai in the Kangxi-Qianlong years. Fukang'an's expedition against the Gurkhas in the early 1790s used the Qinghai route and left a spectacular military record in Qing history.[104] Factually, the Peng-Fan protestation of 1949 was far from an ironclad case.

After receiving Peng's objection, however, Mao did not contest the point but simply returned to his original idea of assigning the task of occupying Tibet to the Second Field Army in the Southwest, which had just concluded the Battle of Chengdu and would continue to clear KMT forces out of Yunnan and Xikang in the next three months. Still in Moscow, on January 2, 1950, Mao sent a telegram to the CCP Central Committee to transmit Peng's report to officials in the Southwest. Directing southwestern officials to study the report, Mao nevertheless stressed in his telegram: "Even without a big population, Tibet occupies an extremely important international position. We must occupy the land and reform it into a people's democratic Tibet."[105] Notably, throughout the "war of liberation," the CCP leadership did not designate any other territory, not even Taiwan, for "liberation" because of its "international position."

In swallowing Peng's grievances about "insurmountable difficulties" that the Northwest Bureau would face, Mao decided finally to assign both the military and political responsibilities for Tibet to the Southwest Bureau. However, as will be discussed in chapter 2, the shared-responsibility formula was not completely abandoned. Now, Mao wanted troops to begin marching into Tibet in mid-May and to occupy the entire region by October 1950.[106] When Mao's telegram arrived at the Southwest Bureau, people there, in Deng's words, were so busy with taking over Chongqing that "everyone is out of breath." But they managed to answer Mao in less than a week, "agreeing completely that entire Tibet be occupied by September of this year." Deng chose Zhang Guohua and his Eighteenth Army for the task.[107] Thus, forty years after the Qing court sent troops into Tibet for the last time, and eight years after Chiang Kai-shek planned for a military invasion, a military expedition aimed at Lhasa was afoot again.[108]

✳ ✳ ✳

At the end of 1949, the CCP Central Committee sent a message to the country, pledging to liberate Tibet along with Taiwan and Hainan Island in order to "eliminate the last remnants of the Chiang Kai-shek bandits, to complete the cause of unifying China, and to deny the aggressive force of American imperialism any foothold in our territories."[109] In one stroke, Tibet was identified as a battleground for three "wars"—the oldest one over the geo-body of the Chinese nation, the recent one over the political destiny of the Chinese society, and the newest one over the international alignment of the Chinese state, or the Cold War.

In *The Resurgence of East Asia*, a group of leading scholars in East Asian studies propose that the trajectory of East Asian development be evaluated in three "temporalities," or three perspectives, covering 500 years, 150 years, and 50 years, respectively.[110] Such a multitemporality approach is beneficial to all historical investigations. In considering the attributes of the Tibetan question in modern times, the four timescapes discussed in the introduction to this study covered 250, 100, 40, and 5 years, respectively, as of 1950. Thus, when Beijing decided to replace its patient political approach to Tibet with an urgent military agenda, this change of mind was not due merely to those incidents, personalities, and the domestic and international circumstances of the late 1940s. The Sino-Tibetan relationship entered a precarious new era because several old and recent threads of historical developments converged. That is, when the CCP picked up the geopolitical landscaping and territoriality transformation from its Manchu and Nationalist predecessors, pushed resolutely its brand of sociopolitical revolution into all purportedly Chinese territories, and entered the Cold War as an opponent to the predominantly Western international order, Tibet began to lose its luxurious status quo as a peaceful land of the Buddha. The next chapter details how, having decided to use military force to awe Lhasa, CCP leaders developed a set of stratagems designed to cajole the Tibetan ruling elites to follow their lead.

CHAPTER 2

THE "DALAI LINE"

In the sixteenth century, Niccolo Machiavelli of Italy gave power holders some pragmatic advice on how to control newly acquired states that had different languages, customs, and laws. Among the various types of states that would require different ways of controlling, Machiavelli identified "ecclesiastical principalities." These, according to Machiavelli,

> are sustained by the ancient ordinances of religion, which are so all-powerful, and of such a character that the principalities may be held no matter how their princes behave and live. These princes alone have states and do not defend them; and they have subjects and do not rule them; and the states, although unguarded, are not taken from them, and the subjects, although not ruled, do not care, and they have neither the desire nor the ability to alienate themselves.[1]

In the middle of the twentieth century, Tibet seemed one of few places in the world that to some extent met this peculiar Machiavellian qualification. In 1950, the newly founded Communist power in China was poised to acquire Tibet, a land that had lived under the "ancient ordinances of religion" for centuries and outside the political influence of China in the previous decades.

In contrast to what constituted political control in Machiavelli's time, Beijing intended not just to hold Tibet but also to bring a set of new political and social systems to the Himalayan country, which would eventually mean overturning the ancient Tibetan theocracy. Mao Zedong characterized Beijing's Tibetan policy in the 1950s as *xian li hou bing, bing hou you li* (peaceful means before resorting to force, and peaceful means again after using force).[2] The actual events occurred this way: In 1950, Beijing first used force to coerce the Tibetan government to negotiate a settlement in a seventeen-point "Agreement on Steps for Peaceful Liberation of Tibet," concluded in May 1951. Then came a period of relative peace in Tibet as well as in areas of Sichuan, Gansu, and Qinghai where ethnic Tibetans were concentrated. Next, in the mid-1950s, a reform war in the Tibetan areas of western Sichuan had an impact on Tibet and other neighboring provinces. Finally, when a revolt broke out in Lhasa in March 1959, Beijing used force again over the next few years to establish total control of Tibet. The struggle between Beijing and its Tibetan opponents was simultaneously over domestic and international security, sovereignty, social changes, and international alignment.

This chapter considers how, in the early 1950s, the CCP leadership, despite its accumulated political acumen and experiences, struggled to introduce Communist as well as Chinese influence into Tibet within the frame of the Seventeen-Point Agreement. With limited knowledge about Tibet, Beijing sought to use the Tibetan establishment centered around the Dalai Lama to infiltrate Tibetan society. The goal was eventually to win over the minds and hearts of the Tibetan "laboring masses." This delicate and ultimately class-based stratagem was marred from the outset by a scheming calculation, at various levels of the CCP, that the Panchen Lama, supposedly more "patriotic" and willing to collaborate with Beijing, could be used to undermine or pressure the current Tibetan theocracy, enabling the CCP to achieve its revolutionary goals more easily. During the first few years of the PRC, this constant "second opinion," along with a quarrel-prone bureaucratic setup of the CCP apparatus and a disposition to micromanage Tibetan affairs, made Beijing's efforts in Tibet a bumpy process.

Envisioning a "Bridge"

On October 6, 1950, the Eighteenth Army of the People's Liberation Army (PLA) under General Zhang Guohua started the Battle of Chamdo. By crossing the Jinsha River, the de facto divide between Chinese and Tibetan political influence, the Chinese Communist force officially entered Tibet. This happened thirteen days before Chinese troops entered the Korean War by crossing the Yalu River—a much more familiar episode in Cold War history. Over the next eighteen days, the Eighteenth Army had more than twenty engagements with the Tibetan army and killed, wounded, and captured about 5,700 Tibetan troops. Lhasa's effort to block the PLA invasion failed, and negotiations between Beijing and Lhasa followed.

Before advancing toward Lhasa, troops of the Eighteenth Army went through the usual preoperation political mobilization. They learned that they were going to attack "a small number of Tibetan feudal rulers," who were conspiring with British and American imperialists to sell out the motherland and permanently enslave the Tibetan people.[3] After the Battle of Chamdo, Liu Shaoqi, the emerging number two leader of the CCP, proclaimed: "The Battle of Chamdo had the similar significance as the Huaihai Campaign [of the Chinese Civil War in 1948–49], and it laid the foundation for liberating Tibet. The Tibetan revolution is a continuation of the Chinese revolution and an inevitable result of struggles between two classes."[4] Yet afterwards, the CCP neither agitated for a "Tibetan revolution" nor pursued class struggle in Tibetan society. Because Beijing's aim was to use military leverage to seek a political solution of the Tibetan question, before the Battle of Chamdo Mao Zedong cautioned the CCP's propaganda apparatus against using words that might be considered offensive to the Tibetan ruling circles.[5] After the battle, Zhang Guohua found himself explaining to his officers that now they had to implement a "lenient" policy toward lamas and feudal aristocrats who, in other circumstances, might well be considered "class enemies." The reason, according to Zhang, was that the Tibetan question was a *minzu wenti*, or "nationality question," and unless the PLA worked with *shangceng*, or the upper strata of Tibetan society, and used them as a "bridge" to reach the masses, the PLA would not be able to take root in Tibet.[6]

The instrumental role assigned to the Tibetan power establishment was essential to Beijing's Tibetan policy in the 1950s. Though unique, this policy was not completely out of sync with Beijing's nationwide orientation in the early years of the PRC. Starting as a state based on the Marxist notion of class struggle as well as on anti-imperialism, during its formative years the PRC went through a period of relative moderation dubbed New Democracy and did not fully display the sharp edge of class struggle. In this period, the CCP leadership sought to promote multiclass cooperation using a seemingly inclusive conception, "people," which was officially defined to include workers, farmers, petty bourgeoisie, and "national bourgeoisie." Those excluded from the "people" category were "bureaucratic bourgeoisie," landlords, and other counterrevolutionary elements. These "non-people" groups were still "citizens" of the new China but had to reform themselves before being accepted into the "people." When extended to non-Han communities, and especially those frontier regions of single or multiple *shaoshu minzu*, or "minority nationalities," this "people's republic" was promoted as a "great family of various nationalities' friendly cooperation."[7] According to Zhou Enlai, premier of the PRC, this differed from all previous unifications in Chinese history because it was "unification by the people," not by the people's oppressors. A question, therefore, was whether the upper classes of the non-Han "nationalities" should be excluded from this "people's unification."[8] At the time, Beijing considered all Tibetan social classes, "oppressors" and "oppressed" alike, as part of the "Chinese people."

In conceptualizing a new Chinese state, CCP leaders had gone through an intellectual journey from accepting to rejecting the Chinese nationalist notion that China's ancient tributary system was morally superior to Western colonialism in dealing with weak peoples. Mao Zedong was typical in this regard. In his early education, Mao subscribed to the idea that imperial China had always treated its dependencies generously. But by the late 1930s, when China sank into a deep national crisis, Mao clearly stated that, in dealing with minority nationalities, the "old approach of controlling with mollification and loose rein" (*huairou jimi de lao banfa*) could no longer work. Instead, he offered the formula of a unitary state in which all "nationalities" enjoyed equal rights.[9] During China's war against Japan, the CCP suspended its ideological commitment to the Leninist principle of a right to self-determination for minority nationalities in favor of a centralizing Chinese nationalism. In fact, Mao was always opposed to applying the principle of self-determination to Tibet, which, he believed, could only benefit British imperialism.[10]

At the beginning of 1950, in deciding to take Tibet as soon as possible, Mao wanted to achieve two things: first, to "occupy the land," and second, to "reform it into a people's democratic Tibet," sociopolitically abreast with the rest of the PRC.[11] As discussed in the previous chapter, Mao's decision was motivated by a perceived imminent threat from the outside. Meanwhile, the reformation of Tibetan society was a long-term goal. An ethnopolitical tie between China's Tibetan and Mongolian affairs resurfaced, but not in the military/religious sense of the Qing time. Rather, Beijing intended to use the Inner Mongolian Autonomous Region as a model for all China's ethnic frontiers, including Tibet. "Regional autonomy for minority nationalities" was first entered into the Common Program of 1949 as a general policy and then, in 1951, was included in the Seventeen-Point Agreement.

Inner Mongolia was an "autonomous region" in the sense that its regional leadership was Mongolian, but the leadership was completely in line with Beijing in implementing "democratic" and "socialist" changes in the region. Having gone through waves of spontaneous and partisan movements for autonomy during the first half of the twentieth century, by 1949 Inner Mongolia had already been channeled into the orbit of the Chinese Communist movement. Ulanhu, the highest ranking Inner Mongolian member of the CCP, until his dismissal from office at the beginning of Mao's Cultural Revolution in the mid-1960s, would continue to act as the spokesman simultaneously for Inner Mongols in the PRC and for CCP policies in Inner Mongolia.[12] At the beginning of the PRC, Inner Mongolia began to go through radical changes that, according to Ulanhu, would eventually abolish all privileges of feudal classes and lamas.[13] The model of Inner Mongolia, however, was useful for the

CCP's Tibetan enterprise only in the long run. Tibet had not been infiltrated by Chinese Communism, nor did it have a powerful native partisan force that was willing to collaborate with the CCP. Channeling the region and its people into the CCP orbit would have to follow a path rather different from that of Inner Mongolia.

The CCP's search for a Tibetan path to national integration began at the local level. Mao's formula for shared responsibility between the CCP's Northwest and Southwest Bureaus led to separate investigations of Tibetan affairs by CCP apparatuses in Qinghai and the Sichuan-Xikang region. Starting in November 1949, Fan Ming's study group, or "Tibetan seminar," under the Northwest Bureau, worked closely with the CCP Central Committee's intelligence personnel in the Northwest.[14] In the Southwest, the Eighteenth Army set up an Office for Studying Policies Toward the Tibetan Question. Wang Qimei, deputy commissar of the Eighteenth Army, was in charge of that office, which included some of China's best scholars in Tibetan studies.[15] In Chongqing and Chengdu, some of the leading officials of the Southwest Bureau, including Liu Bocheng and He Long, conducted interviews with scholars, Buddhist monks, and former KMT officials to learn about Tibetan affairs.[16]

Lacking an authoritative CCP figure in Tibetan affairs similar to Ulanhu in Inner Mongolia, the CCP leadership prepared its Tibetan policy by tapping into two rather different sources of information: one was a set of perceptions closely associated with the Panchen Lama group that had sat in Qinghai and borne a grudge against Lhasa for decades; the other was modern Chinese scholarship on Tibet that had become concentrated in Sichuan during China's war against Japan.[17] As a result, Beijing received different policy suggestions from its two regional bureaus. The disagreement on Tibetan affairs between Fan Ming's group in the Northwest and the Eighteenth Army in the Southwest would soon become entangled in Beijing's management of Tibetan affairs and cause enormous turbulence in Tibetan policy.[18]

Initially, Beijing contemplated using the Panchen Lama in Qinghai to facilitate its Tibetan enterprise. As discussed in chapter 1, Mao Zedong, out of a sense of urgency, initiated a strategic scheme for moving the PLA into Tibet from the Northwest. The Panchen Lama and his entourage, alienated from Lhasa, presented a ready political asset to the CCP. In the fall of 1949, when Mao's directive on protecting and respecting the Panchen Lama reached Peng Dehuai's headquarters, CCP officials in the Northwest understood it as a strategic decision for solving the Tibetan question.[19] The decision was so important that it was conveyed to the Soviets. At the end of 1949, when conversing with the Soviet chargé d'affaires P. A. Shibaev, Liu Shaoqi talked about the PLA's pending advance into Tibet. From this conversation, Shibaev learned that the CCP was using the Panchen Lama in Qinghai to foment religious discord within Tibet and weaken Lhasa's influence in Ngari, the northwestern part of neighboring Xinjiang.[20] Liu also learned something from his conversation with Shibaev. The next day, he cabled Peng Dehuai and the Northwestern Bureau: "The Panchen [Lama] will be very important to our solution of the Tibetan question. Soviet comrades advised us to pay close attention to not allowing the Panchen [Lama] to be poisoned to death."[21]

This northwestern stratagem was soon tabled as Mao, in early 1950, changed his mind about the division of labor between the Northwest and Southwest Bureaus and reassign the Tibet task to the latter. As a result, the Sichuan-Xikang milieu became the principal intellectual ground from which CCP policymakers would obtain their initial knowledge and ideas about how to handle the Tibetan question. Among senior CCP officials in the Southwest, He Long, who had been transferred from the Northwest to the Southwest in late 1949 and ranked number three after Liu Bocheng and Deng Xiaoping, was the first to question the wisdom of using the Panchen Lama to upset the extant Tibetan establishment. In January 1950, He Long pointed out to the CCP leadership in Beijing:

> Whereas the Dalai [Lama] is the highest leader of the government, the Panchen [Lama] is in charge of some of the monasteries. The Panchen [Lama] has the same kind of influence as the Dalai [Lama] in Lamaism [*lamajiao*], but in term of political power he is under the Dalai [Lama]'s leadership. . . . Politics, economy, and culture are all entangled with religion, and the situation is extremely complicated. The decisive key is whether or not the issue of religion can be handled properly. Therefore, we must be very cautious. It is generally believed that marching forward is easier than logistics in the rear, and military operation is easier than political settlement. The Kuomintang failed in Xikang and Tibet because it did not handle well the religious issue internal to the Tibetans. The issue cannot be settled at all by promoting a Panchen [Lama] who is not in Tibet.[22]

Starting with He Long's contention, a consensus soon emerged among CCP officials of the Southwest Bureau that the "Dalai clique" (*Dalai jituan*) should be the principal object of the CCP's work in Tibet.

He Long's report carried weight in Beijing as well. At the time, both Mao and Zhou Enlai were in Moscow negotiating with the Soviets for a treaty of alliance, leaving Liu Shaoqi in charge of the government's operations in Beijing. On January 22 and 24, Liu sent telegrams to both the Southwest and Northwest Bureaus. While still stressing the importance of "winning over" the Panchen Lama group, Liu admitted:

> Because we know very little about the internal situation of Tibet, we are not clear about the difference between the Dalai clique's and the Panchen clique's influence over the Tibetan people. Furthermore, since the KMT government

had over the years used the Panchen clique to counterbalance the Dalai clique, we need to be very cautious in taking practical steps to facilitate discords inside the reactionary power of Tibet in order to achieve the established goal of liberating Tibet.

Liu directed officials in the Southwest and Northwest to investigate further and then make suggestions to Beijing.[23]

In January 1950, Fan Ming's study group prepared what Fan would later claim to be the first CCP investigative report on political conditions in Tibet, titled "Organizations and Personnel of the Tibetan Government." The gist of the report was that the Dalai Lama and the Panchen Lama used to be heads of two separate theocracies in "Front Tibet" (*qianzang*) and "Rear Tibet" (*houzang*), respectively, and that the thirteenth Dalai Lama extended his control to "Rear Tibet" only after the ninth Panchen Lama was forced out of Tibet in the 1920s. In August, this view was conveyed to leaders in Beijing in a document titled "Steps for Tibetan Liberation and Plans for Political and Religious Organizations." In name, the document was prepared by representatives of the Panchen Lama group who were on their way to Beijing to pay their respects to the new Central People's Government. In reality, since the document was dispatched via Peng Dehuai's headquarters, Fan Ming was heavily involved in drafting the document, with Peng's endorsement. As envisioned in the document, the PLA should launch simultaneous attacks on Tibet from Yunnan, Sichuan, Qinghai, and Xinjiang. The Panchen Lama group would advance into Tibet along with PLA troops. After liberation, Tibet would be reorganized in one of these three ways:

1. Organize "Front Tibetan People's Government" under the Dalai [Lama], "Rear Tibetan People's Government" under the Panchen [Lama], and a Ngari administrative district under a "Tibetan People's Autonomous Committee" based in Gyantse [Jiangzi].
2. Organize a Tibetan coalition government in Gyantse to include the Chinese Communists, the Panchen [Lama], and the Dalai [Lama]; the Panchen [Lama] and the Dalai [Lama] would continue to preside over religious affairs in Rear and Front Tibet separately from Shigatse and Lhasa.
3. Divide Tibet into two autonomous regions separately under the CCP's Southwest and Northwest Bureaus; Front Tibet plus Chamdo would be administered by the Dalai [Lama] under the guidance of the Southwest Bureau, and Rear Tibet plus Ngari by the Panchen [Lama] under the Northwest Bureau.[24]

The key to all three proposals was the Panchen Lama's marching into Tibet along with the PLA and achieving a status equal to and parallel with that of the Dalai Lama, which would constitute a direct challenge to the status quo of Tibet and cause bitter grievances against Beijing. By this time, Lhasa had already conveyed its concerns to Beijing in at least two communications. In January 1950, the Tibetan "National Assembly" in Lhasa sent a message to the CCP authorities, stressing that

> the Tibetan people worship the Dalai Lama, and the Dalai Lama is the sole supporter and sacred leader of the Tibetan people. As long as he is in charge of the government, Tibet would be at peace internally, Tibetan people would enjoy happiness, and the problems between China and Tibet could be settled and friendship achieved in an amicable and glorious way.

Soon after, the Tibetan authorities issued an "or else" message via the airwaves:

> The clerical and secular people of Tibet are devoted to the successive Dalai Lamas and believe in them as the genuine Buddha.... The Tibetan people do not have any disagreement in religion as well as in politics and will strive as one and with their life for self-governance [*zizhu*].[25]

To avoid a head-on confrontation with Lhasa, Beijing would need a better set of ideas than that proposed by its Northwest officials. In March 1950, Wang Qimei's research office in the Southwest completed a series of lengthy position papers. These documents discussed issues that the Eighteenth Army would face when entering Tibet, and proposed political, economic, social, and foreign policy measures for administering Tibet afterwards. Among these, a paper titled "Preliminary Opinion on Various Policies Toward Tibet" proposed an approach different from the tactics favored by the Northwest. Before conditions in Tibet became ripe for reforms, the document contended, the current theocracy should continue. In the meantime, Beijing's leadership over Tibet could be realized through a military-administrative committee above the Tibetan government.[26] During the initial years of the PRC, military-administrative committees had been used as a transitional structure for establishing the CCP's military control of various territories. Where the formula of "peaceful liberation" was implemented, they were organized at provincial level, such as in Suiyuan and Hunan. More eye-catching, however, were those military-administrative committees that administered large regions encompassing several provinces. At the time, there were six such large regions—Northwest, Central South, Southwest, Northeast, East China, and North China—corresponding to the CCP Central Committee's regional bureaus and military regions.[27] The proposed military-administrative committee for Tibet would differ from these in keeping the extant Tibetan government system intact.

As for the thorny relationship between the Dalai Lama and the Panchen Lama, the "Opinion" disagreed completely with the Northwestern position:

> The Dalai [Lama] is the highest political and religious leader of the Tibetan people, enjoying supreme authority over and worship by the Tibetan people. We should therefore respect the Dalai [Lama]'s status. In the event that the Dalai [Lama] runs away once our troops enter Tibet, according to the Tibetan tradition the Panchen [Lama] must not replace the Dalai [Lama] lest such step cause major discords and Tibetan people's misgivings.... In Tibet, the Panchen [Lama] and the Dalai [Lama] are two top religious leaders, but the Panchen [Lama] does not interfere in government affairs and his religious status is also lower than the Dalai [Lama]'s. In the past the KMT reactionary government incited discords between the Dalai [Lama] and the Panchen [Lama] and tried to control Tibet by using the ninth Panchen [Lama] to oppose the thirteenth Dalai [Lama]. This policy resulted in the ninth Panchen [Lama]'s exile and death in the interior.

In pointing out the ongoing controversy between Lhasa and the Panchen Lama group in Qinghai over the incarnation of the tenth Panchen Lama, the "Opinion" opposed the idea of the Panchen Lama's marching into Tibet along with the invading PLA, lest this mislead Lhasa into believing that the PLA was taking the Panchen Lama's side against the Dalai Lama and the Tibetan government.[28]

The "Opinion" also discussed the physical arrangement for Tibet after its "liberation." Contradicting the Northwest's idea that a separate domain for the Panchen Lama be established inside Tibet, CCP officials in the Southwest promoted unitary governance for Tibet and also contemplated a unified larger "Tibetan Autonomous Region" in the future, combining Tibet with the Tibetan areas of Yunnan, Xikang, Sichuan, Qinghai, and Gansu.[29] In treating Tibet as a Dalai Lama–centered unitary entity, the document bore clear marks of cautionary advice from intellectuals and religious figures in the Southwest.

Yet, oddly, a month later when Zhang Guohua went to Beijing to meet with Mao, he brought with him a plan for dividing Tibet into several smaller regions. Titled "Tibet Work Committee's Proposal for Administering Tibet," the document proposed that, because of Tibet's remoteness and lack of qualified minority cadres, the area be divided "into regions according to old Tibetan customs, religious sects, realms, blood relations, geographic terrains, and needs of national defense." Learning from the "divide and rule" (*fen er zhi zhi*) stratagem used by many dynasties in the past, Beijing could administer these regions separately by "using Tibetans to rule Tibetans." Allegedly, such a divisive approach would not only allow the CCP to use contradictions internal to

Tibet to facilitate its work but could also let both the Northwest and Southwest Bureaus contribute to the liberation and construction of Tibet.[30]

It is unclear what motived the Eighteenth Army and the Tibet Work Committee (TWC), both headed by Zhang Guohua, in presenting to Beijing two apparently contradictory policy recommendations. Whereas extensive scholarly involvement in drafting the earlier "Opinions" is evident in its detailed discussion of the social and political conditions of Tibet, the same cannot be said about the second "Proposal," which is basically a treatise on political strategy. Published sources do not agree on how the "Proposal" was produced.[31] It is possible that when Zhang Guohua came to Beijing to meet with top CCP leaders, he needed a plan that was more accommodating to the CCP leadership's original notion of adding the Panchen Lama to the political equation. The "Proposal" could also reduce the burden on the Eighteenth Army by shifting some responsibilities to PLA units in the Northwest. Actually, a few months later, Liu Bocheng himself would propose to Beijing that the PLA of the Northwest take over the military and political responsibilities for Ngari and "Rear Tibet."[32] Thus, the "Proposal" indicated that, at this juncture, the policy stances of the CCP's two regional bureaus were not in stark contrast. Yet the proposed division of labor between the Southwest and Northwest Bureaus would inevitably result in separating the Dalai Lama and the Panchen Lama into two bureaucratic domains and rendering the Dalai Lama–centered unitary governance of Tibet meaningless. Allegedly, Mao rejected the proposal once he saw it.[33]

Whatever the reason behind the two contradictory policy suggestions from Zhang Guohua's headquarters, these were tactical options for dealing with established Tibetan elites. While claiming that the goal of the PLA was to "liberate genuinely" the Tibetan people "from imperialist aggression and feudal oppression and exploitation," the policy proposals from the CCP's regional apparatuses were untypically lacking any reference to measures for mobilizing "laboring" Tibetans and waging class struggle.[34] Zhang Guohua's "bridge" metaphor was to the point: in preparing the Tibetan society for eventual transformation, the PLA had to associate itself with one or more of the Tibetan religious and political factions.

Making a "Hat"

Before applying any stratagem for changing Tibet in the future, Beijing first had to convince Lhasa to let the CCP into its region. Because Beijing's chosen strategy was not initiating an all-out attack but using military leverage to coerce Lhasa into accepting a political settlement, CCP policymakers had to find a formula that could simultaneously satisfy their basic objectives and reduce Lhasa's resistance to the minimum.

In May 1950, Beijing received two different agendas for negotiating with the Tibetans. The CCP authorities in Qinghai organized a delegation to Lhasa to persuade Tibetan leaders to accept a political settlement. The mission was abortive, but the delegation's six-point proposal for negotiating with the Tibetans was initially endorsed by Beijing. The six points in effect demanded that the Tibetan authorities capitulate under conditions of the Common Program of the PRC. Although "freedom of religious beliefs" would be protected, Tibetan leaders were sternly warned that if they refused to support "peaceful liberation," they would be punished and their property confiscated. In early May, after receiving these points from Zhang Zhongliang, CCP chief of Qinghai, Liu Shaoqi approved them on behalf of the CCP leadership.[35] The Southwest Bureau immediately objected, contending that the forthcoming negotiation for a political settlement with Lhasa must be based on proper and feasible conditions, and that communications with Lhasa should be conducted from the direction of Xikang in the Southwest. In a message to Beijing dated May 11, the Southwest Bureau pointed out that the British and Americans were trying to influence the Tibetans' negotiation with Beijing and continuing to send weapons to Lhasa. Under these circumstances, the "work of political suasion" had to be strengthened. The Southwest Bureau set forth four points, which were "more generous and easier to achieve," in place of the six points from the Northwest:

1. Expel British-American imperialist influence from Tibet, and return the Tibetan people to the great family of the People's Republic of China.
2. Implement the Tibetan nationality's regional autonomy.
3. Maintain the status quo of all existing systems of Tibet for now; decide the issue of reform in Tibet through consultation and according to the will of the Tibetan people.
4. Practice freedom of religion, protect monasteries, and respect religious beliefs, customs, and habits of the Tibetan people.[36]

Beijing approved this new formula on the ground of tactical merit and directed the Southwest Bureau to develop a fleshed-out document to be used in talks with the Tibetans. As a result, the Southwest Bureau prepared a ten-point document that explicitly responded to Lhasa's central concern about preserving the Dalai Lama's religious and political positions. New content was added with respect to cultural and economic development of Tibet. A specific promise was made about forgiving those Tibetan officials who had associated themselves with foreign imperialism and the KMT in the past, if they were now willing to rally to the PRC. Another key point: PLA troops must enter Tibet. In the next few months, as the PLA applied military pressure on Tibet, this document served as Beijing's political inducement for Lhasa to accept "peaceful liberation."[37]

Establishment of the Dalai Lama–centered approach to a political settlement in Tibet did not mean that Beijing gave up the Panchen Lama as a political asset. In early August, Mao cabled Peng Dehuai: "In the end we should properly arrange the Panchen [Lama]'s position."[38] In September, in Beijing, Mao received the Panchen Lama's salutary delegation from Qinghai. The meeting resulted in Beijing's agreeing to take a series of measures to shore up the organizational and material strength of the Panchen Lama group. These included financial support and personnel training, constant contact between the two sides, and, most important, organization of a "Tibetan National Liberation Army" of three thousand to five thousand troops. In a telegram to the Northwest and Southwest Bureaus, the CCP Central Committee pointed out:

> Because of historical reasons the Panchen clique is promoting our policies and willing to cooperate with us. This is a wonderful and important development. No matter in what form Tibet will be liberated and how the Dalai clique will change, we must actively strive for cooperation with the Panchen clique and the people under its influence.[39]

Consequently, CCP officials in both the Northwest and the Southwest accepted the notion that the Panchen Lama group was an "anti-imperialist and patriotic force." Although the timing of the Panchen Lama's return to Tibet had to be determined in Beijing's negotiations with Lhasa, in the winter of 1950 and the early months of 1951 Beijing instructed its regional apparatuses to make active preparations for such an operation.[40] When the Seventeen-Point Agreement was concluded in May 1951, "preservation of Panchen Erdeni's original status and authority" was included in the agreement, thus opening the door for the Panchen Lama's return home.[41]

Ngabö Ngawang Jigmé, a key figure in the Beijing-Lhasa relationship of the 1950s, once said that the Seventeen-Point Agreement of 1951 was a "custom-made hat for the Tibetan head," alluding to Beijing's awareness of the unique conditions of Tibet.[42] In a certain sense, the Seventeen-Point Agreement was indeed reminiscent of the Qing court's "ordained patronage" of Tibet before the nineteenth century and also echoed the spirit of the "New Policies" that tried to substantiate Qing power in Tibet at the beginning of the twentieth century. The way the CCP installed the Seventeen-Point Agreement did not differ much from that used by Qing emperors, from Kangxi to Qianlong, in bestowing *zhangcheng* (ordinance) to Lhasa: in both cases, such written regulations were adopted only after military maneuvering on Beijing's part.

The Seventeen-Point Agreement was not the first interethnic agreement in twentieth-century Chinese history. In the late 1940s, the Chinese Nationalist government had concluded agreements with a Soviet-supported separatist movement in Xinjiang, and the CCP had also negotiated agreements with a powerful Eastern Inner Mongolian autonomous movement. Yet the cases of Xinjiang and Inner Mongolia involved situations rather different from that of Tibet in 1951. Therefore, the Qing emperors' "ordained patronage" remains a better comparable precedent. A fundamental commonality between the 1951 agreement and those imperial ordinances of the eighteenth century is that they were compromises premised on an asymmetric balance between the military prowess of the centralizing authority in Beijing and the magnitude of the Tibetan geo-ethno-religious complex. They were momentary stalemates or mismatches between, to use conceptions of our own time, hard and soft power. The comparison ends here, however. Whereas, on each occasion, Qing rulers conceived their ordinance for Tibet as a permanent arrangement, CCP leaders intended to use the 1951 agreement merely as a temporary stop in a phased transformation of Tibet. In other words, as far as Beijing's policy was concerned, the 1951 agreement signaled the first round of a waiting game.

Although the 1951 agreement took the form of a bilateral contract, it was really a political arrangement designed by the CCP side. The document began with a preamble that was a typical CCP narrative about liberating China and correcting the Tibetan government's previously "non-patriotic" stance of not rejecting foreign imperialist aggression. Despite their CCP wording, most of the articles in the document could have been acceptable to the CCP's Manchu and Nationalist predecessors. Ten of the seventeen articles were about establishing the Chinese central government's domestic and international sovereignties, and five were about maintaining the Tibetan religious/political systems and developing Tibetan cultural and economic life.[43] As far as Beijing was concerned, the most important and immediate effect of the agreement was to recognize Chinese sovereignty in Tibet, in the modern sense, as well as to set up a legal frame under which the Chinese Revolution could be consummated geographically.

For the Tibetan side, a soothing portion of the agreement was article four: "The Center [i.e., Beijing] will not change the current political system of Tibet. The Center will not change the original status and authority of the Dalai Lama. Officials at various levels will remain in office." The Tibetans most feared the PLA's entry into their land, which was nevertheless stipulated in article two. But, potentially, the most destabilizing part of the agreement was article eleven: "The Center will not impose anything on Tibet. The local government of Tibet ought to carry out reforms voluntarily. When the people demand reforms, the issue should be solved through consultation with leading figures of Tibet." Accordingly, from the very beginning of the Beijing-Lhasa compromise, the Tibetan side came under an obligation to transform itself. Inevitably, though not stated explicitly in the agreement, Beijing would decide the scope and direction of such changes. CCP leaders certainly did not expect the Tibetan authorities to change the Tibetan sociopolitical systems voluntarily.

As masters of organizing and mobilizing the masses, CCP leaders were apparently confident that, by working through the "Dalai bridge," they would sooner or later be able to reach the Tibetan people and win over the lower classes of Tibetan society to their agenda. The 1951 agreement was therefore a formula of interethnic cooperation hatching class struggle, even though the length of the hatching period was not spelled out. Ngabö was therefore naïve in believing that the Tibetans would be able to wear the "hat" of the Seventeen-Point Agreement forever.

In embedding a Chinese Communist revolution in a compromise with an antiquated Tibetan system, the 1951 agreement constituted a unique and unprecedented step in the CCP's dealing with frontier affairs and interethnic relations. This was not highlighted, however, in CCP propaganda. A few days after the Seventeen-Point Agreement was concluded, Mao was keen to make the point, in an editorial in the *People's Daily*, that the formula for Tibet's "voluntary reform" should be applicable to all minority areas of China.[44] Thus, just as the CCP had departicularized the autonomy of Inner Mongolia by nationalizing the system of "nationality regional autonomy" in the Common Program of 1949, Mao offered the "Tibetan hat" rhetorically to all other minority nationalities of China. The content of the Seventeen-Point Agreement, of course, would not be applied elsewhere. For a short while, the CCP would just maintain moderation in the Tibetan areas outside Tibet.[45]

For Beijing, an operational question was how long the Tibetan elites would be needed as a "bridge" to reach the Tibetan masses. In the spring of 1950, Zhou Enlai told a group of Tibetan trainees in Beijing quite disarmingly: "All of us should learn from Chairman Mao. Things that will be needed tomorrow but not today (meaning socialist society) should be put aside for now."[46] From CCP leaders' statements like this, established Tibetan elites could learn that "today" Beijing wanted to work with them. However, they could not know when "tomorrow" would come. In May 1951, when reporting to Mao on how his troops had digested the CCP's policy toward Tibet, Zhang Guohua said that the Tibet work would progress as slowly as a turtle climbing a mountain. Mao responded: "That would be too fast!"[47] Yet when such apparent patience with Tibet was quantified, the "turtle" in Mao's mind was not so slow after all. In July 1951, in a directive to the TWC, Deng Xiaoping quoted Mao as suggesting that reforms would start in three years.[48] This timetable was not conveyed to the Tibetan side.

A test of Beijing's patience came in 1952. In mid-March, friction arose between CCP personnel and a "people's assembly" in Lhasa backed by some Tibetan officials. In early April, the PLA's newly organized Tibet Military Region (TMR) got intelligence that the Tibetan side was planning a military attack. Fan Ming, who was then ranked number three in the TWC and was in charge of military intelligence, alleged years later that around April 1 Mao sent to Zhang Guohua a secret directive, instructing the TWC to "use this opportunity to strike hard and destroy as many Tibetan troops and rebellious bandits as possible, and accomplish liberation [of Tibet] by force for the second time."[49] No other source has corroborated Fan's revelation. Since Fan did not provide the complete text of the message, it is not clear whether Mao meant for the PLA to launch an offensive or a counterattack in the event that the Tibetans attacked. According another source, the PLA indeed made preparations for a counterattack. On April 11, the TMR issued an order to PLA troops and laid out an "operational orientation": "We will let the enemy attack our camps, and let them fire the first shot. Our troops must not fire first. Then the enemy will lose political ground and we will be able to achieve political advantage."[50] The goal of this stratagem of *hou fa zhi ren* (gaining mastery by striking only after the enemy has struck) was to achieve "comprehensive victory both militarily and politically." It was consistent with the CCP tradition in such situations and, as will be discussed in chapter 6, would be fully implemented in 1959.

It turned out that in the spring of 1952 neither side wanted to start an armed conflict. The first crisis for Beijing's post-Agreement Tibetan policy was soon over. The crisis was, however, educational for leaders in Beijing, giving them pause as to the length of the waiting period. On April 1, amid the crisis, Mao sent a telegram to the TWC and the Southwest Bureau. Here is the passage concerning the issue of timing:

> Your work in the Tibetan region must insist on the implementation of the [Seventeen-Point] Agreement. In the meantime, you should learn about conditions of various aspects, base your work on such conditions, and achieve the goal of implementing the Agreement steadily and through several necessarily tortuous steps. Long and systematic work should be done to support those who are close to the Center (such as Ngabö), win over those in the middle, and isolate the diehard conservatives (such as the two *sicao*). You have paid attention to the orientations above, but the Center hopes that you can be even more conscious about these issues in every step taken, especially because at the moment we have not been able to control the Tibetan area completely in political and military senses. Inflation in Lhasa and some other places is serious; the Kangzang [Xikang-Tibet] Highway cannot be completed anytime soon; the troops will not be able to achieve self-sufficiency through production this year; for a while we will not be able to improve the welfare of the Tibetan people's material life. In sum, at present and in the next one or two years our position in Tibet is and will remain unstable. Therefore, we must adopt an extremely cautious attitude politically, and make progress steadily. Only after the highway is getting through, self-sufficiency based on production is achieved, and the material interests of the Tibetan people are enhanced, can certain significant reform measures be considered.[51]

The message spelled out the material changes the CCP leadership anticipated for consolidating PLA troops' position in Tibet, thus enabling them to start working on reform. In retrospect, however, even Mao's "extremely cautious" expectation to start reform in 1954 was excessively optimistic.

Beijing's optimism corresponded to anxiety among PLA troops in Tibet. The Eighteenth Army accepted the Tibet assignment with tremendous reluctance. Having participated in the "war of liberation" from northern to southern China, troops of the Eighteenth Army advanced into Sichuan thinking that this rich province would be their final destination. After the Tibet assignment came, a fear of Tibet's allegedly desolate and barbarous conditions overwhelmed the troops. Liu Bocheng found it necessary to remind officers of their duty as soldiers:

> An old saying in Sichuan goes like this: "Brewed in the pot, tofu has to be made." . . . Now that Chairman Mao and the Central Military Commission made the decision and ordered the Eighteenth Army to march into Tibet, the task must be accomplished no matter how grave the difficulties will be.[52]

In mobilizing his officers and troops, Zhang Guohua tried to boost their morale by glorifying the new mission, but, depending on the mind-set of the listener, his message could be either inspiring or saddening: "We will go to Tibet and serve the Tibetan compatriots as long-term hired hands (*changgong*)."[53] Furthermore, the Eighteenth Army did not enter Tibet simply as a military force but, under the framework of the Seventeen-Point Agreement, entered an unfamiliar environment to accomplish a task totally novel to any unit of the PLA: spreading revolution without making revolution.

A time-honored formula of the CCP's military and political strategy—mobilization of the lower-class masses to wage class struggle—was now taboo for Zhang Guohua's troops. It took some time for Zhang and his associates to realize that their military success would not necessarily pave the way for their political work in "raising the Tibetan people's consciousness."[54] Mao personally admonished Zhang that "the Tibetan affairs must be settled with a good job." For the time being, Mao's advice to Zhang was to consider *minzu* (nationality) and *zongjiao* (religion) first in dealing with every issue, which to Zhang meant temporary tolerance of the backwardness of Tibet. Deng Xiaoping, in his typical pragmatic manner, also had this advice for Zhang: "You should cross a river by feeling the rocks [*mo zhe shitou guohe*] and not expect to achieve great results in one stroke."[55] It was, however, most bewildering for the troops, who had been indoctrinated with the notion of class struggle and had a strong sense of mission about liberating poor people. In their new assignment, unfamiliar factors like nationality and religion seemed to have turned the familiar logic of class relations upside down. They were now required to support the lower classes by not struggling against but "uniting with the upper classes." Officers of the Eighteenth Army and cadres of the TWC were told to treat a "united front" as the highest priority and to carry out work in this regard "vigorously," meaning to cultivate empathy among established Tibetan leaders and elites. In addition to explaining tirelessly to Tibetan aristocrats Beijing's "nationality policy" and good intentions, senior officers of the Eighteenth Army were also assigned to make personal friends with notable Tibetan figures on a one-on-one basis.[56]

In the meantime, "mass work," which was fundamental to the PLA in the rest of China for maintaining its very nature as a "People's Army," was reduced to a vague idea of "doing good deeds."[57] Typical "good deeds" included opening schools and medical clinics, reminiscent of Western missionaries' similar approaches in China. In Lhasa, PLA troops cleaned streets, built public restrooms, and even tried unsuccessfully to solve the nuisance of stray dogs.[58] These activities were intended to impress Lhasa residents with the troops' niceness but did not address the central concern of the usual "mass work"—rallying ordinary people politically to the CCP. Perhaps concerned about the integrity of the CCP's mass work (*qunzhong gongzuo*) in general, Zhou Enlai coined a term for the pseudo-mass work in Tibet: "mass-affecting work" (*yingxiang qunzhong gongzuo*).[59] The term, however, just highlighted what the "good deeds" were unable to achieve. In the past, the CCP had gained Chinese lower classes' affection by catering to their interests—for instance, using the issue of land to win over the peasants. This approach was denied to CCP officials in Tibet. In May 1952, the TWC proposed to Beijing that connections with lower-class lamas be cultivated in order to isolate those high-positioned lamas who still wanted to separate Tibet from China. Beijing's reply sternly forbade the proposed move and instructed the TWC to remain focused on forging a united front with the upper-class circles of Tibetan society.[60]

In not rushing into the work for "awakening class consciousness" among lower-class people, in the early 1950s the TWC's work fell under a general CCP policy of moderation in the minority areas of Southwest China.[61] In Tibet, however, religion was a peculiar concern. From the outset, CCP leaders received cautionary advice that PLA troops would encounter their greatest difficulty in the spiritual realm of Tibet. In January 1950, in Chengdu, He Long and a group of CCP senior officials conversed with Ren Naiqiang, a leading scholar of Tibetan studies at the Sichuan University. In the two-hour meeting, Ren identified three obstacles to PLA operations to "liberate" Tibet. One was the difficult climate and terrain for lowlanders. Another was the language barrier that would likely render the PLA's "people-loving practices" meaningless to the Tibetan people and also prevent the PLA from learning about the Tibetan people's aspirations. The greatest barrier, however, was the "fundamental contradiction between the Han and the Tibetan cultures." Ren told CCP officials that "Lamaism has dominated the Tibetan mind for more than a thousand years, and the religion is deep-rooted and unshakable." Therefore, it would be easy to liberate serfs and poor herdsmen physically but difficult to liberate the Tibetans spiritually. In hearing this, He Long asked: "Will not it be enough if we declare freedom of religious belief?" Seeing that He did not get his point, Ren used numerous successful and failed examples in ancient and recent Chinese history to stress that the PLA should not compete with the Tibetan religion. Instead, it would be advisable for the PLA to respect the tenets of Tibetan Buddhism, protect monasteries and clerical personnel, and preserve traditional Tibetan customs. These remarks did not evoke any comment from He Long and other CCP officers, who simply asked Ren to move to another topic.[62]

Beijing heeded such cautionary advice as Ren's only to a degree. In late October 1952, after Mao received a letter from the Dalai Lama carried by a salutary delegation from Lhasa, Beijing sent a message to the Southwest Bureau and the TWC, instructing them to deal with religion cautiously. Seeing the Dalai Lama's letter as evidence that the Tibetan establishment was using "the banner of 'religious development' ... to safeguard their feudal power," leaders in Beijing nonetheless reminded CCP officials in Tibet that Tibetan Buddhism had profound influence among ordinary people, and that the question of religion had a lasting and international significance. Their instructions were:

> You must firmly follow and carry out the policy of protecting religions and respecting freedom of religious beliefs. Matters of purely religious nature must not be interfered with by administrative means. Other issues, if involving religion in any manner, must also be handled with extreme caution so as not to cause any misgiving because of religion.[63]

In contrast to Ren's recommendation for permanent accommodation of Tibetan religious practices, the CCP's orientation was one of postponed acculturation. The agenda was so obscure at the time, however, that even some senior CCP officials misunderstood it.

Right after Mao talked with the Tibetan salutary delegation, the highlights of the conversation were broadcast by the Central People's Radio Station. Mao had made a reference to the development of Tibetan culture, including religion, in the years to come.[64] This led the Propaganda Department of the CCP Qinghai Committee to believe that development of the Tibetan religion was a long-term policy. This notion caused serious concerns in Beijing. In April 1953, the Propaganda Department and the United Front Department of the CCP Central Committee felt it necessary to send a joint message to their subordinate departments in the Northwest and to all the CCP's regional bureaus, clarifying how Mao's words should be understood:

> In the years to come the Tibetan religion will develop considerably because children in Tibet will still believe in Lamaism during a considerable length of time. This will be a natural development. In the meantime, these points must be noted:
>
> (1) Such development differs by nature from development of the other aspects of the Tibetan culture. In the past, the other aspects of the Tibetan culture were extremely underdeveloped and will from now on develop from scratch and expand immensely. By contrast religion was highly developed in Tibet in the past. It will continue naturally in the future but will not be able to expand because in Tibet everybody already beliefs in religion and everything is already dominated by religion. Therefore, Chairman Mao's words about underdeveloped Tibetan culture in the past and its development in the future should not be understood to mean that because the Tibetan religion did not grow under reactionary oppressions in the past, it should be developed in the future. This is factually inaccurate. Underdeveloped culture means underdevelopment in matters such as schools and newspapers.
>
> (2) ... At the present, we must of course not handle the question of religion with undue haste. The Propaganda Department of the Qinghai Party Committee understands this completely correctly. But we must not accept in principle that at any time in the future ideological struggles for religious reformation, for separation between government and religion, and against religious superstition should not be carried out in any form (for now this point should be understood only within high-level offices but must not be propagated).[65]

As indicated in the last sentence, for the moment the CCP's long-term orientation about Tibetan Buddhism had to be kept secret lest it disturb Tibetan society. This secrecy, however, was not helpful to PLA troops, who were put into an unfamiliar environment to implement an intricate policy. Some clever minds among them used two Chinese idioms to describe the situation in which they were caught: at high altitudes of the Tibetan Plateau, they were *ku xiao bu de* (unable to either cry or laugh) for lack of oxygen, and in implementing Beijing's policy, they were *zuo you wei nan* (hesitant to turn either left or right) for lack of precise guidance.[66] Under the circumstances, "mistakes" by CCP personnel in Tibet were inevitable; such "mistakes" were often censured by Beijing with the label "great Han chauvinism." To avoid mistakes, officials of the TWC dared not make frequent contact with the "masses" but limited themselves to the united-front work with the upper classes, which usually involved social gatherings and dinner parties. In observing the situation, the troops made up more jokes about what their officers were doing on a daily basis.[67]

For the time being, as the Tibetan side poised uncomfortably under the "hat" of the Seventeen-Point Agreement, Zhang Guohua and his troops remained uncertain how to cross the "bridge" of the Tibetan establishment.

Southwest Versus Northwest

Feasibility aside, Beijing's delicate project for eventually invalidating the traditional Tibetan establishment by way of an expedient alliance with that very establishment required intensive and consistent management. During the crisis in the spring of 1952, Mao reminded the TWC that Beijing's goal in Tibet was to "transform the economic and political systems of Tibet bloodlessly and gradually in several years."[68] According to Mao's calculation, Beijing's goal could be accomplished once the CCP gained "material basis," "mass basis," and "elite basis" in Tibet. After the Qingzang (Qinghai-Tibet) Highway and the Kangzang (Xikang-Tibet) Highway were completed in December 1954, the PLA's material conditions in Tibet were significantly enhanced. Yet the CCP's "mass base" and "elite base" did not improve, and even deteriorated. The goal of building trust in the Tibetan society proved much more difficult to achieve than that of overcoming the treacherous terrain of the Tibetan Plateau. In retrospect, therefore, it is surprising that Beijing started its Tibet project with a messy managerial setup full of bureaucratic confusions and infighting.

In contrast to the Qing practice of using residential *amban* to represent the emperor's authority, the CCP started typically with a plan for installing a *weiyuanhui* (committee) in Lhasa to represent the authority of the Central People's Government. The idea of a military-administrative committee (*junzheng weiyuanhui*) for Tibet first appeared in the planning documents of the Eighteenth Army, which did not recommend that Beijing have its revolutionary cadres participate in or give advice to the Tibetan theocracy. The proposed military-administrative committee would instead be above the Kashag, the powerful governing council consisting of three secular and one clerical officials who collectively made policy recommendations for the Dalai Lama to consider. The committee would represent Beijing's authority while serving as a transitional mechanism before the Tibetan Autonomous Region was established.[69] Officials in Beijing accepted this conception and incorporated it into the Seventeen-Point Agreement of 1951. As conceived by Li Weihan, chief negotiator on the Beijing side, the chairmanship of the planned Tibetan military-administrative committee would be held by a *datouzi* (big boss), and the deputies would include the Dalai Lama, the Panchen Lama, and some CCP officials. The committee would thus be an office of tremendous veneration headed by a high-ranking CCP figure, and it would be responsible, as defined by the *People's Daily*, for "guiding the implementation of all the items in the [seventeen-point] agreement according to actual conditions of Tibet."[70]

After the Tibetan delegation brought the agreement back to Lhasa, however, Beijing changed the plan and decided that the Dalai Lama should be the chairman of the military-administrative committee. This change caused suspicions and resistance from the Tibetan side. Questions were raised about Beijing's motives and the appropriateness of assigning a new position to the Dalai Lama. Even Ngabö, the staunchest supporter of the Seventeen-Point Agreement among Tibetan officials, did not believe that the Dalai Lama should shoulder this responsibility at such a young age. The Panchen Lama group was also upset, believing that not Beijing but some scheming CCP officials in the TWC had changed the original plan. Now they demanded that, for the sake of fairness, the Dalai Lama should become the "first" chairman of the planned committee and the Panchen Lama the "second." This, in turn, caused even stronger objections from Kashag officials, who were opposed to the Panchen Lama's deputy position on the committee in the first place.[71] Information about Beijing's reason for changing the original plan is unavailable. It might have been a well-intentioned improvisation for giving the Dalai Lama a new lofty title and not installing a Chinese official on top of him. But to suspicious Tibetan officials, the new arrangement looked more like a scheme for laying a trap for the Dalai Lama and destabilizing the Tibetan theocratic order. Beijing's unilateral change of mind about a mutually accepted arrangement certainly did not help foster trust on the Tibetan side. As a result, in the early 1950s, the military-administrative committee remained a controversial subject, until Beijing abandoned the idea entirely. Eventually, CCP leaders turned cancellation of the idea into a gesture to show the Tibetans that they were accommodating their feelings, or "fear" in Mao's word.[72] Without a military-administrative committee, Beijing's presence in Tibet became purely military.

Yet, covertly, the CCP had set up its committee for Tibet even before sending the Eighteenth Army across the Jinsha River. In January 1950, the CCP leadership decided to organize a *Xizang Gongwei* (Tibet Work Committee, or TWC), consisting of leading officers of the Eighteenth Army. The TWC would later be expanded and become the leading organ of the CCP inside Tibet to carry out Beijing's policies. The TWC, however, was not part of the Seventeen-Point Agreement and did not have a legitimate position in the Beijing-Lhasa relationship. In fact, during several years after the Seventeen-Point Agreement was concluded, the TWC in Lhasa and its subordinate organizations in different parts of Tibet had to work undercover and use names that sounded like branches of the Eighteenth Army.[73] In late 1951, Tibetan official Wangchen Gelek Surkhang asked Zhang Guohua why, given that the *amban* of the Qing time had only had a *yaman* (office) in Lhasa, so many PLA troops had to be there. He warned that if eventually PLA troops had to leave Tibet for lack of food, the situation would be worse than a military defeat. Officers of the Eighteenth Army took Surkhang's words as a veiled threat. However, they overlooked a big question mark in Surkhang's remark about who, or what office, represented Beijing's authority in Tibet.[74]

During the Qing dynasty, the central concern of the Manchu court in its ordained patronage of Tibet was to clarify the *amban*'s authority as a supervisor of Tibetan affairs on behalf of the emperor. In working with the *amban* according to those written imperial ordinances, the Tibetan authorities accepted the patronage of *dahuangdi*, or the grand emperor in Beijing. After Tibet was incorporated into the PRC under the framework of the Seventeen-Point Agreement, Beijing's authority over Tibet became bifurcated. In September 1952, an Office of the Assistant in Foreign Affairs to the Representative of the Central People's Government was set up in Lhasa, taking over Tibetan external affairs and asserting the PRC's diplomatic sovereignty.[75] However, because of the post-Agreement dynamics between Beijing and Lhasa, neither a military-administrative committee nor an *amban*-type official existed in Lhasa to embody the PRC's domestic sovereignty.

The so-called "representative of the Central People's Government" was an improvised solution on Beijing's part. In June 1951, Zhang Jingwu, director of the General Office of the CCP Central Military Commission and a member of Beijing's negotiating team with the Tibetans, went to Dromo (Yadong) to meet the Dalai Lama, who had moved there earlier to evade the invading PLA. At the time, Zhang's official title was "Central Representative *Going to* Tibet" (*zhongyang fu zang daibiao*), and his task was limited to persuading the Dalai Lama to return to Lhasa and accept the Seventeen-Point Agreement. Then, in March 1952, concerned with internal friction in the TWC between two groups of officials from the Southwest and the Northwest Bureaus, CCP leaders in Beijing decided that Zhang Jingwu should remain in Lhasa and replace Zhang Guohua as the first party secretary of the TWC. Yet his number one position among the CCP officials in Lhasa was not made public until two and half years later. In the meantime, Zhang Jingwu's capacity in dealing with the Tibetans also changed into "Central Representative *Residing in* Tibet" (*zhongyang zhu zang daibiao*).[76]

Some Chinese accounts have characterized Zhang Jingwu as the "*amban* of the new China."[77] This characterization is probably meant to stress Zhang's key role in the Beijing-Lhasa relationship. Yet Zhang was not installed in Lhasa by design, and unlike Qing *ambans*, whose authority was defined by imperial ordinances, he was only vaguely identified as a "central representative." After his appointment was changed from "going to Tibet" to "residing in Tibet," neither side of the relationship had a clear idea what Zhang's authority would be vis-à-vis the Dalai Lama and the Kashag. In the early 1950s, Beijing made concessions over certain articles of the Seventeen-Point Agreement, such as the military-administrative committee and reorganization of the Tibetan army, retreating from a unilaterally designed scenario to a mutually acceptable impermanence. Zhang Jingwu's appointment was part of that impermanence, even though at the time he functioned as the chief manager of Beijing's Tibet enterprise. During the crisis of 1952, Zhang was the official face of Beijing to Tibetan officials and inevitably harvested personal acrimony from the Tibetan side. In a letter to the Dalai Lama dated March 8, 1953, Mao provided the only known clarification of Zhang's position and function:

> Comrade Zhang Jingwu represents not only the Central People's Government but also the Chinese Communist Party.... You may consult with him about any question and he will do his best to assist you. Hopefully you can find more opportunities to talk with him face to face. He can also transmit to me any message that you want to send to me directly.[78]

Mao's description of these functions of representing, consulting, assisting, and transmitting did not do much to clarify Zhang's specific authority in Tibetan affairs. On the other hand, the notion that he was the link between Mao and the Dalai Lama gave Zhang's position an aura of old imperial commissioners. At the time, Mao's note was actually an abortive effort to salvage Zhang's relations with the Tibetans. In the next year, when the Dalai Lama visited Beijing, Mao accepted the Tibetan leader's request that Zhang Jingwu not return to Lhasa.[79]

Thus, after vigorously legalizing its sovereignty over Tibet in the Seventeen-Point Agreement, Beijing fell into an ancient mode of mismanagement of frontier affairs in its confusing and ad hoc way of appointing a chief official for Tibet. Wang Yangming, a Confucian strategist of the Ming dynasty, had some advice for his emperor to avoid mistakes in selecting a chief manager of frontier affairs. Because frontier societies tended to be eventful and hard to stabilize, an official assigned to the task of managing frontier affairs had to have three qualities: first, he must be loyal, determined, and wise in making judgments in order to pacify frontier unrest swiftly; second, he must be familiar with frontier social customs and frontier people's temperaments in order to win over the local people's hearts; third, he must be physically healthy and strong in order to endure difficult climates and strange lifestyles while stationed on frontiers.[80] Needlessly to say, Wang's qualifications are Sinocentric and open to criticism from various modern points of view. The point here is that Zhang Jingwu's appointment had an even narrower, party-centric basis and, other than his loyalty to the CCP and impeccable revolutionary credentials, went against most of Wang's qualifications.

In 1951, Zhang was forty-five years old and in poor health. Between 1951 and 1959, he would be absent from Lhasa at vital moments for political and health reasons. A Hunanese like Mao Zedong, Zhang had not met Mao in person until the eve of his trip to Dromo in 1951. Mao's familiarity with Zhang must therefore have been limited. Allegedly, Zhang was chosen for the Tibetan mission because of his experience in united-front work, having participated in peace negotiations with the Nationalists during the Chinese Civil War of the late 1940s. This, however, was a far cry from the situation Zhang would face in Lhasa. Nothing in his background connected him to non-Han peoples and frontier regions. Zhang did have an important credential for the CCP's Tibet work in the early 1950s, though: his career bridged the CCP organizations in the Southwest and the Northwest, and he was sent directly by the CCP "Center," not by one of its two regional bureaus. When he went to Dromo in 1951 to meet with the Dalai Lama, Zhang Jingwu, as the chief of staff of the Central Military Commission that Mao chaired, carried with him some endearing concerns for the Tibetan leader from Mao himself. But afterwards, when residing in Lhasa, Zhang got his assignment for reasons that concerned internal politics of the CCP more than the ethnopolitics of Tibetans.[81] The intramural friction between the CCP's northwestern and southwestern personnel was a problem of Beijing's own creation and had nothing to do with Beijing's authority vis-à-vis the Dalai Lama and the Kashag. Indeed, as soon as the CCP's Tibet work began, serious policy disagreements and personality conflicts arose inside the TWC. Zhang Jingwu thus became a much-needed mediator between two factions of CCP officials. Beijing, therefore, appeared to choose Zhang Jingwu for the right reason for rectifying its party apparatus in Lhasa, but the wrong one for managing its Tibetan enterprise.

The infighting within the TWC mystified even its own members. Many years later, Xu Danlu, a member of the TWC whose career in Tibetan affairs ended suddenly because of the infighting among leading TWC officials, asked these questions in an unpublished memoir:

Why did these people become so excited and unwilling to yield their grounds whenever internal disagreements were mentioned? Why did not they consider how such internal discords would impact the already very serious conditions around us? Why did they not follow their superiors' repeated instructions and earnest admonitions?[82]

A mid-echelon official, Xu could raise questions only about the divisive behavior of his immediate superiors in the TWC. Actually, the scope of the problem exceeded what Xu dared to imagine. Mao's decision to use two regional bureaus to run the Tibetan enterprise created a policy mechanism with a built-in tendency to bifurcation. While the PLA's multipronged advance toward Lhasa appeared an advantage at the beginning, the resultant bureaucratic confusion proved hard to redress in the long run. As a military-political organization, the CCP always had inner factions that channeled personal loyalty and structured routine party operations. The factional affiliations linking TWC officials to either the Southwest or the Northwest Bureau did not disappear, even when they were together dealing with a culturally alien and politically hostile environment. For a while, such affiliations actually became accentuated because of the officials' entanglement with the contest between the so-called Dalai clique and the Panchen clique.

The "Southwest faction" formed around Zhang Guohua, commander of the Eighteenth Army. A country boy from Jiangxi, Zhang joined the Red Army in the late 1920s and then survived the Long March. In 1950, the Southwest Bureau assigned the Tibet task to Zhang and his Eighteenth Army because in the past Zhang had established himself as an able military commander and a political operative capable of functioning independently. In addition, Zhang was known for being collegial and working smoothly with people from PLA units other than his own. In late May 1951, when discussing with Zhang his Tibet assignment in the years to come, Mao personally affirmed Zhang's leading position among CCP officials in Tibet, as both party secretary and commander in chief. Zhang's political acumen and interpersonal skills, however, evaporated once he met his Northwest counterpart, Fan Ming, on the Tibetan Plateau. The two got off on the wrong foot over secondary issues, such as how the troops should greet Fan's team, which arrived in Lhasa on the heels of the Eighteenth Army but demanded a glamorous reception. At the beginning, the tensions between Zhang and Fan just reflected the usual irritations between two competitive military units, but more serious policy disagreements grew. After Beijing decided to throw another Zhang (Jingwu) into the fray, Zhang Guohua was immensely disappointed. He almost resigned, questioning Zhang Jingwu directly as to why Beijing had changed his original position as both the military and party chief in Tibet. When Deng Xiaoping received a report on the affair, he expressed surprise that his old subordinate should have developed such "individual heroism," a CCP term for egoism.[83]

Like Zhang Guohua, Fan Ming was also born in 1914, but he joined the CCP movement by following a path rather different from Zhang's. Born as Hao Keyong, Fan received a traditional education in his home province of Shaanxi before attending the Fudan University in Shanghai and then the Northeastern University in Manchuria. After the Sino-Japanese war began, Fan became an underground CCP operative in the Nationalist army in Shaanxi. In 1942, after his Communist identity was discovered by the KMT authorities, Fan fled to Yan'an. Allegedly, Fan reported his work on the Nationalist side directly to Mao, and Mao advised him that, as a rule, underground CCP operatives should change their names after leaving Nationalist areas. Henceforth, the name "Fan Ming" replaced "Hao Keyong." Later, Fan would receive more designations from Mao. In the early 1950s, Mao called him a *hanlin* (imperial academician), praising his good use of his education. Once Mao also called Fan a *shaozhuangpai* (the up-and-coming), encouraging his radical stance in Tibetan affairs. But it was also Mao who blocked removing a "rightist" label from Fan in the 1960s.[84]

In February 1951, the Northwest Military Political Council appointed Fan as its representative to the Panchen Lama's residency in Qinghai, where Fan reported receiving the same kind of treatment that the Tibetans used to accord to an *amban* from the Qing court. At the end of 1951, having taken a leading role in arranging the Panchen Lama's return to his traditional site in Shigatse, Fan arrived in Lhasa. At first, he assumed the number two position in the TWC after Zhang Guohua. Then, when the TWC was reorganized in March 1952, the self-appointed "amban" was pushed down to the number four position after Zhang Jingwu, Zhang Guohua, and Tan Guansan. Yet Fan's responsibilities for intelligence and united-front work gave him both the sources and legitimate reasons to write lengthy reports on policy issues, which more often than not contradicted the two Zhangs' ideas.[85]

In July 1952, a serious policy disagreement arose at a TWC meeting. The main issue was the relationship between the two theocratic establishments under the Dalai Lama and the Panchen Lama. The two Zhangs criticized Fan for harboring an ambition to become the "king of *Houzang* [Rear Tibet]" and following the Nationalist approach of "divide and rule" in handling the Tibetan situation. Afterwards, Fan drafted a lengthy dissenting report titled "A Few Tactic Issues in the Current United Front Work for the Tibetan Region." In the report, Fan characterized the Tibetan question as "in essence one of imperialism and classes, but in appearance one of inter-nationality barriers." Using a series of incidents to prove that the Dalai clique had never really given up seeking international help to drive the PLA out of Tibet, Fan contended that Lhasa's acceptance of the Seventeen-Point Agreement had only created a false impression of its cooperating with the Central People's Government. Fan believed that the Dalai clique could still be won over from the side of American-British imperialism, but that the key was to create some common interests between "them" and "us." To that end, Fan proposed a series of measures. Financially, the Tibetan currency should be made exchangeable with Chinese currency in order to tie the Tibetan aristocrats' pockets to the rest of China. Economically, interest-free or low-interest loans should be provided to Tibetan power holders and aristocrats, enabling them to develop capitalist commercial and industrial enterprises, thereby orienting them economically toward the central government in Beijing and weakening their "feudal" economic basis. Politically, within the frame of the Seventeen-Point Agreement, various official positions should be created to give upper-class figures "high places with handsome salaries" and thus make them politically indebted to the CCP. Following Mao's démarche of "gaining unity through struggle," Fan also offered steps of "struggle" that would supposedly guarantee the effect of these luring measures. Since the Dalai Lama was a banner that could be used by either the feudal classes or the proletariat, a "flank struggle" should be waged to purge pro-imperialist elements from the side of the religious leader. This flank struggle should be preceded by steps such as forceful reorganization of the Tibetan army, restoration of Beijing's "original power" on personnel matters within the Tibetan government, and creation of an "intense atmosphere of anti-imperialism" among the Tibetans.[86]

As part of this stratagem, Fan clarified his most controversial idea about what stance the TWC should take on the relationship between the Dalai Lama and the Panchen Lama. Although admitting that historically the Dalai Lama was the highest ruler of Tibet and occupied a stronger position than the Panchen Lama in every aspect of the Tibetan life, Fan contended that the situation had drastically changed since the "peaceful liberation." Now Chamdo in the east, Bomê in the southeast, and the land of the so-called thirty-nine clans of Nagqu in the north were "liberated areas"; in "Rear Tibet," the Panchen Lama's influence covered about 60 percent of the area; and Ngari was under the Lhasa regime but was too remote to be actually controlled. Thus, the Dalai Lama's ruling power in Tibet actually covered less than two-thirds of the population and less than one-third of the territory. Under the circumstances, the liberated people of Chamdo, Bomê, and Nagqu and the patriotic people of "Rear Tibet" must not be forced into a phony unification with the "pro-imperialist-separatist faction" centered in Lhasa. According to Fan, the correct policy was to "use the progressive to push the backward" and to "gain unification through separate administrations," meaning that genuine unification of Tibet could be achieved only in a revolutionary manner and at the moment when the Dalai Lama became genuinely patriotic as well. Fan believed that such a policy was completely in line with article five of the Seventeen-Point Agreement on "maintaining Panchen Erdeni's original status and official position."[87]

After Mao had reaffirmed a "slow and steady" strategy for Tibet, Fan appeared rather audacious in promoting such an aggressive line of action. His flamboyant personality aside, Fan may have felt encouraged by a recent development. Shortly after Fan was criticized at the July meeting of the TWC, Mao instructed the TWC to investigate a complaint from the Panchen Lama group that the TWC branch in Shigatse had violated a previous understanding and used PLA units to replace the Panchen Lama's personal guards. In his telegram to the TWC, Mao reprimanded the TMR, demanding that CCP officials in Tibet "adjust our relationship with the Panchen clique swiftly so that it can increasingly become intimate but not estranged." Mao designated Fan to head the investigation. Since Zhang Guohua was in charge of military affairs, he took the blame and made self-criticism to Beijing. Although the episode emboldened Fan, he did not dare to question Mao's verdict on the CCP's lack of strength and influence inside Tibet. Instead, Fan chose to emphasize, as favorable conditions for taking bolder steps in Tibet, the PLA's "absolute superiority" in terms of military force, the CCP's supposedly popular nationality policy, and the "supportive strength of the powerful motherland."[88]

Although others in the TWC may have shared Fan's impatience and his confidence in the material strength of the PRC in dealing with Tibet, the TWC nevertheless tabled Fan's report for its obvious deviation from the established orientation. This decision may actually have protected Fan, who had already enraged Mao once in 1951 over the issue of divided administration for Tibet.[89] However, in July 1953, a year after criticizing Fan for unduly promoting the Panchen Lama group, the TWC accepted his idea of luring Tibetan aristocrats to the CCP side by financial means and suggested to Beijing that the Tibetan currency be unified with the Chinese *renminbi*. Zhang Guohua, Fan's nemesis in the TWC, was at the time in charge of the TWC's financial work. Beijing did not like the idea at all. In a message to the TWC dated August 12, the Central Committee of Finance and Economy headed by Chen Yun questioned the assumption that Tibetan aristocrats would welcome monetary unification with the rest of China. More important, the TWC was advised, "our financial and economic foundation is not yet solid enough and we should not prematurely shoulder the financial burden of the Tibetan government. Bartered trade between the heartland [*neidi*] and Tibet will therefore continue for a considerable period, and there is no need for currency unification now."[90]

Financially and economically, just as in the political arena, Beijing's preference was to wait it out. So far, Beijing had limited its involvement to importing consumer goods from India and injecting some Indian rupees into the Tibetan market to buy back the silver dollars that PLA troops had spent. Both measures were adopted to reduce the inflation caused by the PLA's entry into Tibet. State trading companies also bought Tibetan wool, which had become overstocked because of recent political developments in Tibet on cross-border trade. In all these measures, however, Beijing followed a principle of doing everything through Tibetan traders and the Tibetan authorities, with no direct involvement by any Chinese authorities. In March 1955, the State Council did contemplate gradually suspending the circulation of Tibetan currency, but then abandoned the idea because of objections from the Kashag. In November 1955, Mao circulated a letter among CCP leaders in charge of state economic affairs, suggesting that because Tibet was a unique case even in comparison to Xinjiang and Inner Mongolia, a special approach must be adopted for developing the Tibetan economy. Mao brought up the idea of long-term subsidy by the Central People's Government. Yet, after the issue was discussed at an enlarged Politburo meeting, CCP officials could not come up with a long-term economic plan for subsidizing the Tibetan economy beyond transporting into Tibet 12,500 tons of grains to stabilize prices and 12,000 tons of materials to construct an airport.[91]

While Beijing acted cautiously to a fault, its apparatus in Lhasa was in a messy situation that could not be tidied up easily. In appearance, Zhang Guohua and Fan Ming and their respective supporters in the TWC became entangled with the chronic sectarian discords between the Dalai Lama and the Panchen Lama. In reality, these officials were caught in an intricate political process created by the CCP itself. After Beijing incorporated Tibet into the PRC, the content of the Tibetan infighting changed: the theocratic establishment around the Dalai Lama tried to sideline the Panchen Lama lest Beijing use him to make inroads into the Tibetan status quo; the Panchen Lama group strived to gain a status of parity with the Dalai Lama in the traditional, theocratic, and Tibetan sense as much as in a revolutionary, political, and Chinese sense. CCP leaders consistently followed a Dalai Lama–centered approach to solving the Tibetan question, never seriously entertaining the notion of waging a revolution in Tibet with the Panchen Lama as their chief collaborator. But, always prepared for different contingencies, Beijing did have an option in the Panchen Lama. As mentioned earlier, before the Battle of Chamdo, when the Dalai Lama's cooperation with Beijing was not yet ascertained, the CCP leadership appeared sympathetic to the Panchen Lama group's idea about how to restructure Tibet politically and religiously and also approved their plan for organizing a Tibetan National Liberation Army.[92] After the Seventeen-Point Agreement was concluded, such steps became neither necessary nor proper. But the "patriotic," "anti-imperialist," and "progressive" labels affixed to the Panchen Lama group would not change; the Panchen Lama would continue to occupy a special position in Beijing's Tibetan policy.

At the end of 1951, Xi Zhongxun, then ranked number two in the Northwest Bureau, told CCP cadres assigned to Tibet: "In Tibet the Panchen clique is a progressive force, similar to the three districts, Yining and so on, of Xinjiang. They are suppressed in Tibet and will have to rely on us and cooperate with us to the end." Xi stressed that the "enemy," meaning the current Tibetan regime, must not be allowed to lure even a single person from the "Panchen clique."[93] The "three districts" referred to a Uighur-Kazakh separatist movement in Xinjiang that started to challenge the Chinese Nationalist regime in 1944 but was absorbed into the PRC after 1949. The movement was supported by the Soviet Union, and several of its principal leaders were actually trained by the Soviets.[94] The Panchen Lama and the "three districts" were therefore hardly comparable in terms of their political persuasions. Nevertheless, Xi's words clearly indicated a quasi-comrade identity assigned to the Panchen Lama group by high-ranking CCP officials. In the politics of national integration, in which many Lhasa officials were reluctant participants whereas the Panchen Lama group appeared willing, "revolutionary seniority" was significant. The so-called three-district revolution of Xinjiang and the Inner Mongolian autonomous movement were both legitimized by the CCP as "part of the Chinese revolution" before they were integrated with the PRC. The Uighurs and the Inner Mongols therefore enjoyed "revolutionary seniority" over the Tibetans. Inside Tibetan politics, however, the Panchen Lama group was adept in promoting its own "revolutionary seniority," an arena that the Lhasa regime did not even want to enter.

In late summer 1952, the Tibetan government was organizing its first salutary delegation to Beijing. After the unpleasant confrontation between the Kashag and the TWC in the spring crisis, the delegation would be a symbolic centripetal gesture by the Tibetans. The matter, however, just caused one more round of rivalry between the two Tibetan leaders, as well as discord within the TWC. The Panchen Lama group, through the TWC branch committee in Shigatse, insisted that the delegation should have two heads, from the Dalai Lama's side and the Panchen Lama's side, respectively. Che Jigmé, chief executive of the Panchen Lama group, contended that the Panchen Lama had been "patriotic" for twenty years and deserved a position higher than the Dalai Lama. Rejecting the two-head notion and sending the delegation away with just one leading official from the Kashag, the TWC, however, presented two opinions to Beijing: one was its directive to the TWC branch committee in Shigatse, titled "On the Question of the Orientation for Tibetan Unification"; the other was a lengthy dissenting document drafted by Fan Ming, in consultation with the Shigatse branch committee, titled "Opinion on the Question of the Orientation for Tibetan Unification." The two documents took different stances on "unification" and "separate administration" of Tibet, but the crux of the debate remained the same: whether the Panchen Lama group should be integrated into the current Tibetan theocracy, so that Beijing could gain the trust of principal Kashag officials and especially the Dalai Lama, or keep its "progressive" distance from Lhasa so that Beijing could maintain leverage over the Kashag in addition to the PLA presence in Tibet.[95]

In its own long struggle with the Chinese Nationalists, the CCP had worked both inside and outside the KMT under the united-front policy, and both the inner and outer tactics had proven useful under different circumstances. In applying the united-front approach to the Tibetan case, at first Beijing used its Northwest Bureau to promote the Panchen Lama as an outside pressure on, if not a substitute for, the Lhasa regime. Then Beijing used its Southwest Bureau to foster a working relationship with the Lhasa regime in which the Panchen Lama would serve as an inner leverage. By late 1952, however, Beijing found that its two hands in the Tibetan affair were arm-wrestling between themselves.

After receiving the TWC's directive to its Shigatse branch, Beijing cabled the TWC to approve its plan for working gradually toward the unification of Tibet. Fan Ming's formula for "separate administration leading to unification" was explicitly rejected. "Winning over the Dalai clique" remained the highest priority, and nothing must be done that would be detrimental to that goal. Although admitting the value of the Panchen Lama group in being progressive "within a certain limit and to a certain degree," CCP officials in Beijing did not believe this value outweighed the fact that "the Dalai [Lama]'s status and influence inside Tibet and for the entire Tibetan nationality are higher than the Panchen [Lama]'s."[96] Yet, after seeing Fan's long "Opinion," which the TWC did not transmit to Beijing until November 2, CCP leaders seemed to begin to doubt that the two Zhangs in Lhasa were following Beijing's orientation correctly. Fan's "Opinion" made a strong argument that, historically, the Panchen Lama had been under the *amban* from the central government of China but not under the Kashag. Therefore, the TWC's attempt to persuade the Panchen Lama group to accept the leadership of the current Kashag was historically wrong and politically unwise. Before the Dalai Lama could be won over, the TWC's orientation would probably ruin the CCP–Panchen Lama relationship. Fan's opinion led Beijing to issue a new directive on November 19, asking the TWC to investigate further "the Panchen [Lama]'s original status and official positions" and then offer a "basically correct and unanimous opinion." Before completing its investigation and reaching a consensus, Beijing cautioned, the TWC must not rush the Panchen Lama group into negotiations with the Kashag over the issue of unification.[97] Thus, eager to advance their political agenda in Tibet, leaders in Beijing unwittingly created a paralyzing condition for their officials in Tibet: their demand for "consensus" between two sharply opposing factions of the TWC would prove unattainable.

Soon, unable to make a judgment on the Tibetan situation, leaders in Beijing began to worry whether the TWC, as structured, could continue to function smoothly. During the visit of the Tibetan salutary delegation in Beijing, Deng Xiaoping, Xi Zhongxun, and Li Weihan personally interviewed TWC officials who accompanied the delegation. Deng and Xi had recently moved to their new posts in Beijing. Deng was appointed vice-premier of the Government Council; Xi, appointed chief of the Propaganda Department of the CCP Central Committee, would soon become the secretary-general of the Government Council. From these interviews, CCP officials in Beijing learned for the first time how serious was the internal division of the TWC. When talking to Zhang Xiangming, one of the TWC officials who came to Beijing with the Tibetan delegation, Li Weihan pointed out that the disagreements within the TWC went beyond policy issues and reflected unhealthy personal misgivings. In Li's opinion, the two Zhangs and Fan Ming all had their shares of responsibility for the internal quarrels, but Zhang Jingwu, as the leading member of the TWC, should have settled the problems.[98] In October 1953, a Tibetan work conference was held in Beijing, where leaders had the chance to learn firsthand about the thorny question of Tibet and the factional contests inside the TWC. The CCP had entered Tibet; now Tibet, in turn, entered the party politics of the CCP.

The "Center" and the TWC

Embodying state authorities, the Central People's Government of the PRC was a bureaucratic front that could not have functioned without an intricate CCP, or party, mechanism for making and executing policies. In the spirit of the Qing's Lifan Yuan (Board of Dependency Management) and the Nationalists' Mongolian-Tibetan Affairs Commission, after 1949 the PRC established a Nationality Affairs Commission under the Government Council. But until a Preparatory Committee for the Tibetan Autonomous Region was established in Lhasa in 1956, the Government Council rarely made decisions about Tibetan policies. It was the CCP *Zhongyang*, or "Center," that was in charge of Tibetan affairs. In the 1950s, the Center appeared a monolithic collective leadership of the CCP. At the beginning of the PRC, a small group of top CCP leaders made policy decisions for the new state and directed its daily operations. The group included Mao Zedong, Liu Shaoqi, Zhu De, Ren Bishi, Zhou Enlai, and Chen Yun. They were members of the Central Secretariat of the Standing Committee of the Politburo and had a division of labor among themselves. Mao was responsible for the Military Affairs Commission, Liu the Propaganda Department, and Zhou the United Front Department, the Social Department (in charge of intelligence), and foreign affairs. In the meantime, all reports and telegrams from the CCP's regional organizations would go through Mao.[99] In the 1950s, Mao, Liu, and Zhou all drafted or revised policy directives on Tibetan affairs in the name of the Center. The CCP's Central United Front Department (CUFD), then headed by Li Weihan, was a central office responsible for Tibet-related operations and, sometimes, also for drafting the Center's directives for top leaders' approval. All these leaders concurrently held official positions in the Central People's Government. Li, for instance, was also the director of the Nationality Affairs Commission between 1949 and 1954. But his dealing with the Tibetan question as the chief of the CUFD really reflected the nature of Beijing's policy, which was conceived more as a party project than a state practice.[100]

While managing its Tibetan enterprise with such a dual bureaucratic structure, Beijing continued to recognize the "gray" character of Tibet within the PRC; that is, through most of the 1950s, Tibet remained a twilight zone between China's foreign and domestic affairs. Talking to members of PRC diplomatic missions abroad in 1952, Zhou Enlai exhorted:

> We stress heightened and conscientious discipline befitting the Party's interests. Individualistic tendencies are not permitted. Acting and speaking indiscreetly will cause troubles. Diplomacy is about state-to-state relations. In diplomatic work, instructions must be requested before any action can be taken, and reports must be filed after each action.

The usual sensitivity of interstate relations was just one reason for such tight control. More important was that many PRC diplomats were stationed in nonsocialist countries, defined by Beijing as "antagonistic states" (*diqing guojia*). Hence Zhou's admonition about "limited authorization" in foreign affairs was legendary among Chinese diplomats of the Mao years.[101] Although Tibetan affairs became "domesticated" under the framework of the Seventeen-Point Agreement, the very framework also accommodated the political environment of Tibet that, as perceived by Beijing, was similar to that faced by PRC diplomats.

Yet, initially, Beijing fully authorized its regional bureaus to deal with Tibetan affairs. In late 1949, PLA troops' early encounters with Tibetans in northern and western Sichuan caused Liu Shaoqi to send a telegram to the Northwest and Southwest Bureaus:

> This type of minority nationality affairs must be handled carefully, otherwise their suspicion and fear of us will increase. But, because the Center is far away from them and unclear about their situation, the Center cannot appropriately deal with their problems. Therefore, the Northwest and the Southwest Bureaus should deal with all their problems.... Even for those issues that the Center must handle directly, the two bureaus should make suggestions for the Center to adopt.[102]

Several months later, however, incidents between PLA troops and minority peoples in frontier regions alarmed leaders in Beijing. These relations appeared too delicate to be left to local officials and troops to handle. In a June directive, Liu informed the CCP's regional bureaus that from now on all policy decisions concerning minority nationalities "must not be made at local levels and a report system must be insisted." Troubled especially by the prospect that CCP troops and cadres might push social and cultural changes deemed offensive by the Hui and the Tibetans, Liu cautioned against imposing on Islamic and Tibetan schools curricula that taught "how monkey changed into human beings."[103] Shortly before Liu's telegram, Mao had already negated a plan for managing Tibet from Zhang Guohua's headquarters. Afterwards, following Mao's instruction, Zhang prepared a new plan in consultation with Li Weihan and Liu Geping, deputy director of the CUFD. After Zhou Enlai endorsed the plan, Zhang brought it back to the Southwest for Deng Xiaoping to consider. Deng, in turn, proposed a ten-point plan in the name of the Southwest Bureau, and this served as the basis of negotiations for the Seventeen-Point Agreement.[104]

Such a circular way of making policy continued, but increasingly Beijing not only provided guiding principles but also became closely entangled with TWC operations in Tibet. Originally, the Southwest Bureau under Deng Xiaoping shouldered the principal responsibility for supervising the TWC's work in Tibet. Then, during the spring crisis of 1952, Deng made a peculiar request to Beijing that since settlement of the current crisis would have enormous ramifications, Beijing should guide the TWC directly. The Southwest Bureau would continue to offer suggestions to Beijing but would not answer any question from the TWC. Beijing's response, drafted by Mao himself, was no less astonishing:

> We concur with the Southwest Bureau's opinion that the unrests in Lhasa be handled directly by the Center. The Center has also decided that from now on all negotiations, consultations, and settlements of incidents between our side and the Tibetan side, including political, military, diplomatic, commercial, religious, and cultural issues, would be centralized and handled by the Center. The TWC will report directly to the Center while informing the Southwest Bureau. The Southwest Bureau should offer the Center its opinions on these issues. The Southwest Bureau and the Southwest Military Region will continue to be in charge of the internal affairs of the Party, and the Tibet Military Region in charge of such issues as personnel, deployment, training, production, construction, logistics, and so on.

In the same telegram, Mao criticized the TWC for not reporting to Beijing some of its recent activities in Tibet.[105]

It can only be speculated what Deng and Mao, the two most original political minds in the PRC history, were thinking at the time. By way of comparison, the Inner Mongolian Autonomous Region was not under any CCP regional bureau but reported directly to Beijing. In 1953, when Beijing planned to implement regional autonomy in Xinjiang, the precedent of Inner Mongolia was followed.[106] Direct control by the CCP central leadership was therefore a norm of Beijing's management of the three old ethnic frontiers bequeathed by the Qing. Yet Deng's shedding of responsibility was unusual because it took place when the CCP's Tibetan operation was in the thick of a serious crisis. Both Deng and Mao indicated that the seriousness of the Tibetan situation was the reason for structural readjustment on the CCP's side. But the readjustment was made not for the sake of speedy reaction to or precise management of crises in the Tibetan frontier. It was made for the sake of implementing unmistakably a policy line formulated in Beijing.

At the time, Deng appeared a self-admitted obstacle to Beijing's orientation. On April 6, the day before asking Beijing to take over the direct responsibility for managing the Tibetan crisis, Deng sent a message to Beijing criticizing himself for an unrelated matter: The Southwest Bureau had approved execution of an unidentified number of "economic criminals" in its region without Beijing's sanction. Deng was obviously responding to an earlier censure from Beijing, admitting that the bureau had committed the mistake because of its eagerness to push forward the "Three-Antis" campaign and its misunderstanding of relevant directives from Beijing.[107] Deng was certainly not so fragile that he could not stand being reprimanded by CCP leaders in Beijing. Yet the "Three-Antis" case may have compounded the divergence between Deng's understanding of the Tibetan crisis and Mao's.

In his two previous directives to the TWC, dated April 2 and 5, Deng analyzed the political crisis in Tibet through a three-wing perceptual frame typical of the CCP's united-front work. He urged the TWC to take countermeasures that could unite the "progressives" and the "middle elements," and to expose, isolate, and strike against "reactionaries" behind the scenes. Deng classified the Dalai Lama as the leader of the middle elements and believed that in the current crisis they should be "actively protected and supported" so as to encourage them to take a firm stance against the reactionaries. Mao had no problem grouping Tibetans under these labels, but he did not believe the Tibetan protest against the CCP in Lhasa was merely agitation by a small number of bad elements. Instead, in his telegram to the Southwest Bureau and the TWC, Mao identified the crisis as a "representation to us by the majority of the Dalai clique," suggesting that "we should therefore accept in essence (not just in form) this petition and postpone the implementation of the whole [17-point] agreement."[108] Clearly, Mao's understanding of the Tibetan crisis and his "procrastination" orientation differed significantly from Deng's. Consequently, Deng offered to bench the Southwest Bureau, meaning himself, so as not to interfere with Mao's delicate strategy. Mao, never harboring any doubt about his ability to judge a political situation, took over responsibility for Tibet once and for all, probably to avoid unnecessary bureaucratic formalities. From then on, the TWC would become the first recipient of Beijing's directives on Tibet, and the Southwest Bureau the second.

Meanwhile, Mao's confidence in Deng as an able administrator was undiminished. In July, Deng was summoned to Beijing and became part of the central leadership of the PRC. Before he left the Southwest, Deng took another action that would prove vital to the development of Tibetan affairs in the next few years. He organized the reunification of Sichuan, which until then had been administered as four provinces, as a single province. Three years later, Sichuan would become even larger by incorporating the Xikang Province or, to Tibetans, the southeastern part of Kham. Li Jingquan, who had come to the Southwest with He Long in 1949, was installed as governor and party secretary of this augmented Sichuan. In the years to come, Li would fully display his enthusiasm in following Mao's frenzied "continuous revolution."[109]

If Inner Mongolia set a precedent for Beijing's direct supervision of an ethnic frontier, the readjustment of the CCP's organizational responsibility for Tibet in 1952 made such supervision a rule. Beijing began trying to micromanage

TWC operations and demanded, sternly and repeatedly, that every item of the Tibet work must be reported to Beijing in advance and must not be implemented without Beijing's approval. In 1952 the TWC was censured several times for violating the new rule. The issues involved ranged from setting up an elementary school in Lhasa to attempting to establish a branch military region. The situation mirrored Beijing's micromanagement of the PRC's foreign affairs. As Zhou Enlai told PRC diplomats, "there are no trifles in diplomacy"; after 1952, CCP cadres in Tibet learned that nothing was too trivial as far as Tibet was concerned. At the end of the year, after learning that the TWC had created a "department of agriculture and pastoral work" without Beijing's approval, Mao asked Deng to make the TWC understand that Beijing, not the Southwest Bureau, was directly in charge of Tibetan affairs. Since the TWC appeared so obtuse in getting the point, in January 1953 Beijing sent another stern telegram to the TWC, asserting its direct control over Tibetan affairs.[110]

Actually, the Southwest Bureau and Beijing had confusions of their own. When Deng was called to Beijing, Mao initially intended him to work in Beijing only two or three months. Deng would therefore remain the secretary of the Southwest Bureau, with Song Renqiong as his first deputy to attend to daily operations. After Deng left for Beijing, the Southwest Bureau approved independently the creation by the TWC of a "department of agricultural and pastoral work," indicating Deng's deputies' unawareness of their limited role in Tibetan affairs.[111] In another instance, Beijing appeared to speak in two voices. In late July, the Central Military Commission (CMC) approved the TWC's request to set up branch military regions under the Tibet Military Regions, contradicting an earlier telegram from Mao that explicitly instructed the TWC not to reorganize the Tibetan army and not to establish branch military regions. Mao chaired the CMC and could not possibly have contradicted himself. The misstep may therefore have happened under Peng Dehuai, one of the vice-chairs of the CMC who had returned not long before from the Korean War to take charge of the CMC's daily operations. This incident led Li Weihan to propose a new procedure: from now on, all telegrams processed by the ministries and committees in Beijing would have to be examined by the CCP Central Secretariat if they concerned Tibet.[112] As will be discussed in chapters 5 and 6, this meant that the Central Secretariat would become a powerful policymaking body concerning Tibet. It would also reestablish Deng Xiaoping as a decisive voice with regard to Tibet.

As the PRC took shape in its formative years, the CCP control of the state also became an increasingly elaborate operation. During the first few months of his participation in the central leadership, Deng attended several enlarged meetings of the Central Secretariat and also frequented "Mao's place" to attend top leaders' meetings called by Mao to discuss various policy issues. One of Deng's new duties was to draft, on behalf of the Center, directives that were to be sent to CCP apparatuses at lower levels after being approved by Mao or Liu. On March 10, 1953, Beijing adopted a decision for strengthening the party leadership over various aspects of the Central People's Government. Aside from Mao and Liu, who had overall responsibilities, and Zhu De, who was semiretired, a new division of labor was established among senior CCP officials who operated at the Center: Gao Gang was in charge of state planning; Dong Biwu, Peng Zhen, and Luo Ruiqing of public security and law; Cheng Yun, Bo Yibo, Deng Zihui, Li Fuchun, Zeng Shan, Jia Tuofu, and Ye Jizhuang of finance and economy; Xi Zhongxun of culture and education; and Zhou Enlai of foreign affairs. Deng Xiaoping was responsible for all other aspects of party-state operations not included in these five categories, such as supervision and inspection, minority nationalities, and personnel. At the time, Deng's position in the government was vice-premier of the Government Council, but it was his party position without portfolio that groomed him to become a chief executive of the CCP.[113] Especially interesting is that Deng, having benched himself in Tibetan affairs at the regional level, became a leading player in Tibetan affairs in particular, and nationality affairs in general, at the Central level.

At the beginning of October 1953, Li Weihan wrote a letter to Deng, suggesting that a Tibet work conference be held in Beijing to settle the internal discords of the TWC. Deng endorsed the idea and asked Li to preside over the conference if Mao and Liu agreed to it. Both Mao and Liu soon gave their approval.[114] A year before, Li had told Zhang Jingwu that, as the party chief of the TWC, he had to maintain internal unity among TWC officials. Since then, Zhang had achieved little in this regard, and Beijing now decided to intervene directly.

Like the TWC, however, the CCP central leadership consisted of individuals of different temperaments and convictions. The Tibet work conference would be held under the aegis of Li's CUFD, which would be represented at the conference by a number of its principal officials. Together with Li, these officials were supposed to function more effectively than Zhang Jingwu as mediators in solving internal discords of the TWC. Yet these officials in Beijing were divided among themselves over the Tibetan question. The so-called nationality work was just one component of the multifaceted responsibility of the CUFD. Before 1953, a Nationality Division was in charge of the department's nationality work. Then, in 1953, Zhou Enlai personally nominated a heavyweight Nationality Work Committee to work directly under the CCP Central Committee. The plan changed, however, and the Nationality Work Committee was put inside the CUFD, thus superseding the function of the original Nationality Division. The director of the committee was Wang Feng; its members included Li Weihan, Ulanhu, Liu Geping, Liu Chun, Yang Jingren, and Zhao Fan. In early 1954, the Nationality Division and the Nationality Work Committee were merged into the Nationality Policy Research Office of the Central Nationality Affairs Committee.[115] These officials were top CCP experts in interethnic affairs. Most of them had been involved in policymaking with respect to the Inner Mongols and the Hui during the CCP's Yan'an period. Ulanhu and Liu Chun, especially, contributed to the CCP's "overcoming" the Inner Mongols' autonomous movements during the Chinese Civil War. Ulanhu was an Inner Mongol; Liu Geping and Yang Jingren were Hui. All of them except Zhao Fan were or would be ministerial- or provincial-level officials. As for Zhao, before 1949 he was a CCP underground operative for a period, after which he returned to join the party's united-front work. His special qualifications for working on Tibetan issues remain unclear. In 1953, Zhao was in charge of the Tibetan desk inside the CUFD but was already in disagreement with his immediate superior, Yang Jingren.

The Tibet work conference in Beijing lasted more than three months, from October 1953 to January 1954. Zhang Guohua, Fan Ming, and three other members of the TWC participated in the conference. After six decades, information about the conference remains scarce. Two of the conferees, Fan Ming and Zhao Fan, mentioned the conference briefly in their memoirs. What is presented here is therefore a sketchy impression constructed from available bits of information.

Deng Xiaoping famously and bitterly compared the conference, which turned into a series of inconclusive quarrels, with the marathon negotiations for ending the Korean War in Panmunjom. Deng's role in relation to the conference, however, is unclear. On the other hand, Xi Zhongxun appears to have stood behind Fan outside the conference and pressured some TWC officials, such as Ya Hanzhang, also from the Northwest, to close ranks with Fan. At the outset, the two factions of the TWC provided the conference with written memos reiterating their respective stances. Neither side changed its position as a result of the conference. As far as CUFD officials were concerned, Zhao expressed discontent with Li Weihan's leadership of the conference, which appeared to waver between the two opposing views. Zhao's own presentation at the conference, which supported Zhang Guohua's stance and questioned the sincerity of the Panchen Lama group's pro-Center attitude, enraged Fan Ming, and other CUFD officials criticized Zhao for erroneously involving himself in the Zhang-Fan controversy.[116]

As a popular saying in China in the 1940s and 1950s went, "the KMT had a lot of *shui* (taxes) and the CCP a lot of *hui* (meetings)." After 1949, Beijing was a capital of meetings. Between late 1953 and early 1954, the Tibet work conference was only one of many meetings taking place in Beijing. A conference that was mainly about the internal problems of the TWC did not seem to have a high priority on the agenda of top CCP leaders such as Mao, Liu, and Zhou. During the conference, Zhou met with Zhang Guohua and Fan Ming only once to discuss issues concerning India's relations with Tibet.[117] Meanwhile, as

Beijing tried to help the TWC solve its internal discords, the CCP was experiencing its first leadership crisis after 1949. When the CCP leaders decided to end the New Democracy period earlier than originally expected, the so-called Gao (Gang)-Rao (Shushi) affair ensued. It appeared to begin with Gao Gang's challenge to Liu Shaoqi's number two position in the party and ended with Gao's suicide after he was criticized by other senior CCP officials. Between February 6 and 10, 1954, the fourth plenum of the Seventh CCP Central Committee was held in Beijing. Liu Shaoqi presided over the meeting on behalf of Mao and delivered a keynote speech condemning Gao and Rao for engaging in irregular activities.[118]

Much of the Gao-Rao affair remains unknown and deserves serious examination by historians. Most interesting for this study, however, is its impact on the Tibet work conference. Decades later, in his unpublished memoir, Zhao Fan accused Fan Ming and his supporters in the CUFD of being members of the Gao-Rao clique and trying to use the issue of the Panchen Lama to provoke the Dalai Lama into rebellion against Beijing.[119] In view of Zhao's personal vendettas against Yang Jingren and Wang Feng, this accusation is neither credible nor comprehensible. Yet the Gao-Rao affair did affect the Tibet work conference in two ways. First, because of the magnitude of the affair, the Tibet work conference had to be suspended in January 1954. The TWC's internal discords were dwarfed by the factional struggle among top CCP leaders. Shocking as the affair was to all CCP cadres, it had a sobering effect on officials involved in the Tibet work conference, especially on those from the Northwest whose paths had crossed Gao's in the past. Although a large-scale organizational purge did not happen this time, in an internal speech Zhou Enlai did mention "some very high-positioned comrades who were inexplicably misled" by Gao's activities before "returning to the correct path." Zhou named Xi Zhongxun as one such person. In the wake of the Gao-Rao affair, the CCP leadership stressed "unity," "collective leadership," and "prestige of the Center," all cautionary to the divisive and quarrelsome TWC. The wrangling at the Tibet work conference was therefore no longer permitted. Deng Xiaoping, using his Panmunjom analogy, ordered the participants to stop quarreling.[120]

Second, because the Gao-Rao affair was officially characterized as a plot to split the CCP, internal unity became one of the most important themes stressed at all levels of the party. This emphasis may have prevented Beijing from undertaking some surgical measures to solve the divisiveness of the TWC. At least one source indicates that at a Politburo meeting Deng Xiaoping admitted a change of plan by the top leaders: during the Tibet work conference, the central leadership had originally intended to take Fan Ming out of Tibet, but in the end, this did not happen.[121] This change may well have been a "unity" gesture on Deng's part, in the wake of the Gao-Rao affair, toward TWC officials of Northwest background. Given that Fan Ming was a subordinate of

Xi Zhongxun's and maintained contact with Xi during the Tibet work conference, Deng's gesture was probably more meaningful to Xi than to anybody else. Deng and Xi had come to Beijing as regional chiefs of the Southwest and the Northwest. Because Xi returned to the "correct path" in the Gao-Rao affair, he did not suffer afterwards. Deng, on the other hand, was in the forefront of the struggle against Gao Gang and Rao Shushi. In the wake of the Gao-Rao affair, Deng not only replaced Rao as the chief of the CCP's Department of Organization but was also promoted to the position of secretary-general of the Central Secretariat. Two years later, Deng would join the six-member standing committee of the CCP Politburo, and his humble secretary-general title would be converted into a powerful position: general secretary of the CCP Central Committee.[122]

As the power dynamics were changing in Beijing, the Tibet work conference, after fifty-nine sessions, produced its conclusion. Since Beijing already had an established orientation in Tibet and the purpose of the Tibet work conference was to enable the TWC to implement it more effectively, the conference did not produce anything new as far as policy was concerned. Rather, because the Gao-Rao affair, in a twisted way, blocked organizational measures that could have solved the TWC's internal rift, the Tibet work conference became just another mediating effort. Although it carried much more authority than Zhang Jingwu's similar function, eventually it proved similarly ineffective. To prepare a concluding document, a drafting committee was formed, including Zhang Guohua, Fan Ming, and their respective supporters at the conference. This guaranteed another round of quarreling. Yet, under the atmosphere of Beijing after the Gao-Rao affair, the committee muddled through and produced a lengthy "conclusion" dated February 10, 1954.

It was an odd and self-contradictory document. While reaffirming the established policy of administering Tibet as a unitary entity and focusing on winning over the Dalai Lama group, the document labeled the Dalai Lama a "centrist" and the Panchen Lama a "leftist." As to the Dalai-Panchen relationship, the document stated, "The Dalai [Lama] group and the Tibetan local government represent the whole of Tibet," but then went on to say:

> However, the Dalai [Lama] cannot represent the Panchen [Lama]. And the Panchen [Lama]'s Labrang is also not subject to the Kashag. In order to promote unity between the Dalai [Lama] and Panchen [Lama] groups and to avoid quarrels, we should try our best to use the names of both the Dalai [Lama] and Panchen [Lama] when we deal with the issue of entire Tibet.[123]

The logic embedded in this statement had a precedent in the CCP's own relationship with the KMT government during China's war against Japan. At the time, the CCP supported the KMT government as the legitimate authority for the whole of China while jealously guarding its own autonomy from the KMT regime. In the Tibet statement, the positions of the Panchen Lama and the Dalai Lama echoed those of the CCP and the KMT. As the two TWC factions and their respective supporters were stuck in a debate about the absolute truth and absolute falsity of each other's stances, leaders in Beijing wanted to endorse just a kernel of truth in each. The two opposing opinions inside the TWC had to become mutually supplementary in formulating a functional strategy.

Zhao Fan believed that such a compromising conclusion was "incomplete" and would leave unsolved problems to TWC officials. He wrote a dissenting opinion to Liu Shaoqi, and Liu brought it to an enlarged meeting of the Politburo. Both Xi and Deng were present at the meeting. Whereas Xi fully supported the conclusion, Deng agreed with Zhao but wanted to adopt the document for the sake of unity.[124] Thus, with the Northwest beating a retreat and the Southwest making a magnanimous gesture, unity in the TWC was supposedly restored. In this peculiar context, Zhang Guohua emerged from the Tibet work conference as an actual winner in a twisted way. Although Zhang had Deng's support in Beijing, it was Zhang, not Fan Ming, who, after returning to Lhasa in July 1954, made self-criticism and took the blame for the discord within the TWC. The twist would be untwisted, or doubly twisted, four years later when a "rectification campaign" inside the TWC labeled Fan Ming an "ultra-rightist" and stripped him of his party membership and all his official positions inside the CCP and the PLA.[125]

In the internal politics of the CCP, "ultra-rightist" was a label for party officials who had behaved ostentatiously as "leftists" before falling out of favor. Between the "patriotic" Panchen Lama group and the "non-patriotic" Dalai Lama group, Fan Ming sided unrelentingly with the former and was constantly on the "left" side of the CCP's Tibetan politics, which in the eyes of Beijing leaders was admirable as a political stance but unwise as a tactical approach. In the CCP's management of the political-religious dualities of Tibet, balance was the key. When dealing with the Panchen Lama group directly, Beijing stressed to them that "Rear Tibet" was part of Tibet and that unity with the Dalai Lama must be achieved. In practice, however, Beijing maintained the parallel statuses of the two Tibetan leaders by allowing both to communicate with the Center directly. In March 1953, not long after endorsing the TWC's refutation of Fan Ming's formula for "separate administration leading to unification," Beijing approved the establishment of the Khenpos (also Kampus, or abbots' assembly) Committee under the Panchen Lama, and thus officially put the Panchen Lama administration based in Shigatse directly under the Government Council of the PRC.[126]

Beijing did not balance Lhasa just with the Panchen Lama group. After taking Chamdo by force, Beijing never returned the area to the Kashag.

Between December 27, 1950, and January 3, 1951, the first "people's congress" of the Chamdo area held meetings and elected a "Liberation Committee of the Chamdo Area" headed by Wang Qimei, deputy commissar of the Eighteenth Army. After the Seventeen-Point Agreement was signed, Lhasa strongly demanded that Chamdo be returned to its administration. Beijing did not relent, on the ground that the military-administrative committee stipulated by the Seventeen-Point Agreement had to be established first. In the meantime, Beijing supported the TWC's opinion that Chamdo should not be turned into an "autonomous region" prematurely lest Lhasa be offended.[127] Thus, although after 1951 the issue of Tibetan unification often took the form of historical discord between the Dalai Lama and the Panchen Lama, Beijing added its own piece, "liberated" Chamdo, to the game board of Tibetan politics. Having served as the doorway for the PLA to enter Tibet, Chamdo was able to stay out of the internal fray of Tibet simply because it was already a bona fide CCP operation.

In 1954, having kept its shaky partnership with Lhasa alive and fine-tuned its operational mechanism inside Tibet, Beijing was ready to move the Tibetan enterprise a step forward by incorporating the Dalai Lama and the Panchen Lama personally into the structure of the Central People's Government. In July, the two Tibetan leaders accepted Beijing's invitation and came to the PRC capital to attend the first meeting of the First National People's Congress. Chamdo also sent its own delegation to Beijing. Immediately, the futility of the Tibet work conference, which had ended just months before, was exposed: the Tibetan leaders' journey to Beijing became another occasion for the Dalai Lama and the Panchen Lama to compete for status. Inevitably, factional friction inside the TWC was rekindled. Continually frustrated by the infighting of the TWC, and unable to deal with the new round of the Dalai-Panchen contest, Zhang Jingwu called on Beijing for help. At Mao's request, Li Weihan drafted a detailed directive on "Orientations about Receiving and Hosting the Dalai [Lama] and the Panchen [Lama] and about the Propaganda Concerned." On August 2, the directive was sent to the TWC and to relevant CCP regional bureaus.[128]

For the first time after 1951, because of the two Tibetan leaders' tour to Beijing, the Tibetan question arrived in provinces beyond Tibet. In the August 2 directive, Beijing stressed to its provincial officials that their receiving and hosting of the two Tibetan leaders must embody the essence of Beijing's Tibetan policy:

> The Dalai [Lama] and the Panchen [Lama] are coming to Beijing to attend the National People's Congress, showing that Tibet is getting closer to the motherland and the Center. The political significance is enormous. But the Han-Tibetan barriers remain serious. Imperialism and the Chiang Kai-shek

clique are still trying to incite discord between Tibet and the Center (one of their fabrications is that the Center is supporting the Panchen [Lama] and suppressing the Dalai [Lama], and intends to substitute the Dalai [Lama] with the Panchen [Lama]). Furthermore, the relationship between the Dalai and the Panchen cliques is by no means friendly. The two sides both suspect that the Center is biased toward the other. We must therefore adopt an extremely cautious attitude in dealing with the Dalai-Panchen relationship. We should do our best to handle such matters properly. We must avoid upsetting either side or causing their suspicions. In the meantime, we should promote discreetly unity between them.

Now that, as the directive implied, Tibetan politics had changed direction and became centripetal, the key issue in the Dalai-Panchen relationship was their relative statuses vis-à-vis the Central People's Government.

The Center's orientation is to make a step forward in realizing unified regional autonomy in the Tibetan region. Under the principle of treating the Dalai [Lama] as number one and the Panchen [Lama] number two, and the Dalai [Lama] the chief and the Panchen [Lama] the deputy, the patriotic forces in both the Dalai [Lama] and the Panchen [Lama] groups and in other groups should unite and establish a unified Tibetan autonomous region. It will take many years of complicated and tortuous work to materialize this orientation. In the past few years such work was done but serious difficulties still exist. One of the difficulties is that both groups harbor suspicions of the Center.

To reduce such suspicions, Beijing outlined regulations for local officials to implement in receiving and hosting the two Tibetan leaders. These regulations were in five categories: the proper forms of addressing the Dalai Lama and the Panchen Lama and the theocratic organizations under them; the order of the two's appearance and seating on public occasions; news media coverage; arrangements for welcoming the Tibetan leaders by local CCP officials, the Tibetan populace, and religious figures; and the limitation on circulating the directive inside the party. As a rule, in all places, ceremonies of equal warmth and scale would be accorded to the two Tibetan leaders—*yi shi tong ren* (similar treatments), as expressed in the directive. But whenever they appeared together, the status of the two leaders would be differentiated through delicate ranking arrangements. Beijing named Zhang Jingwu and Fan Ming to accompany the Dalai Lama and the Panchen Lama, respectively, to Beijing. Zhang and Fan should also help local governments in arranging their reception of the Tibetan leaders.[129] Having seen Beijing's directive, the two Zhangs of the TWC expressed their full support. Fan Ming was not satisfied with the proposed arrangements and made a complaint to Xi Zhongxun, without effect.[130]

After the Tibetans arrived in Beijing, the internal politics of the CCP regarding Tibet continued to zigzag between "leftist" and "rightist" policy options. At an internal meeting, Mao brought the disagreement into the open, jokingly calling himself a *lao youqing* (old rightist) and Fan Ming a *shaozhuangpai* (the up-and-coming) because of Fan's inclination toward a hard-line approach in using the Panchen Lama to push changes in Tibet.[131] The Tibetan leaders', especially the Dalai Lama's, journey to Beijing in 1954 indicated that under the 1951 agreement, Beijing's patient Tibetan policy had worked to a certain degree. The Tibetan leaders' visit in Beijing was historic, differing from that of all previous Tibetan visitors in the ancient capital of China. Before leaving Beijing for tours in other Chinese provinces, the Dalai Lama was elected vice-chairman of the Standing Committee of the National People's Congress and the Panchen Lama vice-chairman of the National People's Political Consultative Conference. Unmistakably, Tibet had entered the "national" era of Chinese politics.

Nevertheless, Beijing's strict principle of parallel but differentiated treatment for hosting the Tibetan leaders was reminiscent of the Qing court's handling of the Tibetan tributary missions sent once every two years, alternately, by the Dalai Lama and the Panchen Lama.[132] For instance, the expenses for the Tibetan visitors were established in advance. While all the personal daily expenses of food and other items for the Dalai Lama and the Panchen Lama would be fully covered by the CCP government, those for Tibetan officials in their entourages would be reimbursed in fixed amounts corresponding to their ranks. Brands of cigarettes of different qualities would be provided to Tibetan officials according to rank: *Zhonghua* for officials of the fourth rank and above, *Daqianmen* for lower-ranked officials, and *Hengda* for ordinary retinue.[133] The two Tibetan leaders' dietary habits were carefully investigated. Here is what CCP officials in Sichuan learned about the Dalai Lama's dietary preferences:

> The Dalai [Lama] likes to eat rice, noodle, steamed twisted roll, and steamed bread. For non-staple food he eats meat (various kinds of meats), chicken, duck, eggs, and seafood, and in general the Sichuan style of cooking is suitable. He does not like Western-style food and vegetables. For drink he mainly drinks milk, Tibetan buttered tea (self-made), but not soda.

And, because of the Dalai Lama's concern about personal security, all his food and drinks must be tested in advance for poison.[134] Such details could be considered by the Protocol Department of the Chinese Ministry of Foreign Affairs in receiving a foreign dignitary, but not in the treatment of any provincial official traveling inside China. This, therefore, set the Tibetan leaders apart from all other local officials of the PRC, even those from Inner Mongolia and Xinjiang.

***

The years 1954 and 1955 saw a transition in Beijing's Tibet question. Again, Ngabö's "hat" metaphor was revealing. Ngabö used the metaphor not just for the Seventeen-Point Agreement but also in a completely different meaning. In October 1951, shortly before the Kashag accepted the Seventeen-Point Agreement in the Dalai Lama's name, Ngabö explained to Zhang Jingwu how "imperialism" was trying to incite distrust of Beijing among the Tibetans. The notion, according to Ngabö, was that the CCP tended to offer sweet deals at first but then replace them with bitterness. Ngabö said: "This hat can fit perfectly on the head of Tibet. During the first ten years the PLA can be good, but it can still be suspected in the eleventh year." After the first encounter between the two sides in 1950–51, ordinary Tibetans did indeed ask "Will the PLA be this good forever?"[135] The issue of "being good" was a tricky one for both the PLA and the Tibetans. The PLA's entry into Tibet initiated not only an interethnic contact of massive scale but also an intersystemic fusion, or friction, in the most profound sense. From the outset, "being good" was an issue of mutual perception, but the CCP also defined "goodness" for both sides. In these years, Beijing believed that the PLA would favorably impress the Tibetans by doing good deeds and leaving the Tibetans alone. As for the Tibetan elites, who were the main targets of the TWC's effort, a definition of "good" Tibetans was constantly debated among CCP cadres, who applied various labels to Tibetans as individuals or groups. CCP officials had no question about the Tibetans' "backwardness," which was taken for granted in both cultural and Marxist senses. But, as clarified by the infighting of the TWC and Beijing's interventions, the ultimate standard for a Tibetan to qualify as "good" was that he or she appear "patriotic," or supportive of the CCP's efforts in Tibet. In 1954 and 1955, therefore, CCP leaders in Beijing entertained and hosted two "good" Tibetan leaders.

The criteria of "being good," however, were about to change for both the PLA and the Tibetans. The CCP itself was becoming more radical, or "better" in Beijing's own terms, replacing New Democracy with socialism. As the CCP led the country in an effort to catch up with the most advanced powers of the world, Tibet was pushed to keep up with the rest of China. In March 1955, before the Tibetan leaders returned to Tibet, the State Council decided to establish a Preparatory Committee for the Tibetan Autonomous Region.[136] The State Council also adopted new measures for helping economic and cultural development in Tibet. Shortly afterwards, Beijing authorized the TWC to come out into the open and also upgraded the Tibet Military Region as one of the twelve large military regions of the PRC. At a State Council meeting in early March, at which Tibetan representatives were present, Zhou Enlai proclaimed triumphantly that the work in Tibet was entering a "new phase." Zhou identified two tasks for Tibet to accomplish in the years to come: first, "democratic reform," and second, reduction of people's burdens in life.[137]

In this new phase, the mutual images of the CCP and the Tibetans would change again. The next chapter discusses a drastic turn in Beijing's relations with the Tibetans in the mid-1950s. Having executed a seemingly successful reception of the two Tibetan leaders in the heartland of China, CCP officials both in Beijing and at the local level felt that the waiting in Tibet had run its course and an era of reform had arrived. Ngabö's anxiety about conditions of the Sino-Tibetan relationship in the "eleventh year" proved prescient, though the "eleventh year" came sooner than that. With the relationship barely entering its fifth year, reconceptualization of "being good" on both sides began. It happened first outside the political realm of the Dalia Lama and in those Tibetan areas that had already been incorporated into Chinese provinces.

CHAPTER 3

A TIME TO CHANGE

In early February 1949, resigned to the CCP's military victory in China, U.S. secretary of state Dean Acheson informed President Harry Truman that a consensus in the Department of State considered China an "area of lower priority." It was so, according to Acheson, because the CCP had seized from its Nationalist predecessor something that "had been merely a façade in China, with a rough equilibrium maintained among feudal barons." "It is only a fiction," Acheson asserted to his president, "that China is called a nation today. Consequently, when the [Nationalist] Government collapses now China would be back where it had been many times before. Before the communists could do anything, they would have to create something."[1] Although dismissive of the incoming communist power in China, the Department of State did not completely rule out the possibility of a "communist-initiated rapprochement," which would mean the CCP's adoption of domestic policies in a "less doctrinal light" and, more importantly, renunciation of its pro-Soviet international orientation. For Washington, despite the obvious "antagonism between prevailing political philosophies" in the United States and Communist China, the possibility of American-CCP cooperation was based on the historical stream of time:

> US political philosophy is not unsympathetic to many of the immediate national aspirations of the Chinese communists. The US, as historic advocate of a free and prosperous China, agree in principle with the communist aims of territorial integrity of China, full Chinese sovereignty, and improved standard

of living, although objecting to the communist approach to the realization of those aims.²

In Washington, empathy toward the Chinese Communist Revolution lingered even after the PRC was officially launched. At the end of 1949, a major position paper of the U.S. National Security Council stated: "The Asians share poverty, nationalism, and revolution." In this "have-not and sensitively nationalistic area," the U.S.-Soviet competition would in the long run favor the "side which succeeds in identifying its own cause with that of the Asian peoples and which succeeds in working in harmony with the dominant motivating forces in Asia today and in influencing these forces rather than attempting by direct or impatient methods to control them." Therefore, "it would be inappropriate for the United States to adopt a posture more hostile or policies harsher toward a communist China than towards the USSR itself."³

Such empathy toward Asian societies' efforts to temporally catch up with the West, however, left out Tibet. Exactly because of its apparently archaic social conditions and physical isolation from the dynamic rest of Asia, Tibet assumed a dubious value in the emerging Cold War struggles. In early 1947, an internal State Department memorandum mentioned a "facetious" opinion voiced by some Joint Chiefs of Staff officers, who envisaged two possible functions of Tibet in current and future international politics: it might serve "as a country offering great waste areas in which rockets could be tested, or as a final retreat (Shangri-La) to which peace-loving people could flee when atomic war breaks, for Tibet is too remote to be of significance in any war."⁴ In the next few years, as the Chinese Communists were extending their influence to China's Inner Asian borderlands, State Department officials did not wish to see this Tibetan frontier of international politics being disturbed by either China's or India's interference.⁵

"Shangri-La," the famous fantastic land, was not unreal at all to some. A British political officer stationed in Sikkim, A. J. Hopkinson, gave his image of "Shangri-La" in these words:

> [If] happiness, contentment, self-sufficiency, and liberty mean anything, the modern world has more to learn from Tibet than to teach. Self-sufficiency in almost all essentials, Tibet is one of the few countries in the world that has no shortages, no rationing, no queues. You rarely see anyone under-nourished, under-clad. . . . Tibet's continued welfare depends on its maintenance. . . . Certainly, we should not go out of our way to thrust modernization on to Tibet.⁶

At the time, Hopkinson's admonition against Western powers' attempt to modernize Tibet was historically irrelevant because the moment for the West to effect or prevent any change in Tibet—if such a moment had ever existed—was already past. The CCP would soon take up the role as an agent of change in Tibet. Experienced observers of Tibetan society, including British, Indian, and Tibetan officials, were almost unanimous in pointing out that the conditions of Tibet could not make the land a stronghold against the tide of Chinese Communism. Just the opposite: living under feudal conditions for such a long time, the Tibetan people might prove to be a "fertile ground for communist propaganda." A high-positioned Tibetan official admitted to a visitor from India: "The only reason that Tibet had not already gone communist, in the light of the depressed condition of so many Tibetans, was the universal reverence of the Tibetan people for the Dalai Lama."[7]

But would the Dalai Lama be a harbinger of modernization or a mainstay of the status quo? Frank Bessac, after his tragic journey into Tibet with Douglas Mackiernan, reported to the State Department:

> The [Tibetan] government has recognized the necessity of land reform, but no action will be taken until the Dalai Lama comes of age. The discontent amongst the Tibetans is concentrated in the nobility and a very few of the educated clergy. Their discontent is a result of the backwardness of Tibet and the danger they think threatens Tibet as a result of her lack of modernization. This discontent is directed against the present government. Their hopes are placed in the young Dalai Lama. This 16-year-old youngster, besides being possessed of a remarkable personality, is extremely intelligent and capable. He is a very patriotic Tibetan.[8]

As the Tibetan situation unfolded in the years to come, the young Dalai Lama's "patriotism" was a major factor in shaping the way Tibet was to change. During the first few years of the PRC, however, policymakers in both London and Washington fixed their attention on power politics with Beijing, not social politics within Tibet. The British did not see the "loss of a very anachronistic Tibet" to communist China as a big deal. It might even be a sensible "material price" to pay "if the eyes of India can be opened" by such a development. Officials in London expected that as the PLA moved closer to the Indian border, New Delhi would become more amenable to the Western powers' view about the true nature of communist China.[9]

Officials in Washington were similarly interested in "exploiting the subject of Chinese communist actions in Tibet." In their opinion, the incorporation of Tibet into the PRC could not be impeccably repudiated from the stance of international law, especially after the conclusion of the Seventeen-Point Agreement between Lhasa and Beijing. Yet the archaic nature of Tibetan society—a "stage of development" comparable to "that of Europe about 1,000 years ago"— became Tibet's best defense against the Chinese Communists. An internal State Department memorandum suggested: "If Tibet cannot be depicted as the victim of external Chinese communist imperialism and colonialism, it may be possible to develop a useful case against the communists for destroying local and traditional systems of government and denying to the Tibetan people the rights of self-determination and self-government."[10]

Thus, for policymakers in London and Washington, modernization was a moot point as far as Tibet was concerned because, beneficial or not for the Tibetans, any change imposed on Tibet by the Chinese Communists could only be bad. Tactically, for a while, Beijing was in agreement with American and British officials that the local and traditional systems of Tibet must not be destroyed by outside force. But whereas London and Washington hoped that the Tibetan establishment would be an insurmountable barrier to CCP expansion into Tibet, Beijing, as chapter 2 shows, felt conversely that the Tibetan theocracy around the Dalai Lama could serve as a ready "bridge" for the CCP to cross and reach the Tibetan people en masse.

In this chapter, our story makes a detour on the route to Lhasa and sheds light on the situation of eastern Kham, administered as Xikang during the initial years of the PRC. In 1955, the region was incorporated into Sichuan and became the province's western frontier with Tibet. The Tibetan areas outside the political realm of the Dalai Lama, known to Tibetans as Amdo and Kham, assumed different degrees of importance in Beijing's policymaking. The eastern part of Kham, separated from Tibet by the Jinsha River, stood out both because historically the area served as a geo-ethnopolitical buffer between the Chinese and the Tibetan authorities and because, after 1951, Beijing wanted to use developments in the area to induce changes inside the Dalai Lama's political domain. Unlike the region under the Dalai Lama that was covered by special stipulations of the Seventeen-Point Agreement, from the outset those Tibetan communities not ruled by Lhasa belonged to the general category of "minority nationality areas" in Beijing's policymaking, even though CCP officials vacillated briefly between the notion of a unified large Tibet and an experiment of setting up a number of separate Tibetan autonomous regions. Eastern Kham's incorporation into Sichuan in 1955 ended the administrative uncertainty. As the following narrative shows, considering eastern Kham as a region simultaneously subject to the CCP's general policy toward minority nationalities *and* exemplary for Tibet under the Dalai Lama, Beijing started its social engineering in the region with tactful measures but ended up with a bloody war. Throughout the process, CCP leaders always understood that their policies and practices on the eastern side of the Jinsha River would have "positive" and "negative" effects on the other side of the river.

"Smart Class Struggles"

While most Western observers saw the CCP as an outside force destructive to Tibetan society, there were also individuals who desired that the CCP crack the Tibetan society open. In June 1950, E. E. Beatty, a Scottish missionary of the China Inland Mission, left Dartsédo (Kangding) after being stationed there for decades. When Beatty was passing through Hong Kong, the American Consulate General in Hong Kong interviewed him for information about the situation along Tibet's eastern border. What Beatty told the Americans was an astonishing piece of "intelligence" that mixed misinformation, hearsay, and facts. Beatty told the Americans that he had witnessed many PLA troops advancing toward Tibet. The morale of the troops appeared high, and they talked about marching into India after Tibet was secured. Allegedly, a PLA intelligence officer had told Beatty that the PLA had taken Chamdo and captured two Westerners: an Englishman with a radio and an Austrian who was a former prisoner of war escaped from India. Actually, PLA troops would not take Chamdo until months later. At the time, they indeed captured a Briton named Robert Ford who was in Chamdo operating radio for the Tibetan authorities. The Austrian was meant to be Heinrich Harrer, who tutored the fourteenth Dalai Lama in Lhasa but never traveled to Chamdo. It would be futile to speculate whether Beatty or the "PLA intelligence officer" fabricated the story, or if the whole thing was Beatty's somewhat prescient fantasy.[11] Beatty, who had tried but failed to enter Tibet, certainly did not feel dismayed by the PLA's advance toward Lhasa. In an article for the December 1950 issue of his mission's journal, *China's Millions*, Beatty wrote:

> The armies of China may be used of God to break the tyrannical yoke of taxation with which Tibetan temples throughout the centuries have burdened the life of the Tibetan people from birth to death. . . . Today the armies of Communist workmen are building a motor road across Tibet on which ten-wheel trucks already are moving toward Tibet's capital, Lhasa. We believe, hope and pray that this road, in the wisdom and power of God, will become a way of advance for those who proclaim the Christian gospel and way of life.[12]

One hundred and ten years before Beatty, American missionaries in China had used similar words to greet British gunboats coming to the Chinese shores: "God in His power may break down the barriers which prevent the gospel of Christ from entering China."[13]

Beatty's prayer for the Christian gospel would not be answered anytime soon. For a while, even his prediction about Beijing's breaking the Tibetan theocratic "yoke" seemed misplaced. Before the PRC's Tibetan affairs turned violent in the mid-1950s, the CCP, as discussed in chapter 2, endeavored to maintain a "good" image in Tibetan society. This was not an isolated effort; though unique, it was not at odds with Beijing's policies in other minority areas. The drastic turn of Tibetan affairs after the mid-1950s, therefore, must be understood in the context of the gradual radicalization of Beijing's general ethnopolitical orientation, which immediately affected the Tibetan communities on the eastern side of the Jinsha River.

As symbolized in the PRC's Common Program of 1949, the central message that Beijing wanted to disseminate in China's ethnic borderlands was about commonality. In the words of Ulanhu, then a leading member of the Nationality Affairs Committee of the CCP Central Committee as well as the party chief of Inner Mongolia, the CCP's goal was to achieve a "realm of great harmony consisting of all nationalities."[14] As for the recent expansion of Chinese Communist influence into the borderlands, all the consequences entailed were wrapped in an official rhetoric about "help." According to Zhou Enlai, talking in the context of Inner Mongolia, because "the Han people abound in gifts of nature [*de tian du hou*] and break into the lead in development [*kai fenghua zhi xian*]," they, as the "advanced," were obligated to "help the backward" minority nationalities. In October 1953, when talking to a group of Tibetan visitors, Mao Zedong insisted that development of Tibet must be achieved mainly by the Tibetan people and their leaders, and that the central government in Beijing "will only help" the Tibetans in the endeavor.[15]

Mao's stressing of Tibetan agency and his assertion about the seemingly secondary role of Beijing in "developing" Tibet reflected a general orientation of the CCP's ethnic policies in the early 1950s. The "Key Policies of the People's Republic of China in Implementing Nationality Regional Autonomy," adopted by the Central People's Government in early August 1952, stipulated that "internal reforms in nationality autonomous regions will be implemented according to the will of the majority of the people and leading figures who have connections with the people."[16] This duplicated the exact wording of the Seventeen-Point Agreement between Beijing and Lhasa, thus elevating the agreement into a general policy for all the minority nationalities of the country. An immediate question was whether the CCP's policy formula for Inner Mongolia or for Tibet should serve as a model for China's other minority areas. Earlier, in mid-October 1950, shortly after the PLA crossed the Jinsha River and began to advance toward Lhasa, Ulanhu told delegations from various minority areas that they had "only one way to achieve their complete liberation, which is to do the same as Inner Mongolia in following Mao Zedong's banner."[17] In 1952, however, the Tibetan model seemed to overshadow that of Inner Mongolia.

In the next few years, when discussing the socioeconomic development of Inner Mongolia, Ulanhu would continue to vacillate between "keeping pace with the whole country" and using less radical measures to continue the "uniqueness" of the region, especially in the pastoral areas of Inner Mongolia.[18] His specific concern for Inner Mongolia aside, Ulanhu's apparent flip-flopping was entirely in concert with the CCP's ethnic policy at the time, which was designed to induce national minorities' conformity with the "Chinese Nation" by accommodating selected ethnic attributes. Typically, the policy emphasized conformity and accommodation alternately for the sake of advancing the CCP's agenda at any given time. In the early years of the PRC, Beijing endeavored to reconnect China's central authorities with ethnic frontiers that had stayed aloof since 1911. This ethnopolitical agenda not only produced the Seventeen-Point Agreement with Tibet but also fostered an inviting atmosphere for suspicious ethnic minorities in general. Under the circumstances, Ulanhu was able to proclaim openly: "The land and pastures of Inner Mongolia belong to the Inner Mongolian nationality." By 1954, with Beijing's support, Inner Mongolia incorporated Suiyuan Province, rolling back the expansion of the Chinese province system in the Republic of China period. In the same year, Ulanhu replaced Li Weihan as the director of the CCP's Nationality Affairs Committee.[19]

All of this happened as part of Beijing's "help" project. Zhou's talk of the Han people's "gifts of nature" can be seen as reminiscent of Confucian superiority, comparable to Euro-American ideology about the "white man's burden" and almost identical to Sun Yat-sen's Han-centered assimilation project. But above all, the confident and righteous overtone of CCP leaders' "help" discourse was sustained by their conviction that communism was transformative in immunizing them against all kinds of bigotries and prejudices with which their "feudal," "reactionary," "bourgeois," and "imperialist" adversaries were diseased.

Beijing's confidence could not, however, be readily translated into action in the field. Initially, when the CCP encounter with peoples of ethnic frontiers did not go as smoothly as hoped, local party operatives were blamed. In the summer of 1950, reacting to "rebellions and killings among minority nationalities," the CCP Central Committee issued a directive that forbade its local apparatuses to initiate socioeconomic reforms in minority regions. More than two years later, seeing little effect in rectifying the "very irregular local relations among nationalities," Mao raised Beijing's censuring of local party officials to a new level. In an internal directive, Mao asserted that irregularities in internationality relations were caused by an "almost omnipresent" and "massively existent great Han chauvinism" among CCP cadres, which was allegedly a reactionary outlook bequeathed by the KMT and feudal-bourgeois classes.[20]

Yet an undeniable, paradoxical fact was that local CCP officials committed this "reactionary crime" of thought when implementing Beijing's revolutionary agenda in minority areas. As party cadres were the foot soldiers of the CCP's "help" project, their morale was fundamental to Beijing. Thus, a few months after Mao penned his harsh "internal" criticism of local officials, the

People's Daily publicized the problem of "great Han chauvinism" in an editorial, which was a much milder admonition to the CCP's local operatives. According to the editorial, symptoms of the problem mainly consisted of rushing forward in carrying out reform policies and "mechanically" transplanting experiences from the Han areas to minority communities. The editorial insisted that "great Han chauvinism" no longer existed systematically in the PRC, but its "remnants" continued to bedevil CCP members. The party's work in the minority areas could not progress without overcoming "great Han chauvinism," but, the editorial instructed its readers, overcoming the problem would be a long-term effort that could not be accomplished in one stroke. Above all, correction of the problem must not be done in a way that could hurt "Han cadres' enthusiasm."[21]

During the initial years of the PRC, the CCP's Han cadres, with "enthusiasm," were carrying out land reform in minority areas. This was a major step for the CCP to advance into China's largely rural frontiers. In the summer of 1950, Liu Shaoqi reported to the People's Political Consultative Conference that after continuous implementation of land reform in the next two years, only a small number of minority areas, with their population of twenty million, would remain unchanged. In 1952, when Xinjiang was added to Beijing's agenda for land reform, Liu instructed the CCP Xinjiang Branch Bureau: "This is a determined revolutionary offensive and any hesitation is not permitted."[22]

In all ethnic frontier areas, if there was one thing that could make Beijing hesitant in unleashing the "Han cadre's enthusiasm" for carrying out such "revolutionary offensive," it was the "mass's consciousness" (*qunzhong juewu*), or the ordinary people's willingness to support CCP policies and practices. "Mass's consciousness" was a magic term in all CCP operations. Mao once said that "mass work" must be the CCP's daily undertaking (*tian tian zuo*) and "mass line" the daily maxim (*tian tian jiang*).[23] Prior to 1949, when still struggling against the KMT state power, the CCP had relied on "mass support" to redress its material weakness vis-à-vis the KMT. After 1949, as the CCP transitioned into a power-holding party and changed its relationship with Chinese society, "mass line" remained a fundamental orientation for the CCP in its social engineering. In minority regions, as typified by Tibet, both the historical weakness of Chinese authorities and the CCP's messianic ideology underscored the need to reach the masses. Without the masses' gaining their "consciousness"—meaning substantial indoctrination by the CCP—Beijing felt forbiddingly handicapped in extending its programs into these areas.

In competing with traditional local establishments for "mass support" in minority areas, the CCP's initially weak position was comparable to its situation in KMT-controlled areas before 1949. In 1950, in a letter to a foreign communist party, which was revised by Mao himself, Liu Shaoqi explained how, before

1949, "three principles of justifiability, advantage, and restraint [*youli, youli, youjie*] guided the [CCP's] mass struggle in 'white [KMT] areas' ":

> First, [the struggle] must be viewed by the majority of the people as just and reasonable and can gain sympathy and endorsement from the majority, but must not be viewed by the majority as unreasonable so that its participants become isolated. This is the principle of justifiability. Second, [the struggle] must be advantageous to the mass in terms of comparison of power between our side and the enemy, and must be able to win victory. It must not be an unprepared struggle without certainty for victory, and not a risky undertaking against the enemy under circumstances unfavorable to the mass. This is the principle of advantage. Third, the struggle must be conducted with restraint, with appropriately and flexibly organized offensive and retreat. The struggle cannot continue endlessly so as to put the mass in predicament and frustration. This is the principle of restraint.[24]

These principles were included in a document titled "Conclusions on the Principal Experiences of the Party's Work Among the Minority Nationalities in the Past Few Years," which Beijing circulated in October 1954. At once cautionary against rushing into actions and emphatic about moving toward the CCP's goals, the document marked a point of departure for Beijing's policies in the minority areas. Two developments should be noted as the background of the "Conclusions." First, although circulated in 1954, the document was drafted in the previous year, when the PRC started its "transition to socialism." Second, Beijing decided to circulate the document among its local apparatuses at a time when the Dalai Lama and the Panchen Lama were visiting in Chinese provinces and seemingly vindicating the CCP's orientation of working with the Tibetan establishment.

The "Conclusions" was the final product of a national conference on united-front work held in July 1953. The conference had a broad agenda, but its main task was to review the CCP's "nationality work" during the first four years of the PRC. The "Conclusions" was based on a careful consideration of 192 reports from all over the country. As such, its authoritativeness and significance for broad application was beyond question. In thirty-two pages, the document set out to censor "incorrect" conceptions and practices among CCP officials and to prescribe "correct" ones for "bringing those backward nationalities up to the level of advanced nationalities so that they can complete transition to socialism."[25]

In asserting the necessity of social reforms, the "Conclusions" put Beijing's "help" orientation into perspective:

> Neither national liberation and equality nor assistance by advanced nationalities can thoroughly liberate minority nationalities. This is because, without

social reforms, the vast laboring masses of minority nationalities cannot gain complete and thorough emancipation from the oppressions that they have been enduring, social progress cannot be made, and transition to socialism cannot possibly be achieved.

Although this "liberation" mission was typical of CCP operations, the familiar approach of mobilizing the masses via violent class struggles was not to be used, for two reasons. First, in minority areas, "class polarization [*jieji fenhua*]" was yet to take place, and traditional social and religious leading figures still enjoyed tremendous support. Second, because many of these areas were located along China's international borders, they remained estranged from the central government and harbored centrifugal tendencies, which could be exploited by foreign imperialists. Thus, a new approach was in order:

> On the one hand, we should win over and unite all upper-stratum [i.e., upper-class] individuals who can be won over and united, and continue the orientation of long-term unity and cooperation with them. For this purpose, we should prepare to spend money to provide for such individuals so that in return they can concede and endorse transformation of old systems. . . . Surely upper-stratum people of minority nationalities can be reformed, and we should strive to reform the majority of them. On the other hand, revolutionary force should be developed gradually (including laboring people's armed forces) so that new and progressive elements can grow gradually in political, economic, and cultural and educational work. . . . After a period of such effort, a situation will be created in which the upper strata have to agree to abolish those old systems, such as the feudal serfdom, and to establish some new systems, such as farmer's ownership of land via land redistribution. These will be implemented in a top-down manner and through government ordinances. This approach is still one of class struggles (it has to be a class struggle) but not reformist charity. Yet this is a kind of smart [*qiaomiao de*] class struggle in a different form.

It was expected that these "smart class struggles" would produce six specific preconditions for land reform:

> (1) Stable social order; (2) sound inter-nationality relationship; (3) accurate analysis of social and economic conditions and class relations based on investigation and study; (4) demand [for reform] by the vast majority of the people of the nationality in question; (5) endorsement by social elites and leaders of the nationality in question who have connections with the people, and internal unity of the nationality; (6) existence of revolutionary activists and necessary personnel from the nationality concerned.

Following these six conditions, the "Conclusions" listed seven policy measures that should be implemented during reforms. Wherever these steps had been closely implemented in the past, according to the document, reforms went smoothly. Otherwise, whenever ignoring these steps, CCP cadres had committed serious errors. A consequence of such errors was to cause rebellions in minority areas, which had been numerous in the past three or four years. According to the "Conclusions," the most serious conflicts took place in Qinghai, Gansu, Sichuan, Yunnan, Xikang, and Xinjiang, involving Kazak, Hui, Yi, and Tibetan peoples. Although blaming KMT agents and other counterrevolutionary elements for inciting rebellions in minority regions, the "Conclusions" admitted that CCP cadres' erroneous practices in certain areas had caused rebellions or created opportunities for counterrevolutionaries.

Religion stood out among those issues that often got CCP operatives into trouble. In the "Conclusions," Beijing stressed that religion was not merely a personal concern but a "nationality-wide" phenomenon in most minority regions. In China before 1949, the document reasoned, minority peoples used religion to unite themselves in resisting national oppression. Today, "Islam and Buddhism have basically remained religions of the oppressed colonial peoples of the Orient." Therefore, the CCP must "respect religion" for both domestic and international reasons. Nevertheless, in discussing rebellions against CCP policies by those ethnically, religiously, and geographically integrated minority groups, the "Conclusions" was forthright that "small class struggle" must be buttressed with force:

> Rebellions in [minority] nationality areas are naturally inseparable from upper-stratum figures of minority nationalities. But such rebellions are often nationalistic and popular in nature as well, and they must not be treated as banditry or identified with ordinary counterrevolutionary rebellions. Therefore, rebellions in such areas should not be handled in the same way as problems of banditry and counterrevolutionary rebellions, but should be treated as nationality questions. Except for some unique circumstances, these should be handled with political means. . . . This is because military suppression can easily create inter-nationality barriers, and these barriers are easy to make but difficult to overcome. In the meantime, full military preparations are imperative, without which political work would not be able to proceed effectively, and the means for decisive victory would be missing when and where force must be used.

Although characterized as "smart class struggle," this orientation was not entirely unique in Chinese history. The CCP's dynastic and nationalist predecessors had worked with local sociopolitical establishments for the sake of appeasing China's ethnic frontiers. The so-called smartness of the CCP orientation lies in the fact that, at least in the early 1950s, Beijing was confident that traditional establishments in ethnic frontiers could be manipulated into willingly accepting the demise of their social existence. This set the CCP apart from its Manchu and Nationalist predecessors, but when and if these minority establishments proved unrelentingly perseverant, the CCP would forcefully abolish them anyway.

In the early 1950s, CCP officials in frontier regions were not as confident as Beijing about achieving the effect of "smart class struggle." Several months before Beijing circulated the "Conclusions," the Southwest Bureau had called its own conference on nationality work and also produced its own report on a policy orientation for the years to come.[26] In contrast to Beijing's "Conclusions," which emphasized the "nationalistic" characteristics of the conditions in minority areas, the Southwest Bureau contended that "spontaneous class struggles" by the laboring masses of minority nationalities were central to the question of how minority areas could advance into socialism along with the rest of the country. While admitting that relatively mild and circuitous means should be used to bring about reforms in areas along China's international boundaries and close to Tibet, the Bureau's report deviated from the preconditions for reforms set in Beijing's "Conclusions." The report reduced Beijing's six conditions to four, deleting "sound inter-nationality relationship" and "accurate analysis of social and economic conditions and class relations based on investigation and study." It also replaced the "stable [*wending*] social order" prescribed by the "Conclusions" with a "pacified [*anding*] social order" and a parenthetical phrase, "military force must exist in frontier regions." The report did include "agreement by the upper stratum" as a precondition for reforms, but such "agreement" was qualified as "forced" (*beipo*). The "most fundamental condition," according to the Bureau, "is the growth of revolutionary force among the minority people."[27]

The Southwest Bureau's dissenting voice was by no means subtle. In contrast to the "smart class struggle" proposed in Beijing's "Conclusions," the Southwest Bureau advocated for a familiar, forceful, and mass-oriented approach that would focus on seeking, fostering, and expanding pro-CCP, lower-class elements in minority societies. Such not very "smart" class struggle could completely dispense with caution about those "nationalistic" bounds that had so far defined the ethnicity of a minority people. Circulating the "Conclusions" months after the Southwest Bureau had voiced its opinion, top CCP leaders indicated that they wanted to stick with the "smart class struggle" orientation. By the end of 1954, the Southwest Bureau disappeared as a level of CCP policymaking. As one of the consequences of the "Gao-Rao affair," in April 1954 Beijing decided to abolish all its regional bureaus, which by now had become too powerful and unwieldy.[28] The Northeast and Northwest Bureaus, both of which had historical connections with Gao Gang, were among the first to go; the Southwest Bureau lasted till December. Yet, as the ethnopolitics of the PRC unfolded, the sentiment expressed in the Southwest Bureau's report would persist within the CCP. For a while, local CCP operatives remained subject to Beijing's "smart" restraint, but their artless approach would not be rejected by leaders in Beijing permanently.

"Unification of Tibet"

A key point made in the Southwest Bureau's report was that the degree of "smartness" in pushing for social changes in minority areas should be measured in terms of these areas' physical proximity to international boundaries and social intimacy with Tibet. Tibet, therefore, was deemed unique even by radical elements of the CCP. In this sense, as of 1954, a consensus existed at all levels, from Beijing to the TWC in Lhasa, that the "smart class struggle" approach should definitely continue in Tibet. Yet, in contrast to Beijing's practice years later of using "Tibet" only to refer to the area directly under the Dalai Lama's government, there was a brief period in which the CCP viewed *Xizang* (Tibet) as a socioeconomic and geopolitical amorphism, more complex than a dichotomy between a "political Tibet" and an "ethnographic Tibet."[29] At the time, it was the Tibetan authorities in Lhasa who wanted to limit the meaning of "Tibet" to the area directly under their rule, or the so-called political Tibet. In 1949, the Tibetan authorities wrote to CCP leaders and asked them not to send PLA troops in Qinghai to cross the "border" and enter "Tibet." Tibetan officials were also anxious about a scenario, as described to American diplomats in India, in which Tibetans on the eastern side of the "border," or in eastern Kham, develop a friendly relationship with the returned "Great [Long] Marchers" and then affect Tibetans on the western side.[30] At the time, Lhasa evidently wanted to stay away from those "ethnographic" Tibetan areas that had already became parts of the Chinese provinces of Qinghai, Gansu, Sichuan, and Yunnan. The connection between Beijing's policies for the Tibetan areas inside and outside the Tibetan "border," therefore, was one of the most crucial issues in the Beijing-Lhasa relationship in the 1950s.

As mentioned in chapter 2, before the Seventeen-Point Agreement was concluded, CCP officials held diverse and nuanced sociopolitical imageries about Tibet. For instance, in early 1950, the research office of the Eighteenth Army favored "in principle" the idea of a unified autonomous Tibetan government for all Tibetans. Typical of the CCP thinking at the time that accused old "reactionary" regimes of China of oppressing minority peoples with a "divide and rule" scheme, the notion of a unified Tibet was also in line with Beijing's support of a unified Inner Mongolia. However, a unified Tibet did not happen. In May 1950, for supposedly tactical reasons, the TWC became in favor of "divide and rule" in Tibet: not only should Kham remain separate from Tibet, but even *Xizang benbu*, or "Tibet proper," should also be divided into two sectors along the Yarlung Tsangpo River that ran through the region from west to east.[31]

Beijing did not approve such outright division of the region under the Dalai Lama. But, in general, differentiated treatment of minority regions was an established CCP practice. In mid-September 1950, Mao learned that the CCP Xikang Committee had set up an "eastern Tibetan autonomous region." Surprised, Mao wanted to know whether the step had been approved by Beijing and what would be the relationship between such a "region" and the province of Xikang. He wrote to other senior CCP leaders: "Among Tibet, Qinghai, Ningxia, Xinjiang, Gansu, Xikang, Yunnan, Guangxi, Guizhou, Hainan, and Xiangxi [western Hunan], some of these places will need to establish governments for large regions as in Inner Mongolia, but some others will need to establish governments for smaller regions involving several counties, or one county or district." Mao asked Li Weihan to investigate the issue.[32] In late 1951, reporting on behalf of the Nationality Affairs Committee, Li clarified three types of autonomous regions for minority nationalities in the PRC: regions of one nationality, those of one big nationality plus several smaller ones, and those of several nationalities.[33] Li's was a top-down perspective that focused on formulating three types of regional nationality administration. Many minority peoples, however, Tibetans included, were in a fourth condition—one nationality divided into several administrative units.

While committing ostentatiously to an "unshakable orientation" for a "unified Tibet," meaning only the region under the Dalai Lama, Beijing decided against applying the Inner Mongolia precedent to the Tibetan case, or unifying all Tibetans in one territory and under one government. Furthermore, the so-called unshakable orientation did not mean that Tibet had to be treated as a sociopolitical monolith. While strictly forbidding CCP officials in Shigatse and Chamdo to establish autonomous regional governments in their areas, Beijing was also adamant that, having changed as a result of recent events, these areas should politically reunify with Lhasa only "gradually." Thus, on the one hand, Lhasa would not have a clear case to complain about CCP violation of the Seventeen-Point Agreement, and on the other, the "more progressive" Shigatse and Chamdo, separately under the Panchen Lama and a "liberation committee," could continue their "current work for implementing progressive measures so that they can push and influence progress inside Tibet."[34] Having pledged in the Seventeen-Point Agreement not to impose reforms upon Tibet from the outside, Beijing had to come up with the "smartest" form of class struggle in order to achieve its ultimate goals in the political realm of the Dalai Lama. The different shades of politics in Shigatse and Chamdo necessarily became part of the stratagem.

CCP influence in Shigatse and Chamdo marked the degree to which Beijing was able to crack the Tibetan establishment from the inside. Then, after the mid-1950s, the physical and legal segregation between Tibet covered by the Seventeen-Point Agreement and those Tibetan areas in neighboring Chinese provinces ceased giving comfort to Lhasa. These areas became another means that Beijing could use to influence Tibet's internal situation from the outside. From the outset, these areas were subject to the CCP's "smart class struggle," but to a lesser degree. As such, they were destined to complete "democratic reform" and "transition to socialism" ahead of Tibet. An unstated territorial scheme underlying the Seventeen-Point Agreement was to negate any possible intention on Lhasa's part to extend influence into Amdo and eastern Kham. Meanwhile, it left the door open for Beijing to cultivate "progressive" Tibetans in Amdo and Kham who could use their ethnic connections to influence the Tibetans under Lhasa. For CCP officials in ethnic frontiers, territorial demarcation concerning minority areas was first and foremost about division of labor with respect to their "nationality work." For instance, in the early 1950s, Beijing could not decide which provincial authorities, those of Gansu or Sichuan, should take charge of Golok (Guoluo) and Ngawa (Aba), both ethnographically Tibetan areas. The Northwest and Southwest Bureaus reached a temporary understanding: Golok would be under the northwestern leadership and Ngawa the southwestern, and their final affiliations would be determined by the results of the two bureaus' respective "work" in these areas.[35] In such friendly intramural competitions among the CCP's regional organizations, those minority areas that made "progress" earlier and faster would hold an advantageous edge within the PRC system over those that lagged behind.

As the CCP authorities in Beijing and in the Qinghai-Sichuan-Xikang frontiers methodically deliberated and arranged hard and soft divides inside and outside Tibet, they made decisions swiftly on consolidating and expanding Sichuan Province. Initially, a plan was contemplated for dividing Sichuan into two provinces. Then, a year after the Seventeen-Point Agreement was concluded, the plan was abandoned in favor of "restoration of the old Sichuan province." As Deng Xiaoping explained to Mao in a letter dated July 9, 1952, the Southwest Bureau abandoned the original plan because the bureau was unable to find suitable candidates for two provincial party chief positions and also because the CCP leadership in Beijing was in favor of the one-province option. It took only four days for Beijing to approve the new plan and appoint Li Jingquan, who ranked number three in the Southwest Bureau after Deng moved to Beijing, as Sichuan's party chief and chairman of the provincial government.[36]

In the past, depending on the viability of China's ruling authorities sitting in the eastern half of the country, Sichuan had alternately played the role of a rear area or that of a frontline. In the 1950s, the province was again at the forefront of the Chinese authorities' effort to manage the Tibetan frontier. A native of Jiangxi, Li Jingquan had had a bout of ethnic frontier experience in Inner Mongolia during China's war against Japan. In the CCP's post-1949 relationship with Tibet, Li was a radical pusher for reforms in the Tibetan areas. Behind Li, a more powerful hand was his old superior Deng Xiaoping. In August 1950, even before Beijing had finalized its orientation in dealing with Lhasa, Deng instructed CCP officials in Xikang to establish an "eastern Tibetan autonomous region" as soon as possible. When the news reached Beijing, Mao appeared surprised and uneasy about the initiative from below.[37] In the next two years, however, the Northwest Bureau seemed to get ahead of the Southwest in setting up a string of "Tibetan autonomous regions" in Qinghai.[38] Thus, after Li got his appointment in Sichuan, one of his first moves, in December 1952, was to set up a Tibetan autonomous region within the province. As early as August, Deng indicated his support for Tianbao to hold concurrently the chairmanship of the Tibetan autonomous regions in both Sichuan and Xikang, foreshadowing the merge of the two provinces in 1955. The name of the autonomous region in Sichuan was not decided right away. At first Deng named it "Western Sichuan Tibetan Autonomous Region." When the autonomous region was finally launched in late December, however, its name was simply "Tibetan Autonomous Region of Sichuan Province," explicating to Lhasa a "progressive" Tibetan counterpart on the eastern side of the Jinsha River.[39]

The official report of the autonomous region's inaugurating conference was typical of CCP united-front operations, hailing the event for executing correctly the party's "upper-stratum" orientation toward frontier minority nationalities. Among the 363 representatives, 145 were local chieftains, tribal leaders, lama and secular officials, and notables. In view of such a presence by established social and political elites, the alleged "consensus" at the conference sounded rather impressive. Of course, according to the report, such consensus was reached only after a struggle between two opinions held by people of different class backgrounds. Although upper-class figures did not oppose the idea of an autonomous government, they wanted that government basically to continue the political status quo. In particular, they "demanded to emulate Tibet [*xiang Xizang kanqi*] and to adopt policies according to the [seventeen-point] agreement for peaceful liberation of Tibet." This opinion "did not win the majority's sympathy but on the contrary caused bitter refutations." The report stressed that most of the "middle-stratum" representatives joined the rebuttal. A Tibetan representative was quoted: "All minority nationalities should emulate the Han big brother, and the people of the whole country should emulate the Soviet Union. This should be our path and direction." Another: "Chairman Mao is in Beijing. Even Tibet has to emulate Beijing, and therefore we can no longer emulate Tibet." Allegedly, after a few days of discussion, all conference participants reached agreement on these points: "establishment of the Tibetan autonomous region is not for independence or separation from the leadership of Chairman Mao and the People's Government but for even closer unity around Chairman Mao and the People's Government"; "whereas religion can still follow Tibet, the path of people's life must follow Beijing"; "the positions of chieftains and tribal leaders and related systems should be decided by people's demands and leading figures' will, but the worst elements in the systems must be changed." With such "consensus," the conference was declared a success.[40]

But, the report admitted, "serious defects or even mistakes" existed. The conference paid too much attention to the upper-class participants and overlooked or slighted middle- and lower-class representatives, some of whom complained that their contribution to the CCP's war of liberation in the past few years had been made in vain. When making such self-criticism for overlooking "class contradictions" among the Tibetans, Li Jingquan's team in Sichuan promised that more radical policies would follow. In 1955, as Xikang was merged into Sichuan, in one stroke Beijing lifted nearly a half-million Tibetans out of a frontier province and incorporated them into a long-standing Chinese province.[41] As a result, the layered Tibetan frontier was further simplified, and the Jinsha River became the sole barrier left between a "socialist" Sichuan and, as British officials put it, a "very anachronistic" Tibet.[42]

In the confrontational international circumstances of the 1950s, especially after the Korean War, Tibet was a concern to CCP leaders not only because of its anachronism but also because of its twilight position between the "two camps" of international politics at the time. In September 1954, in a directive on "national public security work," the Ministry of Public Security pointed out that nine neighboring countries of the PRC in the Middle East and South Asia were affiliated with imperialism. In China's borderlands, taking advantage of interethnic and religious barriers between these areas and the rest of China, foreign imperialists and KMT agents were engaged in espionage and counterrevolutionary activities. The ministry classified these borderlands into three categories in terms of their security liabilities. Class one included areas where people's governments had been established and land reform carried out, such as Inner Mongolia, the ethnic Korean area of Yanbian in Jilin, most of Xinjiang, and the advanced part of Yunnan. Class two covered areas where the laboring masses were not yet mobilized and little reform had been implemented, including the Yi, Hui, and Tibetan areas of Sichuan, Xikang, Yunnan, Qinghai, and Gansu. Class three, the least secure category, consisted of Tibet, Chamdo of Xikang, and the Kawa areas of Yunnan, where "old power has continued, imperialism has deep roots, and our public security work does not exist." Emphatically, the ministry identified lama monasteries and Muslim mosques as centers that, aside from religious functions, conducted subversive political activities. These establishments exercised tight internal control and also served as safe havens for counterrevolutionaries.[43]

In viewing Tibet not only as a backward place for China's socioeconomic development but also a weak link in China's international struggle, CCP leaders had to decide how long they could afford to allow the status quo of Tibet to continue. The Seventeen-Point Agreement did not provide any clue about Beijing's timetable. Despite the wording about reforms by the Tibetans themselves, Beijing did not expect that these would take place automatically. Reforms in Tibet would have to be a result of the CCP's work, or "political struggle" conducted according to the three *you* principles limned by Liu Shaoqi. Before that, in Liu Shaoqi's words, what the CCP should achieve was to "take a steady foothold in Tibet."[44] When talking to some Tibetan dignitaries in October 1952, Mao used "fear" to characterize the Tibetan reluctance to implement changes in accordance with the Seventeen-Point Agreement. Mao promised that as long as such fear continued, changes would not be made.[45]

A "fear" factor, as the Ministry of Public Security's directive indicated, also existed on Beijing's side—an apprehension of sabotage by foreign, mainly American, imperialism. Therefore, Beijing's patience with the Tibetan status quo was rather limited. In 1952, Mao was resigned to the idea that "at least for two or three years" land reform could not be carried out in Tibet.[46] In the next few years, as the rest of China was making strides in the "transition to socialism," Beijing's patience for keeping a foothold in Tibet would be replaced with active search for ways of expanding the CCP's political ground. Under the framework of the Seventeen-Point Agreement, however, the offensive had to start from outside Tibet.

"No Need to Wait for Tibet"

After the Seventeen-Point Agreement was signed, Beijing praised the Tibetans as an "unconquerable nationality" (*buke zhengfu de minzu*) for not allowing foreign imperialism to vanquish them during the long separation between Tibet and China. In the CCP's public discourse, such credit could go only to the "Tibetan people," not the ruling elites who in the past had committed "non-patriotic" mistakes.[47] This class logic would continue to run through CCP deliberations at various levels about carrying out "democratic reform" in Tibetan areas, in which the "laboring" Tibetans were considered natural supporters of reforms and the "upper-stratum" Tibetans obstacles, even though for the moment Beijing's policy treated the latter's attitude as a key factor in deciding the timetable for reform. In the spring of 1954, the Southwest Bureau, while continuing to heed Beijing's policy of cooperating "sincerely" with upper-class Tibetans and religious figures, contended that correctly handling "spontaneous class struggles" from below was central to the realization of Beijing's goal of transition to socialism. In contrast, a work group dispatched to Xikang by

Beijing concluded that the question of whether reforms could be implemented peacefully in the area would hinge on a few local headmen's satisfaction with their treatment by the CCP.[48]

By the mid-1950s, CCP officials working in minority areas began to lose patience with "smart class struggles," increasingly eager to keep these areas abreast with the rest of China, which was changing with dazzling speed. This was especially the case for CCP officials in Xikang and the Tibetan areas of Sichuan, which were lagging behind even Qinghai, Gansu, and Yunnan in terms of reform. As Beijing did not have a uniform policy for all the Tibetan areas, Qinghai, Gansu, and Yunnan decided their own reform agendas and schedules for their Tibetan and other minority populations. In Qinghai, for instance, the Tibetans totaled more than 412,000, accounting for about 30 percent of the province's population. The CCP provincial leadership decided not to have a special policy for the Tibetans, lumping the seven non-Han peoples of the province together as one "minority nationality question." Because of Muslim warlords', or the Ma brothers', long-term rule in the province before 1949, Qinghai Tibetans harbored a deep hatred against the Hui, or Chinese Muslims. In the early 1950s, when the CCP endeavored to mobilize ordinary people to participate in state-sanctioned sociopolitical movements, some Tibetan communities drove Hui population out of their areas in the name of "liberation." Such interethnic conflicts prompted the CCP authorities to follow an evenhanded approach in dealing with various non-Han communities in the province. Initially, the CCP Qinghai Committee was cautious in differentiating the Han from minority communities as far as social reforms were concerned. Such differentiation disappeared, however, in 1952, when a provincewide land reform movement began. While encouraging minority peoples to struggle against landlords of their own ethnicities, CCP officials found in the process that once their "class consciousness" was awakened, minority laboring mass could become extremely active in demanding rapid reforms. In Qinghai, land reform affected those mosques and lamaist monasteries that owed farmlands, though leaving out the province's nomadic population for a while.[49]

CCP officials in Xikang and Sichuan, therefore, felt that they were behind their northwestern comrades for a few years. In January 1955, the CCP Xikang Committee adopted an "outline for discussing the question of democratic reform in the Tibetan autonomous region," which initiated Xikang's reform agenda. In August, the Committee filed another report on the "Situation of the mass' spontaneous struggles in Garzê Tibetan autonomous prefecture," according to which poor peasants rose against and even killed landlords in the name of the CCP. Such "intensified class struggles," the Xikang Committee contended, constituted clear evidence that reforms should begin immediately.[50] Leaders in Beijing endorsed the initiative. On August 21, Liao Zhigao, chief of the CCP Xikang Committee, informed his colleagues that Deng Xiaoping, who was already part of the central leadership in Beijing, had instructed the Xikang Committee to prepare a reform plan for Beijing to consider. Since Xikang would soon merge with Sichuan, the plan was intended as a preliminary reform agenda for the Tibetan areas of Sichuan as well. Liao also conveyed encouraging words from Liu Shaoqi: "Reform [in Tibetan and Yi areas] must be carried out. Do not fear: We communists never conceal our intentions and we frankly state them. We said this in the spring of 1953 and now we openly talk about reform." As for Tibet in Xikang's western neighborhood, Deng told Xikang officials not to worry too much: "Would reform in the Tibetan areas [of Xikang] necessarily impact Tibet? Among our country's 10 million minority nationality population, only 4 million have not yet experienced reform. And most of these are in the southwest."[51]

In the next four days, two teams of the CCP Xikang Committee discussed reform plans separately for the Tibetan and Yi areas of the province. The "Tibetan group," headed by Fan Zhizhong, included Ren Mingyuan, Zhang Chengwu, Miao Fengshu, Wei Huang, and Tianbao. Tianbao was the sole ethnic Tibetan in the group; all the others were Han.[52] Notably, the group's discussions mentioned just once the "pre-conditions" for reform and the notion of "smart class struggle" set in documents previously circulated by Beijing. The group's task was to answer not when but how "democratic reform" should be carried out in the province's Tibetan areas. Therefore, its discussions focused on issues like the conditions of land ownership, usurious loans, degree of exploitation, class classifications, and mass struggles, all typical of CCP land reform operations in the Han areas.

Tianbao voiced his strong doubts. During the first day of the group's deliberation, pros and cons of two reform approaches were considered. One was for rapid and massive operations to achieve surgical results, the other for smaller operations to accumulate piecemeal effects, or, in CCP officials' words, "peel a layer of the skin at a time [*bopi*]." Tianbao opposed the former:

> It would be even more thorough [meaning radical] than [measures taken] in the Han areas in terms of speed and methods. The advantage is faster. But in a time of one year it would be difficult to gather ten thousand Tibetan activists [meaning people who would willingly and actively participate in CCP operations]. They of course can be recruited from other regions but they may not remain active once they enter [the Tibetan areas]. In the meantime, the issue of lamas is huge and has international ramifications. Maybe monasteries should be exempt for now lest the number of enemies increase significantly—landlords, rich farmers, lamas, and especially the mass under lama's influence.

To support his point, Tianbao cited the Dalai Lama's comment: "The true religious believers are not in Lhasa but in Xikang." Another issue was guns in the society that, according to Tianbao, "mostly involved middle-stratum people who view guns as their life."⁵³

Fan Zhizhong disagreed with the piecemeal approach, which in his opinion could not effectively mobilize the masses, create enough pressure on upper classes, and enable the Tibetan areas to catch up with the rest of the country in socialist construction. Zhang Chengwu supported Fan by quoting Liu Shaoqi: "Mobilization of the mass has to be achieved in an integral way but not bit by bit." Tianbao was not convinced, contending that a one-stroke solution would be advantageous only if the CCP state were strong enough to do so, a condition that did not exist at the time. He made four points: first, transportation of troops was not ready; second, the masses could not be mobilized in a short time; third, military force could not prevent landlords from fleeing into other areas to make trouble; fourth, Beijing had indicated that under special circumstances, concessions should be made over the timing of reforms. Tianbao thought his Han colleagues underestimated the danger of armed resistance by the Tibetans, who could fight either for religion or because of hidden enemies' agitations. His warning was ominous:

> Differing from the Yi, all Tibetans are connected and still quite powerful. Without many small battles, it would have been impossible to start the Huaihai Campaign just in one stroke. I am especially concerned about monasteries. . . . 3 percent of the population being landlords, 4 percent being rich farmers, and plus monasteries and backward masses: These are a lot of enemies.

The Huaihai Campaign was one of the CCP's three decisive military operations during the Chinese Civil War of 1945–49. Tianbao's Huaihai analogy, however, did not work on this occasion. Although conceding to Tianbao's concern about monasteries, Fan insisted that the fundamental question was "whether or not reform should be carried out and can be carried out." With respect to the possible impact on Tibet, Fan stated: "If our conditions are ready [for reform], we do not need to wait for Tibet. The question of impact [on Tibet] also depends on whether or not we can achieve good results." In Fan's opinion, all reforms, even one through the patient approach of "peeling a layer of the skin at a time," would upset upper classes; "a so-called peace [peaceful reform] would actually still involve sharp and violent struggles." These words basically ended the debate. The conclusion of the day was that "democratic reform" would be carried out in three stages and completed in three years. The Tibetan group continued to confer for three more days, during which Tianbao again pleaded for moderation without effect. In the group's discussions, "directives from Commissar Deng [Xiaoping]" were mentioned a few times, indicating Beijing's close involvement.⁵⁴

In late August, based on the Tibetan group's work, the CCP Xikang Committee produced a reform plan, which went through several revisions before being jointly adopted by Xikang and Sichuan in late September.[55] The document, entitled "Preliminary Plan for Implementing Democratic Reform in the Agricultural Tibetan Areas of Sichuan," had three parts: "basic conditions," "questions regarding the policy orientation for carrying out democratic reform," and "time and steps of the reform." The first part laid out the rationales for reform, showing a significant radicalization of CCP policymaking with respect to the Tibetans:

> The two Tibetan autonomous prefectures, Garzê [Ganzi] and *Shuaijinsi* [sic, Shuajinsi, capital of Ngawa, or Aba], of Sichuan Province have a population of 930,000. Among these about 220,000 live in pastoral areas, and . . . about 400,000 live in agricultural areas where Tibetans [are] concentrated. While some of these areas are in the stage of feudal society, most are just in the initial phase of feudal society. Farmlands are controlled by chieftains, headmen, and lamaist monasteries, and cannot be traded. The vast majority of farmers are fettered to "assigned land" and exploited severely, and more than 90 percent of them owe usurious debts that they cannot pay back in several life times. . . . As a result, more than 10 percent of the population are farmers who have lost their "assigned land," and these plus farmers who have little land account for more than 60 percent of the population. At the moment, the class ratio is like this: landlords, 5 percent; rich farmers, 3 percent; middle farmers, 30 percent; poor farmers, 50 percent; farmworkers, 10 percent; others, 2 percent.
>
> In general, the Tibetan areas have a self-sufficient natural economy, but capitalism has also grown. Some feudal lords and monasteries are involved in commerce. . . . Lamaist monasteries are the important pillar of the feudal system of the Tibetan areas and seriously blocked Tibetan people's political, economic, and cultural development. The two prefectures currently have 672 monasteries and 70,000 lamas, and 60 percent of these are permanent lamas.
>
> Feudal lords and monasteries control a great number of guns. The Tibetans have 80,000 guns. Although 70 percent of these belong to the mass, most are actually controlled by feudal lords and monasteries. They have their own courts, prisons, and a set of administrative institutions and systems. They use these to force farmers to contribute labor service and tributes, and they have even sentenced farmers to death. To maintain their feudal power, they have often used inter-nationality and inter-tribal discords from history to provoke conflicts, inter-clan fighting, and even large-scale warfare.
>
> In the past five years or so we have followed the Center's directives and thoroughly carried out nationality policies. . . . Tibetan people's charges against feudal lords and spontaneous struggles in various forms have increased day by

day and these have happened in many places. This is a gigantic torrent and will certainly submerge the fortress of feudal lords once it is unleashed, organized, and channeled. If staying aloof from or trying to stop the mass' enthusiasm, we would seriously alienate the mass, damage national unity, and make all aspects of our work hard to proceed.

In the meantime, we should realize that further development of capitalism in the Tibetan areas would increase difficulties for socialist transformation in these areas in the future. Commercial capitalism in the Tibetan areas on the one hand has grown on the basis of the feudal system . . . and on the other it has connections with foreign imperialist economy. Since the Kangzang Highway was completed, such connections have increased. The data about Garzê shows that in 1954 the total commercial sales are 262.8 percent of the number for 1951. In the first season of this year imports of British and Indian goods increased more than ten times of the same period last year. If democratic reform is not carried out, the mass cannot be mobilized and organized to support implementation of the policy of "using, restraining, and reforming" private commercial enterprises. The number and capital of such enterprises will continue to expand and create more difficulties for socialist transformation in the future. In the countryside of eastern Xikang, rich farmers have been thriving in the past few years. If reform is further delayed, the same will happen in other areas and set obstacles for socialist transformation. In addition, without reform the mass cannot possibly be emancipated from the influence of religion, cultural and educational causes cannot progress, inter-clan fighting provoked by the upper stratum cannot be completely stopped, hidden bandits and enemy agents cannot be purged, united-front work with the upper stratum can be more difficult, and the state plan for large-scale migration into the Tibetan areas cannot be carried out. In sum, all these indicate that democratic reform in the Tibetan areas cannot be postponed any longer. Procrastination is highly unfavorable to us. As for the Tibetan upper stratum, by nature they are opposed to reforms, and currently quite a few of them are engaged in sabotage activities. The struggle will surely become even sharper and more complicated. But, because the masses have enhanced class consciousness and because our struggle has progressed every day, upper-stratum figures have realized that their ruling position is shaking. More and more of them hope to find out what future they may have in the wake of reform. Under the influence of our party and army and also because of our united-front work in the past few years, considerable split took place among these people. The Garzê Autonomous Prefecture has about a thousand upper-stratum figures, and they are holding different political attitudes: about 20 percent of them are close to us politically and are compelled to support reform; about 60 percent are in the middle and accept reform reluctantly; about 20 percent are resisting reform and a very small number of these people are firmly opposed to reform and may possibly conduct rebellion. But as long as we thoroughly mobilize the mass... and struggle firmly against all reactionary activities, even more serious split may occur among upper-stratum figures. Thus, we would be powerful and resourceful enough to force most of them to accept "peaceful" reform, to isolate a handful of reactionaries so that they cannot start rebellion, and, even if rebellions take place, to suppress them rapidly.

Reform in the Tibetan areas [of Sichuan] must be conducted with a view on its impact on Tibet. We believe that after reform is implemented in the Tibetan areas of our province, the laboring people of Tibet will be immensely inspired and our Tibet work will also be facilitated positively. The influence will certainly be good. But at the beginning, the upper stratum and religious circles of Tibet will inevitably become concerned. Yet, as long as we adopt mild and lenient policies and make proper arrangements for the livelihood of the upper stratum and lamas after reform, advance reform measures in stages and periods, set up, if necessary, a buffer zone in areas connected to Tibet, and make great effort to avoid missteps in reform, then the upper stratum of Tibet may probably not be affected so much or even become less worried, and hence they may be put at ease. But if we do not carry out reform or put off reform further, not only our work in these areas is hard to continue but the work in Tibet may also suffer. On the one hand, the near rear area [jin houfang] of Tibet could not be solidified, support from liberated mass could not come into existence, reactionary forces would be able to hide for a long time and carry out frequently subversive activities in collusion with the upper stratum, social order could not be stabilized, and security along the Kangzang Highway could not be assured. On the other hand, the Tibetan people would not be able to see the path they should follow, and the upper stratum of Tibet and those chieftains and headmen in Sichuan's Tibetan areas would support and influence each other and thus would not make progress. The Tibet work would consequently be hindered.[56]

Clearly, in the eyes of Xikang and Sichuan officials, not only were the traditional conditions of the Tibetan areas of Xikang and Sichuan marks of backwardness, but even the post-1949 economic gains of these areas were ideologically dangerous to the PRC. In combination with the PRC's international environment, therefore, "democratic reform" had to be carried out as quickly as possible. In this document, the earlier formula of "smart class struggle" had disappeared and the usual CCP line of mobilizing lower classes in a "mass struggle" was dominant. A year earlier, such a radical proposition would have been rejected right away by Beijing. But times had changed.

On December 5, 1955, Liu Shaoqi presided over a meeting of top provincial officials called by the CCP Politburo. He conveyed to the participants a recent directive from Mao: "Conservatism in every aspect of our work must be opposed so that socialist industrialization and transformation can be achieved ahead of schedule." In preparing his speech, Liu included these talking points: "The atmosphere has changed, and gigantic power of production has come into being, which our comrades could not even imagine a few months ago.... Therefore, the potentials of our work in various aspects are enormous, our cause can speed up, and additional results can be accomplished."[57] Thus, when Beijing was injecting such new thinking into the minds of its local officials, Sichuan and Xikang officials did not feel restrained in making the case for their region's catching up with the rest of China. Now the alleged readiness of the Tibetan laboring masses became the very reason for urgent reform. Internationality harmony and gradual social progress were deprioritized in the CCP policy. Immediate victory over feudalism and preemptive success against capitalism became the battle cry of the day.

Indeed, the Sichuan-Xikang reform plan stipulated that "democratic reform" and "socialist transformation" should take place simultaneously in the Tibetan areas.[58] The two dangerous issues that Tianbao had warned about as essences of Tibetan spiritual and secular life—monasteries and guns—were set up in the plan as two conspicuous targets to be dealt with by reform. Most remarkable in the plan was the paragraph justifying urgent reforms in Sichuan and Xikang by referring to Tibet. The paragraph did not exist at all in the earlier drafts and must have been added to the final version to dispel any concern in Beijing.[59] Fully aware of the close connections between the Tibetan communities on the two sides of the Jinsha River, Sichuan and Xikang officials nevertheless wanted to quash any anxiety in Beijing that Tibet would be negatively affected by radical changes on the eastern side of the river. The plan's conception of "near rear area" was especially revealing. In understanding China's eastern coast as the main front of the PRC's international struggle, the plan put the Tibetan frontier in an integral geostrategic perspective. Conversely, along the Tibetan frontier in the west, the plan proposed to use the Min River, the Yalong River, and the Jinsha River as three natural divides for a phased reform expanding from east to west. In a word, the plan envisioned the Tibetan frontier simultaneously as a cutting edge of the CCP's domestic social engineering and a security cushion for the PRC's international political venture.

With approval from Beijing, Sichuan officials began taking the planned reform steps in various areas in the winter of 1955 and the spring of 1956.[60] In the spring of 1956, as a step toward preparing reform in pastoral Tibetan areas, Sichuan sent an eighty-member delegation to Inner Mongolia to learn from their experiences. The result could be nothing but reaffirmation of Inner Mongolia as the model to emulate.[61] In the meantime, "peaceful reform" in the Tibetan areas of Sichuan and Qinghai would serve as a model for reform in Tibet in the future. For that purpose, at Beijing's request, upper-class figures of Tibet were to visit Sichuan and Qinghai and see peaceful reforms with their own eyes.[62] In their reform plan, Sichuan-Xikang officials used quotation marks for "peaceful reform," indicating a degree of cynicism about the notion. Soon, their prophecy about the impossibility of a reform at once "genuine" and "peaceful" would be fulfilled by their own militant measures in the former eastern Kham, now western Sichuan. "Democratic reform" in western Sichuan was a two-pronged operation targeting simultaneously the Yi and the Tibetan communities. According to official PRC publications, on December 24, 1955, some Yi slave owners of Liangshan fired the first shot to resist reform. Then, in the two Tibetan prefectures of Sichuan, Garzê and Ngawa, rebellions started separately on February 25 and March 13, 1956.[63]

Actually, ever since the beginning of the PRC, the CCP authorities had never stopped "bandit annihilation" (*jiaofei*) in frontier regions. Such "banditry" activities were mainly repercussions of China's regime change in 1949. Starting in the winter of 1955–56, however, the new round of military clashes in western Sichuan had a different sociopolitical background in that they were caused by the CCP authorities' effort to reshape minority societies. "Democratic reform" in minority areas marked the CCP's decisive rejection of one of the administrative legacies from China's long history, *yin su er zhi* (rule according to local customs). The reform also exceeded another legacy of China's frontier management, *gai tu gui liu* (changing native rulers into regular officials), altering the local socioeconomic and even cultural systems. The most recent *gai tu gui liu* along the Tibet-Sichuan frontiers had taken place during the first decade of the twentieth century, when Zhao Erfeng, the Sichuan-Yunnan commissioner of the Qing Dynasty, imposed a series of changes to frontier Tibetan communities, earning the nickname "Butcher Zhao" because of his perverted proclivity for killing people.[64]

The CCP's "democratic reform" in western Sichuan caused social upheavals and interethnic conflicts on a much larger scale than Zhao's havoc. According to official figures from the PRC, during the reform period, rebellions occurred in forty-four of the fifty counties of Sichuan's three Yi and Tibetan prefectures, and a total of 150,000 local people joined rebellions. During the six years of the CCP's *pingpan* (pacification of rebellions) operations, or from 1956 to 1961, sixty thousand PLA troops fought more than ten thousand battles, and "annihilated" (meaning killed, captured, and dispersed) 145,000 rebels (the remaining five thousand escaped to other places). If the estimate of the Tibetan population in the Sichuan-Xikang reform plan can be trusted, the reform-affected agricultural and pastoral areas had 400,000 and 220,000 Tibetan residents, respectively. The Liangshan area had 700,000 Yi people. Official statistics put "annihilated" Yi rebels at 29,231, or about 4.2 percent of the Yi population. This means that those "annihilated" Tibetan rebels totaled 115,769, or nearly 19 percent of the region's Tibetan population. The reported casualties on the PLA side were close to 10,000. Differing from the "bandit annihilation" operations in the early 1950s, which were sustained logistically by hundreds of thousands of farmer-laborers, the operations between 1956 and 1961 were carried out by modernized PLA troops supported by three automobile regiments and an air force.[65]

This was a "reform war." As the fighting spread, polemics defining the nature of the struggle began to unfold on both sides of the conflict, both in the field and within the CCP. The war was certainly more complicated than a conflict between local Tibetan rebels and PLA troops. As soon as reform was afoot, CCP apparatuses in Sichuan at various levels began to make urgent requests for weapons to arm "revolutionary mass" and cadres working in the field. On February 13, 1956, the CCP Sichuan Committee sent this telegram to the General Staff of the PLA:

> To protect smooth development of democratic reform in the minority areas of our province, local cadres, and state enterprises and units urgently need arms. During reform people's armed self-defense forces are to be organized and they also need a lot of weapons. Comrade Tianbao and others already raised this issue during a meeting with the General Staff [of the PLA], and comrade Chen Geng promised to help on the spot. Here are the weapons and ammunitions we need: 9,000 rifles, 70,000 ammunitions for 7.63 Mauser pistols, 2,330,000 ammunitions for 79-millimeter rifles and machineguns, 10,000 ammunitions for 65-millimeter rifles, 16,000 ammunitions for Soviet made 7.62 rifles, 30,000 ammunitions for carbines, and [six-figure number illegible] hand grenades.[66]

In mid-March, the PLA General Staff partially met Sichuan's request and agreed to provide 1,000 rifles, 50,000 rounds of ammunition, and 7,000 hand grenades.[67] At the time, the CCP leaderships in both Sichuan and Beijing expected that local officials of Sichuan would be able to carry out an armed "peaceful" reform without involving PLA troops. The General Staff appeared optimistic in sharply reducing the numbers of weapons requested. During the initial months of the reform, even the Sichuan leadership did not envision an extensive conflict. In mid-March, after distributing 1,500 rifles and thirty-six machine guns to the minority areas, the Sichuan leadership believed that the armament issue was solved.[68]

The atmosphere in the field was rather different. The Yi areas sounded alarms first. Between March 10 and 15, the CCP Xichang Prefecture Committee sent three urgent messages to the Sichuan leadership, describing the situation in the region as "unprecedentedly tense" and "very likely to lead to comprehensive trouble." Since not many PLA troops were present in the region, the CCP Xichang Committee proposed to organize all the cadres of the prefecture into "armed work teams" and to arm "the basic mass of minority nationalities" for self-defense. Reportedly, at the time there was a "nationality self-defense unit" of about a thousand members, which was to be expanded into a militia of several thousand troops. To implement the proposed expansion, Xichang officials put in a request for guns, ammunition, and a hundred tons of grain. The grain was needed to feed militia troops, who were "mostly slaves and semi-slaves."[69]

The Sichuan leadership did its best to satisfy Xichang's demands. But, the initial "rebellions by reactionary headsmen" soon turned into a full-scale war that engulfed the province's Yi and Tibetan populace. PLA involvement thus became inevitable. Soon tens of thousands of PLA troops began to operate in western Sichuan. In late March 1956, the CCP Kangding Area Committee asked the Sichuan leadership to send twenty thousand farm laborers into the Tibetan areas to sustain PLA operations. These laborers would mainly be used to maintain ammunition supplies for PLA troops. Fighting took place in difficult terrain and remote locations, and consequently it was calculated that one PLA soldier would need support by one and two laborers, respectively, in northern and southern Dartsédo [Kangding]. The CCP Kangding Committee explained that such manpower could not be achieved locally because in the thinly populated region many of the able-bodied men had already become involved in the conflicts, either as rebels or as militias and members of a "Tibetan regiment" on the CCP's side.[70] In a report dated April 1956, the Sichuan Public Security Department gave high marks to those Yi and Tibetans who joined the CCP side in the reform war:

> As democratic reform is unfolding, self-defense militia has grown and expanded to facilitate the reform in various areas. The militia has played an important role in mobilizing the mass and assisting [PLA] troops' operations. Especially in high mountains and the chilly climate of minority areas, this force is superior in several aspects. Specifically, they are familiar with the terrains and deft in climbing high and steep ridges. As natives they are familiar with local dialects and customs, and they can easily get information. They lead a simple life, can endure hardship, and can be indifferent to starvation and severe weather. In addition, all of them can shoot the rifle well.

Although not providing an exact number of such minority fighters, the report requested ammunition to supply a militia of "several tens of thousands."[71]

The question is whether or not reports like this should be taken at face value. For the Chinese Communists, their revolution was not only about overturning old sociopolitical systems but also about "liberating" the laboring masses materially and spiritually. In the Tibetan areas of western Sichuan, "democratic reform" would mean nothing if CCP cadres could not prove that the vast majority of the local population enthusiastically embraced the reform. In reporting to their superiors, Sichuan officials usually listed material results of the so-called three movements (readjustment of debts, abolition of *u-lag* or corvée labor, and emancipation of slaves) as evidence of reform progress. In the meantime, they especially highlighted "liberating" effects of the reform that changed ordinary people's sociopolitical identities. For instance, in two counties of western Sichuan, where pilot reform projects were first implemented among a population of 40,800, the reported achievements included emancipating 207 slaves, enrolling 12,059 or 80 percent of adult farmers into peasant associations, training 4,281 (29 percent of the adult farmers) "activists" (meaning enthusiasts for reform), recruiting 174 Youth League members, and enlisting 3,750 members of self-defense militias. Even in other counties where "democratic reform" did not begin until February 1956, membership in peasant associations expanded rapidly, from 30 percent to 80 percent of adult farmers, and the number of militia members reached 10,000. Allegedly, "liberated farmers were very excited and could not stop thanking the party and Chairman Mao. A great number of young farmers wanted to join the army and the Youth League. Even some lamas wanted to join self-defense militias or the army."[72] In early 1960, a PLA report on "militia work" had these numbers: in 1959, the militia membership in minority areas of Sichuan totaled 275,660, or 13.8 percent of the population; in that year, the militias engaged rebels in 1,506 operations, either independently or in coordination with the PLA, annihilating 6,723 enemies, or 31.9 percent of the total annihilated for the year. With these numbers, the report proclaimed "pacification of rebellions" as a "people's war."[73]

This notion of a "people's war," or a class struggle in which laboring Tibetans rose en masse to overthrow the old oppressive and exploitative systems, is as inaccurate as is portraying the conflict as an interethnic struggle in which all Tibetans fought on the same side against the Chinese intrusion. While reports filed by Sichuan officials at various levels were selective about facts and intrinsically class-struggle oriented, they nevertheless revealed tremendous intricacies wrought by "democratic reform." Here are some details from those reports.

In these reforms, as in CCP operations in other provinces, "classes" were arbitrarily classified according to how wide a "scope of strike" (*dajimian*) would be politically appropriate. In certain areas, 10–20 percent of the population were initially classified as "landlords" or "rich farmers" who would be subject to "readjustments" (*tiaoji*). Reactions from these "classes" varied. Some landlords praised reform measures for treating them "very generously," but others rebelled as soon as they learned about the contents of the forthcoming reform. In certain places, landlords and rich farmers kept a low profile but "middle farmers" were "extremely rampant" in opposing reform. In Drakgo (Luhuo County) of northern Garzê, for instance, some villages and townships rebelled in their entirety except those "principal upper-stratum figures" who were either supportive of reform or maintained "neutrality" in the conflict. A case mentioned in CCP documents involved a chieftain who allegedly threatened residents in his area with severe punishment if they dared to join the rebels. From the outset, monasteries occupied a central position in the conflict, but the forms of their involvement varied. The Dajin and Garzê Monasteries (Dargye Gompa and Garzê Gompa) of Garzê were internally divided and asked the CCP authorities not to see their attitudes toward reforms as monolithic. In certain places, after rebellions took place, local chieftains and high-ranking lamas joined CCP work teams to persuade "rebellious masses" (*panzhong*) to give up and return home. But the Shouling Monastery (Drakgo Gompa) of Luhuo rebelled and "coerced" ordinary folks to join the rebellion. When PLA troops attacked the monastery, local "mass activists" also participated in the action. To many, "democratic reform" was a procedure of dispossession. By the end of March, aside from "readjusting" landownership, the CCP authorities "borrowed" more than 4,800 guns and "mobilized without compensation 900,000 kilograms of grains" from the local communities. These "borrowed" guns and "mobilized" grains came not just from those households classified as landlords and rich farmers but also, to an unspecified extent, from those classified as middle farmers. In certain places, gun collection even violated lower farmers. The dispossessing process actually went beyond the usual format of "democratic reform" and adopted a form of "socialism." By early April 1956, about 41 percent of the households of Garzê were organized into "mutual assistance groups," which in the PRC was a preliminary step toward "transition to socialism." Yet, because these "mutual assistance groups" collectivized production resources, labor, management, and distribution, it became clear to Sichuan provincial leadership that local cadres were actually pushing for a more radical form of "advanced cooperatives." Provincial officials feared that "such rush in organizing cooperatives is bound to cause big problems."[74]

Thus, the reform war in western Sichuan in the mid-1950s was a mixture of interethnic and interclass conflicts. At the beginning, a set of socioeconomic changes was initiated by Han CCP cadres, most of whom were not local. The violent continuation of the reform was sustained by both PLA troops and the local Yi and Tibetan population, who became split in the social upheaval because of their various material and spiritual positions in the prereform social setting and the ways in which "democratic reform" affected their lives and beliefs. Anti-Han catchwords and class-struggle slogans were used by rebels and the CCP authorities, respectively, for political advantage. Neither accurately defined the reform war that blurred ethnic and class lines. In February 1956, the CCP Sichuan Committee called a conference of regional CCP chiefs. A finding of the conference was that in launching "democratic reform," Han cadres generally did not trust the "laboring people of minority nationalities."[75] Undeniably, on the side of Han cadres, ethnic bigotry was on open display. On the other side, rebels in southern Garzê held an anti-Han stance because "the Han wanted reform and did not allow us to have religion." In comparison, in northern Garzê, rebellions began with attacking those local Tibetan cadres and activists who promoted reform, but not the CCP authorities and the Han populace. The attack shifted to the latter only after "some Tibetan cadres and activists were terrorized into submission."[76] Situations like these seem to indicate that the rebels were fundamentally antireform but only contingently anti-Han.

As with CCP officials elsewhere, Sichuan cadres' commitment to reforming the two ethnic-frontier societies, Yi and Tibetan, was unconditional. Not necessarily convinced that "democratic reform" had to be spearheaded by war, they did not hesitate to forge ahead when social engineering shed blood. In mid-May 1956, Fan Zhizhong, chief of the CCP Kangding Committee, summarized the developments of the Garzê reform for a regional CCP cadre meeting. Li Jingquan attended the meeting and made occasional remarks during Fan's speech. What emerged from the meeting was the scope and intensity of the reform war and the Sichuan leadership's adamancy to proceed despite the havoc. According to Fan, as "democratic reform" was unfolding during the previous five months, only three of Garzê's twenty counties did not rebel, and eight counties were completely engulfed by rebellions. Of the 470,000 residents of Garzê, 20,000 joined rebellions directly. On the side of reform, Fan asserted, 16,000 local people were armed and 19,000 militia members participated in operations against the rebels.[77] Li had this to say about the situation:

> In a word, the rebels used nationality slogans to oppose us. Some of them ran into Tibet. The Dalai [Lama] said: if [rebellions] involved only a small group, without any doubt they violated the law; but if the majority became involved, the issue should be studied. They [Lhasa] wanted to come to investigate. Let them come. Those who are fighting us include both serf masters and unenlightened farmers. But how many upper-stratum people are really fighting us? (Fan: We have not figured that out yet.)
>
> The work with the upper stratum [of the Tibetans] is the same as that with capitalists. We want to eliminate them but should make them understand as well. Effective work with a person can stop that person's resistance and is therefore beneficial. The buyout policy for the upper stratum cannot work without [support from] the mass and troops. Otherwise even though you want to buy him out, he would not come forward at all. . . . We should do our best to work with the upper stratum. Meetings with them may last for a few days but then they should be allowed to go home. We do not use the stratagem of luring a tiger out of the mountain. Let them rebel if they want to. But we cannot do anything for them if they decline our invitation to join us.
>
> . . . We are not warmongers and we have been forced to fight. All problems should be settled peacefully if they can be settled peacefully. Our troops prefer to strike monasteries because monasteries are easy targets. The training battalion wanted to attack monasteries in Luhuo. After coming to Garzê, they

again wanted to attack monasteries. But monasteries in Garzê are along the main roads and therefore are not easy targets. Later, the Garzê Monastery became internally divided and invited us to step in. It has not been attacked until today. We may work to persuade the monastery to surrender some guns, which would be as good as attacking it. In our view, it would be better not to attack monasteries because such attack can easily get us entangled into religious and inter-nationality issues. Our troops should not calculate their achievements by counting how many people they have attacked. The Litang [Lithang Chode] Monastery is the largest in the Xikang area. The news about its being attacked has had tremendous impact on other places and led to surrendering of guns in Bathang [Batang] and Chaktreng [Xiangcheng]. Some thought that now that attack on the Litang Monastery was permitted, why not other monasteries? If the provincial committee had not set up an approval procedure about attacking monasteries, many more monasteries would have been attacked. . . .

The provincial committee was not fully prepared for developments in the Tibetan areas. Initially we thought that the Tibetans were relatively civilized, politically savvy, and appreciative of the prevalent trends. At a meeting in last winter, the Yi opposed and the Tibetans supported [reform]. Consequently, we were caught in an awkward position. Troops were deployed only after conflicts broke out. Reform arrangements also became overstretched. . . . Our work was overstretched but we did not do enough in splitting the upper stratum in order to reduce resistance. Work arrangements were out of sync and rushed. The idea proved unworkable that "separate upper-stratum figures from their locales for a while in order to mobilize the mass rapidly to create a fait accompli." You may have lured the tigers out but they did not really leave their mountains. They continued to communicate and make contacts with their areas. In sum, we acted somewhat in haste. According to the originally planned steps, pilot projects of land reform should have started in Rongtrak [Danba], the three movements should have been implemented in eastern and northern Xikang, and the status quo should have been maintained in southern Xikang. Fortunately, we took advantage of our mistakes. Fighting broke out even before the training of activists was completed. So, we preserved our strength and did not lose Chaktreng and Bathang. This is one advantage alongside nine disadvantages. . . . Apparently peaceful reform is impossible without backup by force.[78]

Li's rambling revealed how Sichuan cadres' intransigency turned the CCP project for "helping" the minorities into a bloody conquest. His discussion of attacks on monasteries showed especially how "advantage" in such operations was calculated. While admitting that a bit more patience and a bit slower pace in implementing the reform agenda could have avoided the open conflict, Li affixed the responsibility for starting the fight to the uncooperative "upper-stratum" Tibetans. In this way, he justified the "class war" waged by CCP cadres along with an "enlightened" mass.

In late May, the CCP Sichuan Committee sent an upbeat report to Beijing. While admitting that "roughness" and "mistakes of great-Han chauvinism" did exist in reform, the Sichuan report stressed the fundamental "correctness" of those reform measures in the Tibetan-Yi areas of Sichuan.[79] The claim, however, was not endorsed by CCP observers from Tibet and Beijing. After investigating the reform in Garzê, a team sent by the Tibet Work Committee made three points: first, the reform in the minority areas of western Sichuan simply copied methods from the Han regions of China and should therefore not serve as a model for the future reform in Tibet; second, rebellions took place because Sichuan cadres failed to consult with Yi and Tibetan upper classes; third, Sichuan's work teams pushed reform while not prepared to deal with rebellions.[80] Although these findings by the TWC could not have much impact on developments in western Sichuan, the opinion held by a group of officials from Beijing was a different matter.

"Tiger" and "Pigs"

As early as January 1956, the Central United Front Department (CUFD) was already proposing modifications of Sichuan's reform plan. In CUFD's opinion, issues like land, guns, privileges, and usuries of the monasteries should be dealt with through relatively generous and flexible policies, and detailed and differentiated measures should be considered for farmland and pastureland owned by the upper classes.[81] Yet, in view of what happened during the initial months of the reform, the CUFD proposal obviously had no effect on Sichuan's original reform plan. Then, in April, in the thick of the reform war, deputy director of the CUFD Liu Geping went directly to Dartsédo. The Sichuan leadership sent one of their own, Miao Fengshu, to accompany Liu. Liu did not just come to inspect. Having learned about the situation, he began to direct local CCP officials to take steps to stop the fighting.[82] Between May 1956 and February 1957, Liu drafted policy directives and gave talks to CCP cadres as well as to Tibetan and Yi elites for the sake of restoring peace.

Liu's ideas were carried out only in some areas and, in general, were firmly resisted by Sichuan officials. Two years later, in a totally different political atmosphere around Tibetan affairs after to the Lhasa revolt of March 1959, the CCP Garzê Committee denounced Liu's orientation as a "rightist line" that capitulated to the enemy, apologized to the upper stratum, and suppressed the mass's enthusiasm. Thus, Liu was labeled as a "spokesman of serf masters and landlords inside the Party."[83] In 1960, the Garzê Committee compiled a document to further highlight Liu's words and ideas that Garzê officials deemed incriminating and thus, unwittingly, created a record of a dissenting voice inside the CCP leadership. Like Tianbao, Liu understood the two key issues in the region, guns and religion, that the CCP authorities had to face:

> The issue of guns is a nationality question. In history, from the viewpoint of the mass, their own nationalities or tribes have for long engaged in armed struggles against external and internal enemies. They do not feel powerful without guns. In the meantime, guns can be traded freely and constitute a big fortune. . . . Guns have been used for self-defense and for protection of pastures. Trade through traveling cannot be conducted without guns. It is therefore very difficult to ask them to surrender their personal guns. . . . Through our patient and prolonged work, landlords and rich farmers will eventually become willing to hand in their guns. As long as we carry out the Center's policy correctly, we have nothing to fear from the few guns owed by landlords and rich farmers. . . . Monasteries should be allowed to decide by themselves whether or not to sell their guns. It is unnecessary to borrow guns from them in the future.
>
> . . .
>
> We must understand that religion per se is not feudalistic. . . . Lamaism has profound influence in the entire Tibetan nationality, and it played an important role in unifying the Tibetan nationality in history. All Tibetan intellectuals (Geshe and above) live in monasteries. Our work to win over the monasteries, if successful, can significantly facilitate democratic reform, socialist transformation and construction, and national unity. . . . In respect to religion, if the mass criticize us for being rightist, then that would mean a political advantage for us. Yet we must avoid being criticized for being atheists who interfere in other people's religious beliefs. . . . We should see that monasteries engage in trade and act as commercial agents in buying and selling local products. This is already a form of state capitalism. They have started transformation and should be given a retail market in the future. . . . For now, the monasteries should not be touched. Cadres of [reform] work teams should persuade the mass to pay land rent and honor debts to monasteries.

Liu did not believe that the local communities should be held responsible for the current bloodshed:

> The reform has some achievements but has many defects. Many problems have been exposed. Everyone is dissatisfied with the work, and many comrades in provincial, regional, and work committees are dissatisfied. . . . Who should take responsibility? First, I am responsible [Liu recalled that in 1950 Mao sent him here to visit but he failed to discover problems at the time]. Secondly, the

Party is responsible. And thirdly, people dressed in different cloths [meaning various social classes] are responsible. You [meaning upper-class figures] should have told us about the problems but you didn't. Neither did you write to me—your friend, nor write to the Center, Chairman Mao, and the Sichuan Provincial Committee. Next, the Han cadres working here are responsible. You [Han cadres] did not follow Chairman Mao's and the provincial committee's directives. You paid attention only to the interests of peasant mass but not to those of the upper strata. You did not consult with the latter and went beyond policy limitations in violating people's interests other than those of monasteries, landlords, and rich farmers, such as the middle farmers' interests.

What, then, went wrong with the CCP's policymaking? According to Liu:

We did not understand the local conditions. Everyone knew about the principles, such as reliance on poor and hired farmers . . . and struggle against landlords. But how should the landlords be struggled against, who were also objects of our united front? Should the monasteries also be targeted, which were also landlords? Thus, we were confused. This happened because we did not understand the fundamental nature of the society and its production relationship; we became self-contradictory and committed dogmatism. Consequently, heads rolled on the ground and many people got killed. In my view, this is the crux of the problem. . . . Rebellions would not have happened without reform. Our work was defective and provided the rebels with excuses to oppose reform.

Liu's contemplation of the reform crisis touched upon the crux of Beijing's "nationality question," autonomy:

Since the autonomous prefecture was established, the rights of autonomy have not been fully exercised. . . . The Kangding Autonomous Prefecture was established very early and should have been a model. But now it lags behind Tibet. Two highways and railroads will be constructed in Tibet, and there are many other projects. Here we should make plans too and speed up constructions. . . . Reforms must develop smoothly and minority cadres should be fostered and promoted. Indigenization [*minzu hua*] should be achieved as soon as possible. . . . Districts and townships should achieve complete indigenization, which means district party secretaries, mayors, and other officials should be mainly minority cadres. If permitted by conditions, all positions can be theirs. . . . [At the county level] more than 50 percent of the cadres should be minority. At least there should be minority deputy party secretaries. When conditions are ready, minority cadres should be fostered as party secretaries. [CCP] county committees should mostly consist of them.[84]

At the time, Liu, an ethnic Hui, was one of the few minority high-ranking CCP officials who played an important role in Beijing's policymaking in respect to minority nationalities. Another such official was Ulanhu. In late 1955 and 1956, during senior CCP officials' discussions of the situation in western Sichuan, Ulanhu voiced his objection to "pacification of rebellions" by force: "Dealing with minority nationalities with battles is the worst policy choice."[85] Liu in 1960 and Ulanhu in 1966 were labeled "local nationalists" and dismissed from their official positions.[86] But in 1956, both Liu and Ulanhu were still at the peak of their careers and yet to pay a price for their views on the CCP's nationality policies. For Sichuan officials especially, Liu appeared to bring pressure from Beijing to rectify the tumultuous situation in the Tibetan-Yi areas. A new development in Tibet further accentuated Sichuan officials' anxieties: in late April, a Preparatory Committee for the Tibetan Autonomous Region was established, and Beijing sent a huge delegation, the first ever, under deputy premier Chen Yi to Lhasa to celebrate the event. While the authorities in Lhasa and Beijing seemed able to advance their cooperation peacefully, the violent conflict in western Sichuan sounded a dissonant chord. In May, both the Dalai Lama and Chen Yi were sending investigation teams to western Sichuan.[87]

In the summer of 1956, "democratic reform" in the Tibetan-Yi areas of Sichuan arrived at a crossroad. In early July, the CCP Sichuan Committee sent Liao Zhigao (who ranked third in the provincial leadership), Miao Fengshu, and Tianbao to Beijing to participate in the third conference of the Nationality Affairs Committee of the People's Congress. The conference was presided over by none other than Liu Geping.[88] The conference was in session for only a few days, but intensive discussions between officials from Sichuan and those in Beijing would continue until late July, culminating in a report session involving Mao Zedong himself. After returning to Sichuan, Liao recalled the roller-coaster sensation he and his colleagues had experienced in Beijing:

> We arrived in Beijing on July 1 and were greeted in tense air. It was said that democratic reform in Sichuan was a mistake, and was a reform with armed force and Han suppression of minority nationalities. An opinion both outside and inside the Party believed that all went wrong and that we must admit wrong doings. The situation was very tense. The Center learned a lot and understood the whole situation. The reform was characterized with a rise of slaves and serfs against slave masters and feudal lords. We reported to the Center according to the facts, and also made a thorough self-criticism. We submitted a written report and talked for more than nine hours. After we made the report, the issue was discussed at eighteen meetings. At a Politburo meeting Premier Zhou talked for five and a half hours. The issue of guns was solved on the afternoon of the day before yesterday [July 24]. So far, all questions have been clarified,

but it is hard to say that everybody no longer harbors any doubt. Now I am going to talk about Chairman Mao's conclusion on whether or not the reform was a mistake.[89]

Mao made his remarks on July 22, while listening to Li Weihan's report. Also present at the session were a group of senior CCP officials based in Beijing and Liao and his colleagues from Sichuan.[90] The following is a selected translation of a record kept by Liao Zhigao.

> Minutes of Chairman Mao's directive about the reform in Garzê and Liangshan (midnight of July 22)
>
> When comrade Li Weihan was making a report on the reform in Garzê and Liangshan, the Chairman made many important directives by inserting remarks. The contents inside quotations marks below are the Chairman's directives:
>
> I. Garzê
>   1. General conditions:
>   (1) Report about the serfdom—"It more or less resembles the time of the Southern and Northern Dynasties"; after learning that each year on average every serf household must provide one person's free service to feudal lords, "that sounds like in the time of Confucius, the Spring and Autumn and the Warring State periods."
>   (2) ...
>   (3) Report about the rebellions—"*The essential nature of the war is class struggle. On the other side (meaning the western side of the Jinsha River) it should be fought as a national war.*" After learning that the western side of the River sent people over to participate in the fight, "*The other side also joined the fight; they are vitally interrelated [xiu qi xiang guan].*"
>   (4) ...
>   2. Concrete policy issues:
>   (1) Pacification of the rebellions:
>   A. Report about winning over [rebels] politically and ceasefire for negotiations—"Only if they stop fighting."
>   B. "Wherever we did wrong or we did not do well, we should admit mistakes."
>   C. Report about how to treat rebels and whether to punish those who caused public wrath—"No punishment. The mass are now demanding punishment, but after a year the mass will become eased and no longer demand punishment. It would be better to be lenient"; "this also involves many people coming from Tibet, and no punishment is very good. . . ."

(2) Guns:

Report about using methods of borrowing and asking for contributions to solve the problem of guns in the hands of landlords and rich farmers—*"Tiger borrows pigs; scholar borrows books"* [*laohu jie zhu, xiucai jieshu*]

(3) Monasteries:

A. Consensus that monasteries' land will not be touched—"Good."

B. Report about a disagreement over how to handle monasteries' guns; some suggested not touching them for now if monasteries accept certain conditions whereas some wanted to collect them now—"The principle is that you must be victorious"; "in this way we have the initiative because we would be the side to make concessions!" "But we will take the guns if they violate laws"; "you can concede a bit."

C. Report about abolishing monasteries' debts and privileges—"This is fine"; *"Touching two items [debts and privileges] without touching two others [land and guns]." Later, when the issue of religion and monasteries was mentioned again in the context of the issue of Liangshan, it was changed into no touching of all four items.*

(4) When listing to report about collecting surplus productive and living materials like farm tools and animals from the landlords, the Chairman said "It's fine." Then later Tianbao suggested that these should not be touched—*"If Tianbao does not agree, we should do according to Tianbao's opinion"*; "these may be purchased with government funds, and the approach of confiscation should not be applied to properties other than land; we should be more generous toward landlords of minority nationalities, and the government can purchase farm tools and farm animals from landlords and rich farmers and then distribute these among farmers."

(5) Report about not classifying the serfs into poor farmers, hired farmers, and middle farmers—"It's fine."

(6) When listening to report about paying attention to class backgrounds in developing the Party organization, the Chairman gave directives as listed below:

A. "The Party must be developed seriously."

B. *"The cadres should be gradually replaced with minority nationalities, and minorities should gradually replace the Han. This is not to say that all Han cadres will leave. A small number will stay. Most of the business should be run by themselves, and let them understand policies. If we always do things for them, nothing can be accomplished. Minority cadres should increase at every level and gradually take over. In the future, minority cadres should be party secretaries at the prefecture and county levels, and the Han serve as second and deputy secretaries. This cannot be realized easily in the current transitional period. In the future, minority nationalities will play the leading role with the*

Han in assistance. We must keep this in mind and have such a plan. Otherwise this cannot be realized and minority nationalities will not be comfortable. During the current reform period there is no alternative to having an overwhelming number of Han as leading cadres. In the future, after the Han leave and their number becomes smaller, minority nationalities can still ask for retaining a few Han cadres. Currently Han cadres are enduring hardship and cannot leave even if they want to. They have to work there and be prepared for being replaced by minority cadres. Work can proceed smoothly if we have such an orientation and plan. Members of party committees should gradually be replaced with people of the local nationalities and native to the areas (at the point comrade Li Weihan reported that Sichuan had already stipulated that minority cadres should occupy 70 percent of the cadres at the district level and 50 percent at the county level). 90 percent should be minority cadres."

C. "*Ideas of Tibetan cadres should be listened to (Chen Yi: the county secretary must be persuaded to obey the prefecture governor and cooperate well). Native cadres must be trusted. Wrong ideas of theirs should be corrected through persuasion, and wait if they cannot be persuaded for the moment.* The Center used to listen to Gao Gang in northern Shaanxi. Now this person is no longer valid. But at the time whenever Gao Gang was hesitant about something, I would not do it. Who was more knowledgeable? I admitted that Gao was more knowledgeable. I made decisions with Gao's consent because he was a native and more knowledgeable about the place. Then I asked Gao to use the same approach in the Northeast, but he refused. Incorrect ideas of theirs are small in number and should be persuaded to change. Wait if persuasion does not work. Such an orientation can work. It is not good not to trust local cadres. Inter-nationality barriers will exist for a long time. The length of time can be shortened only if we use this orientation."

D. "Opposite views must be permitted. Minority Nationalities should have chance to speak out and to express fully their opinions and complaints."

(7) Report about how to set the landlord–rich farmer ratio when classifying classes—"7–8 percent is a bit too much. 3–5 percent is better. This is for you to consider. During the land reform in the Han areas we made some people happy by giving them a hat of petty land renters. The percentage should be lower for minority nationalities, and the scope of striking should be intentionally narrowed down. The upper stratum should be provided for and can have the right to vote. Although they can no longer be landlords, they may still be officials. This differs from the Han areas." "You need to consider how 3–5 percent can solve the problem. At most the percentage can be 6 percent, but probably 3–5 percent is better."

(8) Report about the mass' production and life, and funds needed for providing for the upper stratum—"It is fine in principle. Money should be

provided. The upper stratum needs money during the transition. The [CCP] provincial committee should make concrete plans." Report about the need to construct a highway from Dartsédo to Bathang—"This is a good undertaking and the road must be built." Report about the need to expand Tibetan militias—"An armed force of minority nationalities is needed and indispensable."

3. Inter-nationality relations

(1) Report about minority nationality cadres' opinions being ignored and suppressed by Han cadres—"We must not impose upon them and force them to do what they disagree. Even good things cannot be imposed upon them."

(2) Report about autonomy being mostly in name without substance or in name only—"This must be reversed completely and their words should be listened to."

(3) Report about the leadership at the Center having not given enough attention to the views of the autonomous regions—"In the future minority nationalities should be allowed to fully express their opinions. There is no need to hold 18 meetings. Several meetings should be adequate." "The approach of setting up opposing views [*chang dui tai xi*] can be used. Meetings should be called successively in this winter and next spring, one meeting for each of these places, Xinjiang, Qinghai, and Inner Mongolia."

II. Liangshan

...

The Chairman's conclusion:

"Reforms in the two prefectures are necessary, and the decision on reform was made correctly. The war has been a war of liberation. Li [Weihan] said that the war was more or less characterized by mass participation. As I see it, this is essentially a class struggle, though this is not completely a class struggle because the upper stratum has deceived a portion of the mass with national slogans."

"Battles were fought in this place to liberate the people. But because the upper stratum deceived a portion of the mass with national slogans, we must be very cautious in such a war. We were forced to fight, and now the fight should be stopped in order to negotiate. We would not fight if they did not, and we mainly use the means of political suasion and give them no excuses. We must seize the banners of religion and nation from them [upper stratum], and correct our mistakes in the past. We should listen to what native cadres have to say. A moment ago, we are all convinced once Tianbao started talking."

"We are not fighting for pillaging. The state spends a lot of money every year not for the sake of oppression and exploitation, but for assistance to, liberation and development of, and self-governance by [minority nationalities]. This is the most important point. Now this is not done well in all places and must be corrected."

Comrade Li Weihan said that it was incorrect to believe peaceful reform must or must not proceed with fighting—"Neither of these scenarios should be suggested as certainty. Fighting may be avoidable under certain conditions. Wherever these conditions were present, fighting did not happen (such as Rongtrak and Yunnan). Under certain circumstances fighting could not be avoided, such as in the south [of Xikang]. They attacked there because they saw a situation in favor of them, and they felt that they could overcome and destroy you. Fighting can start under another circumstance in which reactionary agitations exist or our work makes mistakes. If you deploy troops first, fighting may be avoided. But if you do not have enough troops and the other side makes an accurate estimate of the situation (Li Weihan: rebellion can start easily in such a situation), fighting may start. Yet, attack may not be deterred even if we deploy six regiments. Unless reform does not go ahead, they will certainly want to contest us if reform is carried out."

Slaves' struggles [against slave masters] are mentioned—"Yes! Serfs' rebellion!"

"The war has educated the upper stratum, the farmers, and also Lhasa. This is a correct estimate. This battle has also educated us. The situation would have been better if there had been more careful consultations [with the upper stratum]. *We should strive to avoid fighting with Lhasa, and reform must take this into account. The work orientation for the western side of the Jinsha River should be to avoid fighting. This should be achievable. But we have a small condition: a genuine reform must be implemented. Hence fighting is probably inevitable.* Fighting in certain areas is possible. But it would be the best if there is no fighting at all."

Comrade Li Weihan said that our state's superior position made peaceful reform feasible—"Highways are part of this. Fighting could have been avoided had the highway to southern Xikang been completed. Transportation is part of the situation."

Li mentioned that serious and repeated consultations with the upper stratum were necessary—"If consultations have no results, postpone [reforms]."

Li pointed out that reactionary feudal lords of Xikang were armed and might rebel once provoked—"This was somewhat underestimated."

Li suggested that statements made inside and outside the Party should be in agreement—"Do not develop two sets of ideas. What is decided inside the Party must be able to be talked about outside the Party. . . ."

Li mentioned that concessions had to be made—"If you do not make concessions, the other side would not be interested and would not want to listen to you!"

Li suggested that in cooperation with the upper stratum, first they should be brought along and secondly their legitimate positions should be respected—"We may retreat a bit."

Li talked about what should be done when nationalities did not trust one another—"Distrust also exists within the Han. For instance, during the Yan'an period the orientation of 'learning from past mistakes to avoid future ones and curing the sickness to save the patient' would not be convincing without a prolonged implementation. Now that long-term coexistence has been announced, the democratic parties get excited. . . . This meeting is good and minority nationalities have voiced their opinions. Conditions for setting up opposing ideas must be created. This is to say that cooperation inside the Party should be achieved. Whenever disagreement is concealed, unity is fake and not genuine. Any work imposed on people cannot be good. *Minority nationalities have suffered for long, and we have this Communists' burden: We are Communists, doing neither embezzlement nor exploitation—so let's liberate you. So arrogant! We must admit that consultation was inadequate.*"

"If we had defects and made mistakes, we must admit them. Otherwise we cannot be convincing. We should admit that we did not consult with them adequately."

"*Reform is necessary, and the decision on reform was correct. The war was one of liberation, and in essence was a class struggle. These shortcomings should be admitted: inadequate consultation, estimate, preparations, respect, patience, concession, and flexibility. If we admit these shortcomings, Lhasa would be happy.*"[91] (emphasis added)

While Mao's personal attention attested to the seriousness of the situation in Sichuan, this top-level discussion took place not because of any insurmountable obstacle to Sichuan officials' pushing reform in their province. The discussion happened because of the stark policy disagreement within the CCP. This disagreement had a concealed interethnic connotation in that several high-positioned non-Han CCP officials were questioning the reform war in the Southwest. These officials' dissenting voices, plus Lhasa's grave concern about the eastern side of the Jinsha River, warranted a hearing in front of Mao. Throughout the July meetings in Beijing, Deng Xiaoping and his southwestern subordinates, hard-liners in this policy debate, appeared to be in the hot seat. It should be recalled that, not long before, they were the moderates in a different debate about Tibet with officials from the Northwest.

Despite the whole set of new terms and conceptions deployed in CCP political discourse, Mao's intervention in the policy dispute was reminiscent of imperial frontier management in the past: the emperor had functioned as the last arbitrator in any policy confusion. After Mao talked, both sides of the dispute could claim victory to a certain degree. The hearing was staged in such a way that Li Weihan was able to present to Mao the principal grievances of the reform war's critics, and Mao appeared sympathetic. Ceasefire, consultation, and concessions seemed to become the spirit of the day. For instance, initially Mao endorsed a policy toward the monasteries that would "touch two items without touching two others," but then readily agreed to leave all four aspects of the monasteries' "feudal" power alone. Mao went out of his way to show all present how respectful he was toward Tianbao's opinions. His assertion that minority cadres should eventually take the leading role in their areas must have sounded tantalizing to minority CCP officials, who had complained about being neglected by Beijing. Yet in the unfolding ethnopolitical history of the PRC, Mao's words on this day would assume importance precisely because they did not materialize. The ultimate initiator of China's "continuous revolution," Mao was willing to take a tactical pause and even to compromise momentarily, but sooner or later he would push his revolution into the next phase.

In the long run, therefore, Sichuan officials could feel vindicated. In using the typical, dialectical way of CCP discourse, Mao made it clear that in the main the reform war was positive and necessary and its "shortcomings" were marginal and secondary. The weightiest among all Mao's remarks was his verdict about the war being one of "liberation" and "class struggles." In CCP politics, these were deemed essential for the party's mission. The rest were merely tactical concerns. Typically, in endorsing Sichuan officials' collection of guns from Tibetans, Mao used an unfamiliar Hunan proverb, "tiger borrows pigs; scholar borrows books," to express cynically the same spirit of the three *you* principles outlined by Liu Shaoqi.[92] After Mao's intervention, the issue of keeping reform peaceful became a moot point for CCP officials in the Southwest. The "peaceful reform" of the mid-1950s in the Yi-Tibetan areas of Sichuan would be just as peaceful as the "peaceful liberation" of Tibet in the early 1950s; the reform could be "peaceful" only if implemented forcefully.

For a short while, though, an atmosphere of moderation did appear. On July 24, two days after Mao's hearing of the Sichuan case, Zhou Enlai distilled several points from the meeting and conveyed them, as "the Center's and Chairman Mao's opinions," to a large audience of various backgrounds, including "upper-stratum figures of minority nationalities residing in Beijing." In August, Zhou's speech was circulated as a "Central Document" to several frontier provinces. The speech had a rather conciliatory undertone, calling rebellions in western Sichuan "unfortunate incidents" and promising remedies to redress the situation. Basically, Zhou called for continuing the orientation of "peaceful reform," handling properties of the established classes and monasteries benevolently and cautiously, and differentiating between the nationality and reform questions. With respect to rebels who were still fighting, Zhou challenged Sichuan officials to act more skillfully and farsightedly than Zhuge Liang of the ancient Three Kingdoms period. Invoking Zhuge's precedent of allegedly capturing and releasing a local chieftain named Meng Huo seven times before winning over his heart and pacifying the southern frontiers, Zhou urged Sichuan officials to be prepared to capture and release rebels a hundred times before winning them over to "democratic reform."[93]

As the reconciliatory orientation from Beijing was being circulated and digested throughout the ethnic frontiers of western China, Sichuan officials contemplated how to continue what they had started. In the wake of the Beijing conference, monasteries destroyed by the PLA's air force in Garzê were rapidly repaired and restored.[94] Yet Sichuan officials did not believe that their mission to demolish the old establishments in the minority areas had come to an end. Having brought Mao's "directives" back to Sichuan, Liao Zhigao told his Sichuan colleagues: "Reform should go ahead as usual." Indeed, Liao admitted, consultation with minority officials outside the party had not been adequate in the past. But that was because "we believed in heading toward [a society of] Communism whereas they wanted to keep feudal system and slavery intact."[95] Thus, the "Communists' burden" identified by Mao persisted. When discussing with Sichuan officials how to carry out the orientation of the Beijing conference, Li Jingquan further expressed such messianic sentiment, clearly in responding to Mao's remark about "arrogance": "Abolition of slavery and serfdom is a great cause. The proletarians of the world have not done this, and neither has our Party done this before. Those comrades from more advanced areas may not be able to do things right, but this should not be the reason for us to become arrogant."[96]

Yet, the "great cause" was currently hindered by local resistance entrenched in a popular religion and an armed culture, for which the monasteries served, both symbolically and substantively, as fortresses. Now, attack on these had to be recalibrated under the "not touching" decision from Beijing. As the CCP chief in Sichuan, Li laid out a new line of action for his subordinates:

> We should still follow the spirit of Premier Zhou's words: "Monasteries should not be touched for the moment. What to do in the future?—this should be discussed between monasteries and the mass." The second sentence is rather pregnant [di er ju jiu you wenzhang]. Comrade Tianbao said that this was a correct approach and gave us a good excuse [hao shuohua]: we would not touch [monasteries]; but if the mass want to touch them, we would mediate. . . . In a word, we need to effectuate [fahui] Premier Zhou's two sentences. We must not dampen the mass' enthusiasm, and this is in concert with our principle. First, we say "not touching," secondly, we support the mass, and thirdly, we make the mass raise demands [about reforming monasteries].[97]

If such "effectuating" of Beijing's directives appeared manipulative, the manipulation reached not only the Tibetan communities in Sichuan but also Beijing. Li's words were uttered at the first provincial conference on nationality work after Liao returned. When the conference concluded in late August, the CCP Sichuan Committee made a report to Beijing. According to the report,

> in discussing the Center's and Chairman Mao's directives, all participants were excited and spoke enthusiastically to express their own ideas. They felt unanimously that Chairman Mao's directives, "reform was necessary and the decision on reform was correct" and "the war was fundamentally one of liberation and class struggles," backed us up and strengthened our resolve and confidence in carrying out reforms.

After admitting defects in Sichuan's previous reform measures, the report complained about the new orientations from Beijing in the name of minority cadres:

> Minority cadres of the Liangshan areas were resistant, and the Yi and Tibetan cadres of the Garzê area were especially resistant in their minds. They felt that [under the new orientations] too many concessions would be made to the feudal lords and slave masters. The mass would become discontent and many difficulties would arise to hinder our work.

In particular, while accepting the "not touching for now" orientation in respect to monasteries as a "circuitous and indirect way to liberate the mass under the exploitation of lamaist monasteries," the report contended that the approach might not be feasible:

> An actual situation should be studied and dealt with. According to preliminary investigations, 15 percent of the mass are exploited by lamaist monasteries through land, and 50 percent through debts and labor services. The mass working on the lands of feudal lords and landlords account for 85 percent of the total farming households. . . . When 85 percent of the mass gain victory and liberation through democratic reform that will have abolished various privileges and exploitations of the feudal lords and landlords, they will firmly resist various ways of control and exploitation by the monasteries and will certainly impact those mass under monasteries' control. Therefore, even if we are maintaining the orientation of "not touching for now" about the monasteries, spontaneous mass struggles will certainly take place everywhere. We estimate that such a situation will occur immediately in the wake of the struggles against feudal lords and landlords or even simultaneously in certain areas.

The Sichuan Committee therefore proposed that measures of "mediation" between the mass and the monasteries be prepared now. For this purpose, the report informed Beijing, Miao Fengshu and Tianbao would be sent to Garzê to investigate, and then proper measures would be reported to Beijing for approval. For now, the whole issue would be put on hold.[98]

At the time, Tianbao appeared to experience serious self-doubt about his political career. Having failed to persuade his Han colleagues in the CCP Sichuan Committee to postpone reforms in the Tibetan areas of Sichuan, in December 1955 Tianbao went along with what he believed was a relatively moderate reform agenda. Then a bout of illness and participation in Beijing's Central Delegation to Tibet in the spring of 1956 kept Tianbao away from Sichuan for a few months. While visiting in Lhasa with the Central Delegation, Tianbao was bombarded with questions about reforms in western Sichuan that he was unable to answer. When he returned to Sichuan, Tianbao was shocked by the bloodshed. Seeing violation by reform teams and militia, involving mostly their Han members, of monasteries and upper-class figures who had so far been collaborating with the CCP, Tianbao was troubled by the inconsistency between the CCP's stated policies and actual practices and dismayed by internal quarrels among CCP officials from county to provincial levels. In an internal speech, Tianbao criticized the Sichuan leadership for focusing on the sixty million Han population of the province while overlooking what was happening to the few million minority peoples. Saddened immensely by recent developments, he said: "War started and many ordinary people and PLA troops were killed. I am guilty for letting so many people die." "Among the killed Tibetans," Tianbao added, "very few were actually bad people." He asked the CCP Sichuan Committee to dismiss him from the committee as well as from his position as deputy governor of the province.[99]

Tianbao's Han colleagues in Sichuan did not share his remorse, and the CCP leaderships in both Sichuan and Beijing would not let him fade away from the by now heated Tibetan affairs. Tianbao was thus among the Sichuan officials who attended Li Weihan's report to Mao in Beijing, after which his career began to change. In his July 24 speech, Zhou Enlai recited Mao's remark about the value of Tianbao's opinion, referring him as Mao did by his "Chinese" name, Tianbao. But later, in the officially circulated version of Zhou's speech, Tianbao's ethnic identity was advertised, appearing in his Tibetan name, Sangye Yeshe.[100] From that point, Tianbao became Sangye Yeshe again in Beijing's ethnopolitical affairs. Jolted by the July conference in Beijing, in late July Sangye Yeshe was added to the standing committee of the CCP Sichuan Committee and thus became the only Tibetan member of that body. Then, in September, he was elected as an alternate member of the CCP Central Committee at the CCP's Eighth National Congress.[101]

Sangye Yeshe's position in the PRC's ethnopolitics also changed subtly after Mao stated his deference to "Tianbao's opinion" about the reform in western Sichuan. In reality, after Mao fundamentally endorsed the hasty reform started by Sichuan officials, Sangye Yeshe's dissenting position was no longer tenable.

On the other hand, Mao's ostentatious support of Sangye Yeshe's opinion on specific issues made him part of Beijing's two-pronged effort in managing the reform war: to simultaneously restrain Han cadres and pacify the Tibetans. Li Jingquan and others in the CCP Sichuan Committee embraced Sangye Yeshe's newly gained fame in Tibetan affairs and turned it to their own advantage. On September 28, Sangye Yeshe sent a report to the Central United Front Department and the Central Nationality Committee "to be transmitted to the Center and the Chairman." The report was extraordinary because Sangye Yeshe was not even one of the secretaries of the CCP Sichuan Committee and ranked last among the fifteen members of the standing committee of the CCP Sichuan Committee. This was not an audacious move on Sangye Yeshe's part to bypass his superiors, a CCP member's exercising of his "right" when disagreeing with immediate superiors. Rather, as Sangye Yeshe explained in the report, the document was approved by the CCP Sichuan Committee and sent in his name according to a collective decision by Li Jingquan and three other top-ranking secretaries of that committee. In other words, Li and his principal colleagues intended to send the report to Beijing as a "Tibetan cadre's opinion" that they endorsed. Since Mao himself appeared to esteem this Tibetan cadre's opinion and Zhou identified "comrade Sangye Yeshe's suggestion" as the very basis of Beijing's "not touching" policy about monasteries, there was nothing better than a stratagem of using "Sangye Yeshe's opinion" to preempt Beijing's possible objection to Li's way of "effectuating" the "not touching" orientation.

Necessarily, the report was drafted in first person, and its gist was that after investigating the conditions in Garzê, "Sangye Yeshe" realized there was no way to differentiate those masses exploited by monasteries from those exploited by feudal lords and landlords. In different areas, 80–90 percent of the masses were exploited by feudal lords and landlords, but the rest were exploited by both monasteries and feudal lords. Therefore, both groups would inevitably become involved in reform struggles for liberation. The second group, those who were "partially" exploited by monasteries, would not be satisfied with "partial liberation" from feudal lords but "temporarily" not from monasteries. Therefore, to avoid "isolation from the mass," "Sangye Yeshe" proposed that the masses' land rents, debts, and labor services to the monasteries be adjusted in ways acceptable to both sides and that monasteries' guns not be collected unless they joined rebellions or engaged in lawless activities.[102]

As Sangye Yeshe became a team player in the CCP Sichuan Committee, his hard-line Han colleagues in the CCP Kangding Area Committee made "self-criticism." In October, in an eighty-one-page report, the committee reviewed its reform work since the beginning of the year. In supporting Mao's evaluation of the reform war, the Kangding Committee took responsibility for making numerous mistakes in reform. Allegedly, the committee failed to fully follow policy directives from Beijing and the provincial leadership. Meanwhile, the report reiterated those points in Sichuan's original reform plan for carrying out reform urgently. A difference was that the Kangding Committee could now use graphic descriptions of the masses' "spontaneous struggles" and atrocities attributed to rebels to depict a sharp and violent "class struggle" in western Sichuan. According to the report, the months from February to June were the "most tense period in which the largest number of problems occurred, and most serious mistakes were made"; "on the one hand rebellions took place everywhere and killed many cadres, and on the other many problems occurred in reform everywhere and people inside and outside the Party were screaming." The bedlam came to a halt in August. After discussing with the Sichuan leadership based in Chengdu about what to do in view of what had transpired in recent meetings in Beijing, Fan Zhizhong made a phone call to local cadres in Kangding and informed them of possible policy changes. After that, according to the report, "not much was done as far as reform was concerned and therefore no obvious defects and mistakes occurred." Having identified the roots of their mistakes by labeling themselves with "subjectivism," "bureaucratism," and "great Han chauvinism," Kangding officials concluded their self-criticism with a touch that made sense in CCP internal politics: They quoted a whole passage from Deng Xiaoping's speech at the Eighth National Congress, the spirit of which, if it had been followed, could supposedly have prevented their mistakes.[103]

In this way, the CCP Kangding Committee became the highest level in the CCP organization to shoulder direct responsibility for committing "mistakes" in the reform of western Sichuan. Similar self-criticism did not take place at the provincial level and certainly did not involve Deng in Beijing. In December, Sangye Yeshe became the chief of the CCP Kangding Area Committee and the former party chief Fan Zhizhong became his deputy.[104] Having got his Chinese name Tianbao from Mao after joining the Chinese Communist Revolution, in 1956 Sangye Yeshe restored his Tibetan name and assumed the top position in the Tibetan region of western Sichuan. A historical irony is that "Sangye Yeshe" reappeared in Tibetan affairs only to preside over the bloodiest phase of the reform war.

For a while the violence appeared to subside. In early October, the Central United Front Department held another discussion of the Sichuan reform in Beijing. At that meeting, Li Weihan reaffirmed the original "not touching" orientation toward monasteries and did not endorse Li Jingquan's proposal for "effectuation." Late in the month, Beijing sent a goodwill mission to western Sichuan, led by Wang Weizhou and Liu Geping. The mission was intended to renew good feelings toward the CCP among local Tibetan elites that were lost in reform. Wang was chosen for the mission because, during the prereform years, he had overseen the nationality work of the Southwest Bureau and made many friends among local elites. The mission also functioned to supervise policy readjustment by the Sichuan leadership. In early November, the Sichuan leadership duly called a nationality work conference and, watched by officials from Beijing, clarified policy issues according to Beijing's recent directives. By that time, rebellions in most areas had calmed down. Forgivingly, the CCP authorities referred to participants in rebellions as "rebellious elements" (*canpan fenzi*), not "rebellious bandits" (*panfei*) or "enemies." To facilitate a ceasefire and negotiations, the government promised to treat these people leniently and even expressed a willingness to postpone reform in certain areas.[105]

Nevertheless, information collected by the Public Security Department of the Garzê Autonomous Prefecture indicated mixed feelings about Beijing's reconciliatory orientation among both local elites and local reform activists.[106] The last few months of 1956 were a relatively peaceful interval under Beijing's orientation of "using political suasion as the principal approach and military strike as the supplement." In December, the CCP Kangding Area Committee, which would soon be renamed as the CCP Garzê Tibetan Autonomous Prefecture Committee, initiated a pilot project of "peaceful reform" in Garzê County. In early February 1957, when the project was evaluated, the old policy debate among Sichuan officials broke out again.[107] Again Beijing intervened. This time, however, the Center's directive came from Deng Xiaoping, not Mao.

"The More Thorough Is the Battle . . ."

By September 1956, Mao, who concurrently held the chairmanships of the CCP Central Committee, the Central Politburo, and the Central Secretariat, was ready to share some of his workload. In promoting Deng to the last position, now renamed "secretary-general," Mao listed Deng's qualifications: "He is talented and can get things done; he is considerate, fair, kind, and not intimidating to others."[108] In his new capacity, Deng soon demonstrated how he got things done as far as Tibetan affairs were concerned. In early March 1957, Sichuan officials again brought the issue of reform to Beijing. Mao gave his general endorsement of Sichuan officials' proposed policy before passing the report to Deng for an official response.[109]

In their report, the Sichuan officials posed a simple question to their superiors in Beijing: Should democratic reform in Garzê continue? In weighing the pros and cons, the report offered three options. Its presentation, however, clearly gave Beijing just one choice, which was to continue the reform. Continuation of the reform meant, as Sichuan officials admitted, that the upper stratum of the Tibetan communities on both sides of the Jinsha River would be disturbed, the work in Tibet would become even more difficult, and war on the eastern side of the River would be unavoidable. These problems, in their opinion, would be temporary and could eventually be solved. The benefits, on the other hand, would be enormous: serving the Tibetan people's "fundamental interests" and destroying "feudal armed forces." But "if the Center still considers making concessions to Tibet [meaning Lhasa]," a second option was to continue reform only in the northern and eastern counties of Garzê but halt the process in the south, where "feudal lords" were still in charge and rebellions supported by Tibet were on the rise. The third option was to stop reform completely. There might be some advantages in retreating, such as saving money for the state, reducing local burdens, and ending the current quarrels. But the long-term consequences of retreating would be extremely costly, according to Sichuan officials. The cadres and masses in Garzê would be hurt, whereas the right wing of the upper stratum would feel encouraged. The end of reform would cause greater confusion, alienate the masses, and intensify mutual hatred between the Han and Tibetans. Thus, all revolutionary achievements gained so far would be lost, and many problems would arise in the future, not only for the work in Garzê but also for that in Tibet.[110]

At the time, "democratic reform" in western Sichuan became problematic not only because of the violence in the area but also because of Beijing's recent decision to postpone reform preparations in Tibet. When the Central Secretariat got the assignment from Mao to act on the Sichuan report, Deng and his colleagues had necessarily to consider policies on both sides of the Jinsha River. In early March, the Central Secretariat held a series of meetings to discuss policies concerning the Tibetan societies divided by the Jinsha River. Beijing's policy considerations about the western side of the Jinsha River, or Tibet, will be discussed in the next chapter. It should be noted here, however, that in the early months of 1957, CCP leaders in Beijing deliberated and made important policy decisions affecting all Tibetans living in the PRC, though these decisions emphatically differentiated the two Tibetan regions divided by the Jinsha River.

The issue of reform in western Sichuan was mainly discussed at a Central Secretariat meeting on March 9. Liao Zhigao and Sangye Yeshe were present at the meeting. Several members of the Central Secretariat spoke at the session, but Liao only took note of what Deng had to say. The CCP Sichuan Committee polished Liao's notes before passing the content to officials in Garzê for taking actions accordingly.[111] Taking his cue from Mao, Deng completely endorsed Sichuan's proposed orientation for continuing reform. In Deng's opinion, there was no reason to retreat now. He even raised the bar by insisting that the "democratic reform" must be "genuine," which was a revolutionary criterion meaning the masses' "awakening and standing up" in both economic and political senses. Specifically, Deng said: "A reform without letting [the masses] air their grievances and venting their bitterness can only be a phony one." Deng's demand for a "genuine reform" would soon lead some already reformed areas in western Sichuan to go through the ordeal for a second time.[112] This was also a key point on which leaders in Beijing saw the difference between their policy in western Sichuan and that in Tibet. As Deng put it: "Winning over the upper stratum must be based on mobilization of the mass. We must rely on one of the two ends. In Tibet the Dalai [Lama] is the one to rely on, and in Kangding the basic mass are the ones to rely on even though the upper stratum should be won over as well. We cannot afford to lose both ends."

Yet, for the Tibetan communities in Sichuan, Deng's most consequential remark was his unequivocal assertion of a "war situation":

> The upper stratum will fight as long as we insist on carrying out reform on the eastern side of the [Jinsha] River. Preparations for big battles should be made. The more thorough is the battle, the better will be the result. This must not be forgotten. Do not hesitate. Hesitation can only make the situation worse. We should battle skillfully and mercilessly. Our orientation should be explained to the upper stratum clearly. If you want to fight, let's fight. We are actually fighting now. If we do not fight, they will become more arrogant. Military deployment should be done carefully and the commandership must be strengthened. If troops are inadequate, reinforcement can come from the western side of the River or from the outside. In the southern direction, battles and political suasion should be done simultaneously. We must strike whenever opportunity emerges. This is a war situation. It is not like that because they did not fight yesterday, we cannot fight today. Our force should concentrate and pacify one area at a time. Never let political suasion be separate from military strike. Only military victory can make political suasion work. After the reform is implemented, fighting may continue because of the factor on the western side of the River. [Our policy] should be based on this estimate even though big battles will probably be unlikely.[113]

Thus, having contemplated waging "smart class struggles" and experimented with various stopgap measures for alleviating the violent conflicts that "democratic reform" had provoked, Beijing finally returned to the familiar formula of violent and merciless class struggle based on the "mass line." Although Deng depicted the "war" as one to overcome Tibetan upper classes' resistance to reform, the real fighting, as discussed earlier, was not marked by class divides.

On May 14, Beijing sent a formal response to the CCP Sichuan Committee. After Deng made his pointed remarks, the document, which was brief because Deng wanted to limit it to 400–700 words, served only to complete the formality.[114] Even before sending their formal response to Sichuan, leaders in Beijing took a step to enhance the war effort there. In the spring of 1957, Zhang Aiping, deputy chief of the PLA General Staff, was originally scheduled to inspect military work in the Southwest. The Central Secretariat decided to send

Su Yu, chief of the General Staff, instead. Su's assignment was to recalibrate the military operations in western Sichuan. Su arrived in Sichuan in early April. After listening to a report by the Xichang Branch Military Region, Su criticized the Xichang command for failing to suppress rebellions resolutely and having a "rightist" tendency in carrying out reform. Late in the month, after learning that some 34,000 cadres and 135,000 militias in the field had neither combat experiences nor enough weapons, Su helped arrange for the Chengdu Military Region to dispatch 3,620 officers to western Sichuan as armed work teams and to add 24,440 guns, 90,000 grenades, and 6,955,000 rounds of ammunition to the onslaught. In early May, in Chengdu, Su called a meeting of four neighboring provinces and discussed with local officials how to coordinate their military operations. Su's Sichuan tour also had direct ramifications for Tibet. In February 1958, in a report to the Central Military Commission, Su proposed that active military preparations be made in Tibet, following an orientation of "being intense inside but appearing relaxed outside," but that the PLA avoid firing the first shot. Mao endorsed the proposal heartily, noting in the report's margin, "very good."[115]

Thus, with Su Yu's assistance, beginning in the early summer of 1957, CCP officials in Sichuan launched a "comprehensive struggle" combining "rebellion pacification, democratic reform, and mass mobilization." The struggle now went beyond the agricultural areas and entered the pastoral land that had previously been designated for a moderate policy aimed at maintaining stability.[116] Between May and November, heavy fighting took place in Garzê. The PLA carried out large-scale operations in Derge (Dege), Dengke, and Changtai counties, all along or close to the Jinsha River. In addition, some 260 small operations unfolded in other places. According to a report by the CCP Garzê Prefecture Committee, these operations annihilated 6,261 rebels. Blockhouses were constructed along the Jinsha River to prevent attack from the western side, but the PLA was unable to seal the Jinsha River completely until late April 1958. By that time, the PLA had deployed seven regiments in Garzê and basically controlled the southern half of the area where the rebels had previously dominated.[117]

In the PRC's official chronicle of Sichuan, the year 1956 is marked as a period of "comprehensive counteroffensive" against the Tibetan-Yi rebellions, and the period from March 1957 to the end of 1959 as one of "focused pacification of rebellions."[118] Although the PRC chronicle divides the numbers of rebels evenly between the first and the second periods, or seventy-five thousand for each, undoubtedly the second phase of the reform war was a social-military conflict more violent than the first. On the CCP side, a moderate "Tianbao" became a hard-line "Sangye Yeshe." In March 1957, Sangye Yeshe brought Deng's directive back to Garzê. Very soon, local CCP cadres were ready to "fight a few good battles" while pushing the reform forward. Then, in early

September 1957, Sangye Yeshe wrote an opinion criticizing the current work in the Tibetan and Yi areas. In his view, the reform had not struck widely enough. Consequently, slave owners and landlords had not lost much, and the masses had not been completely mobilized and acted as the ruling force. He demanded that reform must be done thoroughly so as not to leave any feudal force alive, hidden guns uncollected, and the issue of monasteries unsolved. At the time, there was nothing peculiar about such a hard-line policy proposition in the CCP's reform war in western Sichuan. Historically peculiar is the fact that Sangye Yeshe was the one who raised these issues and urged the provincial committee to take action.[119] Policy conformity, if not consensus, was solidly in place on the CCP side.

As the CCP's reform orientation became rapidly radicalized in 1957, the two old obstacles to "democratic reform" in the Tibetan-Sichuan frontiers, guns and monasteries, were forcefully overcome. At the Central Secretariat's March 9 meeting, Deng insisted: "Gun must change shoulders," which was a much clearer command than Mao's "tiger borrows pigs" adage.[120] Yet, the class-struggle undertone of Deng's words was false, for the process was not one of moving guns from feudal lords' shoulders to those of the laboring masses. Before "democratic reform," most of the guns were already in the hands of laboring people. But class categorization in the PRC increasingly depended on political criteria. Any Tibetan, upper or lower class by social definition, could be classified as a "class enemy" if he refused to surrender his gun to the CCP authorities. After the Central Secretariat decided to flex military muscle to accomplish "democratic reform" in western Sichuan, the PLA was facing a situation that was in stark contradiction to its founding principles. In a report dated June 1957, the CCP Ngawa Prefecture Committee noted that PLA troops occasionally alienated the masses because "in a time of war it is hard [for the troops] to differentiate the rebels from the people [*min pan nan fen*]." The situation in the Yi areas was similar. In the summer of 1957, Liao Zhigao demanded that the CCP Liangshan Prefecture Committee correct two situations: (1) the practice of confiscating guns from slaves and ordinary laborers who did not join the CCP organized militia; and (2) willfully killing and arresting [*suibian dasi, suibian zhuabu*] rebels' family members and ordinary masses. In Liao's words, such practices were "highly unpopular" and would "seriously alienate the mass and cause very bad consequences." Liao made it clear that these wrongdoings must stop before the rebellions could be pacified.[121] But when such prevalent practices were part of a general CCP offensive, Liao's calling for tactical nicety could not have much effect.

Information about developments in western Sichuan in 1957 and after is too sporadic to give a full picture. Still, such archival information does exist for the second but not the first phase of the reform war, and it reflects the caution-excessiveness-correction trilogy typical of every sociopolitical campaign that the CCP launched in Mao's time. The March decision by the Central Secretariat clearly opened the door for local reformers to engage in excessive behaviors. In the summer of 1957, reports from Ngawa and Garzê indicated that as the campaign for the lower classes to "vent grievances" assumed momentum in these areas, the masses became so exceedingly enthusiastic that the "struggle was hard to control." Such "struggle" was often conducted in "improper forms," including beating, torturing, and killing.[122] The intensified social relations in 1957 were also evidenced by another phenomenon: in both the Tibetan and Yi areas, some CCP members and cadres of minority backgrounds "betrayed [the CCP] and capitulated to the enemy." As depicted in a document of the CCP Sichuan Committee, such individuals joined rebellions either willingly or reluctantly; some "actively engaged in counterrevolutionary activities, committed crimes, and antagonized the people"; some "colluded with the enemy secretly, collecting money and foodstuff and recruiting troops for the enemy."[123] Such individuals tended to be among the politically most active elements of the frontier societies, who had joined the CCP effort a few years before and now took a political stance for the second time. In general, explanations of such "betrayal" in CCP documents did not go beyond finding defects in the perpetrators' personal characteristics.

During the second phase of the reform war, unlike the gun issue, the issue of religion did not stand out right away. Having learned a lesson from the first phase, the CCP authorities intentionally pushed back the subject in their agenda. At the March meeting of the Central Secretariat, Deng set out two points for Sichuan officials to follow in dealing with monasteries: "The first is not to assist their development and the second is not to let them collapse too fast."[124] The resultant orientation in western Sichuan was "to firmly neutralize religion in order to facilitate destruction of feudal and exploitive systems." Yet in practice, as local officials reported, two extremes occurred. One was "excessive struggle" that made monasteries part of the reform targets; the other was "excessive peace" that "sacralized religion" and let feudal classes use religion to cover their resistance against reform.[125] Aside from these "mistakes" on the reformers' side, "neutralization of religion" was hard to achieve if monasteries refused to stay neutral in the conflict. An example was the Dajin Monastery of Garzê, which in 1956 served as a base for the rebels and had been watched closely by the CCP authorities ever since. In late July 1957, CCP officials in Garzê got information that the monastery was organizing a force of five hundred and collecting many horses. Fearing that a plot was afoot, a local CCP work committee asked a PLA regiment to put the monastery under siege on July 22. In the next few days, the work committee received two contradictory directives from the CCP Garzê Prefecture Committee and the headquarters of the Kangding Branch Military Region, one saying that the PLA action was a mistake whereas the other saying that the troops should not be withdrawn.

Eventually it was decided that a force of battalion size should be stationed close to the monastery while the two sides negotiated. In the meantime, the CCP Sichuan Committee wanted Garzê officials to act cautiously because "we do not yet have a finalized policy in dealing with monasteries."[126]

At the time, the Sichuan authorities learned that in the province there were 727 Tibetan Buddhist monasteries and 81,296 lamas, or about 13 percent of the province's Tibetan population. Among these, 496 monasteries and 65,069 lamas were in the Garzê Tibetan Autonomous Prefecture. Sichuan officials noticed some "achievements" of *gai tu gui liu* (changing native rulers into regular officials) in the late Qing: in the five counties of Garzê untouched by the Qing measure, lamas accounted for 21 percent to 43 percent of the total population whereas in the other thirteen counties, which had gone through *gai tu gui liu*, the lama population was much smaller, about 9 percent of the total. At the end of August 1957, the Sichuan Nationality Work Committee prepared a draft plan for jettisoning the "temporary not touching" policy toward monasteries. The basic goals in solving the monastery question were "to cut the economic ties between monasteries and the mass, reform the majority of lamas into self-supporting laborers, and protect proper religious activity under the precondition that socialist industrialization will not be hindered." Li Jingquan, however, untypically advised caution this time. Before "touching" monasteries, he wanted four questions to be answered: (1) What would be the impact on Tibet? (2) What would be the impact on pastoral areas? (3) Was the timing premature since the reform was not yet concluded? (4) What was the Center's thinking? If any of these questions could not be positively answered, Li indicated to his colleagues, the "not touching" policy should not be changed.[127]

Li's questions did not have a moderating effect, though. In the summer of 1957, as the Anti-Rightist Campaign was in full swing in the PRC, patience and caution were no longer virtuous qualities in CCP policymaking. It was in this new political atmosphere that Sangye Yeshe made his September criticism of the stagnant reform in Garzê. Afterwards, Garzê officials loosened restrictions on attacks against monasteries. Since the "temporarily not touching" orientation had not been officially rescinded, CCP officials continued to inform the Tibetans that "democratic reform" and religion were two "matters of different natures" and that the masses would neither be mobilized nor discouraged to "vent grievances against monasteries." In the meantime, with local CCP authorities' approval, face-to-face struggle against "villainous" religious figures began.[128] In early December 1957, the CCP Garzê Prefecture Committee put the issue of monasteries in a new context: socialist transformation of Garzê. As "democratic reform" was winding up in eastern and northern Garzê and was scheduled to be completed in southern Garzê in 1958, monasteries and "big Tibetan merchants" now stood out as agents of "private commercial capitalism." In Garzê officials' opinion, continuation of such Tibetan establishments would not only "weaken the achievements of democratic reform and directly undermine production and socialist transformation of agriculture" but, "if capitalism develops further," would also "foster [Tibetan] nationalism and centrifugal tendencies, and encourage certain reactionary upper-stratum figures to lean toward reactionaries in Tibet and even rally to imperialists."[129] In other words, when the PRC was marching into socialism, the old Garzê anchored on religion became intolerable: monasteries, in CCP officials' opinion, symbolized not only social backwardness but also political danger.

A frontal attack on monasteries would not begin, however, until the winter of 1958. In November 1958, the CCP Sichuan Committee instructed Garzê officials to start a "four antis" campaign (anti-rebellion, anti–law violation, anti-privilege, and anti-exploitation) aimed to "abolish the monastery system of feudal exploitation and oppression." Originally, the campaign was planned to end in the spring of 1959, but it continued for a year, joined by new conflicts in the wake of the Lhasa revolt in March 1959. In the meantime, once the interdict against attacking monasteries was lifted, "democratic reform" on the eastern side of the Jinsha River came to a speedy conclusion in December 1958, as previously scheduled.[130]

* * *

During the March 1957 discussions of the Central Secretariat about the situation in western Sichuan, Li Weihan expressed his support for the continuation of reform, saying that reform on the eastern side of the Jinsha River would have a positive impact on the western side. At the same time, he also articulated a two-Tibet formula: "Tianbao and the Dalai [Lama] must not invade each other." While "class struggle" was engulfing the eastern side of the river, Li still considered "inter-nationality unity," meaning Beijing-Lhasa cooperation, as the top priority in Beijing's Tibet policy. A caveat, though, according to Li, was that "unity among brotherly nationalities cannot be achieved without class struggles."[131] Thus, after the Seventeen-Point Agreement erased the Jinsha River as a divide of sovereignty between Lhasa and Beijing in 1951, by 1957 the reform war in western Sichuan had the effect of reaffirming the Jinsha River as a sociopolitical divide between the Tibetan and the CCP systems. In the thick of the Cold War, an internal systemic divide like this in the PRC was at once conspicuous and precarious. Whether or not the divide was meant to last is the question to be discussed in the next chapter. Here some conclusive remarks on Beijing's construction of "Tianbao's Tibet" are warranted.

"Tianbao's Tibet" was, of course, an ethnopolitical expression that Beijing used to cover the actual CCP political process during the 1950s. As the CCP authorities advanced into the ancient Tibetan-Yi corridor, they were faced with a social peculiarity almost as unfamiliar to them as Tibet itself, even though the vast area was a constellation of petty local powers not controlled by Lhasa. The same kind of tension existed in CCP policymaking in this area as in Tibet, between the CCP leadership's self-admitted social ignorance and its ingrained political confidence. In the final analysis, the CCP's admission of ignorance about Tibetan society did not become a hindrance to action because CCP officials held the Marxist insight on class struggle as the panacea for all social problems. It was therefore mainly out of confidence—the self-righteousness of the CCP revolution, a sense of the Han people's cultural and material superiority, and the overwhelming power and prowess of the Chinese Communist state over frontier minority communities—that Beijing initially proceeded "peacefully" in this inner frontier with Tibet. The orientation was simultaneously cautious and audacious: it was cautious not to upset the original networks of local societies in which the CCP did not have much influence; it was audacious to believe that the CCP could "smartly" persuade the Tibetan/Yi ruling elites to incapacitate themselves. Such cautious audacity characterized the CCP's "nationality policy" in all ethnic frontiers of the PRC where Beijing endeavored to plant roots of its political authority via expedient collaboration with the old elites.

Between 1956 and 1958, as the reform war increasingly intensified, "nationality policy" as such was superseded by a class-struggle orientation typical of CCP politics. In just two years, the class-struggle orientation changed western Sichuan from one of China's unique ethnic frontiers into an integral part of the PRC system. It was in this familiar mode of CCP operations, however, that PLA troops and CCP authorities encountered what appeared to them a strange phenomenon: a considerable portion of the Tibetan and Yi "laboring mass" joined their own "class enemies" in resisting their Han "liberators." In these years, therefore, the CCP experienced two paradoxical ethnopolitical situations. Initially, when the CCP designed a "nationality policy" for dealing with a minority people as a whole, the policy focused mainly on minority elites. Later, when the CCP switched to a class-struggle orientation against minority elites, the orientation provoked a fight that blurred class divides and engaged a minority people across the board.

Thus, in contemplating policies toward the minorities, CCP leaders tended to understand nationality/ethnicity as elite properties and rarely recognized ethnic attributes of the ordinary or lower-class people. As disciples of Marxism, CCP leaders used a nationality/ethnicity frame of analysis only as a pragmatic, supplementary tool for understanding the unfamiliar "class situation" of minorities. When their class struggle–oriented perception was contradicted by ethnopolitical realities, such as the issues of religion and guns in the Tibetan communities of Sichuan, CCP officials had no choice but to blame class enemies for deceiving the "unenlightened mass."

CCP policymaking was, of course, not a monolithic process. As violence spread in western Sichuan, alleviating measures were proposed by officials who were either ethnic minorities themselves or directly responsible for the party's "nationality work." Their voices were heard in Beijing and did have an impact on the process of the reform war. But, eventually, their preferred soft-pedaling of CCP programs turned out to be just a bubble in the violent torrent that the CCP managed to unleash. In retrospect, these officials' relatively "soft" approach could not have worked because it fell into the same delusion as Beijing's initial demarche of cautious audacity. In the 1950s, the CCP was in a vital stage of its history, trying to establish itself as a ruling party domestically and internationally. Unlike in either the pre-1949 period, when the CCP was struggling for survival and for power, or the post-1978 years, when the CCP refocused on economic development as a means to relegitimize itself, during the first decade of the PRC the CCP had a lot of items on its plate but was unwilling to compromise over any. As a newly established revolutionary regime in its radical phase, Beijing forged ahead, peacefully if possible and violently if necessary. Among old Tibetan/Yi elites, it was recognized that the advance of the Chinese Communist system into their areas was unstoppable, just as "it is impossible to cover the sun with hands or to block daybreak with a quilt." These local figures, however, could not comprehend why the system, which was supposed to benefit all, had to come with such brute force.[132]

Western Sichuan was just an inner layer of the PRC's Tibetan frontier. The PLA's crossing of the Jinsha River in October 1950 and the concluding of the Seventeen-Point Agreement in May 1951 made Tibet part of the PRC without integrating Tibet into the CCP's ideological and sociopolitical systems. In the eyes of Beijing leaders, Tibet remained an alien place. As Beijing's orientation in western Sichuan changed from one of "smart class struggles" to one of "good battles," the region's demonstration role for the western side of the Jinsha River remained unchanged. The next chapter explores how Beijing managed its relationship with Lhasa while pushing forward radical changes on the eastern side of the Jinsha River.

CHAPTER 4

A NEW PHASE

In waves of "class struggles" during the Mao years, the CCP leadership tended to characterize its own political steps as *yangmou*, or "overt stratagems," and its adversaries' as *yinmou*, or "covert plots."[1] A *yangmou* was righteous, constructive, and totally justifiable as far as the CCP was concerned. A *yinmou* was just the opposite and, historically, constituted a vain attempt to stop the unstoppable Chinese Communist revolution. The reform war of 1956–1962 in western Sichuan was clearly started by the CCP's sociopolitical assault on the old establishments and customs of Tibetan society in the region. The assault was originally intended as a peaceful operation of liberation to be welcomed by lower-class and swallowed by upper-class Tibetans. That the operation turned violent was not unexpected by the CCP leadership. As early as 1951, Mao Zedong pointed out that CCP reform imposed upon the Tibetans or any ethnic minority of China would surely cause "nationality antagonisms" (*minzu fangan*).[2] The intensive military preparations for reform, described in chapter 3, showed that from the outset CCP officials in both Beijing and Sichuan anticipated armed conflict. As Mao said during the reform war, "war may not be avoided . . . unless there is no reform."[3] Because "democratic reform" constituted a *yangmou* on the CCP's part, Beijing was unapologetic for the consequent bloodshed and massive fighting, even though admitting "errors" in implementing certain specific policies. In executing its *yangmou*, the CCP could also afford to be lenient for a while and did not classify the rebels, those who "could not understand" the CCP's "righteous cause," as counterrevolutionary "bandits" or "enemies."[4]

Yet the logic of class struggle required identification of some perpetrators of *yinmou*, deemed by the CCP to be the root cause of irregular activities against the PRC authorities. In October 1956, the CCP Kangding Area Committee reported these findings to its superiors:

> Incited and directed by Kuomintang bandits and secret agents, some of the feudal lords and landlords started preparations for rebellions against revolutionary and democratic reform a long time ago . . . Investigations and a great number of captured letters and other materials can prove conclusively that [rebellions] were incited and directed by Kuomintang bandits and secret agents. For instance, rebels in Bathang had radio transmitters. They openly displayed the British banner and set up a "Kuomintang Commanding Headquarters for Xikang and Tibet." Kuomintang agent Duan Juxian (a Han living Buddha) was the actual plotter and commander. The Kuomintang banner appeared in Litang, and five Han counterrevolutionaries were identified among the captured rebels. The rebellions under the Shouling Monastery [Drakgo Gompa] of Luhuo, *Chongwang Langjia* [充旺郎加] of Zongmai, and Rinzin Thondup of Seda were all started under the direction of counterrevolutionary Zhang Hang.[5]

The two "KMT agents" identified in the document would not appear in CCP literature again, for they would soon lose their usefulness in the CCP's historical narrative. Yet in the mid-1950s, they served as evidence for the CCP's unequivocal assertion about a continual struggle with its archenemy, the KMT. In contrast, CCP documents dating from this period do not in any way implicate Lhasa for inciting Tibetan rebellions in Sichuan. During both the planning and reviewing stages of "democratic reform" in western Sichuan, CCP officials considered the Lhasa regime and the Tibetan society on the western side of the Jinsha River as recipients of influence from the eastern side of the River. The questions they asked were how the reform in western Sichuan would "positively impact" Tibet and what precautions should be taken to reduce negative impact.[6] After rebellions began in Garzê, Lhasa's concern, especially the Dalai Lama's personal inquiry, became inconvenient for CCP reformers. As rumors traveled as far as southern Gansu, one of which said that the Dalai Lama had gone to India to borrow troops to fight the Communists, Sichuan officials had to prepare themselves for receiving investigation teams from both Beijing and Lhasa.[7]

When meeting with Sichuan officials in July 1956, Mao talked about Lhasa's reactions. But the records kept by various officials show two rather different versions of Mao's remarks. In one version, Mao allegedly said that "common interests" on the two sides of the Jinsha River led the western side to send people to join the fight on the eastern side. In another Mao said: "Lhasa heard about the war and made a lot of fuss. But they were unable to come to the help [of the rebels]. They wanted to start armed rebellions but realized that they could not do it. Soon or later landlords' and monasteries' armed forces have to be wiped out no matter how Lhasa cried."⁸ The sources of Mao's information about Lhasa's reaction cannot be ascertained. Archival materials do show that a year after Mao made his remarks, CCP officials in Garzê reported a move by Lhasa. Allegedly, in May 1956, the rebellious Dajin Monastery contacted Tibetan officials in Lhasa and asked for assistance. This led to two Tibetan army officers' visiting and staying in the Dajin Monastery until September.⁹ Such intelligence, even if available to Mao in July 1956, would have been too trivial to support his judgment about Lhasa's intention. In any case, although the two versions of Mao's talk contradict each other with respect to Lhasa's involvement in the Tibetan rebellions in Sichuan, both show that Mao was talking about Lhasa's demeanor *after* the rebellions started. In the same vein, in a 1956 report, the Central United Front Department suggested that, whereas "democratic reform" was not yet scheduled for Tibet, the region *would nevertheless be influenced* by the examples of the reform in the Tibetan areas of Qinghai and Sichuan.¹⁰

This chapter begins with the *yangmou/yinmou* binary of CCP discourse and information from Chinese archives dating from the mid-1950s, paving the way for a discussion of two major issues in relevant historiography. One is the relationship between Lhasa and the Tibetan rebellions in western Sichuan. Relevant publications in the PRC are unanimous in accusing the "Dalai clique" for inciting rebellions in western Sichuan, whereas studies outside the PRC have not been able to clarify the relationship one way or the other. Another is Beijing's policy intentions about and responsibility for reform preparations in Tibet in 1956. These preparatory measures assumed such magnitude that they almost ruined the delicate Beijing-Lhasa relationship under the frame of the Seventeen-Point Agreement. PRC publications and some studies in the West have blamed some hard-liners in the TWC for rushing forward reform and thereby undermining Beijing's gradualist approach. Information from Chinese archives shows a rather different situation.

Spreaders of a "Sweet Rain"

The past happened in one way, but "history" has been written in many different ways. A historiographic issue concerning both the PRC and Tibet is whether, or to what extent, Lhasa was responsible for the rebellions in western Sichuan in the mid-1950s. In other words, was the reform war a result of Beijing's *yangmou*, or Lhasa's *yinmou*? In contrast to what is revealed by CCP documents dating from the mid- to late 1950s, which can be termed an "internal party narrative," the established historical narrative in the PRC today, the "public party narrative," ironically gives full agency to Lhasa for agitating and causing rebellions in western Sichuan in the mid-1950s. According to this public narrative, between early May and early June 1955, on his way back to Lhasa from his Beijing visit, the Dalai Lama lingered in Garzê for some twenty days. During this time, allegedly, Surkhang Wangchen Gelek, a member of the Kashag, and Trijang Lobsang Yeshe, the Dalai Lama's junior tutor, went separately to the north and the south to incite local headmen and lamas to wage resistance against the CCP's reform. Such agitations were therefor responsible for starting rebellions in western Sichuan. This public narrative, as will be shown later in this chapter, began to take shape after the Lhasa revolt of March 1959 but was not finalized until the end of the century. In 1995, when the official chronicle of Sichuan, *Sichuan Shengzhi*, was being prepared, the compilers hesitated about whom to identify as agitators of the rebellions in western Sichuan. An initial edition for "internal discussion" included, aside from Trijang, three other "reactionary Tibetan living Buddhas": the head lamas of the "White Sect," the "Red Sect," and the "Flower Sect" of Tibetan Buddhism. But when the chronicle was issued in 1999, only Surkhang and Trijang were identified as the villains.[11]

In his autobiography, published in 1962, the Dalai Lama does admit that he sent the three highest lamas of his entourage to areas he himself was unable to visit. But he has also been consistent, in the autobiography and in interviews given over the years, that his message to the Khampas was about peace, patience, and cooperation with Han cadres because, having just talked to CCP leaders in person, he still cherished the hope of working with Beijing. When some Khampa leaders approached him with an idea about Tibetan independence, the Dalai Lama was astonished and alarmed.[12] Depending on their adopted frames of interpretation, previous works of historical scholarship outside the PRC, written in English or in Chinese, have taken various stances on the public party narrative within the PRC, ranging from outright rebuttal to simple dismissal to reserved acceptance.[13] None of these, however, is supported with archival information.

A number of questions may be asked about the allegation made in the public party narrative. First, in view of the CCP leadership's careful arrangements for escorting the Dalai Lama group back to Lhasa, what chance was there for members of the group to incite Khampas without being detected by their CCP escorts? When sending the Dalai Lama group back to Lhasa, Beijing put three persons in charge: Liu Geping, Phüntso Wangye, and Xu Danlu. The first two stopped at Changdu, and Xu continued all way back to Lhasa. When the group reached Xikang's capital city, Ya'an, in pursuance of Zhou Enlai's directive on tightening security, the original escorting team from Beijing was expanded to a huge band of more than five hundred people and a hundred cars. Xu Danlu, Kang Nai'er (deputy governor of Xikang), and Qin Chuanhou (security chief of Sichuan) formed a new three-member leading group that was responsible for the lap from Ya'an to Chamdo. Xu kept a journal throughout the trip, which recorded the Dalai Lama group's religious activities from Kangding to Chamdo but mentioned nothing about suspicious moves made by members of the group.¹⁴

Xu's journal is consistent with official documents generated by the CCP apparatuses at regional and county levels in Xikang, which assumed direct security and intelligence responsibilities when the Dalai Lama's deputies visited different places. On January 31, 1955, the CCP Kangding Area Committee transmitted to its superiors in Ya'an a letter from the Dalai Lama group to the Xikang Tibetan Autonomous Region:

> When leaving Lhasa in this [lunar] year, [the Dalai Lama] promised to the three monasteries and the people that he would return to Tibet in a year. Therefore, [the Dalai Lama] cannot stretch his journey back too long and cannot stay for too many days in your region. [The Dalai Lama] wishes to meet the mass in areas not connected to the highway but will not be able to do so because of time restraint. Therefore, Trijang Rinpoche, Karmapa Rinpoche, and Mindrolling Rinpoche are requested to act as the Dalai Lama's representatives to visit various places in order to satisfy the wish of religious and secular people alike. The Dalai Lama will personally visit only the areas along the highway.¹⁵

The planned visitations by the Dalai Lama's three representatives needed approval from the highest authorities in Beijing, who not only approved the plan but also provided financial assistance. In late January, the Central Nationality Committee sent to Tianbao a billion yuan (old *renminbi*), half of which was for Trijang and the other half to be divided between the Karmapa Lama and Mindrolling Trichen.¹⁶ In early February, the State Council officially notified CCP officials of Xikang about the three's itineraries and instructed them to make proper preparations. The separate arrangements for the three were that, after arriving in Kangding in late February, Trijang would proceed to Litang, Bathang, Chaktreng, and other counties in the south; in the northern direction, the Karmapa Lama would go to Derge (Dege), and Mindrolling Trichen to Garzê (county) and Xinlong. The CCP Kangding Area Committee informed relevant county officials: "The Dalai [Lama]'s representatives will carry out purely religious activities." While the visitations should be considered beneficial to CCP policy in the context of the Dalai Lama's recent visit in Beijing and participation in the National People's Congress, the leading CCP officials of these counties, the Kangding Committee cautioned, must realize that the Dalai Lama group would use the opportunity to expand its influence under the "banner of the [Tibetan] nationality and religion" and also to "extort a fortune" from the local people. In receiving the three, county officials should pay special attention to their guests' physical security and living accommodations.

The officials ought to behave properly so that their demeanor not arouse the visitors' suspicion about the CCP's policy toward religion. In the meantime, intelligence must be collected to find out how various local circles reacted to the visitations.[17]

When visiting the designated locations, the three rinpoches were free to decide their agendas and daily activities. In the meantime, they were under careful and constant watching by the security personnel assigned to them. The Trijang team had ten members and was escorted by thirteen government guards, the Karmapa team of thirteen by seven guards, and the Mindrolling team of six by nine guards. The three conducted their activities separately in the southern and northern halves the Xikang Tibetan Autonomous Region (Garzê Tibetan Autonomous Prefecture after 1955) from early March to late April and then, in either Derge or Chamdo, rejoined the Dalai Lama, whose visit in Xikang began on May 5.[18] CCP security personnel accompanying the three rinpoches, ad hoc CCP work committees, and public security apparatuses in the counties concerned all sent regular reports to their regional and provincial superiors. After the Dalai Lama group left Xikang, the Public Security Department of the Xikang Tibetan Autonomous Region submitted a concluding report to the General Office of Public Security of Xikang Province.

All these reports convey a clear impression that, except for some minor irregularities, the Dalai Lama's and his three representatives' visitations in Xikang constituted a successful propaganda tour beneficial to the CCP. When preaching, Trijang told his audience that they could not have met him without Chairman Mao, and that they should treat Han cadres nicely. He also told local Tibetan officials that working hard for the people and accepting the Han's assistance would be as good as getting an audience from him and the Dalai Lama.[19] The Mindrolling Trichen, a leading figure of the Red Sect (Nyingma) of Tibetan Buddhism, preached in a way that was almost comparable with CCP officials' public speeches.[20] He talked about the resolutions of the recent National People's Congress and the new constitution of the PRC, reflected on his tour in eastern provinces, discussed subjects like the liberation of Taiwan and opposition to the atomic bomb of American imperialism, exhorted monasteries not to engage in criminal trade of drugs and arms, and asked the people to concentrate on production. He praised the "new society" of the PRC for interethnic unity and freedom of religious beliefs, and even promoted the new edition of renminbi that had just been issued.[21] Among the three, the Karmapa Lama (Rangjung Rigpe Dorje), head of the White Sect (Kagyu), appeared the least political in public and limited his preaching to religious affairs, admonishing lamas to behave becomingly and monasteries to work together regardless of sectarian differences. In private, however, he took advantage of traveling together with CCP cadres to complain about the inadequate attention that Beijing had paid to him. The Karmapa Lama contended to CCP officials that, having associated neither with the British nor with the Kuomintang, he had a cleaner background than both the Dalai Lama and the Panchen Lama. He also offered to mediate between two local factions in Derge or to go abroad to facilitate the relationship between Beijing and Bhutan, Nepal, and India.[22]

To leaders in Beijing, the most important thing, of course, was what the Dalai Lama had to say during his tour in Xikang. The Public Security Department of the Xikang Tibetan Autonomous Region acquired the content of a conversation between the Dalai Lama and some local Tibetan officials in northern Xikang, which did not sound feinted and probably reflected the Dalai Lama's actual thinking at the time:

> (1) The [Communist] Party's nationality policy is to let minority nationalities learn to walk with their own legs. You do not work for the Han but for your own nationality. Han cadres came here not to occupy offices but to help us. You should trust the Communist Party and its members. (2) Unity among nationalities and within a nationality must be strengthened. In the past, problems detrimental to unity did exist among Kham, Front Tibet, and Rear Tibet. For instance, the Khampas [*Kangren*] said that the Tibetans [*Zangren*] were too cunning and the Tibetans said that the Khampas were backward and savage. (3) In the past, I was also suspicious of the [CCP's] policy of freedom of religious beliefs. I am now totally convinced after participating in the discussion of [the PRC] constitution and visiting various places. You should all be convinced as well. (4) Religion does not need assistance from the Han, but economic and cultural assistance should be welcomed. Religious activities must not contradict state policies. Our Tibetan cadres have worked for the government, and some lamas have to spend less time than before in studying the sutras. You have my approval. (5) The Soviet Communist Party and the Chinese Communist Party are both working for the ordinary people, and there is no reason to fear them. We should all take a long-term view and see for thirty, twenty, or at least five years.

According to the report, the Dalai Lama and his representatives conveyed this general message to their audience:

> Religion will thrive if all monasteries maintain unity among them and within themselves, work well with the government, and keep connected with the mass. The Communist Party will not act against religion if the monasteries are completely devoted to the belief and not involved in misdemeanors. The supreme law of the state has legally confirmed the policy of protecting freedom of religious beliefs. In the future, any fear will be groundless that the Communist Party wants to destroy lamaist monasteries.[23]

Local CCP cadres accompanying the Tibetan dignitaries would have failed in their duty, however, if they had not reported the Tibetans' irregular behaviors. Intelligence reports in this category mentioned sectarian discord among Tibetan lamas and also noted some secular Tibetan officials' loose sexual contacts with local women. More serious were a series of "secret conversations" that the Dalai Lama and his representatives held with local headmen and high-ranking lamas. Some of these conversations took place "behind closed doors," some "in midnights," and some in other ways for evading CCP personnel. Local CCP authorities had no clues about the contents of most of these conversations but did manage to learn a bit about two of them. In one, Trijang suggested to local headmen that in the future every county on the eastern side of the Jinsha River send a permanent representative to Lhasa in order to keep close contact between the two sides. In another, he urged local Tibetan officials to visit Chinese provinces in the east. When reporting such conversations, local CCP cadres did not appear surprised or alarmed by the Tibetans' secretiveness. In following their superiors' instructions about being good hosts, local CCP officials gave their visitors freedom of movement while reporting to their superiors how, in their eyes, Trijang and others acted either affectionately or affectedly.[24] Also included in their reports were some "rumors" that arose during the three rinpoches' tours. For instance, in Bathang, two members of Trijang's entourage used a sort of ominous language in talking about how the People's Liberation Army was weak and unable to liberate Taiwan and how awesome America's atomic bomb was. Land reform was also a concern. In some southern counties of Xikang, land reform in Yunnan was rumored to be a precedent for Tibetans in these areas. The concern existed in northern Xikang as well. In his meeting with local personalities, the Mindrolling Trichen was questioned about whether the Dalai Lama had asked Chairman Mao not to introduce land reform into the Tibetan areas. In the south, however, CCP cadres could not establish a connection between Trijang's team and the rumor about land reform, and in the north, CCP cadres were satisfied with the way the Mindrolling Trichen handled his questioners. Not saying anything about what had been discussed in Beijing about reform in western Sichuan, the Mindrolling Trichen simply reaffirmed his confidence in the CCP's policies.[25]

Actually, the local CCP officials focused their attention on what danger their Tibetan guests might encounter, not what potential threat these Tibetans might pose. In early March, Beijing instructed relevant provincial officials to "strictly prevent penetration and sabotage by bandit agents [*feite*, meaning agents of Taiwan]" during the Tibetans' visit. Accordingly, the Xikang authorities arranged extremely tight security measures for controlling some identified "counterrevolutionaries and ordinary criminals" in their region. Throughout the Tibetans' tours, however, there was just one case of some importance, involving a "bandit agent" named Zhang Xing. Zhang had evaded

CCP authorities for some time, and CCP security officials were concerned that Zhang might join the Karmapa Lama's team in disguise and escape abroad via Tibet.[26] Zhang deserves attention because later, in 1956, he would be identified by CCP authorities as one of the few "enemy agents" who had agitated Tibetans to start rebellion in western Sichuan.

The Tibetans' tours in Xikang were the last leg of the Beijing-directed operation of winning over the Tibetan leadership. Fully aware of the delicate nature of their task, Xikang officials made great efforts in taking care of their visitors. However, they assumed the host's role only partially, for local monasteries provided accommodations most of the time and contributed to security measures as well. CCP officials must have watched ambivalently how the local people mobbed and worshipped the Dalai Lama and his representatives, hearing the "mass" express gratitude to Chairman Mao and the Communist Party for letting them meet in person with these "living Buddhas." In total, the Dalai Lama and his representatives held about 130 preaching sessions to an audience of more than a hundred thousand people. The Dalai Lama personally visited six counties, and his representatives, according to the CCP Kangding Area Committee, "traveled throughout the region except the most remote areas like Derong and Shique."[27] CCP officials of Xikang understood that these religious activities had to have political connotations, but the question was to whose benefit. In July, in making a final report about his mission of escorting the Dalai Lama, deputy governor Kang Nai'er remarked: "In my view this [whole event] is more beneficial than harmful. . . . In the opinion of the mass, the Dalai [Lama] is a good lama who has joined the revolutionary work and preached throughout his journey to propagate the [CCP] Center."[28] In view of what the post-1959 CCP narrative has to say about the Dalai Lama group's tour in Xikang, these words from the CCP Kangding Area Committee's concluding report are worth quoting:

> Because they had visited Beijing, participated in the National People's Congress, and witnessed the great construction in various places of the motherland, the Dalai [Lama] and his officials were educated by facts, achieved a better understanding of the Party's nationality policy, and enhanced their patriotic ideas. Consequently, in their activities they propagated the Party's policies and influenced some upper-stratum individuals and the vast mass immensely. . . . Yet, on the other hand, we should note that they also engaged in political activities through religious activities, such as rectification of monasteries and inquiry with some upper-stratum individuals about the conditions of work in this region. In Derge [the Dalai Lama] met with Jago Topden seven times . . . We learned that Jago Topden was uneasy about prospective social reforms in our prefecture and asked the Dalai [Lama] for advice about how to handle the situation in the future. It was quite common that upper-stratum personalities

in various places used their contacts with Tibetan officials accompanying the Dalai [Lama] to expand their own influence. Some careerists were especially active. During this period, there were signs that some such individuals' attitudes turned to the worse. For instance, Jago Topden's attitude became abnormal lately. . . . Rumors appeared in various places: "The Communist Party was battling the United States but could not prevail. Therefore, they invited the Dalai [Lama] to Beijing for advice." . . . In addition, the Dalai [Lama]'s activities brought tremendous economic losses to the mass. . . . In total, the mass lost more than a million yuan. In other words, the results of several years' production were almost all taken away.[29]

In sum, according to the intelligence information collected and the conclusions reached by Kangding officials, the Dalai Lama group's touring in their region was a success with mixed consequences. At the time, these officials did not show any concern about a Tibetan plot for starting armed resistance against reform in Xikang.[30]

There were indeed reform-related anxieties among local aristocrats, though. According to CCP intelligence, such anxieties were caused by the newly adopted PRC constitution that included minority areas in the country's reform agenda. In the case of Jago Topden's consultation with the Dalai Lama about the possibility of reform in Xikang, whatever the Dalai Lama said to him, Jago Topden took steps in the next few months to relocate to Tibet, which reflected an attitude of resignation to but not resistance against the inevitable.[31] Jago Topden emerged as a focus of CCP intelligence for good reason. Born in 1900, Jago Topden was the chieftain of Derge and a typical frontier personality who had survived the intricate and multilateral political struggles on the Tibetan-Sichuan frontiers in the twentieth century. According to the official chronicle of the PRC, before 1949 Jago Topden maneuvered among Sichuan warlords, the KMT regime, Lhasa, and the CCP, while competing constantly with other local Khampa headmen. During the CCP's Long March in the 1930s, Jago Topden had a skirmish with the Red Army; he was captured and then released to become a member of a local Tibetan government organized by the Red Army. After the Red Army marched northward, Jago Topden resumed his collaboration with the KMT regime. Then, in 1950, he again changed with the times; he asked the PLA to "liberate" his area and aided the PLA's military advance toward Lhasa. Because of his contribution to the CCP's cause of liberation, Jago Topden became one of the most important local figures in the CCP's united-front work, continually holding a deputy chairmanship in the Tibetan autonomous region governments of Xikang and Garzê.[32] In the mid-1950s, slick as ever, Jago Topden sensed that another turn of affairs would soon happen to his area, necessitating a reevaluation of his relationship with the CCP.

In any case, Jago Topden's disappointing behavior did not become a reason for CCP officials to be suspicious of the Dalai Lama group. Instead, the group impressed Xikang officials favorably because of another, unrelated episode. During the Dalai Lama's visit in Xikang, five "people's representatives" traveled from Tibet to meet him and ask him to deliver a letter to Mao. The letter demanded Tibetan independence. The Kashag had tried but failed to stop them in Lhasa. In Kangding, the Dalai Lama group voluntarily informed CCP officials of the group's arrival and dissuaded them from delivering the letter. Therefore, in general, the Dalai Lama group appeared to act in Xikang to soothe, not incite, the Kampas' anxieties.[33]

In retrospect, the Beijing-Lhasa détente peaked in 1955, though years later the Dalai Lama would recall numerous times how, in a meeting in Beijing, Mao "startled" or "scared" him by telling him that religion was poison. In 1955, the Dalai Lama was confident enough to offer Mao a dose of that "poison": having returned to Lhasa, the Dalai Lama composed a long ode praising Mao in Buddhist terms.[34] The ode compared Mao with "Brahma who created the world," and Mao's "campaign for peace" with "Mani's white umbrella that shields the heavens, the earth, and the people with pleasant coolness." After eulogizing the Buddha—"Shakyamuni's religion of goodwill is like the clear and cool radiance of the infinite rays from the bright pearly moon"—the ode continued: "Your [Mao's] will is like a mass of clouds and your call is like the sound of thunder. A sweet rain constantly emanates from them to unselfishly refresh the world." The ode ended with a prayer: "May the benevolence of Buddha, the supernatural power of Dharmapala and the true words of God of Success make all my fine wishes come true!"[35] As the Dalai Lama was receptive to Mao's "sweet rain," his positive remarks about the CCP in Kangding made him a spreader of Mao's message. In stark contrast to how years later the Dalai Lama in his exile would describe his feelings toward Mao as far as religion was concerned, his 1955 prayer did reflect a cautious, albeit misplaced, optimism within the upper echelon of the Tibetan clergy that their religion would be able to manage under Mao.[36]

"Plotters of Many Rebellions"

Although Xikang and Kangding officials' factual findings and concluding remarks in 1955 may well agree that their Tibetan guests helped spread the "sweet rain" of the CCP, these have not been used to construct the official historical narrative in the PRC. The current official narrative about the Dalai Lama is a post-1959 reconstruction. In 1959, a major revision of the internal party narrative about the 1955 events took place; it had little to do with what the CCP authorities actually knew about the Dalai Lama's Xikang tour in 1955 but everything to do with what happened in Lhasa in March 1959. In mid-April 1959, a month after the Lhasa revolt, Zhang Jingwu delivered a speech about the recent events in Lhasa, which at the time was classified as *juemi* (top secret) within the CCP system. The venue and occasion of Zhang's speech are not clear. The speech was obviously intended to dispel any doubt about the correctness of Beijing's Tibet policy that might exist among CCP officials after the recent collapse of the Beijing-Lhasa relationship. Zhang, without naming names but meaning Fan Ming and his supporters within the TWC, attacked an "anti-Party clique" within the CCP that had questioned the wisdom of Beijing's 1956 decisions about reforming Tibet. In the meantime, Zhang's speech was the earliest official accusation against the Dalai Lama group for starting rebellions in various places outside Tibet: "The rebellions of last year and the year before the last in places like Xikang, Qinghai, Gansu, and Yunnan were all supported and started by upper-stratum reactionary cliques like the Dalai [Lama] group."37 Very soon, this narrative appeared publicly in the *People's Daily* and in a chronology of important events in Tibet compiled by the Minzu Chubanshe (Nationality Publisher) in Beijing.38

Zhang's speech was just the beginning of a historical retuning of the party rhetoric about Tibetan affairs. In the process, as Zhang repudiated an "ultra-leftist" policy orientation favored by Fan Ming's "anti-Party clique," CCP officials in Garzê got their chance to attack a "rightist" line imposed on them by Liu Geping in 1957. At the end of 1959, in a sixty-one-page document titled "Basic Conclusions on the Democratic Reform in the Garzê Tibetan Autonomous Prefecture (first draft)," the CCP Garzê Prefecture Committee asserted that, opposing Liu Geping's intervention, most of the Han cadres in Garzê had since 1956 insisted on a correct line for "revolutionary" and "thorough" reform. In the document, all the "problems" and "mistakes" that had occurred during the "democratic reform" in western Sichuan were attributed to a line of "phony reform," which was allegedly promoted by "comrades within the Party who were holding rightist and opportunistic views."39

Now that CCP officials on the two sides of the Jinsha River had separately blamed their "ultra-leftist" and "rightist" comrades for past mistakes in the Tibet work of their respective regions, they acted remarkably in sync in accusing the Dalai Lama group as the culprit behind the rebellions in all Tibetan areas. More than Zhang Jingwu, the Garzê Committee provided some necessary details to the public party narrative in the years to come:

Based on a great number of documents and items captured in the war, such as radio transmitters, telegrams, letters, and other types of papers, it has been fully proven that the rebellions were planned as early as in the summer of 1955. *At the time, when the Dalai Lama's group passed through our prefecture after attending the National People's Congress in Beijing, Tibetan upper-stratum reactionaries*

> *Surkhang, Trijang and others used the opportunity to plan and make systematic arrangements for launching armed rebellions.* Imperialism, Kuomintang reactionaries, and the Tibetan upper-stratum reactionary clique planned and directed the rebellions. Many reactionary lama monasteries served as staff departments and commanding centers that plotted and organized concrete steps of the rebellions.[40] (emphasis added)

In referring to "great number of documents" allegedly captured in the reform war during and after 1956, Garzê officials actually confirmed that CCP intelligence in 1955 had yielded no evidence connecting the Dalai Lama group to the rebellions in western Sichuan. As for the "documents and items captured in war," neither archival research nor publications in the PRC have so far yielded any convincing specifics.

Whereas Garzê officials' vendetta against Liu Geping and his moderate policy would remain an internal affair of the CCP, their accusation of the Dalai Lama group for plotting Tibetan rebellions in western Sichuan was adopted nationwide through various CCP channels. The December 1959 issue of *Gong'an Jianshe* (Construction of public security), a "top secret internal periodical" of the Ministry of Public Security issued to the county level, circulated an article by the Social Department of the TWC, titled with a slogan, "Thoroughly Beat Back and Expose the Treacherous Crimes of the Tibetan Upper-Stratum Reactionary Clique to Protect the Vast Laboring People's Struggle for Liberation." In line with the Garzê officials' presentation, the article provided an account of how, in a prolonged period, the "Tibetan reactionary upper-stratum" had prepared and eventually launched the Lhasa revolt of March 1959. The article asserted that Tibetan reactionaries had attempted not only to detached Tibet from China but also to establish their rule in the five neighboring provinces—Sichuan, Xikang, Yunnan, Gansu, and Qinghai. As for the Dalai Lama's Xikang tour, the article added new details:

> Among the rebellions planned and organized [by the "Dalai clique"], the largest was the Khampa rebellion in the Tibetan areas of Sichuan in 1956. To plan this rebellion, in 1955, when returning to Sichuan after following the Dalai [Lama] to participate in the National People's Congress, *Surkhang Wangchen Gelek and Trijang Lobsang Yeshe travelled separately to the south and the north of the Garzê Tibetan Autonomous Prefecture to incite and direct rebellions. Surkhang went to Kangding, Garzê, and Derge, and Trijang to Xiangchang, Daocheng, and Litang before meeting in Chamdo.* At the time Surkhang told reactionaries in these areas: "*You upper-stratum people must maintain internal unity. Communist and imperialist countries of the world have many contradictions. We Tibetans will not perish. You must do your best to postpone and block reform. You should start*

armed resistance if reform begins. But Tibetan independence can be achieved only if connections with foreign powers are established. In the Tibetan areas of Xikang you may propose unification with Tibet. If you have difficulties, I can offer assistance." Afterwards, reactionaries in these places held meetings and sent people to Tibet to maintain contacts with Surkhang and others.

Rebellions in Garzê actually began shortly after [bujiu] Trijang and Surkhang left the area. The Litang Monastery and the Dajin Monastery, where Trijang and Surkhang stayed separately, were the first to start rebellions [shouxian faqi panluan] and became rebellious centers. Using religious preaching as a cover, Tibetan upper-stratum reactionaries continued to send people to Kham to incite rebellions. In certain places rebellions began right after the preachers left.[41] (emphasis added)

The "top secret" classification of this document does not automatically make it a piece of trustworthy information. Like Zhang Jingwu's secret speech and the Garzê officials' report discussed above, the article was prepared with the clear intention of rectifying and streamlining CCP members' understanding of the recent developments in Tibet. The goal was to incriminate the Dalai Lama group, and the developments in western Sichuan were just used to complete a narrative. In this undertaking, informational accuracy was the least of the drafters' concerns. In the first place, those words attributed to Surkhang in the article are highly problematic. Terms like "upper stratum," "imperialist countries," and "Tibetan areas of Xikang" were commonly used by CCP cadres but unlikely to be used by Surkhang or any Tibetan official. In addition, as discussed earlier, the two-pronged travel involving the Dalai Lama's three religious representatives took place between early March and late April 1955. But in the article, Surkhang appears to have traveled simultaneously with Trijang, replacing the Karmapa Lama and the Mindrolling Trichen who had actually traveled northward. The fact is that Surkhang never left the Dalai Lama, who arrived in Xikang in early May and crossed the Jinsha River late in the month. Surkhang served as the liaison of the Tibetan side with the CCP escorts. Throughout the journey, the CCP escorts reported their bickering with Surkhang over the Dalai Lama's travel and accommodation arrangements.[42] In late June, after the Dalai Lama group left Xikang, the Derge chieftain Jago Topden was unwilling to go to Beijing to attend a conference of the National People's Congress. CCP officials in Garzê suspected that his decision might have been affected by a meeting with Surkhang. Not knowing what had been discussed between Surkhang and Jago Topden, Garzê officials nevertheless speculated that Surkhang might have connections with American intelligence and might have urged Jago Topden not to proceed to Beijing.[43] Such intelligence contradicted Surkhang's alleged whereabouts in the TWC article of 1959 and added little to his alleged role of inciting rebellions.

In tying the Dalai Lama group's 1955 visitation in western Sichuan to the rebellions of the region, the TWC article also used time sequence to suggest causation. Yet the time factor in the article is vague and twisted. The term *bujiu* (soon) in the article blurred a duration of more than eight months between the Dalai Lama group's departure from western Sichuan, in late May 1955, and February 15, 1956, when the "first shot" of the rebellions was fired. And, according to an official chronicle of Garzê Prefecture published in 1997, the "first shot" was fired by neither of the monasteries identified in the article but by a local headman in Seda County. Although following the public party narrative, the Garzê chronicle nevertheless uses dates from historical archives and puts the beginning of Litang Monastery's rebellion on March 9, 1956. Meanwhile, it does not even name the Dajin Monastery as one of the rebellious monasteries.[44] An April 1956 report from the CCP Sichuan Committee to Beijing had this to say about the Dajin Monastery:

> Lama monasteries are internally divided. The Dajin and Garzê Monasteries of Garzê have become increasingly divided internally. For instance, upper-stratum lamas of the Dajin Monastery who are close to the government have approached us and asked us to take measures immediately to prevent rebellion by a small number of lamas in the monastery.[45]

The inconsistence between the cited pre- and post-1959 CCP documents, both part of "archival information" to today's researchers, have inevitably created difficulties for compilers of the public party narrative. In the mid-1990s, when Sichuan Province prepared its official chronicle, the compilers put down these words about the rebellions of 1956:

> Incited by Kuomintang bandit agents and the Tibetan reactionary clique, upper-stratum reactionaries started armed rebellions in the Garzê Tibetan Autonomous Region. *In the summer of 1955, Tibetan reactionary living buddha Karmapa (head of the White Sect), Mindrolling (head of the Red Sect), and Jangtsiling (head of the Flower Sect), and Trijang (tutor of the Dalai Lama)* entered separately various monasteries and engaged in activities of inciting opposition to democratic reform.[46] (emphasis added)

Except for moving the Tibetans' activities from the spring to the summer of 1955, this passage still followed the pre-1959 archival records in naming all the high-positioned lamas who visited southern and northern Xikang ahead of the Dalai Lama, including Jangtsiling, who arrived in Kangding ahead of the Dalai Lama to check on local preparations. When revising their drafts, however, compilers of the Sichuan Chronicle corrected this "error" and replaced the three non-Gelug sects' leaders with Surkhang:

In May 1955, when the Dalai Lama was on his way of returning from the heartland to Tibet, officials in his entourage, junior tutor Trijang Lobsang Yeshe and First Kalon Surkhang entered separately monasteries in southern and northern Xikang, inciting local headmen and religious upper-stratum to oppose democratic reform.[47]

Modification of the story would continue. The most recent version of the story appears in an authoritative publication, *Zhongguo Gongchandang Xizang Lishi Dashiji, 1949–2004* (Important historical events of the Chinese Communist Party in Tibet, 1949–2004), compiled by the Office of Party History of the CCP Committee of the Tibetan Autonomous Region:

> May [1955], on the Dalai [Lama]'s way back to Tibet, Trijang and Surkhang incited rebellion in the Tibetan areas of Sichuan. Members of the Dalai [Lama]'s entourage, junior tutor Trijang Lobsang Yeshe and Kalon Surkhang Wangchen Gelek, in the name of conducting religious activities along the southern and the northern routes, went separately to Litang and Ganzi of the Ganzi Tibetan Autonomous Prefecture and the Litang and Dajin Monasteries. They called together local chieftains, headmen, and upper-stratum lamas and incited them to oppose democratic reforms, oppose the Communist Party, and start armed rebellions. Trijang and Surkhang even said: "You should organize armed rebellions. The Kashag can provide weapons and assist you."[48]

Thus, the Dalai Lama's journey back to Lhasa in 1955, a cooperative operation carefully managed by both the Dalai Lama group and the CCP authorities at the time, has since 1959 been presented as an unscrupulous offensive by the Tibetan side. The various versions of the story assert the same point: the old Tibetan establishment around the Dalai Lama was responsible for starting the rebellions in western Sichuan.

This verdict had Mao Zedong's personal sanction. In January 1961, when talking to the Panchen Lama in Beijing, Mao talked about why in the past decade the CCP had followed the "Dalai line." It was a pragmatic approach, Mao explained, because most of the Tibetan people worshiped the Dalai Lama. But Beijing had known for some time that "the Dalai [Lama] used the Khampas to conduct rebellions." Mao said: "The Dalai [Lama] began his rebellious conspiracy in 1955 right after he left Beijing. He came back from India in early 1957 and continued to make preparations for two years till 1958."[49] At the time, Mao's accusation against the Dalai Lama for personally directing subversive activities was not publicized. But two years later, a campaign for openly "exposing the Dalai [Lama]'s crimes of treason" began in all Tibetan areas. The Dalai Lama's alleged crimes included personally advocating for Tibetan independence on his way back to Lhasa in 1955 and orchestrating all the troubles in Tibet, as well as in other Tibetan areas, ever since 1951.[50]

The question is why the CCP authorities had to go through the trouble of creating a second narrative. The narrative cannot be squared with the CCP's own historical records and has, in a twisted way or by upholding a "conspiracy" scenario, exaggerated and distorted Lhasa's agency in the reform war. Surely, in blaming the Dalai Lama group for the reform war, hard-line officials of Garzê and Sichuan could feel exonerated from the 1956 verdict about their mistakes and vindicated in their debates with moderates like Liu Geping and Tianbao (Sangye Yeshe). Such factional significance did not exist for the western side of the Jinshan River. As mentioned earlier, Fan Ming had been removed from the TWC months before the incrimination of the Dalai Lama group began, and, without Fan Ming, the TWC was able to speak in one voice about its work in the wake of the Lhasa revolt of March 1959.[51] Yet the construction of the party narrative after 1959 was motivated not by such internal frictions of the CCP but by a more fundamental concern: to exculpate Beijing from any responsibility for the collapse of the Seventeen-Point Agreement. Undeniably, the violent events on the two sides of the Jinsha River between 1956 and 1959 were closely connected. Although the CCP's epochal, sociopolitical assault on the Tibetan frontier constituted the principal cause of the violence, the public party narrative was to construct a sequence of events that could exonerate the CCP from any violation of the spirit or substance of the Beijing-Lhasa peace arrangement made in 1951. Thus, the overblown agency that the public party narrative attributed to Lhasa served to fix the CCP record on the eastern side of the River as well as to obscure what the CCP did on the western side after the mid-1950s.

"Tibet Is Backward Too"

Most strikingly, in the second, public party narrative, the originally triumphant Beijing, advancing its *yangmou* (overt stratagem) of "liberation," appears to have taken a reactive and defensive role in its relationship with Lhasa. The latter, with a string of alleged *yinmou* (covert plots), becomes the side that attempted to upset the status quo. As of March 1959, the so-called status quo of Tibet had a legal definition in the Seventeen-Point Agreement. As mentioned in chapter 3, in the summer of 1955, when planning "democratic reform" for the Tibetan areas of Xikang and Sichuan, CCP officials used the Min River, the Yalong River, and the Jinsha River as three landmarks for a phased reform offensive. Although concrete reform steps for the western side of the Jinsha River were beyond Xikang and Sichuan officials' jurisdiction, they nevertheless included Tibet in their policy deliberations because of the obvious connections between the two sides of the river. As far as Beijing was concerned, the entire ethnographic Tibetan region was subject to an integral gradualist approach to sociopolitical transformation. In comparison to the Tibetan areas east of the river, Tibet was unique only in a sense that the region was designated as the last to change. Because of the standing Seventeen-Point Agreement, it also meant that Beijing had to take a direct role in creating conditions for change in Tibet.

Lhasa was not completely inactive as far as "reform" was concerned. In 1952, probably goaded by the reference to "reform" in the Seventeen-Point Agreement, the Kashag organized a reform bureau to consider reform-related issues. In January 1954, the Kashag issued a "Public Notice on Reforming the Social System of Tibet in Accordance with [the Seventeen-Point] Agreement." This broad reform agenda touched upon various aspects of Tibet's social life, such as lands illegally possessed by aristocrats, excessive fees, services, and taxes extracted from ordinary people, social ethics, education, Han-Tibetan relations, and conditions along the borderlines.[52] While there is no evidence as to how Beijing perceived Lhasa's reform agenda at the time, the CCP formula for "democratic reform" differed significantly from the Kashag's plan. Beijing wanted to accomplish nothing less than integrating Tibet with the rest of China in both administrative and sociopolitical senses.

In the next two years, Beijing took big strides in cajoling Lhasa to head in that direction. When the Dalai Lama and the Panchen Lama visited Beijing in early 1955, Mao advised them that although the ordinary Tibetan people did not oppose social improvements, the two Tibetan leaders would have to work patiently with conservative elements of Tibetan society. According to Mao, China was a "very backward country" and hence in need of a social revolution. What Mao really meant to tell his Tibetan guests was: "Tibet is backward too, and this must be admitted.... We will not approve if you do not make progress at all." In October, Mao received another Tibetan delegation in Beijing, consisting mainly of aristocrats. Mao urged Tibetan aristocrats to rid themselves of fear about reform, promising that their postreform life could only become better than their current one. But now, Tibetan aristocrats had to consider whether they wanted to become obstacles to reform. Mao told his Tibetan guests: "You must make up your own minds about reform. If you do not want reform, we will not do it. Reform can be carried out only with support from aristocrats and lamas. We cannot make the decision for you." In rhetorically sticking to the script of the Seventeen-Point Agreement, Mao nevertheless conveyed an unmistakable message to his guests. A member of the delegation later remembered that Mao actually asked "living Buddhas and aristocrats" to "take the lead in the democratic reform."[53]

Changes planned for Tibet were set in motion not merely by Mao's words. As mentioned in chapter 2, on March 9, 1955, at a meeting of the State Council about Tibet, Zhou Enlai announced that the Tibet work was entering a "new phase" of making preparations for establishing the Tibetan Autonomous Region. Such a "new phase" entailed the tasks of carrying out reform and enhancing the Tibetan people's standard of living. Zhou praised Tibetan leaders' desire to develop their economy speedily but emphasized that "democratic reform" was the necessary precondition for such development. The meeting took a crucial step in planning a new government structure, a Preparatory Committee for the Tibetan Autonomous Region (PCTAR). The planned new body, to be headed by the Dalai Lama, would be an "organ of political power" directly under the State Council. It would assume leadership over the three existing administrative authorities inside Tibet, based separately in Lhasa, Shigatse, and Chamdo. The State Council decided that establishment of the PCTAR was warranted because the Tibet work had achieved "remarkable progress" and hence the circumstances had changed significantly since the conclusion of the Seventeen-Point Agreement. The same meeting made two additional decisions, one on establishing a Tibetan Bureau of Transportation and Communication under the PRC Ministry of Transportation and Communication, and the other on dispatching technicians to Tibet to establish eleven projects for economic and cultural development.[54]

Now that the earlier restraints against changing Tibet had been lifted as far as Beijing was concerned, the process of integrating Tibet with the rest of China, beginning with interethnic exchanges, happened even faster than Beijing expected or desired. Just six months after the State Council took steps to pave the way for transforming Tibet, leaders in Beijing felt it necessary to urge the neighboring provinces of Tibet to rein in their enthusiasm. In a circular issued to Sichuan, Gansu, and Qinghai, the State Council instructed these provinces to stop providing *jieshaoxin* (letters of introduction) for Han people (*hanren*) to enter Tibet. According to the circular, since the Kang-Zang (Xikang-Tibet) Highway was opened at the end of 1954, "a considerable number of Han people" bearing such letters had entered Tibet. These people could not be put to good use, however, because social reforms and economic construction were yet to begin inside Tibet. Some Han migrants' bad behaviors, such as theft, swindle, and violation of Tibetan social customs, had already disturbed social stability and caused interethnic grievances. Nevertheless, the State Council stopped short of categorizing these Han people as "aimless drifters" (*mangliu*), a term for illegal internal and mostly rural migrants, because they differed from the usual "aimless drifters" in two counts. First, most of them were "workers," and second, they carried *jieshaoxin* issued by their local authorities, which was a required document for traveling legally inside the PRC. Therefore, while directing the neighboring provinces not to unleash Han migrants any more, the State Council asked the TWC to do its best to find jobs for those who had already come. Meanwhile, the State Council authorized the TWC, when needed, to request and approve Han migrants to enter Tibet from the neighboring provinces. Such a tepid measure proved ineffective in preventing Han migrants from trickling into Tibet. A few months later, the TWC made a plea to its counterparts in neighboring provinces to stop the flow of renminbi into Tibet. Obviously, the currency could not have entered Tibet without its bearers.[55]

The relationship between Tibet and its neighboring provinces during the first decade of the PRC is yet to be fully investigated. One thing is clear, however: no matter how differently CCP officials inside and outside Tibet might value an "opened" Tibet, they agreed at the time on ending Tibet's seclusion through "democratic reform." As a matter of fact, when the Dalai Lama was visiting in the eastern provinces of China, TWC officials already sensed that the time for reform in their region was arriving. In November 1954, trying to grasp the depth and scope of a forthcoming reform in Tibet, they sent a question to Beijing as to "what would be the nature of reform in Tibet today (including land reform in the future)." To officials in Beijing, the question was somewhat premature. They did not formulate an answer until ten months later, after the Dalai Lama's visit in Beijing and the eastern provinces appeared a success. In a directive dated September 4, 1955, the CCP leadership reaffirmed the uniqueness of Tibet and pointed out that reform in the region would take more time and assume a form different from that in other places. Thus, reform in Tibet would be "democratic" but not "socialist." At the same time, Beijing was unequivocal that because the PRC had begun the transition to socialism, "any reform of the Tibetan nationality will have to be part of the general task of the country during the transitional period"; "just like other advanced nationalities at home, the Tibetan nationality must and should be able to take the socialist path of development."[56]

Before the year ended, the CCP central leadership informed the TWC of its own estimate of the Tibetan situation: since the Tibetan leaders' visit in Beijing and the completion of the Chuan-Zang (Sichuan-Tibet) and the Qing-Zang (Qinghai-Tibet) Highways, conditions in Tibet had significantly improved.[57] Beijing's displayed its confidence in Tibetan "progress" not only in words. On July 1, 1955, the CCP's birthday, the TWC came out into the open, shedding its previous disguise under a code name for PLA troops. Two months later, Beijing approved the first ever delegation of foreign journalists, representing ten foreign communist parties, to visit Tibet for forty-five days.[58] During a period of more than a year, from the late spring of 1955 to the late summer of 1956, Beijing changed its previously snaillike move in Tibet with a series of foxtrot steps.

The Dalai Lama's meetings with senior CCP leaders in Beijing in the mid-1950s produced good rapport between the two sides. Mao and Zhou intended to use this asset fully to facilitate the task ahead.[59] Yet the CCP leadership also realized that the young Tibetan leader's commitment to reform would need continuous encouragement and that he would not be able to bring the entire

Tibetan establishment around without some direct assistance from Beijing. For this purpose, during the early months of 1956, Beijing carefully organized a Central Delegation to Tibet to congratulate the scheduled establishment of the PCTAR in April. The Central Delegation to Tibet, according to Zhou, had no precedent in Chinese history. The thirty-one delegates represented eighteen nationalities and came from fourteen provinces that "have frequent relations with Tibet." Zhou made it clear that such assorted membership of the delegation was not for ceremonial purposes but for making the widest contacts possible in order to get Beijing's messages across to Tibetan society. To lubricate its operation, the delegation was accompanied by a dance troupe, a Beijing opera troupe, a team of acrobats, and a film crew. The delegation was also joined by journalists, doctors, car drivers, cooks, and security troops. In total, this corps of suasion included more than eight hundred people. They were going to perform on stage, in meeting halls, and in sitting rooms. They were going to present gifts, give alms, circulate documents such as the PRC constitution, and distribute photos showing the Dalai Lama, the Panchen Lama, and CCP leaders together and, necessarily, badges of Mao Zedong.[60]

Before the Central Delegation left for Lhasa, Mao again personally promoted reform in Tibet. During the lunar new year of 1956, Mao received a group of Tibetan officials and aristocrats in Zhongnanhai, the CCP headquarters in Beijing. In the conversation, Mao made a clear connection between the establishment of the PCTAR and "democratic reform":

> The PCTAR will be established when it is ready. Are you still afraid? Do you support land reform? Land reform in the Tibetan region will be implemented in a different way, like that in Yunnan . . . where land reform was carried out with means of peaceful consultation, and both the people and the chieftains were satisfied. In a word, the life of aristocrats will not change but remain the same or become even better. Religious beliefs will also remain the same. . . . For now, the task in Tibet is not to organize collectives but to implement democratic reform. You should decide when to start. After the PCTAR is established, you may study this issue. The Dalai Lama and the Panchen Erdeni need to make up their minds. Secular and clerical Tibetan officials, lamas, and khenpos in monasteries should make decisions. A period of deliberation is necessary, one, two, or three years during which minds can be persuaded through discussions. . . . After returning [to Lhasa], you should carry out such work among aristocrats and lamas. . . . With regard to democratic reform, I must make it clear here lest you bring a wrong message back saying that I want to carry out land reform in Tibet now. I just want you to study the issue after you return, and to report to the Dalai [Lama] and the Panchen [Lama]. If doable, do it. But if you all disagree, there is nothing I can do. I cannot command you to do something, and I just want to make some suggestions. It is up to you to accept

them or not. This should not be misunderstood. . . . After returning to Tibet, you should seek meetings with the Dalai Lama more frequently, listen to his instructions, and increase your knowledge.[61]

Despite his disclaimer about not "commanding" the Tibetans, Mao unmistakably impressed his Tibetan guests when talking as the supreme leader of China from inside the old imperial residency. The Tibetans certainly learned this much: reform in Tibet was part of Beijing's agenda now and would happen after a grace period not longer than three years.

On the same day, after talking to the Tibetans, Mao clarified for Chen Yi what his mission to Lhasa was about:

China is not the only country that pays attention to Tibet, and the Tibetan question may attract the gaze of the world. Tibet would have no future without reform, but the means of reform should differ from that used in the heartland [*neidi*], such as the means of buying out. *On this trip, you should bring to Tibet the Center's policies of insisting on reform* [*Zhongyang jianchi gaige de zhengce*] *and inter-nationality unity. You should reason with them all the time, do good deeds, and do not impose our views on them.*[62] (emphasis added)

A month later, Mao talked to Chen Yi, Zhang Jingwu, and Wang Feng again, advising them on their mission to Tibet:

The Han-Tibetan estrangement cannot be overcome in one or two days, and we should be mentally prepared to use ten to twenty years. *The principal task of your trip* to Tibet is to celebrate the establishment of the PRTAG, but not to do many other things. We should mainly oppose Han chauvinism. Only by opposing Han chauvinism can we persuade other nationalities to give up their local nationalism. This order cannot be reversed. *The tasks of this trip* should not be too many and we should not hope for too much, and issues like land reform, women's question, and price stabilization should be processed according to circumstances but not in haste.[63] (emphasis added)

While continuing his rhetoric about patient and peaceful change in Tibet, Mao was nevertheless unequivocal about forthcoming reform. The most interesting feature of this conversation is the distinction that Mao made between an apparent "principal task" of the mission and ancillary ones; in reality, the mission's ceremonial task was secondary.

By the early months of 1956, Tibet had clearly been "upgraded" in Beijing's agenda of social engineering, which was noticeably synchronized with the initiation of "democratic reform" on the eastern side of the Jinsha River. Subtle but important evidence of the upgrading was a change in Beijing's way of issuing directives to provincial officials. Previously, since the issue of "democratic reform" was deemed premature for Tibet, Beijing had not sent reform-related directives to the TWC. In late February 1956, issuing a directive about reform in pastoral areas of minority nationalities, for the first time Beijing included the TWC among the intended recipients. In the directive, Beijing instructed officials in Gansu, Sichuan, Qinghai, and Xinjiang to learn from Inner Mongolia how to achieve a peaceful transition to socialism in pastoral areas. As for Tibet, the directive suggested that upper-stratum people be organized to visit western Sichuan and Qinghai to observe "peaceful reform" there.[64]

Closely following the directive, at the end of February, the Central United Front Department adopted a reform schedule for all minority areas of the country. This was probably the first Central Document of the CCP that set up a clear timetable for reform in Tibet. The plan envisioned a period of twelve years for all minority areas to complete the transition to socialism, including those areas where socioeconomic development was supposedly at a level much lower than that of the Han areas. The pastoral areas of Tibet were earmarked for completing both "democratic reform" and the "transition to socialism" in twelve years. Although not providing a separate deadline for the agricultural areas of Tibet to complete reform, the plan stipulated that "those minority agricultural areas yet to carry out democratic reform should use means of peaceful consultation to complete reforms in two, three, or five years according to local conditions."[65]

Thus, under a cautious optimism, in early 1956 Beijing set a maximum of five and twelve years, respectively, for the agricultural and pastoral areas of Tibet to be fully incorporated into the socialist system of the PRC. Of course, Beijing still needed a way to translate this unilateral planning into a bilateral formula that would supersede the Seventeen-Point Agreement. Very soon, however, the optimism was dampened by Chen Yi's findings in Lhasa. Archival research has yielded two reports to Beijing drafted by the Party Leading Group of the Central Delegation in Lhasa. According to the first report, dated April 18, 1956, the second day after the Central Delegation arrived in Lhasa, because of the recent conflict in western Sichuan and the planned organization of the PCTAR, the delegation entered a "very tense" political atmosphere. The arrival of the delegation caused a lot of rumors, and "pro-imperialist reactionaries" and "lamas of certain monasteries" "were very aggressive in plotting." The Dalai Lama talked to Phüntso Wangye "very sincerely," advising the CCP authorities to pay close attention to Chen Yi's safety. He also apologized for not having joined Lhasa residents to greet Chen Yi personally the previous day, citing strong objections inside the Kashag as the reason.[66]

As the Central Delegation's first impression of the situation in Lhasa, the report already signaled serious troubles for Beijing's Tibet policy. First, the reform in western Sichuan had been predicted to have a "positive" impact on

Tibet, but the actual effect appeared just the opposite. Second, and more fundamentally, Beijing's "Dalai line" appeared ineffective: although it had made a correct decision in supporting the Dalai Lama establishment as the political center of Tibet and achieved remarkable results in cultivating good feelings with a "sincere" fourteenth Dalai Lama, Beijing had made little progress in winning over leading members of the Dalai Lama group. This grave political reality was most clearly revealed by a ceremonial matter, the Dalai Lama's inability to join Chen Yi in the welcoming procedures. These two points were amplified and further clarified in the delegation's second report.

The Central Delegation spent about one and a half months in Tibet, and, on May 31, its principal members flew back to Beijing from the newly constructed Damxung Airport of Lhasa. During their sojourn, Chen Yi and his associates engaged in various activities in cultivating good feelings among Tibetans, but they conducted their most important business between April 22 and early May, when meetings and discussions were held in Lhasa for launching the PCTAR.[67] Having accomplished its central task, the delegation sent its second report to Beijing, excerpts of which are translated below:

1. When the Central Delegation arrived in Lhasa, news about the rebellions in the Tibetan areas of Sichuan had already reached here. . . . Shock and fear were therefore widely felt among upper-stratum lamas and aristocrats in Lhasa. *They suspected that the establishment of the PCTAR and the arrival of the delegation meant to start reform. Consequently, their attitudes toward the PCTAR and the delegation suddenly changed from one of enthusiastic welcome to one of suspicion, aloofness, and fear. Such change also happened to left-wing personalities such as Ngabö. In the first half of April, for instance, Ngabö feared that he would lose his official position and property and would be "struggled" against. Anxious about his future, for a while he became passive and silent.* The Tibetan aristocratic clique had a sense of guilt and feared that once the people were mobilized to settle accounts with them, they would not be able to pass the test. . . . Incited by a handful of reactionary and extremely conservative upper-stratum elements, a few monasteries became involved in activities of preparing and organizing rebellion. . . . The political atmosphere of Lhasa remained very tense . . . [and] guns stored in the Potala were secretly distributed among lamas as rumors ran wild. *The situation was explosive.*

Under the circumstance, we decided to reassure the public first. After entering Lhasa, we conducted extensive activities such as courtesy calls, visitations, interviews, meetings, gift presentations, banquets, and almsgiving to lamas in monasteries. . . . The public anxieties caused by the rebellions in the Tibetan areas of Sichuan have not been completely assuaged, though. . . . *Yet, the attitudes of left-wing personalities such as the Dalai [Lama] and Ngabö are stable; the Panchen [Lama] clique supports us firmly; the Tibetan people are in favor of the achievements of our work in Tibet in the past few years.* . . . Even though rampant in conspiring, counterrevolutionaries have so far dared not to take hasty actions. Now that the PCTAR inaugural conference has concluded victoriously, it can be expected that as our work continues, the situation of Lhasa can become further stabilized.

2. *In the near future, four issues are most salient in the political life of Tibet, which will cause most frequent struggles between us and Tibetan lamas and aristocrats, as well as between the Dalai [Lama] and Panchen [Lama] cliques. These are the rebellions in the Tibetan areas of Sichuan, reform in Tibet, the future of religion, and the relationship between the Dalai [Lama] and Panchen [Lama] cliques.*

(1) After rebellions started in the Tibetan areas of Sichuan, certain monasteries in the rebellious areas, such as the Litang Monastery, sent letters to the Dalai [Lama] and monasteries in Tibet, demanding assistance and support with sentences like this: "We will soon be eliminated by the Han, but you still do not take action." In the meantime, some rinpoches and lamas escaped into Tibet or came here to make contacts. Lamas and merchants of the Kham background also spread various stories based on information from their homeland. *According to a prevalent view, the rebellions were caused by (a) struggles against the upper stratum, (b) confiscation of guns, (c) taxation, and (d) destruction of religion. Those holding this view can back up their stories with many facts.* Ngabö, [Dege] Kelsang Wangdu, and Dorje stated this view in public and even in front of us. Banda Dorje said: "If the rebellions are explained with counterrevolutionaries' spreading discords and making agitations but nothing about mistakes in [the Party's] work, I personally cannot feel satisfied with such an explanation." A few days ago, the Dalai [Lama] also expressed his opinion: "If the rebellions in Kham involve just a handful of people, they should be suppressed firmly. But the situation is worth careful consideration if the majority of the mass are involved." *In sum, either in terms of class relations or of inter-nationality feelings, the events in the Kham areas have shocked and agitated them greatly. Furthermore, they do not believe that the real situation is like what we have told them. They therefore suspect that our words and deeds are different, and they even believe that we are still practicing nationality oppression.*

In response, we followed the Center's instructions in making repeated explanations, informing them that the Center was doing its best in trying to bring this unfortunate event to an end. We emphasized that as long as the rebels repented and rallied to the government, they would be treated leniently. We accepted the Dalai [Lama]'s request for sending his people to the Kham areas to assist the government's placating activities. . . .

(2) At the moment, the issue of reform in Tibet has the following aspects. *On the one hand, many aristocrats realized that reform was inevitable, and they were also convinced with the Center's policies—"reform must be done through*

peaceful consultations and must produce good but not bad results," and *"[reform] should not affect their [aristocrats'] political positions or worsen their living conditions."* They therefore support reform. During this conference, the Panchen [Lama] and Che Jigmé on behalf of the Khenpos Assembly, and Banda Dorje on behalf of Chamdo, demonstrated positive attitudes toward reform. They expressed confidence in and support to the Center's policies and were willing to start reform experiments in Rear Tibet and Chamdo in due course after the conference (the Panchen [Lama]'s written speech indicated the winter of this year and the spring of next year), and they requested endorsement by the conference for sending their plans to the State Council for approval. In conversations with us, Ngabö also proposed proactively that land reform should be considered at a proper time. He said: "Before the issue of land is settled, every aspect of construction in Tibet is difficult. This is because schools and factories must be constructed on land but not in midair. At the moment the greatest difficulty is about land ownership." *On the other hand, the vast majority of upper-stratum clergymen and aristocrats still worry greatly about reform.* The monasteries are very anxious about their incomes. During our almsgiving activities in the monasteries, they made a common demand that the Center guarantee not to change monasteries' incomes. Aristocrats are reluctant to give up exploitation on the one hand and are nervous on the other about how they will be provided for and how their living conditions will not worsen [after reform]. They are also scared of being struggled against and "suppressed" [*zhenya*, meaning execution]. A few days ago, Surkhang said to us: "After years of personal experiences, I and many others have implicit faith in the Communist Party's nationality policy. But the recent events in the Tibetan areas of Sichuan have scared us instantly. We fear that in the future ordinary people will be mobilized in the same way as that in Sichuan to struggle against us, or armed force will be used to suppress us." The feeling revealed by him exists widely among upper-stratum personalities (Ngabö and Lalu admitted to us that they had committed crimes and therefore were fearful of struggle and suppression).

Among the upper-stratum lamas and aristocrats of the Dalai [Lama] clique, many were displeased with the Panchen [Lama]'s reform proposal made at the conference. *In appearance, they criticized the Panchen [Lama] for not consulting with them and vying for making the proposal ahead of others; they also contended that reform in Tibet could not be carried out without the support from the vast majority of the people and their leaders lest negative consequences be produced. In essence they wanted to delay reform as long as possible.* Originally, they prepared to launch voluminous attacks on the Panchen [Lama] during the discussions on the 30th. Had the attacks taken place, the conference would have fallen into a stalemate or even a dangerously divisive situation. *On April 29, we invited officials above the third rank from the Dalai [Lama], Panchen [Lama], and Chamdo sides to have a discussion together. At the meeting comrade Chen Yi* thoroughly explained the significance of reform and the Center's policy, reiterating responsibly the spirit and methods of the Center's guarantee for maintaining their political positions and living standard. After the meeting Kashag officials agreed voluntarily to revise their original drafts of speeches that opposed the Panchen [Lama]'s reform proposal. Nevertheless, when speaking to the conference on May 1, Khenpo [Duwa] of the Drepung Monastery, after stating his support to socialism and the Center's policy about reform, still said: "If reform is not peaceful and pushed forward without the people's and their leaders' endorsement, unthinkable consequences will take place."

In our opinion, under such circumstances democratic reform in Tibet should neither rush forward nor delay for too long, and conditions for reform must first be created. When returning from Shigatse to Lhasa, we plan to study carefully with the TWC the timing of reform and specific policy measures necessary for implementing the Center's established orientation [jiding fangzhen]. The resultant suggestions will be reported to the Center.

(3) In addition to a concern that after reform the sources of monastery incomes will disappear, the monasteries also fear that reform will lead to reduction of the number of lamas and decline of religion. The three principal monasteries pointed out to us that according to established practices, each year fixed numbers of people from Mongolia, Qinghai, and Sichuan would come to the three monasteries to study Buddhist sutras, but the numbers had decreased in past few years. They hoped that the government could permit enough lamas from these places to come according to schedule. *Yesterday, Xiasur solemnly expressed his hope that the Center's policy about protecting and developing religion would not change. He asserted that this issue was vital to the rise or fall of the Tibetan nationality, and that he was making a petition on behalf of the entire Tibetan people.*

(4) Since the Dalai [Lama] and Panchen [Lama] returned from Beijing, the relationship between the two sides has improved immensely. Now the personal relationship between the Dalai [Lama] and the Panchen [Lama] is rather cordial, and officials on both sides admit this. But many misunderstandings and discords between the two cliques still exist. . . . The biggest complaint of the Dalai [Lama] side is that some officials on the other side want equality between the Panchen [Lama] and the Dalai [Lama] in every aspect. The Dalai [Lama] once said: "The Panchen [Lama] side is patriotic and supportive of the Center, and they also care for Tibet's destiny and have long-term visions. We should have been able to unite more closely and promote the cause of Tibet as one. But they often fuss over small things and impair the big picture." *Ngabö regards the Dalai [Lama]–Panchen [Lama] relationship as an issue very hard to deal with and even believes that this is the most difficult problem in Tibet.* Many people in the Dalai clique suggested that this problem might cause big trouble in Tibet if not solved properly. *But the Dalai [Lama] does not share this view. In his*

opinion, unity with Rear Tibet and Chamdo can be achieved relatively easily, but resistance from hard-line conservatives within the clerical and aristocratic clique of Lhasa is the most difficult to overcome. (At present upper-stratum clergymen and aristocrats control the Dalai [Lama]'s every move. Their stratagem seems to be like this—"all obey the Dalai [Lama], the Dalai [Lama] obeys the system, and we control the system. . . .") As for the Dalai [Lama]–Panchen [Lama] relationship, we are doing our best to mediate with a principle of "the big takes care of the small and the small supports the big, uniting to serve the people."

3. In the forthcoming week, we plan to continue visitations and discussions in Lhasa, and, especially, to hold talks with a number of right-wing personalities. We will also greet troops stationed near Lhasa and deliver two political reports for Party and non-Party cadres. On May 8 and 9 our branch delegations will leave for Shigatse, Chamdo, and Ngari. Around May 10 the Central Delegation will visit Shigatse and return to Lhasa around May 20 in order to discuss upcoming work with the TWC. The branch delegations to Shigatse and Gyantse will return to Lhasa around May 25, and they will leave Tibet before the end of the month. Their returning routes will be decided according to security conditions of Sichuan at the time.

The original plan for almsgiving, with a budget of 150,000 yuan, included the three principal monasteries and the Tashilhunpo Monastery. After giving the plan some thought, we decided that small monasteries and other sects (red, flower, and white sects) should be treated equally so as to enlarge the Center's influence and forestall misgivings from them. They will receive the same amount of alms (three yuan per person). Therefore another 250,000 yuan is needed (400,000 yuan in total). In addition, because of increased numbers of gifts and security troops from Qinghai, the budget for the delegation is in red. This is a preliminary report. A complete report on increased budget will be sent to the Center when it is ready.

One more issue is that the Dalai clique wants to send Trijang Rinpoche and others to the Tibetan areas of Sichuan as a delegation to assist the local Party and governmental organizations in carrying out propaganda and placating work. We agreed to the plan but please instruct us about what time will be advantageous for the delegation to go.

Generally speaking, this time the Tibetan right wing and those hidden elements colluding with imperialism did not dare to disturb the Han-Tibetan relations, to respond to the rebellions in Kangding, and to directly object land reform. They instead focused their effort on attacking the Panchen [Lama] and spreading discords between the Dalai [Lama] and the Panchen [Lama]. This is the stratagem adopted by pro-imperialist and right-wing elements. Because of the Center's correct policies and the accomplishments of our work in Tibet, our strength is strong and has discouraged them from staging direct resistance. Their circuitous stratagem is flimsy and constitutes the easier side of the problem. The other side of the problem will need long and patient work, which is to unite the Dalai and Panchen cliques on their gradual path into peaceful reform. Work for winning over people on the right and those in the middle ought to be strengthened; pro-imperialist elements must be isolated but encouraged to repent; left-wing people need to get more education and support; steady policy of buying out should be applied to religion and aristocrats. *[Our contacts with] the laboring people should be gradually expanded from current spots and lines [dian xian] into large groups [mian]. Cultivation of Tibetan cadres should be the central focus of our work. Rushing ahead should be objected and the proper policy should be one of promoting unity while conducting struggle.*[68] (emphasis added)

This remarkable document reflects how, in a crucial moment of the Beijing-Lhasa relationship, the CCP leadership worked with the Tibetans and what Beijing learned about the conditions of Tibet in the closest possible manner. Indeed, before Beijing-Lhasa cooperation collapsed in 1959, Chen Yi's visit was the only time that senior CCP leaders sent one of their own to Tibet to investigate.

Clearly, what caused the tense situation in Lhasa was the issue of "democratic reform." As reflected in the preceding report, Tibetans in Lhasa had a clear grasp of the reform war in western Sichuan and did not have many illusions about the prospect of reform in Tibet. Since the Central Delegation focused its work on upper-class Tibetans and Tibetan officials, the Tibetan fear of reform in the report assumed a class character: Tibetan elites' worry about the political and economic precariousness they would face in the CCP's reform operations. Nevertheless, the anxiety about the future of religion was certainly shared throughout the Tibetan society. Chen Yi and his associates gave a rather sympathetic hearing to the "prevalent" Tibetan view about the causes of the reform war in western Sichuan, which, as mentioned in chapter 3, would help bring about a serious review of the reform policies and practices in western Sichuan by CCP leaders in Beijing in July 1956.

Mao appeared receptive to the sentiment of Chen Yi's report. One May 11, Mao transmitted the report to leading party officials of Sichuan and Kangding. In the name of the CCP central leadership, he instructed Sichuan officials to receive "warmly" a forthcoming team from the Dalai Lama and inform the team "truthfully" (*laolaoshishi*) of the causes of rebellions and mistakes in CCP policies. Mao especially called Sichuan officials' attention to the four causes of rebellion listed as the "prevalent" Tibetan view in Chen's report, asking them to analyze these causes and explain the facts to the Dalai Lama's delegates.[69]

In the late spring of 1956, the Tibetan question entered a crucial phase not only because of the reform war on the eastern side of the Jinsha River but also because of the newly inaugurated preparatory work for reform on the western side. Despite the Central Delegation's efforts to convince the Tibetans that "democratic reform" in Tibet would be peaceful and would not take place right away, Tibetan elites did not misunderstand the signs of what was coming. In this regard, their fatalist prescience was matched by TWC officials' enthusiastic projection. A member of the TWC recalled years later:

> In February [1956], we began to contemplate the issue of the PCTAR. The focal point of our deliberation was that democratic reform in Tibet would take place simultaneously with the establishment of the PCTAR. We planned to start democratic reform first with pilot projects, and nobody objected this approach. . . . At the time comrade Zhang Guohua, Fan Ming, and Tan Guansan were in charge. As I remembered, all of us cheered every reform proposal when it was put forward. In Tibet, cadres like us had nothing else to do except promoting united front. We were very anxious and could not wait to start reform in Tibet. We approached the Panchen [Lama] first, and he was willing to start pilot projects for reform in Shigatse. Chamdo of course had no problem and the Liberation Committee there could also start pilot projects. Thus, we decided to launch pilot projects of democratic reform simultaneously with the establishment of the PCTAR.[70]

This was the very reason that Chen Yi and his associates spent so much energy on April 29 dissuading those Tibetan officials from attacking the Panchen Lama's proposal for starting reform experiments in his domain. The effort was made not just to maintain a harmonious relationship between Lhasa and Shigatse; the Panchen Lama was actually the front person of the TWC's tactic to launch reform in Tibet. Chen faithfully carried out Mao's instructions. In Lhasa, he "insisted on reform" while working tirelessly to promote "inter-nationality unity," as in his lavishing alms on monasteries. As reflected in the Central Delegation's report, implementing his work of suasion with the Tibetans, on no occasion did Chen delink the PCTAR from reform. Instead, Chen and his associates tried consistently to assuage Tibetans' anxiety about reform. Notably, in problematizing Khenpo Duwa's insistence on "Tibetan people's and their leaders' endorsement" as a precondition for reform, which was in concert with the Seventeen-Point Agreement, the Central Delegation's report assumed that in 1956 CCP policymaking had already entered a new phase as far as reform in Tibet were concerned.

Yet, in suggesting to Beijing that reform in Tibet be neither delayed nor rushed, Chen and his associates took an ambiguous approach to timing. They were realistic in admitting that, after working inside Tibet for five years, the CCP still lacked support in Tibetan society. CCP influence among the ordinary people was limited to "spots and lines," and upper-stratum clergymen and aristocrats remained suspicious and fearful of the future that Beijing prescribed for them. In their report, Chen and his colleagues made it abundantly clear that the reform war in western Sichuan had almost ruined the bit of trust and confidence in Beijing among the Tibetan elites, "left wing" and "right wing" included. As for the Dalai Lama himself, the findings of the Central Delegation cast serious doubt on Beijing's optimism derived from his recent visit in eastern China. Although putting the Dalai Lama in a rather positive light and characterizing him as "sincere," "reasonable," and "progressive," the report made it clear that Beijing's cultivation of the Dalai Lama's goodwill had so far failed to break the intricate Tibetan triad consisting of "all Tibetans," "the Dalai Lama," and the "system," over which the young Dalai Lama did not necessarily hold supreme authority. In this regard, Chen Yi and his associates did not have any new solution except reiterating the CCP canon about achieving unity through struggle.

Thus, as the Central Delegation discovered, the CCP's two-pronged advance on the two sides of the Jinsha River proved self-contradictory. The reform war in western Sichuan caused inflammable social anxieties in Tibet. The question for CCP leaders in Beijing was how much longer the delicate equilibrium inside Tibet could last. The Jinsha River proved a porous divide between the nervous Tibetans on its two sides. Refugees and rebels continued to cross the divide, and, at least in one occasion, a PLA airplane made an incursion into the sky over the western bank and terrified the locals.[71]

A "Small Condition"

In July, during CCP officials' discussion in Beijing of the reform war in western Sichuan, Mao said these words about reform in Tibet:

> We should strive to avoid fighting with Lhasa, and reform must take this into account. The work orientation for the western side of the Jinsha River should be to avoid fighting. This should be achievable. But we have a small condition: genuine reform must be implemented. Hence fighting is probably inevitable. Fighting in certain areas is possible. But it would be the best if there is no fighting at all.[72]

Mao's words raise a question as to how the ongoing reform war in western Sichuan and Chen Yi's troublesome findings in Lhasa may have affected Mao's thinking about Tibet. While the CCP's "smart class struggles" in western Sichuan had failed to produce a peaceful reform, Chen's findings significantly dimmed Beijing's hope that "democratic reform" on the western side of the Jinsha River would be able to unfold peacefully. While continuing to dangle the old inducement to Lhasa that peaceful "democratic reform" in Tibet was "achievable," Mao displayed his tough pragmatism in pointing out that "genuine reform" would "inevitably" lead to armed conflict. In this way, Mao was moving away from the preconditions for reform stipulated in the 1951 agreement. Now, CCP leaders wanted reform to take place in Tibet according to their schedule, peacefully if possible and forcefully if necessary. During most of 1956, despite concerns inside the CCP about the reform war in western Sichuan and its negative impact on Tibet, Beijing's general euphoria about the prospect of reform in Tibet continued. Preparations for reforms began frantically in the summer of 1956 and then, suddenly, stopped in early 1957.

An unsettled question in historical literature is who was responsible for pushing reform in Tibet in the summer of 1956. The most recent official historical narrative in the PRC adopts a double-mistake formula. On the one hand, Fan Ming is blamed for committing a "mistake" in violating Beijing's cautious approach and launching a so-called Great Development (*da fazhan*) scheme in the summer of 1956, and on the other, the TWC leadership is criticized for making a "mistake" in labeling Fan as the head of an "anti-Party faction" in 1958.[73] Melvyn Goldstein's study also holds Fan responsible for pushing reform in 1956.[74] In his memoir, Fan admits that he was in charge of the TWC between June and October 1956 and was therefore responsible for the "rushed advance and wastes" in that period. Meanwhile, Fan defends himself fervently, insisting that in doing so he was following Beijing's directives and should not be blamed personally.[75]

Circumstantial evidence seems to lend support to Fan's self-defense. For instance, according to Zhang Xiangming, a TWC official of Southwest background who strongly disliked Fan, preparations for the PCTAR and planning for reform began simultaneously in early 1956, when Zhang Guohua was still in charge of the TWC operations. In his otherwise highly partisan memoir, Zhang appears rather evasive about Fan's personal responsibility for pushing reform afterwards, stating that in the summer of 1956 he did not pay much attention to what Fan was doing in his Great Development and how Beijing "corrected" his mistakes later.[76] At the time, Zhang was deputy director of the TWC's United Front Department. It is hard to believe that Zhang was an uninformed bystander in the whole process. Apparently, for some reason, in writing his memoir, Zhang wanted neither to contradict nor to confirm the official narrative.

In defending himself, Fan provides a clear timeline of events in his memoir, showing how the reform preparations began in Tibet.

On July 31, 1955, Zhang Guohua attended a conference of provincial party secretaries, at which Mao spoke on the issue of agricultural cooperation and criticized a conservative tendency in the party as "walking like a woman with bound feet." Mao's idea for a speedy cooperativization in agriculture would become a resolution at the sixth plenum of the Seventh CCP Congress in early October, which Zhang also attended. Later, Zhang brought the spirit of the two conferences back to Lhasa and talked about speeding up the CCP's work in Tibet with a "whip" if necessary (like urging a horse on with a whip). Emulating Mao, Zhang also criticized rightist and conservative thinking among TWC officials.

Sometime in the winter of 1955, before Zhang returned to Lhasa, Mao told him to get ready for reform in Tibet. Mao stressed that reform preparations must be based on the likelihood of armed resistance by Tibetan aristocrats. If fighting started, some of the aristocrats would be destroyed and some would run away. It would not be a big deal, Mao told Zhang, if a few more people ran to Hong Kong or Kalimpong and cursed the CCP from these places. At the time, Fan was in charge of the TWC in Zhang's absence and learned about the conversation from Zhang via a security phone line. But, for some reason, Zhang did not inform other TWC members of Mao's directive after he returned to Lhasa.

On January 13, 1956, the TWC sent a report to Beijing, reporting its work in the winter of 1955 and outlining a work plan for the first season of 1956. The plan included establishment of the PCTAR in April. Then, from mid-January to early February, a conference of CCP representatives in Tibet was held in Lhasa. Zhang delivered to the conference a report drafted by Fan, outlining twelve items in the year's work, mainly about reform preparations. Soon after, CCP leaders in Beijing approved the report, adding two points: (1) twelve thousand cadres would be moved into Tibet from other provinces to help with reform preparations, and (2) the TWC should make a plan for enhancing CCP influence in 1956.[77]

In April 1956, Chen Yi and the Central Delegation arrived in Lhasa. Chen brought five points from Beijing: (1) insisting that reform begin with pilot programs and be completed in three years; (2) enhancing unity between the Dalai Lama and the Panchen Lama and between Han and Tibetans; (3) reaffirming Mao's three-item orientation of "patriotism, unity, and progress"; (4) implementing reform on the political front while relaxing it with respect to religion (Chen conveyed these words from Mao to the Tibetans: "Long live the Dalai [Lama], and long live the Panchen [Lama]! Tibet should thrive both politically and religiously to achieve prosperity!"); (5) taking good care of all monasteries by the government after reform. In addition, Chen said that to guarantee the implementation of these items, a railroad would be built in the next five years. It was under Chen's instruction that Zhang Guohua and Fan Ming endeavored separately to persuade the Dalai Lama and the Panchen Lama to support reform.[78]

Since Fan had a grave personal stake in constructing such an account and the details of his account cannot be corroborated with other information, Fan's story has to be read with caution. At the same time, his story should not be dismissed. Aside from Zhang Xiangming's recollection, which attests to a degree to the credibility of Fan's account, Fan's "facts" are not inconsistent with those found in archival materials, such as Zhou Enlai's announcement of Tibet's entering a "new phase" and Chen Yi's activities in Lhasa. An unmistakable impression from these pieces of information is that, as of the summer of 1956, CCP leaders in Beijing and leading TWC officials in Lhasa were as one in pushing reform in Tibet.

In addition, Fan's account does not stray from the general political atmosphere in Beijing in late 1955 and early 1956. At the time, Mao was pleasantly surprised by the speedy and relatively peaceful completion of cooperativization in China's countryside. Consequently, in Mao's view, the CCP's previous orientation had been "overly cautious" in planning China's socialist construction. On this issue, Liu Shaoqi sided with Mao, but Zhou Enlai had to criticize himself for letting the State Council lag behind Mao's thinking. At the end of 1955, at an internal meeting of senior CCP officials, Zhou admitted that the government's work had been conservative, derogating himself with these words: "My misunderstanding of Chairman Mao can be summarized with a couplet. The upper verse is: objective possibilities exceed subjective cognition; the lower verse: subjective efforts lag behind objective needs. The new continent [*xin dalu*] has always been there but we discovered it too late."[79]

The question, however, is to what extent the mood of rushing forward in Beijing affected CCP leaders' policies toward Tibet, which until then had been treated as a unique case. As already suggested in the aforementioned CCP directive of September 4, 1955, Tibet should not be left out of the PRC's transition to socialism. Chen Yi's mission to Lhasa in 1956, despite its dire findings, certainly did not exclude Tibet from Zhou's allegorized "new continent." The Central Delegation's report to Beijing mentioned that Chen had discussed with the TWC "issues of the upcoming work." Thus, Chen may well have helped TWC officials launch the next stage of their reform preparations.

In mid-June, as a cautionary step in reform preparations, the TWC commanded its subordinate units to conduct a review of their recent "nationality work." The review process appeared rather perfunctory, serving merely as a prelude to the TWC's reform planning. At the end of the month, the TWC filed with Beijing a "Preliminary Opinion About the Five-Year Plan for the Tibet Region from 1956 to 1960." According to the "Opinion," starting in the spring of 1957, pilot reform projects would begin in Chamdo and the Panchen Lama's domain while propaganda for reform would move into high gear. In following Mao's constant admonishment about the importance of training minority cadres, the TWC gave top priority to personnel preparation: 4,000–6,000 people would be added to the current security police force, and 2,400 to the "people's armed force" and economic police; 40,000–60,000 Tibetan cadres and 50,000–70,000 Tibetan workers would be recruited and trained; 20,000–30,000 Tibetans would be induced into the CCP and 30,000–50,000 into the Communist Youth League; 60,000 Han personnel of various skills and specialties would come from other provinces; labor unions and organizations for women and youth would be established or expanded. In total, during the initial four years, reform in Tibet would mobilize into action from 156,400 to 198,400 people, plus the PLA troops that were already in Tibet.[80] In July, the TWC reported to Beijing its work plan for the next two seasons, asserting:

> Democratic reform in Tibet has already been entered into our work agenda. The Dalai [Lama] and the Panchen [Lama] proposed reform at the PCTAR, and their proposals were approved and assumed actually the form of law. In the past, we underestimated the possibility of such a development and must now seize the opportunity to propagate reform vigorously and push forward the work of pilot reform projects.[81]

At the inaugural conference of the PCTAR, the Panchen Lama, instigated by Fan Ming, proposed to start pilot reform projects in the Shigatse area. The Dalai Lama, in contrast, merely expressed a positive attitude toward "top-down reform" while advising the PCTAR to wait for the "proper timing" to start "peaceful consultation" about how to proceed.[82] Between the inaugural conference and early July, the standing committee of the PCTAR held six meetings. Although these could have been occasions for the Dalai Lama to make additional statements about reform, the contents of these meetings remain unknown. Specific information about an unequivocal statement by the Dalai Lama to support reform, which could have corroborated the TWC's previous assertion, has never surfaced from any publication in the PRC in the past six decades.[83]

For leaders in Beijing, the question of whether the Dalai Lama genuinely supported reform was extremely delicate. In mid-July, in a telegram to the TWC, Zhou Enlai seconded what Chen Yi had found out in Lhasa: "Until today the Dalai [Lama] has been in a powerless position, and his every move has been under aristocratic officials' control and interference." This was not a situation that Beijing could change anytime soon because, as Zhou pointed out, any hasty effort by the TWC to beef up the Dalai Lama's power position would result in "the Dalai [Lama]'s complete isolation from the people around him."[84] At the time, Beijing still hoped that the Dalai Lama could carry most of the Tibetan ruling elites with him in his ostensible cooperation with the CCP. Hijacking the Dalai Lama's will for the sake of pushing through reform, which the TWC's July report seems to have been doing, was probably not a tactic preferred by Beijing. In this regard, Sichuan's butchered "consultations" with local Tibetan elites served as a bad precedent. In the meantime, Beijing did not stop what the TWC was doing either.

On top of the confusion and anxieties caused by the fighting on the eastern side of the Jinsha River, in the summer months of 1956 the TWC's bold moves began to reshape the political landscape of Tibet. Beijing's initial reactions were ambivalent. On the one hand, in late July, the CCP Organizational Department under Deng Xiaoping met the TWC's need by moving thousands of Han cadres into Tibet. In early August, the TWC took steps to replace its hitherto stringent "supplied finance" (*gongji caizheng*) with a "construction finance" (*jianshe caizheng*) that could meet the need of rapid economic development. Such a change would not have been possible without Beijing's approval.[85] On the other hand, CCP leaders soft-pedaled what the TWC was doing in their communications with the Dalai Lama.

Between July and August, Mao Zedong, Liu Shaoqi, and Zhou Enlai all wrote letters to the Dalai Lama. Liu wrote a letter in his capacity as the president (chairman) of the PRC and, in his typical orthodox style, encouraged the Dalai Lama not to rush forward but to take a step at a time in making "social reforms," as if the Dalai Lama were the one who was pushing reform in Tibet. Among the three CCP leaders, Liu conveyed the clearest message to the Dalai Lama that "democratic reform" was about to begin in Tibet. In contrast, the messages from Mao and Zhou, both of whom had been more closely involved in Tibetan affairs than Liu, remained rather vague as far as reform was concerned. In replying to a letter from the Dalai Lama, Zhou just implied reform in advising the Tibetan leader to work patiently in "doing things beneficial to the people." Concerning himself mainly with the foreign-relations aspects of Tibetan affairs, Zhou, who was then concurrently premier and minister of foreign affairs of the PRC, praised a recent decision by the Dalai Lama to decline foreign invitations to visit India and Nepal. Zhou also tried to put the Dalai Lama at ease in separating him from some of his family members abroad who were allegedly under American-British influence. In his previous letter to Zhou, the Dalai Lama enclosed three petals. A consummate diplomat, Zhou reciprocated with a flower and a maple leaf.[86]

The most tactful letter, dated August 18, came from Mao, which is partially translated here:

> The Preparatory Committee for the Tibetan Autonomous Region has already been established, which is supported by all nationalities and satisfactory to all. *I learned that the issue of social reforms in Tibet was discussed openly. This is very good. Now it is not yet the time to implement reform. The issue should first be widely discussed so that people can be fully prepared in their minds. When everybody becomes receptive to the idea and various arrangements are made, then reform can start.* In this way disturbances can be reduced, and it would be the best if no disturbance happens at all. Sichuan encountered some troubles mainly because of instigations by pro-imperialist elements and remnants of the Kuomintang. But our work was not flawless either. I hope that disturbances can be avoided in Tibet. Vice-Premier Chen Yi brought back your opinion.

> We all understand you well and trust that you can do a great job for Tibet. *I however have a constant concern that the Han people there do not cooperate well with you and are not gaining Tibetans' trust. Please take the responsibility for rigorously educating those Han who make mistakes, and please treat Han cadres as your own.* . . . Can you read and comprehend this letter? There are still too many cursive characters in it, fewer than my last letter though. Whenever difficulties happen, be patient. Difficulties can always be overcome gradually. Hope to see you again.[87] (emphasis added)

The last a few lines of the letter give the letter an aura of fatherly advice. The letter certainly conveyed Mao's perseverance with the "Dalai line" at the moment. On the other hand, although unequivocal about the inopportuneness of reform at the moment, Mao made it crystal clear that mental and material preparations for reform should proceed in Tibet. In asking the young Tibetan leader, who according to Zhou could not even control Tibetan officials around him, to "educate" those seasoned CCP officials in Lhasa, Mao was not telling a crude joke but advising the Dalai Lama to take TWC officials into his confidence.

Yet the distinction made carefully by CCP leaders between "reform" and "reform preparations" may not have mattered to the Tibetans. Even before Mao wrote his letter to the Dalai Lama, "disturbances" had already begun in Tibet. Ironically, armed conflict erupted first in Chamdo, which was the area first "liberated" by the PLA in 1950 and therefore the most "progressive" on the western side of the Jinsha River. On July 21, Chime Gombo, headman of the Jomda (Jiangda) *dzong*, rebelled right after attending a PCTAR meeting at which his *dzong* was designated as one of those for pilot reform projects. His violent objection to reform was symbolic because he also had a "progressive" capacity as the director of the Jomda People's Liberation Committee. Chime Gombo's people caused quite a stir by attacking PLA troops repeatedly along the Kang-Zang Highway. One of the attacks almost caused an international incident as it targeted a geological inspection team from the Soviet Union.[88] Yet more significantly, the situation of Jomda immediately put to the test Beijing's reform policy for Tibet. Now that fighting had started on the western side of the river as reform was just being prepared, the question facing leaders in Beijing was whether they should continue pursuing Mao's "small condition" or suspend the newly initiated "new phase" of the CCP work in Tibet. In the next few months, policymakers in Beijing reacted to the Jomda rebellion as they considered the TWC's assertive "legal" justification for reform in Tibet. They first tried to hold the line, but then decided to retreat after some new developments emerged.

The first sign that Beijing was having second thoughts a the "new phase" in Tibet was a directive sent to the TWC dated September 4. The document would be controversial within the CCP in the years to come. Here is a partial translation of the document:

> *Democratic reform in the area of Tibet must be peaceful.* Reform can be carried out peacefully only after preparations with the Tibetan upper stratum are completed. Such preparations include mainly two aspects. First, consultations with leading Tibetans in various circles should be accomplished. *Consultations must be done repeatedly to gain their genuine, not reluctant, agreement. Before they express genuine support, reform must not begin forcefully.* Secondly, arrangements for the upper stratum should be satisfactory. In accordance with the principle of not lowering the political positions and living standards of all clergymen and aristocrats, especially their leading members, proper arrangements should be made through consultations. . . . *Democratic reform in Tibet should be implemented in peaceful means and should be decided by the will of the Tibetan people and their leaders.* This has been clearly established in the [Seventeen-Point] Agreement on peaceful liberation of Tibet, Chairman Mao's numerous conversations with upper-stratum Tibetan figures, and comrade Liu Shaoqi's report on the draft constitution. *Not honoring this in respect to reform, we would lose credibility.* It would be extremely disadvantageous to us if we lose credibility in Tibet over such a vital issue. . . .
>
> *In view of the current status of our work in Tibet, cadre condition, upper-stratum attitude, and recent events in Chamdo, conditions for reform in Tibet are not ready. Neither is it possible for us to complete our preparatory work within one or two years. Therefore, democratic reform will certainly not take place during the First Five-Year Plan. It may possibly not happen during the Second Five-Year Plan and may even possibly be postponed to the time of the Third Five-Year Plan. Over the issue of democratic reform in Tibet we have waited for years, and now we must continue waiting.* This should be regarded as a concession [rangbu] to the upper stratum of the Tibetan nationality. We believe that such a concession is necessary and correct, for, until today, the Tibetan nationality does not completely trust the Han and the Center, meaning us. It is a very important task of the Party to use necessary and proper means to remove the Tibetan nationality's suspicion. . . .
>
> *Of course, our waiting is not passive. On the contrary we must work actively. Starting from now till the beginning of reform, we must strengthen united front with the upper stratum, foster Tibetan cadres, recruit members for the Party and the [Youth] League, assist the mass in production, do our best in improving the life of the mass (including reduction of certain burdens of theirs), and gradually democratize the political power of the autonomous region [zizhiqu zhengquan de zhubu minzhuhua].* Achievements should be made in these key aspects so that conditions for reform can be achieved.

> As for your proposed pilot reform projects, they should certainly be suspended for now. The work for propagating reform should also be readjusted properly and reduced.
>
> ....
>
> The TWC should offer its opinion after reconsidering democratic reform and related preparatory work in Tibet in accordance with the gist of the above. The Central United Front Department may also invite Zhang Jingwu, Zhang Guohua, and other comrades of the TWC who are attending the Eighth Party Congress to study the issue with comrades in relevant departments [of the Central People's Government]. Their opinion should be reported to the Center.[89] (emphasis added)

Among important CCP documents concerning Tibet in this period, this one is highly unusual. A curious feature is that the authorship of the document cannot be ascertained. None of the published *nianpu* (chronicles of life) of Mao Zedong, Liu Shaoqi, Deng Xiaoping, and Zhou Enlai, the four CCP leaders most likely to have had anything to do with this directive, makes any reference to its subject's having drafted, revised, discussed, or even read the document. Between late July and early September 1956, first in Beidaihe and then in Beijing, all these leaders were busy with preparing the CCP Eighth Congress. Mao wrote his letter to the Dalai Lama on August 18 and did not return to the subject of Tibet until early November. On September 4, Mao discussed with other CCP leaders the draft political report for the Eighth Congress and also received a delegation from Japan.[90] Liu, who was the one to deliver the political report at the CCP congress, immersed himself in drafting and revising the report in consultation with Mao and others in the summer months.[91] Zhou had been involved in arranging the Central Delegation's visit to Tibet and also in discussions of the rebellions in western Sichuan from April to late July. But in August and September, Zhou appeared fully preoccupied with his dual responsibilities of setting goals for the PRC's Second Five-Year Plan and communicating with foreign dignitaries.[92] Deng, in his capacities as chief of the CCP Organizational Department and secretary-general of the CCP Central Committee, assumed major responsibility for preparing the CCP congress. In late August, he told officials around him: "Now the Center focuses energy on the documents for the Eighth Congress and for the moment cannot carefully consider any other issue."[93]

"Any other issue" obviously included Tibet, which, although troublesome at the moment, did not assume such magnitude as to divert CCP leaders' attention from the forthcoming Eighth Congress. It is therefore very likely that the September 4 directive was produced by Li Weihan's Central United Front Department, sanctioned by one of the four leaders, and then sent out. Li's imprint in the document can be recognized in three places. First, in invoking the Seventeen-Point Agreement, the directive stressed the CCP's credibility with the Tibetans, which actually amplified what Li had said in his report to Mao about the Sichuan situation on the night of July 22. On that occasion, when discussing the prospect of peaceful reform in Tibet, Li said: "We should do according to what we say, and we should keep our political credibility."[94] Second, the repeated use of "Tibetan nationality" (*Xizang minzu*) as the object of Beijing's policy followed Li's, not Mao's, track of thinking about the Tibetan question. Until this point, Mao had used the concept of "Tibetan nationality" only twice, once in his public speech celebrating the conclusion of the Seventeen-Point Agreement in 1951 and a second time in one of his conversations with the Dalai Lama during the latter's visit to Beijing in the mid-1950s. As far as can be seen in available information, Mao never used the term in Beijing's internal directives. Mao's preferred term was "Tibetan people" (*Xizang renmin*) or, if the Tibetans had to be referred to in connection with the Han, he usually used "Tibetan ethnicity" (*Zangzu*).[95] As can be seen in their discussion of the reform war in Sichuan on July 22, Mao and Li diverged somewhat on whether the war was an interclass struggle or an internationality conflict. It is not surprising that in 1962, when Li was subject to severe criticism inside the CCP leadership, his alleged errors included theoretical thinking and policy orientation since 1956 that had confused the two issues of class and nationality.[96] And third, the directive ended by charging Li's Central United Front Department with orchestrating the downgrading of the CCP's "new phase" in Tibet—a task that, as will be shown in chapter 5, would soon be taken over by a higher level of the CCP establishment.

The September 4 directive is unusual also because of the way it was used inside the CCP afterwards. In stressing the necessity of Tibetan elites' "genuine, not reluctant, agreement" to reform, the directive clearly negated the TWC's assertion that reform could now begin on a "legal" basis. The crucial point, aside from reiterating emphatically Beijing's desire for a peaceful transformation of Tibet, was what the directive intended to do about the "new phase" of CCP work in Tibet. Pilot reform projects, a direct cause of the Jomda rebellion, had to stop. Large-scale propaganda for reform, which could easily provoke social anxieties, also had to be scaled back significantly. Otherwise, the directive actually reaffirmed the original definition of the "new phase," which was a period of "working actively" to prepare "conditions for reform." Notably, the directive said nothing about suspending personnel movement into Tibet from other provinces and continued to urge the TWC to recruit "activists" from the Tibetan populace as "cadre" or CCP and Youth League members.

The recruiting constituted a landmark departure from the pre-1956 practices of the TWC. In the context of PRC ethnopolitics, in addition to the standard qualifications for Communist Party membership, a non-Han member of the CCP was also required to "oppose nationalism and feudal reactionary influence of his own nationality, insist on cooperation with the Han when contacts with the Han take place, ... and welcome Han cadres sent to his area to help and other forms of assistance from the Han."[97] Surely, such an ethnopolitical requirement for CCP membership would cut deeply into the old social fabric of a non-Han community. It became applicable to Tibet only after the TWC and its branches came out into the open as CCP apparatuses, on July 1, 1955. Expansion of the CCP organization was afterwards implemented as one of the key measures of the "new phase." Actually, twenty days after the September 4 directive, the CCP leadership approved the TWC's plan for continuously recruiting CCP members from Tibetan society, lower and upper classes included.[98] Another "key aspect" identified by the September 4 directive in the TWC's work, "democratization" of political power of the "autonomous region," was also unprecedented in naming Tibet as such and presaging steps of reorienting the TWC's attention toward lower-class people. This was a typical CCP approach of unrooting the entrenched old establishment in areas that newly came under the CCP's control. In Tibet, the approach already constituted a move of "democratic reform."

Indeed, in contrast to the first September 4 directive of 1955, partially quoted earlier in this chapter, this second September 4 directive replaced confidence with caution. Yet, in terms of its policy content, the directive was neither a green light letting the TWC go ahead with its reform steps nor a red light suspending the "new phase" in midair. Rather, it was a blinking yellow light warning the TWC that advance should be made with great care. As for the length of such cautious preparations, the directive mentioned tentatively the Second Five-Year Plan (1958–1962) or the Third (1963–1967) as a "possible" time to start reform, meaning that the period of "active" preparations could either last for three years at the shortest or eleven years at the longest. Such tentativeness is also shown in the last paragraph of the directive, which kept the door open for further policy deliberation between the TWC and officials in Beijing.

But the meaning of the directive became blurred in late December 1956, when Deng Xiaoping sent a message to Zhang Jingwu in Lhasa and gave a rather different reading to the September 4 directive:

> On September 4, the Center already issued a directive about not undertaking democratic reform in the region of Tibet during the Second Five-Year Plan. According to this decision, the orientation for work arrangements in the coming year is not one of intensification but one of contraction. Therefore, a number of cadres should be sent back, induction of Party members and cadres should be stopped, and projects not yet set up should no longer continue.[99]

Among all the interpretations of the September 4 directive made by CCP officials, then and later, Deng's message is certainly the most authoritative yet twisted one. Deng actually added new contents to the directive in light of what happened in Tibetan affairs after September 4. His message definitely turned on a red light for the TWC, but what Deng wanted to stop had been authorized in the September 4 directive for the TWC to continue. Available information does not shed light on why Deng misread the September directive and thus blamed the TWC for not carrying out Beijing's policy. The course of the CCP leadership's switching from the blinking yellow to the red light between September and December of 1956 can, however, be roughly documented. In suspending completely its reform work in Tibet, Beijing did not return to its pre-1956 orientation. Beijing would indeed resume its waiting for conditions to mature so that Tibet could enter "democratic reform," but, starting at the end of 1956, Beijing's Tibet policy entered its waiting game round two, immensely different from round one. This policy shift will be discussed in the next chapter.

CHAPTER 5

A WAITING GAME

Time was always a crucial element in the relationship between Beijing and Lhasa. As illustrated in previous chapters, every phase of that relationship after 1949 was characterized by incompatibility between the temporal perspectives on the two sides—one resolving to keep the eternal "land of Buddha," and the other insisting on revolutionizing a "backward" borderland. In 1958, the rest of China made a "Great Leap Forward," an initially thrilled dash toward a communist society. A slogan during this frenzied campaign, broached first by Liu Shaoqi but attributed to Karl Marx, was "one day is equal to twenty years."[1] Just like all revolutionaries before them in world history who were committed to making fundamental social changes, the Chinese Communists deemed control of life's pace a core component of their revolution. Vital to the CCP's legitimacy, therefore, was a promise to the Chinese people that the temporal gap between China's dire reality and the nation's dream about wealth and power would be erased by the Communist Revolution. In the eyes of CCP officials, when the rest of China was "leaping forward," an unreformed Tibet became even further lagged behind.

In his insightful study of time, social psychologist Robert Levine contends that "time is power." Levine identifies several "rules of the waiting game." Two of Levine's rules are especially germane to the situation between Beijing and Lhasa in 1957 and 1959. One is, "the more powerful control who waits," and the other, "waiting can be an effective instrument of control."[2] Between 1957 and early 1959, Beijing set up the second round of its waiting game about Tibet with a prescription of "no reform for six years." In appearance, Beijing was the side in waiting. But since the suspense and its tempo were set up by Beijing in the first place, there was no question as to who was dominating the game. In the end, the Lhasa revolt in March 1959 brought the "six years" formula to a premature conclusion, asserting a frustrated Tibetan agency in the time contest. Although failing to achieve their goals, rebellious Tibetans did exert influence on the tempo of their political life after all. Afterwards, Beijing celebrated its victory of "pacifying rebellions" in Tibet as a way of bringing the region abreast with the rest of the PRC in socialist transformation. Yet a historical assessment of the abrupt termination of the waiting game reveals a more complicated process than a linear advance of Chinese Communism in Tibet. The dynamics of the waiting game between 1957 and 1959 revealed historical possibilities, with the result that neither Beijing nor Lhasa achieved what they set out to achieve.

This chapter dissects a scheming yet hesitant process in which CCP officials in Beijing laid out a waiting strategy with respect to Tibet. Aside from Mao Zedong, whose intentions were decisive, Deng Xiaoping left a heavy personal mark on the strategy. In dealing with the Tibetan case in the late 1950s, Deng appeared much less patient than he would be decades later when setting up the "one country, two systems" formula for Hong Kong. Change of times, however, not any alteration of Deng's personality, set the two cases apart.

"No Reform for Six Years"

In 1956, two days after the TWC received Beijing's September 4 directive, a Tibetan delegation of 120 people, the largest so far, left Lhasa for Beijing. Included in the delegation were aristocrats, high-ranking lamas, educators and technicians, and rural agents from the Kashag and the Panchen Lama's quarters.[3] In organizing the delegation this way, the TWC wanted the operation to be both a united-front event and a learning process for Tibetans who would participate in reform in the future. At the time, neither the TWC nor leaders in Beijing saw any inconsistency between the delegation and Beijing's September 4 directive. In mid-October, the TWC sent to Beijing a report on its work during the third and fourth seasons of the year, expressing "complete support" of Beijing's instruction on appropriately reducing propaganda about reform while "actively continuing the preparatory work in various aspects." The TWC would continue to oppose "conservatism in the work of fostering Tibetan cadres," and, during the fourth season, it would complete the original plan of recruiting fifteen thousand cadres and inducting two thousand CCP members and five thousand Youth League members for the year 1956.[4]

In Beijing, the CCP's Eighth Congress was convened on September 15. Liu Shaoqi delivered a political report on behalf of the CCP Central Committee.

According to Liu's report, of the country's total minority nationality population of thirty-five million, areas that accounted for twent-eight million had completed socialist transformation, areas that included 2.2 million were going through socialist transformation, and areas of two million were going through democratic reform. Thus, there remained only a few areas, totaling three million people, that had not yet started democratic reform. Liu asserted: "To grow into modern nationhood, minority nationalities, aside from undertaking social reform, must develop modern industries in their areas. This is a key issue of fundamental importance."[5] At the conference, Ulanhu, then chairman of the State Nationality Affairs Commission, declared triumphantly that the CCP had successfully resolved the nationality question (*minzu wenti*) at home. As for the three million minority population singled out by Liu, Ulanhu stated: "Obviously, these not yet reformed minority areas must and will inevitably undertake various democratic reforms, like land reform and emancipation of slaves, and socialist transformation." He told his audience that it would be naive for any area to believe that it could enjoy the benefits of socialism and high-speed development without reform and within old class relations and exploitive systems.[6]

Without question, Tibet was the largest area in China that was not yet engulfed by this wave of CCP social engineering. Tibet was nevertheless affected. At the time, all principal officials of the TWC, except Fan Ming, were in Beijing to attend the Eighth Congress. Fan remained in Lhasa in charge of the TWC's daily operations. At the conference, TWC officials represented one of the most "backward" areas in terms of advancing the CCP's policy goals. On September 20, after Ulanhu's triumphant proclamation, Zhang Guohua made a speech. While pointing out that Tibet had made progress in launching the PCTAR and having all classes interested in reform, Zhang admitted that long-term preparations must be completed before reform could begin.[7] In a speech a few days later, Li Weihan reminded his audience that the CCP had achieved the peaceful liberation of Tibet with the united-front approach, exhorting the party to see that Tibet transform peacefully as well: "Peaceful reform is a special form of class struggles, which relies on the laboring people, unites all forces possible, and achieves the goals of democratic and social revolution through circuitous methods."[8]

It was remarkable that after Sichuan officials had butchered the "smart class struggle" orientation in their reform war, in late 1956 Li should continue to stick to "special form" and "circuitous methods" of class struggle with respect to Tibet. By that time, CCP leaders had already come to the point of facing directly the question of whether their goals in Tibet could be achieved peacefully. As a matter of fact, when discussing the reform war in western Sichuan in late July, policymakers in Beijing had already come very close to admitting that conflict of some sort could not be avoided in Tibet as long as the CCP was determined to implement its reform agenda, intended peacefully or not.[9] Then, suddenly, in the winter months of 1956, two developments led Mao and others in Beijing to decide not only to postpone reform but also to rescind the preparatory "new phase" in Tibet.

One development was the Dalai Lama's lingering in India. On November 2, Zhou Enlai informed the Dalai Lama and the Panchen Lama that Beijing would not oppose their acceptance of invitations from India and Nepal to attend the celebration of the Buddha's 2,500th birth anniversary in those countries. Zhou suggested that they visit India first and then go to Nepal before returning to Tibet.[10] Earlier, in April, the Chinese Ministry of Foreign Affairs had declined an invitation from the Indian government. On that occasion, India had invited eight leading Buddhists in China, including the Dalai Lama and the Panchen Lama. Beijing's excuse was that most of these people, especially the two Tibetan leaders, could not leave their hectic work and some were too old to travel.[11] The Dalai Lama, at the TWC's advice, sent a message to the Indian government in the same vein. At the time, Beijing appeared determined to shield the Dalai Lama from expatriate Tibetans' influence in India and possible American plots. Beijing had information that Kalimpong was such a nesting place for subversive activities against China. But later, when the Indian government sent an invitation again for the two Tibetan leaders to visit, Beijing relented, even though knowing that the Dalai Lama would want to visit Kalimpong as well on his journey.

Tsering Shakya and Melvyn Goldstein, the two best-informed scholars of recent Tibetan history, agree that Beijing approved the visit both to reassure the Indians, whose friendship was a valued asset in Chinese foreign affairs, and to placate the Dalai Lama, who was becoming increasingly dissatisfied with developments in both western Sichuan and Tibet. The two scholars diverge, however, on the meaning of the event to Beijing's Tibet policy in general, interpreting differently a speech made by Mao on November 15. In that speech, at the Second Plenum of the CCP's Eighth Central Committee, Mao discussed the Dalai Lama's India trip in these words:

> In addition, I want to talk about the Dalai [Lama] question. The Buddha died 2,500 years ago [sic], and now the Dalai [Lama] wants to make a pilgrimage to India. Should we let him go or not? The Center believes that we'd better let him go and that it would not be good to stop him. He will leave in a few days. We have advised him to travel by air, but he is unwilling and wants to take a car to go through Kalimpong. In Kalimpong there are spies of various states and also secret agents of the Kuomintang. We should foresee that possibly the Dalai [Lama] would not want to come back. Not only so, he may curse every day, saying "the Communists invaded Tibet" and other things. He may even declare "Tibetan independence" in India. He may also direct reactionaries of

the Tibetan upper stratum to call for a great upheaval so as to drive us out. Then he can evade responsibility by referring to his absence. Such a possibility is the worst-case scenario. I would be happy too if this happens. Our TWC and troops should make preparations in constructing strongholds and accumulating a lot of food and water. We do not have many troops there and anyone can act freely anyway. If you fight and attack, we will defend ourselves. We never attack first and let them to be the first to attack. Then we will counterattack and crush thoroughly the attackers. Should I feel sad if a Dalai [Lama] runs away? I would not even if nine more, ten in total, run away. We have had an experience: it was not bad that Zhang Guotao ran away. Tying a man and a woman together cannot make them into a couple. He does not love your place anymore. Let him go if he wants to. What is so bad for us if he runs away? Nothing at all, except that he may curse us. We Communists have been cursed for thirty-five years with baloneys no other than that the Communists "are extremely vicious and utterly evil," "communizing property and women," and "cruel and inhumane." It's not a big deal if one more person, the Dalai [Lama], joins the cursing. Let them curse for another thirty-five years or make it seventy years. In my opinion, a person should not be afraid of being cursed. Some are concerned that secrets may be leaked [by the Dalai Lama]. Zhang Guotao knew a lot of secrets, but I have not heard that our work was ruined because Zhang leaked secrets.[12]

Goldstein contends that Mao's harsh words about the Dalai Lama did not mean to jettison the "Dalai line" but constituted a face-saving ploy anticipating the possibility of the Dalai Lama's staying abroad. In contrast, Shakya detects a change of direction in Beijing's policy, suggesting that Mao might have been preparing for a showdown in Tibet.[13]

Mao certainly wanted to prepare his colleagues mentally, but the speech also signified a change in his attitude. Until this point, as reflected in their writings and statements concerning Tibet, Mao and other leaders in Beijing appeared to consider the Dalai Lama as an educatable young man who could not control his immediate environment. In this speech, Mao for the first time treated the Dalai Lama as someone who harbored ill will toward the CCP and could harm the party's Tibetan enterprise. Mao's comparison of the Dalai Lama with Zhang Guotao, a traitor in official CCP chronicles, was not made casually. Mao's choice of such extraordinarily harsh words could mean that his judgment of Tenzin Gyatso (the fourteenth Dalai Lama) as an individual changed drastically in the last months of 1956; or that he had never genuinely had confidence in the Dalai Lama; or that in Mao's eyes, the Dalai Lama symbolized the Tibetan establishment more than he behaved as a free-will agent.

According to a source knowledgeable about internal matters of the TWC, Mao was receiving conflicting information from TWC officials. In his speech, Mao talked harshly about the Dalai Lama because he chose to believe Fan Ming's allegation that the Dalai Lama group was making secret contact with American and Kuomintang agents in Kalimpong.[14] A different source, also with access to information internal to the TWC, identifies Zhang Jingwu as Mao's source of information during these crucial days. More than a year before, Mao had taken Zhang out of Tibet at the Dalai Lama's request.[15] After Beijing decided to let the Dalai Lama visit India, Mao sent Zhang back to Lhasa. Zhang arrived on November 6 and delivered a personal message from Mao to the Dalai Lama. The note included four items. First, Mao explained that Zhang Guohua could not return to Tibet at the moment because of health reasons and therefore he had to send Zhang Jingwu instead. Second, the Dalai Lama need not worry about the issue of reform. Third, after the solution of the recent troubles in Poland and "counterrevolutionary conspiracy" in Hungary, "everything is getting better" in the socialist camp. Fourth, Zhang Jingwu would also convey "other information" in person.[16] Whatever feelings Mao may have harbored toward the Dalai Lama in his November 15 speech, Zhang Jingwu's reports about his conversations with the Dalai Lama must have served as a factual basis.

Certainly, Mao did not call the Dalai Lama's attention to the events in Poland and Hungary just to update the young Tibetan leader's awareness of international affairs. Neither would the general welfare of the "socialist camp" concern the Dalai Lama in any direct way. The two East European events sent shock waves through the entire communist world, and CCP leaders were compelled to review China's domestic conditions in that context. At the time, the reform war in western Sichuan and unrest in Tibet were the most disturbing situations in the PRC. Less than two months after Mao mentioned Hungary to the Dalai Lama, Zhou Enlai would actually juxtapose Hungary and Tibet in his conversation with Indian prime minister Nehru, asserting that unlike the Hungarian situation, in Tibet "our inimical countries are trying to carry out subversive activities, but they will not be successful."[17] Depending on Mao's judgment of the Dalai Lama's loyalty to the PRC, his reference to Poland and Hungary could either be an effort to reassure the Tibetan leader about the soundness of the PRC or a veiled warning against any Tibetan attempt to follow the bad precedents in Eastern Europe. The "other information" that Zhang Jingwu delivered to the Dalai Lama indicates that Mao's words may have been intended for the latter. Zhang told the Dalai Lama that, while trusting him completely in his decision about visiting India and not sending anyone to accompany him on the trip, CCP leaders advised the Dalai Lama not to travel by land and not to pass through Kalimpong. It is not clear to what extent the Dalai Lama's dislike of Zhang affected his reaction to the message he delivered. He did not say much to Zhang, but afterwards Zhang learned that the Kashag insisted on the Dalai Lama's using ground transportation to travel to India. Zhang believed that the

Kashag must have been plotting something and reported to Beijing accordingly.[18] In not responding positively to Zhang's message, the Dalai Lama was actually rejecting advice from Mao himself, which could only aggravate Mao's bitterness. Although it cannot be ascertained when exactly the Dalai Lama changed from an asset to a liability in Mao's strategy for resolving the Tibet question, the Dalai Lama's ignoring of Mao's advice could at least have been a contributing factor. Nor did Mao just put out empty words in asking the TWC and PLA troops to be prepared for Tibetan attacks. Two days after Mao's speech, Beijing directed the TWC to make substantive preparations for Mao's worst-case scenario.[19]

On November 20, three leading TWC officials, Zhang Jingwu, Fan Ming, and Li Jue, bade farewell to the Dalai Lama in Lhasa. On the same day, the Dalai Lama joined with the Panchen Lama in Shigatse. Two days later, the two entered India through Dromo (Yadong). The TWC assigned two officials to escort the Tibetan leaders until they crossed the border.[20] In entering India in a way that displeased Mao, for the first time since 1951 the Dalai Lama personally contradicted Beijing. He would not have risked offending Mao over a minor issue of traveling if he had not planned to do something else that, should it become known to Beijing, would have sent CCP leaders into a rage.

The Dalai Lama arrived in New Delhi on November 25; he talked with Jawaharlal Nehru the next day and then again on November 28. According to Nehru's notes, in these conversations the Dalai Lama expressed his grievances against Chinese Communist policies. These included partitioning Tibet into three sections (the "eastern area liberated by force," "Central Tibet" under the Dalai Lama, and "Tsang Tibet" under the Panchen Lama); making preparations for land reform that aroused the Tibetan people's opposition; presenting a potential threat to Tibetan religion; and "tightening their grip gradually" of Tibet in violation of the 1951 agreement. The Dalai Lama also complained that when he visited Beijing in 1954, Mao and other CCP leaders tried to convert him to communism over his objection. According to the Dalai Lama, most people in Tibet did not believe that the Chinese could be forced out. Therefore, the only hope was foreign support, and the "hope lies in India." To the Dalai Lama's disappointment, Nehru tried to convince him that he should not resist but take the lead in land reform because this was a program adopted by all progressive parties of underdeveloped countries, including India. Believing that the Dalai Lama was still thinking in terms of Tibetan independence, Nehru advised him to accept Chinese "suzerainty" and "secure the maximum internal autonomy." Nehru made it clear that India, or any other country, was in no position to help Tibet, and that India would be most useful to Tibet only by keeping a friendly relationship with China. Unconvinced, the Dalai Lama countered that "internal freedom" in Tibet was impossible under the Chinese, but he pledged to use peaceful means to gain freedom.²¹ Not included in Nehru's notes but revealed by the Dalai Lama years later, during his first "real talk" with Nehru, the Dalai Lama expressed his wish to stay in India until "there was some positive sign of a change in Chinese policy." In response, Nehru urged the Dalai Lama to go back and carry out the Seventeen-Point Agreement.²²

The Dalai Lama's conversation with Nehru revealed an ugly schism between Lhasa and Beijing after the two sides had tried for years to find a solution. Both promoting "social progress" and "autonomy" of Tibet and desiring to settle their differences peacefully, Beijing and Lhasa could not agree on details. In the ethnopolitics of the Tibetan frontiers in the 1950s, Beijing pushed "social progress" by way of transplanting the CCP system into Tibet, whereas Lhasa sought "autonomy" meaning Tibet's practical segregation from the rest of China. By the end of 1956, the two stances had not come closer and proved hard to bridge. Soon, to avoid an explosion of the Tibetan situation, policy-makers in Beijing would decide to suspend their agenda for piecemeal change in Tibet and reorient drastically toward an even more patient gimmick. As for the Dalai Lama and his advisers, hopelessly devoted to preserving the status quo of Tibetan society, the self-reform strategy proposed by Nehru was out of the question. Consequently, they had no other game to play except Beijing's. In the meantime, the spell of peace was already broken. Some local headmen decided to do what was impossible in the Dalai Lama's opinion—to force the Han out.

Coincident with the Dalai Lama's arrival in New Delhi, Phurpa Bum Tsering Gyaltsan, headman of the *Ningjing dzong* (宁静宗, today's Markham County) and deputy director of the Department of Agriculture and Animal Husbandry of the Chamdo People's Liberation Committee, led an attack on a PLA platoon guarding a bridge on the Lancang River. The fighting continued for four days. The rebels killed twenty-one PLA soldiers, took all the platoon's ammunition, and then escaped before PLA reinforcements arrived.²³ This was the second rebellion in Chamdo after the one led by Chime Gombo. In early December, in reporting to Beijing about the recent fighting in Ningjing and some other counties in southern Chamdo, the TWC and the TMR admitted that these recent rebellions reflected the upper classes' discontent about reform, which was ominously shared by Banda Dorje (aka Tobgyal Bangdatsang), a member of Bangdatsang, one of the richest Tibetan merchant families. Banda Dorje served in the KMT government in Xikang before 1949 but began to cooperate with the CCP in early 1950. In April 1956, he became the deputy secretary of the Preparatory Committee of the Tibetan Autonomous Region and, in December, the director of the Chamdo People's Liberation Committee.²⁴ Thus, Banda Dorje was the most important supporter of the CCP in Chamdo. Because a great number of ordinary Tibetans fought PLA troops, the TWC qualified the rebellion as a "nationalistic and popular riot" incited by the reactionary ruling class in the name of the "Tibetan nation" and religion. The TWC proposed to Beijing that the situation be dealt with by political means buttressed by military preparations. On December 13, Beijing allowed the TWC to proceed, while cautioning TWC officials against any impatient move. CCP leaders also advised the TWC to put Banda Dorje in charge of the security work in southern Chamdo, so as to use his political influence among Tibetan chieftains and also to make him responsible for local stability.[25] Later, the same stratagem would be applied to the Kashag, which the TWC would require to assume responsibility for quelling rebellions in the area under its control.

Controlled by a "people's liberation committee" since 1950, Chamdo had maintained a position parallel to Lhasa and Shigatse in Beijing's Tibet enterprise.[26] The region served as a testing ground for reform in 1956 just as it had served as a base for the PLA advance toward Lhasa in 1950. In Beijing's policymaking, Chamdo was differentiated from Lhasa until March 1959 when, scandalously, most Tibetan members of the "people's liberation committee" rebelled. In late 1956, although the unrest in the Chamdo area was alarming, the situation was not grave enough to cause CCP leaders to revisit their policy in Tibet as a whole. But then, on December 12, the TWC sent to Beijing an urgent message about the political situation in Lhasa:

> The Center:
>
> According to intelligence we obtained recently, Tibetan reactionaries will likely start riot in Lhasa and other areas around December 17. We will file another report about emergency measures for dealing with this. If riots begin, the Dalai [Lama] may either make an excuse for not returning to Tibet or may be prevented from returning, and this may put Ngabö under danger of being detained or assassinated. This would be a serious loss to us. If Ngabö can come back either before or after riots take place, it will be useful for both pacifying riots and stabilizing the situation. Therefore, we ask the Center to consider calling Ngabö to Beijing as soon as possible and then to send him back to Tibet.
>
> The Tibet Work Committee
>
> 12 o'clock, December 12, 1956[27]

Beijing's reaction to this "triple-twelve" message, made in a directive dated December 16, differed drastically from its December 13 directive to the TWC that focused narrowly on the Chamdo situation. This lengthy telegram, addressed to the TWC, Zhou Enlai, and the Chinese embassy in India, would afterwards be distributed to all provincial committees of the CCP, hence establishing the nationwide importance of the Tibetan situation. The telegram is translated below:

> *The Tibet Work Committee, Premier Zhou via the embassy in Burma, and the embassy in India:*
>
> *The TWC telegram of the 12th about possible riots [baoluan] by reactionaries around the 17th and comrade Jingwu's telegram of the 11th about the political situation in Tibet were both learned. At the present, you should fully and practically make military and material deployments and preparations. In the meantime, you should consciously keep a calm attitude and do whatever possible to avoid causing unnecessary anxieties. Please continue to investigate in depth the situation as it unfolds and report to the Center timely.*
>
> *Under the current circumstances, the TWC ought to work even harder on the religious and secular upper stratums in Lhasa. The work on Gadrang [Lobsang Rigzin], Xiasur [Jikmé Dorje], and Neushar [Tupten Tarpa] should especially be intensified. These individuals and all those religious and secular upper-stratum people who could be won over should be won over with the greatest effort possible. Attention should also be paid to the work on Yuthok [Tashi Dhondup]. The information about possible riots by reactionaries should be measuredly disclosed to Gadrang, so that we can enlist their cooperation in preventing riots. They should also be informed that for coping with such sudden incidents, we have already made necessary preparations. We certainly do not want to start war, and we are willing to settle whatever problems through peaceful consultations. But, if reactionaries follow foreign direction in provoking rebellions, causing unrest, and attacking the PLA, we are not afraid of war. The consequences would not benefit reactionaries.*
>
> *In view that in the past year the Tibetan upper stratums resented and feared greatly reform, and that reactionaries often used opposition to reform as the biggest reason for agitating misgivings against us and even inciting riots, now the Center believes it necessary to thoroughly clarify our attitude toward the issue of reform in Tibet for the Tibetan religious and secular upper stratums. The Center and Chairman Mao have always believed that reform must be approved by the Dalai [Lama], the Panchen [Lama], and other clerical leaders, and reform should be implemented only after conditions in various aspects become ready. At present neither the conditions among the upper stratum nor those among the people are ready. Therefore, reform cannot be implemented in the next few years. The Center does not believe that reform can be implemented during the Second Five-Year Plan. A decision [on reform] for the Third Five-Year Plan*

will have to be made according to circumstances as well. But if foreign-directed reactionaries reject consultations and are resolved to destroy the Seventeen-Point Agreement and smash the status quo in Tibet, then it will be possible that the laboring people be provoked to rise up to overthrow the feudal system and establish a people's democratic Tibet.

At present the orientation of no reform for six years should be widely transmitted within the Party and conveyed to the Tibetan upper stratum. In the near future, the TWC should invite the principal officials of the PCTAR and the Kashag to have a talk, explaining to them the Center's orientation above. Hopefully, by means of the PCTAR, Buddhist associations, and other ways, these people can convey the Center's orientation widely to aristocratic officials in Lhasa and other places, upper echelon of the monasteries, and Tibetan army officers.

In the Center's opinion, it would be inappropriate to call Ngabö back now. Our work for winning over the Dalai [Lama] would lose an important force if Ngabö is moved away, and the Dalai [Lama] would become suspicious as well. As for what to do next with regard to the Dalai [Lama], the Panchen [Lama], and Ngabö, it will depend on developments to come.

In the future comrade Jingwu should still work in Tibet. The question regarding a Center's representative [in Tibet] will be considered later.

The Military Commission has already replied to you separately in respect to military deployment.

The Center

December 16, 1956[28] (emphasis added)

Although its contents remain unknown, Zhang Jingwu's December 11 message was likely a detailed analysis of the political situation of Tibet. That was why Beijing responded in referring to several Tibetan names. These Tibetans were all members of the PCTAR holding high positions in the Kashag. As the Dalai Lama and his closest advisers were absent from Lhasa, these individuals' attitudes were crucial to the precarious situation in Tibet. This directive arrived on Mao's desk on December 16 and was sent out after Mao added or rewrote the italicized parts.[29] At this juncture, Mao apparently made up his mind about suspending reform preparations in Tibet for the sake of placating the Tibetan elites. As for the "orientation of no reform for six years," it made a tentative idea in the September 4 directive into a firm policy. Apparently, "peace," "status quo," and "cooperation" with the Kashag in preventing riots were the intended targets of the orientation. Yet, as will be discussed later in this chapter, as the orientation was deliberated further among CCP leaders, it evolved into a more complex strategy than its initial form in the December 16 directive.

December 16 was a Tibetan day for Mao. In addition to revising the directive, Mao did three things in relation to Tibet. After 3:00 P.M., he telephoned Zhang Jingwu and asked him about the situation in Lhasa. Then, at 6:50 P.M., he called Zhou Enlai, who had just arrived in Yunnan from his recent visit in Burma. Mao informed Zhou of the Tibetan situation and asked him to go to India after his visit in Pakistan and Nepal. In the evening, Mao called a meeting in Zhongnanhai to discuss the Tibetan situation and also the drafting of a major editorial for the *People's Daily*.[30] Zhou had just made a state visit in India in November, but he would return there at Mao's request, mainly to deal with the Tibetan question—specifically, the Dalai Lama's lingering in India in light of the most recent developments in Lhasa.

Dalai Lama's "Divine Air"

Based on what Zhou Enlai said to the Dalai Lama at the end of December, it can be ascertained that when talking to Zhou via telephone on the afternoon of December 16, Mao asked him to convey to the Dalai Lama Beijing's new orientation of "no reform for six years." The meeting in Zhongnanhai on that evening was therefore just a formality to confirm what Mao had already decided. The December 16 directive marked a major reorientation of Beijing's policy since the September 4 directive that had allowed the TWC to continue stumbling ahead with the dilapidated "new phase." Because of Mao's revision, the new directive changed the previous policy in two respects. First, unlike the previous directive that reaffirmed the "new phase" in supporting "active" reform preparations but was vague about how long "democratic reform" should be postponed, the December 16 directive clearly established the six-year time frame and omitted any reference to reform preparations. Second, unlike the September 4 directive that stressed necessary concessions on the CCP's part for the sake of maintaining the party's credibility, in the December 16 directive Mao shifted the burden of credibility to the Tibetan side, warning that the Seventeen-Point Agreement could no longer restrain Beijing from extending "people's democracy" to Tibet if the Tibetan situation continued to deteriorate. Mao was not bluffing. It is telling that having finished revising the December 16 directive, Mao had the document circulated among several CCP officials who were respectively in charge of the state's financial, diplomatic, united-front, and military functions. The two PLA officers included in the loop were Peng Dehuai and Tan Zheng.[31] Peng was then the defense minister, and Tan was in charge of the PLA Political Department.

Deng Xiaoping's name was conspicuously missing from those who participated in the Zhongnanhai meeting and those among whom Mao circulated the directive. The official *Nianpu* of Deng omits Deng's activities between December 2 and 24, and the two most recent biographies of Deng do not shed light on these days either.³² Then, on December 25, Deng reemerged and presided over a meeting of the Central Secretariat of the CCP Central Committee. Tibet was one of the subjects discussed on the occasion. Deng told those present:

> As for Tibet, the Center's original orientation was to carry out reform. Then, after further deliberations, the Standing Committee of the Politburo decided that reform would not be implemented and the status quo [of Tibet] might be preserved for ten, twenty, or thirty years. We have laid foundations in Tibet and reform can be implemented. But we will not do it and will only work on united front with the upper stratum.³³

Deng's these words are crucial in clarifying three issues. First, despite the CCP's vague conception of "reform preparations" and CCP leaders' soft-pedaling of the notion of reform to Lhasa, Deng's words confirmed that in 1956 Beijing had an established orientation for starting reform in Tibet. Second, Deng hinted at the time of Beijing's policy change in referring to "deliberations" by the Standing Committee of the Politburo. After the Eighth Congress, the Standing Committee of the Politburo had six members: Mao Zedong, Liu Shaoqi, Zhou Enlai, Zhu De, Chen Yun, and Deng Xiaoping. Both Chen and Deng were newly elected members of this top decision-making body. Very likely the committee's "deliberations" mentioned by Deng referred to the meeting called by Mao on the evening of December 16, at which all standing committee members were present except Zhou and Deng. Before the meeting, Mao had already consulted with Zhou on the phone, so Deng was the only one uncounted for in the "deliberations." Thus, the decision to suspend reform in Tibet might have been news to Deng, and in the passage just quoted Deng was breaking the news to his colleagues in the Central Secretariat. Third, Deng did not use the "no reform for six years" phrase but said that the Tibetan status quo could last as long as thirty years, which sheds light on the sentiment of the Politburo meeting. Interestingly, even at this late date, Deng still believed that Tibet was ready for reform. As will be shown below, Deng would implement Beijing's new decision with determination. His expressed conviction that Tibet was ready for reform may have revealed a feeling, or a reluctance to retreat, shared by many senior officials in Beijing at the time. As mentioned earlier, at the end of December, Deng called Zhang Jingwu about rearranging the TWC's work in accordance with Beijing's new policy, indicating that Deng and his Central Secretariat were now in direct command of the CCP operations in Tibet. In doing so, he curiously referred to Beijing's policy change anachronistically as if it were already part of the September 4 directive.³⁴

With the Central Secretariat in charge of the Tibet work, Beijing was poised to take a second look at its hitherto largely successful operations in Tibet.

Two years before, having successfully hosted the Dalai Lama and the Panchen Lama, Mao confidently recommended the CCP's experience in Tibet to the Burmese prime minister U Nu, who was then visiting in Beijing. On that occasion, discussing the general world situation and also domestic conflicts in Burma involving the Burmese Communist Party, Mao encouraged his guest to seek a "compromise" with domestic opponents:

> Our method toward Tibet may be for your reference. We are preparing to negotiate with the local Tibetan government for a very long period and consult with them. As far as social reforms in Tibet are concerned, we do not insist on implementation right away. If, after consulting with them, they say okay, we will take a small step. If they say no, we will not make a move for the moment. Of course, the experience of China is merely for your reference because the domestic conditions of our two countries are rather different. Every country must handle its problems according to its own conditions.[35]

While it is astonishing that Mao compare Burma's communist problem with Beijing's Tibetan enterprise, at the time Mao had good reasons to believe that he had a firm grip on Tibetan affairs. In the next two years, however, the Tibetan situation did not go well as Mao expected. The "peaceful" reform in the Tibetan areas of western Sichuan turned into a bloody war, the "new phase" in Tibet was crumbling, and the linchpin of Mao's Tibetan stratagem, the Dalai Lama, was lingering in India. Under the circumstances, Mao could not possibly still hold the same rosy expectations about Tibet as he had conveyed to U Nu. As far as Tibetan affairs were concerned, the winter months of 1956 constituted a watershed for Mao as the ultimate decision maker of the CCP, when he appeared to degenerate from a visionary strategist into a fatalist tactician.

Previously, within the framework of the Seventeen-Point Agreement, the CCP had endeavored to achieve several intertwined agendas of different historical origins. In incorporating Tibet into the Chinese state in a legal form, the CCP followed its Manchu and Nationalist predecessors, though the geostrategic significance of such "unification" was understood in the context of the Cold War in the 1950s. In projecting an eventual socialist transformation of Tibetan society and systems, the CCP was both advancing its "revolutionary cause" and extending domestic sovereignty of the central government authorities. Yet, being both Han and communist, CCP leaders realized from the outset that they appeared even stranger to the Tibetans than previous modern state builders dressed either as Manchu monarchists or Chinese Nationalists. It was therefore particularly important for Beijing to keep the Dalai Lama on its bandwagon before the CCP could, via the Dalai Lama, reach ordinary Tibetans. In late 1956, as indicated in Beijing's December 16 directive, CCP leaders still wanted to "win over" the Dalai Lama and were keen to get him back to Lhasa.

For one thing, the Dalai Lama's lingering in India, given his obvious grievances against recent CCP policies in western Sichuan and Tibet, could be incendiary to an already explosive situation in Lhasa. For another, whatever new stratagem Mao and his comrades intended to use in Tibet, they would need the appearance of normality to continue, and for that the Dalai Lama's presence in Lhasa was key.

The task of persuading the Dalai Lama to return to Lhasa fell on Zhou Enlai. After getting Mao's urgent request for him to go back to India in mid-December, Zhou took on a punishing schedule to accomplish his mission. According to Zhou's Tibetan-language interpreter, during a daylong conversation with the Dalai Lama, Zhou had to take naps during the intervals while his words were being translated into Tibetan.[36] During that winter, Zhou talked to the Dalai Lama three times, once on November 29 during his first visit in India, and twice more on December 30 and January 1 (1957) during his second visit. After his November meeting with the Dalai Lama, Zhou also talked with the Dalai Lama's two older brothers, Gyalo Thondup and Thubten Norbu. To facilitate his mission of suasion, in early January 1957 Zhou also met with principal officials of the Dalai Lama's entourage.

There are no reliable records of Zhou's conversations with the Tibetans.[37] Based on published "minutes" of Zhou's conversations with the Dalai Lama and participants' recollections, Zhou's strategy of suasion had three elements: reassuring the Tibetans, discrediting China's adversaries, and predicting the Dalai Lama's future. When talking with the Dalai Lama in late November, Zhou reaffirmed Beijing's rhetoric that "democratic reform" in Tibet would not be carried out without the Tibetan leaders' consent, and that now was not the time for reform. As for the Dalai Lama's return, without showing any sign of urgency, Zhou conveyed a suggestion from Mao that the Dalai Lama visit Beijing first before returning to Lhasa. When the two met again at the end of December, the Dalai Lama's return became the focus of the conversation. Three times Zhou urged the Dalai Lama to consider an "early return" to Lhasa lest certain wicked elements there take advantage of his absence and start rebellions. Informed of Beijing's December 16 decision, Zhou told the Dalai Lama for the first time:

> Now Chairman Mao wants me to tell you that reform will not be considered in the Second Five-Year Plan at all. Even if reform becomes possible after six years, the issue should still be decided by you according to conditions and circumstances. At the moment, there is no need to discuss how to reform in the future because such discussions may cause unnecessarily misunderstandings and suspicions.[38]

Besides reassuring the Dalai Lama that reform would not reach Tibet any time soon, Zhou also refuted an idea attributed to the Dalai Lama's brothers that the Tibetans might receive assistance from India or the United States for achieving independence. Zhou told the Dalai Lama and his officials that Nehru maintained a friendly relationship with the PRC, recognized Tibet as part of China, and did not permit any anti-Chinese activities in Indian territories. As for the United States, the idea of American assistance was but a hoax. The United States was far away and could not airlift aid materials to Tibet over the air space of India. So, the Americans could only brag with empty words. Zhou went a step further in describing a prospect for the Dalai Lama should he still decide to stay abroad. Perhaps having in his mind a Chinese proverb, "The monk can run away but the temple cannot" (*paodeliao heshang paobuliao miao*), Zhou reasoned that since the Dalai Lama's temple was in Lhasa, if he stayed abroad, the Dalai Lama would not only lose political influence inside Tibet but also his "divine air." Admitting that the Dalai Lama would be valuable to the PRC's adversaries if he were willing to curse the Chinese Communists, Zhou nevertheless predicted that such value would dwindle over time.[39]

While trying different angles of reasoning to persuade the Dalai Lama and his officials to return to Lhasa, Zhou regarded the Indian prime minister Nehru as an even more important target because Nehru could deny asylum to the Dalai Lama. However, Zhou made an erroneous judgment about Nehru, and his attempts at persuasion would prove costly to the Chinese-Indian relationship a few years later. As shown in Nehru's conversations with the Dalai Lama in November 1956, from the outset he did not harbor any intention of keeping the Dalai Lama in India. Zhou, however, was suspicious. The Dalai Lama seemed to confirm that suspicion when he told Zhou in November that he sensed a great "pulling force" from the Indian side.[40] On December 31, 1956, and January 1, 1957, Zhou and Nehru held long talks. Since the records kept by the Chinese side remain classified, the contents of these conversations can be known only through published Indian records. The two leaders started their conversation with a lengthy discussion of recent developments in the Middle East and East Europe. But the focus of the conversation soon shifted.[41] Clearly, Tibet was the most important issue on Zhou's mind. At one point, Nehru mentioned that in his recent visit in the United States President Eisenhower had indicated a willingness to allow American journalists to visit the PRC if Beijing would release the ten American prisoners from the Korean War. Zhou did not want to pursue this topic without first reaching an understanding with Nehru about Tibet. In a long monologue that followed, Zhou described Tibet's historical relationship with China, Beijing's policy of giving "a large measure of autonomous rights" to Tibet, and Beijing's current "attitude of waiting and seeing" toward the issue of improving conditions of the region. Zhou admitted that understandably some Tibetans were nervous about how their life and religion would be affected, and "there is also a minority under foreign influence" who wanted independence. While not complaining to Nehru about the Indian government's invitation to the Dalai Lama and the Panchen Lama, Zhou told Nehru that from the very beginning Beijing had known trouble would start once the Tibetan leaders left their region. According to Zhou, instigated by American and KMT agents, the Dalai Lama's brothers and Tibetan expatriates wanted the Dalai Lama to visit Kalimpong and would very likely keep him there. Then this would create an opportunity for certain people back in Lhasa to cause serious trouble.

In responding, Nehru professed innocence, saying that he knew little about Tibet, never heard about the Dalai Lama's plan to visit Kalimpong, and was surprised by Zhou's information about a huge number of Tibetans in Kalimpong. Although admitting that Kalimpong was known to be a "nest of spies," Nehru insisted that the Dalai Lama's visit in Kalimpong was a "matter primarily for Your Excellency and the Dalai Lama to decide" and "it would be embarrassing for us to say anything either way." Nehru's noncommittal attitude worked on Zhou's anxiety and induced him to switch gears. Unable to invoke Nehru's goodwill in helping Beijing with the Dalai Lama dilemma, Zhou hoped to appeal to Nehru's sense of India's self-interest. So, when Nehru asked him to clarify Beijing's view on the historical status of Tibet in China's administrative system, Zhou confirmed that Tibet had never been made into a province of China. Then he brought up a topic to which Nehru had to respond:

> When I said that India knew more about Tibet, I meant about the past history. For example, I knew nothing about the McMahon Line until recently when we came to study the border problem after liberation of China.

It was Nehru's turn to become nervous. Yet he chose his words carefully:

> We recognize that China has, in law and in fact, suzerainty over Tibet even though it may not have been exercised sometime. As Your Excellency has said, Tibet has behaved in an autonomous way and was cut off from other countries. The criterion of an independent state is that the state should have independent foreign relations and Tibet had no foreign relations except with England.
>
> The McMahon Line was put forward in the 1913 [sic] Conference between the Chinese, the Tibetans and the British. That Conference decided not only the McMahon Line but also two other points. The Chinese Government raised objection only to the other two points. Surely, the Chinese Government always knew about it (i.e. the McMahon Line).
>
> As regards [the] Dalai Lama, we do not want any incident to take place about [the] Dalai Lama in Kalimpong or while he is in India. We will do as Your Excellency and [the] Dalai Lama decide. What kind of incident does Your Excellency fear might happen? If you can give some specific idea about the trouble, we can prevent it.

The Chinese stance would typically have raised objections to Nehru's use of "suzerainty," not "sovereignty," in defining China's right over Tibet and also to his account of the official Chinese attitude toward the McMahon Line. Zhou let these issues pass, however, because he had heard what he came to hear—Nehru's clear promise to help with the Dalai Lama problem. He told the Indian leader that if the Dalai Lama went to Kalimpong and if Tibetans there attempted to detain him, the Indian government had the power to intervene. Zhou next clarified how the issue of the McMahon Line was connected to that of the Dalai Lama's return to Lhasa:

> Perhaps U Nu might have told Your Excellency that we studied this question and although this Line was never recognized by us, still apparently there was a secret pact between Britain and Tibet and it was announced at the time of the Simla Conference. *And now that it is an accomplished fact, we should accept it. But we have not consulted Tibet so far.* In the last agreement which we signed about Tibet, the Tibetans wanted us to reject this Line; but we told them that the question should be temporarily put aside. . . . But now we think that we should try to persuade and convince Tibetans to accept it. This question also is connected with Sino-Burmese border and *the question will be decided after [the] Dalai Lama's return to Lhasa*. So, although the question is still undecided and it is unfair to us, still we feel that there is no better way than to recognize this Line. (emphasis added)

After this crucial exchange, Zhou and Nehru proceeded to discuss Zhou's recent visits in Burma and Pakistan and also returned to the issue of Sino-U.S. relations brought up by Nehru earlier.[42]

As shown in the preceding quotations, Zhou presented the issues of the Dalai Lama's return and the McMahon Line in terms of a quid pro quo: New Delhi's cooperation in sending the Dalai Lama back to Lhasa would be rewarded with Beijing's positive attitude toward the McMahon Line. It is unclear whether this tactic was agreed upon by Mao and Zhou when the two conversed on the phone on December 16. The flow of the Zhou-Nehru conversations indeed seems to indicate that the tactic worked. Yet in reality, Beijing's suspicion of Nehru in relation to Tibet was misplaced. Given Nehru's policy priorities at the time, which included a good relationship with the PRC, and his encouragement for the Dalai Lama to continue cooperating with the CCP, Zhou's quid pro quo was unnecessary. That is, although Zhou's unexpected reference to the McMahon Line got on Nehru's nerve and induced him to promise cooperation with respect to the Dalai Lama's visit, Zhou's tactic did not affect New Delhi's established policy about Tibet. As a matter of fact, after talking to Zhou, Nehru did not see any connection between the conversation and his own willingness to prevent Tibetan expatriates from using the Dalai Lama's visit to conduct anti-PRC activities in India. In a postconversation memorandum to a number of Indian officials, Nehru detailed his talks with Zhou but did not even hint at a connection between the McMahon Line and the Dalai Lama's visit.[43] In the future, Zhou's oral consent to accept the McMahon Line would become a point of contention between Beijing and New Delhi.

At the beginning of 1957, however, Beijing's priority was the Dalai Lama's return to Lhasa. On January 1, after conversing with Nehru, Zhou immediately conveyed Nehru's attitude, which the Tibetans already knew, to the Dalai Lama and his entourage.[44] This was Zhou's last meeting with the Tibetans in India. At this point, Zhou was by no means confident that his words would produce the expected results. On January 2, Zhou sent a telegram to Beijing, informing Mao and others: "If he [the Dalai Lama] insists to go to Kalimpong, I cannot stop him. If troubles happen, he will likely not be able to return to Tibet. Then the Dalai [Lama] and the Indian government will have to take responsibilities."[45] That was, Zhou advised Beijing to prepare for the worst-case scenario. From January 8 to 10, Mao was having intensive discussions of China's economic issues with CCP officials in the Yinian Hall of Zhongnanhai. On the evening of January 11, heeding Zhou's warning, Mao called a special meeting with Liu Shaoqi, Chen Yun, and Deng Xiaoping in the Yinian Hall. There was only one agenda item for the meeting: the Dalai Lama's expected journey to Kalimpong.[46]

When Zhou sent his telegram off, he did not realize that his worst-case scenario would not happen. On late evening of January 1, Nehru met with the Dalai Lama and, for the second time, clarified for the Tibetan leader his attitude toward the Tibetan question. The following is Nehru's own record of what he said to the Dalai Lama on that occasion:

> 10. I told the Dalai Lama that his brother at Kalimpong often spoke very foolishly and it seemed to me that he was rather unbalanced. I told him that as he had already agreed by a Treaty [the Seventeen-Point Agreement] to Tibet being part of China but autonomous, it was not easy for him to break this agreement. Indeed, any attempt to do so would result in a major conflict and much misery to Tibet. In an armed conflict, Tibet could not possibly defeat China. I also pointed out that we had a treaty with China in regard to Tibet. Our position all along had been that sovereignty rested with China but Tibet should be autonomous. Therefore, the best course for the Dalai Lama to adopt was to accept this sovereignty but insist on full autonomy in regard to internal affairs. He would be on strong ground on this, and he could build up the Tibetan people under his leadership.
>
> 11. I told the Dalai Lama also that I have been surprised to learn that some people had advised him to remain in India and not return to Tibet. That would be the height of folly and it would harm him as well as Tibet. This was not the

way to serve the cause of Tibet. He must be in his own country and give a lead to his people. He listened carefully to what I said and did not say much himself. I am likely to meet him again a week or so later.[47]

In talking about the "cause of Tibet," Nehru urged Dalai to return to Lhasa for reasons different from those with which Zhou had tried to convince the Tibetans. But Nehru and Zhou agreed on the "height of folly" in the Dalai Lama's contemplation of not returning to Tibet. In November 1956 and January 1957, Nehru twice showed the Dalai Lama that his hope of India, either as a supporter of Tibetan independence or an asylum for the Dalai Lama, was misplaced. Although this was not part of a deal Nehru made with Zhou, Zhou's barrage on the Dalai Lama problem during the previous two days certainly affirmed Nehru's belief that this was the right thing to do. The Dalai Lama would still go to Kalimpong, against Zhou's advice. But, after talking to Nehru, the Dalai Lama also realized that he had no choice but to return to Lhasa. On January 3, he met with Pan Zili, the Chinese ambassador to India. During the conversation, the Dalai Lama criticized himself for being easily swayed by the opinions of those Tibetans in India.[48] Before leaving for Kalimpong, the Dalai Lama performed an official function on behalf of Beijing. On January 12, he presented to Nehru two books by Xuan Zhuang, the famous Buddhist monk of the Tang dynasty. Either on this or on a different occasion, the Dalai Lama informed Nehru that he had decided to go back to Lhasa because of Nehru's advice and Zhou's promises. Still, Nehru decided to take some "special steps" to forestall any trouble in Kalimpong while the Dalai Lama was visiting there.[49]

The Dalai Lama arrived in Kalimpong on January 22 and stayed there for about a month. No trouble of the kind feared by Beijing and Nehru took place. On February 25, the Dalai Lama crossed the border and arrived in Dromo (Yadong), and on April 1 he reached Lhasa.[50] The dynamics in Tibet were no longer the same. By flirting with the idea of remaining abroad at a vital moment in Beijing's policymaking with regard to Tibet, the Dalai Lama had effectively halted the "new phase," or the CCP's preparations for "democratic reform" in the region. Two days after the Dalai Lama crossed the border and reentered Tibet, Mao, in his capacity as the chairman of the Central People's Government of the PRC, delivered his famous speech, "How to Handle Correctly Internal Contradictions of the People," at the eleventh enlarged Supreme Conference on State Affairs (*zuigao guowu huiyi*). In the speech, Mao included a statement about the CCP's policy of not implementing reform in Tibet for six years, or during the Second Five-Year Plan.[51] Under this publicly promulgated state policy, it was less clear what would come next in Tibet. In the eyes of CCP leaders, the Beijing-Lhasa relationship had changed in some subtle ways. In late January, the Ministry of Foreign Affairs planned to send Yang Gongsu, chief of the ministry's office in Lhasa, to India to accompany the Dalai Lama on his way back to Lhasa. The TWC also planned to hold a welcoming party for the Dalai Lama, which, according to the TWC's original idea, should be "even warmer" than the one sending the Tibetan leader off to India. But Beijing did not want to celebrate the Dalai Lama's return. Accordingly, Yang would not go to India but would just greet the Dalai Lama on the Chinese side of the border, and the TWC's welcoming party would be conducted in the same manner as the earlier one.[52]

Since 1950, developments in Chamdo had served as a weathervane for the rest of Tibet. But in early 1957, the significance of events there could not be divined clearly. In mid-January, a southern headquarters of the Chamdo Security District of the Tibet Military Region was established, and Banda Dorje was appointed its commander. Banda Dorje's appointment was based on his social connections with upper-class figures in the area and motivated by the CCP's orientation of "political suasion assisted with military strike," which was a familiar formula in the reform war on the eastern side of the Jinsha River.[53] In the meantime, CCP leaders were awaiting the Dalai Lama's return to resume his role in their political suasion scheme about Tibet. For a while, rebellions in the Chamdo area subsided but did not end completely. As the reform war on the eastern side of the River expanded, a new waiting game was about to begin on the western side.

"Tibet as a Buffer Zone"

The decision to wait on Tibet for at least six years was made by Mao, and all the important elements of the waiting game were either decided by Mao personally or adopted with his approval. Meanwhile, the specifics of Beijing's political strategy during the interval between an unsatisfactory present and a desirable future in Tibet were articulated at a series of discussions between Central Secretariat members and TWC officials in the early months of 1957. Not every idea or opinion broached in these discussions was shared by all discussants. The records of these discussions thus constitute a rare opportunity to see divergent intentions and bare-knuckle calculations of top-echelon CCP officials who faced the Tibetan dilemma, which cannot be seen in the resultant policy directives sugarcoated with the usual party jargon.[54] Between February and May 1957, the Central Secretariat held a dozen meetings about Tibet. Deng Xiaoping always took the lead in these discussions. Other Central Secretariat members involved in the discussions were Li Xiannian, Peng Zhen, and Tan Zhenlin. In addition, senior CCP officials Chen Yun, Li Weihan, Song Renqiong, and Xi Zhongxun attended some of the meetings and commented on various aspects of the CCP's work in Tibet.⁵⁵ TWC officials attending some or all of these meetings were Zhang Jingwu, Zhang Guohua, Fan Ming, Zhou Renshan, Wang Qimei, Ya Hanzhang, and Mu Shengzhong. For the sake of clarity, the following discussion considers seven issues deliberated at the Central Secretariat's meetings in early 1957.

1. What Went Wrong?

Many years later, the CCP literature would characterize reform preparations made in Tibet during the second half of 1956 as *dafazhan* (great development). The term is not derogatory, but in the CCP history about Tibet it means a rushed and erroneous policy move in Tibet two years ahead of the disastrous *Dayuejin* (the Great Leap Forward) in the rest of the PRC. The term was, however, not mentioned even once in the Central Secretariat's discussions in 1957. What had happened in the previous year did not have a name, and certainly Zhou Enlai's term, "new phase," was not used to characterize CCP activities in Tibet in 1956. The participants in the meetings just agreed that excessive measures had been used to push changes in Tibet. Too many people had been moved into Tibet from the outside, too many Tibetans recruited into government works, too much money spent, and too many projects launched.

The reform preparations involved a tremendous swelling of the rank and file of the "revolutionary work" in Tibet, moving thousands of Han cadres and workers into Tibet and recruiting many local Tibetans. According to Zhang Jingwu's report to the meetings, the personnel expansion resulted in putting more than 45,600 Han and Tibetans into 406 "government units," many of them newly created. Among these, 15,519 were Han, including 10,142 cadres and trainees and 5,377 workers. As for the Tibetan personnel, 8,970 were cadres and trainees, 19,170 workers, and 2,000 upper-class people who accepted the CCP's "arrangements" for them. The total number of Tibetan recruits was 30,140, or more than 3 percent of the Tibetan population. In addition, about a hundred "government established and supplied" elementary schools enrolled more than seven thousand students, all receiving stipends from the government. Originally, for the year of 1956, the TWC planned to recruit ten thousand Tibetans as government workers and trainees, but the CCP Organizational Department under Deng Xiaoping increased the number to fifteen thousand. The task of recruitment was assigned to local authorities at different levels, each of which had a quota to fulfil. Such rapid induction of large numbers of local Tibetans into the CCP's Tibet work was more than the Tibetan society could bear. As a result, some five hundred children were included among the new recruits, and three hundred to four hundred prostitutes, thieves, ruffians, and jobless wanderers were enlisted from the streets to attend training sessions at cadre schools. The personnel expansion caused labor shortages in the society, and the inclusion of children and those unruly social elements among the new recruits became a laughingstock to the local people. Even the proreform Panchen Lama complained to the TWC: "We know the number of Tibetan intellectuals. You should have considered the population ratio when expanding the personnel."[56]

The personnel expansion was sustained at huge expense. According to Zhang, the planned expenditure for 1956 was 74.37 million silver dollars, but 106.19 million was actually spent, including more than 40 million in foreign currencies. The planned budget for 1957 was even bigger, and expenditures reached 128 million yuan. On average, each Han cadre received a yearly salary of 2,700 yuan and each Tibetan trainee, 960 yuan. Daily wages for manual and skilled Tibetan laborers ranged from three to eight yuan. Even each elementary school student received a thirty-five-yuan payment each month. As salaried personnel increased rapidly, the market crashed. High inflation and panic buying became inevitable. In his report, Zhang gave a couple of examples: a silver yuan could buy just two *jin* (= a kilogram) of firewood or eight *jin* of cow dung; twenty-eight *jin* of barley costed seventeen silver yuan. Housing conditions in Lhasa and Shigatse were also affected. In these places, the government bought 80 percent of the houses under aristocrats' names, resulting in the aristocrats' eviction of their poor tenants. These developments caused across-the-board discontent in Tibetan society. Yet, in such an atmosphere, the TWC still decided to begin pilot reform projects in the winter of 1956 and spring of 1957. In Zhang's words, CCP cadres "forced the Chamdo people's representative conference to adopt [reform] resolutions." Consequently, the three monasteries in Lhasa made petitions opposing reform, and "the centrifugal tendency of the Dalai clique increased."[57]

These developments would at worst have been "defects" in the TWC's "reform achievements" if Beijing had wanted to continue the "new phase." But now, following the new orientation of suspending reform in Tibet, Deng and his colleagues appeared shocked by these facts. Aside from the scandalous recruiting of elements of social vices into the reform work, even the payment to elementary school students sounded incredulous to CCP officials in Beijing. Deng raised the issue to another level:

> We are full of ideas about standardization [*zhengguihua*], but they [Tibetans] did not want standardization. Our way of doing things in Tibet would ruin the state [*wangguo*] in three years. This was [a mistake of] subjectivity, and such a superstructure was incompatible with that social foundation. . . . We put more than fifty officials in a *dzong* but each *dzong* used to have just one or

two officials in the past. Only in this fact we may see that the Dalai [Lama]'s system is better than ours. If we follow the same way in the country, the whole country would demise.⁵⁸

Yet, no matter how Deng stressed the seriousness of the CCP's erroneous endeavors in the previous year, all the problems identified in the Central Secretariat meetings were considered tactical in nature. No one questioned fundamentally the "party line" about reform. Probably that was why, without involving "party line," the issue about who was responsible for the 1956 fiasco was treated lightly by the Central Secretariat.

2. Whom to Blame?

Nevertheless, the question as to who was responsible for the 1956 "mistakes" of "great development" has been fiercely polemical inside the CCP ever since 1958. The current official historical narrative in the PRC firmly assigns the blame to Fan Ming, but this is vehemently rejected in Fan's memoir and also equivocated in some other TWC officials' recollections.⁵⁹ In many historical cases of "policy mistakes" openly acknowledged by the CCP, the alleged perpetrators of such "mistakes" were often scapegoated for the sake of maintaining the impeccable image of the CCP leadership or Mao himself. Fan Ming, for all his faults, was no exception. In 1958, Fan was denounced for his "anti-Party activities" by the TWC so that Beijing could turn a page in its relationship with Lhasa. Some twenty years later, the Central Organizational Department of the CCP would have to reconsider the verdict in the spirit of "correcting unjust, false, and wrong cases" of the reform era. In its draft report for rehabilitating Fan, the Organizational Department attributed the "great development" to a decision made collectively by the TWC. But in its final conclusion on the Fan Ming case, the Organizational Department simply stated that Fan had made the mistake of "rushing forward" in implementing "great development," leaving out the questions of whether the "great development" itself was wrong and who should be held responsible for it.⁶⁰ Indeed, during the meetings of the Central Secretariat in the spring of 1957, neither Fan individually nor the TWC collectively was held responsible for the "erroneous" developments of 1956.

In a February report to the CCP central leadership and in Zhang Jingwu's oral presentations in Beijing in March, the TWC did initially make self-criticism. The TWC admitted that in 1956 it had "rushed forward" and, as a result, caused a "situation of 'blowing strong wind ahead of the storm'" with respect to reform.⁶¹ It was, however, Deng Xiaoping who set the tone for assigning responsibility for the 1956 "mistakes." In a conversation with TWC officials in February, Deng suggested that the TWC should indeed examine problems in its work because the Center had not issued directives on those steps of expansion. On the other hand, the TWC "should not alone be held responsible" for the situation. In Deng's opinion, the orientation for reform was not wrong. The main problem was that, because of the poor conditions of communication and transportation, Tibet was still too far away from the Han "heartland" (*neidi*) and a reformed Tibet could not have been sustained. Whereas Deng talked about the sustainability of a Tibet reformed by whatever means, Li Weihan stayed close to the publicized CCP scripts, putting Tibet's geographical remoteness into historical and social perspective. Li noted that, historically, Tibet had been "independent" (*duli*) of China for a very long period, and the Seventeen-Point Agreement, despite the CCP's efforts in the past six years, had neither altered the Lhasa administration nor changed Tibetan society. Since both the upper stratum and the mass remained "deeply alienated from us," conditions for peaceful reform did not exist in Tibet. Therefore, in Li's words, "the problem about last year is not that too much was done too quickly," implying that a more fundamental misjudgment had been made above the level of the TWC.[62] In May, at a Politburo meeting, Peng Zhen put the matter in even plainer terms:

> Reform or not was not the issue. The issue was that conditions for reform were not ready. Ngabö was right on target in saying: "[Reform] was feared by those at the top [of the Tibetan society] and unwanted by those at the bottom." The Tibetan question is about nationality as well as religion. What advantages could be gained with reform? Currently this is the situation for our work. As for the change of the orientation, it dawned upon us only gradually. Nobody ought to be held responsible [for the "mistakes" of 1956]."[63]

Thus, in the spring of 1957, senior CCP officials in Beijing came very close to admitting that, in launching a "new phase" in Tibet in 1955 and 1956, the CCP leadership had collectively misjudged the Tibetan situation. Reform preparations for synchronizing Tibet with the rest of China should not have been attempted prematurely. A logical conclusion, however, was never articulated: what happened in 1956 was mainly a strategic error made in Beijing, not a tactical mistake committed by the TWC in the field. During the Central Secretariat's deliberation, because of this unstated understanding, neither Fan nor other TWC officials were censured for being overzealous in pushing reform. Throughout the Central Secretariat's deliberation, Fan enjoyed the Center's trust just as did the other TWC officials. During a meeting on March 6, Deng made a special point that discussion of concrete steps for discontinuing reform in Tibet should wait for Fan's arrival in Beijing. In May, Fan even participated in a Politburo meeting on Tibet and brought Beijing's decisions back to Lhasa.[64]

3. Why Retreat?

Now that pulling back from Tibet became necessary, the Central Secretariat was tasked with providing an explanation to the party in particular and to the country in general. Deng identified four causes of the Tibetan predicament. First, historical segregation: "the Tibetans have never been conquered by the Han, and no change whatsoever took place during the Kuomintang period." Second, the Dalai Lama–Panchen Lama discord: although returning the Panchen Lama to Tibet was the right thing to do, mutual grievances between the two Tibetan cliques had continued. Third, discontent and malicious agitation in society: people who were "deeply religious" or harboring "ideas for independence and nationalist emotions" were manipulated by agents of hostile governments who wanted to provoke a war against the CCP. Fourth, the Indian government's intention: although Nehru might want only to encourage centrifugal tendencies within Tibet and not to support Tibetan independence, the policy carried out by his subordinates could be more dangerous. Therefore, given domestic and international conditions combined, at the moment Tibet could not carry out reform without risking war. During the discussions, more than once Deng said: "The Tibet question does not just concern our state but also has international ramifications. We must not change our idea about reforming Tibet. But carrying out reform now would certainly start a war. War can be won but is not worth the effort. What is the advantage to reform [with war]?" Always mindful of cost efficiency, Deng stressed: "The most important point is not to fight a war for the sake of reform. Let's keep this system of 1.2 million serfs, and it will not hinder our construction of socialism."[65]

In terms of the CCP's mass-oriented politics, Deng's remark sounded almost callous in leaving more than a million Tibetan "laboring people" to their own devices in the supposedly miserable life of "serfdom." CCP leaders' commitment to transforming Tibet into a "people's democracy" and overturning Tibetan "serfdom" reflected the Marxist vein of CCP ideology. Because of the unique conditions of Tibetan society, Beijing had pragmatically delayed its revolution in Tibet for six years under the Seventeen-Point Agreement. In 1957, as the CCP was about to launch the rest of China into a frenzied "leap forward," it was extraordinary that Beijing again showed willingness to postpone its mission of "liberating" the Tibetan people. Deng's remark was indictive that the Seventeen-Point Agreement had actually allowed Tibet to remain an outsider to the PRC system, and that advancement of the CCP program in the rest of the PRC was always the top priority. Now that convergence between medieval Tibet and socialist China appeared premature, the awkward coexistence between the two systems had to continue for a while.

Still, CCP leaders felt it necessary to justify the halting of their "liberation" mission in Tibet with some historical precedents of autonomy. The two precedents brought up in the Central Secretariat discussions had nothing in common: one was Emperor Qianlong's Twenty-Nine-Article Ordinance of the late eighteenth century; the other was the Far Eastern Republic of Soviet Russia in the early 1920s. In CCP officials' opinion, Tibet in the mid-1950s was actually more "progressive" than the Soviet Far Eastern Republic. Deng admitted that the CCP leadership had not had any idea about Qianlong's ordinance when the Seventeen-Point Agreement was drafted. But now, in 1957, he asserted that except for its reference to reform, the 1951 agreement was more lenient than Qianlong's ordinance.[66] Obviously neither precedent was comparable to Beijing's waiting game in 1957. In the wake of World War I, Russian Bolsheviks created the makeshift Far Easter Republic to fend off foreign intervention from the direction of Northeast Asia, not to deal with the ethnopolitical aspirations of a frontier people. Qianlong's ordinance was, by contrast, a supposedly permanent arrangement in the tributary age of East Asian history. Nevertheless, the two precedents, one from international communist history and one from Chinese history, satisfied CCP leaders' proclivity toward the justificatory use of history.

4. How to Retreat?

Aside from attesting to the ideological and tactical correctness of Beijing's retreat in 1957, the Central Secretariat brought up the Far Eastern Republic and Qianlong's ordinance also to establish a criterion of minimal control over Tibet. Neither, however, provided a ready formula for Beijing's retreat. Participants in the March discussions in Beijing had to decide whether they wanted to just slow down the CCP's sociopolitical advance in Tibet or to beat a drastic retreat. Initially, the TWC intended the former. In its February report to Beijing, the TWC stated that its orientation for 1957 would combine "measured contraction, consolidation and improvement, and steady advance." This proposition was overly optimistic to leaders in Beijing. What should be adopted, in Deng's words, was an "orientation of determined contraction."[67] This would mean, first and foremost, a significant reduction in CCP personnel. The TWC's original plan was to reduce Han cadres and trainees to four thousand. But soon this plan had to be revised according to a message from Mao himself. In Deng's words, "A reduction to 3,000 [cadres] would be a big move of dismount [*xiama*], but the Chairman wanted to keep even less."[68] Hence the TWC revised its numbers: 13,422 Han cadres and workers would leave immediately, and eventually 1,797 would remain; the number of Tibetan cadres and trainees would be reduced from 8,000 to 2,000; 13,000 PLA troops would stay, stationed in 12 locations. Yet Deng proposed even smaller numbers, suggesting that eight thousand troops and only five hundred cadres should stay in Tibet permanently. Many years later, information published in the PRC indicates that the so-called "great dismount" (*da xiama*) in 1957 reduced Han and Tibetan cadres, workers, and trainees from 45,000 to 3,700, or by 92 percent. As for PLA troops, 70 percent were pulled out and fewer than thirteen thousand remained in various locations in Tibet.[69]

Such massive evacuation of personnel was consequential. Not only would the 1956 reform preparations be abolished, but some results of the TWC's work in previous years would also be scaled back. The Central Secretariat expected that many offices would be closed and many projects and enterprises discontinued, contracted, or turned over to the Preparatory Committee of the Tibetan Autonomous Region.[70] In other words, culturally, economically, and financially speaking, the CCP authorities would become maximally disengaged from Tibetan affairs. There were, however, two exceptions. First, having gleaned from Tibetan society several thousand "cadres," who were young, relatively educated, and supposedly willing to work for reform, the CCP authorities would not let them perish in a political environment of Tibet that could be expected to turn even more "reactionary" than before. As Deng put it, in the future, the party would no longer interfere with personnel issues inside Tibet, but for now, all the Tibetan cadres and trainees recruited in 1956 should be allowed to go to the heartland. They should come on a voluntary basis and be allowed to return to Tibet anytime. In Chinese provinces, they could enter schools or take up jobs. In Deng's words, "For those who come to the heartland, we will take care of them to the end. If reform does not happen in the next fifty years, we will take care of them till their death." In the summer of 1957, this decision resulted in more than three thousand young Tibetans' being enrolled in schools or training programs in Sichuan, Gansu, and Beijing. Most of them would return to Tibet two years later when "democratic reform" began along with the PLA's suppression of Tibetan revolts.[71]

Second, coal and borax mines in Tibet would continue to operate. Borax in particular was a strategic mineral in high demand during the Cold War years. It was indispensable for aviation, rocket, and nuclear technologies and consequently became one of the key links between Soviet interest and Tibet. A string of lakes in northern Tibet had rich deposits of borax. During the three tumultuous years 1957–1959, production and export of borax from Tibet grew steadily. In 1957, 1,200 tons were produced, and in the next two years, 28,050 and 43,813 tons, respectively, were transported out of Tibet. In 1960, as the Sino-Soviet relationship was deteriorating, borax became one of the means Beijing used to repay its debts to Moscow. Zhou Enlai personally asked Zhang Guohua to accomplish the task of producing and transporting 100,000 tons of borax in 1960, an amount larger than the total for the past three years. By the end of the year, 110,106 tons were moved out of Tibet, a "miracle" not uncommon in Mao's China—a "political triumph" achieved at the expense of rational economic and financial calculations, with ingenuity and individual sacrifice of the rank and file who participated in the operation. In that year, rushed transportation caused 589 traffic accidents, wounding 172 and killing 27.[72]

Although officials at the Central Secretariat meetings agreed that a retreat of massive scale was necessary, for a while they could not reach a consensus on the scope of the retreat. While *jigou xiama* (institutional dismount) and *shiye xiama* (enterprise dismount) were to be carried out, should *zhengzhi xiama* (political dismount) be implemented as well? As "democratic reform" was to be postponed to the west of the Jinsha River for a lengthy period, should reform be suspended as well to the east of the river?

Initially, the idea of "political dismount" was broached for the purpose of discontinuing TWC branches at the *dzong* level and abolishing CCP organizations in locations where PLA troops would no longer be stationed.[73] Then, at the meeting on March 5, Li Weihan suggested that both "enterprise dismount" and "political dismount" be considered. Deng appeared in agreement: "The Dalai [Lama], Panchen [Lama], and Chamdo [areas] should all be considered [for retreat] in political terms. We will retreat in practice, and the form of our retreat should be acceptable to them as well." Li put "political dismount" in two concrete steps: reinstatement of the two *sicao* (acting Silön, or executive ministers of the Kashag), whom the Dalai Lama had dismissed in 1952 at the TWC's request, and legalization of the "people's assembly" that had been banned simultaneously with the *sicao*'s dismissal. The symbolic significance of such measures would be enormous. The Tibetans could understand them to mean, in Deng's words, that "we [CCP] were defeated and kicked out by them." The Central Secretariat was understandably hesitant in moving in that direction. Xi Zhongxun's question was typical: "Even though our general purpose is to get out of the current predicament, should we give up what has already been gained politically?" The meetings on March 5 and 6 could not reach a conclusion about "political dismount" and had to leave the subject for further deliberation.[74]

The Central Secretariat was also vexed by the apparent discrepancy between Beijing's plan for retreating from Tibet and the ongoing reform war in western Sichuan. Originally, Beijing had intended to use reform on the eastern side of the Jinsha River to encourage changes on the western side. As far as Tibet was concerned, however, the intended function of the reform model in western Sichuan was never certain. Initially CCP officials imagined the reform in western Sichuan as a beneficial inducement to Lhasa. Soon after the reform turned into a war, the situation of western Sichuan stood as a warning to Lhasa for having a "genuine reform." In 1957, however, Beijing had to contemplate resynchronizing its policy steps on the two sides of the Jinsha River the other way around—that is, how the new no-reform policy in Tibet would reshape the reform policy in western Sichuan. At the March 5 meeting, when reporting the TWC's plan for retreat from Tibet, Zhang Jingwu suggested that because the regions on the two sides of the river were actually "in one" (*yiti*) in terms of religion and ethnicity, policy orientations and measures in respect to reform in these areas ought to be kept "generally in concert" (*dati yizhi*). In supporting Zhang Jingwu's contention that the two Tibetan regions had strong mutual influence, Zhang Guohua pointed out that, according to Ngabö, who had talked to Tibetan expatriates during his recent trip to India, the rebellions in western Sichuan were directed by Kalimpong and Lhasa. To the two Zhangs' remarks, Deng's immediate reaction was, "the so-called 'generally in concert' could mean the orientation of no reform for six years (on the western side of the river as well as the eastern side)." But should this orientation really be applied to western Sichuan? Deng did not have a definitive answer right away but expressed willingness to "consider the issue of Xikang [western Sichuan] from the angle of Tibet." Other senior officials' opinions varied. For instance, whereas Song Renqiong was opposed to stopping the reform in western Sichuan, Peng Zhen suggested that a choice could be made among a real retreat, a "phony reform" (*jia gai*), and a continued reform in the region. Li Weihan was ambivalent. Although admitting that all areas of the "Tibetan nationality" must be considered together, Li contended that the east (western Sichuan), the middle (Chamdo), and the west (area under the Kashag) did not have to follow the same set of policies. In particular, "the conditions on the eastern side of the River are different," and "it would be hard to explain [*hen nanshuo*] why the eastern side of the River could not be reformed."[75]

Sichuan officials did not participate in the March discussions in Beijing. They nevertheless played a key role in affecting Beijing's decision on the two difficult issues just described. Obviously privy to the retreating mood of the Central Secretariat meetings, as mentioned in chapter 3, on March 5 the CCP Sichuan Committee filed a report with Beijing that made a strong argument for continuing the reform in western Sichuan. In listing reasons about how the "fundamental interest of the Tibetan people" would be served by continuing the reform in western Sichuan, Sichuan officials suggested that "if the Center still considers making concessions to Tibet," then the southern half of Garzê might postpone reform to a future time. But, they contended, a complete stop of "democratic reform" would have serious consequences not only for Garzê but also for Tibet on the other side of the river.[76] On March 7, Deng went to Mao's place to report what had transpired at the Central Secretariat meetings. On the same day, after reading the Sichuan report, Mao put his opinion in writing: "I believe that [we] should agree with this orientation [proposed by Sichuan officials]."[77]

Mao's opinion was final not only for the reform in western Sichuan but also for the notion of "political dismount" in Tibet. At the meeting the next day, Deng declared: "The question about continuation of the reform in Xikang [western Sichuan] has been settled, and the Tibet work must be considered in the context of continued the reform in Xikang." A delicate change occurred in the atmosphere of Central Secretariat discussions. Having learned about Mao's opinion, participants in the discussions realized that concessions to Lhasa must not go too far. "Political dismount" was consequently removed from their agenda. As Deng clarified, the two dismissed *sicao* should be won over and could be appointed to positions in a proposed Tibetan political consultative council, but they must not be reinstated and the Tibetan "people's assembly" must not be legitimized, no matter what. Li Weihan was also unequivocal: "As for the issue of the eastern side of the River, I support continuation of the reform. As for the issue of Tibet, the general goal is national unity. But class struggles must be carried out in dealing with hostile classes, and national unity cannot be achieved without class struggles."[78]

5. How Long to Wait?

Having planned for a nearly comprehensive retreat from Tibet, the Central Secretariat also had to decide how the remaining work in Tibet should continue in the years to come. Deng characterized the task as *chongxin bushu, lingqi luzao* (redeployment to make a fresh start).[79] *Lingqi luzao*, literally "to start a new kitchen," was interestingly reminiscent of Mao's famous prescription for PRC diplomacy in 1949.[80] Whereas in 1949 Mao meant to separate PRC foreign relations from those of the ROC, in 1957 Beijing reoriented its Tibet policy in a search for continuity. In this case, no "new kitchen" would really be started. As Li Weihan indicated, "The retreat from Tibet should not go beyond the [Seventeen-Point] Agreement. The Agreement was surpassed [*chaoguo*] in the past few years, but retreat must not be made where such surpassing did not occur."[81] So the "old kitchen" of the Seventeen-Point Agreement would be kept. But because it was precisely under the old formula that Beijing had reached the current impasse in Tibet, what would a fresh start really mean?

Actually, Li's point about returning to the 1951 agreement was moot. Beijing's new orientation of "no reform for six years" already surpassed the Seventeen-Point Agreement. The 1951 agreement, lacking a timetable for reform and a date for its own expiration, appeared to connote a timeless tolerance of the Tibetan status quo. The question in 1957, then, was how to time the new round of the waiting game. For CCP leaders, the publicized "six years" conception was neither clear nor final. In early 1957, in setting China's territorial sovereignty over Tibet as the bottom line of their concessions, top CCP officials appeared ready to accept that such sovereignty could remain just nominal for a period much longer than the publicized "six years."

At the Central Secretariat meetings, both Deng and Chen Yun mentioned that, in Mao's opinion, reform in Tibet could be postponed to the twenty-first century. As Deng put it, such a long delay was necessary not only because conditions for reform did not exist in Tibet but also because "Southeast Asia can hereby be reassured for a considerable period." At one point, Deng used a Chinese idiom to depict the situation: *liu de qingshan zai, bupa mei chai shao* (while there is life, there is hope; or, literally, as long as green mountains are still there, one need not worry about lack of firewood). In Chinese culture, the idiom is usually applied to a most desperate situation. Obviously CCP leaders were extremely disheartened by the retreat from Tibet, but they were still resolved to carry it out. Their privately expressed willingness to live with the old Tibet for another "fifty or a hundred years" has left room for scholarly speculation about historical possibilities.[82] What if the first generation of PRC leaders had put this idea into practice?

Counterfactual speculations in this regard cannot go very far, though. Although a majority of top CCP leaders supported Mao's notion of not reforming Tibet during the twentieth century, this was an "internally understood" orientation that has since remained a secret.[83] In other words, Mao and his comrades did not even rhetorically demonstrate their willingness to tolerate Tibet's unique existence within the PRC for a meaningfully lengthy period. Imaginably, a promise of "no reform for fifty years" could have had a much stronger soothing effect on the anxious Tibetan society than Beijing's promise of "no reform for six years." The reasons for CCP leaders' keeping their rather liberal timetable to themselves cannot be documented. Sensible speculations can, however, be attempted. First, the idea of no reform in the twentieth century, if publicized, would have been out of sync with Beijing's social revolutionary agenda and too difficult to explain to the CCP's domestic and international allies. Otherwise, the promise of "no reform for six years," or even no reform during the Third Five-Year Plan, still included Tibet in the CCP's general timetable for socialist construction in China. Second, bent on making revolutionary changes in Tibet as well as in the rest of China, bringing about a range of practical advantages for the CCP, Mao and his associates naturally preferred the flexibility provided by the "six years or longer" formula to the restraints embedded in a "fifty to a hundred years" promise. Third, the notion of not reforming Tibet in the twentieth century may just have reflected CCP leaders' reluctant, momentary resignation to the Tibetan reality more than a carefully deliberated long-term strategy. In a word, in dealing with the Tibetan question in the late 1950s, CCP leaders had a mind-set rather different from Deng Xiaoping's in the 1990s, when he would formulate a "no change for fifty years" orientation for Hong Kong.

In 1957, CCP leaders preferred to administer a short intermission in the Tibetan melodrama. Given the tumultuous conditions on the two sides of the Jinsha River, even the six-year waiting period might not run its course. In the CCP's dialectical reasoning, a premature termination of the six-year formula would be at once the worst-case and best-case scenario. A consensus reached at the Central Secretariat discussions was that during the next six years the Central People's Government had to continue to control diplomacy and national defense as far as Tibet was concerned. It was anticipated, however, that such control would be difficult to enforce because, to a certain degree, Tibet would return to its previous isolation from the rest of China. It was agreed that the Qing-Zang Highway must be protected and continue to operate because of its importance for transporting borax. But the Kang-Zang Highway was a different matter. Actually, Deng desired to see it fail, saying, "It would be the best if the Kang-Zang Highway collapses." In particular, "it would be beneficial to us if they [Tibetans] attack and destroy the Kang-Zang Highway." Deng estimated that, spared the burden of maintaining the highway, Beijing would be able to save eighteen million yuan each year. But financial considerations were merely secondary to Deng and his comrades. They focused on the possibility that the Tibetans would initiate an armed revolt in spite or because of Beijing's retreat.[84]

Indeed, revolt was the only type of Tibetan agency that CCP officials could envision for the next interval. Deng talked repeatedly at the meetings about the possibility of war:

> Tibet may serve as a buffer zone, but it will be entirely a different matter if war breaks out. Reform will not be implemented for a long period, but if war breaks out we will fight to the end. They [the Tibetans] should be the side to start war against us.
>
> ... If they make war for establishing an independent state, reform will have to be implemented.
>
> ... Under the current orientation [of no reform], some people will raise their tails ten thousand *zhang* [one *zhang* = 3.3333 meters] high, but they cannot get out of the palm of our hand. It does not matter if they fight a big war for independence. They may also possibly fight a small war.
>
> ... Independence is not permitted. We must fight over this issue. We must fight [over this issue] even after retreat. In the wake of a war a few more Ngabö may emerge.[85]

At the time Ngabö Ngawang Jigmé was the CCP's most trusted Tibetan official in the Kashag. At one of the meetings, Zhang Guohua conveyed a piece of intelligence from Ngabö: reactionary Tibetans knew that they would not be able to gain independence by means of war, but they nevertheless wanted to provoke fighting in order to embarrass Beijing internationally and to get more American dollars from secret American agents.[86]

The issue of war evoked a most interesting ambivalence among CCP officials. Whereas military power was always Beijing's trump card in dealing with Lhasa, in the spring of 1957 CCP leaders held the notion that they would be able to regain "political initiative" (*zhengzhi zhudong*) in Tibet only if armed conflict was avoided.[87] This notion was not convincing, however, because of the ongoing reform war on the eastern side of the Jinsha River. Deng's words, quoted previously, left the door to war wide open: What if political initiative could be regained through war? By keeping the "internally understood" long waiting period to themselves and advertising a much shorter interval, Beijing nearly forfeited the luring effect of a waiting game. As the waiting side, Beijing did not appear very patient; as the waited side, the Tibetans were not given a decent opportunity for procrastination. Especially because, between 1951 and 1957, the Tibetans had already had six years of close contact with the CCP, Beijing's promise of waiting for six more years could hardly have sounded reassuring to the anxious Tibetan society. The Tibetans might indeed not want to sit on their hands for six more years and, as Deng expected, would overturn the waiting game by revolting. What if, after correcting its "errors of excessiveness," the CCP was still presented with a war started by the Tibetans? In such a contingency, Beijing would gain political advantage in two counts: it could shed much more easily the responsibility for demolishing the by now enervated Seventeen-Point Agreement, and the war would usher "democratic reform" into Tibet.

6. What to Wait For?

Ultimately, the question about Beijing's new waiting game was: What were the CCP leaders waiting for this time? For the new waiting period, the CCP leadership planned to take a stance in Tibet neither seeking nor evading war. But in what direction would the Tibetan situation go? How should the CCP continue to work in Tibet after the retreat? How should the CCP react differently to a "big war" or a "small war"? Specifically, what would be a *casus belli* for the PLA in Tibet? All these questions, arising from Beijing's policy deliberations in early 1957, pointed to a deferral strategy significantly different from Beijing's gradualist approach in the previous period.

In the CCP's policy analyses, the Tibetans were never viewed as a monolithic group. The Central Secretariat, therefore, tried to predict who among the Tibetans would make what move in the years to come. In the Central Secretariat discussions, the Tibetans were categorized into three types of clusters: first, "leftist, centrist, and rightist"; second, "upper, middle, and lower"; and third, "eastern, central, and western" (*zuo, zhong, you; shang, zhong, xia; dong, zhong, xi*).[88] The first was a category of political stances, a measure of "patriotism." The second was one of social classes. The third included the three political zones on the western side of the Jinsha River, with the Chamdo area as the eastern zone, the Lhasa area the central, and the Shigatse area the western. These categories reflected a familiar trichotomy of the CCP's united-front strategy, which usually set out to rely on the leftist activists to mobilize the lower classes in a struggle both to win over the centrist groups and middle classes and to defeat the rightist enemies and upper classes.

This norm of CCP operations was, however, not what the Central Secretariat recommended for Tibet in the years to come. Because the usual steps of "mass mobilization" and training of activists, including recruiting members for the Youth League and the Communist Party, would be suspended during the waiting period, the Central Secretariat professed continuation of "mass work" but could not enumerate specifics except literacy education. Thus, as Deng put it, in the years to come the political tasks of the TWC would be limited to working on "foreign affairs and united front with the upper stratum." As for those political, class, and geographical clusters identified by the Central Secretariat, the TWC would pursue conservative goals with respect to the "leftists," "lower classes," and relatively "progressive" areas of Chamdo and Shigatse, which meant providing some protection and consolation to these groups. In the meantime, the "centrists" and "rightists," middle and upper classes, and Lhasa would be watched closely. What emerged from the Beijing discussions were two possible scenarios that could end the waiting game: either a war started by "reactionary elements" or "internal discords of hostile classes." As for the latter, Li Weihan suggested that "internal contradictions in Tibet be fostered." Peng Zhen predicted that "as the Han-Tibetan contradiction becomes eased, internal contradictions in Tibet will naturally grow." Deng was consistently a ruthless tactician: "We cannot be responsible for the internal problems [of Tibet]. Let it rot so that we can put things back in order afterwards [*rang ta fulan, lan le zai shoushi*]."[89] Gone was the spirit of cooperation embedded in the Seventeen-Point Agreement.

The "no reform for six years" stratagem, therefore, did not mean a fixed six-year interval before Beijing would renew reform in Tibet. It was an open-ended ploy anticipating missteps by Beijing's adversaries. As Li Weihan put it, "no reform for six years" was both a "central idea" and an "excuse."[90] The stratagem was to kick the ball into the Tibetans' court. It was expected that Beijing would then resume reform in Tibet either via suppression of an anti-CCP Tibetan revolt or through interference in an internally disintegrated Tibet. Either way, in the minds of CCP leaders, Beijing would regain "political initiative." This line of action emerged in the March discussions but would never be articulated in any "Central directive." Instead, it became an understood orientation. At the end of October, Deng called another meeting to discuss the Tibetan question, which included officials of the Central United Front Department, the State Nationality Affairs Commission, and the TWC. If there were still questions among CCP operatives as to what to do in Tibet, Deng gave them an unequivocal answer: "The struggle with feudal aristocrats cannot be overly honest and straightforward and should let them fight over their internal contradictions." More specifically, the key was to wait patiently for chaos to happen in Tibet:

> Let reactionaries show their faces, the more exposed the better. They cannot strike us out, and we can reenter even if stricken out. The British and Americans will not send troops to Tibet. Tibet is a Chinese territory and India cannot take it away, though India may flirt with [Tibetan] aristocrats. Our posts are still too many and can be reduced. We do not have many people there, but some more can be reassigned to the heartland. Do not launch class struggle, and do not set up Party and Youth League cells in the society. Training of troops should be intensified. Our cadres should be told: first, not to fear; second, be patient. Do not be nervous and do not fear chaos. Do not seek clarification of the Tibetan situation anytime soon. They would ask us for money and for construction as soon as the situation becomes clarified. If the situation of Tibet calms down, we would be put in a disadvantageous position and the aristocrats would have a good life. Chaos would be advantageous to us, in which the aristocrats would not be able to have a good time. "No reform for six years" should be upheld and must not be rushed. The Kashag wants to centralize power, which can be achieved with our support. Our support would mean to let them assuage internal contradictions, but we should take advantage of their internal contradictions. As for those patriotic, pro-unity, and progressive forces, our support should be frequently expressed. Those pro-imperialist and reactionary elements all joined the pseudo "people's assembly," and this only made them even more unpopular. When reform begins in the future, they will be dealt with according to their political attitudes. As the reactionaries behave rampantly to a certain degree, they will enrage the mass. Take a long-term view.[91]

With these words, Deng outlined an "antagonistic gradualism" fundamentally different from the "cooperative gradualism" intended by the Seventeen-Point Agreement of 1951. Now, constructive cooperation with the Tibetan establishment around the Dalai Lama, which had been central to the 1951 agreement, was replaced with a devious hands-off approach underneath the "no reform for six years" promise. Deng's calling for further reduction of the CCP personnel in Tibet was aimed at one effect: emboldening the Tibetans with the appearance of CCP weakness.

7. The Final Decision

Deng's antagonistic stratagem was almost sabotaged. The Central Secretariat concluded its discussions of the Tibetan question on March 9. Then Deng left Beijing on March 11 and spent the next month or so inspecting a number of northwestern provinces.[92] Deng, however, left some loose ends, one of which was an unconvinced Fan Ming. Having admitted that he tried erroneously to rush forward the "great development" in 1956, in early 1957 Fan was granted a break from the frenzied Tibet work. Yet, having barely started his vacation in Nagqu (Heihe), Fan was urgently summoned to Beijing, arriving on March 8 when the Central Secretariat discussions had already been in session for a few days. Dismayed with the retreat plan set by the previous discussions, in his first but the Central Secretariat's last meeting on March 9, Fan voiced his objection to dismantling all the achievements of reform preparations in 1956 and to discontinuing every reform preparation measure. Years later, Fan recalled the tense air he caused in the meeting: "Zhang Guohua pulled my coat and asked me to sit down and stop talking. [Li] Weihan and [Xi] Zhongxun also gestured me to stop, but I did not. Not responding to what I said, Deng Xiaoping pushed over some documents on the table and said that everything had been decided already. Then he left."[93]

Fan was not intimidated by Deng. In next two weeks, while participating in a quarrelsome process of drafting concluding documents for the Central Secretariat discussions, Fan took an audacious step. On March 22, he wrote a letter to Mao to express his dissenting opinion. Neither stopped by warnings from Zhang Jingwu and Zhang Guohua against defying Deng, nor mollified by Li Weihan's reading of his letter to a small circle of officials as an alternative to delivering the letter to Mao, Fan insisted that his letter be delivered to Mao. Having failed to restrain Fan, eventually Li conceded that he had no right to withhold Fan's letter and agreed to send it.[94] In his letter, Fan contended that overestimating the difficulties of the Tibetan situation, the Central Secretariat was proposing to take excessive measures to scale back the Tibet work and adopting a passive attitude toward reform preparations in the future. Such an orientation, according to Fan, would only embolden Tibetan reactionaries and sadden Tibetan progressives, which was "unfair to the Tibetan people" and constituted "big-nationality chauvinism." As for the waiting strategy formulated by the Central Secretariat, it appeared that Fan did not comprehend or appreciate it: "It would be a paternalistic approach of kicking out a good-for-nothing son for now and expecting a prodigal's return [*langzi huitou*] in the future."[95]

Fan Ming was not opposed to Beijing's readjusted approach toward the "Dalai clique," which was long overdue in his opinion. In the new approach, he could not accept the apparent, albeit temporary, abandonment of those Tibetans who, in his opinion, were truly patriotic and progressive, mainly the

Panchen Lama group. Mao's reaction to Fan's letter remains unknown. But what happened next seems to indicate that, just as he balanced radical Sichuan officials with a moderate Tianbao amid Sichuan's reform war in 1956, Mao opted to balance the Central Secretariat consensus with a dissenting Fan Ming in the retreating scheme for Tibet in 1957. Some time in early April, Li Weihan brought the Center's, obviously Mao's, decision back to those officials who had already worked over four versions of the Central Secretariat's concluding document about the "big dismount." According to Fan's recollection years later, Li told the group that instead of a document about the "big dismount," the Center now wanted to have a new document, the "TWC's decision on the Tibet work in the future," and to append to it a TWC plan for scaling back its previous work. Fan was named the leading drafter of these documents. In addition, Li conveyed another pregnant message: "the Central Secretariat could not represent the Center." It must have been a pleasant day for Fan.[96]

On May 14, a Politburo meeting, presided over by Liu Shaoqi, approved the new documents. Mao was in Beijing at the time but did not participate in the meeting. In contrast to his personal direction of the discussion about Sichuan's reform war the previous year, Mao's absence from this important meeting on a retreat from Tibet left room for the historian to speculate.[97] At the meeting, Zhou Enlai and Liu Shaoqi made comments, translated below, that shed additional light on CCP leaders' thinking about the Tibetan question at the time:

> *Zhou:* We should link the notion of a greater Tibetan autonomous region with that of [Tibetan] independence. *Apparently, the right wing started the idea of a greater Tibetan region. The idea may lead to independence. This is a circuitous way followed by reactionaries. We can influence the western side of the [Jinsha] River only if it is separated from the eastern side. Advocacy for a greater Tibetan region is a step toward independence. The idea of greater Tibet must be repudiated according to history. Xikang already became a province in the wake of gai tu gui liu [i.e., bureaucratization of native chieftains]. The Simla Conference [of 1914] recognized China as the suzerain state [zongzhuguo] of Tibet as well.* The constitution [of the PRC] has relevant stipulations and cannot be changed. The minorities wear a big hat that is called the People's Republic of China whereas the Han people wear a small hat. The big includes the small and vice versa, and the two sides are mutually equal. We do not want to learn from the federation approach of the Soviet Union. According to the regulations of the State Council, the east, middle, and west [i.e. the Chamdo, Lhasa, and Shigatse areas] are included [into Tibet], but the western [sic; eastern] side of the River is not included. The idea to include the western [sic; eastern] side of the River must be blocked. The purpose of reforming the eastern side [of the River] is to influence the western side. Large-scale assistance must go slowly.
>
> ...

Liu: Reform should not be mentioned if we do not want to do it, and reform can be carried out only under mature conditions. *Historically the Soviet Union helped Outer Mongolia to reform, but the reform did not bring many benefits because conditions were not yet ready.* Reform must be implemented with ready conditions and experiences. For now, contractions cannot be avoided. *Too many people entered [Tibet] in the past, and various branches of the Central Government behaved a bit anarchically.* In the future, an office should be designated to supervise personnel matters when various places and government agencies send their people to work in Tibet. Rebellions took place on the eastern side of the River because of reform. Reform on the western side would most likely cause rebellions as well. *We should hold them [Tibetan upper classes] responsible for the contraction: you wanted reform in the past and we sent people in; now you do not want reform and hence the contraction.* What is happening now is a contraction, but not our failure or inability to hold our ground. All the problems come down to reform. *Our work for several years has benefited the mass somewhat and has also gained some support from the mass. But the mass and the upper stratum have not yet become mutually antagonistic. We should make clear explanation to the mass: we have difficulties, but your difficulties are even greater. Massacre of a massive scale will probably not happen. The mass should be told to learn how to act underhandedly, and the mass should be led to complain about the right wing.* How can it be sustained when each student is offered thirty silver dollars? We retreat not because we cannot hold our ground, or the situation is deteriorating, but because conditions for reform are not ready. Long-term but indirect preparations should be made. The state cannot afford to take care of 70,000 people [working in Tibet]. Now we should just make friends and provide some medical services. This will make the right wing happy. Some of them will however not be happy because they can no longer make money. It is unnecessary for all the students to come to the heartland. But if the upper stratum wants to keep people and vehicles, we will carry out reform. *Reform will be carried out wherever rebellions take place. Reform can be carried out relatively easily wherever rebellions take place.* Intelligence work should not be secretive but should be done through the united-front work. The document prepared by the [Tibet] Work Committee can be approved in principle. The policy toward the Panchen [Lama] will not be changed; neither will the wording of the policy. *If our counterpart starts war, we may react. The People's Liberation Army will not stand by. If we fight, we will fight a comprehensive war.*[98] (emphasis added)

Zhou spoke in his two capacities as the principal diplomat and chief administrator of the PRC, probably reacting to a piece of intelligence from the Chinese Embassy in India. According to the embassy, before leaving India, the Dalai Lama explained to expatriate Tibetans his decision on continuing cooperation with Beijing, suggesting that he would be able to set up a greater Tibetan autonomous region for now and a Tibetan state in the future.[99] Despite the fact that CCP leaders had considered the intraethnic connections among all the Tibetan areas before, for the first time Zhou characterized "greater Tibet" as a "reactionary" notion harmful to the PRC. His reference to the Simla Conference at this juncture was also revealing. Having had his recent exchanges with the Indian leader Nehru, Zhou obviously understood the legal significance of the conference: it was a double-edged sword in recognizing limited Chinese authority over Tibet, on the one hand, and Tibetan autonomy, on the other. In the spring of 1957, as CCP leaders decided to allow Tibet to maintain its unique status within the PRC, Zhou's invocation of the Simla Conference indicated the extent to which, albeit briefly, Beijing was willing to retreat even in legal terms from its established relations with Lhasa.

Liu was the one who made concluding remarks for the Politburo meeting. His words, therefore, carried special authority. He added two elements to Beijing's collective deliberation of the Tibetan question. One was cognitive and one tactical. Until that time, the CCP leadership had upheld Inner Mongolia as a successful model of the party's handling of the ethnic minority question. But, in discussing Tibet at the Politburo meeting, Liu chose to use Outer Mongolia instead as a failed precedent of the Soviets' treatment of a satellite state. Although Liu's comparison of Outer Mongolia with Tibet should not be overinterpreted, his reference to Outer Mongolia and Zhou's to Simla seem to have revealed the same cognitive shift in CCP leaders' understanding of the Tibetan question—that Tibet ought to be treated as an outer realm for some time. Liu's criticism of central government agencies' chaotic involvement in Tibet in 1956, meanwhile, admitted one more time that the TWC alone should not be blamed for the rushed reform preparations in Tibet.

The tactical element in Liu's remarks was his spinning of the class politics in Tibet. During the Central Secretariat discussions, all present accepted the reality that in Tibet neither the upper classes nor the lower classes wanted reform. Liu nevertheless set the tone for Beijing's official rhetoric in the years to come: the Tibetan upper stratum should be held responsible for rejecting progress. In addition, his words on how to prepare the Tibetan masses for the party's retreat were reminiscent of typical pre-1949 CCP propaganda for preparing poor peasants in an area that the CCP was about to abandon to the KMT. Finally, Liu's concluding words reaffirmed the nucleus of the Central Secretariat's proposed stratagem: wait until the Tibetan side provides Beijing with its *casus belli*.

Following the meeting, Beijing issued a directive to the TWC—drafted, according to Fan Ming, by Xi Zhongxun and Li Weihan—to formalize its new orientation for the future.¹⁰⁰ After explaining Tibet's unreadiness for "peaceful reform," the directive stated:

> In areas of minority nationalities, the approach of using war to mobilize the mass and carry out reform can only be the last resort. Because of historical and current reasons discussed above, plus its distance from the heartland and inconvenient conditions of transportation and communication, Tibet, put into a long-term view, is not an area suitable for this approach: it would be politically disadvantageous and militarily unworthy. This approach should therefore be avoided. It would be another thing if troops have to be used to pacify armed rebellions incited by imperialists and traitors of the state.¹⁰¹

For the CCP's work in Tibet over the next six years or longer, the directive listed a number of things as either "doable" or "undoable." The "doable" category included five items: control of matters pertinent to national defense, foreign relations, and important highways; fostering of Tibetan cadres; united-front work with the upper stratum; economic or cultural enterprises welcomed by the Tibetans; and certain forms of patriotic education. None of these would have any direct function in preparing Tibet for "democratic reform" in the future because the "undoable" category was unequivocal about ending all CCP practices in relation to reform. The directive instructed the TWC:

> To reduce Tibetans' suspicion of the Han to the greatest extent, and to relax tensions in Tibet, we must firmly realize these: First, stop and end all preparations for reform. Second, not interfere in internal affairs of Tibet. Third, not recruit Party members in the society. Fourth, not initiate construction projects that are not urgently needed and supported by the upper and lower stratums of Tibet.¹⁰²

To Fan Ming, these "five doables" and "four undoables" constituted the very essense of the Center's decision on retreating from Tibet while "not contracting the [Tibet] work comprehensively." The decision therefore nullified the "big dismount" notion of the Central Secretariat. This was a policy for "indirect reform preparations" in Tibet in the years to come. In the "TWC's decion on the Tibet work in the future" that Fan helped draft, such "indirect reform preparations" were articulated along with "more can be achieved in Chamdo and the [Panchen Lama] Khenpo area." Thus, the May 14 meeting was another moment of Fan's vindication. Zhou Enlai praised the "five doables" and "four undoables" as a good example of dialectic thinking, Peng Dehuai lauded Fan Ming for having political insight and being vigorous and experienced in nationality work, and even Deng Xiaoping had good things to say about the documents' drafting process and expressed his support for preventing "big nationality chauvinism" in the CCP's Tibet policy.[103] Fan's personal convictions and feelings aside, these elements in the May 14 decision may have reflected whatever "positive thinking" about Tibet remained in the minds of CCP leaders.

The "indirect reform preparations" insisted upon by Fan, however, would not take place. Before he brought the Center's new decision back to Lhasa, Fan Ming had a conversation with Deng Xiaoping in the latter's home. Deng let Fan narrate his general view about the Tibet question without expressing his own opinion. Instead, Deng's advice for Fan was completely about the value of compromise in CCP internal politics: "Your view and opinion may constitute the best approach while theirs [the two Zhangs'] may not be as good, but they are the faction with real power [*shilipai*]. Without their support, your best approach would just be empty words." A few months later, Deng let Fan realize what kind of real power he was dealing with. In September, a telegram from the Center instructed the TWC to stop all reform preparations, direct *and* indirect. In Lhasa, Fan could not do anything except use the code of the telegram to trace the message back to the Central Secretariat.[104] The background of the September telegram renains unclear, and the political maneuvering in Beijing can only be imagined. Nevertheless, the effect of the telegram was to decisively clear the path for Beijing's antagonistic waiting game in Tibet, the one already outlined by the Central Secretariat in March 1957. Ironically, having always contended that the Dalai Lama and the Kashag were not reliable partners in the CCP's effort in Tibet, in 1957 Fan almost undermined Beijing's preparation for a showdown with Lhasa.

On May 14, besides sending its directive to the TWC, the Politburo also issued a directive to the CCP Sichuan Committee, instructing Sichuan officials to "firmly continue" reform in the Garzê area and be fully prepared to beat back rebellions on an even larger scale by "Tibetan upper-stratum reactionaries."[105] Before long, the same "fighting and reforming" approach would be applied to Tibet when CCP leaders believed that "political initiative" had returned to their hands.

"Huge Amount of Foreign Goods"

While the new waiting period was nerve-racking for the Tibetans, neither was Beijing relaxed. On the night of August 1, Mao lost sleep. He read two poems by the Song poet Fan Zhongyan and then wrote a commentary for his wife Jiang Qing and daughter Li Ne.[106] Mao pointed out that Fan's poems combined the *wanyue* ("graceful and restrained") and the *haofang* ("bold and uninhibited") schools and therefore "never bored his readers." Then Mao launched into a commentary about human nature: "Man's mood is complex, which can be biased toward one side but is still complex. So-called complexity means unity between two opposing sides. Man's mood always contains mutually opposing elements, which is never unitary and can be dissected."[107] It cannot be known whether the Tibetan question was on Mao's mind when he was writing these words. But Beijing's Tibetan policy in 1957 combined *wanyue* and *haofang* as well: "restrained" on the western side of the Jinsha River and "uninhibited" on the eastern side.

As Mao pondered human nature via Song poems, Zhou Enlai was carrying out a complex approach to the Tibetan situation. At a symposium on nationality issues held in Qingdao in July and August, Zhou made a speech promoting "natural" and "mutual" assimilation between the Han and non-Han peoples of China for common prosperity, contending that it would be "unequal" for any ethnic group if that group were to be left in its "backward" condition and excluded from the "construction of our socialist industrial country."[108] In the meantime, at the same symposium, Zhou spoke softly with Ngabö. Zhou praised Ngabö for acting correctly in recent events and told him that he had the party's complete trust. Zhou also pointed out that the key in the Tibet work was to respect and protect the Dalai Lama. As for reform, Zhou admitted that, for the moment, Beijing "did not have a good plan." Probably encouraged by Beijing's retreat from Tibet, Ngabö made a suggestion that the region under Chief Derge, the largest administrative unit of Kham on the eastern side of the Jinsha River, be incorporated into the Tibetan Autonomous Region. Zhou rejected the idea, explaining to Ngabö that all the Tibetan areas in Sichuan, Qinghai, and Gansu should remain in these provinces so that reform in these areas would not disturb Tibet on the western side of the Jinsha River. The line between "restrained" and "uninhibited" was thus firmly drawn and could not be changed.[109]

Ngabö's suggestion was significant because it echoed what happened both inside Tibet and in the Tibetan areas of the neighboring provinces. Beijing's new orientation of "no reform for six years" had a strong impact on the Tibetan areas outside Tibet. In May, shortly after Beijing finalized its waiting policy for Tibet, the CCP Kangding Area Committee reported that the "mass" in the area were agitated by a rumor from Tibet. It was said that the Dalai Lama did not permit reform and used troops from India to beat the PLA back to Chamdo. The CCP Sichuan Committee also reported to Beijing that recently "rebellious feudal lords and slave masters" had made unreasonable demands in negotiations for suspending reform forever and withdrawing PLA troops from their areas. Two months later, a few hundred people from Qinghai, Sichuan, and Yunnan gathered in Lhasa and asked the Dalai Lama to extend Beijing's no-reform policy to all Tibetan areas.[110] Clearly, Beijing's new waiting policy caused excitement and expectations among Tibetans in all these areas, intensifying conflicts between the CCP authorities and local communities.

As Beijing's May 14 directive to Sichuan indicated, the CCP leadership had anticipated such developments. Yet, outside Tibet, the CCP wanted neither to retreat nor to wait. In 1957 and 1958, the CCP's differentiated treatments of Tibet and those Tibetan areas outside Tibet appeared even more conspicuous than before. Inside Tibet, the TWC completed all the steps of retreat by August 1957. To make the retreat authoritative, Mao sent a reassuring letter to the Dalai Lama via Ngabö, praising the Dalai Lama's return from India, admitting errors in the CCP's work in the past year, and affirming Beijing's policy of not carrying out reform in Tibet during the Second Five-Year Plan. Thus, reform in Tibet was decisively tabled. The TWC would continue to make perfunctory plans for its work in the years to come, but in practice it entered a period of dormancy.¹¹¹ In the process of discontinuing reform preparations, the TWC requested neighboring provinces to accept and train the small number of Han cadres who were designated to stay in Tibet during the waiting period, for there would not be much for them to do inside Tibet in the next six years. For these provinces, receiving and reassigning thousands of cadres withdrawn from Tibet were by no means an easy task.¹¹²

In the meantime, the CCP offensive on the eastern side of the Jinsha River was building momentum. When the so-called great dismount began in Tibet in May 1957, CCP officials in Sichuan were toggling between two supposedly erroneous stances with respect to the Tibetan religion, one being "excessive struggle" and the other "excessive peace." By the end of August, the hesitancy ended. As the TWC became dormant in Tibet, the CCP Sichuan Committee, in contrast, quickened its steps and decided that the time had arrived to end the "not touching" policy with respect to lamaist monasteries. As Sichuan officials put it, "the main object of our struggle" was to "thoroughly solve the problem of Lamaism and gradually liberate the Tibetan people from religious exploitations and spiritual enslavement."¹¹³

What Sichuan officials were doing was in sync with Beijing's general orientation in the rest of China. In early October, as the CCP's Anti-Rightist Campaign was in full gear, Ulanhu, then director of the Central Nationality Affairs Commission, called for a counteroffensive against "rightists" in nationality affairs. A week later, Beijing issued a directive about how the campaign should unfold in minority areas, though renaming the campaign as one of "rectification and socialist education among minority nationalities." In 1958, the ideological thrust of the Anti-Rightist Campaign became merged with the economic frenzy of the Great Leap Forward. In minority areas, according to Liu Shaoqi, "local nationalism," "bourgeois rightists," and "separatists" were the three targets of the dual campaigns. But in CCP propaganda, the relatively integrated Xinjiang, not the actually segregated Tibet, was used as an example to illustrate what Beijing meant by "local nationalism." In October 1958, the *People's Daily* declared victory of the two campaigns in minority areas, announcing: "There should be no more question about the certainty of minority regions' ability to construct socialism in the highest speed." Allegedly, with Han people's assistance, the minority regions were "catching up" with the Han regions and "countless miracles" had been achieved in the process.[114] In such a general atmosphere, hesitation, caution, and balancing stratagems disappeared from the CCP's reform in the Tibetan areas outside Tibet.

In the summer of 1958, Zhang Jingwu and Zhang Guohua met with Mao, reporting that they had received criticisms from CCP officials elsewhere for acting very slowly in Tibet as the whole country was making a great leap forward. Mao responded that Tibet must not participate in the "leap" no matter how things in the rest of China were turned upside down.[115] The TWC was not spared "rectification," however, though the campaign was kept an "internal" one. Between November 1957 and the early months of 1958, under the name of "internal rectification," a vicious debate took place between Fan Ming and the two Zhangs. The "rectification" ended with Fan's purge for allegedly leading an "anti-Party faction." Among the numerous crimes Fan was accused of, the most serious included his responsibility for the "great development" in Tibet in the summer of 1956, opposition to Beijing's "Dalai line" in handling the Tibetan question, and resistance to "no reform for six years" in his March 22 letter to Mao.[116]

Personality conflict between Fan and the Zhangs (mainly Zhang Guohua) aside, Fan's misfortune in party politics attested to the momentary insulation of Beijing's Tibet policy from that for the rest of China. In insisting that the crux of the Tibetan question was a struggle between unifying and splitting the Chinese nation, Fan would have been a "correct" party official if he had served in a minority area other than Tibet. Just as Fan was repudiated in the TWC, Wang Feng, deputy director of the Nationality Affairs Commission, delivered a speech at an enlarged meeting of the commission. Titled "Following Socialism or Nationalism?," Wang's speech declared that although "great Han chauvinism" among Han cadres should continue to be criticized, currently the main task was opposition to "local nationalism among minority nationalities." Wang asserted that American and British imperialists were scheming with reactionary elements among minority nationalities to establish an independent Tibetan state, launching an "eastern Turkistan movement" in Xinjiang, and using the Hui areas of Qinghai and Gansu to create a "Taiwan within the mainland."[117] Wang's speech did not save Fan's political career. Yet his question, "socialism or nationalism?," would soon appear in the relations between Tibet and its neighboring provinces. Beijing could insulate "backward" Tibet from the frenzied socialist construction in the rest of China only up to a point. The sociopolitical divide that Beijing wanted to maintain for a while between Tibet and the rest of China was first ruptured by an unexpected factor—trade.

When devising the waiting strategy for Tibet, the Central Secretariat considered the issue of trade but did not foresee any trouble arising from this sector. In the "no reform" period, both domestic and foreign trade were expected to be left in the hands of Tibetans. State companies in Tibet would only take care of the needs of PLA troops and government personnel. The only exception was the tea trade, which would be "assisted" by the state because tea was consumed daily by ordinary Tibetans. Beijing's principal concern was the commercial relationship between Tibet and the inner provinces. In the process of retreat, the TWC did make the point that foreign goods should be prevented from entering Tibet, but because the PLA did not control the Tibetan borders, and Beijing did not maintain custom services along the borders, the TWC could not do anything about goods crossing the internal and external boundaries of Tibet.[118]

If trade spearheaded economic force and societal interests, it was certainly not a docile companion of state politics even in Mao's China. In Cold War international relations and China's revolutionary politics, the political effects of trade were often wrongly predicted in advance and misconceived afterwards, though trade tended to be the first victim of political discord.[119] Before the British Empire withdrew from South Asia, British Indian officials were convinced that while Tibet should be kept as a "substantial" buffer or a perfect "political vacuum" between China and India, Tibetan trade should be drawn into the Indian orbit. The Indian authorities continued the same orientation after the British left.[120] After 1949, when the United States government inserted itself into Himalayan politics, its perception of trade differed drastically from that held by the British. The United States had a very limited trade interest in Tibet, a stake of about two million dollars in Tibetan wools. American officials were actually worried about the commercial relations between Tibet and its neighbors, fearing that such relations could be used by the Chinese Communists to infiltrate into Nepal, Bhutan, and eventually India. While the drama of "peaceful liberation" was unfolding between Beijing and Lhasa in the early 1950s, the U.S. Department of State contemplated briefly using trade and other economic measures to strengthen Lhasa's resolution in resisting Beijing. But by the end of January 1952, the U.S. government decided to subject Tibet to the same foreign assets control regulations as were applied against areas controlled by the Chinese Communists. Thus, commercially and economically, Washington officially consigned Tibet to the communist side of the Cold War.[121]

This was certainly not how the Chinese Communists saw the situation. In their eyes, Tibet remained a gigantic opening through which wind of the capitalist world blew into China. In early 1954, Gansu officials reported that products of Western countries such as brand-name watches, pens, and woolen goods were entering their province via Tibet and affecting the market. For instance, an Omega watch was priced at 3,800,000 yuan (old renminbi) but was sold at 5,500,000 yuan by private merchants. At the time, Gansu officials were mainly concerned about government control of foreign currency and foreign trade, but the issue was soon put on a political platform.[122] This was done first in Sichuan. In the late summer of 1955, in its petition to Beijing for starting "democratic reform" in the province's Tibetan areas, the CCP Sichuan Committee pointed out that completion of the Kang-Zang Highway had significantly enhanced private Tibetan trade, and during the first season of the year importation from India had increased ten times. This thriving trade was interpreted as one of the augmented obstacles to the construction of socialism.[123] In early 1957, as CCP officials prepared a big retreat from Tibet, stopping the "huge amount of foreign goods flowing inward from Tibet" was listed as a task for the TWC and Tibet's neighboring provinces to accomplish.[124]

In Beijing, officials at the Ministry of Commerce saw the situation from the same "socialism versus capitalism" angle. Thinking in the same way as their counterparts in the Ministry of Public Security, Commerce officials also put minority areas into categories based on varied growth of socialism. Thus, in areas such as Inner Mongolia and Yanbian (Korean area of Jilin Province), socialist commerce, meaning state-controlled commerce, was dominant, renminbi were circulating and squeezing foreign currencies and silver dollars out, and private merchants operated only on small scales. The next category included Yi, Dai, and Yao areas of Yunnan and Guangxi, where state commerce was weak and trade still relied on small Han retailers. The Tibetan areas of Tibet, Qinghai, Sichuan, and Gansu constituted the third category. In these places, state-run commercial enterprises were rare and weak; Tibetan, Hui, and Han private merchants were quite active; but the most powerful traders were Tibetan wholesalers of foreign goods backed by aristocrats, chieftains, and monasteries. Whereas in Tibet Beijing forbade the use of the renminbi lest it disturb local finance, in other Tibetan areas foreign currencies and silver dollars circulated together with the renminbi and caused tremendous confusion in the market. At the time, Beijing's orientation toward Tibetan merchants was to limit private commerce "with great caution," aiming mainly to persuade those in foreign trade to focus on goods meeting local people's daily needs and to prevent large amount of foreign goods from entering inner provinces.[125] This approach soon became unattainable as "socialist construction" further widened the gap between Tibet and the rest of China.

In 1957, Beijing's new waiting strategy suspended expansion of the socialist economy into Tibet. Moreover, by keeping Tibet as a twilight zone between the socialist PRC and its "capitalist" neighbors, Beijing unwittingly made the region probably China's largest entrance for foreign goods and Western material influence. As CCP cadres and Han workers were leaving Tibet, the newly established Chinese postal service and transportation facilities were also scaled back.[126] Yet, ironically, as the CCP's revolution was retreating from Tibet, foot soldiers of the revolution brought "capitalism" back to PRC provinces and whetted Chinese consumers' appetite for more. In late August, just as the TWC wound up its work of discontinuing reform preparations, the Tax Bureau of Gansu received a report that cadres and workers returning to the province from Tibet were bringing back foreign goods like watches and woolen products exceeding the limitations permitted by the TWC. Similar situations occurred in other provinces that had sent cadres and workers to Tibet in 1956. Since there were no established regulations and laws on how such goods should be tariffed, some provinces started to collect tariffs on their own and some waited for Beijing to provide guidance.[127] Two months later, the problem appeared so serious that the Central Secretariat had to call a special meeting. At the meeting, Deng Xiaoping warned that if such "smuggling" from Tibet was not brought under control, Sichuan, Qinghai, Yunnan, Shaanxi, Gansu, and Xinjiang would be adversely affected. As for the "smugglers," or the official personnel of the PLA, public security apparatuses, and other states agencies involved, Deng wanted to punish them severely.[128]

Soon it became clear that these revolutionary "smugglers," most of whom took foreign goods out of Tibet just once and mainly for personal consumption, were by no means the real problem. In October, Beijing received an urgent report from Sichuan about a recent discovery: silver dollars were flowing from the province to Tibet in huge amounts. Reportedly, in 1955, 1.05 million yuan of silver were deposited in banks of Garzê and 270,000 yuan were withdrawn. In 1956, the figures were 180,000 and 210,000, respectively. The situation in the first half of 1957 was quite alarming: zero was deposited while 280,000 yuan went out. According to the Sichuan report, Tibetan merchants, monasteries, and upper-class people used yaks and sometimes trucks to transport unknowable huge amounts of silver dollars into Tibet. This money flow caused confusion in the market and economy on the eastern side of the Jinsha River. These people did not always ask for permission, and when they did, they said that the monies were for almsgiving or religious studies. In fact, a great portion of the money was used for trading purposes. On the one hand, Sichuan officials did not feel that such operations could be banned altogether because of religious reasons and the CCP relation with Tibet. On the other hand, the amount was too large to be ignored.[129]

"Silver drain" was a familiar and alarming concept in recent Chinese history. During the first decades of the nineteenth century and under completely different circumstances, the Qing court's fear of an opium-related "silver drain" finally led to the Opium War. In the late 1950s, although the problem of silver was not as serious to Beijing as it had been to the Qing court a century before, it nevertheless posed a threat to Communist power. In November 1957, the State Council adopted regulations and the CCP Central Committee also circulated a directive to deal with this new aspect of the

Tibetan question. As revealed in these documents, in the previous few months private merchants and speculators from various provinces had evaded state control of foreign trade and rushed to Tibet to buy luxury foreign goods to make exorbitant profits in the markets of various provinces. This spontaneous commercial movement was deemed detrimental to the PRC on three counts. First, it caused the country's silver dollars to flow abroad in great amounts; second, a huge volume of foreign goods entered China, undermining the domestic market and socialist construction; third, in taking advantage of this sudden upsurge of trade activities, some "bad elements," such as prostitutes, politically unreliable individuals, and people who simply wanted to escape from "socialist transformation," spirited themselves into Tibet. On the last point, the TWC reported that such newcomers had already upset Tibetan society and seriously hindered the CCP's work.[130]

A bizarre case of this type involved a certain Ouyang Hongzhi, who went to Lhasa from Lanzhou with a caravan of three trucks in May 1957 and then disappeared with the trucks after arriving in Lhasa in early July. Ouyang was a "bad element" because he had been arrested during the *Sufan* (purging counterrevolutionary) campaign in 1955. According to his confession, Ouyang joined Dai Li's secret police before 1949 and then stayed in the PRC as an undercover KMT agent. The most serious of Ouyang's confessed crimes was participation in plotting the famous yet abortive attack of Tiananmen on the PRC national day in 1950. But because his confession could not be verified, Ouyang was soon released and put under long-term surveillance until his successful escape in 1957.[131]

Just as such "bad elements" became entangled with consumerists within the CCP in disturbing Beijing's delicate waiting scheme in Tibet, the line between "trade" and "smuggling" was blurred as far as Tibetan commerce was concerned. The former was the legal flow of goods between Tibet and Chinese provinces that was subject to government regulation, but the latter, as Deng suggested, was illicit and punishable. In the late 1950s, when CCP officials pondered the issue of commercial activities involving Tibet, they typically prioritized political effects over legal niceties. Different conditions and CCP policies on the two sides of the Jinsha River made the issue of trade extremely complicated. Under Beijing's no-reform policy for Tibet, the Chinese authorities could do nothing along the Tibetan borders with neighboring countries and not much with regard to merchants based in Tibet. At the same time, the CCP tried a range of political, legal, and economic measures to shut off the newly thriving Tibetan trade from the side of the Chinese provinces.

Continuation of reform in western Sichuan was a case in point. According to Sichuan officials, "commercial capitalism" in Garzê Prefecture was a force of 2.5 million yuan, 72 percent of which was controlled by monasteries. Big Tibetan merchants, monasteries, aristocrats, and foreign capitalists were all interconnected, and this network of capitalist commerce was the principal obstacle to socialist development in the region. Sichuan officials, however, advised against a frontal attack. Although these merchants were involved in speculation and even illegally traded drugs and arms, their role in facilitating economic exchanges between the agricultural and pastoral areas of the province was irreplaceable at the moment. Furthermore, since the beginning of reform, many Tibetan merchants had moved their capital to Tibet or abroad, and, therefore, the CCP authorities should not take any drastic step now lest more capital be scared away. Accordingly, Sichuan officials recommended an approach that would weaken Tibetan merchants gradually through regulations and a carefully deployed "encirclement."[132]

Whereas Sichuan officials treated Tibetan merchants as a long-standing issue and did not highlight the recent flow of foreign goods into the province, Gansu officials had a different perspective. To Gansu, "imported British and Indian goods from Tibet" had increased in both kind and volume in the previous few years. In a brief period of July and early August 1957, for instance, several hundred Tibetan merchants came to Lanzhou and sold imported goods. These Tibetans were part of a much larger army of private importers including also Uyghur, Hui, and Han merchants and PLA and government personnel. These assorted traders brought to Gansu a wide range of foreign items, from daily and luxury consumer goods to materials such as steel, rubber, and leather. To Gansu officials, the problem was one of how to collect "tariff on merchandise imported from Britain and India." Lack of customs control along the inner border of Tibet, ambiguous regulations and irregular practices regarding duty exemption for government personnel, and language barriers with or resistance from Tibetan and Uyghur merchants were the specifics of the problem.[133]

In late November, the Ministry of Public Security held a symposium to discuss measures for implementing the CCP Central Committee's directive on dealing with problems caused by foreign goods from Tibet, which put the problem of Tibet into a national context. The symposium involved principal security officials from twenty provinces and municipalities, indicating the geographic extent of the problem. The symposium revealed that in that year, Lanzhou of Gansu and Xining of Qinghai discovered "smuggled" foreign goods worth 1.2 million and 4 million yuan, respectively, both exceeding those in previous years. Chengdu, the capital city of Sichuan, saw the same development. Unrelated to developments in Tibet, activities of smuggling in provinces along China's southeastern coasts and northeastern borders also multiplied. Although Guangdong was the most obvious route for smuggled foreign goods, security officials suspected that a significant volume of foreign goods entered inner provinces through Tibet without being detected. At the symposium, Tibet was considered together with Hong Kong and Macao, or categorized as an external base from which smuggled goods originated. Yet, unsurprisingly, officials at the symposium agreed that Tibet's "internal borders" with the PRC were not as rigid as the PRC's "external borders" with Hong Kong and Macao, and that the routes through Tibet provided the best gateways for smugglers to reach Chinese provinces. Reportedly, foreign goods smuggled through these places resurfaced in cities like Beijing, Tianjin, Shanghai, Shenyang, and Xi'an. It was estimated that in that year, two to three hundred million yuan of contraband entered China. Among the smuggled goods, the favorite items for urban buyers were watches, pen, cameras, bicycles, auto parts, razors, cigarette lighters, nylon toothbrushes, woolen fabrics, and medicines. More menacing than these consumer goods were alloy steel, narcotic drugs, telecommunication equipment, weapons, and explosives.

In this nationwide picture, Tibetan "smugglers" were profiled as rich merchants, lamas, aristocrats, and officials. In smuggling, they were joined by Han farmers, fishermen, border residents, PLA officers and government cadres, returned overseas Chinese, Koreans and Vietnamese residing in border areas, and foreign service officers of those Asian and Western countries that had diplomatic relations with the PRC. Allegedly, this army of smuggling seriously undermined state policies regarding taxation, finance, and foreign and domestic trade, harmed state enterprises producing similar goods, corrupted a small number of CCP officials, and depopulated or even ruined some agricultural cooperatives. In listing these consequences, the public security symposium believed that this smuggling was affecting the very vitality of the PRC:

> By nature, smuggling activities are not just an economic concern but have affected the political and ideological realms as well. In essence, this is a serious struggle between socialism and capitalism that will be long and complicated. The result of this struggle will have direct or indirect impact on our cause of socialist construction and reform as well as on our country's security and stability.[134]

Yet, even though CCP officials depicted the smuggled foreign-cum-Western goods as a serious threat to the PRC, Beijing was slow in establishing a stern ban against foreign goods. Actually, "smuggling" was not the real threat to socialist China, but private foreign trade was. The fact was that after eight years in power, the CCP had not yet abolished a free market in "foreign," mostly Western, goods in China. While evasion of custom duties was a type of smuggling, such activities took place along China's northeastern and southeastern borders because they were sustained by a normal free market at home. To this odd situation, Tibet made its unique contribution. After 1951, Tibet became a PRC borderland without the usual international border establishments. Neither did Tibet have a functioning administrative divide with neighboring Chinese provinces. In 1957, because of Beijing's suspension of reform preparations in Tibet, these features along Tibet's peripheries suddenly became highlighted. While "construction of socialism" was in high gear in the rest of China, Tibet became the country's last open frontier. Naturally, profit-pursuing people rushed to this last chance to make money. The public security symposium of 1957 indeed reflected Beijing's serious concern, but it mischaracterized the problem: the public security establishment of the PRC could not jump into the fray until and unless private foreign trade was outlawed.

Unsurprisingly, in mid-December 1957, or shortly after the security symposium, private foreign trade became illegal in the PRC. In pursuance of a State Council decision, the Ministry of Commerce issued a secret directive to its provincial branches, which began with this provision: "All foreign goods entering the heartland through Tibet and other border areas ought to be purchased and sold by the state, and the free market of foreign goods is now abolished."[135]

At the time, the State Council and Commerce Ministry did not treat privately imported foreign goods as contraband and did not stipulate their confiscation. The purchase-and-sale policy was designed to eventually eliminate such foreign goods from both the supplier's and the consumer's ends. State purchasing stations would be set up at port cities, international borders of Yunnan, and, notably, the *inner* boundaries between Tibet and its neighboring provinces. All privately imported foreign goods arriving at these fault lines between capitalism and socialism would be subject to duties and related taxes and then be sold to the Chinese state at prices that would just cover their cost and freight. In the case of luxury goods and items that PRC producers could adequately provide for the domestic market, the purchase prices would be protectively lower than their cost and freight. The principle of the purchasing policy was to render foreign goods *wuliketu*, or unprofitable. Then the purchased goods would be sold in designated stores at high prices in order to protect similar goods of Chinese brands. Second-hand shops would be prohibited from deaing in foreign goods, and the number of shops authorized to deal foreign goods would also be significantly reduced. Silver dollars would no longer circulate in provinces other than Tibet. Unless approved by county-level authorities, no private citizens or organizations other than the People's Bank of China would be permitted to take silver dollars into Tibet. All vehicles and individuals, Tibetan dignitaries included, crossing the boundaries between Tibet and its neighboring provinces would be subject to rigorous inspection, and vehicles owned by Tibetans would not be allowed to come to inner provinces. In the meantime, "legitimate commerce" between Tibet and Chinese provinces, defined as trade involving special local products, would be encouraged and facilitated to bring Tibet economically closer to the rest of China. It was anticipated that after these measures became effective, the free flow of foreign goods would gradually stop but smuggling would continue for even steeper profits. That would be a long struggle in which the public security apparatuses could play a key role.[136]

Aside from controlling the flow of goods from abroad, Beijing also took steps to reduce border crossing by ethnic Tibetans. At the end of 1957, the Tibet Office of Foreign Affairs (TOFA) under the TWC reported to the Ministry of Foreign Affairs that from August to November, more than 1,100 Tibetans had applied for and received travel permits to go to India, and that the vast majority of these people were from areas outside Tibet. In the past, the TOFA had usually granted foreign travel permits to Tibetans, especially to those Tibetan merchants with established trade connections in India. In light of Beijing's new policy of preventing foreign goods from entering Chinese provinces through Tibet, the TOFA proposed to tighten the issuance of travel permits, especially to Tibetans from outside Tibet. The office made two points: first, these Tibetan travelers from outside Tibet could obviously take advantage of the duty-free Tibetan boundaries and bring foreign goods back to their home provinces; and second, some of these travelers might be "bad people" trying to escape from "democratic reform" in their home areas. In July 1958, having consulted with the provinces concerned, the Ministries of Foreign Affairs and Public Security and the Central Commission on Nationality Affairs issued a joint directive on restricting ethnic Tibetans' travel to Tibet from neighboring provinces.[137]

These measures were intended to close Tibet as an entrance point for foreign goods, but their effectiveness was problematic. The desire for foreign products in Chinese society continued despite the government's association of foreign brand names with evil capitalism. After the State Council's policy of state monopoly of foreign trade became effective, commercial branches of local governments in many areas began to dispatch government purchasing agents into Tibet to buy foreign goods. These agents' achievements must have been varied, but the practice persisted throughout 1958. This led the Ministry of Commerce to issue a nationwide notice in January 1959, asking its local apparatuses to stop sending purchasing agents into Tibet; as a result of Beijing's no-reform-for-six-year policy, the ministry asserted, importation of foreign goods was basically suspended and there was not much to buy in Tibet.[138] As far as the ministry's trading firm in Tibet was concerned, the importation of foreign goods was suspended, but this was certainly not the case for the general Tibetan market. Even after Beijing took measures to shut down private foreign trade, Tibet would remain for years an attraction to audacious individuals and opportunist provincial authorities seeking either profit or foreign luxury items.

This lingering commercial significance of Tibet can be seen in a January 1965 report by the Ministry of Foreign Trade:

> On November 19, 1957, the State Council issued "regulations on controlling strictly foreign goods entering the heartland through Tibet and other border regions." Afterwards, governmental branches concerned in various areas took effective measures to improve market administration. By 1959, the once thriving free market of foreign goods and serious smuggling in various big and medium-size cities of the inner provinces were fundamentally under control. Then, in May 1962, custom services were set up in Tibet, beginning inspection of travelers' luggage, personal items, and goods entering and exiting the region. The Tibetan Autonomous Region also exercised control over foreign goods in the market. In recent years, foreign goods flowing inward from Tibet have been scarce. In view of this development, in September last year, the Finance and Public Security Departments of Qinghai withdrew their inspection stations from the Tangla [Tanggula] Mountains and Golmud [Ge'ermu], no longer checking on Tibetans and vehicles passing through.
>
> . . .
>
> Having consulted with the Ministry of Finance and the Central Bureau of Industrial and Commercial Administration, we propose the following: in view of the changed situation, in the future, any foreign commodity entering the heartland from Tibet, if being smuggled from abroad, will still be treated as such by the customs according to law (by tax bureaus where customs does not exist); foreign goods transported privately from Tibet for sale, or foreign goods brought into the heartland for personal consumption but sold privately, will be treated as violation of market regulations and handled by industrial and commercial administrations concerned. As far as unconfiscated goods are concerned, tax agencies should collect provisional commerce taxes according to regulations.[139]

The dates in the report are most interesting, indicating that until the eve of Mao's Cultural Revolution, Tibet had maintained "private" commercial connections with the outside world and was not completely integrated with the PRC's socialist economy.

During most of the Mao era, the PRC was economically segregated from the West. In particular, the daily life of ordinary people lacked material connections with the West. This situation, however, did not begin in 1949. In 1957, Beijing decided to postpone the timetable for Tibet to enter socialism, and, consequently, the question "Socialism or Nationalism?" posed by Wang Feng to all other minority areas was not applicable to Tibet. In fact, Wang's question was unexpectedly reversed: delaying socialism for Tibet had the effect of decelerating the Chinese society's material disconnection from the West.

By the mid-1960s, Tibet was finally shut off as an unwanted gateway of the PRC to the West. At the time, this development was in concert with the general direction of Beijing's policies, though two decades later, the PRC under Deng Xiaoping would strive for economic reintegration with the outside world, especially with the more advanced West.

* * *

Because of Beijing's efforts to shut the West out through Tibet and other border regions in 1957, a paper trail was created in PRC archives that showed the extent to which Chinese society was materially connected to the West as of the late 1950s. In 1957, the customs of Qinghai Province got the assignment of compiling a list of dutiable values of foreign goods entering Chinese provinces through Tibet. It must have been a tedious and complicated task, for the Qinghai authorities were not able to complete the list until July 1959, four months after conditions in Tibet had been fundamentally changed by the Lhasa revolt in March. The list of twenty-seven pages put foreign goods into twelve categories: watches and clocks, bicycles and parts, photographic equipment, fabric products, rubber and plastic products, metal products, cosmetics, medicines, stationery and instruments for sports and entertainment, tools, sewing machines, and nutrients. In total, 118 brand names of watches from several Western countries were listed. Bicycles made in England, cameras made in Germany, and garments made in India, England, and Italy occupied much of the list. While some small items in the list, such as nail clippers, syringes, and watch belts, were identified as made in the United States, the American presence was mainly represented by brand-name products including Kodak films, Parker pens, Evans tools, and Singer sewing machines.[140] All these would soon become unknown to a generation of Chinese citizens growing up under Mao Zedong. In the late 1950s, however, these Western brand names found in Chinese society served as a reminder to Mao and his comrades: the waiting game in Tibet was not just about the Tibetans.

Beijing's policymaking in the 1950s treated Tibet as a unique case not because the region was relatively insulated from the rest of China but because the region was constantly relevant to the CCP's nationwide undertakings in a unique way. The year 1957 was a watershed for Beijing's tactical orientation in dealing with this unique case. Before that year, taking a phased approach to state building and social engineering for the PRC and switching from New Democracy to socialism, Beijing managed its relationship with Lhasa on the platform of the Seventeen-Point Agreement and worked with constructive intentions for integrating the Tibetan establishment into the PRC system. In this period of benevolent waiting, CCP leaders adopted two parallel tactics. One was to use class cooperation and political suasion inside Tibet to condition the Tibetan establishment for the communist destiny toward which the PRC was heading. The other was to accomplish sociopolitical changes via "smart" or forceful class struggles around Tibet, especially in the Tibetan areas of the neighboring provinces. In combination, these tactics were intended to demonstrate to Lhasa that the only choice available for old systems was their demise, either peaceful or violent. In 1957, as Mao Zedong's "continuous revolution" entered high gear in the rest of China, remarkably Beijing scaled back its efforts inside Tibet. Newly available information from the PRC, as shown in this chapter, indicates that continuing to recognize the uniqueness of Tibet, CCP leaders displayed extraordinary patience with Lhasa in 1957 precisely because they were no longer interested in integrating the Tibetan establishment into their "new China." Instead of returning to their original orientation of benevolent waiting, CCP leaders' thinking switched to a mode of antagonistic temporizing, which followed well the established "unity-struggle" alteration of CCP strategy. While setting up a rapid transition to socialism for the rest of China, which would soon turn into a frenzied "leap into communism," CCP leaders appeared willing to let the sociopolitical gap between Tibet and the rest of China become even wider, tolerating Tibet as an isolated domain untouched by their revolution and an opening to capitalist influence. But under Beijing's perseverance was a bitterly suppressed annoyance. What CCP leaders were waiting for was an opportunity to take the Tibetan establishment out of the political equation of the Tibetan question. The next chapter discusses how this expected opportunity came in an unexpected way, and sooner than Beijing anticipated.

CHAPTER 6

THE SHOWDOWN

When CCP leaders entered a new round of the waiting game in Tibet, they were pursuing a diametrically opposite orientation for the rest of the PRC: the Great Leap Forward. In May 1958, launching the country into a dash toward communist utopia, Mao Zedong harked back to a *People's Daily* editorial published in 1957, which had used "leap forward" to define the CCP's economic programs. The background was a policy discord between Zhou Enlai's caution against "rush forward" in 1956 and Mao's "anti-anti-rush forward" stance in 1957. Now Mao praised the editorial for using a positive conception to articulate his double negative stance. In Mao's inflated words, "the achievement deserves a credit equal to that for Yu [ruler of the Xia Dynasty who was credited for putting the flooding Yellow River under control]. If a doctoral degree can be awarded, I'd like to propose to grant the highest doctoral degree to that (or those) scientist who invented this great slogan (i.e. leap forward)." It turned out that this doctorate-deserving person was the previously cautious Zhou. In a letter to Mao, Zhou humbly identified himself as the author of the phrase who, before seeing the chairman's remark, had been unaware of its political significance. Zhou therefore suggested that the venue that published the phrase, the *People's Daily*, deserved credit as well.¹

No matter how this notorious period of the PRC got its name, 1958 was unmistakably a year of extreme optimism as far as the CCP leadership was concerned. Not only did Mao famously promoted the idea of China's "surpassing" Great Britain and "catching up with" the United States in economic development, but he also believed that the PRC could do better than its ideological mentor and enter communism ahead of the Soviet Union.² Zhou put the tasks of the PRC into more specific yet nevertheless universal terms: socially, the PRC aimed "to conclude class struggles during the first half of human history"; technologically, the PRC would enter "the era of inter-planet communication started by the three Soviet man-made satellites."³ This was a time when CCP cadres were required to see the world according to Mao's assessments: "Easterly wind is overwhelming westerly wind," and "the enemies are rotting day by day and we are thriving day by day." Furthermore, these assessments must be understood in "absolute," not "relative," terms.⁴ In his lengthy career of political writing, Mao accumulated some favorite expressions that he used more than once. In May 1941, Mao published an article for reestablishing national and international confidence in China's ability to vanquish Japan eventually, titled "In today's world, please see who is the real master of all under heaven!" (*qingkan jinri zhi yuzhong, jingshi shuijia zhi tianxia*).⁵ In 1958, a Chinese diplomat's analysis of the situation of the "Western world" inspired Mao to come back to his proclamation made seventeen years before:

> Huan Xiang was correct. Falling apart—this is the situation of the Western world. The process of falling apart is happening, not yet complete, and heading toward the inevitable end. The process may continue for a long time and certainly not conclude just overnight. The so-called unity of the West is an empty word. Unity is indeed a goal that [John F.] Dulles is trying to achieve. But this "unity" is to demand, with atomic bomb, his big and small partners to rally toward the United States and to come under American domination. By unity, the Americans mean that the others should surrender tributes and do hard kowtow to submit to the United States. Such a situation will definitely lead to the opposite of unity: falling apart. In today's world, comrades, please see who is the real master of all under heaven.⁶

Such breezy confidence about the superiority of the "socialist camp" in the Cold War was entirely consonant with the CCP leadership's elevated optimism that year about "socialist construction" at home. The question was, how could the seemingly discordant note of Tibet fit Beijing's marching melody? Was the deteriorating situation inside Tibet really undesirable to leaders in Beijing? Although Tibet was a unique case as far as Beijing's policymaking was concerned, there was a fundamental continuum between Beijing's policy in the rest of the PRC and that for Tibet. When the Lhasa revolt took place in March 1959, it effectively concluded the suspenseful condition of Beijing's Tibetan question. Yet the final collapse of the flimsy cooperation between Lhasa and Beijing should be understood in a larger context: Beijing's "leap forward" in strengthening control over the ethnic frontiers of northwestern and southwestern China.

248 The Showdown

This chapter shows how, while preparing for eventually bringing the "backward" Tibet abreast with the rest of the PRC, Beijing got its *casus belli* in the Lhasa revolt of March 1959.

"Entering Heaven in One Step"

In a sense, Communist power in China's frontiers in the early 1950s was comparable with Nationalist power in China after 1928. Having claimed "central" authority in Nanjing in 1928, the Nationalist government maintained domestic sovereignty over a huge portion of Chinese territory only by arranging a temporary military-political truce with local warlords. In the early 1950s, Beijing's control over PRC territories was much more substantiated than that of its Nanjing predecessor, but along the frontiers, Beijing maintained authority by arranging a socioeconomic truce with local ethnic elites. By the late 1950s, the truce was rescinded. In 1958, with the reform war in western Sichuan now two years old, widespread conflicts began in Gansu and Qinghai.

First, in March, rebellions broke out in five counties of the Gannan Tibetan Autonomous Prefecture of Gansu. Then, in August, six counties of the province's Linxia Hui Autonomous Prefecture also rebelled.[7] Before the year ended, at a public security conference of northwestern China, public security officials in Gansu reported their "achievements" in suppressing various sorts of adverse force. According to these reports, during the eight months prior to the rebellions, 74,741 "landlords, rich farmers, counterrevolutionaries, and bad elements" were subject to "strikes" by state public security apparatuses. After the Great Leap Forward began in the province in April, another 62,774 "enemies of various kinds" were suppressed. Gansu officials carefully separated these figures from that of suppressed "rebels," who numbered 44,986 for the period from March to August. Without including the "rebels," the first two suppressed groups accounted for a rather small percentage of the province's total population, a mere 1.1 percent. Hence Mao's assessment proved right: "Counterrevolutionaries still exist but their number is not large." Gansu officials put those more recent "rebellions" into a different category, and, like their counterpart in Sichuan, attributed the rebellions to "scheming by American and Chiang [Kai-shek] agents and the Tibetan reactionary clique."

Gansu officials' reporting revealed that rebellions in their province took place in connection with Beijing's phased revolutionary strategy: several rebel leaders were county- or prefecture-level officials of the new Communist government who had been secular or religious elites of the old establishment before 1949. These people had cooperated with the CCP during the initial years of the PRC but became opponents when Beijing pushed its revolution into a more radical phase. As Gansu officials put it, the recent rebellions provided an opportunity for "turning a bad situation into a good one," so that some long-standing issues in minority areas, Tibetan and Hui included, could now be solved once and for all. These issues were summarily termed "systems of exploitation and feudal privileges." Another set of figures shows how "rebellion suppression" was really a fundamental change of the local social structure. By the end of October, the public security apparatuses of Gansu arrested more than 60 percent of the imams of the Linxia Hui Autonomous Prefecture and 65.3 percent of the headmen of the Gannan Tibetan Autonomous Prefecture. While such decapitation of the Hui and Tibetan societies served to justify the CCP rhetoric on class liberation, these suppressed imams and headmen totaled around 3,080, or merely 6.8 percent of the reportedly suppressed "rebels." Similar to the situation in western Sichuan, guns in Tibetan tribes and religions in both Tibetan and Hui communities were two of the major issues that provoked mass resistance in Gansu. Yet in 1958 neither CCP officials in Gansu nor CCP leaders in Beijing showed any hesitance in collecting weapons from the society and closing mosques and lamaist monasteries. In this way, the reform war of Sichuan was duplicated in Gansu. Before the conflict, Linxia had 1,816 mosques. The CCP Linxia Prefecture Committee planned to keep fourteen of these open, but reportedly the "mass wanted" to have even less. The lamaist monasteries in Gannan totaled 161 originally; only four remained open by the end of 1958. After being closed, these mosques and monasteries were reportedly turned into schools, kindergartens, libraries, dining halls, and storages that served socialist purposes.[8]

The situation of Qinghai was even more violent. A report by the Qinghai Public Security Department indicated that since April, rebellions had become provincewide, involving all six autonomous prefectures, twenty-two counties, sixty-four districts, seventy-nine townships, 154 tribes, and 163 monasteries. The rebels totaled sixty thousand. In CCP officials' "dialectic thinking," this violent turmoil was an excellent development. For, as the report asserted, the province's Tibetan areas changed fundamentally in the process of rebellion pacification: "The entire Tibetan region has jumped over the stages of tribal, slave, and feudal societies and entered socialism, completing a number of phases of revolution in one stroke. It is not exaggerating to say that [the Tibetans] have entered heaven in one step."[9] As a result, Qinghai achieved the highest record in northwestern China in "striking the enemies," or 17.04 percent of the province population. At the time, such records were praised as indicators of a "great leap forward in political and legal work."[10]

Years later, CCP leaders would have second thoughts about such high-speed entry into "heaven." In 1972, when introducing China's experiences in carrying out social reforms to an envoy sent by Pakistan prime minister Zulfikar Ali Bhutto, Zhou Enlai said that if democratic and socialist reforms were implemented simultaneously, too many people would be attacked at the same time and fewer people would be included in the unity. Two separate steps would therefore be advisable and could avoid trouble.[11] Zhou's guest, of course, had no way of knowing the factual basis of Zhou's assertion. In that year, Zhou was initiating a review of "rebel" cases in ethnic frontiers. Central Document No. 22, issued for the purpose, described the problem in language typical of the time:

> The processing of rebel cases, because of resorting to confessions under duress and other erroneous policy practices, led to excessiveness. Resultantly two different types of contradictions [i.e., intra-people and antagonistic] became confused, class divides were blurred, class enemies were covered up, we became self-isolated, and the Party's relationship with the mass and national unity were seriously undermined.[12]

In pursuance of this document, the Ministry of Public Security sent an investigation team to Gansu in the summer of 1973. The team's report provides further information about the damage done by "rebellion pacification" in the province. According to the report, the 1958 rebellions in Gansu were started by counterrevolutionary upper-stratum figures who resisted socialist transformation. The rebellions involved thirteen counties and 67,900 rebels. In total, from 1958 to 1961, the operations for rebellion pacification killed twelve thousand and led to forty-two thousand arrests. Among the arrested, 27,700 were released after "education," and 10,091 died in prison or during "concentrated training." The report pointed out that many of those arrested or sent to "training" camps were ordinary people "coerced" or "tricked" into joining rebellions. In some places, the local authorities, to meet quotas from their superiors, even arrested guides to PLA troops or the CCP's undercover agents sent to the enemy's side. The investigation team from Beijing planned to reexamine the nearly sixty-eight thousand individual cases in four to six months. By the time the team made its report, about a third of these cases had been processed. Of those, 81.44 percent were rehabilitated, and only 10.05 percent of the original verdicts remained unchanged. It should be noted that this review was carried out during the Cultural Revolution, the most radical period of the PRC. While Liu Shaoqi and Lin Biao, both out of Mao's favor by this time, were blamed for the "mistakes" of the past, the Cultural Revolution claimed its own victims. Huang Huoqing, an ethnic Tibetan who was the governor of the Gannan Tibetan Autonomous Prefecture in 1958 and participated in rebellion pacification that year, was absurdly identified in the report as a "rebellious bandit."[13] New rounds of rehabilitations and incriminations would follow in the years to come. A 1981 review indicated that a total of 78,188 people were arrested in connection with the 1958 rebellions, including 1,600 "preemptive" arrests. By that time, after a series of reviews, about three thousand of the 78,188 cases remained unchanged, and all the rest were proved wronged in various ways. In connection with these cases,

13,458 households were confiscated. All these "wrong" or "unjust" cases were attributed to the "leftist thinking" of the late 1950s.[14]

The 1981 review in Gansu was triggered by a Beijing directive to Qinghai. Although relevant Qinghai archives remain classified, a published source in the PRC does reveal the extent of the damages. In late June and mid-August 1961, a three-level cadre conference was held in Qinghai to criticize former Qinghai CCP chief Gao Feng's "leftist adventurism" between 1958 and 1961. Allegedly, Gao was responsible for a "blind leap forward" and excessiveness in conducting rebellion pacification. Because of these "mistakes," 261,538 people, or 10 percent of the Qinghai population, died; 68,000 people, or 2.6 percent of the population, were arrested; 70 percent of upper-class people were arrested or sent to labor camps; 50 percent of livestock died; only 13 of the 1,694 monasteries and mosques remained; and 7.5 percent of cadres were punished for various reasons.[15]

"Leftist thinking" is just one of the pejorative terms in the CCP vocabulary that have no analytical value for historical studies. What happened in the PRC in the late 1950s was that Beijing stopped considering *minzu*, translated alternately as "nationality" or "ethnicity," as an essential category in its policymaking with respect to minority nationalities. In 1958, Beijing endorsed completely Gansu officials' handling of the situation in their province. In an August directive, the CCP leadership advised its local organizations: "Work in minority areas must firmly implement the class orientation according to local conditions. It should be remembered constantly that in a class society, the essence of nationality question is class question. Nationality question cannot be thoroughly solved without grasping its class essence."[16] Thus, Beijing decided to end its hitherto circumspect approach in expanding socialist programs into the non-Han areas of the PRC. At the local level, the orientation shift was understood as the end of the period of "making cautious and steady advance" in minority areas. A new phase began that would stress the "class line" similarly for all nationalities.[17]

In minority areas, a serious consequence of the Great Leap Forward was to put aside "nationality contradictions" while bringing "class struggles" to the fore. Thus, disturbances or resistance in minority areas caused either by "socialist transformation" or plots originating from outside the PRC were put into a new perspective. To Beijing, such unrest became a welcoming development, signaling that forceful measures could now be applied to achieve a thorough solution. Therefore, local upheavals in ethnic frontiers in 1958 were fundamentally structural, not incidental, though the forms of such upheavals differed in various places. For instance, the province of Yunnan did not see large-scale rebellion, but before the year ended, more than 115,000 people fled across the PRC's borders with Burma, Vietnam, and the Laos, either seeking life under a different system or acting out the "art of not being governed."[18]

The upheavals were structural because they were mainly ignited by the CCP's nationwide, radical socioeconomic programs. Two years earlier, Mao had characterized the reform war in western Sichuan as one of "liberation." In 1958, rebellion suppressions in Gansu and Qinghai were also characterized as such. To Beijing, "liberation" of these areas for the second time after 1949 marked the advance of the communist revolution in socioeconomic terms, albeit supported by military means. Therefore, Mao did not share provincial officials' view about "turning a bad situation into a good one," believing that the recent rebellions in Qinghai and Gansu were "extremely good [*jihao*]" because the opportunity for liberating laboring people had come.[19] In Mao's mind, dialectic reasoning was unnecessary here; the developments were straightforwardly positive.

"The Bigger Is the Convulsion . . ."

When discussing the causes of rebellions in their regions, public security officials of Gansu and Qinghai unanimously blamed the "Tibet reactionary clique."[20] This differed drastically from Sichuan officials' analyses of rebellions in their province two years before. In the eyes of CCP officials, Lhasa's political stock had fallen by a wide margin. During the new round of waiting in Tibet, Beijing constantly received intelligence about hostile scheming inside and outside the region. In view of what was happening in Gansu and Qinghai, Beijing had to weigh such intelligence carefully.

Ironically, when Beijing decided to postpone its reform agenda for Tibet, one of the first pieces of information about malicious scheming against the PRC came from the Dalai Lama's quarter. In early April 1957, having just returned from their journey to India with the Dalai Lama, kalons of the Kashag voluntarily surrendered a telegram codebook to the TWC. The codebook had been crafted by Tibetan expatriates in Kalimpong, and the kalons surrendered it to the TWC either to show their innocence or to give up an unconcealable secret. Regardless, Beijing was presented with a piece of material evidence that new troubles were fermenting in Tibet. At the time, a Buddhist scripture allegedly emerged from a Garzê monastery, predicting ominously: "In the Year of Pig (1959) the world will become one of the beasts, and religion will decline. In the Year of Rat (1960) the Heaven will speak, and Bodhisattvas will come from all directions." Rumors also directed the Tibetans' attention to a place where they ought to look for hope: "The United States promised to offer three atomic bombs, one to bomb Xikang and two to bomb locations yet to be decided."[21]

In 1958, Beijing got a series of intelligence reports about recent activities of Tibetan expatriates and Taiwan and American agents with respect to Tibet. Following are synopses of these reports; the italicized dates indicate when Beijing circulated the information among designated CCP officials.

April 15, 1958. *Jiangte* (Chiang Kai-shek's agents) set up secret liaison groups in India and intelligence groups in Kalimpong, and preparations were made for establishing a radio station. These agents were collaborating with the Dalai Lama's older brother Gyalo Thondup in sending secret agents to Tibet and northwestern areas of China. In 1957, the head of *Jiangte* in India selected individuals who had fled to India and planned to train and send them back to northwestern China. At the end of this March, *Jiangte* brought a poisonous drug to Gyalo Thondup from Hong Kong and plotted to carry out assassinations in Tibet. A number of *Jiangte* would go to Kalimpong to intensify the collection of intelligence about Tibet. In the past, *Jiangte* had sneaked into India from Hong Kong, but recently they changed the approach and used Portuguese passports to enter India.[22]

May 24, 1958. In August 1957, Gyalo Thondup asked Nehru to give further support to Tibetan independence. Nehru told him that for the sake of India's relations with China, the Indian government could not openly support them. Gyalo Thondup was displeased with the answer. Then, in October, Gyalo Thondup contacted a Pakistani official in India and asked the Pakistani government to support the Tibetan independence movement and to facilitate a UN observer group to visit Tibet. The Pakistani official agreed to help.[23]

July 2, 1958. Gyalo Thondup, (Wangchuk Deden) Shakabpa, and Lukhangwa (Tsewang Rapten) purchased horses and guns, organizing Tibetan expatriates from Xikang, Qinghai, and Tibet to carry out guerrilla warfare in Tibet. The organization, the Free Tibetan People's Army, had its headquarters in Kalimpong or Kathmandu of Nepal. About two to three thousand Tibetans gathered and planned to enter Tibet on July 1. Gyalo Thondup and associates divided Tibet into three guerrilla areas, to be supplied from three locations: Kathmandu of Nepal, Dawan of Bhutan, and Assam of India. Most of the supplies would come from foreign countries; a small portion would be provided from inside Tibet. The Americans participated directly in military plotting and in providing military guidance to Tibetans. They would give Tibetans military and intelligence training in Kalimpong. Reportedly, the Americans used *Jiangte* to assemble a group of former officers of Chiang Kai-shek's army in Hong Kong, and these agents would enter Tibet via Nepal.[24]

July 4, 1958. In pursuing rebels, PLA troops captured a *Jiangte* radio station in Yajiang, Sichuan. This proved that the Chiang clique in Taiwan had directly commanded the reactionary rebels in the Tibetan areas of Yunnan and Sichuan. Also captured was a codebook created by American intelligence that had been used to receive directives from Taiwan and to maintain contact with Lhasa and India. In this year, the radio station made several urgent requests to Taiwan to send ammunition to rebels in the Tibetan areas of Yunnan and Sichuan.[25]

July 17, 1958. Gyalo Thondup was urging Nehru to visit Tibet in September. He planned to start rebellions in Nagqu (Heihe), *Cuola dzong* (错拉宗 in the document cited, but might be a misnomer for Tsona dzong or today's Cona County), and Kongpo (Gongbu) before Nehru's arrival, so that when Premier Zhou and Nehru arrived in Tibet, the three big monasteries could ask Nehru to mediate between Tibet and Beijing. Reportedly, they planned a rebellion of ten thousand people, and the Tibetan government would supply most of the weapons. *Cuola dzong* would be the center of the rebellion because the location was close to the government's granary in Zayu (Zhaye). The location was also convenient for the rebels to get supplies from Gyalo Thondup's plantation and get foreign support from Assam of India through Bhutan or from eastern Pakistan. Recently, Gyalo Thondup and others had organized a Buddhist Association of the Tibetan People in Kalimpong and set up branches in Darjeeling and Sikkim. They urged young members of the association to return to Tibet to fight, and they threatened those who were reluctant. Reportedly, two hundred people so far were ready to return to Tibet with guns and horses.[26]

August 15, 1958. In the past three months, from 1,500 to 4,000 Tibetans had left Kalimpong for Lhoka (Shannan). They intended to establish a base there for supporting and expanding the rebellions of Xikang. From Lhoka, a Xikang Tibetan Association sent a letter to Lukhangwa in Kalimpong. The letter demanded that all Tibetans in Kalimpong reach Lhoka before July 31, asserting that the Kashag had already ordered the counties nearby to provide help, and Tibetans must not miss this opportunity to serve the Dalai Lama. Recently, the amount of flour transported from Kalimpong to Lhoka had increased abnormally. In just one day, July 6, three thousand bags were transported. Although this might be partially caused by speculating Indian merchants, military supplies were involved, and weapons and ammunition were transported as well. Reportedly, the Dalai Lama's saving account in Gangtok, Sikkim, was used to purchase weapons, and Bhutan agreed to provide grain to Lhoka.[27]

September 26, 1958. Recently, incited by the United States, Bhutan provided assistance continuously to Tibetan rebels in Lhoka that was contiguous with Bhutan. When Rani, the mother-in-law of Bhutanese king Wangchuck, lived in Kalimpong, the United States used Tsarong's close relationship with Rani and convinced Bhutan to help Tibetan rebels in Lhoka. The Bhutanese king and leaders of Tibetan rebels in Lhoka reached an agreement, and afterwards Bhutan delivered a huge volume of grain to the rebels. More would be delivered in September. Bhutanese prime minister Jikmé Dorji was on good terms with one of the rebel leaders, named Sangdak Lochungtra, and issued a visa so he could travel through Bhutan and transport weapons from Kalimpong to Lhoka. At the end of August, Sangdak Lochungtra led eighty rebels from Kalimpong to Lhoka via Bhutan.[28]

Without exception, every piece of intelligence cited here came from Kalimpong. At the time, Beijing's security orientation regarding Tibet was neither to recruit nor to use "special intelligence agents" (*teqing*) inside Tibet but to use such agents in Kalimpong.²⁹ Details like names, numbers, locations, and dates seem to indicate that PRC intelligence had succeeded to a certain degree in infiltrating the Tibetan expatriate community in India.³⁰ From these reports, Beijing could get the following impressions: (1) a group of Tibetan expatriates around Gyalo Thondup in Kalimpong were actively planning to start armed rebellions in Tibet, and in the second half of 1958 they began to implement their plan, transporting weapons, supplies, and fighters back to Tibet; (2) the Kashag and even the Dalai Lama himself were aware of or might have participated in the conspiracy; (3) the designated areas for rebellions were eastern and southern parts of Tibet for the sake of affecting Lhasa, reacting to the reform war on the eastern side of the Jinsha River, and receiving assistance from Himalayan states nearby; (4) all Tibet's Himalayan neighbors became entangled with Tibetan conspirators in various ways, and the Indian government, the most important among these, for the moment maintained an ambiguous attitude toward the Tibetan conspirators inside its territory; (5) the Americans and the Nationalists in Taiwan were the most vicious adversaries of the PRC in this Himalayan contest, inciting the Tibetans to revolt and providing training, military know-how, and diplomatic help to the Tibetan expatriates. An organized separatist movement, sympathetic neighbors, and great-power support (albeit covert) were all necessary ingredients for a perfect recipe of territorial separation in a frontier region, which could be embraced eagerly by an agitated Tibetan society.

In a sense, people in both Beijing and Kalimpong were expecting an explosion of the Tibetan society, but the contacting point between the two forces, Lhasa, remained ambiguous. In late July 1957, the TWC and the Kashag established a joint committee for public security, which assigned the principal responsibility to the Kashag and an assistant role to the PLA. Such a facade of "constructive collaboration" between the two sides would continue into 1958, when Tibet became an undeclared battleground between PLA troops and Khampa fighters.³¹ On Beijing's side, and probably on the Kashag's side as well, it was all about tactics.

Information about CCP leaders' policymaking with respect to Tibet in 1958 is scarce. This is not surprising in view of Beijing's waiting game. In late September 1958, before the second Taiwan Strait crisis was over, Deng Xiaoping spoke to a group of high-ranking CCP officials of Liaoning Province. According to Deng, in current international affairs nothing seemed noisier than what was going on in the Taiwan Strait. But, he added, "Chairman Mao is not paying attention to that situation, which does not deserve much attention and can be looked into just occasionally. What has constantly occupied our attention is [production of] 10,700,000 tons of steel."³² Deng's speech indicated that in 1958 CCP leaders were faced with many urgent issues at home and offshore, and for a while Tibet was on the back burner.

Yet Tibet was certainly not forgotten. On several occasions in late 1957 and 1958, Mao mentioned Tibet. The contexts of these references were quite indicative. In early October 1957, Mao expressed his opinion about the necessity for some foreign communist parties to carry out violent revolutions in their own countries. Mao said: "We have two maxims. First, a gentleman uses his words, not his fists. Second, when attacked by a lowlife, one should certainly fight back." He used the CCP's experiences to make his point: "One battle at Chamdo did not enable us to advance into Lhasa. After Beijing and Tianjin were liberated, the issue of Suiyuan was solved. In general, both maxims should be followed to avoid mistakes."[33] A few months later, when talking about the Anti-Rightist Campaign, Mao said: "Some cadres in Xinjiang are in favor of disunity, and Tibet is for disunity as well. They do not support unity of China's various nationalities and are advocating national disunity. If continuing to take such a stance, they will suffer defeat."[34] Soon, in June 1958, the province-wide rebellions in Qinghai sent the issue of Tibet to Mao's desk. In a report to Beijing, Qinghai officials asserted: "The armed counterrevolutionary rebellions in Qinghai are closely connected with the conspiracy for splitting our country by the Lhasa regime of Tibet, which was under imperialist influence. These rebellions were incited and initiated by the Lhasa reactionary clique and imperialists." In approving actions taken by Qinghai, Mao made his view known to leading CCP officials in all provinces:

> Comrade [Huang] Kecheng please duplicate and circulate this document [Qinghai report] to all the comrades attending the meeting of the Military Affairs Commission. In the meantime, comrade [Deng] Xiaoping please circulate the document among the Party committees of all provinces, municipalities and autonomous regions, and send it to Sichuan, Yunnan, Guizhou, and Tibet first. Everybody should know this development. Reactionaries rebelled in Qinghai. Extremely good! The opportunity for laboring people's liberation has arrived. The orientation of the [CCP] Qinghai Provincial Committee is completely correct. In Tibet, preparations for dealing with a comprehensive rebellion should be made. The bigger are the convulsions, the better. Should the reactionaries of Tibet dare launch a comprehensive rebellion, the laboring people there would be able to achieve liberation sooner. This is absolutely certain.[35]

The year 1958 was not 1956, and Mao's reaction to the armed conflicts in Qinghai differed significantly from his reaction to the reform war in western Sichuan two years before. It should be noted that Mao wrote these words *before* PLA troops were attacked inside Tibet, which would take place about a month later. Mao therefore appeared to welcome "Tibetan reactionaries" to start a large-scale rebellion so that the waiting game could come to an end. But a "comprehensive rebellion" was slow to come in Tibet. In December, a new edition of Mao's collected poems was published. Mao wrote a lengthy comment in his personal copy that included these words:

> Mosquitoes in the mainland have almost been eliminated. Of course, the revolution is yet to complete, and comrades should continue to make effort. In Hong Kong and Taiwan, there are still many mosquitoes. In the Western world, armies of mosquitoes still exist. It would be so great if peoples of the world could wipe out these mosquito armies by learning from Yu Gong's way of moving a mountain![36]

Although not mentioning Tibet, Mao must have seen a few flying "mosquitoes" there as well. As Mao pushed the rest of China into the Great Leap Forward, his patience with Tibet was quickly running thin.

As discussed in the previous chapter, in late 1957 Deng Xiaoping had already admonished CCP officials not to wish for "a quiet Tibet."[37] Mao's wishing for a "big convulsion" in Tibet in mid-1958 further explicated that, in contrast to Beijing's pre-1956 gradualist approach in Tibet, which was one of benevolent anticipation, its post-1957 stratagem was replete with baleful expectations. In the meantime, although leaders in Beijing enthusiastically embraced those "good" rebellions in Qinghai and Gansu and waited for a similarly "good" rebellion to take place in Tibet, their expected scenario for Tibet still differed markedly from the Qinghai-Gansu situation. Rebellions in Qinghai and Gansu were mostly local reactions to the CCP's socioeconomic offensive in the name of the Great Leap Forward, whereas such an offensive was absent in Tibet. In Qinghai and Gansu, the CCP authorities was already solidly in place and were therefore the rebels' direct target. By contrast, in Tibet the Kashag remained the nominal authority and was responsible for maintaining social stability. Thus, the "comprehensive rebellion" anticipated by Mao would have to mean either the Kashag's partaking in rebellions or its loss of control. That was why Deng advised the TWC not to help the Kashag's governance but watch patiently the spread of chaos. Small bands of rebels should not be the PLA's concern, and, in contrast to elsewhere, the TWC was even advised not to worry about foreign imperialist plots. In early 1958, Mao approved Su Yu's suggestion that PLA troops in Tibet adopt a posture of "internal intensity and external relaxation" (*neijin waisong*) and a policy of "not firing the first shot." On the eastern side of the Jinsha River, PLA troops under the Chengdu Military Region were able to seal the river by late April.[38] A key condition was thereby secured for Beijing to carry out different strategies of fighting and waiting, respectively, on the two sides of the river.

On July 11, 1958, to a national conference on united-front work, Deng Xiaoping defined the CCP struggle against "local nationalism" in minority areas as a "communist liberation movement." Democratic reform in these areas was inevitable. As for Tibet, although Beijing would keep its promises about no reform for six years and peaceful reform in the future, the Dalai Lama and the Kashag should realize by now that if war broke out in Tibet, it would lead to an armed, thorough reform. Admitted that Beijing's orientation toward Tibet had never been static, Deng asserted: "Using the same slogan, orientation, and method in different times is not Marxism."[39] Three days later, in response to a TWC complaint about the Kashag's passivity toward rebels in areas under its control, Beijing instructed the TWC to convey the gist of Deng's message to Tibetan officials. Beijing criticized the Kashag for appeasing the rebels, warning Tibetan officials that, as in Qinghai and Gansu, an armed reform might begin if rebellions became out of control. At the same time, the Kashag was invited to act responsibly to secure the prospect of peaceful reform.[40]

While pressuring the Kashag without assisting it in restoring order in Tibet, Beijing had a real management problem with the TWC. Probably feeling it had lagged behind by its peers' "leap forward" in other provinces, the TWC did not seem to have a solid grasp of Deng's game plan of letting rebels wreak havoc and the Kashag shoulder the responsibility. Having just purged Fan Ming, the TWC appeared eager to take actions against rebels in Tibet and get on with socialist work.[41] At the time, the rebels in Tibet were mainly Khampa fighters in a newly formed guerrilla force named Chushi Gangdruk (literally, "four rivers, six ranges"), whose commander was Gonpo Tashi. On July 21, Gonpo Tashi's force ambushed a caravan of PLA trucks. This was the first attack on the PLA in the Lhasa area. Three days later, the TWC and the Tibet Military Region (TMR) made a joint request to Beijing for retaliation. Their plan was to safeguard the Chuan-Zang Highway by striking the rebels along the line from Nyingtri (Linzhi) to Lhasa. Beijing approved the plan with a condition: the PLA might strike only if Gonpo Tashi's main force could be destroyed with one stroke. The operation began on August 2 and lasted for fifteen days, but it was unable to destroy Gonpo Tashi's main force. Right after the operation, Deng summoned Zhang Guohua and his deputy Deng Shaodong, reminding them that PLA troops must not be used casually and they should strike only if victory could be guaranteed. On September 8, Deng had another discussion with Zhang, which was followed by a directive to the TWC against fighting rebels with PLA troops without a guarantee of success.[42]

As the PLA and Gonpo Tashi's fighters had their first clash, Beijing was busy dealing with the situation in the Taiwan Strait. Between August 18 and September 8, Deng attended thirteen meetings called by Mao about starting bombardment of the Jinmen (Quemoy) Island and managing the consequences afterwards. On September 8 and 9, Deng attended meetings with Mao and other CCP leaders, who decided to relax the cross-strait situation. Only then did Deng appear at ease and make his nonchalant remark, mentioned previously, about Mao's not paying attention to the Taiwan Strait crisis.[43] Understandably, in these nerve-racking weeks, Deng and other CCP leaders did not hope to see a flaring up of the Tibetan problem. The TWC was, however, unrelenting. In late August, TWC officials came up with a formula that, if implemented, would have ended Beijing's strategy of waiting. According to the formula, lacking the comprehensive rebellion in Tibet prescribed by Beijing, the PLA should operate to suppress "partial rebellions" (*jubu panluan*) while mobilizing the masses and reforming the old regimes in rebellious areas "to a certain degree" (*shidang de*). During the first half of October, despite repeated cautionary advice from Beijing, the TMR tried and failed again to annihilate Gonpo Tashi's force. In the meantime, the TWC planned to start reform in certain areas of Chamdo.[44]

Beijing sternly objected to such local efforts for partially ending the established waiting scheme. On October 11, in a directive to the TWC, Beijing reaffirmed that if a comprehensive rebellion took place either in Tibet, meaning the area under the Kashag's control, or in Chamdo, it must be suppressed so as to thoroughly liberate the laboring people of Tibet. But under the current situation of localized rebellions, the PLA should take a defensive posture and "must not follow an approach of 'pacifying rebellions wherever they take place' regardless of circumstances, conditions, and likelihood of success." Without a comprehensive rebellion, the orientation of "no reform for six years" would remain firm and must not be replaced with a "piecemeal approach of 'carrying out reform wherever rebellions take place.'" To prevent the TWC from hijacking the Kashag's responsibility for dealing with rebellions and resultant social upheavals, Beijing reiterated to TWC officials its logic behind waiting: "The counterrevolutionary poison of Tibet and Chamdo must be let out eventually. Let it run freely for a while to become fully exposed so that a thorough solution can be achieved more easily. Piecemeal measures will not be able to solve the problem."[45]

This time, the TWC finally got the essence of the "comprehensive rebellion" concept: Beijing had written the old Tibetan regime off from the very beginning of the waiting game, expecting the theocracy either to join rebellions or to be rendered irrelevant by them. From November on, the TWC stopped proposing any military or political step beyond the rules laid out by Beijing. In mid-November, when reporting a Kashag suggestion for sending a delegation to Beijing to "disperse the Center's misunderstanding about the local [Tibetan] government," the TWC commented: "We work to split them when they try to achieve unity, and we throw on them all the responsibilities for public security and for rebellion pacification when they try to evade responsibilities. We will not let them off the hook." Seeing the TWC operating on the right track, Beijing stressed a principle of "monopolizing power" in the TWC's decision-making process, meaning that Zhang Guohua should personally control the direction of the TWC's work to avoid any deviation.[46] As for the Kashag's suggestion, CCP leaders were not interested in changing the tempo of their deferment in

Tibet now. Not until mid-December, a month after Kashag officials made their suggestion, did a response come from Beijing, stating, in effect, that Beijing understood the Tibet situation perfectly and that the Kashag should just do its job.⁴⁷

Thus, the suspense of Tibet continued according to Beijing's script. Years later, official accounts in the PRC would identify a total of twelve armed conflicts between the PLA and the rebels inside Tibet throughout 1958 and during the first two months of 1959. Five of these took place after November 1958, all of them attacks initiated by the rebels.⁴⁸ As the PLA maintained its defensive posture inside Tibet, Tibetan rebellions in the neighboring provinces were being systemically suppressed. In mid-February 1959, directed by the General Staff of the PLA, the Lanzhou Military Region called a site meeting of CCP officials and military officers of Tibet's neighboring provinces. The purpose of the meeting was to exchange experiences of rebellion suppression and reform in the Chengdu, Kunming, Lanzhou, Xinjiang, and Tibet Military Regions in the past year, and to coordinate military operations among these military regions in 1959.⁴⁹ At the time, neither the leaders in Beijing nor the PLA commanders in the field expected the Tibet suspense to end anytime soon.

Although in late 1956 and early 1957 CCP leaders contemplated the possibility of a lengthy period of waiting in Tibet, what happened next—the Anti-Rightist Campaign and especially the Great Leap Forward—seems to have quickened the ticking of Beijing's clock for Tibet. Unlike TWC officials, who were eager to take the rapidly deteriorating Tibetan situation head-on, leaders in Beijing still preferred a circuitous approach for the sake of "political initiative." Nevertheless, a clue about Beijing's new timetable and the way to achieve it can be derived from a hitherto unknown plan for moving several hundred thousand youths into Tibet in the late 1950s. In 1956 and 1957, movement of laborers inside Sichuan was already happening on a large scale.⁵⁰ Then, in early August 1958, to implement Beijing's decision on mobilizing a million youths to migrate to frontier regions, Sichuan officials developed a plan for moving a million youths to the Tibetan areas of the province *and* the western side of the Jinsha River. Because of a shortage of laborers caused by the Great Leap Forward, the provincial leadership decided to move six hundred thousand people to Garzê and four hundred thousand to Chamdo and Bome on the western side of the river in the next five years. These young migrants would be selected from all trades, and they would be physically fit and politically reliable. According to the plan, the young migrants were to serve the goals of national defense and revolution in the Tibetan areas. "In considering the close connection with Tibet and the need in future development, priorities for migration should be given to the areas along the Jinsha River, two sides of highways, frontier regions, and reactionaries' political centers such as Litang [Lithang], Aba [Ngawa], and Ruoergai [Zoige]." Before the year ended, the plan was further substantiated.

In the next three years (1959–1961), six hundred thousand people would move into Garzê and Ngawa, where the original population totaled 770,000. The migrants would be completely subsidized by the state. They would move in as readily organized "people's communes," albeit arranged internally as militias in regiments, battalions, companies, and platoons. It was expected that the young migrants would be able to produce and fight simultaneously.[51]

The details of Beijing's calculation for moving a million youths into the Tibetan areas, including Tibet, remain unknown. The reasons behind the decision should not be too hard to fathom, though. Repopulating these areas devastated by a prolonged reform war, demographically Sinicizing an ethnic minority region, and economically developing a remote frontier could all be achieved with an ageless practice, *tunken* (agricultural settlement), that relied on the huge Han population. "Builders and soldiers of socialism" was the name that the CCP gave to the young migrants designated for frontier areas. Spreading socialism was just the most recent form of central power building that had been going on throughout Chinese history. Sichuan officials originally thought that migration to Chamdo and Bome could begin in 1960 but then decided that, because of the unique situation of Tibet, the timeline had to be pushed back. They were prepared to consult with the TWC and finalize a schedule.[52] Yet the decision was Beijing's to make, and this time Sichuan officials proved overly cautious. In late January 1959, CCP leaders made the extraordinary decision to send two thousand youths to Tibet in the next two years.

On the morning of January 20, 1959, Mao called a meeting in *Juxiang Shuwu* (Study of fragrant chrysanthemum) of Zhongnanhai. It is very likely on this occasion that the issue of the two thousand youths was discussed and decided. On the same day, Deng Xiaoping reviewed a Center's directive to the TWC and the CCP Sichuan Committee and wrote in the margin, "We drafted this based on our discussion. Send this out after it is checked by the Chairman [Mao], Liu [Shaoqi], Zhou [Enlai], Chen [Yun], and Peng Zhen."[53] Available information indicates that the decision was a direct reaction to the expanding rebellion in Tibet. The rebels were now estimated to be nearly ten thousand strong. They sabotaged transportation lines, ambushed PLA vehicles and personnel, and had recently begun to encircle PLA posts. The "two thousand youths" were actually soldiers recently discharged from the Kangding Branch Military Region.[54] Having fought the reform war in western Sichuan, they would cross the Jinsha River and do *tunken* in Tibet. In Chinese history, *tunken* took two forms of state-organized settlement in frontier regions, military and nonmilitary. Whereas the planned migration in western Sichuan would adopt a semimilitary form, albeit termed "people's commune," the two thousand former PLA soldiers would move into Tibet in paramilitary organizations disguised as "state farms." Without going through "democratic reform" first, Tibet could not possibly accommodate a "people's commune," a supposedly communist form of socioeconomic organization. The migration plan for Tibet was therefore a major tactical alteration in Beijing's no-reform strategy: after the "great dismount" of 1957, this was the first time Beijing decided to reinforce its strength in Tibet. The waiting game did not end. The "two thousand youths" would be "farmers," not reformers, though they might function either to help consolidate the PLA's position in Tibet or to provide more targets for the rebels to attack.

On January 22, after reading a report from the TMR that rebels were running rampant and PLA troops were forced to defend themselves, Mao put a remark in the report's margin: "Such warfare is very beneficial in mobilizing the mass and training our troops. It would be the best to fight often like this for five to six or seven to eight years, so that a lot of enemies will be eliminated and conditions for reform become mature."[55] On the same day, Mao reviewed the directive about "the two thousand youths" and amended it as follows, clearly indicating that these young people would go through a period of war, not of peaceful construction, in Tibet:

> In Tibet, during a period from now till several years later, we and the enemy will contest for the mass' support. This will also be a time to test our military ability. Several years later, maybe three to four, or five to six, or seven to eight years later, a general showdown [*zong juezhan*] will certainly take place so that the problem can be thoroughly solved. The rulers of Tibet used to be weak militarily, but now, in having ten thousand armed rebels who are willing to fight, they become our serious adversaries. This, however, is not bad at all. Rather, this is a good development because the problem can be finally solved with war. Yet, in the next few years we must (1) win over the basic mass and isolate the reactionaries, and (2) improve significantly our troops' combat ability. Both should be achieved in our troops' struggle with the rebels.[56]

Two days later, the directive was sent to the TWC and the CCP Sichuan Committee. It should be noted that just a half month before, Beijing had instructed the TWC to stick to the orientation of "five things to do and four things not to do" adopted in May 1957 and to maintain a defensive posture militarily.[57] Now, Mao highlighted just two things for the TWC to do. Although Mao appeared patient enough to wait for another three to eight years, "peaceful reform" was no longer the expected result; it was replaced by a "general showdown" for achieving a "thorough solution" of the Tibetan question.

By early 1959, anticipation of a military showdown in Tibet appeared to be the dominant thinking, if not the consensus, among CCP leaders in Beijing. In late 1958, on a number of occasions, Zhou Enlai criticized Han cadres for not being able to understand the religious feelings of minority nationalities. He also talked about the prospect of peaceful reform in Tibet by way of consultation with Tibetan people and leaders.[58] In saying so, Zhou may have either been counseling moderation or just continuing an established rhetoric. But in 1959, "peaceful reform" disappeared from CCP discourse completely. On February 18, Mao read a piece by the Xinhua (New China) News Agency that sounded the alarm by qualifying the situation in Tibet with the vital term "comprehensive rebellion." Mao did not think the situation should be qualified as such yet, repeating his remark to other CCP leaders that "the bigger is the convulsion in Tibet, the better."[59] The next day, Mao read a report by the Operational Department of the PLA General Staff. Lumping together all the rebellions by various ethnic minorities in Sichuan, Yunnan, Gansu, Qinghai, and Tibet since 1955, the report predicted that rebellions in all these regions except Tibet would be pacified in 1959, and that Tibet, because the PLA adopted a defensive posture, would continue to serve as a haven for rebels who fled out of other areas. Mao wanted the report to be sent to all the regions concerned, especially the TWC in Lhasa, "so that they can learn about the whole picture and have a clear understanding of our orientations." Again, Mao did not let the report circulate without amending it. He added a sentence about the "benefits" of the rebellions and, significantly, changed a sentence about "not fear" rebellions to "not only we do not fear but also welcome such rebellions."[60]

"Let Them Go"

The first group of the "two thousand youths," about a thousand strong, arrived in Chamdo during the second half of March. They found that they were not to be state farmers but must immediately join the fray of the "general showdown" in Tibet—they all became members of the Chamdo Police Brigade in dealing with rebellions.[61] The "general showdown" came much sooner than Mao and his comrades expected. Beijing's waiting period ended with a revolt in Lhasa on March 10, 1959. To Beijing, the timing was a surprise, but not the way in which the Tibet suspense ended.

In the early months of 1959, people in both Beijing and Lhasa sensed that something of great magnitude was approaching. In late January, the TWC decided to relocate all "rightists," or state personnel purged in recent Anti-Rightist rectifications, to Chinese provinces, noting that "they are difficult to control under the current political situation of Tibet."[62] Before February ended, Beijing directed the TWC to send an official to the Dalai Lama to find out where he stood in the murky politics of Lhasa. The TWC's findings were inconclusive, suggesting that the Dalai Lama might either have been used by reactionaries or have already joined them. The Dalai Lama's own warning was more ominous, though. He told the TWC that to implicate Beijing, some bad people might try to harm him while disguising the perpetrators as government cadres.[63] The TWC also got a warning from the CCP's most trusted Tibetan inside the Kashag, Ngabö. Ngabö told the TWC that some Kashag officials were trying to scare the Dalai Lama into running away, with rumors about the Han's intention to destroy religion. If this gambit did not work, these people would then try to create troubles inside Lhasa and abduct the Dalai Lama as soon as the PLA counterattacked. Ngabö made his report to the TWC on March 9.[64]

On the morning of March 10, hundreds of Lhasa residents encircled the Norbulingka, the Dalai Lama's summer palace, to prevent the Dalai Lama from attending a prearranged performance in the quarters of the Tibet Military Region, allegedly protecting him from being abducted by the PLA. This was the beginning of the Lhasa revolt. The events in Lhasa during that vital month, March 1959, are part of a familiar story that has been told many times in different versions.[65] What happened among the local Tibetans and how events inside Lhasa were connected to Tibetan expatriates in other Himalayan countries are beyond the scope of this study. Based on information from PRC archives, the following discussion tries to clarify two related issues. First, at what point and under what circumstances did Beijing decide that a "comprehensive rebellion" had happened and, consequently, that the Tibet question could now be resolved by war? Second, did Beijing decide to let the Dalai Lama leave Tibet and, if so, for what reasons?

These decisions were made during the ten days between March 11 and 21. During these days, Mao was not in Beijing and communicated with the Politburo from locations in southern China. In Beijing, Liu Shaoqi held a series of meetings with Zhou Enlai, Deng Xiaoping, and Peng Zhen, some of which were attended by Peng Dehuai, Chen Yi, Huang Kecheng, Yang Shangkun, Yang Jingren, Xu Bing, and Wang Feng.[66] Surprisingly, neither Zhang Guohua nor Zhang Jingwu, the two principals of the TWC, was in Lhasa in the early months of 1959. An account suggests that for health reasons the two Zhangs went back to Beijing during the winter of 1958 and did not return to Lhasa until the revolt was suppressed. During the most crucial moment of the Lhasa situation, the two Zhangs attended a couple of the meetings in Beijing and at one point were also summoned by Mao to Wuhan.[67] Ever since the Qing government had created the *amban* position for Tibet, it had been rare for the central government's chief official to be absent in Lhasa when a crisis took place. It cannot be ascertained whether the two Zhangs' absence was intentional or incidental. Their presence in Lhasa would not have changed history, however, given that Beijing had by then already adopted a military perception of the Tibetan question.

Details about the meetings in Beijing remain largely unknown. Yet a series of communications between Beijing and the TWC, along with Beijing's information summaries about the developments in Lhasa, both of which were circulated among CCP provincial committees throughout the country, can shed light on the way Beijing embraced the breakdown in Lhasa.

Official accounts of the Lhasa revolt in the PRC have marked March 10, 1959, as the day when "the reactionary clique of the Tibetan local government launched a comprehensive rebellion."[68] This is a retroactive construction. In March 1959, when the Lhasa revolt was taking place, leaders in Beijing did not think immediately that the defining moment, or a "comprehensive rebellion," had arrived. During the first thirty hours of the incident, the TWC sent three telegrams to Beijing, two of which have since been declassified and published. One, the initial report, described a mob scene around the Norbulingka on March 10 and summarized a conversation between General Tan Guansan and Kashag officials on the same day. General Tan, ranked number three in the TWC, was in charge because of the two Zhangs' absence. Despite the stern tone Tan used in his conversation with Kashag officials, the telegram did not show any sign that the TWC tried to qualify the March 10 event as a major rupture in the status quo. The second published TWC report, a telegram sent to Beijing at 2:00 P.M. on March 11, adopted a more alarming tone. It reported a meeting of the Tibetans inside the Norbulingka that demanded Tibetan independence, planned to contact the Indian consulate in Lhasa, and called more rebel forces to Lhasa. The TWC also warned that a plot to abduct the Dalai Lama was possibly afoot. These, according to the TWC, constituted "Tibetan reactionary upper stratum's formal activities for independence."[69]

After holding its first meeting about the Lhasa revolt on March 11, the Politburo dispatched an "extremely urgent and top secret" directive to the TWC as well as all other CCP provincial committees. The directive qualified the events in Lhasa of the previous two days as a "very good development" and an "open exposure of the Tibetan upper stratum's reactionary and treacherous nature." Yet Beijing still wanted to wait and "let them run even more rampant and expose even more" so that "we may have an even fuller justification for pacifying the chaos." Military preparations were already underway at the Central level, but the timing of the PLA's pacification operation would depend on the unfolding situation. Beijing cautioned the TWC that the PLA must not fire the first shot in any form. If attacked, the TWC should hold its line for one to two months or even longer. As for the Dalai Lama, the TWC should expose the reactionaries' plot to abduct him and "continue to work from various aspects to win him over." Nevertheless, "we should not be afraid of the Dalai [Lama]'s being abducted by the reactionaries, which, if done by the enemy with or without the Dalai [Lama]'s consent, would not cause a bit of inconvenience to us." The directive ended with an instruction that the TWC should "collect evidence of treason committed by the other side; even a single piece of paper or a printed word would be useful."[70]

The March 11 directive provided a script for the finale of the Tibetan suspense. It had several features. First, although the long standoff between Beijing and Lhasa had been over the issue of "democratic reform," the upheaval in

Lhasa provided an opportunity for Beijing to redefine the Tibetan situation as one of treason. The theme of treason had not appeared in the CCP's previous discourse about armed conflicts in Sichuan, Qinghai, and Gansu but was now central to Beijing's characterization of the Lhasa revolt. The cries for Tibetan independence amid the Lhasa crisis and the reported collusion among the Kashag, independence supporters, and Khampa rebels gave Beijing reasons to contend that the bottom line for continuing its forbearance in dealing with Lhasa—the PRC's territorial sovereignty over Tibet—had been breached. Just as in 1950 Beijing had used military force to end Lhasa's "non-patriotic" stance and bring Tibet into the "great family" of the PRC, in 1959 Lhasa's alleged crime of treason would again justify Beijing's use of force. In taking such a perspective, leaders in Beijing readily accepted the sequence of events in Lhasa after March 10 as a welcome conclusion of their waiting game in Tibet.

Second, also present in Beijing's new operational plan was a mechanism of tactical delay. The Lhasa revolt did not begin with a direct attack on the TWC and the TMR, which were symbols of Beijing's authority in Tibet. It was by no means certain where the dynamic relationship between an assertive crowd in Lhasa's streets and an equivocal Kashag would be heading. Holding "political initiative" as a sacrosanct rule of operation, as well as worried about PLA posts scattered outside Lhasa, CCP leaders decided that the TWC and the TMR inside Lhasa must serve as physical targets to draw the rebels' firepower. The more rebels they could attract into Lhasa, the better. An obvious militarily advantage of such a development was to enable the PLA to inflict an annihilating strike onto the rebels in the Lhasa area. More important was a required political condition: when PLA troops poured into Lhasa, they must be there to fight armed rebels trying to topple Beijing's authority in Tibet, not to disperse unarmed street folks trying to shield the Dalai Lama.

Treatment of the Dalai Lama was the third and most circumspect component of Beijing's post–March 10 strategy. In the previous decade, CCP leaders had tried to figure out how to situate this terrestrial deity within their new state energized by class struggle. Having exhausted the CCP's usual united-front demarches and also tried a highly unusual affectionate offensive involving Mao himself, CCP leaders had achieved little. At different points, while categorizing the fourteenth Dalai Lama variously as a leftist, a centrist, or a rightist on the spectrum of their class analysis, CCP leaders made little headway in changing the Dalai Lama's position either in ordinary Tibetans' minds and or in the Tibetan theocracy. The Dalai Lama was simultaneously too powerful a spiritual presence in the Tibetan mind and heart to offend and too green a political leader in the Tibetan power structure to be held accountable. In 1950, Beijing began its Tibetan policy with a "Dalai line," intending to use the Dalai Lama as a bridge to reach the Tibetan masses. The Dalai Lama's lingering in India in late 1956 and early 1957 caused serious doubt in Beijing about the validity of the

"Dalai line." By March 10, 1959, Beijing had been contemplating to discard the imaginary bridge but still ran into an actual barrier: the Dalai Lama himself became the reason for Lhasa residents to revolt, but the target of the revolt was Beijing. As CCP officials understood the situation, helplessly insulated inside the Norbulingka, the Dalai Lama let himself be turned into the rallying point for all anti-Beijing forces. Under the circumstances, seasoned political masterminds in Beijing came up with a scheme to turn the tables on their adversaries. Before the crisis began, Ngabö had already offered a piece of intelligence that the Dalai Lama might be abducted abroad. Now, Lhasa residents' effort to prevent an alleged PLA plot to abduct the Dalai Lama readily presented a scenario to Beijing: the "reactionaries" might actually be implementing their plan for taking the Dalai Lama abroad. In 1959, the Dalai Lama's fleeing abroad amid an internal upheaval, for which the TWC's responsibility was limited to inviting the Dalai Lama to a show, would carry a political significance immensely different from that of late 1956, when the Dalai Lama wanted to stay in India because of Beijing's reform efforts in Tibet. Eventually, if the Dalai Lama failed to rally to Beijing's side, his departure with the "reactionaries" would effectively remove him as a barrier between the CCP and the Tibetan masses, whether or not the Dalai Lama left Lhasa of his own free will. The Dalai Lama's departure in this way would provide tremendous room for maneuver to CCP propaganda. Thus, from the very beginning of the Lhasa revolt, a "Dalai's abduction" scenario was a crucial component of Beijing's game plan. That was why, to lay the groundwork for propaganda, Beijing wanted the TWC to collect any and all printed or written evidence.

Again, for Beijing's management of the Lhasa crisis, control of its own policy apparatus was more difficult than letting loose the adversaries. While CCP leaders in Beijing were contemplating the Tibetan situation, Tan Guansan and his comrades in Lhasa became increasingly nervous. At 4:00 P.M. on March 11, the TWC dispatched its fourth telegram, which did not reach Beijing early enough to be considered by the Politburo meeting on that day. In this telegram, the TWC reported that the rebels had fortified themselves and deployed a large force and "many machineguns" along the highway north of the Norbulingka. Evidently, they had attempted to cut the PLA's transportation line. The TMR had already issued a stern demand to the Kashag to undo the fortifications. In the TWC's opinion, there were two possible courses of action for PLA troops inside Tibet: (1) in the event that the reactionaries openly declared Tibetan independence, which would mark the beginning of "comprehensive rebellion," PLA troops could start an offensive to thoroughly destroy the rebels; (2) if for the time being the enemy did not openly claim independence, the PLA could refrain from a comprehensive attack on the rebels but still move to destroy the rebels along the highway. On the same day, the TWC sent to Beijing another telegram on additional reactionary activities inside the Norbulingka. Then, on the morning of March 12, probably to save time, Zhou Renshan, a member of the TWC, made a phone call to the Central United Front Department in Beijing. According to Zhou Renshan, the three big monasteries now openly joined the rebellion, and an alleged representative of the Dalai Lama told rebels inside the Norbulingka that the Dalai Lama supported their effort to gain independence.[71]

Determined to proceed at a steady pace, Beijing had to apply the brakes on the TWC. Zhou Renshan's urgent phone call was not transcribed until two o'clock on the afternoon of March 12, but early enough for a Politburo meeting to consider it late that day. CCP leaders in Beijing again advised patience, admonishing the TWC: "You must not rush and must not adopt a military orientation of gaining mastery by striking first [*xianfazhiren de fangzhen*]. Otherwise we would fall into a politically disadvantageous position and the enemy would have excuses to mobilize more Tibetan people to confront us."[72] Along with the directive, the Politburo sent to the TWC a message from Mao. Written before noon on March 12, the message reflected Mao's initial reaction to the Lhasa revolt.

> *To the Center:*
>
> *I received the TWC reports dated March 10 and 11, the Center's March 11 directive to the TWC, and the directive that invited the Dalai [Lama] and other representatives of the People's Congress to come early to attend the meeting in Beijing. The Center's orientation is completely correct. If the situation continues like this, we may be compelled (such "being compelled" is very good) to solve the Tibetan question earlier than expected. Apparently, the Dalai [Lama] has been colluding with others and is the leader of the reactionaries. The tactics of the counterrevolutionary Dalai clique include:*
>
> *(1) Using the Norbulingka as a stronghold to start a revolt in Lhasa and drive our troops out. Such a step may first come to their minds. Because we have "appeared weak" for a long period and taken a defensive posture, they are convinced that "the Han people are timid" and "the Center is impotent," believing that "it is possible" to drive the Han out.*
>
> *(2) Having actually broken with the Center, this group will probably have to proceed along this path. One scenario is that they will continue to demonstrate and make troubles in Lhasa, hoping to scare the Han away. After a few days or months, when realizing that the Han cannot be scared away, they may either flee to India or set up a base in Lhoka [Shannan]. Either would be possible. During the Dalai [Lama]'s visit in India, Nehru had a policy of persuading the Dalai [Lama] to return to Tibet, believing that turning the Dalai [Lama] back might serve India better than keeping him. Since then this policy may or may not have changed. Nehru has*

detected the intention of Tibetan reactionaries. In the past few days he did three things. (a) Talking to the press. He said that the Khampas had caused the disturbance and that the incident had been exaggerated. He did not say a word about the Tibetans [meaning the Lhasa establishments]. Although clearly it was the Dalai clique that was directing the Khampas' defection and their wreaking havoc in Chamdo, Lhoka, and Shanbei [sic] areas, Nehru pretended that he knew nothing about these and did not utter a word. It seems that he acted this way to confuse us so as to help the Dalai [Lama] realize his idea of expelling the Han when ready. In my opinion, the Dalai [Lama] informed India of his plan for expelling the Han to gain independence. *(b) Kicking a British journalist out of Darjeeling for the same reason. This was to prevent the Dalai [Lama]'s plot from being exposed and becoming known throughout the world so that certain secrets could be kept when the Dalai [Lama] would flee to India for protection.* Actually, Western journalists' spreading of the news about the disturbance in Tibet throughout the world would best serve our forthcoming rebellion pacification. Soon or later, the March 10 incident will be reported anyway. The Dalai clique wants to get the news out so that they may ask assistance from the world. Neither can Nehru restrain reactionaries of India. *(c) Arranging with Bhutanese Prime Minister a contingency plan. It is yet to see whether, when fleeing, the Dalai [Lama] would go to India directly or struggle for a while in Lhoka before going to India. [Nehru] does not think that the Dalai [Lama]'s flight into India will benefit India.* Actually, as far as America, Chiang [Kai-shek], Britain, and India are concerned, the Dalai [Lama]'s fleeing abroad would not be beneficial to any of them. To them the most favorable development would be the Dalai [Lama]'s independence through expelling the Han. At present, the TWC should adopt a policy of maintaining defensive posture militarily and launching offensive politically. *The policy is to achieve: (i) splitting the upper stratum, winning over as many people as possible, including some living buddhas and lamas, to our side, and breaking them into two antagonizing factions; (ii) educating the lower stratum and preparing the mass;* (iii) luring the enemy to attack. When the enemy attacks, initially we should not inflict too many casualties on the enemy and must not launch counterattack. They should better be granted some minor victories and a hope that expulsion of the Han may succeed. Only then can a big battle be fought. *Otherwise, the enemy may run away after fighting some small battles. Such a result would not be too bad but not as good as fighting a big battle.* The Dalai [Lama] and his pack have a contradictory mindset, cherishing both hope for victory and fear of defeat and impossibility to escape. When they try to escape, I think that our troops should not block them. To Lhoka or India, let them go.

> It would be the best if ten to twenty or thirty to forty thousand lamas and other reactionaries flee abroad. Such a situation would of course become unbearable to India, Bhutan, and maybe also Nepal. But, whereas Bhutan and Nepal are different, India will have brought this onto itself and cannot blame us. *We ought to start considering now what political attitude toward the Dalai [Lama] we should take when they run into exile.* <u>Two options may be considered: (1) to identify him as a traitor, which means that he would not be allowed to come back until a moment in the future when he repents his crimes; (2) to declare him as being abducted, with a hope that he could manage to leave the rebels and come back at an early date, which means that his positions in the Norbulingka and the People's Congress would be kept for him.</u>
>
> Mao Zedong in Wuchang, 11:00 A.M., March 12, 1959[73] (emphasis added)

In transferring "Chairman Mao's analyses and directive," Beijing instructed the TWC to "study effectively and execute accordingly" Mao's ideas. Yet Mao's ideas both corresponded to and deviated from the rest of the CCP leadership's. While confirming the effect of Beijing's waiting game of "appearing weak" in bringing out Lhasa's aggressiveness, Mao agreed completely with his comrades in the Politburo that the PLA should continue to adopt an orientation of *houfazhiren* (gaining mastery by striking after the enemy has struck). A consummate tactician in Chinese civil wars, Mao was more specific than the Politburo in laying out steps for "luring the enemy to attack." On the other hand, in highlighting an anti-Han intention on the Tibetans' part, Mao curiously deviated from the current maxim of the CCP discourse about minority nationality affairs: "nationality contradiction is essentially class contradiction." His use of *quhan* (expulsion of the Han), wittingly or not, connected the Lhasa crisis of 1959 with the two historical precedents of 1911 and 1949 that were so named in Chinese literature. Also significant was Mao's conviction that the Indian government was in collusion with the Tibetans in the current crisis, which would have serious consequences for the Sino-Indian relationship.

The most striking feature of Mao's message in contrast to the Politburo's earlier directive to the TWC, however, was Mao's unequivocal labeling of the Dalai Lama as the leading reactionary in Tibet. Mao referred to an earlier invitation by the CCP leadership for the Dalai Lama to come to Beijing to attend the People's Congress. The invitation now appeared superseded by events after March 10. Although essentially endorsing the Politburo's scheme for removing the Dalai Lama from the political equation of Tibet, Mao did not seem to care much about the "Dalai's abduction" coverage. Appearing tired of the "winning the Dalai Lama over" operation, Mao simply wrote the Tibetan leader off by installing him as head of the "enemy." In view of previous characterizations in

CCP reports of the Dalai Lama as a sincere yet indecisive young leader who had no control over his own circumstances, Mao's new version of the Dalai Lama came as a bombshell. No longer differentiating the Dalai Lama from the Kashag, Mao not only lumped the Dalai Lama and Tibetan "reactionaries" together in a "pack" (*Dalai jiqi yiqun*) but also assigned to the Dalai Lama the complete responsibility for planning and executing an anti-Center, anti-Han conspiracy. To Mao, an almost certain scenario was not that the Dalai Lama would be "abducted" abroad but that he would lead Tibetan reactionaries to flee to Lhoka or India. Therefore, in his message, Mao suggested to his comrades in Beijing that the CCP ought to formulate a new attitude toward the Dalai Lama. Mao's verdict about the Dalai Lama, however, did not readily become a consensus among CCP officials.

A member of the TWC recalled years later that after the Lhasa revolt began, the TWC studied the question of the Dalai Lama's involvement. In the TWC's opinion, in 1954 the Dalai Lama's political attitude turned to the left or became in favor of Beijing; then in 1956 he was influenced by American agents in India and would not have returned to Tibet without Zhou Enlai's persuasion. When Khampa rebels gathered in Lhoka and attacked places in Tibet, the Dalai Lama did sternly ask the Kashag to stop the rebels, but the Kashag wanted the PLA to do it in order to provoke rebellions on an even larger scale. Under the circumstances, the Dalai Lama decided to maintain a middle-of-the-road approach, controlling Khampa rebels to satisfy Beijing, on the one hand, but not completely stopping the rebels, on the other.[74] During the chaotic and extremely confusing week leading to the Dalai Lama's exile, the TWC's reporting provided a consistent impression that the Dalai Lama was a besieged if ambivalent religious leader with very limited political power. Based on TWC reporting, between March 13 and 20 Beijing sent a series of top-secret circulars to responsible CCP officials in provinces, which portrayed the Dalai Lama rather differently from Mao's message. Contents of the first three circulars are summarized here.

Circular No. 1, March 13. Around 11:00 A.M., March 10, protests began in Lhasa to prevent the Dalai Lama from going to the headquarters of the Tibet Military Region to watch a performance. It was circulated among monasteries that Kashag officials Surkhang Wangchen Gelek, Liushar Thupten Tharpa, and the Dalai Lama's chief aide Phala Thupten Wöden were among the principal conspirators behind the Lhasa upheaval. According to Ngabö, these people had been actively plotting to abduct the Dalai Lama.[75]

Circular No. 2, March 16. On March 12, Surkhang, Liushar, and Xiasur sent a secretary of the Kashag to Ngabö's home and informed him of the following developments. On March 11, the Kashag delivered a petition to the Dalai Lama, which had earlier been adopted by a meeting among local officials, khenpos of the three monasteries, and the so-called people's representatives. The Dalai Lama gave his directive: What happened on March 10 and the disorderly behavior such as the so-called Tibetan independence movement and meetings in the Norbulingka were completely against his will; especially the deployment of "people's guards" inside and outside the Norbulingka was completely wrong. The Dalai Lama said that he did not see any threat to his safety, but these developments could bring great danger to him. Therefore, he demanded that all "people's guards" inside the Norbulingka leave immediately. The Dalai Lama also said: In the past, the Center (Beijing) had often criticized the Kashag for not doing a good job and for not carrying out its directives, but the Center had never criticized him for messing up a certain matter; now if such irregular meetings took place inside the Norbulingka, the Center would be misled to believe that he was leading these activities; at present there was no need to call meetings, and even if meetings had to be held, they must not be held in the Norbulingka. In the end, the Dalai Lama said that your activities were totally against my will and therefore I would absolutely not lead such activities. The Dalai Lama's directive was conveyed to the meeting the same day. Some wanted to follow the Dalai Lama's "very important and correct" directive and stop. But others believed that since the Tibetan independence movement had already begun, it must continue. The abbots of the Kundeling Monastery suggested that the Dalai Lama's fear of being misunderstood by Beijing was laughable and meaningless. A certain "people's representative" voiced his opinion: Now that the people had stood up, they could not be stopped easily without achieving some results. On March 12, a meeting of Kashag officials and khenpos was held in the "Snow" scripture print workshop, which was also attended by some 860 rebels carrying arms. "People's representatives" censured the officials for coming late and not taking "state affairs" seriously. When the officials tried to leave the meeting, they were stopped at gunpoint. Then the Drungtsi (a body of four drunyichemmo and four tsipön, all religious officials) began to describe recent conditions of the Dalai Lama, who refused to eat or speak to others, became emaciated, and often sighed alone. Drungtsi officials pleaded with the participants at the meeting to consider the consequences of their activities, but reportedly nobody seemed to care about what these officials said. The meeting elected "people's officials" and also, according to Ngabö, sent a list of elected members of a "representative council" to the Dalai Lama via the Kashag. The Dalai Lama refused to endorse these elected representatives but wanted to give audience to all of them.[76]

Circular No. 3, March 18. This circular cited excerpts from the Dalai Lama's three letters to Tan Guansan and quoted in its entirety Tan's letter to the Dalai Lama dated March 15. In his hand-written letters dated March 11 and 12, the Dalai Lama expressed how he felt "embarrassed," "worried and saddened," and caught "in a predicament" by the developments since March 10. He said: "Reactionary bad elements are acting with an excuse of protecting me but they are actually persecuting me. I am trying to pacify this." The Dalai Lama reported what he had said about and tried to do with the "illegal activities of the reactionary clique," which was identical with the information in Beijing's circular no. 2. The most important content of this circular was Tan's letter, a third one under his name to the Dalai Lama. Condemning part of the Tibetan upper stratum for carrying their "activities of treason to an intolerable level," the letter demanded that the "Tibetan local government" change its "erroneous attitude and immediately take up the responsibility of suppressing the rebellion and punishing the traitors." "Otherwise, the Center itself will have to take action to maintain the unity and unification of the motherland." In the meantime, the letter praised the Dalai Lama's "correct attitude" about redressing the damaged relationship between Beijing and Lhasa. The last paragraph of Tan's letter reads:

> We are extremely concerned about your current circumstance and safety. If you believe it necessary and practically possible to get out of your current precarious situation of being abducted by treasonists, we warmly welcome you and your entourage to come to the quarters of the [Tibetan] Military Region and live here for a short period. We shall absolutely guarantee your safety. We leave the decision completely to your discretion as to what would be the most appropriate step to take next.

Upon receiving Tan's letter on the afternoon of March 16, the Dalai Lama wrote back expressing happiness about Beijing's concern for his safety. Appearing more confident than in his first two letters, the Dalai Lama informed Tan that he was using a "smart approach" in differentiating progressive and reactionary officials around him, promising that he would proceed secretly to the TMR once he had accumulated enough reliable people.[77]

Tan's third letter was especially important for understanding Beijing's intention because, unlike the first two letters that he actually drafted, the author of the third letter was Deng Xiaoping.[78] Between March 14 and 23, Deng presided over a series of meetings of the Central Secretariat on Tibet. Just as two years before, when Deng supervised the Central Secretariat in setting up the waiting strategy in Tibet, now the same mechanism was in operation to decide specific steps for ending the waiting game. This was a four-level structure of policy-making and execution. On the spot in Lhasa, the TWC provided the necessary information for leaders in Beijing to make judgments and was also the executor of Beijing's policy decisions. In Beijing, whereas the Politburo presided over by Liu Shaoqi decided the general policy orientation toward Tibet, the Central Secretariat under Deng considered tactical specifics for implementing this orientation and also issued directives to the TWC. On March 14, Deng attended a Politburo meeting on Tibet and presided over a Central Secretariat meeting. These two meetings decided the gist of Tan's third letter.

274 "The Showdown"

At the top of the structure was Mao, who was by chance not in Beijing when the Lhasa revolt took place. Starting February 23, Mao made a tour to provinces in eastern China to assess the initial effects of the "people's commune," a "communist" form of rural organization created by the Great Leap Forward. On the morning of March 10, when Lhasa erupted, Mao was aboard a train to Wuhan, the largest city across the Yangtze River in central China.[79] Mao nevertheless exercised control from afar, endorsing, advising, and modifying policy decisions made in Beijing. Whereas Tan's third letter apparently did not write the Dalai Lama off and still tried to persuade him to come over to the PLA side, Mao's reading of the letter was quite different.

At 4:00 P.M. on March 15, Mao wrote a letter to CCP leaders in Beijing with respect to "Tan's third letter," which Deng had drafted the previous day:

> The letter of the [March] 14th to the Dalai [Lama] in Tan Guansan's name is very good, which gives us political advantage. Let's wait and see how he will react. If he replies with whatever attitude, we should write to him again. From now on we may continue to write letters to him to reciprocate any communication from him. All these letters should be prepared for publication in the future. For this reason, a letter should be drafted to chronicle the Center's magnanimous and patient handling of each disturbance [in Tibet] with a hope that treasonists and splitists would repent. Hopefully the Dalai [Lama] may stick to the Seventeen-Point Agreement and his repeated promises, and act in one with the Center in pacifying rebellions, purging splitists, and restoring national unity. This can bring a glorious future to Tibet. Acting otherwise would bring harm to the Tibetan people and result in his desertion by the people. Please consider the above.[80]

It should be noted that before Mao wrote these comments, Deng's draft letter had already been telegraphed to Tan Guansan.[81] Having no effect on Tan's third letter and holding a slightly more flexible attitude toward the Dalai Lama than his March 12 verdict, Mao nevertheless treated the exchange of letters with the Dalai Lama as a propaganda step anticipating the "final showdown."

On March 16, Mao's idea about how to treat the Dalai Lama changed further after he met with Huang Kecheng, Zhang Jingwu, Zhang Guohua, and Lei Yingfu in Wuchang. Huang and the two Zhangs had participated in the Politburo meeting in Beijing two days before. At Mao's request, they came to Wuchang to make a report.[82] Mao spent four hours with these officials, from 5:45 P.M. to 9:50 P.M. Obviously, Huang and Lei were present because Mao wanted to discuss military issues in relation to Tibet, and the two Zhangs could help Mao verify his information and impression about the Lhasa situation and bring his ideas directly to the TWC.[83] Details of the Wuchang discussion remain classified. What has come out is Mao's opinion conveyed to CCP leaders in Beijing in a monologue fashion:

1. Agree with the Center's orientation, which should continue; the situation is good; we finally gained political initiative.
2. *Do not let the Dalai [Lama] go if possible; having him in our hands, we may easily release him if necessary in the future; but it would not be a problem if by any chance he runs away.*
3. *Troops entering Tibet should encircle Lhasa, maintaining "encirclement without attack," which is useful in causing discords [on the enemy's side]; troops should arrive before April 10. As there is no fighting in Lhasa, a regiment should advance to Lhoka [Shannan] in order to control key points and cut [the enemy's] way of retreat.*
4. Rebellion pacification should focus on Lhasa and Lhoka, and other areas can be dealt with later.
5. Use the term of rebellion pacification [in CCP public statements], but reform should not be mentioned. Reform should be implemented only under pacification operations. Differentiated treatments should be applied [to different areas]: early reform for areas that rebelled first, late reform for areas that rebelled later than others, and no reform for areas that did not rebel.
6. Agree with the Military Affairs Commission's plan for troop deployment in Tibet.
7. Agree with the at-the-selected-location approach of diplomacy.
8. No publication in the press but internal circulation of information; troops entering Tibet should issue a public notice.
9. Migration should not be rushed.
10. *What is the Panchen [Lama]'s attitude? Why there has not been any news from him?*[84] (emphases added)

Whereas Mao's points on military operations, reform, and propaganda are self-explanatory, his points on diplomacy and migration cannot be elaborated without further information. Mao's attitude toward the Dalai Lama remained the central subject of this truncated version of the Wuchang discussion. Mao's guests must have conveyed to him the gist of recent discussions in Beijing, for Mao seemingly made an about-face change on the issue of whether or not the Dalai Lama should be retained. Mao, however, did not change his verdict on the Tibetan leader. His new idea about "not letting the Dalai [Lama] go if possible" was merely an operational notion about how to physically handle the Dalai Lama as an adversary, which carried the same political undertone as the "let them go" idea in Mao's March 12 letter. That is why at the end of the Wuchang meeting Mao asked about the Panchen Lama, the obvious substitute for the Dalai Lama in Beijing's postrebellion policy in Tibet. His specific instruction

276   The Showdown

about troops' maneuvering from Lhasa to Lhoka, as will be discussed below, would be a main factor in starting the fighting inside Lhasa.

It cannot be ascertained to what extent Mao's sudden change of mind about the Dalai Lama's retention compounded the already complex situation that CCP operatives faced in Lhasa. On the afternoon of March 17, the day of the Dalai Lama's flight, Huang Kecheng reported Mao's ideas to a Politburo meeting in Beijing. There is no evidence that Beijing rushed a directive to the TWC after learning about Mao's most recent opinion. The two Zhangs also returned to Beijing and did not proceed to Lhasa until the battle of Lhasa was over.[85] It is possible that the two Zhangs conveyed Mao's points to Tan Guansan in Lhasa before or after they returned to Beijing on March 17, but the TWC, as shown below, did not take any action before the Dalai Lama's flight.

Therefore, despite Mao's close overseeing of Beijing's policymaking with regard to Tibet during the crucial days of March 1959, his specific ideas about the Dalai Lama did not readily become policy steps on the spot in Lhasa. As Beijing's *Circular No. 4* of March 18 shows, on March 16 the TWC managed to deliver Tan's third letter to the Dalai Lama and also took a concrete step via Ngabö to try to get the Dalai Lama out of his "abduction." A letter under Ngabö's name was delivered to the Dalai Lama along with Tan's letter. Ngabö warned the Dalai Lama that a conspiracy was afoot to "steal away the great savior and heart-like treasure." It would be blocked no matter which route the conspirators chose to take, and that would mean war as well as great danger to the Dalai Lama; even if the Dalai Lama were lucky enough to get away, he would then become "a lion of the snow land separated from snow." Ngabö advised the Dalai Lama to stay in a chamber of the Norbulingka with reliable guards and to inform General Tan of his location so that measures could be taken to protect him. In replying to Ngabö, the Dalai Lama stated that he was using a mild approach to find a way out, and he also asked Ngabö to persuade Beijing to find a way to avoid war.[86]

Beijing's last two circulars were issued separately on March 20 and 22. *Circular No. 6* of March 20 contained only two pieces of information. First, "according to Ngabö and investigations with other means, on the evening of March 17 or in the early morning of March 18, the Dalai [Lama] and a group of reactionary upper-stratum individuals left the Norbulingka and took leather boats to flee along the Lhasa River." Second, "according to a TMR report, starting with 3:40 [A.M.] of the 20th, rebel forces launched attack on our troops in the city and in the eastern and western suburbs." *Circular No. 7* of March 22 reported that by 9:00 A.M. of that day, the battle of Lhasa had basically ended, and captured rebels confirmed the Dalai Lama's departure on March 17 for either Lhoka or India.[87]

The CCP Central Committee's circulars constitute just one of several possible sets of historical records that can shed light on the last-moment communications between Beijing and Lhasa before the two sides' decade-long collaboration finally collapsed. An empirical analysis of the two sides' degrees of sincerity and maneuvering tactics in conducting communications will have to wait for further declassification of primary sources. Could the communications have had a different result? Relevant to the question were two inconsequential requests in the Beijing-Lhasa communications. One was Beijing's request for the Dalai Lama to rally to the CCP authorities, either a last-ditch effort to salvage the "Dalai line" or a gesture of *ren zhi yi jin* (exhausting utmost benevolence and patience) for the sake of preparing propaganda for a post–Dalai Lama Tibet. The other was the Kashag officials' request for "peaceful negotiations" with the TWC, either wishful thinking for renegotiating the Beijing-Lhasa relationship or a delaying gambit for the Dalai Lama group's safe exit.[88] Eventually, Beijing and the Dalai Lama group reciprocated each other in not satisfying the other side.

If the departure of the Dalai Lama on March 17 marked the decisive termination of Beijing's "Dalai line" in resolving its Tibetan question, the fighting in the early morning of March 20 signaled the beginning of the "general showdown" anticipated by Mao. As far as the TWC was concerned, by March 15 "the enemy has already put the arrow on the bow and taken the sword out of sheath; the horn for a comprehensive rebellion will be sounded once reactionaries in Lhasa openly declare rebellion or attack us militarily."[89] The same characterization can be applied to the PLA. On March 11, the Central Military Affairs Commission directed the Fifty-Fourth Army of the PLA and the Chengdu Military Region to set up two commanding headquarters, under Generals Ding Sheng and Huang Xinting, respectively, for the purpose of suppressing rebellions in the Lhasa and Chamdo areas. On March 15, the PLA General Staff issued orders about dates and locations of assembly to the four divisions designated for entering Tibet.[90] Yet none of these divisions participated in the battle of Lhasa between March 20 and 22, which was fought between Tibetan rebels and some two thousand PLA troops under the TWC.[91]

The timing of the Dalai Lama's secret departure from the Norbulingka and the beginning of the battle of Lhasa may explain the Dalai Lama's successful escape. According to a publication in the PRC, after receiving Mao's letter of March 12, Tan Guansan informed PLA troops in Lhoka (Shannan), Dromo (Yadong), and checkpoints along the border that if the Dalai Lama and his entourage arrived, they should be allowed to pass. On the late evening of March 17, when the Dalai Lama and his companions crossed the Lhasa River and proceeded to Lhoka, their movement was observed but not stopped by PLA reconnaissance groups posted near a ferry crossing point on the river named Ramagang (Nandukou). Only afterwards, based on its size, direction of travel, and number of armed personnel, did the TMR intelligence made a judgment that the group crossing the Lhasa River on March 17 had to have been the Dalai Lama and his entourage.⁹² On March 19, with this piece of intelligence and also information from Ngabö, the TWC made a report to Beijing about the Dalai Lama's flight, which was included the next day in Beijing's sixth circular.⁹³ In retrospect, the Dalai Lama and Kashag officials made the decision to leave Lhasa just in time: both Beijing's "abduction" scheme and Mao's "let them go" directive were still in effect as far as the TWC was concerned, and Mao's most recent opinion about "not letting the Dalai [Lama] go if possible" was yet to reach TWC officials in Lhasa. More important, acutely mindful of maintaining "political initiative," Beijing sternly ordered PLA troops to take a defensive posture and not to seek a fight. Therefore, the scenario in Ngabö's letter to the Dalai Lama, that the Dalai Lama's attempt to leave Lhasa would be intercepted and would provoke a war, did not occur. After March 20, however, the situation changed completely.

Published accounts in the PRC of the events on March 20 are inconsistent. Some official publications insist that the battle of Lhasa began on March 20 because the rebels started an attack on the PLA in Lhasa.⁹⁴ Some other works, while maintaining that the Tibetan side fired the first shot, concede that in the early morning of March 20, PLA troops attempted to control the Ramagang ferry and block the way out of Lhasa via the Lhasa River. This move provoked the Tibetan rebels' attack.⁹⁵ Zhang Xiangming, a member of the TWC who was in Lhasa during the crisis, attests in his memoir that the battle of Lhasa began on the morning of March 20 after a lengthy discussion among TWC officials the previous day. TWC officials feared that if they waited longer for the arrival of troops from outside Tibet, they would let a great number of rebels escape and thus spoil Mao's plan for destroying as many rebels as possible in Lhasa. So they made the decision to launch a "counteroffensive" without Beijing's authorization, for which Tan Guansan agreed to assume full responsibility at the risk of being disciplined by Beijing.⁹⁶ Whereas Zhang's revelation of TWC officials' concern about implementing Mao's military plan is useful for understanding their decision on March 19, his story probably leaves out a more important reason for the TWC to hold its urgent meeting on that day, which was Mao's more recent "directive" that had emerged from his March 16 talk in Wuchang. In light of the content of Mao's Wuchang talk, it is possible that the PLA movement toward Ramagang in the early morning of March 20, whether called a "counteroffensive" or not, was a belated effort to prevent the Dalai Lama from leaving Lhasa.

It is highly unlikely that by March 19 the content of Mao's conversation with the two Zhangs in Wuchang had not reached TWC officials in Lhasa. Research has not discovered any message from Beijing to the TWC that conveyed the content of Mao's talk. Since Mao had already talked to the two Zhangs, who ranked number one and number two in the TWC, such a message would have been redundant. It is reasonable to speculate that one of the Zhangs conveyed Mao's ideas to Tan Guansan by other means. A piece of circumstantial evidence is the Panchen Lama's message to the TWC dated March 19 that pledged loyalty to Beijing, which was obviously a response to Mao's query at Wuchang about his attitude after the Lhasa revolt.[97] To Tan and his associates in Lhasa, Mao's Wuchang talk made two operational points that they were to implement immediately: (1) to prevent the Dalai Lama from running away, and (2) to send troops into the Lhoka area to "control key points and cut [the enemy's] way of retreat." On March 19, the TWC already had information about the Dalai Lama's escape and made the relevant report to Beijing. Yet, before the information could be verified, Mao's point about intercepting the Dalai Lama remained valid.[98] In terms of military operations, preventing the Dalai Lama's flight and cutting the enemy's way of retreat would basically entail the same move by PLA troops. Hence Tan decided to send troops to Ramagang in order to block the rebels' way to Lhoka. Mao's idea of "encirclement without attack," which was imagined as a systematic deployment of troops entering Tibet from the outside, could not be practically performed by PLA troops from inside Lhasa. According to a source, after receiving General Tan's order of controlling Ramagang, the commanding officer concerned ordered his troops not to fire their guns but to "use shoulders and fists" to squeeze rebels out of their positions.[99] Actually, Mao's master strategy conceived in Wuchang put Tan and his troops in an impossible position in Lhasa: they could neither wait for the arrival of PLA troops from the outside, lest the rebels, and maybe the Dalai Lama himself, slip away; nor seal Lhasa without provoking a fight with the rebels. In the final analysis, therefore, it was Mao's ideas of retaining the Dalai Lama and encircling as many rebels as possible inside Lhasa that broke the delicate military standoff in the city and triggered the battle of Lhasa.

Thus, there is no simple answer to the historical question of how the Dalai Lama and his entourage succeeded in fleeing into exile in India. The Dalai Lama's exile turned a page of modern Tibetan and Chinese history, but it happened neither because of Beijing's intention of "letting them go" nor the Dalai Lama group's skill in getting away. Timing was the key. It would have been very difficult for the Dalai Lama group to leave Lhasa after the battle of Lhasa started on March 20, and once the group left Lhasa on March 17, the day when Mao changed his mind about whether the Dalai Lama should be allowed to go, it became very difficult for PLA troops to intercept them. This is perhaps the historical significance of a marginal figure named Zeng Huishan, an "economic police" stationed in a transportation depot near the Norbulingka, who, without authorization, fired two mortar rounds at the palace on March 17.[100] The two rounds did not hit anyone or anything. But Zeng's nervous action set the plan or notion for the Dalai Lama's escape into motion at a time when PLA troops in Lhasa were not positioned to block the way out of the city.

After the battle of Lhasa began, which at the beginning was a PLA operation to block the way to Lhoka, a great number of PLA troops poured in from neighboring provinces. An internal PLA report of early April 1959 stated that the entire PLA establishment, except for one branch (the navy) and one military region (Inner Mongolia), joined the rebellion suppression in Tibet, that "bombers and transport airplanes went in," and that "soldiers and weapons were everywhere." Although the battle of Lhasa sped up PLA movement into Tibet, the earliest date for outside troops to reach Lhasa was scheduled for March 30, just one day before the Dalai Lama crossed the McMahon Line into India. Furthermore, the same source revealed that both PLA ground troops and air force received restrictive orders. For the moment, the ground troops must neither push to the McMahon Line and then stop, which would be tantamount to acquiescing in the line, nor chase the rebels across the line, which would cause diplomatic disputes with India. And PLA airplanes must stay forty kilometers away from the border.[101] In mid-April 1959, when delivering a top-secret report for CCP officials outside Tibet, Zhang Jingwu did not use Beijing's pre-March 17 position to explain how the Dalai Lama got away, saying instead: "The border is too long to be completely guarded."[102] Thus, without revealing the complete truth, Zhang spared himself the trouble of explaining Beijing's "let them go" orientation prior to March 17 and admitting PLA's inability to intercept the Dalai Lama.

In late April, after the battle of Lhoka ended, the Central Military Affairs Commission ordered PLA troops to seal the border rapidly.[103] As far as the CCP leadership was concerned, the post–Dalai Lama period had begun in Tibet.

Zhang Guotao Fallacy

It may be recalled that in late 1956 Mao Zedong already imagined a Tibet without the Dalai Lama, comparing the Dalai Lama's possible exile with Zhang Guotao's rally to the KMT. Mao asserted at the time: "We have an experience that Zhang Guotao's running away was not a bad thing." Suspecting that the Dalai Lama would not return from India, Mao dismissed any harm that might result from the Dalai Lama's joining with the PRC's international adversaries.[104] This cavalier attitude was modified in Beijing's "Dalai's abduction" scenario that awaited the Dalai Lama's removal from the scene of Tibetan politics without incriminating him right away. As far as Beijing was concerned, the Dalai Lama's escape on March 17 was no abduction at all, but the event must be presented as such. Beijing's relevant directive to the TWC spelled out a short-term expediency:

> For the moment the Dalai [Lama]'s escape should not be announced, and he will not be included in the list of leading treasonists. Rather, propaganda should state that treacherous rebels abducted the Dalai [Lama]. This approach may help frustrate the enemy's attempt of using the Dalai [Lama]'s name to call the mass to rebel.[105]

As a result, the theme of "Dalai being abducted" was established in the PRC news media and in the PLA's "public notice" to the Tibetan populace on its entry into Tibet.[106] While expecting to use the notion to achieve a momentary military effect inside Tibet, Beijing also intended to keep a kindly mien toward the Dalai Lama for a while for political purposes. The Dalai Lama would not be criticized in public, and his positions in the National People's Congress and the Preparatory Committee of the Tibetan Autonomous Region would be kept. In contrast, the CCP had denounced Zhang Guotao as a traitor right after he rallied to Chiang Kai-shek. Mao's Zhang Guotao analogy, therefore, was modified once the Dalai Lama's split with Beijing became reality.

Nevertheless, despite Beijing's public rhetoric that continued to acknowledge the Dalai Lama's "usefulness" in Beijing's Tibetan enterprise after his physical as well as political departure from Tibet, the Zhang Guotao analogy held true in CCP leaders' thinking about a post–Dalai Lama Tibet. CCP leaders believed that not only would their policy in Tibet not be hindered, but it might actually be facilitated by the Dalai Lama's departure. Repeatedly within the circle of high CCP officials, and even when talking to "left wing" figures of the Tibetan upper classes such as Ngabö and the Panchen Lama, Mao expressed a willingness to accept the Dalai Lama if he returned, but with one condition: he must "completely stand on our side" and "change his attitude."[107] Neither was the tactical significance of the "Dalai Lama's abduction" story concealed from midechelon officials. CCP officials and PLA officers learned from "internal reports" that, from the beginning, the CCP leadership "did not harbor any illusion" about the Dalai Lama and the "abduction" story was a "two-faced revolutionary policy" for countering the Dalai Lama's double-dealing.[108]

After the Lhasa revolt was reported in the press and the letters between Tan Guansan and the Dalai Lama were published in the *People's Daily*, united-front and propaganda officials of the CCP surveyed and collected information about reactions from various social circles in major cities and minority areas.[109] Understandably, in minority areas and especially among religious figures, the reported developments in Tibet caused all sorts of emotions, ranging from anger to excitement, fear, and dismay. In cities, government employees, students, factory workers, and social notables also behaved differently. Some embraced completely the official story, and some expressed suspicions and questioned Beijing's past policies. Beijing's story about the Dalai Lama's abduction proved not at all convincing to many. A typical generalization from the surveys was that only a minority of those surveyed believed that the Dalai Lama was innocent in the Lhasa revolt. Meanwhile, the majority either suspected him of duplicity or held him guilty for plotting the rebellion.[110] Politically motivated and often targeted at specific groups or individuals, there is nothing scientific about these surveys. But as far as the "public" suspicion of the official story about the Dalai Lama was concerned, it might actually be an expected effect of Beijing's propaganda. For instance, an internal report of the PLA praised a group of factory workers in Beijing for being "very sharp politically" in seeing through the official story and viewing the Dalai Lama as a double-dealer.[111]

Yet, no matter how people in the Chinese provinces reacted to Beijing's propaganda, they were not the principally intended audience, which were the Tibetans, especially the populace of Tibet itself. The expected propaganda effect in Tibet, different from that in other areas, was to maintain the myth of the Dalai Lama–Beijing amity, for the Dalai Lama's position in the minds of most Tibetans was not shaken even after his exile. In late April, the TWC sent to Beijing its first survey of social attitudes after the Lhasa revolt. With respect to the upper classes of Tibet, the TWC had an established tally of the political attitudes of the individuals concerned. Although behaving differently, leading political and religious figures, classified as "leftists," "centrists," or "conservatives," were ready to embrace or become resigned to forthcoming changes. Most revealing, however, was the survey's description of ordinary people's behaviors and attitudes. After the battle of Lhasa, according to the report, social life gradually returned to normal, one sign of which was the reappearance of laboring people's singing. The report even provided evidence that the masses in Lhasa were assisting the PLA in suppressing the rebels. Yet, as far as the Dalai Lama was concerned, the situation was troublesome to the TWC:

> The mass showed a great concern about the issue of the Dalai [Lama]. Whenever propaganda teams mentioned the Dalai [Lama], many people started to cry. Some pleaded that the Center should find a way to get the Dalai [Lama] back, saying that because the Center arranged the Panchen [Lama]'s return, it must be able to get the Dalai [Lama] back as well. Some believed that without the Dalai [Lama], even reform would not be able to bring about happiness.[112]

Although Beijing's military action in Tibet in 1959 was mainly premised on Tibetan ruling circles' treason, the war actually restored "democratic reform" as the central theme of Beijing's policy in Tibet. As military operations proceeded, Beijing began to carry out "comprehensive democratic reform" to change "the serfdom land of Tibet that was completely incompatible with our big family of socialism."[113] From the recent events in Tibet, Zhang Jingwu derived a conclusion: "Reform could not be implemented without fighting a war. That place had serfdom, and social reforms had to be preceded with mobilization of the mass. Whatever peaceful policy was adopted, it could not change serfdom."[114] Zhang did not ask or want to answer the question of how such a conclusion could be reconciled with Beijing's previous gradualist and "smart" approach. Now that the "Dalai bridge" leading to a peaceful resolution of the CCP's Tibetan question was demolished, war became a necessary device to clear any obstacle in the path of Beijing's reform plan. Still, given the Tibetan people's unshaken belief in the Dalai Lama, Beijing's story about the Dalai Lama's abduction had to remain for a while an integral part of the CCP's mass mobilization in Tibet.[115]

Yet post-1959, mass mobilization in Tibet would no longer be carried out in the Dalai Lama's name. Allegedly, after the battle of Lhasa began, Mao said: "Now we will do a thorough job no matter what [*buguan san qi ershiyi, chedi gaoxiaqu*]."[116] These audacious words reflected a shared confidence among CCP officials when they talked about "comprehensive" changes in Tibet and a "thorough" resolution of the Tibetan question. Whereas, in the Tibetan context, Mao's use of the Zhang Guotao precedent in evaluating the Dalai Lama's lingering influence was fallacious, another CCP fallacy held "class struggle" as the panacea for solving all social and political problems. CCP officials from Beijing to Lhasa saw post-1959 Tibet as a virgin land where the CCP's tested policy formulas, devices, and experiences accumulated in the rest of China could finally be applied. The moment for departicularizing Tibet had arrived. In this deeply religious land, religion would not only be touched but would also be, in Zhang Jingwu's words, "dug to the bottom." This could be done now because the masses' "class consciousness" would be awakened. Zhang's class analysis for Tibet was rather simple: "There are just two classes in Tibet. One is the upper class of aristocrats who wear yellow mandarin jackets [*huang magua*]. Another includes the vast laboring people who have neither house to live nor food to eat."[117]

Mao was not satisfied with Zhang's two-class version of Tibetan society. As the CCP's chief advocate and practitioner of the investigative approach and class-analysis method, Mao wanted to know more about Tibet and the Tibetans in terms of class relations. As mentioned before, in 1950, in preparing for the PLA's advance into Tibet, the Intelligence Department of the Central Military Affairs Commission, the Eighteenth Army, and the Fan Ming group had compiled a series of reports about the conditions in Tibet, but none provided a detailed class analysis. In early April 1959, Mao wanted to fill this gap in his understanding of Tibetan society. He asked the Central United Front Department to provide information to him so that he could study the "overall conditions of all Tibetans," in Tibet as well as in Yunnan, Sichuan, Gansu, and Qinghai. Mao listed thirteen items for which he needed information:

(1) On the western side of the Jinsha River, it is said that the population in Tibet proper [*Xizang benbu*] consisting of Chamdo, *Qianzang* [front Tibet], and *Houzang* [rear Tibet] (including Ngari) is 1.2 million. Is this correct? (2) How many square kilometers is the area? (3) What are the content of serfdom, the relationship between serfs and their masters, and the shares of products for each side? Some people said that it was a 2:8 ratio,

but some other said that in theory all products belonged to aristocrats but, in reality, serfs divided among themselves part of the products not reported to their masters. Is this true? (4) What is the total number of lamas? Is it 80,000, as said by some? (5) In aristocrats' political relationship with the serfs, did they have the right to kill, set up private trial, and use private torture? (6) Situation of monasteries' exploitation and oppression of the serfs under them. (7) Situation of exploitation and oppression inside monasteries. It is said that skinning and sinew plucking were applied to disobedient lamas. Were there really such things? (8) Where did the huge revenue come from for various levels of the Tibetan government and the Tibetan army? Did it come from the serfs or the aristocrats? (9) What is the percentage of the rebels in the total population? Is it 5 percent, or more? Or is it less than five, just one, two, or 3 percent? Which one is accurate? (10) What are the percentages of leftists, centrists, and rightists respectively in the exploitative class? Can the leftists account for a third, or less? What is the portion of the centrists? (11) What is the Tibetan population separately in the four provinces of Yunnan, Sichuan, Gansu, and Qinghai, and the combined total? It is said that in total the four provinces have two to three million of Tibetans. Is that true? (12) How many square kilometers of land are resided by Tibetans in the four provinces? (13) What situations transpired from the *suku* [grievances venting] campaign in monasteries of Qinghai, Gansu, and Sichuan? It is said that many human skins were discovered there. Did this really happen?

Mao gave the provinces concerned one to two weeks to complete the questionnaire and also directed the Xinhua News Agency to undertake a long-term project of investigating and studying conditions in Tibet.[118] Without revealing the origin of the questions, the CUFD conveyed to the provinces all Mao's items except number twelve, which at the time was probably unanswerable.[119]

Obviously, Mao's questionnaire was biased and not intended for a comprehensive social or anthropological investigation. Mao wanted to collect factual information about Tibet not even for the sake of policymaking. Beijing's fundamental policy orientation for Tibet was already set. Instead, Mao needed specific "facts" to substantiate the CCP's class-struggle narrative about Tibetan history. He just needed a certain set of "facts" and asked his questions within the class-struggle frame. His questions already imagined a dark, cruel system dominated by aristocrats and monasteries, under which the vast majority of the oppressed Tibetan people were waiting for emancipation. Meanwhile, the rebels who resisted progressive changes had to be just a tiny minority of the Tibetan population. The provinces answered Mao's questions in time, and, predictably, their answers did not alter even slightly Mao's imagination of the Tibetan communities inside and outside Tibet. On April 15, in his speech to the Supreme Conference of State Affairs, Mao put to use the information he had recently collected. By describing Tibetan Buddhist talismans made of human bones, Mao found a way to justify, at home and abroad, the progressive nature of the CCP's current undertaking in Tibet. In pointing out that more than half the Tibetan population actually resided in the four provinces around Tibet and more than 90 percent of the people inside Tibet did not rebel, Mao depicted a balance of class power utterly in favor of the Tibetan laboring people and their supporter, the CCP.[120] A few days later, in talking to an Italian communist delegation, Mao made the same point about Tibet, suggesting that the situation there was one between twenty thousand "reactionaries" and 1.8 million "Tibetan mass" siding with the PLA. Using Tibet as an example, Mao's advice to his Italian comrades was "class struggle has to be settled with war" and "don't think about getting power without war."[121]

Yet, even answering the CUFD's questionnaire in the class-struggle frame preset by Mao, provincial officials could not completely avoid reporting information that was potentially at odds with Mao's purpose. For instance, the report from Gansu indeed supplied stories about the sorts of tortures used by Tibetan aristocrats and religious talismans made of human skins and skulls. At the same time, the Gansu report also provided numbers about the rebels that were unusable to Mao. According to the report, the Tibetan population in southern Gansu totaled 166,683, of which 32,064, or 19.43 percents, participated in rebellions. In some villages, more than 50 percent of the households joined rebellions.[122] In July, PLA officers of the Political Department of the Lanzhou Military Region tried to understand why, after rebellions in Qinghai and Gansu were successively pacified in 1958, the number of rebels increased to thirty thousand again and many of them were "ordinary mass who joined the bandits for the second time." They posed these questions to themselves: "Why did the struggle situation reverse even under a circumstance that our side was much stronger than the enemy? Why, after being liberated from the feudal yoke, did the poor laboring mass still run away and join the bandits?" There was no other answer but that the "class consciousness" of the masses was still stifled by their "ethnic prejudice and religious ideas." Especially in pastoral areas, these allegedly archaic ideas enabled the rebels to "control almost all the mass last year and to control continually part of the mass this year in confronting us."[123] Obviously, having done his investigation, Mao used the resulting information selectively. The kind of "natural empathy" toward the CCP's undertaking in Tibet and other Tibetan areas that Mao tried to affix to the Tibetan laboring masses in 1959 did not actually exist, even after the Dalai Lama and the Kashag exited from the scene. Yet Mao's propagandist enthusiasm could not be dampened easily. In late April, Mao wrote a piece for the Xinhua News Agency affectionately titled "The People of Tibet Treat the PLA Like Family Members and Support the PLA's Rebellion Pacification." For some reason, the article remained befittingly unpublished at the time.[124]

The effect of propaganda was one thing, and the pursuit of a "thorough solution" of the Tibetan question was another. The "thoroughness" of the solution depended on the way Beijing defined the "Tibetan question." In May, Zhou Enlai delivered a speech at a meeting of the standing committee of the NPPCC, explaining the Tibetan situation to all circles of the PRC's political life. More than Mao, Zhou utilized recently collected information about Tibet in describing a dark feudal system that blended aristocracy and religion. Zhou admitted that not only foreigners but also "political workers like us" did not know much about Tibet. He nevertheless asserted that "no matter how to explain the Tibetan question, by nature the Tibetan question (except Taiwan) was the last violent class struggle in China mainland." According to Zhou, all other major paradigms for interpreting the Tibetan question, which viewed Tibet as a question of "nation" or "religion" or "state," were distorting the class essence of the question.[125] Hence Beijing's particularistic treatment of Tibet came to a decisive end. CCP leaders could convince themselves that the Tibetan question was "thoroughly" resolved when they achieved a total victory in the last battlefield of China's violent class struggle.

While the war between the PLA and Tibetan fighters continued for years after 1959, Beijing took steps for Tibet to catch up with the rest of China in terms of sociopolitical changes. The initial tasks were summarized as "three entries and six measures." Under "three entries," PLA troops would enter Tibet to reinforce national defense, cadres would enter to implement "democratic reform," and migrants would enter to thoroughly develop mineral resources. With "six measures," the Tibetan army would be disbanded, the Kashag abolished, weapons confiscated from the society, religion separated from government, criminals punished, and social reforms realized.[126] On March 28, the State Council issued an order to dissolve the "Tibetan local government," or the Kashag, and transfer its function to the Preparatory Committee for the Tibetan Autonomous Region, which, as the Dalai Lama was still under "abduction," would be chaired by the Panchen Lama. The order also dismissed eighteen PCTAR officials who were accused of conducting rebellion.[127]

In mid-May, Beijing decided that "rebellions in Tibet have been basically pacified, and social reforms will gradually unfold." Fourteen provinces were directed to send cadres to Tibet to help the TWC carry out reform. The first group included five thousand people. Sichuan, Qinghai, and Gansu got the lion's share and were required to make cadres of Tibetan nationality the majority of their dispatched personnel. The other provinces were required to send cadres familiar with nationality work and, in case of the southern provinces, cadres of northern origins.[128] The bias toward northern cadres was not explained, but may have been related to northerners' temperament and physical tolerance of a cold climate. It is interesting to note that the vast majority of the top-echelon leaders of the CCP were southern Chinese and all the leading members of the

TWC were also southerners except the "anti-Party" Fan Ming, who was from Shaanxi.

Thus, Beijing prepared a future for Tibet identical to that of the rest of China, which was to integrate the borderland into the CCP's phased revolution. As Zhou Enlai put it, Tibet would be changed in two steps: first, implementing "democratic reform" and, second, completing socialist transformation. "Democratic reform" would basically duplicate the land reform implemented in the rest of China. Differentiated treatment, however, would be accorded to aristocrats who rebelled and those who did not. As with landlords in the Chinese countryside, the former's lands and properties were to be confiscated and redistributed among poor Tibetans. For the latter, a buyout policy would be applied, comparable to Beijing's policy toward "national bourgeoisie" during "socialist transformation" in other provinces. As for religion, it may be recalled that just a few months before the Lhasa upheaval, Zhou Enlai had criticized Han cadres for lacking empathy toward minority nationalities' religious feelings. Now, in a conversation with the Panchen Lama, Ngabö, and some other Tibetan figures, Zhou told them that although religious reform was an internal matter of Lamaism, the CCP was qualified to demand three things: (1) religion must not be tarnished by feudal serfdom, (2) the Qing dynasty's policy of weakening minorities by way of religion must be opposed, and (3) not all believers of religion had to live in monasteries. For the time being, Beijing's priority was to sever the economic ties between monasteries and the Tibetan people, even if this entailed the government's subsidizing monasteries.[129]

It turned out that Beijing's two-step plan for Tibet to "enter socialism" was not a continuous one as initially envisioned. Overly enthusiastic cadres in Tibet did try to hurry into socialism, but they were stopped by Beijing.[130] In April 1961, Beijing informed the TWC that although democratic reform was completed in Tibet, in the next five years Tibet should not start the transformation to socialism. This grace period would allow the "emancipated serfs" to "taste the benefits brought about by democratic reform, . . . work on their newly obtained lands without anxiety, and recover from the upheaval." Beijing cautioned the TWC against any rush toward socialism because it "would not be understood by them [Tibetans] and could cause tremendous danger." With respect to religion, Beijing conceded that "the prevalent belief in Lamaism among the Tibetan people cannot be changed fundamentally for a long time." But, in citing Mao's writing about Hunan peasants in the 1920s, Beijing expressed confidence that when the "time comes, the peasants will throw away *pusa* [bodhisattva] with their own hands."[131]

Nevertheless, before socialism was installed in Tibet and the Tibetan people showed any sign of discarding divine images and statues as Hunan peasants had done in Mao's story, Beijing decided to remove the highest ranking "living Buddha" from the Tibetan people's hearts. In the summer of 1963, at the TWC's proposal, Beijing launched an education campaign for "exposing the Dalai [Lama]'s crimes of treason" in Tibet, its neighboring provinces, and Xinjiang and Inner Mongolia, where the Dalai Lama's influence remained strong. The TWC contended that ever since his escape, the Dalai Lama had colluded with foreign imperialism, and especially Indian reactionaries, in opposing the PRC. International and domestic counterrevolutionaries had also used his name in conducting all sorts of subversive activities. These developments indicated that the CCP could no longer usefully maintain a harmonious facade concerning its relationship with the Dalai Lama, and that the sooner the Dalai Lama's "true face" was exposed to the Tibetan masses, the better. For this purpose, the TWC compiled a lengthy chronology showing that the Dalai Lama had been personally responsible for all the troubles in Tibet and other Tibetan areas ever since 1951. The education campaign was aimed at convincing ordinary Tibetans that the Dalai Lama was the origin of "all evils" (*wan e zhi yuan*). More specifically, the campaign denounced the Dalai Lama as the "biggest feudal lord," "instrument of foreign imperialism," "traitor of the motherland," and "common enemy of all nationalities."[132]

The goal was difficult to achieve. During a yearlong campaign, CCP officials in Tibetan areas realized that they were in an "extremely sharp and complicated class struggle." For them, an odd phenomenon in the "class struggle" was that while upper-stratum figures seemed divided over the issue of the Dalai Lama, the vast laboring masses continued to worship the Dalai Lama deeply. Pilot programs of the campaign indicated that after going through rebellion pacification and "democratic reform," the masses' belief in the Dalai Lama changed little. Initially, the TWC fancied that the masses continued to worship the Dalai Lama simply because of Beijing's story about his abduction, and that an explanation of Beijing's changed story could reshape their attitude. In the education campaign, however, it was discovered that Beijing's abduction story had not been widely known to ordinary Tibetans. They had always had their own understanding of the Dalai Lama's exile: the Dalai Lama left of his own will; because he was the most powerful figure, nobody could force him to do anything against his will. As reported by local Tibetan cadres, the masses would not denounce the Dalai Lama, and even if they said something disrespectful about the Dalai Lama now, the words "came from above the neck but not from the heart." Allegedly, a typical attitude among ordinary Tibetans was that they wanted both the Communist Party and the Dalai Lama. Such a situation forced the TWC and officials elsewhere to attempt a way of bifurcating the Dalai Lama, or separating his political character from his religious significance. In these resourceful officials' words, the current campaign should aim to achieve a goal of making the Dalai Lama "stink politically" (*cong zhengzhi shang gaochou*), but the goal of making him "stink thoroughly" (*chedi gaochou*) among the Tibetans would have a long and difficult way to go.[133]

Thus, as far as the Dalai Lama was concerned, between 1950 and 1963 Beijing's Tibet policy went through a full circle from de-demonization to re-demonization. In each phase, the Dalai Lama assumed a central role, positive or negative, in Beijing's Tibetan enterprise and was therefore accorded various political "hats" in Chinese Communist terminology. About Beijing's relationship with the Dalai Lama during the first decade of the PRC, the post-1959 CCP discourse was inconsistent, depicting the Dalai Lama variously as one who deceived the CCP, one who constantly wavered, and one whose intentions were seen through by Beijing from the very beginning.[134] Yet consistency in their stories about the Dalai Lama was not a priority for Mao Zedong and his comrades. They were mainly concerned with achieving "political initiative" at every turn of events so as to realize their unalterable goal in Tibet. In the summer of 1965, Tibet had finally "entered socialism" by having its first "people's commune." When the Great Proletarian Cultural Revolution was launched the next year, for the first time Tibet did not lag behind the rest of China and joined Mao Zedong's "continuous revolution" according to Beijing's time standard.[135]

"An Absurd Proposal"

CCP leaders of Mao's generation were social engineers, not social scientists, though they were convinced of their own "scientific analysis" of Tibetan affairs informed by their "proven" revolutionary practice as well as Marxist doctrines. Having conducted their revolution under the Marxist doctrine of class struggle but for the sake of salvaging the "Chinese nation," CCP leaders were conditioned to understand their statecraft as an art of class struggle. After they triumphantly asserted the class-struggle essence of the Tibetan question after March 1959, the political stage of the PRC would no longer accommodate any other possible formula for solving the "nationality question." The CCP's class-struggle solution of the Tibetan question was, however, just the beginning of Beijing's Tibetan problem—an arduous process of integrating Tibetan society with the rest of China.

In October 1962, the postal and telecommunication services between Tibet and the outside world, including places both inside and outside China, were restored after a lengthy interruption by recent violent conflicts in and around the region.[136] This was not a restoration to the old conditions. A top-secret bulletin of the National Conference on Planning, dated September 19, 1963, indicated that by that time, sixty thousand cadres and workers had entered Tibet from various provinces and all of their living and production materials had been transported from outside the region. Each year, at least a third of this corps took a break from Tibet and spent a period of vacation in heartland provinces. There was, therefore, a huge demand for busing these people in and out of Tibet, which usually took seven days for a one-way trip. Reportedly, a consensus among these cadres and workers was that travel on a passenger bus equipped with oxygen would be the best fringe benefit.[137] Beijing was making progress in integrating Tibet socioeconomically and politically with the rest of China, but the place would remain a "frontier" region as far as most Chinese were concerned.

For the CCP leadership, bridging the "Tibetan frontier" and the "Chinese heartland" concerned not only the Chinese population but also, more importantly, the Tibetans. In contrast to the CCP's 1949 displacing of the KMT as the spokesman for the "Chinese nation," Beijing's 1959 "liberation" of Tibet for the second time could not easily replace the Dalai Lama with the CCP as the spiritual pillar for the Tibetan populace. In the early 1960s, still personifying the success of the CCP's regional-autonomy approach in dealing with minority nationality affairs, Ulanhu told a national conference that the crux of regional autonomy was "minority nationalities' being masters of their own business [*dangjia zuozhu*]."[138] The model of Inner Mongolia would remain valid for a while before Ulanhu was deposed on the eve of the Cultural Revolution. In Tibet, after the Dalai Lama's departure Beijing could never find another suitable candidate as a Tibetan "Ulanhu." In Tibet, neither the Panchen Lama nor Ngabö could fill the political and mainly spiritual void left by the Dalai Lama.

Yet when Beijing was still pursuing its "Dalai line," the Dalai Lama was not an "Ulanhu" for Tibet. He was a complex medium between the CCP and the Tibetans. In the wake of the Lhasa clash, Ngabö became too taciturn and the Panchen Lama too excited. Neither was able to satisfy Beijing's policy needs completely, even though both would continue to top Beijing's list of "united-front objects" in Tibet.[139] Once Mao told Ngabö: "We understand you, and we can call you comrade. But the Panchen [Lama] is a monk, and therefore we cannot call him comrade."[140] Mao's words were to reassure Ngabö about Beijing's trust in him but actually revealed a dilemma in the CCP's work in post-1959 Tibet: Was Tibet still unique even after the old Tibetan establishment was abolished? Beijing did not seem to have a clear answer. A related question was not merely who but also what kind of person could serve as the linchpin in Beijing's administration of the Tibetan frontier. After the Dalai Lama disappeared from the political equation, CCP leaders were not able, nor did they hope, to rally the Tibetans around another ethnopolitical/religious figure. But could Beijing use mainly CCP officials and a single-plank platform of class struggle in reorganizing Tibetan society?

That appeared to be the course that Beijing followed after 1959. Resolved to prevent the "class essence" of the Tibetan question from being "distorted" by other factors like ethnicity and religion, until the end of the Mao years, Beijing would unfold the "class banner" in Tibet that obscured, oppressed, and marginalized other aspects of one of the most complicated interethnic relations in modern China. Indeed, during the remaining years before the Cultural Revolution, Beijing acknowledged repeatedly that the "questions of nationality and religion" would continue for a long time and must not be overlooked in the CCP's Tibetan work. Especially, CCP leaders made efforts to convince the Tibetans that Beijing's orientation did not set out to "destroy nationality" and "eliminate religion." Yet "nationality" and "religion" in CCP discourse of this period just camouflaged class struggle. At the end of 1964, Zhou Enlai used these words to welcome the last relatively tranquil year of the Mao era: "Any observation of and decision on the nationality question, if departing from the perspective of classes and class struggles, can only be conducive to national separatism and detrimental to national unity and state unification." About a month before Zhou uttered these words, because of his criticism of CCP practices in Tibet and other Tibetan areas—allegedly an antipeople, antisocialist, and rebellious crime—the Panchen Lama lost his position as the acting chairman of the PCTAR.[141]

Thus, the year 1959 is memorable for being the last moment when opinions about the complexity of the Tibetan question were still openly voiced in Chinese society. Here are three examples that came to the party's attention.

In May 1959, an exhibition was opened in Beijing, which, to expose the darkness of the prereform Tibetan society, displayed graphic evidence of "crimes committed by upper-stratum Tibetan reactionaries." After seeing the exhibition, the historian Gu Jigang wrote a comment on religious talismans made of human bones and tortures used by Tibetan aristocrats. Gu pointed out that the talismans were the Yellow Sect's traditional instruments and every monastery had them. Although showing cruelty, these talismans were not current Tibetan reactionaries' creation and, therefore, their display might make Tibetan Buddhists uncomfortable. In Gu's opinion, these were mainly historical relics that should be displayed in an ethnic cultural museum. As for those horrible tortures used by Tibetan aristocrats, they had been commonly used in many slave and feudal societies in history and were also recorded in ancient Chinese histories. Therefore, a better place to display them would be a historical museum, which could show what the Yin and Zhou times of China actually looked like.[142]

Just as Gu's temporal sense of history was out of sync with the CCP's political presentism, some other historians' spatial sense of history contradicted Beijing's diplomatic rhetoric on the international stage. In a lengthy speech about Tibet in May 1959, Zhou Enlai disputed a British-Indian view that China had suzerainty but not sovereignty over Tibet, contending that ever since the Yuan dynasty "unified Tibet into the great family of our motherland," China had always exercised sovereignty over Tibet.[143] Soon the Central Propaganda Department discovered that a major text on Chinese history, *Zhongguo Lishi Gaiyao* (Synopsis of Chinese history), disagreed with Zhou. This book was coauthored by three leading historians, Jian Bozan, Shao Xunzheng, and Hu Hua, but was actually a collective work by more than ten established historians and was initially intended for a multivolume world history to be published in the Soviet Union. When the book was published in 1956 under the aegis of the Central Propaganda Department, it was acclaimed as one of the first major studies of Chinese history written within the Marxist paradigm, reflecting the most recent Chinese scholarship and commonly accepted views among Chinese historians.[144] The book's presentation of the historical relationship between Tibet and China, however, became problematic after Zhou's speech. An internal publication of the Central Propaganda Department, classified as eyes-only for "leading comrades," pointed out that the book considered the incorporation of Xinjiang and Tibet into China as results of the Manchus' "frenzied expansion" during the Qing dynasty. Notably, the authors used *zongzhuquan* (suzerainty), "exactly the same term currently used by India," to define the relationship between the Qing court and "China's Tibetan area."[145] The case marked a process in the PRC that increasingly blurred the distinction between history writing and political propaganda, especially with respect to "sensitive subjects" such as borderlands and ethnicity.

In the wake of the Tibetan upheaval, there were intellectuals other than historians who were eager to offer policy advice to the CCP. A scientist named Lan Jixi, an associate research fellow of the Institute of Physics of the Chinese Academy of Sciences, wrote a letter to Zhou Enlai in June 1959. According to a top-secret internal journal of the Central United Front Department, Lan made an "absurd proposal for solving the Tibetan question." One of the PRC's pioneer researchers of semiconductors, Lan was probably a recent returnee from either Western Europe or, more likely, the United States. Lan's proposal might have been inspired by reservations for Native Americans in the United States. In his letter, Lan used recent developments in Tibet as evidence that the CCP's "autonomous region" approach had failed to appease Tibet and prevent international disputes. Therefore, Lan proposed, "in order to accommodate the long religious and customary traditions of the Tibetan compatriots," an autonomous prefecture should be set up within the current Tibetan autonomous region. The prefecture should be in the Yarlung Tsangpo River Valley, surrounded by the Gangdise Range in the north, the Jinsha River in the east, and the Himalaya in the south. Given that the Yarlung Tsangpo River Valley was the richest and most beautiful region of Tibet, the "area should be designated for its original residents for whatever reasons, moral, or traditional, or practical." Tibetans in the prefecture would enjoy their habitual self-governance without continuing serfdom and other inhuman customs that had blocked the progress of Tibetan society; they would neither feel threatened by the PLA nor be bothered by migrants and social impact from the rest of the PRC. Such a self-ruling Tibetan prefecture would be able to foster Tibetans' goodwill toward the Chinese society, protect Buddhist culture, and serve as a soothing buffer between the PRC and its neighbors. And, as scientist Lan remarked presciently, the Yarlung Tsangpo River was an international waterway, and tranquility along the river could facilitate international negotiations about water usage in the future.[146]

Of the three examples, only Lan Jixi's proposal explicitly asserted that Beijing's Tibet policy was a failure, thereby earning a mark of "absurdity" from CCP officials. In CCP officials' eyes, though, each was absurd in its own way. The CCP wanted to use Tibetan religious and torture devices as evidence of class crimes and social darkness to incite spectators' strong abhorrence and "class hatred" against the Tibetan ruling class. The just and progressive nature of Beijing's undertaking in Tibet could thereby be vindicated. Gu Jigang was therefore absurd in suggesting dispassionately that these items belonged to a specific period of human history and should not be politicized. On the international scene, the PRC claimed that "ever since ancient times" China had exercised sovereignty over Tibet. This claim needed support with a point ancient enough in Chinese history—the Yuan dynasty, as identified by Zhou Enlai. Jian Bozan and his coauthors were therefore absurd in presenting an authoritative scholarly view that China only began to exercise loose control, not "sovereignty," over Tibet relatively recently. Beijing—simultaneously the national government of China, the center of the Chinese Revolution, and a member of the socialist camp—wanted to exercise full sovereignty in all areas of China, bring socialism to every citizen and each nationality of the PRC, and control effectively China's borders with capitalist neighbors. Lan Jixi, aside from asserting Beijing's policy failure, was therefore the most absurd in proposing that a Tibetan land be preserved as *shi wai tao yuan*, or Xanadu.

EPILOGUE

Tibet and the World, According to Beijing

A historical narrative has to end at some point, often with reluctance and difficulty on the historian's part: reluctance because the end tends to be determined by various objective limitations to the historian's exploration of the past rather than by her/his intellectual curiosity; difficulty because the end is far from conclusive and actually connotes continuities and beginnings. This study, initiated as an effort to piece together tidbits of information about Beijing's Tibetan policy, has run out of materials that can be meaningfully added to the jigsaw puzzle. Nevertheless, the past retrieved has to be explained. Without doubt, the complex developments discussed in this study were among those responsible for reshaping important relationships of the Asia-Pacific world in the mid- and late twentieth century. Initially, this study intended to pursue a hypothetical notion that Beijing's Tibetan enterprise knocked over the first domino in the setup of the PRC's international environment, followed by drastic changes in Beijing's relations with India, the Soviet Union, and the United States. It became clear as the study unfolded that such a mechanical notion, borrowed from the Eisenhowerian thesis about America's Vietnam dilemma in the 1950s, would be too narrow to illustrate the broad and profound ramifications of the Tibetan question.

This study began with the proposition that Beijing's Tibetan question in the 1950s could be understood in four overlapping timescapes, from the most remote to the most recent: geo-ethno-security landscaping, modern transformation of Chinese territoriality, the Chinese Revolution, and the Cold War.

As of 1959, the CCP leadership had dissolved an inherited Tibetan question yet turned Tibet into a problem of its own creation. In the meantime, none of the four historical threads ceased to weave the fabric of the PRC's domestic and international affairs. Indeed, the dynamics concerned appeared even more intertwined than before. They also assumed new directions because of the fallout of the Tibetan situation, which was *frontier* to the PRC in spatial term but by no means *marginal* to Beijing as a sociopolitical issue. Though not a detailed analysis, the following points sketch these further developments to wrap up our story.

"A Lot of Empty Words"

In the 1950s and early 1960s, the United States was the PRC's most vicious adversary in the Cold War. Ideologically, Beijing perceived the United States as the head of a dying capitalist system seeking its way out through wars. Geopolitically, CCP leaders envisioned "three daggers" (Korea, Taiwan, and Vietnam) that Washington put in the eastern side of the PRC, leading Beijing, in Zhou Enlai's words, to push its own "line of national defense to Korea."[1] Yet, despite the profound international ramifications of the Lhasa revolt of March 1959, Beijing's perceptions about the United States did not change much. In the late 1950s and early 1960s, CCP leaders were indeed concerned that the Americans might infiltrate Tibet by plotting from Kalimpong and airlifting agents and weapons into the region.[2] Still, to use Eric Hyer's "strategic dimension" concept about Beijing's geopolitical thinking, the fallout from Tibetan affairs did not change the CCP leaders' view that the American challenges were constantly situated in the direction of the Pacific.[3] Mao never changed his view that the United States was a threat from the east. After the Lhasa revolt, Mao ridiculed Washington's expressed "deepest sympathy" toward the Tibetans as "a lot of empty words."[4] Attesting to Mao's opinion, Chinese intelligence detected that both Washington and London were cautious in reacting to the recent developments in Tibet because they wanted to avoid being accused of interfering in China's domestic affairs. PRC intelligence officials construed the Washington-London stance after the Lhasa revolt as a "reluctant recognition of our [PRC] sovereignty over Tibet: they understand the difficulty to bring the Tibetan question to the United Nations, for neither is China a member of the UN nor the question is external to China and [Beijing's actions] in violation of international laws and [Chinese] constitutions." Allegedly, these Western governments also feared that if they took action over the Tibetan situation, there might be geopolitical repercussions elsewhere, or retaliatory moves by Beijing and Moscow in the Taiwan Strait or West Berlin. Therefore, Washington and London limited their reactions to the Lhasa revolt merely to scoring some propaganda points.⁵

Although in Beijing's view American reactions to the Lhasa revolt constituted no more than a series of inconsequential commotions, the Tibetan situation in 1959 did bring about a significant reshuffling of international relations in China's southwestern neighborhood. The process included Chinese-Indian border conflicts, Sino-Soviet disagreement over an international communist orientation in dealing with India, Soviet-U.S. competition in winning New Delhi's goodwill in the context of the Chinese-Indian conflicts, and readjustments of U.S. relations with Taiwan and Pakistan caused by Washington's recent approach to India. Not all these developments were purely or mainly of Cold War significance, but American policymakers treated the changes in the Himalayan political landscape as an opportunity to fill in a South Asian gap in containing Communist China. Even before the Sino-Indian border war took place in October 1962, Washington already saw "greater convergence of basic interests" between the Unites States and India. When the Chinese and the Indians started fighting along their borders, Washington was uncertain about the legality of either side's territorial claim.⁶ But the matter was secondary to the Americans. The U.S. Department of State hailed the development as one that "has awakened realization in India of [the] aggressive nature of Communism" and the unreliability of the Soviet Union as a friend. In the meantime, Washington was cautious not to push New Delhi into explicit collaboration with the West lest it "trample on this delicate flower of growing awareness" on India's part.⁷

Although the Americans were careful not to upset New Delhi's balancing game of receiving American assistance while maintaining its nonalignment stance in the Cold War, Washington's cultivation of an Indian partnership could not avoid angering its allies in Islamabad and Taipei. American officials discerned "almost traumatic reactions from Pakistan" as the United States was getting closer to India during the latter's conflict with China.⁸ As for Taipei, in late October 1962, after the U.S. government openly endorsed the Indian claim about the McMahon Line, the KMT regime cried "Yalta" and pointed out to Washington that the line was "one of the symbols of imperialist pressure on China and stirs strong anti-British feelings in all Chinese."⁹ While paying these prices for enlisting New Delhi into its Asian strategy, Washington did not perceive the recent crises deep in the Asian landmass as catalysts for causing a diplomatic revolution in the Cold War. While managing to persuade Islamabad and Taipei to put the emerging American-Indian collaboration "in proper perspective," for a while American officials could not find evidence that New Delhi was disposed to enter the anti-communist bloc or that the Sino-Soviet alliance was disintegrating because of the Sino-Indian conflict.¹⁰

"Cold But Not Rigid"

In contrast, Beijing took the recent Himalayan events much more seriously than the Americans. A few months after the Sino-Indian border war, Zhou Enlai told his foreign visitors that India's border disputes with China was already part of Washington's strategic plan. Later, Zhou warned Indian diplomats that, along with America's other clients in Asia, India was now perceived in Washington as part of Kennedy's "new frontier" for encircling the socialist camp.[11] Zhou, however, was just using the Cold War context to accentuate the graveness of a wrecked intra-Asian relationship. By nature, the Sino-Indian relationship was geopolitical more than anything else, and Tibet served as a transit station through which the Sino-Indian relationship went from benign to malignant.[12]

As leaders of a Marxist revolution that had successfully expanded its class-oriented territorial bases throughout China, Mao and his comrades understood geopolitics rather differently than did policymakers in many nation-states. In this regard, they even differed from their counterparts in the Kremlin, who had already retired the notion of world revolution and matched Washington's superpower strategy with their own. Upholding a territorial creed that mixed the notion of worldwide class struggle with that of national sovereignty, CCP leaders held the international boundaries of the PRC simultaneously as a solid "wall" for guarding their domestic revolution and a porous "fence" for maintaining connections with their socialist neighbors and potential revolutions in their capitalist surroundings. In the 1950s, therefore, Beijing viewed India as a neighborly power with "national bourgeois" characteristics.[13] The PRC-Indian relationship began rather auspiciously. New Delhi was among the first group of foreign governments to recognize the PRC, and in a 1954 agreement the two states put aside temporarily the Tibetan question in their bilateral relations. Stressing anti-imperialism as a shared goal with New Delhi, CCP leaders collaborated with the Indians in sponsoring the Five Principles of Peaceful Coexistence, promoted India as the "center for East-West contacts," and encouraged India to work inside the established international community "legally" while the PRC remained, in Mao's words, an international "outlaw."[14]

Yet the Sino-Indian relationship, based on anti-imperialist struggle and the cause of peace, foundered once the Tibetan question returned like a recurring cancer. As it turned out, the People's Republic of China and the Republic of India, successor states of the Qing and British empires, respectively, failed to settle their imperial bequests smoothly. The Tibetan situation in southwestern China was mirrored by ethnopolitical unrest in northeastern India. In May 1962, after visiting the Indian side of the Himalayan frontier, U.S. ambassador John Galbraith reported to President John F. Kennedy:

> In addition to their better-publicized problems with the Chinese, the Indians are having very serious troubles in living with people within their own borders. This is an area with a large number of ethnically separate groups and all are unhappy in their present relations with the Indians. The Nagas are in open revolt and tie down a couple of divisions but they are only the extreme case. A half dozen other ethnic or linguistic groups are asking what they can have in the way of independence, autonomy or self-determination. It is an interesting place to study the problems of neo-colonialism.[15]

Thus, the Tibetan question was part of a historical transformation of the Himalayan frontiers in terms of territoriality. This was only partially obscured by Cold War politics. Beijing and New Delhi were facing similar issues of governing their claimed ethnic frontiers that were directly connected to border demarcations between them.

After the Lhasa revolt, Beijing was quick to blame New Delhi for the incident. At a Politburo meeting on March 17, 1959, Zhou Enlai asserted that the commanding center of the Tibetan rebellion was in Kalimpong, and that while very active backstage, the British and Americans had pushed India to the front. Chinese intelligence concurred, suggesting that having taken a two-faced approach, the Indian government had colluded with "Tibetan reactionaries" for some time and had known all along about the rebellion. In the CCP's worldview, New Delhi's deceptive behavior befitted its "national bourgeois" nature. Therefore, while supporting the "Dalai clique" secretly, "Nehru fears most a decisive rupture of relationship with China" and wanted to avoid "bringing the Cold War into India."[16] Such an understanding of New Delhi's "bourgeois" mind-set may have been behind Mao's decision to bring Beijing's grievances against India into the open. On April 25, Mao ordered a change in Chinese propaganda: the vague accusation in the past against "imperialism, Chiang [Kai-shek] bandits, and foreign reactionaries" for inciting troubles in Tibet was to be replaced with an explicit attack against "British imperialists and Indian expansionists who co-conspired in interfering in China's domestic affairs and attempting to take over Tibet." On the same day, Mao explained to one of his secretaries that, in dealing with New Delhi, he was following a number of ancient Chinese stratagems: *bu wei tianxia xian* (do not make a move ahead of all others under heaven), *tuibi sanshe* (make a retreat when meeting one's adversary the first time), and *li shang wang lai* (follow the rite of reciprocity). Despite Beijing's difficult maneuvering with the Tibetans during the first half of the 1950s, Mao asserted that the CCP's retreat from Tibet in 1957 was to give

India some room to make the first move, and now Nehru found himself caught in a dilemma.[17] As directed by Mao, a barrage of propaganda assaults against India followed. The alleged goal was to use a struggle against Nehru's vacillating bourgeois character to restore Chinese-Indian unity.

While working on New Delhi's bourgeois soul, Beijing could not overlook India's concern about its national geo-body, which would directly affect China's own geo-body. Shortly after the Lhasa revolt, Indian officials admitted to Soviet diplomats that India's concern about Tibet was neither religious nor emotional: loss of Tibetan autonomy meant the disappearance of a buffer zone between India and China, and India felt threatened. The Soviets readily conveyed the message to their Chinese counterparts.[18] The so-called Tibetan buffer had meant a theocratic barrier between Chinese socialism and Indian capitalism as well as a physical distance between the PLA and the Indian Army. In 1957, Beijing carried out a "great dismount" in Tibet and, like New Delhi, entertained the idea of preserving the region as a buffer. This idea disappeared completely from CCP leaders' minds after the Lhasa revolt.

After March 1959, the military distance between China and India disappeared much faster than the expansion of Chinese socialism inside Tibet. Chinese intelligence discovered that after the PLA suppressed the Lhasa revolt, the Twenty-Third Brigade of the Indian Army advanced into Sikkim, and India maintained seventy military posts and stationed 7,206 troops along its borders with the PRC. In the Himalayan frontiers, the situation of "borders without defense" (*you bian wu fang*) on the Chinese side changed as the PLA fought Tibetan rebels. By the end of 1960, along the Tibetan borderline of 3,500 kilometers, the Chinese side set up sixty-three posts, constructed 1,600 kilometers of highways to these posts, and stationed nine regiments.[19] In the meantime, having removed the Tibetan buffer, Chinese leaders tried repeatedly to convince New Delhi that the recent physical contact between the two countries along the Himalayas by no means changed Beijing's defensive orientation focusing on the American threat from the Pacific.[20]

Soon enough, New Delhi's insistence on legitimizing the McMahon Line and Beijing's on historicizing the Sino-Indian boundaries decisively threw their relationship into an unsalvageable situation. The Sino-Indian border conflicts are beyond the scope of this study. It is important to note, however, that as far as Beijing was concerned, the crux of the border issue was the Tibetan question. During the Sino-Indian border war, Zhou Enlai told a British visitor:

> Before Great Britain entered India, India was not unified. Earlier, India had periods of unification but its territories were not always unified even during such periods. This is similar to China's feudal age. A common feature of feudal eras is that borders were not clearly demarcated and moved from time to time. Only after entering the modern age, could states gradually demarcate

their boundaries clearly. As for Tibet, India has inherited British influence and always wanted to turn Tibet into a buffer zone. This is impossible. All these belonged to the past and will not return. Now revolution has happened [in Tibet] and serfdom has been abolished, the Indian government cannot accomplish anything in protecting the Dalai [Lama].[21]

Differing from Beijing's territorial claims usually based on an "ever since ancient time" creed, Zhou's remark was very close to admitting that the "international boundaries" of Asia were the result of modern territoriality transformations. At the same time, Chinese officials perceived India's involvement in Tibetan affairs and its border disputes with China as two components of the same "anti-Chinese conspiracy." In the larger context of the Cold War, Chinese policymakers readily translated these issues into elements of the PRC's international struggle against Western imperialism headed by the United States. Thus, on the one hand, Beijing treated India, along with other Asian "nationalist states," as part of an "intermediate zone" between the socialist and imperialist camps to be won over. On the other hand, because "Indian reactionaries" were actively opposing China, Beijing followed a foreign policy orientation that accorded differentiated treatment to India and to other Asian states. For other states, the policy was to achieve reconciliation and unity, but for India, struggle and isolation. In the Chinese foreign policy community, the orientation toward India in the early 1960s was known as "cold but not rigid" (*leng er bu jiang*). In Zhou's words, the relationship between China and India would be, in the long haul, one of "armed coexistence." After the Sino-Indian border war, while dealing with Tibetan rebels' frequent attacks across the international boundaries of the Himalayas, the Chinese authorities lumped together "American imperialism, Indian reactionaries, and Chiang bandits" as an anti-Chinese clique behind the Tibetan "fifth column."[22]

Among the malicious trio named by Beijing, the "Chiang bandits" on Taiwan stood as the most awkward supporter of the Tibetan rebels. In late 1959, Mao remarked to his comrades rather confidently:

> After the Tibetan question is solved, Taiwan is the only remaining question. Several decades may be needed for Taiwan. More thinking should be done about Taiwan to find a solution."[23]

Clearly juxtaposing Taiwan and Tibet, Mao no longer considered the Nationalist regime in Taipei in the same way as the CCP had viewed the KMT during the two parties' power struggle on the mainland. To Beijing, Taiwan was now simultaneously a problem of territorial unification and one of lingering American influence. In the meantime, the old partisan competition became less relevant.

In contrast, the KMT regime maintained in public a consistent rhetoric about its historical struggle with the Chinese Communists. Soon after the Lhasa revolt, Chiang Kai-shek issued a "Statement to the Tibetan Compatriots," contending that the Tibetan resistance opened a new page of the nationwide "anti-communist revolution." In Taipei, a comparison was made between the "Tibetan revolution" of 1959 and the "Hungarian revolution" of 1956.[24] Tangible steps were taken as well. As detected by Beijing's intelligence agencies, besides sending secret agents and weapons to Tibetan rebels, Chiang also ordered remnant KMT troops in Burma to coordinate with Tibetan operations. The situation was serious enough for Zhou Enlai to make a proposition to the Burmese government that its army destroy KMT troops inside Burma and intercept American airplanes that flew over Burma to drop weapons into Tibet. Beijing also learned that the KMT authorities had started a Yellow Dragon Plan for training and using Tibetans and other frontier ethnic peoples to "undermine comprehensively" the PRC.[25]

Yet there was another kind of intelligence about Taipei that CCP officials did not seem to know how to interpret: a "contradiction" between Chiang Kai-shek's anticommunist politics and Taipei's misgivings about the Tibetan demand for independence. As the relationship between the PRC and India deteriorated over the Tibetan situation and their disputed borders, Beijing's intelligence reported, probably with a degree of amazement, that many KMT officials in Taiwan actually admired PRC policies toward Tibet and India. These Nationalists held the view that "although the CCP was the enemy, its struggle for territorial sovereignty should be welcomed by all Chinese."[26] Taipei's attitude was contradictory in CCP officials' eyes because of the "reactionary" essence that Beijing attributed to the KMT. There was nothing contradictory at all from the point of view of Taipei, however, which continued to claim sovereignty over all of China. Perhaps more than any other subject, the Tibetan question revealed a commonality between the Chinese Nationalists and the Chinese Communists that was deeply rooted in China's long "humiliating" century. This commonality was often obscured or distorted by the two parties' mutual animosity stemming from China's civil wars and their different international orientations in the Cold War.

In Taipei, Chiang Kai-shek kept his habit as a diligent diarist. Had Mao or Zhou read what Chiang brushed during this period, they would have found out that, having switched positions at China's power center and peripheries, the CCP and the KMT were nevertheless of the same mind. Here is an example:

> [Having] annexed our Sikkim and Bhutan and coveted our Tibet, India's immaturity and arrogance are beyond imagination.

... driven by his selfishness and vanity, Nehru of India should unthinkably serve the old enemy and take him as a benefactor, acting shamelessly as the teeth and claws of British imperialism in the East and becoming hostile toward Eastern nations.

These words could well have been written or uttered by leaders in Beijing after 1959, but they were actually written down by Chiang some ten years earlier.[27] As for the status of Tibet, after the Lhasa revolt, Chiang briefly adopted a "revolutionary" stance rather similar to the CCP's in the 1920s and '30s, contemplating giving support to Tibetans' "right of self-determination." Yet very quickly, the indifference of the Dalai Lama group toward Taipei's gestures snuffed out Chiang's ethnopolitical scheme. "In the future," Chiang pondered in his diaries, "the Dalai [Lama] in India will not be able to have any function in our national revolution." In Taipei's policymaking, therefore, Tibet remained an issue of "recovering lost territories."[28] In this regard, Chiang always believed that CCP expansion into Tibet was actually paving the way for his own government. Earlier, when Beijing completed the construction of Lhasa Airport and when the PLA suppressed Khampa rebellions in western Sichuan, Chiang considered both developments beneficial to his government's "state building" in the future.[29]

Ambivalent about Beijing's making headway in Tibet, the biggest disappointment to Chiang after the Lhasa revolt was the attitude of the U.S. government. As Washington forbade Taipei from transferring American materials to the Tibetans and also declined Taipei's offer of cooperation in handling the Tibetan situation, Chiang in his diaries complained about Americans' "ambition of monopolizing the Tibetan affairs." For Chiang, Washington's uncooperative attitude in the wake of the Lhasa revolt was indicative: "Our silent hope ought now to end completely that the United States will launch a counteroffensive [against the CCP in mainland China]." In Chiang's words, the United States was a "most dangerous and unreliable partner because of its inconsistent and ever-changing policy." In late October 1962, after the American Embassy in India gave public support to New Delhi's claim about the McMahon Line, Chiang viewed the development as "one more childish and absurd behavior on the part of the United States." He was "extremely disappointed with the ignorance of the United States as the leader of the free world."[30]

No matter how close the perceptions of Taipei and Beijing became after the Lhasa revolt, they would continue to abuse each other for doing a foreign imperialist's bidding—American and Soviet, respectively. In the 1950s, Chiang Kai-shek's private thinking was consistent with Taipei's official stance, asserting that the CCP's advance in Tibet was part of Soviet aggression against China.[31] Like many observers outside the PRC, however, Chiang and his associates were unaware that, partially because of the Lhasa revolt, the formidable alliance between Beijing and Moscow was starting to crumble.

"Separate But Not Ruptured"

The Sino-Soviet split was one of the most complicated and puzzling developments during the Cold War era. Several studies in the past decade have significantly advanced historical knowledge in this regard, in which the Chinese-Indian border conflicts feature prominently.[32] Chinese Communism was simultaneously a phenomenon from the dynamics of "Eastern" civilization and a trend in China's modern transformation informed by "Western" radicalism. Inevitably, Beijing's dealings with China's two largest neighbors, India and the USSR, combined goals of updating China's imperial domain, building a national state, and supporting "proletarian revolutions" beyond Chinese territories. Moscow and New Delhi could have maneuvered and compromised with Beijing over any one of these goals, but a Chinese foreign policy combining all three was hard for Beijing's onetime ally or friend to comprehend.

The Beijing-Moscow relationship after March 1959 was full of mutually observed absurdities. After the Lhasa revolt, the Soviets showed great interest in the developments in Tibet, and Beijing also diligently kept Moscow informed.[33] In late March 1959, the Soviet leadership received an internal report on the Tibetan situation based on information provided by Beijing. As shown in this Soviet document, CCP officials provided a careful explanation of Beijing's nonreform policy in Tibet before 1959. Still, the Soviets were puzzled by "aspects of CCP policy in Tibet":

> First of all, it is necessary to note that eight years after liberation, Tibetan peasants remain in serf-like dependence, while in other minority regions socialist transformations have already been carried through, with the Party's policy receiving broader social support there. In Tibet the main effort was through peaceful solution of all problems by agreement with the feudal-theocratic circles and their "re-education". In the main, the working masses saw few real results from living in a socialist state.[34]

In May, to remove any doubts in the minds of their foreign comrades, Mao Zedong and Zhou Enlai discussed Tibet with official delegations from several socialist countries, asserting that the essence of the Tibetan question was a serious class struggle to replace a stagnant and backward old society with a vigorous and fast advancing new one. They also insisted that the conflict in Tibet had been provoked by the Tibetan reactionary clique at home and by the Indian big bourgeoisie abroad.[35]

The Soviets remained unconvinced. In October, when Nikita Khrushchev came to Beijing, the first face-to-face clash took place between Chinese and

Soviet leaders. In a meeting on October 2, Khrushchev told Mao that the CCP was at fault in delaying reform in Tibet, letting the Dalai Lama escape ("It would be better if he were in the grave"), and blaming India for the Tibetan situation. Mao's defense of Beijing's waiting strategy was totally beyond the Soviets. Whereas CCP leaders insisted that they had carefully orchestrated and successfully implemented a revolution in Tibet, in the Soviets' eyes Beijing's Tibet enterprise was but an ideologically indefensible and tactically foolish operation. Khrushchev was especially annoyed that, having held Moscow responsible for the Hungarian incident in 1956, Beijing should now blame others for what happened inside its own territory. Ominously, the Beijing-Moscow disagreement about India's responsibility for the Tibetan situation and the border conflicts touched upon a central issue between the two communist capitals—their mutual assessment as a worthy socialist partner. Although the meeting eventually ended with a conciliatory remark by Mao, the Sino-Soviet alliance would never be the same after its central nerve was plucked.[36]

As the post-Stalin leadership of the Soviet Union focused on an intersystem competition with the United States worldwide more than engaging in geopolitical expansion along Soviet boundaries, the CCP was still obsessed with a "base perception" derived from its own career. When struggling for power before 1949, the CCP had created a series of political-military bases resembling autonomous territorial states. In the meantime, the CCP's territorial domain also assumed a "laboring class" character and anticipated, theoretically at least, expansion in a territorial continuum until the world became communized. The shifting boundaries of the CCP's "base-state" were coordinates marking and measuring the balance of not only military power but also class strength between the CCP and the KMT. At least during the early years of the PRC, this base perception and class-state notion did not disappear from Beijing's understanding of state affairs and international politics. Although in the 1950s Beijing was very conscious of its function as a national government and began to settle and clarify China's boundaries with neighboring countries, CCP leaders never stopped viewing such affairs through a lens of class analysis. Accordingly, Beijing expected that the extension of its "class revolution" into Tibet would affect India's "great bourgeoisie." To the CCP leadership, class struggles did not stop at national boundaries. It was therefore quite logical for Beijing to pledge noninterference in India's domestic affairs on the one hand and, on the other, to advise the Communist Party of India on how to conduct its power struggle.[37]

In a conversation with communist delegations from twelve Latin American states in June 1960, Deng Xiaoping articulated most clearly Beijing's view about the connection between class struggles on the two sides of the Himalayan frontier, thereby blurring the divide between the CCP's "domestic" problem in Tibet and the PRC's "foreign" relation with India. Declaring that "peaceful coexistence" was intended only for interstate but not interclass relations, Deng contended:

> All problems become clear if we consider Nehru's bourgeois instinct. In inciting Sinophobia he harbored evil intentions for blocking socialist influence in India. He controlled Tibet through the Dalai [Lama]. We tried for many years to maintain good relations with India, and therefore we intentionally postponed democratic reform in Tibet. . . . Once reform began [in Tibet], Nehru became desperate and provoked incidents along the borders. Was this the most important reason? This was important but not the only reason. The fundamental reason was to solve contradictions inside their own country. The Indian people are suffering terribly. The Indian Communist Party has grown. Principally the border conflicts were started for anti-communist and anti-people purpose. This is truly the essence of the matter. Clearly the [Indian] bourgeoisie has spared no effort in resisting the influence of socialism and suppressing communists and the people.[38]

Deng's tough talk was typical of the CCP discourse in the Mao era. Surely Deng did not intend to achieve merely rhetorical effects. His words reflected CCP leaders' view of the world and the dual nature of the world's states, which were perceived without exception as national and class entities simultaneously. As for whether, how, and when the divides among nations should yield to the interconnection of supranational class struggle, these were tactical issues in Beijing's policymaking dependent on circumstances. Clearly, after 1959, because of recent "class struggles" in Tibet, CCP leaders appeared to pay attention to class struggle in India much more closely than before. Initially, on diplomatic occasions, CCP officials maintained that Beijing's harsh criticism of Nehru after the Lhasa revolt was a stratagem of using "struggle" to win him over.[39] That line was soon abandoned. In 1961, more than a year before the Sino-Indian border war, Beijing decided that Nehru was now an "American product" more than a "British product," a "quintessential bourgeois who rallied to the right wing and reactionaries." Zhou Enlai told the Soviet ambassador that the Indian people could follow the example of the Chinese people and become "revolutionized," and that the Indian Communist Party had a huge responsibility in this regard.[40] A few months after the border war, Zhou predicted to a visitor from Indonesia: "The Indian ruling class will surely fall. It is only a matter of time."[41]

It has been pointed out that Beijing pursued an anti-imperialist revolution in contrast to Moscow's anticapitalist one, and that the two communist powers' different policies toward "neutralist" India in the early 1960s typically highlighted tensions between these two revolutionary models.[42] What should be added is that Beijing did not always oppose New Delhi's international orientation of nonalignment. It took years for CCP leaders' abhorrence of Nehru's policies to grow, a process that kept pace with the development of mistrust between Beijing and Moscow. The Tibetan situation served as a catalyst to bring into the open Beijing's split with both its most important Asian partner and its principal communist ally. As for anti-imperialist or anticapitalist orientation, it should also be noted that in the case of India, Moscow appeared eager to maintain unity between the socialist camp and a leading "nationalist" power in opposing American imperialism. It was Beijing that functioned as a champion of international class struggle in opposing an alleged collusion between Indian "big bourgeoisie" and American capitalism.

Beijing's international class struggle did not stop with India. Soon after Chinese and Soviet leaders quarreled over Tibet and India, Mao told his associates that the PRC, along with the communist parties and workers' movements of the world, was under attack from a "peace wave" pushed by Western monopoly capitalism, reactionary nationalists of Latin America and Asia, and the Soviet Union.[43] Mao's lining up the Soviet Union with China's international adversaries was as remarkable as his equating China with the world's communist and proletarian movements. The international alignments were along class lines, and the USSR and the PRC were not on the same side. To CCP leaders, the PRC was by nature a class-state because it was the result of successful territorial expansion of the Chinese Communist movement. To the established international system, which by now also included the "peacefully coexistent" Soviet Union, Beijing was an outlaw, both self- and other-perceived. In the CCP discourse of the time, *fan hua*, or "anti-China," frequently appeared as a label bestowed on China's international adversaries, whom Beijing perceived as China's national *and* class enemies. This was why, when Moscow told Beijing that the Soviet government would maintain neutrality in the Sino-Indian border disputes, CCP leaders viewed the stance as a violation of class solidarity among socialist states.[44]

Shortly after the Lhasa revolt and amid the Sino-Indian disputes, Beijing accumulated a list of complaints against the Soviet Union.[45] Then, in the wake of the Sino-Indian border war, the Chinese Ministry of Foreign Affairs compiled a top-secret position paper of more than a hundred pages titled "The Soviet Attitude Toward the Sino-Indian Border Issue and the Question of the Soviet-Indian Relations." In its preamble, the document stated:

> The issue of the Sino-Indian borders is an international class struggle between capitalism and socialism. For his needs at home and abroad, Nehru has used the border issue to oppose China. Yet the Soviet Union has taken Nehru's side and ignored the socialist nature of our country, confusing right and wrong in labelling China as the aggressor. . . . The Soviet stance is not neutral at all but has supported and encouraged India to oppose China, which seriously violates the third article of the Sino-Soviet Treaty of Friendship and Alliance.[46]

Fingering Moscow for breaching the Sino-Soviet alliance, albeit secretly at the time, was a grave step taken by the CCP leadership. For the moment, Zhou Enlai defined the current state of the Sino-Soviet relationship as "separate but not yet ruptured" (*fen er bu lie*).[47]

Such a nonruptured condition of the Sino-Soviet relationship did not last. In September 1965, as an armed conflict between India and Pakistan was brewing, Moscow became worried about Beijing's pro-Pakistan stance. Still treating the PRC as their ally in the global contest with the United States, Soviet leaders sent a letter to Beijing expressing their "puzzlement" over Beijing's support for Pakistan in its conflict with India. A month later, Beijing replied, using language that would soon become prevalent in Mao's Cultural Revolution:

> Under the guises of "peace," "unity," and "anti-imperialism," you have actually encouraged aggression, . . . undermined unity among Asian and African countries and among socialist states, opposed socialist China, and served American imperialism and its running dogs.

Noticeably, the Chinese letter was not penned by any top CCP leader but drafted by midechelon CCP officials, indicating that by this time the PRC's rupture with the Soviet Union had already become institutionalized.[48]

Meanwhile, the CCP forged ahead in Tibet. In August 1965, the TWC submitted to Beijing a plan for socialist transformation in Tibet, declaring: "The socialist revolution in Tibet has now entered a new era." Specifically, this meant that "people's communes" would be established in the region. In justifying this radical step, aside from referring to the needs of economic growth and class struggle, the TWC stressed that "communization [*gongshe hua*] is the best way to make preparations for war." Beijing approved the plan before the month ended.[49] Thus, in China's southwestern frontiers, Beijing was completing its operation for "carrying the revolution through to the end." The operation since 1950 had incurred extremely high costs both for Tibetan society and for China's relations with its Asian neighbors. In the mid-1960s, the effect also began to show in the opposite direction. In the early spring of 1966, Ulanhu made a remarkable comment at a party meeting of Inner Mongolia: Inner Mongolia used to be the remotest rear area of China's national defense (*zui houfang*), but now the region had become the "first frontline of anti-revisionism," in the forefront of the country's confrontation with the Soviet Union and its Mongolian satellite.[50] At the time, Ulanhu could not foresee that in only a few months, all of China would be turned into an "anti-revisionist" battleground, and he would be the first provincial CCP official to fall victim to that struggle. Soon after Ulanhu's fall, Deng Xiaoping, the CCP's principal tactician in dealing with the Tibetan question and, along with Liu Shaoqi, a leading executor of the CCP's internal censuring of

Ulanhu's "bourgeois nationalism," also became a prominent victim of Mao Zedong's Cultural Revolution.[51]

* * *

In her Nobel Prize–winning oral history, *Secondhand Time: The Last of the Soviets*, Svetlana Alexievich makes an observation on ex-Soviets: "Everyone thought of themselves as victim, never a willing accomplice."[52] The victim/accomplice question has also been asked in different forms by generations who lived through the Mao era. The questioning is not yet prevalent in the PRC, however, because Mao's passing has not made his era completely a "secondhand time" there. Ultimately, meaningful questions about the Mao era and after will have to be asked and freely debated by the Chinese themselves.

Mao Zedong's China was a timescape of asserted triumphs: the CCP turned China from a victim of centurylong humiliation into a victor of infinite glory; Mao's "continuous revolution" was unfolding from one big success to another even bigger one; all nationalities lived "harmoniously in a great family of the Chinese Nation"; and the PRC enjoyed "friends all over the world." Afterwards, as an era of retuned reforms began under Deng Xiaoping, China's dash toward communist utopia in the Mao era was reassessed as a waste of time with horrendous human costs. Recently, however, in the PRC, both the Maoist past and the Dengist past have gone through a new round of reassessments for the sake of the ever-updating present. As usual, selective memories and collective dementia are at work simultaneously in the process.

Remarkably, the ethnopolitical discourse of the PRC has not gone through such a flip-flop process. Whereas the Mao-brand communist experiments have been either demolished or remolded into something else, the Mao-brand nationalist establishments have remained intact. In the 1980s, as Special Economic Zones appeared in southeastern China to lead the transformation of the entire country, Hu Yaobang spearheaded an ephemeral readjustment for treating Tibet as a special ethnopolitical zone.[53] There was also a scholarly proposition a decade ago that the CCP adopt "second-generation ethnic policies."[54] Both had dubious and eventually minimal effects in altering Beijing's thinking about the "nationality question." In the meantime, historical narratives inside the PRC about the CCP's ethnopolitical experiences in general, and those in connection with Inner Mongolia, Tibet, and Xinjiang in particular, have remained essentially the same, without intervention from a reform-inspired revisionism of historical writing. The situation corresponds fully with the PRC's ethnopolitical system, which, once established under Mao, has changed little.

Nostalgia is part of human nature, a desperate longing to arrest the present that at once advances into the uncertain future and retires into the irretrievable past. Although nostalgia has been invoked in the PRC lately, the Mao era is nevertheless yet to complete its irretrievability as a past. As indicated by the standing narrative in the PRC about the CCP's ethnopolitical "accomplishments," a significant part of the Mao era has become an epistemological fossil blending a fitted past with a desperate desire to stabilize the present. The past is truly over only if the essential properties of the past, beautiful and ugly, become common knowledge and no longer arouse inquisitive minds. As of today, much of the past of the PRC's ethnic frontiers has remained concealed or distorted by opposing political narratives. The recent past of Tibet and other PRC frontiers, therefore, continues to live in the contested present. It is said that since Deng's reforms, Beijing's ethnopolitical orientation has switched from a "class discourse" to an "ethnic discourse."[55] The switch cannot be a clean one when history fails even to clarify the connections between what Beijing inflicted on ethnic frontiers in the name of class warfare under Mao and what Beijing has been trying so hard to hold onto in these frontiers since Deng. When pondering the prospect of the PRC characterized as such a frontier state, one cannot evade a question: Having dropped the communist utopia, can China get out of the nationalist trap?

NOTES

Abbreviations

ACM	Archives of Changchun Municipality
ACMFA	Archives of the Chinese Ministry of Foreign Affairs
AFP	Archives of Fujian Province
AGP	Archives of Gansu Province
AGPf	Archives of Garzê Prefecture
AHP	Archives of Hebei Province
AJP	Archives of Jilin Province
ALC	Archives of Luding County
APCK	Archives of President Chiang Kai-shek
AQP	Archives of Qinghai Province
ASP	Archives of Sichuan Province
EJDX	*Eluosi Jiemi Dang'an Xuanbian* (Selection of declassified Russian archives)
JYLW	*Jianguo Yilai Liu Shaoqi Wengao* (Writings by Liao Shaoqi since the foundation of the state)
JYMW	*Jianguo Yilai Mao Zedong Wengao* (Writings by Mao Zedong since the foundation of the state)
JYZW	*Jianguo Yilai Zhou Enlai Wengao* (Writings by Zhou Enlai since the foundation of the state)
MWWH	*Minzu Wenti Wenxian Huibian* (Collection of documents on the nationality question)
MXGW	*Mao Zedong Xizang Gongzuo Wenxuan* (Selected writings of Mao Zedong on the Tibet work)
MZWH	*Minzu Zhengce Wenjian Huibian* (Collections of documents on nationality policies)
NAUK	National Archives of the United Kingdom

NAUS   National Archives of the United States
PCCM   Personal Collection of Classified Materials
PJFK   Papers of John F. Kennedy
WDCX   *Waijiaobu Dang'an Congshu: Jiewu Lei; Di Wu Ce: Xizang Juan* (Archival series of the Ministry of Foreign Affairs: cluster on boundary affairs, book 5: Volumes on Tibet)
XGWX   *Xizang Gongzuo Wenxian Xuanbian* (Selected documents on the Tibet work)
XWZX   *Xizang Wenshi Ziliao Xuanji* (Selected compilation of Tibetan literary and historical materials)
ZGSD   *Zhongguo Geming Shi Dang'an Wenxian Guangpan Ku* (Collection in CD-ROM of archival materials on Chinese revolutionary history)
ZGXLD   *Zhongguo Gongchandang Xizang Lishi Dashiji* (Chronology of major historical events of the CCP in Tibet)
ZZWX   *Zhonggong Zhongyang Wenjian Xuanji* (Selected documents of the CCP Central Committee)

Introduction

1. Xiaoyuan Liu, *Frontier Passages: Ethnopolitics and the Rise of Chinese Communism, 1921–1945* (Washington, D.C.: Woodrow Wilson Center Press, 2004); *Reins of Liberation: An Entangled History of Mongolian Independence, Chinese Territoriality, and Great Power Hegemony, 1911–1950* (Washington, D.C.: Woodrow Wilson Center Press, 2006).
2. John Powers, *History as Propaganda: Tibetan Exiles Versus the People's Republic of China* (Oxford: Oxford University Press, 2004), 3–8, 157–62.
3. All titles of Chinese documents and scholarly articles cited in the notes appear in their English translations without transliteration of the Chinese characters. This practice is open to criticism but used solely for reducing the length of the citations. Interested researchers should be able to locate these materials by referring to their publication and archival information.
4. Wang Lixiong and Tsering Shakya, *The Struggle for Tibet* (London: Verso, 2009), 91.
5. John Godfrey Saxe, *Poems of John Godfrey Saxe* (Boston: Houghton, Mifflin, 1880), 135–36.
6. Michel-Rolph Trouillot, *Silencing the Past: Power and Production of History* (Boston: Beacon Press, 2015), 51.
7. Hsiao-ting Lin, *Tibet and Nationalist China's Frontier: Intrigues and Ethnopolitics, 1928–1949* (Vancouver: University of British Columbia Press, 2006); Gray Tuttle, *Tibetan Buddhists in the Making of Modern China* (New York: Columbia University Press, 2005).
8. Two pertinent examples are works by Jianglin Li and Melvyn Goldstein. In her books, Li uses published and "internally circulated" printed materials found in the PRC. Goldstein's multivolume study, *A History of Modern Tibet*, uses exhaustively published sources in Chinese, English, and Tibetan languages. His treatment of Beijing's policymaking, however, is based on personal interviews and what he identifies as "Documents from the PRC," a group of CCP documents on Tibet that were allegedly brought to India after Mao Zedong's Cultural Revolution.
9. Martha Howell and Walter Prevenier, *From Reliable Sources: An Introduction to Historical Methods* (Ithaca, N.Y.: Cornell University Press, 2001), 79.

10. During the PRC period, top CCP leaders, including Mao Zedong, drafted and issued directives in the name of the "Center" but rarely in their own names. Appearing as decisions reached consensually among the top leaders, these "Central Documents" (*zhongyang wenjian*) carried ultimate authority within the PRC system.
11. In this category, A. Tom Grunfeld's classic *The Making of Modern Tibet* (Armonk, N.Y.: M. E. Sharp, 1987) leads the way. Warren W. Smith, *Tibetan Nation: A History of Tibetan Nationalism and Sino-Tibetan Relations* (Boulder, Colo.: Westview Press, 1996) and Tsering Shakya, *The Dragon in the Land of Snows: A History of Modern Tibet Since 1947* (London: Pimlica, 1999) are two rather different studies from Grunfeld's, but all three books share a feature in not using archival and published sources in Chinese in their discussions of Beijing's policies. In dissenting from the official Chinese narrative, Wang Lixiong and Li Jianglin are two notable Chinese authors who have written about post-1949 Tibet, and some of their works have been translated into English. Their essayist or literary styles aside, neither Wang's nor Li's works are based on Chinese archival materials. Wang's best-known book about Tibet is *Tianzang: Xizang de Mingyun* (Sky burial: The fate of Tibet) (Brampton, Ont.: Mirror Books, 1998). One of Li's books has been translated into English, *Tibet in Agony: Lhasa 1959* (Cambridge, Mass.: Harvard University Press, 2016).
12. Melvyn C. Goldstein, *A History of Modern Tibet, Volume One, 1913–1951: The Demise of the Lamaist State*; *A History of Modern Tibet, Volume Two, 1951–1955: The Calm Before the Storm*; *A History of Modern Tibet, Volume Three, 1955–1957: The Storm Clouds Descend* (Berkeley: University of California Press, 1989–2014). The fourth volume, published in 2019, is titled *A History of Modern Tibet, Volume Four, 1957–1959: In the Eye of the Storm*.
13. The notion of timescape is borrowed from Christopher Clark, *Time and Power: Visions of History in German Politics, from the Thirty Years' War to the Third Reich* (Princeton, N.J.: Princeton University Press, 2019), 1–2.
14. In *The Landscape of History: How Historians Map the Past* (Oxford: Oxford University Press, 2002), 96, John Gaddis defines the principle: "the greater the time that separates a cause from a consequence, the less relevant we presume the cause to be."
15. Alan M. Wachman, *Why Taiwan? Geographic Rationales for China's Territorial Integrity* (Stanford, Calif.: Stanford University Press, 2007), 47–50, 69.
16. Such cyclical landscaping in Chinese history, of course, is a hypothesis of mine and has not been empirically established. But, for instance, significant differences between a constrained geopolitical realm like the Song dynasty and the spheres of those gigantic dynasties like the Han and the Tang should be obvious.
17. Sun Yat-sen, *San Min Chu I: The Three Principles of the People* (Chungking: Ministry of Information of the Republic of China, 1943), 35, claims that Annam (Vietnam) and Burma, among other places, "were both formerly Chinese territory."
18. "Geo-body" is the insightful conception first introduced in Thongchai Winchakul's *Siam Mapped: A History of the Geo-Body of a Nation* (Honolulu: University of Hawaii Press, 1994).
19. In contrast to traditional Chinese cartographers, Western cartographers before the nineteenth century always portrayed China as a territorial domain with clear boundaries. The David Rumsey Map Collection (https://www.davidrumsey.com) is an excellent site for viewing old Western maps of China. The best collection of Chinese antique maps is Cao Wanru, *Zhongguo Gudai Ditu Ji* (Collection of Chinese antique maps), 3 vols. (Beijing: Wenwu Chubanshe, 1991–97). A shared feature of eighteenth- and nineteenth-century Western maps is to mark out borderlines with China's neighbors in the east and

south, including Korea, Vietnam, *Xianluo* (Thailand), Burma, *Zhemengxiong* (Bhutan), and *Kuo'erka* (Nepal). In 1905, the first Chinese map that presented the Qing state with clearly demarcated international boundaries all around was *Da Qing Diguo Quantu* (Atlas of the Great Qing Empire) (Shanghai: Shangwu Yinshuguan, 1905), which put Manchuria, Mongolia, Tibet, and Xinjiang inside the "Qing Empire."

20. Matthew W. Mosca, *From Frontier Policy to Foreign Policy: The Question of India and the Modern Transformation of Geopolitics in Qing China* (Stanford, Calif.: Stanford University Press, 2013).
21. Max Weber, *The Theory of Social and Economic Organization* (New York: Free Press, 1974), 130–31.
22. Weber, 152–53. For two insightful analyses of the imperial structure of the Qing dynasty, see Pamela Kyle Crossley, *A Translucent Mirror: History and Identity in Qing Imperial Ideology* (Berkeley: University of California Press, 2000), and Mark C. Elliott, *The Manchu Way: The Eight Banners and Ethnic Identity in Late Imperial China* (Stanford, Calif.: Stanford University Press, 2001).
23. John K. Fairbank, *The Great Chinese Revolution, 1800–1985* (New York: Harper & Row, 1987).
24. "Notification of the Chinese Communist Party Central Committee," May 16, 1966, *Renmin Ribao* (People's Daily).
25. Frank Dikotter's trilogy offers one of the bleakest assessments of the Mao years: *The Tragedy of Liberation: A History of the Chinese Revolution, 1945–1957* (New York: Bloomsbury Press, 2013); *Mao's Great Famine: The History of China's Most Devastating Catastrophe, 1958–1962* (London: Bloomsbury Press, 2010); *The Cultural Revolution: A People's History, 1966–1976* (New York: Bloomsbury Press, 2016). The "forest fire" quotation is from Orville Schell and John Delury, *Wealth and Power: China's Long March to the Twenty-First Century* (New York: Random House, 2013), 9.
26. The role of the Chinese Communist Revolution as a model for the world's developing countries was first explored in Mark Selden's classic, *The Yenan Way in Revolutionary China* (Cambridge, Mass.: Harvard University, 1971). This line of inquiry has been significantly expanded in some new studies. See, for instance, Jeremy Friedman, *Shadow Cold War: The Sino-Soviet Competition for the Third World* (Chapel Hill: University of North Carolina Press, 2015); Gregg Brazinsky, *Winning the Third World: Sino-American Rivalry During the Cold War* (Chapel Hill: University of North Carolina Press, 2017); Andrew Mertha, *Brothers in Arms: Chinese Aid to the Khmer Rouge, 1975–1979* (Ithaca, N.Y.: Cornell University Press, 2014); Nicholas Khoo, *Collateral Damage: Sino-Soviet Rivalry and the Termination of the Sino-Vietnamese Alliance* (New York: Columbia University Press, 2011); Bertil Lintner, *Great Game East: India, China, and the Struggle for Asia's Most Volatile Frontier* (New Haven, Conn.: Yale University Press, 2015); Meredith Oyen, *The Diplomacy of Migration: Transnational Lives and the Making of U.S.-Chinese Relations in the Cold War* (Ithaca, N.Y.: Cornell University Press, 2015); Shu Guang Zhang, *Beijing's Economic Statecraft During the Cold War, 1949–1991* (Washington, D.C.: Woodrow Wilson Center Press, 2014).
27. Sun Yat-sen, *San Min Chu I: The Three Principles of the People* (Chungking: Ministry of Information of the Republic of China, 1943), 7.
28. W. A. P. Martin, *The Awakening of China* (New York: Doubleday, Page, 1907), v.
29. Zhang Yintang to Emperor Guangxu, "Memorial That Details Conditions of Tibet and Proposes Programs for Improvements," December 10, 1907, in *Qingchao Zhi Zang Dianzhang Yanjiu* (Study of Qing ordinances and regulations for administering Tibet), ed. Zhang Yuxin (Beijing: Zhongguo Zangxue Chubanshe, 2002), 3:1388–98.

30. Committee on Mongolian and Tibetan Affairs to the Executive Yuan, "Ten Programs for Liberating Slaves in Tibet and Xikang," August 13, 1939, *quanzong hao* (general file number) 141: 3136.
31. Lin Tian, entry on June 30, 1950, *Jinjun Xizang Riji* (Diaries on the expedition into Tibet) (Beijing: Zhongguo Zangxue Chubanshe, 1994), 2.
32. A special issue of the *Journal of Cold War Studies*, vol. 8, no. 3 (Summer 2006), includes three articles on Tibet in PRC foreign policies of the Cold War years: Michael M. Sheng, "Mao, Tibet, and the Korean War," 15–33; Qiang Zhai, "Tibet and Chinese-British-American Relations in the Early 1950s," 34–53; Jian Chen, "The Tibetan Rebellion and China's Changing Relations with India and the Soviet Union," 54–101. Jian Chen's article covers concisely the main events discussed in this study.
33. Odd Arne Westad, *The Global Cold War: Third World Interventions and the Making of Our Times* (Cambridge: Cambridge University Press, 2007), 3.
34. Mao Zedong, "Carry the Revolution Through to the End," *Renming Ribao* (People's Daily), January 1, 1949.

1. A Protracted Agenda

1. Alexander V. Pantsov with Steven Levine, *Mao: The Real Story* (New York: Simon & Schuster, 2012), 354–56.
2. Mao Zedong to Filippov (Stalin), January 17, 1949, in *Eluosi Jiemi Dang'an Xuanbian: Zhong Su Guanxi* (Selected declassified Russian archives: Sino-Soviet relations), ed. Shen Zhihua et al., 12 vols. (Shanghai: Dongfang Chuban Zhongxin, 2014), 1:359 [hereafter cited as EJDX].
3. Henry Kissinger, *On China* (New York: Penguin Press, 2011), 271, 289–90, 334.
4. For the westward expansion of the Qing Empire, see Peter C. Perdue's majestic study, *China Marches West: The Qing Conquest of Central Eurasia* (Cambridge, Mass.: Belknap Press, 2005).
5. This sentence paraphrases one of George Kennan's comments in the documentary *Between the Wars, 1918–1941* (Anthony Landsburg Productions, 1987).
6. Wei Yuan, *Sheng Wu Ji* (A record of sacred military campaigns) (Beijing: Zhonghua Shuju, 1984), 205–6; Huang Yusheng et al., *Xizang Difang yu Zhongyang Zhengfu Guanxi Shi* (History of the relationship between Tibet and the central government) (Lhasa: Xizang Renmin Chubanshe, 1995), 129; Kangxi's decree for grand academicians, academicians, and nine ministers; November, the fifty-ninth year of Kangxi [1720], in *Qingchao Zhi Zang Dianzhang Yangjiu* (Study of the regulations and rules for governing Tibet during the Qing Dynasty), ed. Zhang Yuxin (Beijing: Zhongguo Zangxue Chubanshe, 2002), 1:183–84.
7. Feng Mingzhu, *Jindai Zhong Ying Xizang Jiaoshe yu Chuan Zang Bian Qing—Cong Kuoerka zhi Yi dao Huashengdun Huiyi* (Modern Chinese-British diplomacy and the Sichuan-Tibetan frontier: From the battle of Gurkha to the Washington conference) (Taipei: Guoli Gugong Bowuyuan, 1996), 28–118, offers a detailed analysis of the events involved. For two surveys in English, especially the British connections, see Asad Husain, *British India's Relations with the Kingdom of Nepal, 1857–1947* (London: George Allen and Unwin, 1970), 23–68, and Amar Kaur Jasbir Singh, *Himalayan Triangle: A Historical Survey of British India's Relations with Tibet, Sikkim and Bhutan, 1765–1950* (London: British Library, 1988), 3–6, 165–73, 291–97.

8. Peng Yuanrui et al., *Qing Gaozong Shiwen Shiquan Ji* (Poetry and other writings on the ten perfections of the Qing Gaozong [Qianlong]) (Beijing: Zhongguo Zangxue Chubanshe, 1993; originally issued in 1794), 671.
9. "Memorial to the throne by residential commissioner in Tibet, minister of works, and commander-in-chief He Lin and deputy commander-in-chief Cheng De, the first month of the fifty-ninth year of Qianlong" and "Memorial to the throne by residential commissioner in Tibet, minister of works, and commander-in-chief He Lin, the fifth month (of the fifty-ninth year of Qianlong)," in Zhang Yuxin, 1:199–200. *Mani* and *Ebo* are Chinese renderings of the Tibetan and Mongolian terms, respectively, for stone piles used for prayer purpose. In his reports to Qianlong, He Lin used the two terms alternately to refer to stone boundary markers.
10. "Memorial to the throne by residential commissioner in Tibet, minister of works, and commander-in-chief He Lin, the third month of the fifty-eighth year of Qianlong" and "memorial to the throne by residential commissioner in Tibet, minister of works, and commander-in-chief He Lin and deputy commander-in-chief Cheng De, the ninth month (of the fifty-eighth year of Qianlong)," in Zhang Yuxin, 1:194–98.
11. These maps are reproduced in Feng Mingzhu, 478–96. Historical records indicate that Zhu Yuanzhang, the founder of the Ming Dynasty, once tried to map Tibet, but it is not clear what came of the effort. See *Ming Taizu Shilu* (Veritable records of the Ming's founding emperor), cited in Huang Yusheng et al., 69–70.
12. Zhang Yuxin, 1:5–178, 3:1388–98.
13. Pamela Kyle Crossley, *A Translucent Mirror: History and Identity in Qing Imperial Ideology* (Berkeley: University of California Press, 1999), 327–36.
14. Duojie Caidan (Dorje Tseten), *Yuan Yilai Xizang Difang yu Zhongyang Zhengfu Guanxi Yanjiu* (Study of the relations between Tibet and the central government since the Yuan) (Beijing: Zhongguo Zangxue Chubanshe, 2005), 1:483.
15. "Edict to the grand ministers of state, to be transmitted to Fukang'an et al., about studying carefully and adopting appropriate measures for remedying the remaining problems, the twenty-seventh day of the eighth month of the fifty-seventh year of Qianlong (1792)," in Zhang Yuxin, 1:94.
16. "Twenty-nine-article regulations authorized by the throne for remedying the remaining problems of Tibet," in Zhang Yuxin, 1:131–40; "Memorial by Fukang'an et al. about planned six articles of the regulations for remedying the remaining problems of Tibet; the twenty-first day of the eleventh month of the fifty-seventh year of Qianlong (1792)," Zhang Yuxin, 1:104.
17. Wei Yuan, *Sheng Wu Ji*, 216–17.
18. Zhang Yintang, "Memorial presenting a detailed survey of the Tibetan situation and remaining problems to be remedied; the tenth day of the twelfth month of the thirty-third year of Guangxu (1907)," Zhang Yuxin, 3:1390; Lianyu, "Memorial presenting a detailed explanation of recent situation in Tibet; the fourteenth day of the ninth month of the first year of Xuantong (1909)," Zhang Yuxin, 3:1421.
19. Zhang Yintang, "Memorial presenting a detailed survey of the Tibetan situation and remaining problems to be remedied; the tenth day of the twelfth month of the thirty-third year of Guangxu (1907)," Zhang Yuxin, 3:1388.
20. H. J. Mackinder, "The Geographical Pivot of History," *Geographical Journal* 23, no. 4 (April 1904): 437.
21. Zhang Yintang, "Telegram to the ministry of foreign affairs on tentative suggestions for administering Tibet; the thirteenth day of the first month of the thirty-third year of Guangxu (1907)," Zhang Yuxin, 3:1361–53; Zhang Yintang, "Notice to the Tibetans

on the twenty-four articles for remedying the remaining problems; the second month of the thirty-third year of Guangxu," Zhang Yuxin, 3:1363–68; Zhang Yintang, "Letter to the ministry of foreign affairs on establishment of the nine proposed bureaus and attached draft regulations; the third month of the thirty-third year of Guangxu," Zhang Yuxin, 3:1374–86; Zhang Yintang, "Memorial presenting a detailed survey of the Tibetan situation and remaining problems to be remedied; the tenth day of the twelfth month of the thirty-third year of Guangxu (1907)," Zhang Yuxin, 3:1388–98.

22. James Reardon-Anderson's *Reluctant Pioneers: Chinese Expansion Northward, 1644–1937* (Stanford, Calif.: Stanford University Press, 2005) is an insightful investigation of a counterexpansion by Chinese farmers into the northern borderlands after the Manchus marched southward and conquered China. James A. Millward's *Eurasian Crossroads: A History of Xinjiang* (New York: Columbia University Press, 2007) and Shao Dan's *Remote Homeland, Recovered Borderland: Manchus, Manchukuo, and Manchuria, 1907–1985* (Honolulu: University of Hawaii Press, 2011) are regional histories of grand scope. Wang Xiuyu's *China's Last Imperial Frontier: Late Qing Expansion in Sichuan's Tibetan Borderlands* (Lanham, Md.: Lexington Books, 2011) details Qing efforts in the Tibetan-Yi corridor when the dynasty came to its end. Stephen Kotkin and Bruce A. Elleman, ed., *Mongolia in the Twentieth Century: Landlocked Cosmopolitan* (Armonk, N.Y.: M. E. Sharpe, 1999), contains a number of essays on the conditions in Mongolia at the end of the Qing Dynasty.

23. Daphong David Ho, "The Men Who Would Not Be Amban and the One Who Would: Four Frontline Officials and Qing Tibet Policy, 1905–1911," *Modern China* 34, no. 2 (April 2008), 210–46.

24. About the debate, see my "From Five 'Imperial Domains' to a 'Chinese Nation': A Perceptual and Political Transformation in Recent History," in *Ethnic China: State, Society, and Minorities*, ed. Xiaobing Li and Patrick Shan (Lanham, Md.: Lexington Books, 2015), 3–38.

25. Yang Du, *Yang Du Ji* (Collected writings of Yang Du) (Changsha: Hunan Renmin Chubanshe, 1986), 211.

26. Sun Zhongshan, *Sun Zhongshan Quanji* (Complete works of Sun Yat-sen) (Beijing: Zhonghua Shuju, 1981), 2:1–3; Chai Degeng, ed., *Xinhai Geming Zilao Congkan* (Collection of materials on the Revolution of 1911) (Shanghai: Shanghai Renmin Chubanshe, 2000), 8:30. Xinjiang and the three provinces of Manchuria were among the twenty-two provinces.

27. Sun Zhongshan, 2:382–84, 5:187–88.

28. Sun Zhongshan, 11:309.

29. For two insightful and informative studies of the KMT effort in Tibet, see Hsiao-ting Lin, *Tibet and Nationalist China's Frontier: Intrigues and Ethnopolitics* (Vancouver: University of British Columbia Press, 2006), and Zhu Lishuang, *Minguo Zhangfu de Xizang Zhuanshi* (Nationalist government's special envoys to Tibet) (Hong Kong: Chinese University Press, 2016).

30. Chiang Kaishek, *Xian Zongtong Jiang Gong Sixiang Yanlun Zongji* (Complete works of the late president Chiang Kai-shek), 40 vols. (Taipei: Guomindang Dangshi Weiyuanhui, 1984), 35:16–17.

31. Wu Zhongxin to the Executive Yuan, August 4, 1939, *Shisanshi Dalai Lama Yuanji Zhiji he Shisishi Dalai Lama Zuochuang Dang'an Xuanbian* (Selected archives on the condolence mission for the death of the Thirteenth Dalai Lama and the reincarnation and enthronement of the Fourteenth Dalai Lama), comp. the Chinese Center of Tibetan Studies and the Second Historical Archives of China (Beijing: Zhongguo Zangxue

Chubanshe, 1990), 233–38; Wu Zhongxin to Chiang Kai-shek, August 1939, vol. 63 of Specially Submitted Files: Political: General Frontier Administration, Archives of President Chiang Kai-shek [hereafter cited as APCK].

32. Information about the Tibetan-British collusion submitted by the Department of Europe to the Tibetan affairs conference, November 1944, *Waijiaobu Dang'an Congshu: Jiewu Lei; Di Wu Ce: Xizang Juan1* (Archival series of the Ministry of Foreign Affairs: Border administrations; Book five: volumes on Tibet), comp. Ministry of Foreign Affairs (Taipei: Waijiaobu, 2005), 1:320–22 [hereafter cited as WDCX].

33. Chiang Kai-shek to Xu Yongchang, October 19, 1942, Chou Bi Dang (Hand-written files) 15353, APCK.

34. Xiaoyuan Liu, *A Partnership for Disorder: China, the United States, and Their Policies for the Postwar Disposition of the Japanese Empire, 1941–1945* (Cambridge: Cambridge University Press, 1996), 126–47.

35. Chiang Kai-shek to T. V. Soong, May 25, 1943, and Soong to Chiang, May 25, 1943, "Geming Wenxian, Dui Ri Kangzhan Shiqi; Di 40 Ce: Dui Ying Waijiao" (Revolutionary documents, the period of war of resistance against Japan: Vol. 40: Diplomacy with Great Britain), 140–41, APCK.

36. "Memo by Ouyang Zhongyong of the first section of the Department of Europe on diplomacy with British India in respect to Tibet, November 10, 1945; for the Tibetan affairs conference no. 028," WDCX, 1:345–47

37. Shen Zonglian to the Ministry of Foreign Affairs, October 24, 1946, WDCX, 1:79–81.

38. Melvyn C. Goldstein, *A History of Modern Tibet, 1913–1951: The Demise of the Lamaist State* (Berkeley: University of California Press, 1989), 464–521, offers an authoritative treatment of the Reting conspiracy. Hsiao-ting Lin, *Tibet and Nationalist China's Frontier: Intrigues and Ethnopolitics, 1928–49* (Vancouver: University of British Columbia Press, 2006), 182–98, sheds light on KMT involvement in the abortive coup.

39. Ministry of Foreign Affairs, "Opinion on handling the Lhasa incident, July 26, 1947," WDCX, 1:305–8.

40. "Ambassador to India Luo Jialun's secret message to foreign minister Ye Gongchao about India's encroachment along the Tibetan border and the pending invasion of Tibet by communist troops, December 17 [1949]," WDCX, 1:178–79.

41. I discuss the development of the CCP's perceptions and geostrategies in relation to China's ethnic frontiers in *Frontier Passages: Ethnopolitics and the Rise of Chinese Communism* (Washington, D.C.: Woodrow Wilson Center Press, 2004).

42. Records of these conversations can be seen in EJDX, 1:367–452.

43. Mikoyan's memo on conversation with Mao about Sino-Soviet relations and other issues, February 4, 1949, EJDX, 1:420–25. For a detailed discussion of the issue of Mongolian independence, see my *Reins of Liberation: An Entangled History of Mongolian Independence, Chinese Territoriality, and Great Power Hegemony, 1911–1950* (Washington, D.C.: Woodrow Wilson Center Press, 2006).

44. Mikoyan's memo on his conversation with Mao Zedong about urgent policy issues, February 6, 1949, EJDX, 1:441–46.

45. CCP Central Committee's letter to the CCP Provincial Committee of Sichuan, February 19, 1932, United Front Department of the CCP Central Committee, *Minzu Wenti Wenxian Huibian* (Collected documents on the national question) (Beijing: Zhonggong Zhongyang Dangxiao Chubanshe, 1991; internal circulation), 177–79 [hereafter cited as MWWH]; "CCP Central Committee's proclamation to the Tibetan people of Xikang and Tibet on the struggle program of the Tibetan national revolutionary movement, June 1935," MWWH, 285–91; Zhou Enlai, "Several questions concerning the nationality

policy of our state; August 4, 1957," *Zhou Enlai Xuanji* (Selected works of Zhou Enlai) (Beijing: Renmin Chubanshe, 1984), 2:261–62; Zhou Enlai, "Conversation with Saga, Pujie, and Puyi; June 10, 1961," *Zhou Enlai Xuanji*, 2:319–20.

46. "CCP Central Committee's proclamation to the Tibetan people of Xikang and Tibet on the struggle program of the Tibetan national revolutionary movement, June 1935," MWWH, 285–91; CCP Northwestern Work Committee's program for the Mongolian national question during the war of resistance, July 1940, MWWH, 659, 666–67.

47. Jin Shibai, "Independent Tibetan division of the Red Army remembered," *Hongjun Changzheng Huiyi Shiliao* (Reminiscent materials on the Red Army's Long March) (Beijing: Jiefangjun Chubanshe, 1992), 2:83–88; "Organizing the party," "Organizing government," *Aba Zhouzhi* (Chronicle of Ngawa Prefecture) (Beijing: Minzu Chubanshe, 1994), 850–61.

48. Tianbao, "Red Army's Long March through the Tibetan areas," *Aba Zhouzhi*, 89–96; Zhou Xiyin, "Tianbao—vanguard of the Tibetan people's revolution," *Huiyi Sichuan Jiefang (Xubian)* (Liberation of Sichuan remembered [sequel]) (Chengdu: Sichuan Jiaoyu Chubanshe, 1989), 282–87; "Jiang Anxi," *Batang Xianzhi (Xubian)* (Chronicle of the Bathang county [sequel]) (Beijing: Fangzhi Chubanshe, 2001), 399–403; "Pingcuo Wangjie," *Batang Xianzhi (Xubian)*, 466–74; Melvyn C. Goldstein, Dawei Sherap, and William R. Siebenschuh, *A Tibetan Revolutionary: The Political Life and Times of Bapa Phüntso Wangye* (Berkeley: University of California Press, 2004), offers an autobiographic narrative of Phünwang's remarkable career.

49. "Yunze's opinion about the issue of minority nationalities in the constitution; March 17, 1947," MWWH, 1324.

50. Terebin to Stalin [via Kuznetsov], January 10, 1949, *Cold War International History Project Bulletin* 16 (Fall 2007/Winter 2008): 126; Liu De et al., "Pengxian uprising: record of the uprising led by Liu Wenhui, Deng Xihou, and Pan Wenhua," in *Baiwan Guomindang Jun Qiyi Toucheng Jishi* (Factual accounts of the uprising and rallying by millions of KMT troops), ed. Chang Shun et al. (Beijing: Zhongguo Wenshi Chubanshe, 1991), 2:1202–75.

51. "Arrangements by the Military Commission for nation-wide military advance; May 23, 1949," *Zhonggong Zhongyang Wenjian Xuanji* (Selected documents of the CCP Central Committee) (Beijing: Renmin Chubanshe, 1989–1992), 18:292–93 [hereafter cited as ZZWX (1)]; Stalin to Mao (via Kovalev), May 26, 1949, *Cold War International History Project Bulletin* 16 (Fall 2007/Winter 2008): 166; Ivan Kovalev, "The Stalin-Mao Dialogue," *Far Eastern Affairs*, 1992 (2): 106; Stalin to Mao (via Kovalev), June 18, 1949, EJDX, 2:70; records of Stalin's conversation with the CCP delegation, June 27, 1949, EJDX, 2:71–73; Mao to Peng Dehuai, June 27, 1949, ZZWX (1), 18:349.

52. Mao to Stalin, June 12, 1949, EJDX, 2:64–68; Liu Shaoqi, "Report to the Soviet Communist Party Central Committee and Stalin on behalf of the CCP Central Committee; July 4, 1949," in *Jianguo Yilai Liu Shaoqi Wengao* (Writings by Liu Shaoqi since the foundation of the state) (Beijing: Zhongyang Wenxian Chubanshe, 1998), 1:1–2 [hereafter cited as JYLW]; Mao's cable to Liu for being transmitted to Stalin, July 25, 1949, EJDX, 2:94–95; Zhou Enlai, "Speech outline for the national trade union work conference; July 1949," in *Jianguo Yilai Zhou Enlai Wengao* (Writings by Zhou Enlai since the foundation of the state) (Beijing: Zhongyang Wenxian Chubanshe, 2008), 1:155 [hereafter cited as JYZW].

53. "Chen Xizhang's account of the expulsion by the Lhasa authorities of the personnel of the KMT office in Tibet," *Heping Jiefang Xizang* (Peaceful liberation of Tibet), comp. Committee of the Tibetan Autonomous Region for Collecting Materials on Party

History and Leading Group of the Tibetan Military District for Collecting Materials on Party History (Lhasa: Xizang Renmin Chubanshe, 1995; internal circulation), 209–12; "Tibetan local government's telegram to the KMT government on the expulsion of the personnel of the KMT office in Tibet, July 9, 1949," *Heping Jiefang Xizang*, 237–38.

54. Chiang Kai-shek to Li Zongren, July 30 1949, vol. 39 of Revolutionary Documents: Political: Frontier Administration, APCK.
55. Editorial, "Foreign aggressors' swallowing up of Chinese territory Tibet must not be permitted," *Xinhuashe Dianxun Gao* (Xinhua agency bulletin), September 2, 1949, *Zhongguo Geming Shi Dang'an Wenxian Guangpan Ku* (Collection on CD-ROM of archival materials on Chinese revolutionary history), comp. and produced by Central Archives and Beijing Chaoxing Company, disc B-13 [hereafter cited as ZGSD]; Xinhua News Agency's dispatch from Peiping, "British imperialism and stooge Nehru manufactured the Tibetan incident and attempted to seize Chinese territories," ZGSD; Xinhua News Agency's dispatch from Peiping, "British and Indian democratic newspapers' commentaries on the Tibetan incident, exposing the British-Indian reactionaries' plot to annex Tibet," ZGSD.
56. "Foreign aggressors must not be allowed to annex the Chinese territory Tibet, September 2, 1949," MWWH, 1262–64.
57. Indian Trade Agent, Gyantse, and Officer-in-Charge, Indian Mission, Lhasa [Richardson] to Political Officer in Sikkim, "Report on Indian Mission Lhasa for June, 1949," July 3, 1949, National Archives of the United Kingdom: PRO/FO 371–76315 [hereafter cited as NAUK]; American Embassy London to Secretary of State, September 12, 1949, National Archives of the United States: 893.00 Tibet/9-1249 [hereafter cited as NAUS].
58. Tsering Shakya, *The Dragon in the Land of Snows: A History of Modern Tibet Since 1947* (London: Pimlico, 1999), 9; Goldstein, *A History of Modern Tibet*, 613; *Zhongguo Gongchandang Xizang Lishi Dashiji, 1949–2004* (Chronology of major historical events of the Chinese Communist Party in Tibet, 1949–2004) (Beijing: Zhonggong Dangshi Chubanshe, 2005), 1:2 [hereafter cited as ZGXLD].
59. Chen Xizhang, "Official career in Tibet," in *Jianzheng Bainian Xizang: Xizang Lishi Jianzhengren Fangtanlu* (Witnessing Tibet: Interviews with witnesses of Tibetan history), ed. Zhang Xiaoming (Beijing: Wuzhou Chuanbo Chubanshe, 2004), 58–60; Memo, "Tibetan situation after British departure from India; December 10, 1947," Asia-Pacific Department: File on abolition of the unequal Chinese-British treaties regarding Tibet, Archives of the Ministry of Foreign Affairs, Taipei: 172-1-0011.
60. For instance, the KMT Central News Agency reported in early August that American journalist Lowell Thomas and son were about to enter Tibet to meet with the Dalai Lama. The *New York Times* did not report the Thomas visit until late September. See *Xizang Difang Lishi Ziliao Xuanji* (Selected materials on local history of Tibet) (Beijing: Sanlian Chubanshe, 1963; internal circulation), 376–79; "Lowell Thomas on Litter," *New York Times*, September 26, 1949, 27.
61. "KMT Central Daily's report of the Lhasa incident; August 19, 1949," *Xizang Difang Lishi Ziliao Xuanji*, 373. The *New York Times*, for instance, reported consecutively from July 23 to 25, suggesting initially that it was a revolt against both the Dalai Lama and the KMT regime and might be a communist plot. See "Revolt Against China Is Reported in Tibet," *New York Times*, July 23, 1949, 1; "India to Sift Tibetan Rumor," *New York Times*, July 24, 1949, 24; "Tibetan Revolt Explained," *New York Times*, July 25, 1949, 5.
62. ZGXLD, 1:3.
63. Mao Zedong, "The Chinese people stood up! September 21, 1949," *Jianguo Yilai Mao Zedong Wengao* (Writings by Mao Zedong since the foundation of the state) (Beijing: Zhongyang Wenxian Chubanshe, 1987), 1:4 [hereafter cited as JYMW].

64. Tibetan bureau of foreign affairs to Mao Zedong, November 2, 1949, *Heping Jiefang Xizang*, 241; "Complete transcript of the broadcasting by the Tibetan 'foreign ministry'; January 25, 1950," Archives of the Chinese Ministry of Foreign Affairs, Beijing: 105-00018-01 [hereafter cited as ACMFA].
65. Kovalev's report to Stalin on his conversation with Mao Zedong, May 17, 1949, EJDX, 2:50–53.
66. Stalin's cable to Mao Zedong (via Kovalev), May 26, 1949, EJDX, 2:58.
67. "CCP Central Committee's directive on the personnel and regional responsibilities of South China Branch Bureau, Central China Bureau, and Southwest Bureau; August 1, 1949," ZZWX (1), 18:403; Peng to Mao, He Long, and Xi Zhongxun, August 19, 1949, Peng Dehuai, *Peng Dehuai Junshi Wenxuan* (Selected military writings of Peng Dehuai) (Beijing: Zhongyang Wenxian Chubanshe, 1988), 307–10; "Peng Dehuai's report on the current situation of Qinghai and the work about Tibetans, September 18, 1949," MWWH, 1283.
68. "Zhao Shouyue to the KMT Central Committee reporting the date of the Panchen Lama's death; December 1, 1937," and "Guan Jiyu's congratulatory speech at the ceremony of enthroning the tenth Panchen Lama; August 10, 1949," *Jiushi Banchan Yuanji Zhiji he Shishi Banchan Zhuanshi Zuochuang Dang'an Xuanbian* (Selected archives on the condolence mission for the death of the ninth Panchen Lama and the reincarnation and enthronement of the tenth Panchen Lama) (Beijing: Zhongguo Zangxue Chubanshe, 1991), 3, 379–80.
69. Mao to Peng, August 6, 1949, *Mao Zedong Xizang Gongzuo Wenxuan* (Selected writings of Mao Zedong on the Tibet work) (Beijing: Zhongyang Wenxian Chubanshe, 2001), 1 [hereafter cited as MXGW]; *Qinghai Lishi Jiyao* (Important events in the history of Qinghai), comp. Qinghai Committee on the Compilation of Provincial Chronicle (Xining: Qinghai Renmin Chubanshe, 1987), 515.
70. Fan Ming, *Xizang Neibu Zhi Zheng: Dalai Lama he Banchan Dashi de Maodun, Zhonggong Gaoceng de Fenqi* (Internal controversies of Tibet: contradictions between the Dalai Lama and Master Panchen [Lama] and disagreements among CCP leaders) (Carle Place, N.Y.: Mirror Books, 2009), 95–99; Mao Zedong and Zhu De to the Panchen Lama, November 23, 1949, MXGW, 3.
71. Mao Zedong to Wang Zhen, October 10, 1949, ZGXLD, 1:4.
72. Roshchin's memo on his conversation with Zhou Enlai, November 15, 1949, EJDX, 2:158–61; Roshchin's memo on his conversation with Zhou Enlai, December 5, 1949, EJDX, 2:168.
73. "Commission of Military Affairs' circular about the lessons from the failed attack at the Jinmen Island; October 29, 1949," JYMW, 1:100–101.
74. "Speech at the first meeting of the People's Revolutionary Committee of Military Affairs; October 20, 1949," in *Jianguo Yilai Mao Zedong Junshi Wengao* (Mao Zedong's military writings since the establishment of the state) (Beijing: Junshi Kexue Chubanshe Zhongyang Wenxian Chubanshe, 2010), 1:38–42. The People's Revolutionary Commission of Military Affairs existed between October 1949 and September 1954, and Mao was its chair.
75. Roshchin's memo on conversation with Li Kenong about American espionage activities, November 17, 1949, EJDX, 2:163–64.
76. JYZW, 1:506–7, 557.
77. Jiangbian Jiacuo (Jambey Gyatso), *Li Jue Zhuan* (Biography of Li Jue) (Beijing: Zhongguo Zangxue Chubanshe, 2005), 49–50, indicates that Li Jue, head of the operational department of the Second Field Army in 1949, personally saw Mao's message and was the key figure to add the episode to the history of PLA advance into Tibet more than

four decades later. Li Jue's own recollection, "Peaceful liberation of Tibet remembered," *Zhonggong Dangshi Ziliao* (Materials on the CCP history) 35 (1990): 81, suggests that the CCP Central Committee transmitted Mao's letter to Deng, Liu Bocheng, and He Long in mid-December. This alleged fact did not achieve an authoritative aura until it was adopted by the revised edition of *Zhongguo Gongchandang Xizang Lishi Dashiji* (1:5) in 2005. Since Mao allegedly sent out the letter when passing through Manzhouli, the date can only be December 9.

78. Deng Lifeng, *Xin Zhongguo Junshi Huodong Jishi, 1949-1959* (Record of the military activities of the new China, 1949-1959) (Beijing: Zhonggong Dangshi Ziliao Chubanshe, 1989), 47; *Zhongguo Da Baike Quanshu; Junshi: Zhongguo Renmin Jiefangjun Zhanshi, Zhongguo Renmin Zhiyuanjun Zhanshi Fence* (Great encyclopedia of China: Military affairs: Volume on combat histories of the People's Liberation Army and the Chinese People's Volunteers) (Beijing: Junshi Kexue Chubanshe, 1987), 555–58.

79. Zhou Enlai, "Remarks on Zhang Tiesheng's telegram about the Chiang-American relationship; December 3, 1949," JYZW, 1:612; Zhou Enlai, "Telegram about instigating Liu Wenhui to hold uprising; December 5, 1949," JYZW, 1:628; Roshchin's memo on his conversation with Zhou Enlai, December 5, 1949, EJDX, 2:168; "From the Diary of Roshchin N. V.: 'Memorandum of Conversation with the Chairman of the People's Central Government of the People's Republic of China, Comrade Mao Zedong'; January 1, 1950," *CWIHP Bulletin* 8–9 (Winter 1996/1997): 227–28.

80. "Telegram on dealing with relations with the British and American consulates in Dihua; December 7, 1949," JYZW, 1:637–38.

81. Ted Gup, *The Book of Honor: The Secret Lives and Deaths of CIA Operatives* (New York: Anchor, 2001), 9–42; Thomas Laird, *Into Tibet: The CIA's First Atomic Spy and His Secret Expedition to Lhasa* (New York: Grove Press, 2002), 134–35, 169–70; John Kenneth Knaus, *Orphans of the Cold War: America and the Tibetan Struggle for Survival* (New York: PublicAffairs, 1999), 61–62.

82. "Lowell Thomas on Litter"; "Tibet Fears Told by Lowell Thomas," *New York Times*, October 11, 1949, 21; "Lowell Thomas Back from Tibet," *New York Times*, October 17, 1949, 25; "U.S. May Grant Tibet Recognition in View of Current Asian Situation," *New York Times*, October 25, 1949, 5; "Soviet Sees a Plot in Thomas Tibet Trip," *New York Times*, December 2, 1949, 16.

83. Hu Qiaomu, *Hu Qiaomu Huiyi Mao Zedong* (Mao Zedong remembered by Hu Qiaomu) (Beijing: Renmin Chubanshe, 1994), 447; Wu Lengxi, *Shinian Lunzhan, 1956-1966: Zhong Su Guanxi Huiyilu* (Ten-year polemics, 1956-1966: A memoir on Sino-Soviet relations) (Beijing: Zhongyang Wenxian Chubanshe, 1999), 3–4.

84. "Russians See Paris as 'Turning Point,'" *New York Times*, May 12, 1949, 4.

85. From the Indian Trade Agent, Gyantse, and Officer in Charge, Indian Mission, Lhasa, P.O. Gyantse, Tibet, to the Political Officer in Sikkim, "Report for the Period September first to fifteenth," September 15, 1949, NAUK: FO/371/76315; From U.K. High Commissioner in India to C.R.O. (Commonwealth Relations Office), November 17, 1949, NAUK: FO/371/76314; From U.K. High Commissioner in India to C.R.O., November 8, 1949, NAUK: FO/371/76314.

86. Memo of conversation between State Department officials and Lowell Thomas, Jr., November 9, 1949, NAUS: 893.00 Tibet/11-949; Memo of conversation between Secretary of State and Lowell Thomas, February 17, 1950, NAUS: Rg. 59: Records of the Office of China Affairs, P Files, 1948–55, box 22.

87. The Dalai Lama, cited in Thomas Laird, *The Story of Tibet: Conversations with the Dalai Lama* (New York: Grove Press, 2006), 295.

1. A Protracted Agenda   323

88. Goldstein, *A History of Modern Tibet*, 626, and Shakya, *The Dragon in the Land of Snows*, 16, suggest that publicity and international sympathy were actually the Tibetan authorities' main purposes in receiving the Thomases.
89. A. Tom Grunfeld, *The Making of Modern Tibet* (Armonk, N.Y.: M. E. Sharpe, 1996), 105.
90. Intelligence Department of the Military Commission, *Xizang Gaikuang (Xizang cankao ziliao zhiyi)* (Brief survey of Tibet: Reference materials on Tibet no. 1), January 1950, and *Xizang de Neizheng ji Zongjiao (Xizang cankao ziliao zhiliu)* (Internal contest and religion of Tibet: Reference materials on Tibet no. 6), n.d., Personal Collection of Classified Materials [hereafter cited as PCCM].
91. Zhang Xiangming, *Zhang Xiangming 55 nian Xizang Gongzuo Shilu* (Records of Zhang Xiangming's 55-year work in Tibet) (unpublished internal materials, 2006), 21–22, suggests that after the Battle of Chamdo in October 1950, PLA troops captured two photos of the Thomases and thus provided Beijing with the first material evidence of "American interference." In the CCP literature, the Thomas visit has been consistently treated as the first American step in interfering the PRC's Tibetan affairs. See "Tibet is an inalienable part of our state territory," *Remin Ribao* (People's Daily), April 24, 1959; ZGXLD, 1:1–2.
92. Mao to Stalin (via Kovalev), June 12, 1949, EJDX, 2:64–68; "Ideological work for preparations for military advance into the Southwest; September 13, 1949," Deng Xiaoping, *Deng Xiaoping Xinan Gongzuo Wenji* (Deng Xiaoping's writings on the Southwest work) (Beijing and Chongqing: Zhongyang Wenxian Chubanshe and Chongqing Chubanshe, 2006), 1–3; "Mastering the three most effective methods in overcoming difficulties in the Southwest work; September 20, 1949," *Deng Xiaoping Xinan Gongzuo Wenji*, 4–9.
93. "Telegram to Peng Dehuai about military operations in the Southwest and Northwest; October 13, 1949," JYMW, 1:54–55; Office of Documentary Research of the CCP Central Committee, *Deng Xiaoping Nianpu 1904–1974* (Chronology of Deng Xiaoping's life, 1904–1974) (Beijing: Zhongyang Wenxian Chubanshe, 2009), 2:845–46; Wang Yan, *Peng Dehuai Nianpu* (Chronicle of Peng Dehuai's life) (Beijing: Renmin Chubanshe, 1998), 416–17.
94. "Outline for the report at the first meeting of the Southwest Bureau of the CCP Central Committee; February 6, 1949," *Deng Xiaoping Xinan Gongzuo Wenji*, 92.
95. "Telegram to Peng Dehuai about the issue of liberating Tibet; November 23, 1949," JYMW, 1:152–53.
96. Yang Kuisong, "The personnel policy of the CCP in the initial period of the PRC examined: The origins of 'anti-localism' in the 1950s," *Zhongguo Dangdaishi Yanjiu* (Studies of contemporary Chinese history) 1 (April 2009): 3–39, is an insightful pioneer study of the subject.
97. *Deng Xiaoping Nianpu*, 2:860–69.
98. Roshchin's memo on his conversation with Zhou Enlai, December 5, 1949, EJDX, 2:168.
99. Wang Yan, *Peng Dehuai Nianpu*, 423–24.
100. Xu Dashen et al., *Zhonghua Renmin Gongheguo Shilu* (Veritable records of the People's Republic of China) (Changchun: Jilin Renmin Chubanshe, 1994), 1:136.
101. Fan Ming, *Xizang Neibu Zhi Zheng*, 102–4.
102. Intelligence Department of the Military Commission, *Xizang Gaikuang (Xizang cankao ziliao zhiyi)* (Brief survey of Tibet: Reference materials on Tibet no. 1), January 1950, and *Xizang Jiaotong Gaikuang (Xizang cankao ziliao zhiba)* (Conditions of transportation in Tibet: Reference materials on Tibet no. 8), February 1950, PCCM.

103. H. E. Davies, "Note of conversation with Mr. Hugh Richardson on December third and fourth," NAUK: FO 371/76317.
104. Zhang Yuxin, 3:1125; *Huang Musong, Wu Zhongxin, Zhao Shouyu, Dai Chuanxian Fengshi Banli Zangshi Baogaoshu* (Reports by Huang Musong, Wu Zhongxin, Zhao Shouyu, and Dai Chuanxian about their missions to Tibet) (Beijing: Zhongguo Zangxue Chubanshe, 1993), 189–90; Bate, *Mongguzu Gudai Zhanli Shi* (History of the ancient war cases of the Mongols) (Beijing: Jincheng Chubanshe, 2002), 509–18; Wei Yuan, *Sheng Wu Ji*, 205–6, 229, 234–38; Perdue, *China Marches West*, 227–28, 439–40.
105. Mao's cable to the CCP Central Committee, Peng Dehuai, to be transmitted to Deng Xiaoping, Liu Bocheng, and He Long, January 2, 1950, MXGW, 6–7.
106. "Telegram on planning by the Southwest Bureau for military advance and arrangement of the Tibetan question; January 2, 1950," JYMW, 1:208–9.
107. "Report on the situation of the Southwest work; January 2, 1950," *Deng Xiaoping Xinan Gongzuo Wenji*, 46; "Opinion on military advance into Tibet; January 8, 1950," *Deng Xiaoping Xinan Gongzuo Wenji*, 57.
108. In 1910, the Qing government sent 1,700 troops from Sichuan into Tibet as one of the steps to implement "New Policies."
109. Xu Dashen et al., *Zhonghua Renmin Gongheguo Shilu*, 136.
110. Giovanni Arrighi, Takeshi Hamashita, and Mark Selden, eds., *The Resurgence of East Asia: 500, 150 and 50 Year Perspectives* (London: Routledge, 2003), 2–4.

2. The "Dalai Line"

1. Niccolo Machiavelli, *The Prince* (New York: Simon and Brown, 2016), 28.
2. Jiangbian Jiacuo, *Li Jue Zhuan* (Biography of Li Jue) (Beijing: Zhongguo Zangxue Chubanshe, 2005), 87.
3. *Heping Jiefang Xizang (Neibu Ben)* (Peaceful liberation of Tibet; internal edition), comp. Committee on Collecting Party Historical Materials of the Tibetan Autonomous Region and Leading Group for Collecting Party Historical Materials of the Tibetan Military District (Lhasa: Xizang Renmin Chubanshe, 1995), 59–61.
4. Jiangbian Jiacuo, *Li Jue Zhuan*, 107.
5. Mao Zedong, "On the Issue of Inspecting Broadcasting in Tibetan," May 13, 1950, MXGW, 14.
6. Zhang Xiangming, *Zhang Xiangming 55 nian Xizang Gongzuo Shilu* (Records of Zhang Xiangming's 55-year work in Tibet), unpublished manuscript, 2006, 29. In CCP discourse, *minzu wenti* in the domestic context means a situation involving interethnic relations, in most cases between the Han and one or more non-Han groups.
7. Zhou Enlai, "Special Features of the Draft Common Program of the People's Political Consultative Council," September 22, 1949, JYZW, 1:394.
8. Zhou Enlai, "Great Victory of the People's War," September 30, 1950, JYZW, 3:355.
9. Mao Zedong, "Lecture Notes," October 12, 1913, *Mao Zedong Zaoqi Wengao* (Early writings of Mao Zedong) (Changsha: Hunan Renmin Chubanshe, 1995), 590–91; Mao Zedong, "On the New Phase," October 12, 1938, MWWH, 595.
10. Minutes of the meeting of the Chinese Communist delegation, January 18, 1924, *Liangong (Bu), Gongchan Guoji yu Zhongguo Guomin Geming Yundong, 1920–1925* (Soviet Communist Party (Bolshevik), the Comintern, and the Chinese nationalist revolutionary movement, 1920–1925) (Beijing: Beijing Tushuguan Chubanshe, 1997), 1:469.

11. Mao's cable to the Center, Peng Dehuai, to be transmitted to Deng Xiaoping, Liu Bocheng, and He Long, January 2, 1950, MXGW, 6–7.
12. For autonomous movements of Inner Mongolia during the first half of the twentieth century, see my *Reins of Liberation: An Entangled History of Mongolian Independence, Chinese Territoriality, and Great Power Hegemony, 1911–1950* (Washington D.C.: Woodrow Wilson Center Press, 2006). Uradyn Bulag's *The Mongols at China's Edge: History and the Politics of National Unity* (Lanham, Md.: Rowman and Littlefield, 2002) and *Collaborative Nationalism: The Politics of Friendship on China's Mongolian Frontier* (Lanham, Md.: Rowman and Littlefield, 2010) offer unique insights into interethnic relations of Inner Mongolia during the PRC period.
13. Wang Shusheng and Hao Yufeng, *Wulanfu Nianpu* (Chronicle of Ulanhu's life) (Beijing: Zhonggong Dangshi Ziliao Chubanshe, 1989), 216–17, 305.
14. Fan Ming, *Xizang Neibu Zhi Zheng: Dalai Lama he Banchan Dashi de Maodun, Zhonggong Gaoceng de Fenqi* (Internal controversies of Tibet: Contradictions between Dalai and Panchen and disagreements among CCP leaders) (Carle Place, N.Y.: Mirror Books, 2009), 102.
15. ZGXLD, 1:14. These scholars were Li Anzai, Yu Shiyu, Xie Guoan, Liu Qianli, Zhu Weihan, and Fu Sizhong.
16. He Long, "Report on the conditions of Xikang and Tibet," January 10, 1950, *He Long Junshi Wenxuan* (Selected military writings of He Long) (Beijing: Jiefangjun Chubanshe, 1989), 464; Ren Naiqiang, "Recollection of Discussion with Revered General He [Long] of Liberation of Tibet," *Xizang Wenshi Ziliao Xuanji* (Selected compilation of Tibetan literary and historical materials), comp. Research Committee of Literary and Historical Materials of Tibet, Chinese People's Political Consultative Conference, vol. 22 (2005), 1–13 [hereafter cited as XWZX]; Ji Youquan, *Baixue: Jiefang Xizang Jishi* (White snow: A factual record of liberation of Tibet) (Beijing: Zhongguo Wuzi Chubanshe, 1993), 131–33.
17. Luo Runcang, "Tibetan Studies in Sichuan During the War of Resistance," *Zhongguo Zangxue* (Tibetology of China), 1996 (3): 11–20; Ren Jianxin, "Brief Account of the Society for the Studies of Xikang and Tibet," *Zhongguo Zangxue*, 1996 (3): 21–29.
18. Leaders in Beijing had their own sources of information about Tibet. For instance, the Intelligence Department of the Central Military Commission compiled a set of *Xizang Cankao Ziliao* (Reference materials on Tibet) in January 1950. Although these materials provided detailed information about Tibetan social conditions, government, personalities, and connections with the Kuomintang and foreign influence, they did not offer policy suggestions.
19. Fan Ming, "Account of Escorting the Tenth Panchen Master to Return to Tibet," *Wenshi Ziliao* (Literary and historical materials), published by the Chinese People's Political Consultative Conference, 29:1.
20. Shibaev's memorandum on conversation with Liu Shaoqi about Asian trade unions' and women's conferences, December 25, 1949, EJDX, 2:191–95.
21. Center to Peng Dehuai and the Northwestern Bureau, December 26, 1949, JYLW, 1:191.
22. He Long, "Report on the conditions of Xikang and Tibet," January 10, 1950, *He Long Junshi Wenxuan*, 464.
23. "Center's telegram of January 22 transmitted by the Southwest Bureau," cited in Yang Yizhen, "Historical episodes about the Center's arrangement for military advance into Tibet," XWZX, 22:82–83; Center to the Southwestern Bureau, Northwestern Bureau, He [Long], Li [Jingquan], and Wang Zhen, January 24, 1950, JYLW, 1:329–30.
24. Fan Ming, *Xizang Neibu Zhi Zheng*, 107–11.

25. "Tibetan Full National Assembly to Ambassador Yuan [Zhongxian]," January 18, 1950, ACMFA: 105-00018-09; "Full text of the broadcast by the Tibetan 'Foreign Ministry,'" January 25, 1950, ACMFA: 105-00018-09.
26. Policy Research Office of the Eighteenth Army, "Preliminary opinions on various policies toward Tibet," March 1950, PCCM.
27. *Zhongguo Renmin Jiefang Zhanzheng Junshi Wenji* (Military documents on the Chinese people's war of liberation), comp. Chinese People's Liberation Army Headquarters (Zhongguo Renmin Jiefangjun Zongbu, 1951), book 5 (2): 607–36; Yang Kuisong, "Examination of the CCP's Personnel Policy Early After the State Foundation: Origins of 'Anti-Localism' in 1950," *Zhongguo Dangdaishi Yanjiu* (Studies of Current Chinese History) 1 (2009): 3–11.
28. Policy Research Office of the Eighteenth Army, "Preliminary opinions."
29. Policy Research Office of the Eighteenth Army, "Preliminary opinions."
30. "Tibet Work Committee's proposal for administering Tibet," 1950, PCCM.
31. Zhang Xiangming, *Zhang Xiangming*, 27–28, suggests that Wang Qimei single-handedly came up with the divide-and-rule idea. But Jiangbian Jiacuo, *Li Jue Zhuan*, 80–81, states that the document was drafted after careful collective deliberations within the Policy Research Office of the Eighteenth Army and the TWC. It should be noted that until December 1951, the TWC was a Southwestern setup without officials from the Northwest.
32. *Heping Jiefang Xizang*, 104.
33. Jiangbian Jiacuo, *Li Jue Zhuan*, 80–82.
34. Policy Research Office of the Eighteenth Army, "Preliminary opinions."
35. Liu's telegram to the Northwestern Bureau to be transmitted to the Southwestern Bureau, May 3, 1950, JYLW, 130–31.
36. *Heping Jiefang Xizang*, 75–76.
37. *Heping Jiefang Xizang*, 77–78; Southwestern Bureau to the Center, May 27, 1950, *Xizang Gongzuo Wenxian Xuanbian* (Selected documents of the Tibetan work), comp. Office of Documentary Research of the CCP Central Committee and the CCP Committee of the Tibetan Autonomous Region (Beijing: Zhongyang Wenxian Chubanshe, 2005), 19–20 [hereafter cited as XGWX].
38. Mao to Peng Dehuai, August 3, 1950, JYMW, 1:450.
39. Center's directive on the questions and demands raised by the Panchen salutary delegation, September 23, 1950, cited in Fan Ming, *Xizang Neibu Zhi Zheng*, 115–17.
40. ZGXLD, 32–33; Zhao Shenying, *Zhang Guohua Jiangjun zai Xizang* (General Zhang Guohua in Tibet) (Beijing: Zhongguo Zangxue Chubanshe, 1998), 49–50; Documentary Research Office of the Central Committee of the Chinese Communist Party, *Zhou Enlai Nianpu, 1949–1976* (Chronicle of Zhou Enlai's life, 1949–1976) (Beijing: Zhongyang Wenxian Chubanshe, 1997), 1: 123; Central Military Commission to the Northwestern and Southwestern Bureaus, February 13, 1951, *Zhou Enlai yu Xizang* (Zhou Enlai and Tibet), comp. Office of Party History of the Tibetan Autonomous Region (Beijing: Zhongguo Zangxue Chubanshe, 1998), 13–14.
41. "Agreement between the Central People's Government and the local government of Tibet on the steps for peaceful liberation of Tibet," May 23, 1951, *Heping Jiefang Xizang*, 126.
42. Zhang Dingyi, *1954 Nian Dalai, Banchan Jin Jing Jilue* (Records of Dalai's and Panchen's visit in Beijing in 1954) (Beijing: Zhongguo Zangxue Chubanshe, 2005), 183–84.
43. "Agreement between the Central People's Government and the local government of Tibet," 125–28.

44. Mao Zedong, "Agreement on the steps for peaceful liberation of Tibet must be carried out," May 26, 1951, XGWX, 54.
45. The CCP Center, "Directive on the work in the Tibetan area of southern Gansu," June 29, 1952, Archives of Gansu Province: 91-001-0437 [hereafter cited as AGP].
46. Zhou Enlai, "On the question of nationality policies," April 27, 1950, XGWX, 15.
47. Zhao Shenying, *Zhongyang Zhu Zang Daibiao Zhang Jingwu* (Representative of the Center in Tibet Zhang Jingwu) (Beijing: Zhongguo Zangxue Chubanshe, 2001), 6.
48. Zhao Shenying, *Zhang Guohua*, 63–65.
49. Fan Ming, *Xizang Neibu Zhi Zheng*, 196.
50. Ji Youquan, *Baixue*, 409–10.
51. "CCP Center's directive on the question of the Tibetan work," April 1, 1952, XGWX, 65–66. The author of the telegram is not identified in the publication, but part of the quoted message is included in MXGW, 60. A *Sicao* was an acting *Silön*, or chief executive official of the Kashag.
52. Jiangbian Jiacuo, *Li Jue Zhuan*, 60–67.
53. "CCP Committee of the Eighteenth Army's Directive on the Work of Marching into Tibet," February 1, 1950, *Heping Jiefang Xizang*, 59–61.
54. Zhang Xiangming, *Zhang Xiangming*, 24–25; Lin Tian, *Jinjun Xizang Riji* (Diaries on the expedition into Tibet) (Beijing: Zhongguo Zangxue Chubanshe, 1994), 12.
55. Jiangbian Jiacuo, *Li Jue Zhuan*, 120–21; Zhang Xiangming, *Zhang Xiangming*, 24–25; Zhao Shenying, *Zhang Guohua*, 41, 63–65.
56. Gao Song, "Brief account of the advance team's entry into Tibet," XWZX, 22:23; Center to the Tibet Work Committee, August 18, 1952, *Huihuang de Ershi Shiji Xin Zhongguo Da Jilu: Xizang Juan* (Grand records of the glorious new China in the twentieth century: Volume on Tibet) (Beijing: Hongqi Chubanshe, 1999), 681; Jiangbian Jiacuo, *Li Jue Zhuan*, 158–61.
57. *Xizang Zizhiqu Zhi: Junshi Zhi* (Chronicle of the Tibetan Autonomous Region: Chronicle of military affairs), 251–52, 255–57.
58. Mao to Deng Xiaoping, January 30, 1951, JYMW, 2:93; ZGXLD, 1:61–62; Jiangbian Jiacuo, *Xueshan Mingjiang Tan Guansan* (Snow mountain general Tan Guansan) (Beijing: Zhongguo Zangxue Chubanshe, 2001), 97–105.
59. Fan Ming, *Xizang Neibu Zhi Zheng*, 253, note 36.
60. ZGXLD, 1:58–59.
61. Documentary Research Office of the Central Committee of the Chinese Communist Party, *Deng Xiaoping Nianpu 1904–1974* (Chronology of Deng Xiaoping's life, 1904–1974) (Beijing: Zhongyang Wenxian Chubanshe, 2009), 2:1063.
62. Ren Naiqiang, "Recollection," 2–7.
63. CCP Center to the Southwestern Bureau and the Tibet Work Committee, October 26, 1952, XGWX, 89–90.
64. "Highlights of a conversation with the Tibetan salutary delegation," October 8, 1952, MXGW, 88–89.
65. Central Propaganda and United Front Departments to the Propaganda and United Front Departments of the Northwestern Bureau and the Central Bureaus, "Explanations of the issue of development of the Tibetan religion," April 22, 1953, AGP: 93-001-0026.
66. Jiangbian Jiacuo, *Li Jue Zhuan*, 136.
67. "Center's telegram approving the report by the Tibet Work Committee on implementation of nationality policies in the past two years," May 19, 1953, JYLW, 5:188; Zhang Xiangming, *Zhang Xiangming*, 55.

68. Mao's telegram to the Southwestern Bureau and the Tibet Work Committee to be transmitted to the Northwestern Bureau and the Xinjiang Branch Bureau, April 6, 1952, MXGW, 62.
69. Zhao Shenying, *Zhang Guohua*, 159.
70. Fan Ming, *Xizang Neibu Zhi Zheng*, 131; "Supporting the Agreement on the Steps for Peaceful Liberation of Tibet," May 27, 1951, *People's Daily*.
71. Zhang Jingwu's report on a conversation with Kashag officials, October 14, 1951, PCCM; Zhang Jingwu's report on a conversation with Ngabö in the evening of the 18th, October 19, 1951, PCCM; Zhang Jingwu's report on a conversation with Kashag representative Ngabö, October 22, 1951, PCCM; Zhang Jingwu's report on unity with the Fan Ming detachment and Che Jigmé's demands, December 13, 1951, PCCM. The first document indicates that even Zhang Jingwu did not know about the change of plan before he made the trip to Tibet. He learned about the new arrangement from two Beijing telegrams received in Tibet.
72. Mao's telegram to the Southwest Bureau and the Tibet Work Committee to be transmitted to the Northwestern Bureau and the Xinjiang Branch Bureau, April 6, 1952, MXGW, 61–64; "Highlights of a conversation with the Tibetan salutary delegation," October 8, 1952, MXGW, 88–89.
73. Center to the Southwestern and Northwestern Bureaus and He (Long), Li (Jingquan), and Wang Zhen, January 24, 1950, JYLW, 1:329–30; ZGXLD, 1:52–53.
74. Li Jue, "Peaceful liberation of Tibet remembered," *Zhonggong Dangshi Ziliao* (Materials on the CCP history), 35:110.
75. Zhou Enlai to Zhang Jingwu, June 8, 1952, and Zhou Enlai to Zhang Jingwu and the Tibet Work Committee, August 9, 1952, *Zhou Enlai yu Xizang*, 23–25; ZGXLD, 1:62. The Tibetan government's bureau of foreign affairs was abolished in September 1953.
76. Zhao Shenying, *Zhongyang Zhu Zang Daibiao Zhang Jingwu* (Zhang Jingwu as the Center's representative in Tibet) (Beijing: Zhongguo Zangxue Chubanshe, 2001), 4–5, 62; Zhao Shenying, *Zhang Guohua*, 76; *Dangdai Zhongguo Xizang* (Tibet of contemporary China) (Beijing: Dangdai Zhongguo Chubanshe, 1991), 1:180; Fan Ming, *Xizang Neibu Zhi Zheng*, 180–81, 257–58.
77. Zhao Shenying, *Zhang Jingwu*, 15.
78. Letter to the Dalai Lama, March 8, 1953, MXGW, 93–94.
79. Zhang Xiangming, *Zhang Xiangming*, 66–67; ZGXLD, 1:84; Zhao Shenying, *Zhang Jingwu*, 104.
80. "Memorial on the Lack of talents for the frontiers and recommendation for officials," *Wang Yangming Quanji: Zoushu, Gongyi* (Complete works of Wang Yangming: Memorial and official papers) (Wuhan: Huazhong Kejidaxue Chubanshe, 2015), 3:193–95.
81. Zhao Shenying, *Zhang Jingwu*, 5–9; Xu Danlu, *Fengxue Gaoyuan—Kangzang Diqu Gongzuo Jishi* (Windy and snowy plateau: Account of work in the Xikang-Tibet region), unpublished manuscript, 1996, 185–86.
82. Xu Danlu, *Fengxue Gaoyuan*, 153.
83. Zhao Shenying, *Zhang Guohua*, 6, 25, 34–37, 53–54; Fan Ming, *Xizang Neibu Zhi Zheng*, 257–58; Xu Danlu, *Fengxue Gaoyuan*, 127–28, 185–86; Zhang Xiangming, *Zhang Xiangming*, 42–43.
84. Li Meijie and Zhao Shishu, "General Fan Ming known as being plentiful in six aspects," *Yanhuang Chunqiu*, 2007 (3): 37–42; Fan Ming, *Xizang Neibu Zhi Zheng*, 134, 261, 275.
85. Zhang Xiangming, *Zhang Xiangming*, 101; Zhao Shenying, *Zhang Jingwu*, 62.
86. Fan Ming, "Several tactical issues in the current united front work in the Tibetan region," September 10, 1952, PCCM.

87. Fan Ming, "Several tactical issues."
88. Fan Ming, *Xizang Neibu Zhi Zheng*, 232–40, 244.
89. Fan Ming, *Xizang Neibu Zhi Zheng*, 165–66, 244.
90. Zhao Shenying, *Zhang Guohua*, 83; ZGXLD, 1:69.
91. *Zhou Enlai Nianpu*, 1:231; Documentary Research Office of the Central Committee of the Chinese Communist Party, *Chen Yun Nianpu* (Beijing: Zhongyang Wenxian Chubanshe, 2000), 1:133, 136, 278–79; Fan Ming, *Xizang Neibu Zhi Zheng*, 295; Song Yuehong, "Examining the history of replacing the Tibetan currency with renminbi in Tibet," *Zhongguo Jingjishi Yanjiu* (Studies of economic history of China), 2008 (3): 124–31.
92. CCP Center, "Directive about the questions and demands raised by the Panchen salutary delegation," September 23, 1950, in Fan Ming, *Xizang Neibu Zhi Zheng*, 115–17; CCP Qinghai Committee and Qinghai Government, "Joint directive on recruiting Tibetan national liberation army," March 12, 1951, in Fan Ming, *Xizang Neibu Zhi Zheng*, 145–46.
93. Fan Ming, *Xizang Neibu Zhi Zheng*, 187–88.
94. James Millward, *Eurasian Crossroads: A History of Xinjiang* (New York: Columbia University Press, 2007), 215–34.
95. Zhao Shenying, *Zhang Guohua*, 90–92; Fan Ming, *Xizang Neibu Zhi Zheng*, 245–49; TWC's telegram to the Center to transmit "Opinion on the Question of the Orientation for Tibetan Unification," November 2, 1952, PCCM.
96. "Center's reply to the TWC and the Southwest Bureau on the orientation for unification of Tibet," October 27, 1952, *Huihuang de Ershi Shiji Xin Zhongguo Da Jilu: Xizang Juan*, 681–82.
97. Fan Ming, *Xizang Neibu Zhi Zheng*, 295–97.
98. Zhang Xiangming, *Zhang Xiangming*, 42–46; Xu Danlu, *Fengxue Gaoyuan*, 185–86.
99. "Division of labor in the Central Secretariat," 1949, JYZW, 1:740–41.
100. *Zhou Enlai yu Xizang*, 3–24; *Zhou Enlai Nianpu*, 1: 20–342; "Tibet Work Committee's proposals for governing Tibet," May 20, 1950, PCCM; Song Yuehong, "Oral history: Leaving the whole picture of the peaceful liberation of Tibet for the generations to come," *Zhongguo Minzu Bao* (Journal of Chinese nationalities), December 23, 2011.
101. "Our diplomatic orientations and tasks," April 30, 1952, *Zhou Enlai Xuanji* (Selected works of Zhou Enlai) (Beijing: Renmin Chubanshe, 1984), 91–92; "Report on foreign affairs work in 1951 by our embassy in Burma," December 31, 1951, ACMFA: 117-00151-02; Xiaohong Liu, *Chinese Ambassadors: The Rise of Diplomatic Professionalism since 1949* (Seattle: University of Washington Press, 2001), 22.
102. "Center's Telegram on Dealing Carefully with the Demands by Tibetan Tribes and Monasteries," January 1, 1950, JYLW, 1: 213–14.
103. "Center's directive on how to deal with the question of minority nationalities," June 13, 1950, JYLW, 2:219–21.
104. Jiangbian Jiacuo, *Li Jue Zhuan*, 80–82, 84–86.
105. *Deng Xiaoping Nianpu*, 2:1049; Center to the Southwest Bureau and the TWC, April 8, 1952, MXGW, 65.
106. *Deng Xiaoping Nianpu*, 2:1105–6.
107. *Deng Xiaoping Nianpu*, 2:1048–49. During 1951 and 1952, the CCP carried out the "Three-Antis" campaign (anti-embezzlement, anti-waste, and anti-bureaucracy) and "Five-Antis" campaign (anti-bribery, anti-theft of state property, anti-tax evasion, anti-cheating on government contracts, and anti-stealing state economic information.

330   2. The "Dalai Line"

108. *Deng Xiaoping Nianpu*, 2:1047–48; "Orientation for the Tibetan work," April 6, 1952, MXGW, 61–64.
109. *Deng Xiaoping Nianpu*, 2:1063–65; "Center's telegram on agreeing the Southwestern Bureau's opinion about establishment of the Sichuan Province and personnel adjustment in the Southwest," July 13, 1952, JYLW, 4:328–29; Ministry of Civil Affairs of the PRC, *Zhonghua Renmin Gongheguo Xianji Yishang Xingzheng Quhua Yange* (Changes of administrative divisions above the county level in the People's Republic of China) (Beijing: Cehui Chubanshe, 1986), 1:10.
110. Center to the Southwestern Bureau and the TWC, April 6, 1952, MXGW, 65; Center to the TWC, May 19, 1952, MXGW, 83; Center to the TWC, August 18, 1952, JYLW, 4: 409–10; Center to the TWC and the Southwestern Bureau, December 15, 1952, PCCM; Zhang Xiangming, *Zhang Xiangming*, 45–46; Mao to Deng, December 29, 1952, JYMW, 3:675; Center to the TWC, the TMR, the Southwest Bureau, and the Southwest Military Region, "Center's serious criticism of the Tibet Work Committee's mistake in establishing an agricultural and pastoral department without asking for permission," January 5, 1953, PCCM.
111. Center to Deng, July 13, 1952, JYLW, 4:328; Center to the TWC, the TMR, the Southwest Bureau, and the Southwest Military Region, "Center's serious criticism of the Tibet Work Committee's mistake in establishing an agricultural and pastoral department without asking for permission," January 5, 1953, PCCM.
112. Liu Shaoqi's comments and revision of the Center's telegram to the TWC drafted by the CUFD, August 16 and 18, 1952, JYLW.
113. *Deng Xiaoping Nianpu*, 2:1065–1103.
114. *Deng Xiaoping Nianpu*, 2:1136–37.
115. Zhao Fan, *Zhao Fan Huiyilu*, unpublished manuscript, 1996, 12–13, 16.
116. Fan Ming, *Xizang Neibu Zhi Zheng*, 259–62; Xu Danlu, *Fengxue Gaoyuan*, 214; Zhao Fan, *Zhao Fan Huiyilu*, 17–20, 52–53.
117. *Zhou Enlai Nianpu*, 1:342.
118. Pang Xianzhi and Jin Chongji, *Mao Zedong Zhuan, 1949–1976* (Biography of Mao Zedong, 1949–1976) (Beijing: Zhongyang Wenxian Chubanshe, 2004), 1:265, 276–82; Documentary Research Office of the Central Committee of the Chinese Communist Party, *Liu Shaoqi Nianpu, 1898–1969* (Chronicle of Liu Shaoqi's life, 1898–1969) (Beijing: Zhongyang Wenxian Chubanshe, 1996), 2:313–21; *Zhou Enlai Nianpu*, 1:329–51; *Deng Xiaoping Nianpu*, 2:1137–58. Zhao Jialiang and Zhang Xiaoqi, *Banjie Mubei xia de Wangshi: Gao Gang zai Beijing* (Past events underneath a broken tombstone: Gao Gang in Beijing) (Hong Kong: Dafeng Chubanshe, 2008), offer an account of the Gao-Rao affair that contradicts the official CPP account. Zhao was Gao's secretary and related Gao's side of the story, implicating Mao in Gao's "anti-Liu Shaoqi" plot. Rao Shushi was then the party secretary of the East China Bureau and the chief of the CCP's Department of Organization.
119. Zhao Fan, *Zhao Fan Huiyilu*, 16, 20.
120. *Zhou Enlai Nianpu*, 1:357; Zhao Fan, *Zhao Fan Huiyilu*, 28–29; *Liu Shaoqi Nianpu*, 2:320–21; Zhao Shenying, *Zhang Guohua*, 92.
121. Zhang Xiangming, *Zhang Xiangming*, 46.
122. *Deng Xiaoping Nianpu*, 2:1151–52, 1156–59, 1168, 1318.
123. ZGXLD, 1:71–73, publishes excerpts of the "conclusion." Melvyn C. Goldstein, *A History of Modern Tibet, Volume 2, 1951–1955: The Calm Before the Storm* (Berkeley: University of California Press, 2007), 437–48, offers a complete version of the document.
124. Zhao Fan, *Zhao Fan Huiyilu*, 20.

125. Zhao Shenying, *Zhang Guohua*, 93–95; Zhang Xiangming, *Zhang Xiangming*, 58–59, 71–77; Fan Ming, *Xizang Neibu Zhi Zheng*, 347–55; ZGXLD, 1:116–17.
126. Mao's telegram to Qinghai People's Government to be transmitted to Panchen Erdeni, December 13, 1951, MXGW, 58; Mao's telegram to Zhang Jingwu to be transmitted to Panchen Erdeni, December 4, 1952, MXGW, 90; ZGXLD, 1:67; Fan Ming, *Xizang Neibu Zhi Zheng*, 249.
127. Zhang Xiangming, *Zhang Xiangming*, 27–28; ZGXLD, 1:34; the Southwest Bureau's telegram to the Center transmitting the TWC's opinion on establishing an autonomous government in Chamdo, October 20, 1952, PCCM.
128. Fan Ming, *Xizang Neibu Zhi Zheng*, 264–66; Zhao Shenying, *Zhang Jingwu*, 85–87; Zhao Fan, *Zhao Fan Huiyilu*, 22–24.
129. "Orientations about receiving and hosting Dalai and Panchen and about the propaganda concerned," August 2, 1954, ASP: Jiankang 001-01-2859.
130. Zhao Fan, *Zhao Fan Huiyilu*, 24.
131. Fan Ming, *Xizang Neibu Zhi Zheng*, 274–75.
132. Zhang Yuxin, ed. *Qingchao Zhi Zang Dianzhang Yanjiu* (Study of Qing ordinances and regulations for administering Tibet) (Beijing: Zhongguo Zangxue Chubanshe, 2002), 3:961–72.
133. *Zhonghua*, *Daqianmen*, and *Hengda* were brand names of high-quality cigarettes made in the PRC at the time. While *Zhonghua* was a creation of the PRC, the latter two had longer histories.
134. Hosting Committee of the Nationalities Work Committee of the CCP Sichuan Committee, "Concrete arrangements for Dalai, Panchen, and their entourages when they visit places outside Beijing," n.d., ASP: Jianchuan 012-01-51; Hosting Committee of the Nationalities Work Committee of the CCP Sichuan Committee, "Work plan for hosting Dalai," March 25, 1955, ASP: Jianchuan 012-01-51.
135. Zhang Jingwu's report on a conversation with Kashag representative Ngabö, October 22, 1951, PCCM; Lin Tian, *Jinjun Xizang Riji*, 199–200, 285.
136. After the first constitution of the PRC was adopted in September 1954, the State Council superseded the Government Council.
137. ZGXLD, 1:80–83.

3. A Time to Change

1. "Memorandum for the President," February 4, 1949, President's National Security Files, Harry S. Truman Papers, box 220, Harry S. Truman Library.
2. Division of Research for Far East of the Department of State, "Problems of Domestic and Foreign Policy Confronting the Chinese Communists," OIR Report No. 5011(PV), July 28, 1949, NAUS: 893.000/7-2949, General Records of the United States Department of State Central Files: China, RG 59.
3. NSC 48/1, "The Position of the United States with Respect to Asia," December 23, 1949, NAUS: NSC Policy Papers, Box 6, Records of the National Security Council, RG 273.
4. Memorandum by the Office of China Affairs of the Department of State, March 18, 1947, NAUS: 893.00/3-1847, General Records of the United States Department of State Central Files: China, RG 59.
5. Division of Research for Far East of the Department of State, "Problems of Domestic and Foreign Policy Confronting the Chinese Communists," OIR Report No. 5011(PV),

July 28, 1949, NAUS: 893.000/7-2949, General Records of the United States Department of State Central Files: China, RG 59.
6. A. J. Hopkinson, "Prospect," August 20, 1948, NAUK: FO371-70046.
7. H. E. Davies, "Note of Conversation with Mr. Hugh Richardson on December 3rd and 4th," 1949, NAUK: FO371-76317; J. H. S. Shattock to I. M. R. MacLennan, December 10, 1949, NAUK: FO371-76314; Loy W. Henderson to US Department of State, January 9, 1950, NAUS: 793B.00/1-950, General Records of the United States Department of State Central Files: China, RG 59.
8. H. A. Graves of British Embassy Washington to South-East Asia Department of the Foreign Office, October 30, 1950, NAUK: FO371-84450. This document was transmitting Bessac's "Impression of Military Status of Tibet," obtained by the British embassy from the U.S. Department of State.
9. F. K. Roberts to J. Sterndale Bennett, November 4, 1950, NAUK: FO371-84463.
10. "Extract of Weekly Intelligence Report, Department of the Army; a Survey of Tibet," April 1951, NAUS: Records of Office of China Affairs of the Department of State (RG 59): "P" File, 1948–55, box 22; FE/P: JMH Lindbeck, FE: Miss Bacon, and CA Mr. Osborn to NEA/P Mr. Sanger, and FE/P John L. Stegmaier, May 17, 1955, NAUS: Records of Office of China Affairs of the Department of State (RG 59): "P" File, 1948–55, box 24.
11. Ralph N. Clough to the Department of State, August 21, 1950, NAUS: 793B.00/8-2150, General Records of the United States Department of State Central Files: China, RG 59.
12. E. E. Beatty, "Tibet: A Notable Observation," *China's Millions*, December 1950, 125–26.
13. Cited in Gordon Chang, *Fateful Ties: A History of America's Preoccupation with China* (Cambridge, Mass.: Harvard University Press, 2015), 59.
14. "Common Program," September 29, 1949, *Minzu Zhengce Wenjian Huibian* (Collections of documents on nationality policies) (Beijing: Renmin Chubanshe, 1960) [hereafter cited as MZWH], 1:1; Ulanfu, "Report on the 'Key Policies of the People's Republic of China in Implementing Nationality Regional Autonomy,'" August 8, 1952, MZWH, 1:73–78.
15. Zhou Enlai's conversation with Ulanfu, Liu Lantao, and Su Qianyi about Suiyuan's incorporation into Inner Mongolia, August 20, 1953, Documentary Research Office of the Central Committee of the Chinese Communist Party, *Zhou Enlai Nianpu, 1949–1976* (Chronicle of Zhou Enlai's life, 1949–1976) (Beijing: Zhongyang Wenxian Chubanshe, 1997), 1:320; Mao Zedong's conversation with the representatives of the Tibetan delegations, October 18, 1953, MXGW, 101–2.
16. "Key policies of the People's Republic of China in implementing nationality regional autonomy," August 8, 1952, MZWH, 1:67–72.
17. Wang Shusheng and Hao Yufeng, *Wulanfu Nianpu* (Chronicle of Ulanhu's life) (Beijing: Zhonggong Dangshi Ziliao Chubanshe, 1989), 232, 246.
18. Wang and Hao, *Wulanfu Nianpu*, 248, 305, 324.
19. Wang and Hao, *Wulanfu Nianpu*, 216–17, 231, 267, 273, 283, 306, 319; *Zhou Enlai Nianpu*, 1:349.
20. Internal directive to the party by Mao Zedong, March 16, 1953, MXGW, 99.
21. "Implementing nationality policy and repudiating great Han chauvinism," *People's Daily* editorial, October 10, 1953, MZWH, 1:138–42.
22. Liu Shaoqi, "Report on land reform," June 14, 1950, JYLW, 2:226–27; CCP Center to the Xinjiang Branch Bureau and the Northwestern Bureau, "Telegram on certain orientations in the Xinjiang work," May 17, 1952, JYLW, 4:175.
23. Mao Zedong, "Conversation with the staff of the *Jinsui Daily*," April 2, 1948, *Mao Zedong Xuanji* (Selected works of Mao Zedong), 4:1317–18.

24. Liu Shaoqi, "Historical experience of the Chinese Communist Party," July 19, 1950, JYLW, 2:299.
25. "Center's circular about 'The conclusions on the principal experiences of the party's work among national minorities in the past few years," October 24, 1954, Archives of Sichuan Province: Jianchuan 001-01-328 [hereafter cited as ASP].
26. After Deng Xiaoping went to Beijing in 1952, Song Renqiong, Zhang Jichun, and Li Jingquan were three leading officials of the Southwest Bureau.
27. "Report by the Nationality Work Committee of the Southwest Bureau on the southwestern nationality work conference," transmitted by the Southwest Bureau, April 27, 1954, ASP: Jianchuan 001-01-328.
28. Jin Anping, "Formation of certain principles underlying the center-local relationship in the initial years of the PRC," *Beijing Dangshi Yanjiu* (Beijing Party history studies), 1998 (2): 20–23. The regional bureau system was restored in 1960.
29. For an informative discussion of "political" and "ethnographic" Tibet, see Melvyn C. Goldstein, *A History of Modern Tibet, Volume 3, 1955–1957: The Storm Clouds Descend* (Berkeley: University of California Press, 2013), 79–84.
30. American Embassy in New Delhi to the Secretary of State, November 21, 1949, NAUS: 893.00/11-2149, General Records of the United States Department of State Central Files: China, RG 59; American Embassy to the Secretary of State, November 22, 1949, NAUS: 893.00 Tibet/11-2249.
31. Research Office of the Eighteenth Army, "Preliminary opinions on various policies toward Tibet," March 1950, PCCM; "Tibet Work Committee's proposals for governing Tibet," May 20, 1950, PCCM.
32. Mao to Liu Shaoqi, Zhou Enlai, Zhu De, Ren Bishi, and Li Weihan, September 16, 1950, JYMW, 1:518. The CCP Xikang committee's report was dated September 6, but according to Documentary Research Office of the Central Committee of the Chinese Communist Party, *Mao Zedong Nianpu, 1949–1976* (Chronicle of Mao Zedong's life, 1949–1976) (Beijing: Zhongyang Wenxian Chubanshe, 2013), 1:192–93, Mao did not see the report until September 16.
33. Li Weihan, "A few questions concerning nationality policies," December 21, 1951, MZWH, 1:41–52.
34. Southwest Bureau's communication, "Tibet Work Committee's opinion on the issue of establishing autonomous government in the Chamdo area," October 7, 1952, PCCM; "Center's reply to the Tibet Work Committee and the Southwest Bureau on the orientation about a unified Tibet [excerpt]," October 27, 1952, *Huihuang de Ershi Shiji Xin Zhongguo Da Jilu; Xizang Juan* (Grand records of the glorious new China in the twentieth century; volume on Tibet) (Beijing: Hongqi Chubanshe, 1999), 681–82.
35. Northwest Bureau, "A few points regarding the work in the Tibetan areas of southern Gansu," November 10, 1952, Archives of Gansu Province: 91-001-0437.
36. Deng Xiaoping to Mao, July 9, 1952, JYLW, 4:329, note 3; the Center to Deng, July 13, 1952, JYLW, 4:328.
37. Southwest Bureau to the CCP Committee of Xikang, August 6, 1950, Deng Xiaoping, *Deng Xiaoping Xinan Gongzuo Wenji* (Deng Xiaoping's writings on the Southwest work). Beijing: Zhongyang Wenxian Chubanshe, 2006), 225–26; Mao to Liu Shaoqi, Zhou Enlai, Zhu De, Ren Bishi, and Li Weihan, September 16, 1950, JYMW, 1:518.
38. These were Tibetan autonomous regions of Yushu, Tongren, and Haiyan that were established between December 1951 and November 1952. See *Dangdai Zhongguo Minzu Gongzuo Dashiji, 1949–1988* (Chronicle of important events in the nationality work of contemporary China, 1949–1988) (Beijing: Minzu Chubanshe, 1989), 25, 28, 33.

334   3. A Time to Change

39. Deng Xiaoping to the Central Department of United Front, August 20, 1952, Documentary Research Office of the Central Committee of the Chinese Communist Party, *Deng Xiaoping Nianpu, 1904–1974* (Chronology of Deng Xiaoping's life, 1904–1974) (Beijing: Zhongyang Wenxian Chubanshe, 2009), 2:1067; CCP Committee of Sichuan Province to the Southwest Bureau, November 10, 1952, ASP: Jianchuan 001-01-63; CCP Leading Group of the People's Government of the Tibetan Autonomous Region of Sichuan, "Preliminary conclusive report on the first conference of representatives of all nationalities and all walks of life of the Tibetan Autonomous Region of Sichuan Province," December 1952, ASP: Jianchuan 001-01-63.
40. CCP Leading Group of the People's Government of the Tibetan Autonomous Region of Sichuan, "Preliminary conclusive report."
41. According to a 1953 census of Xikang, the total population of the province was 3,381,064, of which the Han were 54.6 percent, Yi 29.8 percent, and Tibetans 14.2 percent or 480,111. See *Sichuan Shengzhi; Zhengwu Zhi* (Chronicle of Sichuan Province; records of administrative affairs), 279.
42. F. K. Roberts to J. Sterndale Bennett, November 4, 1950, NAUK: FO371-84463.
43. "Central Ministry of Public Security's directive on implementation of the resolutions of the sixth national public security conference in national minority areas," September 18, 1954, *Gongan Jianshe* (Construction of public security), no. 97, 1–7, PCCM.
44. Center to the Tibet Work Committee and the Southwest Bureau, April 11, 1952, MXGW, 67; Center to the Tibet Work Committee and the Southwest Bureau, April 12, 1952, MXGW, 71; "Outline of the report at the third plenum of the first national conference of the youth league," August 26, 1952, JYLW, 4:429–30.
45. "Important points in a conversation with Tibetan delegates," October 8, 1952, MXGW, 88–89.
46. Center to the Southwest Bureau, April 6, 1952, MXGW, 61–64.
47. "Supporting the agreement on peaceful liberation of Tibet," editorial in the *People's Daily* of May 27, 1952, in *Heping Jiefang Xizang* (Peaceful liberation of Tibet), comp. Committee of the Tibetan Autonomous Region for Collecting Materials on Party History and Leading Group of the Tibetan Military Region for Collecting Materials on Party History (Lhasa: Xizang Renmin Chubanshe, 1995), 198.
48. "Report by the Nationality Work Committee of the Southwest Bureau on the southwestern nationality work conference," transmitted by the Southwest Bureau, April 27, 1954, ASP: Jianchuan 001-01-328; Yang Jingren, Li Zijie, and Deng Ruiling, "Report on the basic condition of the Tibetan autonomous region of Xikang province," June 14, 1954, ASP: Jianchuan 012-01-25.
49. People's Government of Qinghai, "Distribution of various nationalities in Qinghai," March 1950, Archives of Qinghai Province: 121–40 [hereafter cited as AQP]; "Minutes of Chairman Zhang Zhongliang's speech at the party-government-military cadres conference," March 1950, AQP: 121–19; Zhang Zhongliang, "Mobilize all party members in launching a large-scale peasants movement, and struggle to complete land reforms in five counties and one municipality," January 25, 1951, AQP: 121–75; "[CCP Qinghai] provincial committee's report to the Northwest Bureau about the current conditions of land reforms," October 15, 1951, AQP: 121–75; CCP Qinghai Committee, "Circular on excerpts from Huangzhong County's report on dealing with the nationality question during the struggle against local tyrants," November 12, 1951, AQP: 121–75.
50. *Ganzi Zhouzhi* (Chronicle of Garzê Prefecture) (Chengdu: Sichuan Renmin Chubanshe, 1997), 46–49; CCP Xikang Committee, "Situation of the mass' spontaneous struggles in Garzê Tibetan autonomous prefecture," August 20, 1955, ASP: Jiankang 001-01-368;

51. Secretariat of the CCP Xikang Committee, "Minutes of nationality work conference," August 21, 1955, ASP: Jiankang 001-01-369.
52. Fan Zhizhong was commander of the Kangding Branch Military Region of the Xikang Military Region and secretary of the CCP Kangding Area Committee. Miao Fengshu was deputy party secretary of Xikang. While information about Ren Mingyuan is unavailable, Wei Huang was head of the Tibetan Office of the Nationality Work Committee of Xikang, and Zhang Chengwu would become secretary-general of the United Front Department of Sichuan.
53. Secretariat of the CCP Xikang Committee, "Minutes of nationality work conference: The Tibetan group," August 21–24, 1955, ASP: Jiankang 001-01-369.
54. Secretariat of the CCP Xikang Committee, "Minutes of nationality work conference: Tibet group," August 21–24, 1955, ASP: Jiankang 001-01-369.
55. CCP Xikang Committee, "Preliminary plan for implementing democratic reform in the Tibetan areas of Sichuan Province," August 29, 1955, ASP: Jiankang 001-01-367.
56. "CCP Sichuan and Xikang committees' preliminary plan for carrying out democratic reforms in the agricultural Tibetan areas of Sichuan," September 22, 1955, ASP: Jianchuan 001-01-549.
57. *Zhou Enlai Nianpu*, 1:524; Documentary Research Office of the Central Committee of the Chinese Communist Party, *Liu Shaoqi Nianpu, 1898–1969* (Chronicle of Liu Shaoqi's life, 1898–1969) (Beijing: Zhongyang Wenxian Chubanshe, 1996), 2:347; Liu Shaoqi, "Outline for a talk at a symposium called by the politburo," December 5, 1955, JYLW, 7:407.
58. In CCP terminology, "democratic reforms" mainly meant demolition of old local political establishments and redistribution of farmland among poor farmers; "transition to socialism" or "socialist transformation" in agricultural areas meant collectivization of private farmland.
59. "CCP Sichuan and Xikang committees' preliminary plan for carrying out democratic reforms in the agricultural Tibetan areas of Sichuan," August 29, 1955, ASP: Jianchuan 001-01-549.
60. *Sichuan Shengzhi; Dashi Jishu* (Chronicle of Sichuan Province; a narrative about important events), 64; *Dangdai Zhongguo Minzu Gongzuo Dashiji*, 73.
61. Nationality Work Committee of the CCP Sichuan Committee, "Tasks, requirements, and matters needing attention for Sichuan provincial inspection delegation to Inner Mongolia," April 18, 1956, ASP: Jianchuan 012-01-97; "Conclusion on visitation and work in Inner Mongolia by Sichuan pastoral areas inspection delegation," June 15, 1956, ASP: Jianchuan 012-01-97.
62. "Center's directive on studying socialist transformation in the pastoral areas of national minorities," February 21, 1956, ASP: Jianchuan 001-01-808.
63. *Sichuan Shengzhi: Dashi Jishu*, 64; *Sichuan Shengzhi: Zhengwu Zhi*, 360–61.
64. *Ganzi Zhouzhi*, 823–31; Wu Guangyao, "Xizang gailiu benmo ji (Records of the process of regularizations in Tibet)," in *Kangqu Zangzu Shehui Zhenxi Ziliao Jiyao* (Selection of rare and valuable materials on the Tibetan society of the Xikang area), ed. Zhao Xinyu et al. (Changdu: Bashu Chubanshe, 2006), 49.
65. CCP Sichuan Committee to the Center, "CCP Sichuan and Xikang committees' preliminary plan for carrying out democratic reforms in the agricultural Tibetan areas of Sichuan," August 29, 1955, ASP: Jianchuan 001-01-549; *Sichuan Shengzhi: Junshi Zhi; Dier Bian: Zhongda Zhanshi (Songshen Gao)* (Chronicle of Sichuan Province: Chronicle of Military Affairs, Part Two: Important Battles [Draft for Approval]), comp. Office of Chronicle of Military Affairs of the PLA Provincial District of Sichuan, 1996, 211, 213–24;

Sichuan Shengzhi: Junshi Zhi (Chronicle of Sichuan Province: Chronicle of Military Affairs), comp. Compiling Committee of Sichuan Provincial Chronicle (Chengdu: Sichuan Renmin Chubanshe, 1999), 295–319, 464–5.

66. CCP Sichuan Committee to the General Staff, February 13, 1956, ASP: Jianchuan 001-01-820.
67. General Staff to the CCP Sichuan Committee and Chengdu Military Region, March 14, 1956, ASP: Jianchuan 001-01-820.
68. Public Security Department of Sichuan Province to the Public Security Offices of Kangding, Xichang, Zhaojue, Leshan, Ya'an, and Ngawa, March 13, 1956, ASP: Jianchuan 001-01-820; Chengdu Military Region to various branch military regions, CCP Sichuan Committee, and Provincial Public Security Department, March 14, 1956, ASP: Jianchuan 001-01-820.
69. CCP Xichang Prefecture Committee to CCP Sichuan Committee, March 10, 12, and 15, 1956, ASP: Jianchuan 001-01-820; CCP Sichuan Committee to CCP Xichang Prefecture Committee, March 17, 1956, ASP: Jianchuan 001-01-820.
70. Li Huafang to Li Jingquan, March 31, 1956, ASP: Jianchuan 001-01-820.
71. Public Security Department of Sichuan, "Report and request for directive on solution of the issue of guns and ammunitions for the militias in national minority areas of our province," April 19, 1956, ASP: Jianchuan 001-01-820.
72. CCP Sichuan Committee to the Center, "Brief on the conditions of the Kangding region," March 19, 1956, ASP: Jianchuan 012-01-102.
73. Headquarters of the Chengdu Military Region, "Basic conclusion on the militia work in nationality areas in 1959," March 22, 1960, ASP: Jianchuan 001-01-1813.
74. CCP Sichuan Committee to the Center, "Brief on the conditions of the Kangding region," March 19, 1956, ASP: Jianchuan 012-01-102; CCP Sichuan Committee to the Center, "Brief on the conditions of the Kangding region," April 11, 1956, ASP: Jianchuan 012-01-102; Li Chunfang to CCP Kangding Regional Committee and CCP Sichuan Committee, "Conditions of Luhuo," March 29, 1956, ASP: Jianchuan 012-01-102; CCP Kangding Regional Committee to CCP Sichuan Committee, "General brief on situation of the work in our region," April 25, 1956, ASP: Jianchuan 012-01-102; CCP Kangding Regional Committee to Garzê Work Committee, Comrade Luo Ming, and also reported to CCP Sichuan Committee, July 29, 1956, appendix: Luo Ming to CCP Kangding Regional Committee, July 27, 1956, ASP: Jianchuan 012-01-102; Liao Zhigao's written comment on CCP Kangding Regional Committee's April 25 report to CCP Sichuan Committee, May 4, 1956, ASP: Jianchuan 012-01-102.
75. "Compiled minutes of the conference of the regional party secretaries of the minority areas," February 28, 1956, ASP: Jianchun 012-01-71.
76. "Minutes of the speeches delivered at the regional (municipality) secretaries' conference, no. 7: CCP Kangding Regional Secretary Comrade Fan Zhizhong's speech," May 16, 1956, ASP: Jianchun 012-01-71.
77. "Minutes of the speeches delivered at the regional (municipality) secretaries' conference, no. 7: Kangding Regional Secretary Comrade Fan Zhizhong's speech."
78. "Minutes of the speeches delivered at the regional (municipality) secretaries' conference, no. 7: Kangding Regional Secretary Comrade Fan Zhizhong's speech."
79. CCP Sichuan Committee to the Center, "Report on work arrangements for the national minority areas," May 30, 1956, ASP: Jianchuan 001-01-818.
80. Zhang Xiangming, "Brilliant policy decision: Chairman Mao's solution of the Tibetan question remembered," *Zhonguo Zangxue* (Chinese Tibetology), 2001 (2): 27–38.

81. The First Office of the Nationality Work Committee of the CCP Sichuan Committee, "Differences between the Central United Front Department's 'Comments on the preliminary plan for implementing democratic reform in the agriculture areas of national minorities of Sichuan Province' and 'Steps for implementing democratic reform in the agricultural areas of certain Tibetan autonomous prefectures of Sichuan province' and 'Steps for abolishing usuries and readjusting debt relations in the Garzê Tibetan Autonomous Prefecture of Sichuan Province,'" January 7, 1956, ASP: Jianchuan 012-01-85.
82. CCP Sichuan Committee to the Center, "Brief on the conditions of reforms in the Dartsédo area," April 11, 1956, ASP: Jianchuan, 012-02-102; CCP Kangding Area Committee, "Report on reviewing of the conditions of democratic reforms and three reform measures in the Garzê Tibetan Autonomous Prefecture," October 1956, ASP: Jianchuan 012-01-88.
83. CCP Garzê Prefecture Committee, "Basic conclusions on the democratic reforms of the Garzê Tibetan Autonomous Prefecture," 1959 (n.d.), ASP: Jianchuan 012-01-196.
84. CCP Garzê Prefecture Committee, "Excerpts of certain ideas and opinions expressed by Comrade Liu Geping when he was working in Garzê Tibetan Autonomous Prefecture," May 10, 1960, ASP: Jianchuan 012-01-224.
85. "CCP North China Bureau's report to the CCP Central Committee on Ulanhu's mistakes," July 27, 1966, in *Neimenggu Wenge Shilu: "Minzu Fenlie" yu "Wa Su" Yundong* (Factual record of the Cultural Revolution in Inner Mongolia: "national splitting" and the campaign of "digging out and purging"), comp. Qi Zhi (Hong Kong: Tianxingjian Chubanshe, 2010), 157.
86. In 1960, Liu was denounced as a "local nationalist" when serving as the first party secretary and chairman of the Ningxia Hui Autonomous Region. Ulanhu was dismissed from his leading position in Inner Mongolia in July 1966 for "splitting the nation and establishing an independent kingdom." See Liu Baojun, "Liu Geping, the first chairman of the Ningxia Hui Autonomous Region," CCP History in Ningxia, the official website of the Office of Party History of the CCP Ningxia Committee, accessed April 26, 2014, www.nxdsyjs.com/a/?c-1-2074.html; and Qi Zhi, 103–18.
87. CCP Central Committee to various provincial, municipality, and autonomous regional committees, and the Tibet Work Committee, "Notice about celebration of the establishment of the Preparatory Committee of the Tibetan Autonomous Region and several issues in organizing a central delegation to visit Tibet," February 7, 1956, ASP: 001-01-830; CCP Sichuan Committee to the Center, the Central Delegation to Tibet, and the Tibet Work Committee, May 14, 1956, ASP: 001-01-830; *Deng Xiaoping Nianpu*, 2:1288.
88. Luo Gangwu, *Xin Zhongguo Minzu Gongzuo Dashi Gailan, 1949–1999* (Survey of important events in the nationality work of the new China, 1949–1999) (Beijing: Huawen Chubanshe, 2001), 194.
89. "Comrade [Liao] Zhigao transmitting Chairman Mao's conclusion about the work of democratic reform in Sichuan," July 26, 1956, ASP: Jianchuan 001-01-808.
90. According to *Deng Xiaoping Nianpu*, 2:1299, those present at the meeting included Mao, Zhou, Deng, Chen Yun, Peng Zhen, Chen Yi, Li Weihan, Liu Geping, Wang Feng, Song Renqiong, Zhang Jingwu, and Zhang Guohua. Liao Zhigao and Tianbao are not mentioned, but obviously they attended the meeting.
91. "Minutes of Chairman Mao's directive about the reforms in Garzê and Liangshan," July 22, 1956, ASP: Jianchuan 001-01-808. *Mao Zedong Nianpu, 1949–1976*, 2:594–95, indicates that the meeting was held in the Yinian Hall of Zhongnanhai, the CCP's headquarters in Beijing, on the evening of July 22. After holding another meeting in the

338   3. A Time to Change

early morning of July 23, Mao and some other CCP leaders left for Beidaihe, a summer resort near Beijing.

92. "Tiger borrows pigs; scholar borrows books" (*laohu jie zhu, xiucai jieshu*) means a way of depriving other people of their possessions in a deceptively disarming manner. A tiger would not return a pig that it "borrowed" from a farm, just as a scholar would be reluctant to return a book borrowed from another person. In this proverb, *xiucai* means a low-level degree holder from China's traditional examination system. In ancient China, and perhaps especially in the cultural milieu of Hunan, book lending and borrowing may have been a rare practice. Goldstein, *A History of Modern Tibet*, 3:259, cites an interview with Fan Zhizhong, who conveyed Mao's words wrongly as "an intellectual depends on knowledge and a tiger depends on legs." Goldstein understands these words to mean "the Tibetans depend on guns, so we need to take them away," missing Mao's cynical endorsement of Sichuan officials' gun collection stratagem.

93. "Notification of the Central Office of the CCP Central Committee about issuing the 'Minutes of Comrade Zhou Enlai's transmitting of the Center's directive about the issue of democratic reform in the Garzê Tibetan Autonomous Prefecture and the Liangshan Yi Autonomous Prefecture of Sichuan,'" August 20, 1956, and "Minutes of Comrade Zhou Enlai's transmitting of the Center's directive about the issue of democratic reform in the Garzê Tibetan Autonomous Prefecture and the Liangshan Yi Autonomous Prefecture of Sichuan," July 24, 1956, ASP: Jianchuan 001-01-808.

94. CCP Kangding Area Committee, "Situation of the work in Bathang County and proposals for future work," July 25, 1956, ASP: Jianchuan 012-01-102.

95. "Comrade [Liao] Zhigao's transmitting of Chairman Mao's conclusion about the work of democratic reform in Sichuan," July 26, 1956, ASP: Jianchuan 001-01-808.

96. "Comrade Li Jingquan's conclusive speech at the nationality work conference," August 10, 1956, ASP: Jianchuan 012-01-72.

97. "Comrade Li Jingquan's conclusive speech at the nationality work conference."

98. "Brief by the CCP Sichuan Committee on the nationality work conference," August 30, 1956, ASP: Jianchuan 001-01-818.

99. "Comrade Sangye Yeshe's speech," n.d., Archives of Luding County [hereafter cited as ALC].

100. At the July 22 meeting, Mao used the name of Tianbao. Zhou did the same when conveying Mao's points to minority figures in Beijing, according to a record kept by a Sichuan official: "Important points from Premier Zhou's speech transmitting Chairman Mao's directives at a reception for national minority upper-stratum figures, afternoon of July 23 [sic]," ASP: Jianchuan 001-01-808. "Tianbao" was changed to "Sang Ji Yue Xi [Sangye Yeshe]" in the Central United Front Department's record of Zhou's speech, which was circulated in the Central Office of the CCP Central Committee: "Notification of the Central Office of the CCP Central Committee about issuing the 'Minutes of Comrade Zhou Enlai's transmitting of the Center's directive about the issue of democratic reform in the Garzê Tibetan Autonomous Prefecture and the Liangshan Yi Autonomous Prefecture of Sichuan,'" August 20, 1956; and "Minutes of Comrade Zhou Enlai's transmitting of the Center's directive about the issue of democratic reform in the Garzê Tibetan Autonomous Prefecture and the Liangshan Yi Autonomous Prefecture of Sichuan," July 24, 1956, ASP: Jianchuan 001-01-808.

101. "Lijie Sichuan shengwei lingdao banzi" (Successive CCP Sichuan committees), accessed May 29, 2014, http://www.phoer.net/history/dangdai/ccp_leader.htm; "Sang Ji Yue Xi," accessed May 29, 2014, http://sc.zwbk.org/MyLemmaShow.aspx?lid=3921; *Aba Zhouzhi* (Chronicle of Ngawa prefecture), 41.

102. Sangye Yeshe to the Central United Front Department and the Central Nationality Committee to be transmitted to the Center and the Chairman, September 28, 1956, ASP: Jianchuan 012-01-88.
103. CCP Kangding Area Committee, "Report on reviewing of the conditions of democratic reform and three reform measures in the Garzê Tibetan Autonomous Prefecture," October 1956, ASP: Jianchuan 012-01-88.
104. *Ganzi Zhouzhi*, 52.
105. "CCP Sichuan Committee's report on the nationality work conference," November 11, 1956, ASP: Jianchuan 001-01-818.
106. Public Security Department of the Garzê Tibetan Autonomous Prefecture, "Summary of the reactions of the upper stratum, religious figures, laboring masses, and cadres after receiving the communication on the Center's directive about democratic reform in the Garzê Tibetan and Liangshan Yi Autonomous Prefectures," November 13, 1956, ASP: Jianchuan 012-01-155.
107. *Ganzi Zhouzhi*, 53.
108. *Deng Xiaoping Nianpu*, 2:1310–11.
109. *Mao Zedong Nianpu, 1949–1976*, 3:95–96.
110. "CCP Sichuan committee's opinion on whether or not democratic reform should continue in the Garzê Autonomous Prefecture," March 5, 1957, ASP: Jianchuan 001-01-1064.
111. Liao Zhigao, "Comrade Deng Xiaoping's conclusions (at the March 9 meeting of the Central Secretariat discussing the issue of reform in the Garzê Autonomous Prefecture)," March 14, 1957, ASP: Jianchuan 012-01-397; CCP Sichuan Committee to CCP Garzê, Liangshan, and Ngawa Prefecture Committees and Xichang, Lishan District Committees, "Principal conclusions of the Central Secretariat's meeting on the issue of reform in the Garzê Autonomous Prefecture," March 15, 1957, ASP: Jianchuan 001-01-1064.
112. CCP Ngawa Autonomous Prefecture Committee to CCP Sichuan Provincial Committee, "Report on fully mobilizing the mass, thoroughly destroying feudalism, and carrying out make-up work in class-two areas like Songpan, Haishui, Ma'erkang, and Zhuosijia," August 26, 1957, ASP: Jianchuan 001-01-1063; *Ganzi Zhouzhi*, 9.
113. CCP Sichuan Provincial Committee to CCP Garzê, Liangshan, and Ngawa Prefecture Committees and Xichang, Lishan District Committees, "Principal conclusions of the Central Secretariat's meeting on the issue of reform in the Garzê Autonomous Prefecture," March 15, 1957, ASP: Jianchuan 001-01-1064.
114. "Center's reply to the Sichuan Provincial Committee's report on continuation of democratic reform in the Garzê Autonomous Prefecture," May 14, 1957, ASP: Jianchuan 001-01-1064.
115. *Su Yu Nianpu* (Chronicle of Su Yu's life) (Beijing: Dangdai Zhongguo Chubanshe, 2006), 604–6, 608–9, 620, 627–28; Nationality Work Committee of Sichuan Province to the CCP Sichuan Committee, April 25, 1957, ASP: Jianchuan 012-01-147. Su's involvement in Tibetan military affairs would end soon. In the summer of 1958, at an enlarged meeting of the Central Military Commission, he was criticized for harboring "bourgeois individualism" and stripped of military command forever. In September, Su, no longer chief of the General Staff, presided over a joint conference of the Lanzhou, Chengdu, and Tibet Military Regions and made his last review of the military situation of all the Tibetan areas in the Southwest.
116. CCP Sichuan Committee to the Center, "CCP Sichuan Committee's report on the nationality work conference and request for instruction on several issues," May 21, 1957, ASP: Jianchuan 001-01-1064.

117. CCP Garzê Prefecture Committee to CCP Sichuan Committee, "CCP Garzê Prefecture Committee's report on holding three-level cadre conference for examining the implementation of the directive by the Secretariat of the CCP Central Committee," November 10, 1957, ASP: Jianchuan 001-01-1064; *Ganzi Zhouzhi*, 768–75.
118. *Sichuan Shengzhi: Junshi Zhi*, 295, 299.
119. CCP Ganzi Prefecture Committee, "Specific plan for carrying out and implementing the directive of the Central Secretariat meeting about the reforms in our prefecture," March 23, 1957, ALC; Sangye Yeshe, "Some suggestions about the work in the Tibetan and Yi nationality areas," September 6, 1957, ASP: Jianchuan 001-01-1063; CCP Kangding Area Committee, "Concrete measures to implement Comrade Sangye Yeshe's suggestions for nationality work in Tibetan and Yi areas in the next half year that have been approved by the provincial committee," October 14, 1957, ASP: Jianchuan 001-01-1063.
120. Liao Zhigao, "Comrade Deng Xiaoping's conclusions."
121. CCP Ngawa Prefecture Committee, "Our opinion on correcting problems that occurred in Tangkun and Anqu," June 11, 1957, ASP: Jianchuan 001-01-1063; Liao Zhigao, "[Issues that] the Liangshan prefecture committee should pay attention to," June 14, 1957, ASP: Jianchuan 001-01-1063.
122. CCP Garzê Prefecture Committee to the Garzê Work Committee and to be reported to the CCP Sichuan Committee, July 17, 1957, ASP: Jianchuan 001-01-1063; CCP Ngawa Prefecture Committee to CCP Sichuan Committee, "Report on fully mobilizing the mass."
123. CCP Sichuan Committee, "Approval and circulation by the CCP Sichuan Committee of the three documents from the organizational departments of the Garzê, Liangshan, and Ngawa Prefecture Committees on disposition of minority nationality party members and cadres who joined the rebellion," December 21, 1957, ASP: Jianchuan 001-01-1063.
124. Liao Zhigao, "Comrade Deng Xiaoping's conclusions."
125. CCP Sichuan Committee to the Center, "Preliminary report on reviewing the execution of nationality policy in the Tibetan and Yi areas of our province," May 28, 1957, ASP: Jianchuan 001-01-1064.
126. CCP Garzê Work Committee to the CCP Garzê Prefecture Committee, "Report on the situation of the Dajin monastery in recent days," July 25, 1957, ASP: Jianchuan 001-01-1063; CCP Sichuan Committee, "Directive on the current work of Garzê County and that regarding the Dajin monastery," August 2, 1957, ASP: Jianchuan 001-01-1063.
127. The Nationality Work Committee of the CCP Sichuan Committee, "Draft plan for settling the issue of lamaist monasteries," August 31, 1957, and Li Jiangquan's note to Liao Zhigao written on page 1 of the document, ASP: Jianchuan 001-01-1068.
128. CCP Garzê Prefecture Committee, "Concrete measures to implement Comrade Sangye Yeshe's suggestions, approved by the provincial committee, for nationality work in the Tibetan and Yi areas in the next half year (from October of this year to March next year)," October 15, 1957, ASP: Jianchuan 001-01-1063.
129. CCP Garzê Prefecture Committee, "Preliminary opinion on carrying out gradually socialist transformation of private commercial capitalism in the Garzê Autonomous Prefecture represented mainly by monasteries and big Tibetan merchants," December 2, 1957, ASP: Jianchuan 001-01-1068.
130. *Ganzi Zhouzhi*, 9, 57.
131. Liao Zhigao, "Comrade Deng Xiaoping's conclusions."
132. "Minutes of an informal discussion (presided by Sangye Yeshe and Huang Jue'an) with the Tibetan and Yi representatives of Sichuan Province to the National Congress," June 12, 1957, ASP: Jianchuan 001-01-1068.

4. A New Phase

1. For instance, in a 1956 speech, Mao described Gao Gang's "anti-party" activities as "blowing wind and setting fire covertly" (*gua yinfeng, shao yinhuo*) in contrast to the CCP leadership's "blowing wind and setting fire overtly" (*gua yangfeng, shao yanghou*). In 1957, during the Anti-Rightist campaign, Mao again asserted that the CCP's reversal of its earlier policy of encouraging criticism to one of suppressing the "rightists" was a *yangmou*, or "overt scheme." See Mao Zedong, "Speech at the Second Plenum of the Eighth Central Committee of the Chinese Communist Party, November 15, 1956," *Mao Zedong Xuanji* (Selected works of Mao Zedong) (Beijing: Renmin Chubanshe, 1977), 5:313–29; "*Wenhui Bao's* bourgeois direction during a period," *Renmin Ribao* (People's Daily), June 14, 1957.
2. Mao Zedong, "Agreement for peaceful liberation of Tibet must be observed, May 26, 1951," MXGW, 50–51.
3. Secretariat of the CCP Sichuan Committee, "Chairman Mao's directive on democratic reform in Garzê and Liangshan (recorded in the midnight of July 22, 1956)," July 30, 1956, ASP: Jianchuan 001-01-808.
4. Ulanhu's speech at the third meeting of the First National Congress, "Achievements of the nationality work and a few policy issues," June 20, 1956, MZWH, 2:30–31; CCP Sichuan Committee, "Current situation in nationality areas and opinions about work in the future," May 11, 1956, ASP: Jianchuan 001-01-818; CCP Kangding District Committee, "Situation of the work in Bathang County and proposals for work in the future," July 25, 1956, ASP: Jianchuan 012-01-102; CCP Sichuan committee, "Report [to the Center] about the conference on nationality work," November 11, 1956, ASP: Jiangchuan 001-01-818.
5. CCP Kangding Area Committee, "Report on the review of democratic reform and results of implementing the three reform items in Garzê Tibetan Autonomous Prefecture," October 1956, ASP: Jianchuan 012-01-88. Zhang Hang was identified in the document as a Han agent of the Kuomintang.
6. Secretariat of the CCP Xikang Committee, "Minutes of the nationality work conference," August 21, 1955, ASP: Jiankang 001-01-369; "CCP Sichuan and Xikang Committees' preliminary plan for implementing democratic reform in the agricultural Tibetan areas of Sichuan," September 22, 1955, ASP: Jianchuan 001-01-549.
7. Public Security Department of Southern Gansu, "Directive on intensifying intelligence work and preventing violent disturbances," April 14, 1956, AGP: 91-008-0059; "Speeches at the regional (municipality) [CCP] secretaries' conference, no. 7: Secretary of Kangding Area comrade Fan Zhizhong's speech," May 16, 1956, ASP: Jianchuan 012-01-71; the Center's telegram to the Tibet Work Committee on an investigative delegation from Lhasa to Kangding, May 6, 1956, in *Deng Xiaoping Nianpu, 1904–1974* (Chronology of Deng Xiaoping's life, 1904–1974), comp. Documentary Research Office of the Central Committee of the Chinese Communist Party (Beijing: Zhongyang Wenxian Chubanshe, 2009), 2:1288; CCP Sichuan Committee to the Center, Central Delegation to Tibet, and Tibet Work Committee, May 14, 1956, ASP: Jianchuan 001-01-830.
8. Secretariat of the CCP Sichuan Committee, "Chairman Mao's directive on democratic reform in Garzê and Liangshan, record taken in the midnight of July 22, 1956," July 30, 1956, ASP: Jianchuan 001-01-808; "Comrade Liao Zhigao's transmitting of Chairman Mao's directive on nationality work, record taken at the provincial committee's nationality work conference," July 29, 1956, ASP: Jianchuan, 012-01-72.

9. CCP Work Committee of Garzê to CCP Committee of Garzê Prefecture, "Report on the recent conditions of the Dajin Monastery," and appendix, "Activities of the Dajin Monastery during democratic reform," July 25, 1957, ASP: Jianchuan 001-01-1063.
10. "Center's directive on studying socialist transformation in pastoral areas of minority nationalities," February 21, 1956, and circular, "Central Department of United Front's report about socialist transformation of animal husbandry in pastoral areas of minority nationalities," February 17, 1956, ASP: Jianchuan 001-01-808.
11. ZGXLD, 1:83; *Ganzi Zhouzhi* (Chronicle of Garzê prefecture), 46–47; Office of Military Chronicle of the Sichuan Military Region, *Sichuan Shengzhi: Junshizhi: Dier Pian: Zhongda Zhanshi (Taolun Gao)* (Chronicle of Sichuan Province: Military affairs: Part 2: Important battles [Draft for discussion]) (unpublished edition for internal discussion, 1995), 27; Committee on Compilation of Local Chronicles of Sichuan Province, *Sichuan Shengzhi: Junshizhi* (Chronicle of Sichuan Province: Military affairs) (Chengdu: Sichuan Renmin Chubanshe, 1999), 295.
12. David Howarth, ed. *My Land and My People: The Autobiography of His Holiness the Dalai Lama* (London: Weidenfeld and Nicolson, 1962), 113–14; Melvyn C. Goldstein, *A History of Modern Tibet, Volume Two, 1951–1955: The Calm Before the Storm* (Berkeley: University of California Press, 2007), 529; Mikel Dunham, *Buddha's Warriors: The Story of the CIA-Backed Tibetan Freedom Fighters, the Chinese Invasion, and the Ultimate Fall of Tibet* (New York: Jeremy P. Tarcher, 2004), 143.
13. For instance, Jiangbian Jiacuo (Jambey Gyatso), *Mao Zedong yu Dalai, Banchan* (Mao Zedong and Dalai and Panchen) (Hong Kong: Xindalu Chubanshe, 2008), 136–37, 142, and Li Jianglin, *Dang Tieniao zai Tiankong Feixiang: 1956–1962 Qingzang Gaoyuan shang de Mimi Zhanzheng* (When iron birds are flying in the sky: The secret war in the Qinghai-Tibetan Plateau from 1956 to 1962) (Taipei: Lianjing, 2012), while offering different views on Mao's and the CCP's policies toward Tibet, suggest that the official view in the PRC is a fabrication. Tsering Shakya, *The Dragon in the Land of Snows: A History of Modern Tibet Since 1947* (London: Pimlica, 1999), 138–40, mentions the Dalai Lama's contacts with Tibetans of Kham *before* he reached Beijing, not *after*. While identifying Trijang as the head of one of the largest monasteries in Kham, Shakya stresses the spontaneity of the rebellions in western Sichuan and Qinghai. Goldstein, *A History of Modern Tibet*, 2:529, mentions the view in the PRC but does not find it credible, suggesting that the Dalai Lama's return trip was apolitical and in general "went well." Warren W. Smith, Jr., *Tibetan Nation: History of Tibetan Nationalism and Sino-Tibetan Relations* (Boulder, Colo.: Westview Press, 1996), 381, mentions in a footnote that Trijang "is indeed rumored to have stirred up resistance to the Chinese in Kham."
14. Zhang Dingyi, *1954 nian Dalai, Banchan Jinjing Jilue: Jian Ji Xizang Zizhiqu Choubei Weiyuanhui Chengli* (A brief account of Dalai's and Panchen's visit in Beijing in 1954: An additional account of the establishment of the Preparatory Committee for the Tibetan Autonomous Region) (Beijing: Zhongguo Zangxue Chubanshe, 2005; internal circulation), 274–75, 351, 354; Xu Danlu, *Fengxue Gaoyuan: Kang Zang Diqu Gongzuo Jishi* (A plateau of snow storms: Factual records of my work in Xikang and Tibet) (unpublished manuscript examined by the Research Desk of Intelligence History of the General Office of the Ministry of State Security, 1996), 221–22.
15. CCP Kangding Area Committee to the CCP Xikang Committee, January 31, 1955, Archives of Garzê Prefecture: 26-2 [hereafter cited as AGPf].
16. The old renminbi was soon replaced with a new edition at a 10,000:1 ratio.

4. A New Phase   343

17. CCP Kangding Area Committee to the CCP Xikang Committee, January 31, 1955, AGPf: 26-2; the CCP Kanding Area Committee, "Directive on issues that should be attended to after the arrival of Trijang, Karmapa, and Mindrolling," February 9, 1955, AGPf: 26-2.
18. CCP Kangding Area Committee to the Work Committee of the Southern Route and the Work Committees of Litang, Chaktreng, Fucheng, and Bathang, February 25, 1955, AGPf: 26-2; Xu, *Fengxue Gaoyuan*, 221.
19. Public Bureau of Xiangcheng County to the CCP Committee of Kangding Region and the Public Security Department of Kangding, March 28, 1955, AGPf: 26-2; Work Team of Xiangcheng County to the CCP Committee of Kangding Region and the Public Security Department of Kangding, April 2, 1955, AGPf: 26-2; CCP Work Committee of Xiangcheng County to the CCP Work Committee of the Southern Route and CCP Committee of Kangding Region, April 7, 1955, AGPf: 26-2.
20. Trichen Jurme Kunzang Wangyal, the eleventh Mindrolling Trichen, was born to the tenth Mindrolling Trichen in 1930. The tenth Mindrolling Trichen died in 1937, but the eleventh was not formally enthroned until 1962. See "Kyabje Mindrolling Trichen—Mindrolling International," accessed June 8, 2019, https://www.mindrollinginternational.org/lineage-and-history/kyabje-mindrolling-trichen/.
21. CCP Work Committee of Xinlong County to the CCP Committee of Kangding Region, the CCP Work Committee of the Northern Route, and the CCP Committee of Xikang Province, "Special report on the activities of Dalai's representatives in our county," April 9, 1955, AGPf: 26-2.
22. Guo Jianmin of the General Office of Public Security of Xikang to the CCP Kangding Area Committee, the Public Security Department of Kangding, and the General Office of Public Security of Xikang, March 13, 1955, AGPf: 26-2; Guo Jianmin of the General Office of Public Security of Xikang to the CCP Kangding Area Committee, the Public Security Department of Kangding, and the General Office of Public Security of Xikang, April 20, 1955, AGPf: 26-2.
23. Public Security Department of the Xikang Tibetan Autonomous Region, "Materials about local reactions to the transit and religious activities of the Dalai [Lama], Trijang, the Karmapa [Lama], and the Mindrolling [Trichen]," June 24, 1955, AGPf: 26-2.
24. CCP Work Committee of the Southern Route to the CCP Kangding Area Committee and the Public Security Department of Kangding, March 5, 1955, AGPf: 26-2; the Public Security Bureau of Xiangcheng County to the CCP Kangding Area Committee and the Public Security Department of Kangding, March 24 and March 28, 1955, AGPf: 26-2; Xiangcheng County Work Team to the CCP Kangding Area Committee and the Public Security Department of Kangding, April 2, 1955, AGPf: 26-2; the CCP Xiangcheng Counter Work Committee to the CCP Southern Route Work Committee and the CCP Kangding Area Committee, April 7, 1955, AGPf: 26-2; the CCP Kangding Area Committee to the CCP Derge Work Committee, Guo Jianmin, and the CCP Xikang Committee, April 13, 1955, AGPf: 26-2.
25. Xiangcheng County Work Team to the CCP Kangding Area Committee and the Public Security Department of Kangding, April 2, 1955, AGPf: 26-2; Public Security Bureau of Bathang County to the CCP Kangding Area Committee and the Public Security Department of Kangding, April 20, 1955, AGPf: 26-2; CCP Xinlong County Work Committee to the CCP Kangding Area Committee, the CCP Northern Route Work Committee, and the CCP Xikang Committee, "Special report on the activities of the Dalai [Lama]'s representatives in our county," April 9, 1955, AGPf: 26-2.

26. Center to the CCP Shanghai Bureau, Tibet Work Committee, CCP Committees of Zhejiang, Hubei, Shanxi, Gansu, Qinghai, Sichuan, Xikang, Guangdong, and of the Central-South, Southwest, and Northwest Military Region, transmitting the Central Nationality Committee, "Plan for arranging the visitations and religious activities of the Dalai [Lama], the Panchen [Lama], and their entourages," March 8, 1955, AGPf: 26-2; Public Security Department of the Tibetan Autonomous Region of Xikang, "Plan for the work of guarding the Dalai [Lama]," March 19, 1955, AGPf: 26-2; the CCP Northern Route Work Committee and the Work Team of the General Office of Public Security of Xikang to the CCP Kanding Arear Committee and Public Security Department of Kangding and the General Office of Public Security of Xikang, March 4, 1955, AGPf: 26-2.
27. CCP Committee of Kangding Region, "Report on the Dalai [Lama]'s religious activities and our opinion on dealing with the aftermath," July 5, 1955, AGPf: 26-2.
28. "Deputy Governor Kang's report on escorting of the Dalai [Lama]," July 1955, AGPf: 26-2.
29. CCP Kangding Area Committee, "Report on the Dalai [Lama]'s religious activities and our opinion on dealing with the aftermath," July 5, 1955, AGPf: 26-2.
30. Fan Ming, in *Xizang Neibu Zhizheng: Dalai Lama he Banchan Dashi de Maodun, Zhonggong Gaoceng de Fenqi* (Internal controversies of Tibet: Contradictions between Dalai and Panchen and disagreements among CCP leaders) (Carle Place, N.Y.: Mirror Books, 2009), 285–87, provides a detailed account of the Dalai Lama group's alleged conspiracy for achieving Tibetan independence by peaceful means if possible and by force if necessary. According to Fan, such a plan had been afoot for some time and the Dalai Lama group even held a meeting in Beijing to discuss concrete steps. In agreeing with the public party narrative with respect to the group's agitation for rebellion on its way back to Lhasa, Fan adds another detail. Allegedly, a secret code was set up between conspirators in Lhasa and those in western Sichuan for the latter to start a rebellion once they received an order from the former. Fan asserts that in his capacity as party secretary of the Intelligence Committee of the TWC, he reported relevant intelligence to his superiors both in Lhasa and in Beijing, including Mao. Yet not only did the Center not take countermeasures, but the piece of intelligence also became evidence of Fan's own plot to frame the Dalai Lama. Consequently, all intelligence investigations targeting the Tibetan upper stratum in␣Lhasa were suspended. Fan's Intelligence Committee was also dissolved, and Xu Danlu, the intelligence liaison from Beijing, was recalled. Coming from the central figure in a factional struggle within the CCP apparatus in Tibet, the reliability of Fan's account is questionable. Zhang Xiangming, *Zhang Xiangming 55 nian Xizang Gongzuo Shilu* (Records of Zhang Xiangming's 55-year work in Tibet), 2006, 46, suggests that Xu Danlu's recall indeed came suddenly, but the reason was his problematic role in the friction between Fan Ming and Zhang Guohua. According to another insider's unpublished account, Zhao Fan, *Zhao Fan Huiyilu* (Zhao Fan's memoires), 1992, 30, during the Cultural Revolution, Fan Ming made an allegation through some Red Guards' "big-character posters" that before 1959 he reported to Deng Xiaoping that "the Dalai was rallying to the brightness [meaning the CCP] in appearance but turning to the darkness in his heart." Deng, according to Fan, tabled the report in order to support Zhang Guohua's faction. None of this can be verified with archival information.
31. CCP Northern Route Work Committee of the CCP Kangding Area Committee, "General report on the conditions of various social strata in Garzê, Derge, Xinlong, Dengke, Drakgo, and Shiqu Counties from January to March, 1955," April 18, 1955,

AGPf: 26-2; the Public Security Department of Kangding, "Summary report on the recent activities of Jago Topden," December 7, 1955, AGPf: 26-2; the CCP Sichuan Committee to the CCP Kangding Area Committee and the Center for transmitting to the TWC and the TMR, December 25, 1955, AGPf: 26-2.
32. *Ganzi Zhouzhi*, 455–57; *Sichuan Shengzhi: Renwu Zhi* (Chronicle of Sichuan Province: chronicles of personalities), 232–33.
33. Temporary Party Group for Escorting the Dalai Lama to the CCP Xikang and Sichuan Committees, Tibet Work Committee, and the Central Department of United Front, May 8, 1955, AGPf: 26-2.
34. The Dalai Lama, *My Land and My People: The Autobiography of His Holiness the Dalai Lama of Tibet* (London: Weidenfeld and Nicolson, 1962), 118; the Dalai Lama, *Freedom in Exile: The Autobiography of the Dalai Lama* (New York: HarperCollins, 1990), 98–99; Goldstein, 2:521; Thomas Laird, *The Story of Tibet: Conversations with the Dalai Lama* (New York: Grove Press, 2006), 326.
35. *Xizang Lishi Dang'an Huicui* (A collection of historical archives of Tibet), comp. Archives of the Tibetan Autonomous Region (Beijing: Wenwu Chubanshe, 1995), 107/1–107/8. The volume includes the Tibetan original of the ode and its Chinese and English translations.
36. Matthen Kapstein, "A Thorn in the Dragon's Side: Tibetan Buddhist Culture in China," in *Governing China's Multi-Ethnic Frontiers*, ed. Morris Rossabi (Seattle: University of Washington Press, 2004), 236–37.
37. General Office of the CCP Hebei Committee, "Comrade Zhang Jingwu's report on the Tibet question (transcribed version)," April 16, 1959, Archives of Hebei Province: 855-5-1563-31 [hereafter cited as AHP].
38. Zhou Zuyou and Li Desen, "Truth about the 'Kham rebellion,'" *People's Daily*, April 26, 1959, republished in *Xizang Wenti Zhenxiang* (Truth about the Tibetan question) (Hong Kong: Shiyan Chubanshe, 1959), 51–52; Guo Ziwen, *Xizang Dashiji (1949–1959)* (Chronology of important events of Tibet, 1949–1959) (Beijing: Minzu Chubanshe, 1959), 14.
39. CCP Garzê Prefecture Committee, "Basic conclusions on democratic reforms of the Garzê Tibetan Autonomous Prefecture," [end of] 1959, ASP: Jianchuan 012-01-196.
40. CCP Garzê Prefecture Committee, "Basic conclusions on democratic reforms of the Garzê Tibetan Autonomous Prefecture," [end of] 1959, ASP: Jianchuan 012-01-196.
41. Social Department of the TWC, "Thoroughly beat back and expose the treacherous crimes of the Tibetan upper-stratum reactionary clique and protect the vast laboring people's struggle for liberation," September 11, 1959, *Gongan Jianshe*, no. 38 (December 25, 1959): 24–30. This "Surkhang statement" would be cited repeatedly in the public party narrative. Fan Ming also cites it in his *Xizang Neibu Zhizheng*, 285–87, and claims that the intelligence work under him discovered such agitations.
42. Center to the CCP Xikang and Sichuan Committees, Liu Geping, the TWC, and the TMR, April 28, 1955, AGPf: 26-2; Temporary Party Group for Escorting the Dalai Lama to the CCP Kangding Region Committee, the CCP Xikang Committee, the Central Department of United Front, the Central Committee on Nationality Affairs, and to be conveyed to the TWC and the CCP Sichuan Committee, May 22, 1955, AGPf: 26-2; Xu, *Fengxue Gaoyuan*, 221–22.
43. Fan Zhizhong to the CCP Xikang Committee and CCP Kangding Area Committee, June 29, 1955, AGPf: 26-2.
44. *Ganzi Zhouzhi*, 49–58; CCP Sichuan Committee, "Brief report on the conditions of the Kangding Region," March 19, 1956, ASP: Jianchuan 012-01-102.

45. CCP Sichuan Committee, "Brief report on the recent conditions of the Kangding Region," April 11, 1956, ASP: Jianchuan 012-01-102.
46. Office of Military Chronicle of the Military Region of Sichuan Province, *Sichuan Shengzhi, Junshizhi: Dier Pian: Zhongda Zhanshi (Taolun Gao)*, 26. The White, Red, and Flower sects refer separately to the Kagyu, Nyingma, and Sakya sects of Tibetan Buddhism.
47. Office of Military Chronicle of the Military Region of Sichuan Province, *Sichuan Shengzhi: Junshizhi: Dier Pian: Zhongda Zhanshi (Songshen Gao)* (Chronicle of Sichuan Province: Chronicle of military affairs: Part 2: Important battles [draft for approval]) (Unpublished manuscript, September 1996), 214; *Sichuan Shengzhi: Junshizhi*, 294–95.
48. ZGXLD, 1:83.
49. MXGW, 213–20.
50. Central Propaganda Department and United Front Department, "Transferring the TWC's 'Propaganda materials for exposing Dalai's crimes of treason,'" December 26, 1963, ASP: Jianchuan 012-01-325; CCP Garzê Prefecture Committee, "Transferring the conclusive report by the prefecture united front department on the education among national and religious upper-stratum figures for exposing Dalai's crimes of treason," February 23, 1964, ASP: Jianchuan 012-01-325.
51. Zhang Xiangming, *Zhang Xiangming*, 70–79, 99–103.
52. Lawudare Tudandanda (Lhaudara Tubdain Daindar), "Reform office established by the Tibetan Local Government for implementing the Seventeen-Point Agreement," XWZX, 9 (May 1999): 22–25; "Public notice on reforming the social system of Tibet in accordance with the [17-point] agreement," XWZX, 9 (May 1999): 134–38.
53. "Conversation with the Dalai Lama and Panchen Erdini," February 23, 1955, in MXGW, 109–11; "Conversation with the Tibetan Regional Delegation and the Tibetan Youth Delegation," October 29, 1955, MXGW, 124–30; Sangding Duojipamu (Samding Dorje Pakmo), "Premier Zhou's kindness will never be forgotten," *Zhou Enlai yu Xizang* (Zhou Enlai and Tibet), comp. Office of Party History of the Tibetan Autonomous Region (Beijing: Zhongguo Zangxue Chubanshe, 1998), 352–55.
54. Documentary Research Office of the Central Committee of the Chinese Communist Party, *Zhou Enlai Nianpu, 1898–1949* (Chronicle of Zhou Enlai's life, 1898–1949) (Beijing: Zhongyang Wenxian Chubanshe, 1989), 1:456; "State Council's decision on establishment of the Preparatory Committee for the Tibetan Autonomous Region, March 9, 1955," *Zhou Enlai yu Xizang*, 40–42; "State Council's decision on the issue of transportation and communication in Tibet, March 9, 1955," *Zhou Enlai yu Xizang*, 42–44; "State Council's decision on assisting Tibet to implement constructive projects, March 9, 1955," *Zhou Enlai yu Xizang*, 44–45.
55. State Council, (*shen*) No. 6, "Circular on preventing Han people's drifting into the area of Tibet, September 15, 1955," AGP: Document 128–0001; General Office of the People's Committee of Gansu, general office secretary's file 0359 (1956), March 31, 1956, and appendix: TWC, "Notification about limiting Renminbi's entering into Tibet," January 10, 1956, AGP: 128-005-0075.
56. "The CCP Center's answer to the question about the nature of current reform in Tibet," September 4, 1955, XGWX, 141–43.
57. ZGXLD, 1:87.
58. ZGXLD, 1:84.
59. Ni Fuhan, "Senior's wisdom and art of suasion," *Zhou Enlai yu Xizang*, 400–401; Mao Zedong, "Letter to the Dalai Lama, November 24, 1955," MXGW, 132.
60. *Zhou Enlai Nianpu, 1898–1949*, 1:558; CCP Center, "Notification on several issues concerning the establishment of the Preparatory Committee for the Tibetan Autonomous

Region and organization of a Central Delegation to Visit Tibet," February 7, 1956, ASP: Jianchuan 001-01-830; "Approval for increasing representatives from various parties and organizations, January 24, 1956," *Zhou Enlai Shuxin Xuanji* (Selected communications of Zhou Enlai) (Beijing: Zhongyang Wenxian Chubanshe, 1988), 522.
61. "Conversation with Tibetan personalities," February 12, 1956, MXGW, 136–39.
62. Documentary Research Office of the Central Committee of the Chinese Communist Party, *Mao Zedong Nianpu, 1949–1976* (Chronicle of Mao Zedong's life, 1949–1976) (Beijing: Zhongyang Wenxian Chubanshe, 2013), 2:527. Melvyn C. Goldstein, *A History of Modern Tibet, Volume Three, 1955–1957: The Storm Clouds Descend* (Berkeley: University of California Press, 2014), 294, quotes Mao's remarks from Central Office of Document Research, *Chen Yi Zhuan* (Biography of Chen Yi) (Beijing: Dangdai Zhongguo Chubanshe, 2006), which provide an identical version of the conversation. Goldstein's English version, however, omits the term *jianchi* (insisting on) from "Center's policies of insisting on reforms and nationality unity" and hence dilutes Mao's message about reform.
63. *Mao Zedong Nianpu, 1949–1976*, 2:548.
64. "The Center's directive on study of socialist transformation in the pastoral areas of minority nationalities," February 21, 1956, ASP: Jianchuan 001-01-808.
65. CCP Central United Front Department, "Outline plan for minority nationality work from 1956 to 1967 (draft)," February 29, 1956, ASP: Jianchuan 0012-01-64.
66. Leading Party Group to the Center, "Brief report on the delegation's situation after arriving in Lhasa," April 18, 1956, ASP: Jianchuan 001-01-830.
67. Liu Shufa et al., *Chen Yi Nianpu* (Chronicle of Chen Yi's life) (Beijing: Renmin Chubanshe, 1995), 2:702–7; ZGXLD, 1:92–94.
68. "The Center's communication on a report by the Leading Party Group of the Central Delegation to Tibet about the political conditions of Tibet and work done by the delegation after its arrival in Lhasa," May 11, 1956, ASP: Jianchuan 001-01-830. The delegation's report was dated April 29, an obvious clerical error.
69. "The Center's communication on a report by the Leading Party Group of the Central Delegation to Tibet about the political conditions of Tibet and work done by the Delegation after Its Arrival in Lhasa," May 11, 1956, ASP: Jianchuan 001-01-830; *Mao Zedong Nianpu, 1949–1976*, 2:577.
70. Zhang Xiangming, *Zhang Xiangming*, 67–68.
71. Propaganda Group of the Central Delegation to Tibet to Chengdu Military Region and the Center, April 29, 1956, ASP: Jianchuan 001-01-830; PLA General Staff to the Central Delegation to Tibet and the Chengdu Military Region, May 10, 1956, ASP: Jianchuan 001-01-830.
72. "Minutes of Chairman Mao's directive about the reforms in Garzê and Liangshan," July 22, 1956, ASP: Jianchuan 001-01-808.
73. ZGXLD, 1:116–17.
74. Goldstein, *A History of Modern Tibet*, 3:306–34.
75. Fan Ming, *Xizang Neibu Zhizheng*, 370–71.
76. Zhang Xiangming, *Zhang Xiangming*, 67–70.
77. Fan Ming, *Xizang Neibu Zhizheng*, 331, 370.
78. Fan Ming, *Xizang Neibu Zhizheng*, 332.
79. Shen Zhihua, *Zhonghua Renmin Gongheguo Shi: Disan Juan: Sikao yu Xuanze: Cong Zhishi Fenzi Huiyi dao Fan Youpai Yundong, 1956–1957* (History of the People's Republic of China: Volume 3: Reflection and choice: From intellectual conference to the anti-rightist campaign, 1956–1957) (Hong Kong: Chinese University Press, 2008), 154–58.

80. ZGXLD, 1:95–96.
81. ZGXLD, 1:96–98. The TWC report, dated July 10, 1956, was titled "General report on the work during the second season of 1956 and work arrangements for the third season."
82. *Xizang de Minzhu Gaige* (Democratic reform in Tibet), comp. Committee of the Tibetan Autonomous Region for Collecting Materials on Party History and Leading Group of the Tibetan Military Region for Collecting Materials on Party History (Lhasa: Xizang Renmin Chubanshe, 1995), 49–52.
83. Fan Ming, who was in charge of the TWC at the time and responsible for the report, admitted two years later that, after consulting the Dalai Lama but without the Center's authorization, he decided to make reform the central topic at the second meeting of the PCTAR. Fan Ming, *Xizang Neibu Zhizheng*, 397.
84. *Zhou Enlai Nianpu, 1898–1949*, 1:600.
85. ZGXLD, 1:97–98.
86. *Xizang Gongzuo Wenxian Xuanbian* (Selected documents of the Tibet work), comp. Office of Documentary Research of the CCP Central Committee and the CCP Committee of the Tibetan Autonomous Region (Beijing: Zhongyang Wenxian Chubanshe, 2005), 165–67, 180–81.
87. MXGW, 150–51.
88. Zhang Xiangming, "Brilliant policy decision: Chairman Mao's solution of the Tibetan question remembered," *Zhongguo Zangxue* (Tibetology of China), 2001 (2): 27–38; ZGXLD, 1:97.
89. XGWX, 182–84.
90. *Mao Zedong Nianpu, 1949–1976*, 2:595–615, 3:23.
91. Documentary Research Office of the Central Committee of the Chinese Communist Party, *Liu Shaoqi Nianpu, 1898–1969* (Chronicle of Liu Shaoqi's life, 1898–1969) (Beijing: Zhongyang Wenxian Chubanshe, 1996), 2:373–74.
92. Documentary Research Office of the Central Committee of the Chinese Communist Party, *Zhou Enlai Nianpu, 1949–1976* (Chronicle of Zhou Enlai's life, 1949–1976) (Beijing: Zhongyang Wenxian Chubanshe, 1997), 1:607–15.
93. *Deng Xiaoping Nianpu, 1904–1974*, 2:1300–1311.
94. MXGW, 148.
95. MXGW, 43, 116.
96. Ye Xuexian, "The first director of the United Front Department of the new China," accessed August 19, 2015, http://dangshi.people.com.cn/n/2014/0416/c85037-24903218-3.html.
97. Liu Shaoqi, "Struggle for higher qualifications of a Communist Party member," April 9, 1951, JYLW, 3:261.
98. "CCP Center's reply to the TWC about party construction in the society of Tibet," September 24, 1956, ZZWX (2013), 24:286–87.
99. *Deng Xiaoping Nianpu, 1904–1974*, 2:1333.

5. A Waiting Game

1. "Liu Shaoqi's work report at the second meeting of the eighth national congress of the CCP, May 5, 1958," ZZWX (2013), 28:13; He Zhaoxia, "Examination of the original meaning of 'one day is equal to twenty years,'" *Shanghai Dangshi yu Dangjian* (Shanghai Party history and construction), March 2010, 8–9.

2. Robert Levine, *A Geography of Time: The Temporal Misadventure of a Social Psychologist, or How Every Culture Keeps Time Just a Little Bit Differently* (New York: Basic Books, 1998), 101–27.
3. ZGXLD, 1:99.
4. ZGXLD, 1:101.
5. Liu Shaoqi, "The CCP Central Committee's political report to the Eighth Congress," September 15, 1956, MZWH, 2:33–35.
6. Ulanhu, "The Party's victorious solution of the nationality question at home," September 19, 1956, MZWH, 2:39–48.
7. ZGXLD, 1:99–100.
8. Li Weihan, "Continue to strengthen the Party's united front work," September 25, 1956, MZWH, 2:36–68.
9. "Minutes of Chairman Mao's directive about the reforms in Garzê and Liangshan," July 22, 1956, ASP: Jianchuan 001-01-808.
10. *Zhou Enlai yu Xizang* (Zhou Enlai and Tibet), comp. Office of Party History of the Tibetan Autonomous Region (Beijing: Zhongguo Zangxue Chubanshe, 1998), 75–76.
11. "Consultation with the Indian side about arrangements for the Dalai [Lama] and Panchen [Lama] to visit India," April 11, 1956, ACMFA: 105-00328-02.
12. MXGW, 152–53. During the CCP's Long March in the mid-1930s, Zhang Guotao was the commander of the Fourth Front Army of the Red Army. He disagreed with the rest of the CCP leadership about the northern direction of the march and took his troops southward to Xikang. Although later Zhang rejoined the rest of the Red Army in northern Shaanxi, he was subjected to severe criticism inside the CCP, which caused his defection to the Kuomintang in 1938.
13. Tsering Shakya, *The Dragon in the Land of Snows: A History of Modern Tibet Since 1947* (London: Pimlica, 1999), 150–51; Melvyn C. Goldstein, *A History of Modern Tibet, Volume Three, 1955-1957: The Storm Clouds Descend* (Berkeley: University of California Press, 2014), 339.
14. Jiangbian Jiacuo, *Mao Zedong yu Dalai, Banchan* (Mao Zedong and Dalai and Banchen) (Hong Kong: Xindalu Chubanshe, 2008), 172–73.
15. Zhao Shenying, *Zhongyang Zhu Zang Daibia Zhang Jingwu* (Zhang Jingwu as the Center's Representative in Tibet) (Beijing: Zhongguo Zangxue Chubanshe, 2001), 111–12. According to Zhang Xiangming, after the Dalai Lama complained about Zhang Jingwu, Mao appointed Zhang as director of the General Office of the PRC Chairman while kept his capacity as party secretary of the TWC and the Center's representative in Tibet in name. Zhang Xiangming, *Zhang Xiangming 55 nian Xizang Gongzuo Shilu* (Records of Zhang Xiangming's 55-year work in Tibet), 2006, 66–67.
16. Mao's note, dated November 4, 1956, is quoted in Goldstein, 3:332.
17. Jawaharlal Nehru, *Selected Works of Jawaharlal Nehru: Second Series* (New Delhi: Jawaharlal Nehru Memorial Fund, c. 1984–), 36:591.
18. Zhao Shenying, *Zhang Jingwu*, 111–12.
19. *Zhongguo Gongchangdang Xizang Lishi Dashiji Dashiji, 1949-2004* (Chronology of major historical events of the Chinese Communist Party in Tibet, 1949–2004), comp. Party History Research Office of the Tibetan Autonomous Region Committee of the Chinese Communist Party (Beijing: Zhonggong Dangshi Chubanshe, 2005), 1:101–2.
20. Zhao Shenying, *Zhang Jingwu*, 113; ZGXLD, 1:102.
21. "7. Talks with Dalai Lama," November 26 and 28, 1956," in *Selected Works of Jawaharlal Nehru*, 35:520–22.

22. The Dalai Lama, *My Land and My People: The Autobiography of His Holiness the Dalai Lama of Tibet* (London: Weidenfeld and Nicolson, 1962), 132–33. In his recent memoir, *The Noodle Maker of Kalimpong: The Untold Story of My Struggle for Tibet* (New York: PublicAffairs, 2015), 160, 163, Gyalo Thondup accuses Nehru of going back on his promise to grant asylum to the Dalai Lama. According to Gyalo Thondup, before his brother, the Dalai Lama, arrived in India, he reached an agreement with Apa Pant, the Political Officer of Sikkim, that the Indian government would grant asylum to the Dalai Lama and also persuade the Chinese to withdraw troops from Tibet. Nehru's personal connection with the agreement is unclear.
23. ZGXLD, 1:102; Du Bin, "Account of rebellion suppression and democratic reform in the Chamdo area," *Zhongguo Zongjiao Minzu Wang* (website of Chinese religions and nationalities), accessed August 28, 2015, http://www.mzb.com.cn/html/report/116466-1.htm. Ningjing became a county in 1912 and was renamed as Markham in 1965.
24. Meilang Zongzhen (Monlam Tsundrub), *Jindai Xizang Jushang "Bangdacang" zhi Bangda Duoji de Zhengzhi Shangya yu Shangye Licheng* (Political and commercial career of Banda Dorje of Bangdatsang, the tycoon family of modern Tibet) (Lhasa: Xizang Renmin Chubanshe, 2008), 89–100, 114–16; Carol McGranahan, "Tobgyal Bangdatsang," *The Treasury of Lives*, February 2016, accessed August 9, 2018, https://treasuryoflives.org/biographies/view/Tobgyal/TBRC_P1TD8.
25. ZGXLD, 1:103; Meilang Zongzhen, 114–20.
26. According to Song Yuehong, "Study of the direct administration by the Central People's Government of the Chamdo People's Liberation Committee," *Zhonggong Dangshi Yanjiu* (Study of Chinese Communist history), 2011 (4): 55–63, from December 1950 to April 1956, Chamdo was directly under the State Council. After the PCTAR was established, the Chamdo People's Liberation Committee merged its work with the PCTAR's but remained under the State Council.
27. The Center to the party committees of various provinces, municipalities, and the Shanghai bureau, "The issue of possible riots in Lhasa and other places," December 19, 1956, appendix 2, AHP: 855-3-0868-14.
28. The Center to the party committees of various provinces, municipalities, and the Shanghai bureau, "The issue of possible riots in Lhasa and other places," December 19, 1956, appendix 1, AHP: 855-3-0868-14.
29. According the compilers of MXGW, note 1, 154–55, Mao "added" these words to the draft directive, and according to Documentary Research Office of the Central Committee of the Chinese Communist Party, *Mao Zedong Nianpu, 1949–1976* (Chronicle of Mao Zedong's life, 1949–1976) (Beijing: Zhongyang Wenxian Chubanshe, 2013), 3:51, Mao "rewrote" this part.
30. *Mao Zedong Nianpu, 1949–1976*, 3:53. Those present at the Zhongnanhai meeting were Liu Shaoqi, Zhu De, Chen Yun, Zhang Wentian, Lu Dingyi, Wang Jiaxiang, Tan Zhenlin, Yang Shangkun, Hu Qiaomu, and Zhang Hanfu. The editorial, "More on the historical experience of proletarian dictatorship," was published in the *People's Daily* on December 29, 1956.
31. *Mao Zedong Nianpu, 1949–1976*, 3:52. These officials were Liu Shaoqi, Zhu De, Chen Yun, Peng Dehuai, Tan Zheng, Xu Bing, Zhang Wentian, and Zhang Hanfu.
32. Documentary Research Office of the Central Committee of the Chinese Communist Party, *Deng Xiaoping Nianpu, 1904–1974* (Chronology of Deng Xiaoping's life, 1904–1974) (Beijing: Zhongyang Wenxian Chubanshe, 2009), 2:1331–32. See Ezra Vogel, *Deng Xiaoping and the Transformation of China* (Cambridge: Belknap Press, 2011), and Alexander Pantsov with Steven Levine, *Deng Xiaoping: A Revolutionary Life* (Oxford: Oxford University Press, 2015).

33. *Deng Xiaoping Nianpu*, 2:1332.
34. Deng's anachronism in this matter is apparent in *Deng Xiaoping Nianpu*. But, in view of the ongoing controversy inside the CCP about reform in Tibet in 1956, it cannot be ruled out that the compilers of the *Nianpu* practiced anachronism so that the responsibility for "excessiveness" could be pinned on Fan Ming.
35. *Mao Zedong Nianpu, 1949–1976*, 2:321.
36. Li Zuomin, "A Role Model That Has Benefit My Whole Life," in *Zhou Enlai yu Xizang*, 326–38.
37. Both *Zhou Enlai yu Xizang* (1998), 142–55, and XGWX (2005), 185–88, 190–95, published "minutes" of Zhou's three conversations with the Dalai Lama, but the latter publication deleted certain paragraphs contained in the earlier one without any indication of omission or explanation, which raises a question about the reliability of the earlier version as well.
38. Documentary Research Office of the Central Committee of the Chinese Communist Party, *Zhou Enlai Nianpu, 1949–1976* (Chronicle of Zhou Enlai's life, 1949–1976) (Beijing: Zhongyang Wenxian Chubanshe, 1997), 1:642–43, 650–51; "Minutes of Zhou Enlai's conversation with the Dalai [Lama], November 29, 1956," and "Minutes of Zhou Enlai's conversation with the Dalai [Lama], December 30, 1956," *Zhou Enlai yu Xizang*, 142–51; Zhou Enlai, "Conversation with the Dalai Lama, November 29, 1956," and "Conversation with the Dalai Lama, December 30, 1956," XGWX, 185–88, 190–92.
39. Li Zuomin, "A role model that has benefitted my whole life," in *Zhou Enlai yu Xizang*, 326–38; Ngabö Ngawang Jikmé, "Monumental achievement in history and everlasting grace," in *Zhou Enlai yu Xizang*, 271–81.
40. "Minutes of Zhou Enlai's conversation with the Dalai [Lama], November 29, 1956," *Zhou Enlai yu Xizang*, 142–48.
41. The following discussion is based on "3. Talks with Chou En-lai—I [December 31, 1956 and January 1, 1957]," in *Selected Works of Jawaharlal Nehru*, 36:583–603.
42. "4. Talks with Chou En-lai—II [January 1, 1957]," in *Selected Works of Jawaharlal Nehru*, 36:603–9.
43. "5. Talks with Chou En-lai—III [January 1, 1957]," in *Selected Works of Jawaharlal Nehru*, 36:610–16. These Indian officials were N. R. Pillai, secretary-general, Ministry of External Affairs; R. K. Nehru, Indian ambassador to China; and Apa Pant, political officer in Sikkim.
44. "Minutes of Zhou Enlai-Dalai [Lama] conversation, January 1, 1957," *Zhou Enlai yu Xizang*, 151–55; Ngabö Ngawang Jikmé, "Monumental achievement in history and everlasting grace," *Zhou Enlai yu Xizang*, 271–81.
45. ZGXLD, 1:106.
46. *Mao Zedong Nianpu, 1949–1976*, 3:61–62.
47. "6. Talks with Chou En-lai—IV [January 1, 1957]," in *Selected Works of Jawaharlal Nehru*, 36:617–19. This was Nehru's second note about his talks with Zhou, addressed to N. R. Pillai, secretary-general, Ministry of External Affairs; R. K. Nehru, Indian ambassador to China; and Apa Pant, political officer in Sikkim.
48. "Ambassador Pan Zili's report to the Center about his conversation with the Dalai [Lama]," January 3, 1957, *Pingxi Xizang Panluan* (Pacifying the rebellion in Tibet), comp. Committee of the Tibetan Autonomous Region for Collecting Materials on Party History and Leading Group of the Tibetan Military Region for Collecting Materials on Party History (Lhasa: Xizang Renmin Chubanshe, 1995), 116–17.
49. "6. The Relics of Huen Tsang [January 12, 1957]," in *Selected Works of Jawaharlal Nehru*, 36:185; "6. Talks with Chou En-lai—IV [January 1, 1957]," in *Selected Works of Jawaharlal Nehru*, 36:617–19. In his autobiography, *My Land and My People*, 137–38, the Dalai Lama indicates that he informed Nehru of his decision in his "final interview" with the Indian leader.

50. ZGXLD, 1:109.
51. *Mao Zedong Nianpu, 1949–1976*, 3:80; Mao Zedong, "On the question of minority nationalities," February 27, 1957, XGWX, 196. In the Mao era, the Supreme Conference on State Affairs was the supreme forum for the PRC chair to outline important state policies for the country. According to the PRC constitution of 1954, meetings of the conference would be called and presided over by the chairman of the People's Central Government whenever necessary. Of the twenty meetings of the conference held between 1954 and 1964, the eleventh had the largest attendance of some 1,800 people.
52. Ministry of Foreign Affairs to the TWC, January 18, 1957, and the Center to the TWC, January 24, 1957, ACMFA: 105-00480-03. Yang Gongsu's recollection is inconsistent with archival information. Yang's memoir, published when he was eighty-nine years old, *Cangsang Jiushinian: Yige Waijiao Teshi de Huiyi* (My life for ninety years: The recollections of a special diplomatic envoy) (Haikou: Hainan Chubanshe, 1999), 275, states that after the Dalai Lama reached Kalimpong, Yang flew there to accompany the Dalai Lama on his flight back to Lhasa. The Dalai Lama did not fly back to Lhasa because, according to Yang, the Dalai Lama insisted on traveling on horseback. Although Yang would live to 105, his memory could still have mistaken what was planned for what really took place more than forty years before.
53. ZGXLD, 1:106; Meilang Zongzhen, 115–18.
54. Goldstein, 3:444–65, with limited access to some of these meetings, differs from the account here, concluding that as a result of these discussions, Beijing just continued Mao Zedong's gradualist approach in Tibet.
55. At the time, Chen Yun was in charge of the CCP's financial work, Li Weihan was the director of the United Front Department, Song Renqiong was the deputy director of the CCP's Organization Department and also the director of the Third Ministry of Mechanical Industry, and Xi Zhongxun was the secretary-general of the State Council. The Central Secretariat also included Huang Kecheng, Li Xuefeng, Tan Zheng, and Wang Jiaxiang, plus alternate members Liu Lantao, Yang Shangkun, and Hu Qiaomu. These officials' names, however, do not appear in the records of the meetings.
56. "Discussion of the Tibetan question by the Central Secretariat, brief summary (1)," March 5, 1957, ASP: Jianchuan 012-01-397; "Records of the Central Secretariat meeting on March 5, 1957," *Zhou Renshan Riji* (Zhou Renshan's diaries), PCCM. Zhang Jingwu's presentation erroneously put the total of Han personnel at 15,159, but should be 15,519 based on the numbers of Han cadres and workers.
57. "Discussion of the Tibetan question by the Central Secretariat, brief summary (1)," March 1, 1957, ASP: Jianchuan 012-01-397. In the report, Zhang said: "One *ke* (25 *jin*) of barley costed 17 yuan." Obviously, Zhang used the Tibetan measurement *ke* here, which equaled about 28 *jin* or 14 kilograms, not the Chinese term *ke* for a gram.
58. "Record of the Central Secretariat meeting on March 6, 1957," *Zhou Renshan Riji*; "Record of the Central Secretariat meeting on March 8, 1957," *Zhou Renshan Riji*.
59. See ZGXLD, 1:101, 116–17; Fan Ming, *Xizang Neibu Zhizheng: Dalai Lama he Banchan Dashi de Maodun, Zhonggong Gaoceng de Fenqi* (Internal controversies of Tibet: Contradictions between Dalai and Panchen and disagreements among CCP leaders) (Carle Place, N.Y.: Mirror Books, 2009), 389–92; Zhang Xiangming, *Zhang Xiangming*, 70–79; Miao Peiyi, *Miao Peiyi Huiyilu* (Memoirs of Miao Peiyi) (Lhasa: Xizang Renmin Chubanshe, 2005), 260.
60. Central Organizational Department of the CCP, *Guanyu Fan Ming tongzhi youpai fandang jituan wenti de fucha baogao (caogao)* (Draft report on the reexamination of the issue of comrade Fan Ming's rightist and anti-party clique), November 13, 1979, and

Guanyu Fan Ming tongzhi youpai fandang jiduan wenti de fucha jielun (Conclusion on the reexamination of the issue of comrade Fan Ming's rightist and anti-party clique), May 7, 1980, PCCM.

61. The TWC, "Basic conclusions on the work of 1956 and work orientations and tasks for 1957," ZGXLD, 1:106–7; "Discussion of the Tibetan question by the Central Secretariat, brief summary (1)," March 5, 1957, ASP: Jianchuan 012-01-397.
62. Zhang Guohua, *Zhongyang lingdao tanhua jilu* (Minutes of a central leader's talk), February 11, 1957, PCCM; "Record of the Central Secretariat meeting on March 8, 1957," *Zhou Renshan Riji*.
63. "Speeches at the Politburo meeting on May 14, 1957, as conveyed by Fan Ming on June 1, 1957," *Zhou Renshan Riji*.
64. "Record of the Central Secretariat meeting on March 6, 1957," *Zhou Renshan Riji*; "Speeches at the Politburo meeting on May 14, 1957, as conveyed by Fan Ming on June 1, 1957," *Zhou Renshan Riji*.
65. Zhang Guohua, *Zhongyang lingdao tanhua jilu*; "Record of the Central Secretariat meeting on March 8, 1957," *Zhou Renshan Riji*; "Speeches at the Politburo meeting on May 14, 1957, as conveyed by Fan Ming on June 1, 1957," *Zhou Renshan Riji*.
66. Zhang Guohua, *Zhongyang lingdao tanhua jilu*; "Record of the Central Secretariat meeting on March 6, 1957," *Zhou Renshan Riji*.
67. TWC, "Basic conclusions on the work of 1956 and work orientations and tasks for 1957," ZGXLD, 1:106–7; "Record of the Central Secretariat meeting on March 9, 1957," *Zhou Renshan Riji*.
68. *Xiama*, literally meaning dismounting from a horse, is a typical CCP expression about discontinuing a project.
69. "Discussion of the Tibetan question by the Central Secretariat, brief summary (1)," March 5, 1957, ASP: Jianchuan 012-01-397; "Notes on central leaders' directive, March 4, 1957," *Zhou Renshan Riji*; *Dangdai Zhongguo de Xizang* (Tibet of contemporary China) (Beijing: Dangdai Zhongguo Chubanshe, 1991), 1:233; ZGXLD, 1:109. This means that before the pullout, more than forty-three thousand PLA troops were stationed in Tibet. The twelve locations where PLA troops stayed were Lhasa, Chamdo, Shigatse, Ngari, Nagqu, Dengqen, Zhamo, Dromo, Damxung, Jomda, *Gangduo* (岗多), and *Tuoba* (托巴).
70. Since the Preparatory Committee of the Tibetan Autonomous Region was itself set up in anticipation of reform in Tibet, its status became an interesting question after the 1957 retreat. The TWC turned over these enterprises to the PCTAR: three experimental farms, five veterinary teams, three power plants, a blood plasma center, ironworks, and all the hospitals, cadre schools, elementary schools, movie-projecting teams, and art troupes. The abolished units were TWC branches in Lhasa, Shannan (Lhoka), and Tagong (Lhagang), all the CCP committees at the *dzong* level, the transportation bureau, the geological bureau, the food bureau, an office of waterpower inspection, the general team of water conservation, forest stations, an observatory of earth physics, the wired broadcast station, a pig farm, a Shaanxi opera troupe, and logging mills. This information is from "Discussion of the Tibetan question by the Central Secretariat, brief summary (2)," March 6, 1957, ASP: Jianchuan 012-01-397.
71. *Dangdai Zhongguo de Xizang*, 1:233–34; "Record of the Central Secretariat meeting on March 6, 1957," *Zhou Renshan Riji*.
72. *Xizang Gonglu Jiaotongshi* (History of Tibetan highway and transportations) (Beijing: Renmin Jiaotong Chubanshe, 1999), 195–205.
73. Zhang Guohua, *Zhongyang lingdao tanhua jilu*; "Notes on central leaders' directive, March 4, 1957," *Zhou Renshan Riji*.

74. "Records of the Central Secretariat meeting on March 5, 1957," *Zhou Renshan Riji*; "Record of the Central Secretariat meeting on March 6, 1957," *Zhou Renshan Riji*; "Discussion of the Tibetan question by the Central Secretariat, brief summary (1)," March 5, 1957, ASP: Jianchuan 012-01-397.
75. Zhang Guohua, *Zhongyang lingdao tanhua jilu*; "Discussion of the Tibetan question by the Central Secretariat, brief summary (1)," March 5, 1957, ASP: Jianchuan 012-01-397; "Record of the Central Secretariat meeting on March 6, 1957," *Zhou Renshan Riji*.
76. "CCP Sichuan Committee's opinion on whether or not democratic reform should continue in the Garzê Autonomous Prefecture," March 5, 1957, ASP: Jianchuan 001-01-1064.
77. *Mao Zedong Nianpu, 1949–1976*, 3:95–96; *Deng Xiaoping Nianpu*, 3:1350.
78. "Records of the Central Secretariat meeting on March 8, 1957," *Zhou Renshan Riji*.
79. "Records of the Central Secretariat meeting on March 5, 1957," *Zhou Renshan Riji*.
80. *Mao Zedong Waijiao Wenxuan* (Selected writings of Mao Zedong on diplomacy) (Beijing: Zhongyang Wenxian Chubanshe, 1994), 79, note; *Zhou Enlai Nianpu, 1949–1976*, 1:235.
81. "Li Weihan's directive of May 19, 1957, as conveyed by Fan Ming," *Zhou Renshan Riji*.
82. Zhang Guohua, *Zhongyang lingdao tanhua jilu*; "Record of the Central Secretariat meeting on March 8, 1957," *Zhou Renshan Riji*.
83. Zhang Guohua, *Zhongyang lingdao tanhua jilu*; "Record of the Central Secretariat meeting on March 5, 1957," *Zhou Renshan Riji*.
84. Zhang Guohua, *Zhongyang lingdao tanhua jilu*; "Record of the Central Secretariat meeting on March 5, 1957," *Zhou Renshan Riji*.
85. Zhang Guohua, *Zhongyang lingdao tanhua jilu*; "Discussion of the Tibetan question by the Central Secretariat, brief summary (1)," March 5, 1957, ASP: Jianchuan 012-01-397; "Record of the Central Secretariat meeting on March 8, 1957," *Zhou Renshan Riji*.
86. "Discussion of the Tibetan question by the Central Secretariat, brief summary (1)," March 5, 1957, ASP: Jianchuan 012-01-397.
87. *Zhengzhi zhudong* was a cherished item in CCP political stratagems. It does not denote "right of taking political action" but a position of justifiable advantage. Although the closest English translation is "political initiative," the connotation of the term is more moral than political.
88. Zhang Guohua, *Zhongyang lingdao tanhua jilu*; "Record of the Central Secretariat meeting on March 4, 1957," *Zhou Renshan Riji*; "Record of the Central Secretariat meeting on March 8, 1957," *Zhou Renshan Riji*.
89. Zhang Guohua, *Zhongyang lingdao tanhua jilu*; "Record of the Central Secretariat meeting on March 5, 1957," *Zhou Renshan Riji*; "Record of the Central Secretariat meeting on March 8, 1957," *Zhou Renshan Riji*; "Record of the Central Secretariat meeting on March 6, 1957," *Zhou Renshan Riji*.
90. "Record of the Central Secretariat meeting on March 6, 1957," *Zhou Renshan Riji*.
91. *Deng Xiaoping Nianpu*, 3:1400; "Central leader's directive, conveyed by Zhang Jingwu, November 13, 1957," *Zhou Renshan Riji*.
92. *Deng Xiaoping Nianpu*, 3:1351.
93. Fan Ming, *Liunian bugai, shidang shousuo (Fan Ming huiyilu)* (No reform for six years and contraction to a certain degree (Fan Ming's recollection), PCCM; *Fan Ming tongzhi tan 1957 nian zai Beijing de Xizang gongzuo huiyi* (Comrade Fan Ming's talk about the meeting on the Tibet work in Beijing in 1957), October 12–14, 1984, PCCM.

94. Fan Ming, *Liunian bugai, shidang shousuo*; *Fan Ming tongzhi tan 1957 nian zai Beijing de Xizang gongzuo huiyi*.
95. *Zhonggong Xizang Gongwei kuoda huiyi guanyu kaichu fandang jituan touzi Fan Ming de dangji he junji de jueyi* (Resolution of the enlarged CCP Tibet Work Committee meeting on expelling Fan Ming, head of an anti-party clique, from the party and the army), August 3, 1958, PCCM. Fan Ming's letter is partially cited in the document as the eighth of Fan's fifteen alleged crimes.
96. Fan Ming, *Liunian bugai, shidang shousuo*; *Fan Ming Tongzhi tan 1957 nian zai Beijing de Xizang gongzuo huiyi*.
97. According to *Fan Ming tongzhi tan 1957 nian zai Beijing de Xizang gongzuo huiyi*, at the meeting Deng Xiaoping refused to sit together with Liu Shaoqi and Zhou Enlai on the rostrum. A document circulated during the Cultural Revolution, Shanxi Red Liason Headquarters for Repudiating Liu (Shaoqi) and Deng (Xiaoping), "How did the Tibetan rebellion take place? —Exposing the chief culprit Deng Xiaoping, June 26, 1967," portrayed Deng as a very angry person at the Politburo meeting.
98. "Speeches at the Politburo meeting on May 14, 1957, as conveyed by Fan Ming on June 1, 1957," *Zhou Renshan Riji*.
99. "Ambassador Pan Zili conveyed to the Center Consul Ye Chengzhang's report on the Dalai [Lama]," February 11, 1957, *Pingxi Xizang Panluan*, 118–19.
100. Fan Ming, *Liunian bugai, shidang shousuo*.
101. "CCP Center's directive on the orientation of democratic reform and contraction in Tibet," May 14, 1957, XGWX, 198–99.
102. "CCP Center's directive," 200.
103. Fan Ming, *Liunian bugai, shidang shousuo*.
104. Fan Ming, *Liunian bugai, shidang shousuo*; *Fan Ming tongzhi tan 1957 nian zai Beijing de Xizang gongzuo huiyi*.
105. "Center's reply to the Sichuan committee's report on continuation of democratic reform in the Garzê Autonomous Prefecture," May 14, 1957, ASP: Jianchuan 001/01/1064.
106. The pronunciation of Mao's younger daughter's name (李讷) is in dispute. The second character 讷 has been pronounced by many as *na*, but the accurate pronunciation should be *ne*. See the Chinese linguist Tan Yuwei's blog, "Accurate pronunciation of these names, Chen Yinke, Jia Pingwa, Li Ne, and Liu Bei," accessed August 12, 2018, http://blog.sina.com.cn/s/blog_4b6668a10100cyxb.html?tj=1.
107. *Mao Zedong Nianpu (1949–1976)*, 3:195.
108. "Several questions about our state's nationality policies," August 4, 1957, *Zhou Enlai Xuanji*, 2:247–71.
109. "Minutes of Premier Zhou Enlai's conversation with Ngabö (excerpts): Qingdao, the afternoon of August 3, 1957," *Pingxi Xizang Panluan*, 120–24; *Zhou Enlai Nianpu, 1949–1976*, 2:65–66. These sources were published in 1995 and 1997, respectively. Neither contains a complete record of the conversation, and many inconsistencies exist between the two versions.
110. CCP Kangding Area Committee, "Summary of conditions," May 25, 1957, ASP: Jianchuan 012-01-155; ZGXLD, 1:111.
111. ZGXLD, 1:114; "Letter to the Dalai Lama," August 18, 1957, MXGW, 162.
112. Central Organization Department, "Notice on training lower- and middle-echelon cadres for Tibet," May 18, 1957, AGP: 92-005-0018-0072; "CCP Central Committee circular: The leading Party group of the Labor Department's opinion on the procedures of resettlement and reassignment regarding the personnel withdrawn from Tibet," April 24, 1957, ZZWX (2013), 25:276–78.

113. "CCP Sichuan Committee's preliminary report on reviewing the execution of nationality policy in the Tibetan and Yi areas of our province," May 28, 1957, ASP: Jianchuan 001-01-1064; Nationality Work Committee of the CCP Sichuan Committee, "Plan for settling the issue of lamaist monasteries (draft)," August 31, 1957, ASP: Jianchuan 001-01-1068; Office of the Nationality Work Committee of the CCP Sichuan Committee, "A few preliminary proposals for dealing with the issue of monasteries (minutes of an informal discussion; for reference only)," September 17, 1957, ASP: Jianchaun 001-01-1344.
114. Wang Shusheng and Hao Yufeng, *Wulanfu Nianpu* (Chronicle of Ulanhu's life) (Beijing: Zhonggong Dangshi Ziliao Chubanshe, 1989), 378; "The CCP Center's directive on carrying out rectification and socialist education among minority nationalities," October 15, 1957, ZZWX (2013), 26:268–78; Liu Shaoqi, "CCP Central Committee's work report to the second meeting of the 8th national representative conference," May 5, 1958, MZWH, 3:1; "Editorial: Why should local nationalism be opposed?," *People's Daily*, June 27, 1958, MZWH, 3:23–26; "Editorial: Minority nationalities are advancing in high speed," *People's Daily*, October 19, 1958, MZWH, 3:33–36.
115. Jiangbian Jiacuo, *Mao Zedong yu Dalai, Banchan*, 245–46.
116. *Zhonggong Xizang Gongwei kuoda huiyi guanyu kaichu fandang jituan touzi Fan Ming de dangji he junji de jueyi*; ZGXLD, 1:114–17; Fan Ming, *Xizang Neibu Zhizheng*, 351–52, 389–92, 396–99.
117. Wang Feng, "Socialism or Nationalism?," February 9, 1958, MZWH, 3:2–22.
118. ZGXLD, 109; "CCP Tibet Work Committee's decision on its work in Tibet in the years to come (excerpts)," June 6, 1957, *Huihuang de Ershi Shiji Xinzhongguo Da Jilu; Xizang Juan* (Grand records of the glorious new China in the twentieth century: Volume on Tibet) (Beijing: Hongqi Chubanshe, 1999), 686–87; "CCP Center's directive to the TWC on Tibetan trade and finance after the completion of the highways," March 11, 1955, ZZWX, 18:283–85.
119. For an insightful study of this subject, see Shu Guang Zhang, *Beijing's Economic Statecraft During the Cold War, 1949–1991* (Washington, D.C.: Woodrow Wilson Center Press, 2014).
120. Secretary to the Government of India in the External Affairs Department to the Secretary of External Department, Indian Office, London, "Policy towards Tibet," September 19, 1945, Indian Office Records, the British Library: IOLR-L-WS-1-1042; Political Sikkim (A. J. Hopkinson) to Foreign Secretary, New Delhi, April 16, 1946, NAUK: PRO-FO371-53614; "Economic Cooperation with Tibet," record of Nehru's talk with the Tibetan trade mission on January 8, 1949, *Selected Works of Jawaharlal Nehru*, 9:470–72.
121. Howard Donovan, Counselor of American Embassy in New Delhi to Secretary of State, "American Policy toward Tibet," April 12, 1949, NAUS: 893.00 Tibet/4-1249; memo by W. W. Start, "Informal Outline of Present Thinking Respecting Tibet," June 16, 1950, NAUS: 793B.00/6-1650; Embassy in New Delhi to the Secretary of State, September 1, 1951, NAUS: 793B.00/9-151; memo by W. O. Anderson, "Tibetan Wool," November 6, 1951, NAUS: Record Group 59: Records of the Office of China Affairs, P Files, 1948–55, box 23; John Allison, Acting Assistant Secretary for Far Eastern Affairs to the Secretary of Treasury, January 4, 1952, NAUS: Record Group 59: Records of the Office of China Affairs, P Files, 1948–55, box 24; Elting Arnold, Acting Director, Foreign Assets Control, to Chief of the Monetary Affairs staff, att.: Chester Carre, Department of State, January 31, 1952, NAUS: Record Group 59: Records of the Office of China Affairs, P Files, 1948–55, box 23.

122. Department of Commerce of Gansu to the Central Commerce Ministry, "The issue of managing and controlling watches imported through Tibet," February 8, 1954, AGP: 192-001-0008-0647.
123. CCP Sichuan Committee and CCP Xikang Committee to the Center, "Preliminary plan for implementing democratic reform in the agricultural Tibetan areas of Sichuan," September 22, 1955, ASP: Jianchuan 001-01-549.
124. "The Chinese Communist Party Tibet Work Committee's decision on the Tibet work in the future, March 19, 1957," cited in Fan Ming, *Liunian bugai, shidang shousuo*.
125. CCP Center's circular, "Joint report by leading Party groups of the Ministry of Commerce and the National Affairs Commission on basic conditions of trade in the minority regions in past few years and opinions on future work," December 15, 1955, ZZWX (2013), 21:447–62; TWC, "Notice on preventing the RMB from entering Tibet," January 10, 1956, AGP: 42-002-0017-0427.
126. Chen Yang, "The postal administrative bureau of Tibet's report on work in 1955 and opinion about work in the future," April 7, 1956, AGP: 161-002-0014-0649; Ministry of Postal and Telecommunication Services, "Notice on cancelation of the postal line by vehicles from Chamdo to Lhasa along the Sichuan-Tibet Highway and ways of sending mails to Tibet," July 5, 1957, AGP: 161-001-0007-0740; PLA General Department of Logistics and Ministry of Food, "Joint notice on the task of transporting foodstuff to Tibet," July 18, 1957, AGP: 180-001-0017-0181.
127. Tax Bureau of Lanzhou to Tax Bureau of Gansu, "Report on tax exemption on goods brought back by personnel returning from Tibet," August 23, 1957, AGP: 179-001-0002-0503.
128. *Deng Xiaoping Nianpu*, 3:1399.
129. "CCP Committee of Sichuan's request for directive about large amount of silver dollars' flowing into Tibet," October 30, 1957, ASP: Jianchuan 001-01-818.
130. State Council, "Regulations on controlling strictly foreign goods that have been entering the interior from Tibet and other border areas," November 19, 1957, AGP: 192-005-0002-0210; CCP Central Committee, "Reply to the TWC's opinion on dealing with private merchants who came to Tibet and engaged in speculative trade," November 29, 1957, AGP: 192-002-0001-0203.
131. Branch Party Group of the Commerce Department of Gansu, "Report on a Tibetan issue," July 18, 1957, AGP: 192-002-0004-0217. The Tiananmen case involved three Italians, a Japanese, a German, a French, and a Chinese, all accused of being agents of the CIA. The case was publicized in 1951 and also served as the basis of a Chinese movie, *Guoqing Shidianzhong* (Ten o'clock of the national day). For two Chinese narratives of the case, see Zhu Zhen Cai, *Jianguo Chuqi Beijing Fanjiandie Da'an Jishi* (Factual account of important counterespionage cases in Beijing during the early years of the PRC) (Beijing: Zhongguo Shehui Kexue Chubanshe, 2006), 95–118; Bai Xi, *Da Zhenya* (Great suppression) (Beijing: Jincheng Chubanshe, 2000), 2:575–89.
132. Nationality Work Committee of Sichuan, "Preliminary opinion about gradually achieving socialist transformation of the private commercial capital mainly controlled by monasteries and big Tibetan merchants," December 3, 1957, ASP: Jianchuan 001-01-1068.
133. Tax Bureau of the Financial Department of Gansu, "Opinion on the issue of collecting retroactively tariff on imported British and Indian goods from Tibet that did not pay duty," 1957 (n.d., but after September), AGP: 179-001-0013-0483.
134. "Center's approval and circulation of the leading group of the Ministry of Public Security's measures for implementing the Center's directive on controlling strictly

foreign goods that entered interior provinces via Tibet," November 29, 1957, appendix: "Report by the leading Party group of the Ministry of Public Security," November 22, 1957, AGP: 192-002-0002-0203.
135. Ministry of Commerce, "Directive on implementation of the State Council's regulations about controlling strictly foreign goods that entered the interior via Tibet and other border areas," December 16, 1957, AGP: 192-005-0003-1988.
136. State Council, "Regulations on controlling strictly foreign goods that have been entering the interior from Tibet and other border areas," November 19, 1957, AGP: 192-005-0002-0210; Ministry of Commerce, "Directive on implementation of the State Council's regulations about controlling strictly foreign goods that entered the heartland via Tibet and other border areas," December 16, 1957, AGP: 192-005-0003-1988.
137. Ministry of Foreign Affairs to the People's Committees of Gansu, Qinghai, Sichuan, and Yunnan, "The issue of tightening restrictions of traveling abroad by Tibetans in areas other than Tibet," Janury 20, 1958, appendix: Tibet Office of Foreign Affairs, "Request for directive on a number of problems in issuing permits for foreign travel," December 31, 1957, AGP: 128-002-0003-0243; Ministry of Foreign Affairs, Ministry of Public Security, and Commission on Nationality Affairs to the People's Committees of Sichuan, Qinghai, Yunnan, and Gansu and the Tibet Office of Foreign Affairs, "The issue of tightening restrictions of traveling abroad by Tibetans in areas other than Tibet," July 25, 1958, AGP: 128-002-0004-0243.
138. Ministry of Commerce, "Notice to governmental branches of commerce in various places on not sending agents to Tibet to buy goods in the future," January 23, 1959, AGP: 192-002-0008-0573.
139. Ministry of Foreign Trade, "Report for instruction on the issue of administering foreign goods entering into the heartland from Tibet," January 15, 1965, AGP: 192-005-0032-1733.
140. Tax Bureau of the Finance Department of Gansu, "Circular from the Beijing Customs of the People's Republic of China: A newly compiled chart by the customs work group of Qinghai listing dutiable values of the foreign goods imported through Tibet," September 6, 1959, AGP: 179-003-0013-0151.

6. The Showdown

1. Mao Zedong's note to an enlarged meeting of the Politburo, May 26, 1958, and "Comrade Zhou Enlai's letter: On the origin of the term 'leap forward,' " May 26, 1958, Archives of Jilin Province: 1-1-14-75 [hereafter cited as AJP].
2. Mao's speech at the second meeting of the Eighth National Assembly of the CCP, May 17, 1958, AJP: 1-1-14-59.
3. "Premier Zhou's report on the current struggle situation in the Taiwan Strait and our tasks," November 10, 1958, AJP: 1-1-14-94.
4. Chen Yi, "On a few questions in current international situation and work concerning foreign affairs," March 7, 1959, Archives of Changchun Municipality: 1-1-12-48.
5. "In today's world, please see who is the master of all under heaven," editorial from *Jiefang Ribao* (Liberation Daily), May 18, 1941, *Mao Zedong Ji* (Collected writings of Mao Zedong) (Tokyo: Suo Suo Sha, 1983), 7:301–5.
6. Mao's remarks in "Huan Xiang on the falling apart of the Western world," in *Guanyu Jiefang Taiwan Wenti Zhongyao Zhishi Huibian* (Collection of important directives on the issue of liberation of Taiwan), comp. Central Department of Investigation, Archives of Fujian Province: 101-12-160 [hereafter cited as AFP].

7. *Gansu Shengzhi, Di Shi Juan: Junshi Zhi* (Chronicle of Gansu Province, volume 10: Chronicle of military affairs) (Lanzhou: Gansu Renmin Chubanshe, 2001), 1:805–6; *Gansu Shengzhi, Di Wu Juan: Gongan Zhi* (Chronicle of Gansu Province, volume 5: Chronicle of public security) (Lanzhou: Gansu Renmin Chubanshe, 1995), 598; *Gansu Shengzhi, Di Qishi Juan: Minzu Zhi* (Chronicle of Gansu Province, volume 70: Chronicle of nationalities) (Lanzhou: Gansu Renmin Chubanshe, 2003), 34–35.
8. "The Center's approval and circulation of a report to the Center by the Gansu provincial committee on solving the problem of Gannan rebellions," April 11, 1958, AHP: 989-4-44-11; "Speech by comrade Liu Lanting of the Public Security Department of Gansu (excerpts), November 17, 1958," *Gongan Jianshe*, no. 73 (December 16, 1958): 12–17; "Developments in using extensive mass movement to suppress counterrevolutionaries in minority areas: Speech by comrade Li Jiman of the Gansu Public Security Department (excerpts)," *Gongan Jianshe*, no. 73 (December 16, 1958): 19–24.
9. "Developments in pacifying counterrevolutionary armed rebellions and mobilizing the mass to vent their grievances and participate in the movement of suppressing counterrevolutionaries: Speech by comrade Yi Zhulin of the Qinghai Public Security Department (excerpts)," *Gongan Jianshe*, no. 73 (December 16, 1958): 62–66.
10. "Comrade Tan Zhengwen's conclusive speech at the conference on the political and legal work in the northwestern region," November 19, 1958, *Gongan Jianshe*, no. 73 (December 16, 1958): 2–8.
11. Documentary Research Office of the Central Committee of the Chinese Communist Party, *Zhou Enlai Nianpu, 1949–1976* (Chronicle of Zhou Enlai's life, 1949–1976) (Beijing: Zhongyang Wenxian Chubanshe, 1997), 3:517.
12. Political Department of the Revolutionary Committee of Gansu's notice, September 25, 1973: Appendix: Study and Investigation Team of the Ministry of Public Security to Gansu, "Report on investigation of Gansu Province's processing problems left by the struggle of rebellion pacification," July 30, 1973, AGP: 129-006-0005-0094.
13. Political Department of the Revolutionary Committee of Gansu's notice, September 25, 1973.
14. United Front Department of CCP Gansu Committee, "Report on processing remaining issues from the excessive rebellion pacification and anti-feudal struggle in 1958," September 22, 1981, AGP: 95-003-0002-0124.
15. *Qinghai Shengzhi: Dashiji* (Chronicle of Qinghai province: Important events), 259.
16. "The Center's approval and circulation of the report by the Qinghai provincial committee on lessons from the counterrevolutionary armed rebellion in the Xunhua Sala Autonomous County," August 27, 1958, AHP: 855-4-1311-14.
17. "Meng Dingjun's speech at a conference on rebellion pacification," February 28, 1959, AGP: 95-001-0005-0527.
18. "A serious situation of Yunnan border residents' fleeing abroad," *Waishi Dongtai*, no. 59 (February 6, 1959); James Scott, *The Art of Not Being Governed: An Anarchist History of Upland Southeast Asia* (New Haven, Conn.: Yale University Press, 2010).
19. "Chairman Mao's approval and circulation of Qinghai Province's 'Directive on province-wide suppression of rebellions,' " June 24, 1958, AHP: 989-4-44-12.
20. "Speech by comrade Liu Lanting of the Public Security Department of Gansu (excerpts), November 17, 1958," *Gongan Jianshe*, no. 73 (December 16, 1958): 12–17; "Developments in using extensive mass movement to suppress counterrevolutionaries in minority areas: Speech by comrade Li Jiman of the Gansu Public Security Department (excerpts)," *Gongan Jianshe*, no. 73 (December 16, 1958): 19–24; "Developments in suppressing counterrevolutionary armed rebellions and mobilizing the mass to vent their grievances

and participate in the movement of suppressing counterrevolutionaries: Speech by comrade Yi Zhulin of the Qinghai Public Security Department (excerpts)," *Gongan Jianshe*, no. 73 (December 16, 1958): 62–66.

21. ZGXLD, 109; CCP Garzê Prefecture Committee to CCP Sichuan Committee, April 17, 1957, appendix: Public Security Department of the Garzê Tibetan Autonomous Prefecture of Sichuan, "Brief report of March on pacifying rebellion," April 5, 1957, ALC; CCP Garzê Prefecture Committee to CCP Sichuan Committee, "Report on holding three-level cadre conference to examine the execution of the directive of the Secretariat of the CCP Central Committee," November 10, 1957, ASP: Jianchuan 001/01/1064.
22. *Qingbao Jianxun* (Intelligence briefs), no. 11 (April 15, 1958).
23. *Qingbao Jianxun*, no. 20 (May 24, 1958).
24. *Qingbao Jianxun*, no. 30 (July 2, 1958).
25. *Qingbao Jianxun*, no. 31 (July 4, 1958).
26. *Qingbao Jianxun*, no. 35 (July 17, 1958).
27. *Qingbao Jianxun*, no. 51 (August 15, 1958).
28. *Qingbao Jianxun*, no. 63 (September 26, 1958). The name of the Bhutanese king's mother-in-law was Mayeum Choying Wangmo Dorji; she was also known as Rani Choying Wangmo Dorji.
29. "Resolution on public security work in national minority areas adopted at the ninth national conference on public security," August 16, 1958, in *Gongan Jianshe*, no. 69 (December 5, 1958), 13–15. Michael Schoenhals, *Spying for the People: Mao's Secret Agents, 1949–1967* (Cambridge: Cambridge University Press, 2013), is the best study of PRC public security operations. According to Schoenhals (p. 175), 207 ethnic Tibetans were recruited into a public security training class in 1956 and then transferred to Beijing in July 1957. It is not clear from which Tibetan areas they were recruited, and they were not put into operation until the Lhasa revolt of March 1959.
30. These intelligence reports paid close attention to the Dalai Lama's brother Gyalo Thondup, but Gyalo Thondup's memoir, *The Noodle Maker of Kalimpong: The Untold Story of My Struggle for Tibet* (New York: PublicAffairs, 2015), cannot corroborate the details in these reports.
31. ZGXLD, 1:112, 120.
32. "Comrades Deng Xiaoping and Li Fuchun's speeches at a meeting of leading party cadres of Liaoning Province and the Shenyang Military Region," September 27, 1958, AJP: 1-1-14-75.
33. Mao Zedong's speech at the third plenum of the Eighth CCP Central Committee, October 9, 1957, AJP: 1-13-1-19-57.
34. Mao Zedong's speech at the second meeting of the Eighth National Assembly of the CCP, May 17, 1958, AJP: 1-1-14-59.
35. "Chairman Mao's approval and circulation of Qinghai Province's 'directive on province-wide suppression of rebellions,' " June 24, 1958, AHP: 989-4-44-12.
36. Documentary Research Office of the Central Committee of the Chinese Communist Party, *Mao Zedong Nianpu, 1949–1976* (Chronicle of Mao Zedong's life, 1949–1976) (Beijing: Zhongyang Wenxian Chubanshe, 2013), 3:559–60. "Yu Gong," or the Old Fool, is a figure in an ancient Chinese fable who symbolizes perseverance as he tries to move a mountain with a spade.
37. Documentary Research Office of the Central Committee of the Chinese Communist Party, *Deng Xiaoping Nianpu, 1904–1974* (Chronology of Deng Xiaoping's life, 1904–1974) (Beijing: Zhongyang Wenxian Chubanshe, 2009), 3:1400; "Central leaders' directives conveyed by Zhang Jingwu," November 13, 1957, *Zhou Renshan Riji* (Zhou Renshan's diaries).

38. *Su Yu Nianpu* (Chronicle of Su Yu's life) (Beijing: Dangdai Zhongguo Chubanshe, 2006), 620; *Ganzi Zhouzhi* (Chronicle of Garzê prefecture), 768–75.
39. "Comrade Deng Xiaoping's speech at the national conference on united front work," July 11, 1958, AHP: 855-4-1276-1.
40. "CCP Center's telegram replying the TWC on the issue of possible rebellions in the areas of Tibet," July 14, 1958, ZZWX (2013), 28:247–48.
41. In the catalog of the Archives of Yunnan Province, this author saw an entry about a letter from the TWC to the Yunnan leadership in the summer of 1958. Although the archivist did not allow me to see the contents of the letter, the catalog indicated that it was a request for advice on how to implement socialism in a minority region. Obviously, while engaging Tibetan rebels, the TWC's "constructive" thinking had already surpassed the phase of mere "democratic reform."
42. ZGXLD, 1:119–20; *Pingxi Xizang Panluan* (Pacifying the rebellion in Tibet), comp. Committee of the Tibetan Autonomous Region for Collecting Materials on Party History and Leading Group of the Tibetan Military Region for Collecting Materials on Party History (Lhasa: Xizang Renmin Chubanshe, 1995), 66, 217–18; *Deng Xiaoping Nianpu*, 3:1451; ZZWX (2013), 29:16.
43. *Deng Xiaoping Nianpu*, 3:1448–52.
44. ZGXLD, 1:120; Ji Youquan, *Xizang Pingpan Jishi* (Account of rebellion pacification in Tibet) (Lhasa: Xizang Renmin Chubanshe, 1993), 49–55.
45. "Center's directive on a few issues in current work in Tibet (excerpts)," October 11, 1958, *Pingxi Xizang Panluan*, 68–69.
46. ZGXLD, 1:122–23; "Center's reply to the TWC and directive on the Tibet work in the future (excerpts)," January 6, 1959, *Pingxi Xizang Panluan*, 70.
47. "CCP Center's reply to the TWC on the issue of the Dalai clique's plan to send a delegation to Beijing," December 16, 1958, ZZWX (2013), 29:339–40.
48. ZGXLD, 119–26; *Pingxi Xizang Panluan*, 211–20.
49. Lanzhou Military Region, "Notice on holding a site meeting for reviewing rebellion suppressions," January 16, 1959, AGP: 95-006-0003-0394.
50. Leading Party Group on Political and Legal Affairs of the People's Committee of Sichuan Province to the CCP Sichuan Committee, February 26, 1958: Appendix: Department of Civil Administration, "Request for directive on a few issues concerning the migration work in 1958," February 14, 1958, ASP: Jianchuan 001-01-1456.
51. Leading Party Group on Political and Legal Affairs of the People's Committee of Sichuan Province, "Preliminary plan for migration toward the Garzê and Ngawa Tibetan Autonomous Prefectures," August 3, 1958, ASP: Jianchuan 001-01-1456; CCP Garzê Prefecture Committee to CCP Sichuan Committee, "Report on preliminary arrangements for settling migrants in the Garzê Autonomous Prefecture," November 13, 1958, ASP: Jianchuan 001-01-1456; Leading Party Group on Political and Legal Affairs of the People's Committee of Sichuan Province, "Preliminary plan for carrying out the Center's and Provincial Committee's directives about mobilizing a million youths in our province to move to the Tibetan areas to participate in socialist construction," December 12, 1958, ASP: Jianchuan 001-01-1456.
52. Leading Party Group on Political and Legal Affairs of the People's Committee of Sichuan Province, "Preliminary plan for migration toward the Garzê and Ngawa Tibetan Autonomous Prefectures," August 3, 1958, and "Preliminary plan for carrying out the Center's and Provincial Committee's directives about mobilizing a million youths in our province to move to the Tibetan areas to participate in socialist construction," December 12, 1958, ASP: Jianchuan 001-01-1456.

53. *Mao Zedong Nianpu*, 573; *Deng Xiaoping Nianpu*, 3:1482. Aside from those named in the text, the other participants at the meeting were Chen Yi, Tan Zhenlin, Zhang Wentian, Kang Sheng, and Liao Chengzhi.
54. Miao Peiyi, *Miao Peiyi Huiyilu* (Memoirs of Miao Peiyi) (Lhasa: Xizang Renmin Chubanshe, 2005), 266.
55. *Mao Zedong Nianpu*, 574.
56. *Mao Zedong Nianpu*, 575.
57. "Center's reply to the TWC and directive on the Tibet work in the future (excerpts)," January 6, 1959, *Pingxi Xizang Panluan*, 70.
58. *Zhou Enlai Nianpu*, 2:185; "Premier Zhou's speech on the current struggle in the Taiwan region and the Chinese people's anti-imperialist task," November 11, 1958, AFP: 101-12-160.
59. "Remarks in *Qingkuang Jianbao* about the rebellions in Tibet," February 18, 1959, JYMW, 8:46. Note 1 on the same page identifies *Qingkuang Jianbao* (Information brief) as an internal circular compiled by the General Office of the CCP Central Committee, which carried the Xinhua piece dated February 2.
60. "Remarks in and revisions of the report by the Operational Department of the General Staff on the developments of rebellion suppression," February 19, 1959, JYMW, 8:47–48.
61. *Miao Peiyi Huiyilu*, 266.
62. Center to the TWC and CCP committees of all provinces, municipalities, and autonomous regions, "The Center's approval of the TWC's opinion on how to dispose rightists in the Tibet region," January 27, 1959, AHP: 855-5-1563-7.
63. TWC to the Center, "Some information from Chen Jingbo's reporting to the Dalai [Lama] about certain issues since the Monlam festival," February 27, 1959, *Pingxi Xizang Panluan*, 71–73.
64. Zhang Xiangming, *Zhang Xiangming 55 nian Xizang Gongzuo Shilu* (Records of Zhang Xiangming's 55-year work in Tibet), 2006, 81; ZGXLD, 1:127.
65. For two detailed accounts of the event, see Stephan Talty, *Escape from the Land of Snows: The Young Dalai Lama's Harrowing Flight to Freedom and the Making of a Spiritual Hero* (New York: Crown, 2011), and Jianglin Li, *Tibet in Agony: Lhasa, 1959* (Cambridge, Mass.: Harvard University Press, 2016).
66. Documentary Research Office of the Central Committee of the Chinese Communist Party, *Liu Shaoqi Nianpu, 1898–1969* (Chronicle of Liu Shaoqi's life, 1898–1969) (Beijing: Zhongyang Wenxian Chubanshe, 1996), 2:452–53.
67. According to Zhao Shenying, *Zhang Jingwu Zhongyang Zhu Zang Daibiao Zhang Jingwu* (Zhang Jingwu as the Center's Representative in Tibet) (Beijing: Zhongguo Zangxue Chubanshe, 2001), 122–27, and *Zhang Guohua Jiangjun zai Xizang* (General Zhang Guohua in Tibet) (Beijing: Zhongguo Zangxue Chubanshe, 1998), 116–17, the two Zhangs were resting separately in Guangzhou and Hainan when the Lhasa revolt happened.
68. ZGXLD, 1:128.
69. "TWC's report on reactionary upper stratum's inciting the mass to petition for preventing the Dalai Lama from going to the [Tibetan] Military Region," March 10, 1959, ZZWX (2013), 30:319–21; TWC's report to the Center, "Development of the Tibetan reactionary upper stratum's formal activities for 'independence,' " March 11, 1959, *Pingxi Xizang Panluan*, 77–78.
70. Center's extremely urgent and top-secret telegram, March 11, 1959, no. 159 of telegrams received by the General Office of the CCP Hebei Committee, AHP: 855-5-1563-20; "CCP Center's directive to the TWC on countermeasures after the Tibetan upper stratum openly exposed their nature of treason," March 11, 1959, ZZWX (2013), 30:318–19.

71. "TWC's follow-up report on reactionaries' activities," March 11, 1959, "TWC's report about five resolutions adopted by a reactionary meeting inside the Norbulingka," March 11, 1959, and "TWC party secretary Zhou Renshan's report via telephone about the rebellion situation in Lhasa," March 12, 1959, ZZWX (2013), 30:330–33.
72. Center's extremely urgent and top-secret telegram, March 12, 1959, no. 160 of telegrams received by the General Office of the CCP Hebei Committee, AHP: 855-5-1563-22; "CCP Center's reply to the TWC on the orientation of dealing with the rebellion of the Tibet reactionary upper stratum," March 12, 1959, ZZWX (2013), 30:329–30.
73. Center's extremely urgent and top-secret telegram, March 12, 1959, no. 157 of telegrams received by the General Office of the CCP Hebei Committee, AHP: 855-5-1563-21. The underlined content is not in the archived version of Mao's message but curiously appears in *Mao Zedong Nianpu*, 3:630. The reason for the discrepancy is unknown.
74. Zhang Xiangming, *Zhang Xiangming*, 81.
75. CCP Central Document No. 241 (59), "Center's circular summarizing conditions in Tibet from March 10 to March 12," March 13, 1959, AHP: 855-5-1563-23.
76. "(Top secret) Center's circular summarizing conditions in Tibet from March 11 to March 14 (2)," March 16, 1959, AHP: 855-5-1563-24. According to Tsepon Wangchuck Deden Shakabpa, *One Hundred Thousand Moons: An Advanced Political History of Tibet* (Leiden: Brill, 2010), 81, Drungtsi was an eight-member committee consisting of four monk secretaries and four lay accountants. Its responsibility was to communicate with the Dalai Lama and the Kashag on behalf of the Tibetan National Assembly.
77. CCP Central Document No. 262 (59), "CCP Central Committee (circular): Conditions of Tibet (3)," March 18, 1959, AHP: 855-5-1563-25.
78. Jambey Gyatso, *Xueshan Mingjiang Tan Guansan* (Renowned snow mountain general Tan Guansan) (Beijing: Zhongguo Zangxue Chubanshe, 2001), 140–46; ZGXLD, 1:131–32.
79. *Mao Zedong Nianpu*, 3:596–628.
80. *Mao Zedong Nianpu*, 3:633.
81. MXGW, 166, note 2.
82. *Deng Xiaoping Nianpu*, 3:1496.
83. Huang Kecheng was the chief of General Staff of the PLA and Lei Yingfu was in charge of the Operational Department of the PLA General Staff.
84. Yang Shangkun, *Yang Shangkun Riji* (Yang Shangkun's diaries) (Beijing: Zhongyang Wenxian Chubanshe, 2001), 366; *Mao Zedong Nianpu*, 3:635–36.
85. *Yang Shangkun Riji*, 366; Zhao Shenying, *Zhang Guohua*, 118; Zhao Shenying, *Zhang Jingwu*, 132.
86. CCP Central Document No. 263 (59), "CCP Central Committee (circular): Conditions of Tibet (4)," March 18, 1959, AHP: 855-5-1563-26.
87. "Center's circular on the situation of Tibet (6)," March 20, 1959, AHP: 855-5-1563-28; "(Top secret) Situation of Tibet (7)," March 22, 1959, AHP: 855-5-1563-29.
88. "(Top secret) Center's circular summarizing conditions of Tibet from March 11 to March 14 (2)," March 16, 1959, AHP: 855-5-1563-24, and CCP Central Document No. 263 (59), "CCP Central Committee (circular): Conditions of Tibet (4)," March 18, 1959, AHP: 855-5-1563-26, indicate that the notion of "peaceful negotiation" was raised at a meeting inside the Norbulingka on March 12 and was conveyed to the TWC in the name of the Kashag on March 15. There is no evidence that Beijing ever considered a response to the idea.
89. "TWC's opinion about carrying out the Center's March 11 directive," March 15, 1959, *Pingxi Xizang Panluan*, 85–87.
90. Ding Sheng, *Luonan Yingxiong: Ding Sheng Jiangjun Huiyilu* (Ill-fated hero: General Ding Sheng's memoirs) (Hong Kong: Thinker Publishing, 2009), 139.

91. Jambey Gyatso, *Tan Guansan*, 150.
92. Jambey Gyatso, *Mao Zedong yu Dalai, Banzhan* (Mao Zedong and Dalai and Panchen) (Hong Kong: Xindalu Chubanshe, 2008), 209; Ji Youquan, *Xizang Pingpan Jishi* (Account of rebellion pacification in Tibet) (Lhasa: Xizang Renmin Chubanshe, 1993), 88, 92, 111.
93. ZGXLD, 1:134. Yang Shangkun's diary entry on March 19, *Yang Shangkun Riji*, 1:367, indicates that according to the TWC, the Dalai Lama fled either on March 16 or 17. As mentioned previously, the time of the Dalai Lama's flight in the Center's sixth circular is the late evening of March 17 or the early morning of March 18. This discrepancy may be caused by a clerical error on Yang's part.
94. For instance, ZGXLD, 1:134–35, suggests that the battle began with rebels' shooting at PLA troops stationed in Ramagang on the early morning of March 20, but *Mao Zedong Nianpu*, 3:636, asserts that Tibetan rebels launched a full-scale attack on PLA troops in Lhasa on the evening of March 19.
95. *Xizang Zizhiqu Zhi (Junshi Zhi)* (Chronicle of the Tibetan Autonomous Region: Chronicle of military affairs) (Beijing: Zhongguo Zangxue Chubanshe, 2007), 484; Ji Youquan, *Xizang Pingpan Jishi*, 95–101; Jambey Gyatso, *Tan Guansan*, 151–53.
96. Zhang Xiangming, *Zhang Xiangming*, 85–86.
97. The Panchen Lama to Tan Guansan and Zhou Renshan, March 19, 1959, *Pingxi Xizang Panluan*, 88. In the message, the Panchen Lama expressed gratitude to the TWC for showing concern about his well-being, which proves that the Panchen Lama did not initiate the communication but was responding to a query from the TWC.
98. Ji Youquan, *Xizang Pingpan Jishi*, 111, suggests that after reporting the Dalai Lama's flight to Beijing, Tan and associates remained uncertain about the Dalai Lama's departure from the Norbulingka and were hesitant for a while in authorizing PLA troops' bombardment of the palace. "(Top secret) Situation of Tibet (7)," March 22, 1959, AHP: 855 5 1563 29, indicates that the Dalai Lama's departure was verified at the battle of Lhasa.
99. Ji Youquan, *Xizang Pingpan Jishi*, 100.
100. ZGXLD, 1:132.
101. *Guanyu Pingpan Wenti* (On the issue of rebellion pacification), 1959, PCCM. This is a report delivered by an unknown high-ranking PLA officer, probably from the PLA General Staff. The report indicates that he made the report on behalf of Huang Kecheng; "Central Military Affairs Commission on the operational deployment of troops for rebellion pacification and their command relationship (excerpts)," March 20, 1959, *Pingxi Xizang Panluan*, 91–92.
102. "Comrade Zhang Jingwu's report on the Tibet question (version based on notes)," April 16, 1959, AHP: 855-5-1563-31.
103. "Central Military Affairs Commission's directive on rebellion pacification in the Lhoka area and the current work," April 23, 1959, *Pingxi Xizang Panluan*, 99–101.
104. MXGW, 152–53.
105. "Center's directive to the TWC on the issue of not announcing the Dalai [Lama]'s escape for the moment," March 20, 1959, *Pingxi Xizang Panluan*, 89.
106. "PLA Tibet Military Region's public notice," March 20, 1959, *Pingxi Xizang Panluan*, 134–35; "About issuing a communiqué on the rebellion in Tibet and other issues," March 27, 1959, MXGW, 168; "Xinhua's press release on the rebellion in Tibet," March 28, 1959, MZWH, 3:118–23.
107. "About rebellion pacification in Tibet," April 15, 1959, MXGW, 175–80; "Policy orientations after rebellion pacification in Tibet," May 7, 1959, MXGW, 195–200,

108. "Comrade Zhang Jingwu's report on the Tibet question (version based on notes)," April 16, 1959, AHP: 855-5-1563-31; *Guanyu Pingpan Wenti*, 1959, PCCM.
109. The CCP leadership circulated its documents and directives to different levels of society according to the nature of the matters involved. The county level in the PRC administrative system and the regiment level in the PLA were the lowest ones that its directives would reach directly.
110. "Some upper-stratum democratic figures' reactions to the incident of Tibet rebellion," and "Reactions of some democratic figures in Shanghai to the incident of Tibet rebellion," *Lingxun* (Miscellaneous information) 59, no. 0036 (April 1, 1959): 1–7; "Reactions of students, workers, and cadres of provincial and municipality offices to the rebellion of the Tibetan local government," and "Reactions of the provincial and municipality political consultative councils, democratic figures, and industrial and commercial circles to the rebellion of the Tibetan local government," *Sixiang Dongtai* (Trend of thoughts), comp. Propaganda Department of the CCP Yunnan Committee, no. 20 (April 2, 1959): 1–6; "Reactions to the Tibet question," and "Symposium on the Tibet question in the Xinjiang Teacher's College," *Sixiang Dongtai*, comp. Propaganda Department of the CCP Committee of the Xinjiang Autonomous Region, no. 6 (April 2, 1959): 2–6; "General survey of reactions on the rebellion pacification in Tibet from non-partisan figures in various circles in a number of cities," *Lingxun*, (59) 0037 (April 4, 1959): 1–6; "Reactions of upper-stratum figures of various national minorities in Yunnan to the incident of Tibet rebellion," *Lingxun*, (59) 0039 (April 7, 1959): 2–4.
111. *Guanyu Pingpan Wenti*, 1959, PCCM.
112. "Center's communication on a TWC report on the situations and attitudes of various social strati of Tibet," April 29, 1959, AHP: 855-5-1563-32.
113. *Deng Xiaoping Nianpu*, 3:1496; *Zhou Enlai Nianpu*, 2:213.
114. "Comrade Zhang Jingwu's report on the Tibet question (version based on notes)," April 16, 1959, AHP: 855-5-1563-31.
115. Clearly leaders in Beijing did not think the Dalai Lama was abducted on March 17, 1959. Yet, according to a piece of CCP intelligence, *Qingbao Jianxun*, no. 18, dated May 27, 1959, the Dalai Lama told Nehru that in the last few hours before his flight, he was forced by people around him to accept the decision. The same intelligence also said that the Dalai Lama professed respect for leaders in Beijing and wanted to return to Lhasa, but he was stopped by his entourage.
116. *Guanyu Pingpan Wenti*, 1959, PCCM.
117. "Comrade Zhang Jingwu's report on the Tibet question (version based on notes)," April 16, 1959, AHP: 855-5-1563-31.
118. *Mao Zedong Nianpu*, 4:12–13.
119. Central United Front Department, "Notification about collecting materials on basic conditions of the Tibetan areas," April 8, 1959, AGP: 95-001-0527.
120. "On rebellion pacification in Tibet," April 15, 1959, MXGW, 175–80. According to *Mao Zedong Nianpu*, 4:13, in April 1959 all the designated provinces except Yunnan submitted reports in response to the Central United Front Department's inquiry on Mao's behalf. In late April, Mao directed Hu Qiaomu to republish an article from *Guangming Ribao*, titled "Backward, dark, reactionary, and cruel social system of Tibet," in *People's Daily* and in a Xinhua news release, saying that it was needed both in China and abroad. MXGW, 192.
121. "Conversation with the Italian communist delegation," April 19, 1959, MXGW, 183–85.
122. CCP United Front Department of Gansu, "Report on the basic conditions of the Tibetan areas in our province," April 14, 1959, AGP: 95-001-0527.

123. Political Department of the Lanzhou Military Region, "Situation of the rebellion pacification struggle in Gansu and Qinghai in this year and our opinion for the future," July 10, 1959, AGP: 91-008-0250.
124. "People of Tibet treat the PLA like family members and support the PLA's rebellion pacification," April 28, 1959, MXGW, 189–90.
125. "Premier Zhou's speech at the first meeting of the Standing Committee of the Third National Committee of the Political Consultative Conference," May 12, 1959, ASP: Jianchuan 012-01-342.
126. *Guanyu Pingpan Wenti*, 1959, PCCM.
127. ZGXLD, 1:138–39.
128. "Center's notification on assigning cadres to Tibet," May 13, 1959, AHP: 855-5-1564-4. The fourteen provinces were Gansu, Sichuan, Qinghai, Anhui, Hebei, Henan, Hubei, Hunan, Jiangsu, Jiangxi, Shaanxi, Shandong, Shanxi, and Zhejiang. Beijing was careful not to include cadres of nationalities other than Han and Tibetan in the forthcoming work in Tibet. Therefore, Yunnan, one of Tibet's neighbors, and those "autonomous regions" were not required to send cadres, even though "nationality work" was their daily undertaking.
129. *Zhou Enlai Nianpu*, 2:22, 226–27; "Center's directive on the draft decisions of the TWC about several issues in the current work of suppressing rebellions," May 31, 1959, AHP: 855-5-1563-33.
130. When talking to Zhang Guohua in December 1960, Zhou Enlai told Zhang that land certificates must be issued to former serfs and forced organization of cooperatives must be stopped. *Zhou Enlai Nianpu*, 2:375–76.
131. "Center's directive on the orientation of the Tibet work," April 21, 1961, *Zhou Enlai yu Xizang* (Zhou Enlai and Tibet), comp. the Office of Party History of the Tibetan Autonomous Region (Beijing: Zhongguo Zangxue Chubanshe, 1998), 90–100.
132. "TWC's request for directive in respect to education among the people of all strata for exposing the Dalai [Lama]'s crimes of treason," May 26, 1963, ASP: Jianchuan 012-01-303; CCP Center, "Reply to the TWC's request for directive in respect to education among the people of all strata for exposing the Dalai [Lama]'s crimes of treason," June 14, 1963, ASP: Jianchuan 012-01-303.
133. "TWC's request for directive in respect to education among the people of all strata for exposing the Dalai [Lama]'s crimes of treason," May 26, 1963, ASP: Jianchuan 012-01-303; "CCP Sichuan Committee's transferring of the provincial nationality work committee's opinion about carrying out the Center's directive about the TWC's 'Education among the people of all strata for exposing the Dalai [Lama]'s crimes of treason,'" July 31, 1963, ASP: Jianchuan 012-01-303; "CCP Garzê Prefecture Committee on carrying out the provincial nationality work committee's opinion about 'Education among the people of all strata for exposing the Dalai [Lama]'s crimes of treason,' transferred by the provincial committee," August 1963, ASP: Jianchuan 012-01-303; Propaganda and United Front Departments of the CCP Garzê Prefecture Committee, "Important points to be implemented in exposing the Dalai [Lama]'s crimes of treason among the people of all strata," September 7, 1963, ASP: Jianchuan 012-01-303; TWC's leading group on exposing the Dalai (Lama)'s crimes of treason transferring the Chamdo Branch Committee of the TWC's work team in Jialin Village, "Report on the educational campaign for exposing the Dalai [Lama]'s crimes of treason among the mass," October 28, 1963, ASP: Jianchuan 012-01-325; CCP Sichuan Nationality Work Committee to CCP Garzê and Ngawa Prefecture

Committees and various county committees, transferring "Opinions about several issues in the current education for exposing the Dalai [Lama]'s crimes by the TWC leading group on exposing the Dalai [Lama]'s crime of treason," November 18, 1963, ASP: Jianchuan 012-01-325; Central Propaganda and United Front Departments' transferring the TWC, "Propaganda materials for exposing the Dalai [Lama]'s crimes of treason," December 26, 1963, ASP: Jianchuan 012-01-325; CCP Garzê Prefecture Committee's transferring the prefecture united front committee, "Conclusive report on carrying out education among nationality and religious upper-stratum figures for exposing the Dalai [Lama]'s crimes of treason," February 23, 1964, ASP: Jianchuan 012-01-325.

134. "Zhou Enlai's conversation with the Panchen [Lama] and others (excerpts)," July 24, 1962, *Zhou Enlai yu Xizang*, 229–30; "Comrade Li Weihan's report at the nationality work conference," May 23, 1962, ASP: Jianchua 012-01-451; *Guanyu Pingpan Wenti*, 1959, PCCM.
135. ZGXLD, 1:224, 238.
136. Leading Party Group of the Gansu Administrative Bureau of Post and Telecommunication to the CCP Committees of the Lanzhou Municipality Bureau of Telecommunication and the Post Office and the Party branches of the post offices at various levels of the province, October 26, 1962, AGP: 161-001-0013-0575.
137. "On the issue of communication and transportation in the area of Tibet," *Quanguo Jihua Huiyi Jianbao* (Bulleting of the national conference on planning), no. 15 (September 19, 1963): 1–3.
138. Wang Shusheng and Hao Yufeng, *Wulanfu Nianpu* (Chronicle of Ulanhu's life) (Beijing: Zhonggong Dangshi Ziliao Chubanshe, 1989), 493.
139. "Center's communication on a TWC report on the situations and attitudes of various social strata of Tibet," April 29, 1959, AHP: 855-5-1563-32.
140. Dorje Tseten, "Esteemed Premier Zhou remembered," *Zhou Enlai yu Xizang*, 294.
141. "CCP Center's directive about the summary of the first nationality work conference of the northwestern region," December 6, 1961, ZZWX (2013), 38:376–77; Deng Xiaoping's comments on behalf of the Center on a "Report about the nationality work conference," June 20, 1962, *Deng Xiaoping Nianpu*, 3:1711; Zhou Enlai's conversation with Panchen and Ngabö, July 24, 1962, *Zhou Enlai Nianpu*, 2:490–91; "Zhou Enlai's report on the government work delivered to the first meeting of the third National People's Congress (excerpts)," December 21–22, 1964, *Zhou Enlai yu Xizang*, 237; Chen Mingyi, "Several of Premier Zhou Enlai's important directives during the 'Cultural Revolution' remembered," *Zhou Enlai yu Xizang*, 287.
142. "Democratic figures' reactions after seeing the exhibition on the crimes of upper-stratum Tibetan reactionaries of Sichuan, Gansu, and Qinghai," *Lingxun*, (59) 0072 (May 18, 1959), 8.
143. "Premier Zhou's speech at the first meeting of the Standing Committee of the Third National Committee of the Political Consultative Conference," May 12, 1959, ASP: Jianchuan 012-01-342.
144. Zhang Chuanxi, "Hu Hua and *Synopsis of Chinese History*," *Bainian Chao* (Century tide), no. 9 (2011): 42–47.
145. "*Synopsis of Chinese History*'s narrative about Tibet," *Xuanjiao Dongtai* (Trends of propaganda and education), no. 46 (June 24, 1959): 14.
146. "Lan Jixi's absurd proposal for solving the Tibetan question," *Lingxun*, (59) 0088 (July 9, 1959): 7–8.

Epilogue

1. Documentary Research Office of the Central Committee of the Chinese Communist Party, *Mao Zedong Nianpu, 1949–1976* (Chronicle of Mao Zedong's life, 1949–1976) (Beijing: Zhongyang Wenxian Chubanshe, 2013), 1:230; "Premier Zhou Enlai's report at the foreign affairs conference of 1953," June 5, 1953, ACMFA: 102-00110-01.
2. Documentary Research Office of the Central Committee of the Chinese Communist Party, *Zhou Enlai Nianpu, 1949–1976* (Chronicle of Zhou Enlai's life, 1949–1976) (Beijing: Zhongyang Wenxian Chubanshe, 1997), 2:4; Chinese Ministry of Foreign Affairs' note to the Indian Government, July 10, 1958, *Pingxi Xizang Panluan* (Pacifying the rebellion in Tibet), comp. Committee of the Tibetan Autonomous Region for Collecting Materials on Party History and Leading Group of the Tibetan Military Region for Collecting Materials on Party History (Lhasa: Xizang Renmin Chubanshe, 1995), 125–27; Central Investigation Department of the CCP, *Qingbao Jianxun* (Intelligence brief), no. 13 (April 13, 1959); Ministry of Public Security of the PRC, *Gongan Gongzuo Jianbao* (Brief on public security work), no. 4 (January 21, 1960); CCP Committee of the Lanzhou Military Region, "Report about the Xining symposium on rebellion suppression," September 15, 1960, AGP: 91-009-0002-0067.
3. Eric Hyer, *Pragmatic Dragon: China's Grand Strategy and Boundary Settlements* (Vancouver: University of British Columbia Press, 2015), 263.
4. *Mao Zedong Nianpu, 1949–1976*, 3:262–63, 658.
5. Research Bureau of the Central Investigation Department of the CCP, *Diaocha Ziliao* (Investigative materials), no. 12 (April 11, 1959).
6. "Memo for McGeorge Bundy," June 26, 1962, Papers of John F. Kennedy, box 107: National Security Files; Countries: India, general [hereafter cited as PJFK]; John J. Czyzak to Grant, "China-India Border Disputes," November 2, 1962, PJFK, box 108: National Security Files; Countries: India, general.
7. State Department to U.S. embassies in Karachi and London, "CENTO and SEATO," October 31, 1962, PJFK, box 107: National Security Files; Countries: India, general; Dean Rusk to U.S. embassies in Phnom Penn and Djakarta, November 1, 1962, PJFK, box 108: National Security Files; Countries: India, general.
8. Dennis Kux, *The United States and Pakistan, 1947–2000: Disenchanted Allies* (Washington, D.C.: Woodrow Wilson Center Press, 2001), 115–46, offers a detailed account of American policy toward Pakistan in the context of the Sino-Indian border war.
9. William H. Brubeck, "Memorandum for Mr. McGeorge Bundy," November 3, 1962, PJFK, box 108: National Security Files; Countries: India, general; Kirk to Secretary of State, October 27, 1962, PJFK, box 107: National Security Files; Countries: India, general; U.S. embassy in Taipei to Secretary of State, October 29, 1962, PJFK, box 107: National Security Files. As suggested in Bruce Riedel, *JFK's Forgotten Crisis: Tibet, the CIA, and the Sino-Indian War* (Washington, D.C.: Brookings Institution Press, 2015), 120, Kennedy's White House went around the State Department in supporting India's territorial claim.
10. Rusk to the American embassy in Taipei, October 29, 1962, PJFK, box 107: National Security Files; Countries: India, general; Thomas Hughes to Rostow, June 25, 1962, PJFK, box 107: National Security Files; Roger Hilsman to Secretary of State, October 26, 1962, PJFK, box 107: National Security Files; Carle Kaysen, "Record of Meeting with the President," October 26, 1962, PJFK, box 107: National Security Files; Galbraith to Secretary of State, October 29, 1962, PJFK, box 107: National Security Files.

11. *Zhou Enlai Nianpu*, 2:545; record of Zhou Enlai's conversation with Indian chargé d'affaires P. K. Banerjee, December 3, 1963, ACMFA: 105-01855-01.
12. The best study of the PRC-Indian relationship is John W. Garver, *Protracted Contest: Sino-Indian Rivalry in the Twentieth Century* (Seattle: University of Washington Press, 2002).
13. I have discussed the CCP's territorial ideology in "The genesis and development of the Chinese Communist Party's territorial ideology, 1921–1949," *Ershiyi Shiji* (Twenty-First Century), 2017 (4): 13–34, and Beijing's policy analyses regarding India in "Friend or Foe: India as Perceived by Beijing's Foreign Policy Analysts in the 1950s," *China Review* 15, no. 1 (Spring 2015): 117–44.
14. "Goals and plans for Premier Zhou Enlai's visit in India," June 22, 1954, ACMFA: 203-00005-01; "Minutes of Chairman Mao's first conversation with Nehru," October 19, 1954, ACMFA: 204-00007-01; "Minutes of Chairman Mao's third conversation with Nehru," October 26, 1954, ACMFA: 204-00007-17; "Premier Zhou Enlai's conversation with newly appointed Indian ambassador to China R. K. Nehru in respect to Sino-American relations and other issues," November 5, 1955, ACMFA: 105-00062-02; "Minutes of Chairman Mao's conversation with Indian ambassador Nehru and Mrs. Nehru," January 23, 1958, ACMFA: 105-00372-02.
15. John Galbraith to Kennedy, May 7, 1962, PJFK, box 106a: National Security Files; Countries: India, general. According to Bertli Lintner, *Great Game East: India, China, and the Struggle for Asia's Most Volatile Frontier* (New Haven, Conn.: Yale University Press, 2015), 40–79, Beijing made contacts with the Naga rebels after the 1962 border war with India.
16. *Zhou Enlai Nianpu*, 2:212; "Foreign reaction to the Tibetan rebellion and our countermeasures," *Waishi Dongtai*, no. 31 (March 25, 1959); "Possible steps and existent worries of India after the Dalai [Lama]'s escape to India," *Diaocha Ziliao*, no. 10 (April 10, 1959).
17. *Mao Zedong Nianpu, 1949–1976*, 4:28–29.
18. Chinese Embassy in India to the Ministry of Foreign Affairs and the Central Investigation Department, May 6, 1959, ACMFA: 109-01354-04.
19. "Kalimpong is the commanding center of the Tibetan rebellion," *Qingbao Jianxun*, no. 12 (April 4, 1959); TWC and TMR, "Conclusions on the work of border defense in 1960," June 2, 1961, ACMFA: 118-00955-12.
20. *Mao Zedong Nianpu, 1949–1976*, 4:48–49, 52–53; *Zhou Enlai Nianpu*, 2:274.
21. "Premier Zhou Enlai's second interview with the former British High Commissioner to India McDonald and conversation about Chinese-British relations, the 'two China' question, and the issue of Sino-Indian borders," October 31, 1962, ACMFA: 110-01107-06.
22. Foreign Affairs Office of Tibet, "Assessment of and suggested countermeasures against current Indian activities about Tibet," March 29, 1961, ACMFA: 118-00955-05; TWC and TMR, "Conclusions on the work of border defense in 1960," June 2, 1961, ACMFA: 118-00955-12; "Indian Secretary of Foreign Affairs R. K. Nehru's visit in China (6): Minutes of the conversation between Nehru and Premier Zhou Enlai and Vice Premier Chen Yi during their meeting and a banquet," July 16, 1961, ACMFA: 105-01774-03; "New trends of India's external expansion," November 24, 1961, ACMFA: 105-01456-02; *Zhou Enlai Nianpu*, 2:490; "TMR's regulations for rewarding rallied rebellious bandits, and the related directives from the Central United Front Department and the General Political Department of the PLA," October 21, 1963, ACMFA: 105-01277-03.
23. *Mao Zedong Nianpu, 1949–1976*, 4:235–36.

24. Chiang Kai-shek, "Statement to the Tibetan compatriots," *Xizang Zai Zhandou Zhong* (Tibet is fighting) (Taipei: Haiwai Chubanshe, 1959), 29; Tao Xisheng, "Influence and development of the Tibetan revolution," *Xizang Zai Zhandou Zhong*, 72.
25. "Chiang Kai-shek sent people to India secretly to comfort Tibetan rebels," and "The Chiang clique directed the Chiang bandit troops fleeing into Burma to increase harassments along our borders so as to coordinate with the Tibetan rebellion," *Qingbao Jianxun*, no. 15 (April 30, 1959); "Under the direction of Jiang Jingguo, Chiang's secret agencies made a 'yellow dragon plan' for sabotaging us comprehensively," *Qingbao Jianxun*, no. 23 (July 2, 1959); "Rebels increased significantly in the Chamdo area," *Gongan Gongzuo Jianbao*, no. 8 (January 26, 1960); *Zhou Enlai Nianpu*, 2:304–5.
26. "The Chiang clique already felt it difficult to take advantage of the Tibetan rebellion," *Taiwan Qingkuang* (Conditions of Taiwan), no. 2 (April 23, 1959); "Chiang's attitude toward and plot about the Chinese-Indian borders and the Tibetan question," *Taiwan Qingkuang*, no. 11 (September 22, 1959); "The Chiang clique admired our stance about Tibet and India," *Qingkuang Jianbao*, no. 1 (January 10, 1960).
27. "Reflections about last week," July 31, 1949, *Chiang Kai-shek Diaries* (Hoover Institution, Stanford), box 47: folder 15; "Chronicle of important events in the 39th year of the ROC," January 15, 1950, *Chiang Kai-shek Diaries*, box 48: folder 1.
28. Entries for March 22, 25, 29, April 3, 11, and May 31, 1959, *Chiang Kai-shek Diaries*, box 67: folders 7–9.
29. "Reflections about last month," May 31, 1956, *Chiang Kai-shek Diaries*, box 65: folder 6.
30. Entries for March 21, 25, 26, 29, and April 11, 1959, *Chiang Kai-shek Diaries*, box 67: folders 7–8; entry for October 29, 1962, *Chiang Kai-shes Diaries*, box 69: folder 16.
31. "Chronicle of important events in the 39th year of the ROC," January 15, 1950, *Chiang Kai-shek Diaries*, box 48: folder 1; "Reflections on last week," November 19, 1950, *Chiang Kai-shek Diaries*, box 48: folder 12.
32. The best studies include Shen Zhihua et al., *Zhong Su Guanxi Shigang, 1917–1991* (Outline history of the Chinese-Soviet relationship, 1917–1991) (Beijing: Xinhua Chubanshe, 2007); Lorenz M. Luthi, *The Sino-Soviet Split* (Princeton, N.J.: Princeton University Press, 2008); Sergey Radchenko, *Two Suns in the Heavens: The Sino-Soviet Struggle for Supremacy, 1962–1967* (Stanford, Calif.: Stanford University Press, 2009); Austin Jersild, *The Sino-Soviet Alliance: An International History* (Chapel Hill: University of North Carolina Press, 2014); and Jeremy Friedman, *Shadow Cold War: The Sino-Soviet Competition for the Third World* (Chapel Hill: University of North Carolina Press, 2015).
33. *Mao Zedong Nianpu, 1949–1976*, 4:32–33; Chinese embassy in Moscow to the Ministry of Foreign Affairs about Soviet reactions to the Tibetan situation, March 27, 1959, ACMFA: 109-01354-04; Zhang Wentian's telegram to the Ministry of Foreign Affairs about his conversation with Andrei Gromyko, May 5, 1959, ACMFA: 109-01354-04.
34. "Report by Yuri Andropov, 'On the Situation in Tibet,' " March 31, 1959, History and Public Policy Program Digital Archive, TsKhSD, f. 5, op. 49, d. 238, ll. 42–48 (R. 8929), translated from Russian by David Wolff and published in Cold War International History Project (CWIHP) Working Paper No. 30, http://digitalarchive.wilsoncenter.org/document/118751; EJDX, 8:337–39.
35. *Zhou Enlai Nianpu*, 2:224; MXGW, 203–4. These briefings took place on May 6 and 10, 1959.
36. "Record of Conversation of N. S. Khrushchev with CC CCP Chairman Mao Zedong, Deputy Chairman Liu Shaoqi, Zhou Enlai, Zhu De, Lin Biao, Politburo members Peng Zhen and Chen Yi, and Secretariat member Wang Jiaxiang," October 02, 1959, History and Public Policy Program Digital Archive, Archives of the President of the

Russian Federation, copy on Reel 17, Volkogonov Collection, Library of Congress, Washington, D.C., translated by David Wolff. http://digitalarchive.wilsoncenter.org/document/118883.
37. *Mao Zedong Nianpu, 1949–1976*, 3:648–49, and 4:201–3.
38. "Record of conversation of Deng Xiaoping with brotherly party delegations from twelve Latin American states," June 30 1960, ACMFA: 102-00036-14.
39. Zhang Wentian's telegram to the Ministry of Foreign Affairs about his conversation with Andrei Gromyko, May 5, 1959, ACMFA: 109-01354-04.
40. "Premier Zhou Enlai's discussion of Laos and India with Soviet ambassador Chervonenko," May 9, 1961, ACMFA: 109-03757-01.
41. "Record of conversation of Premier Zhou Enlai and Vice Premier Chen Yi with Indonesian Vice Prime Minister and Foreign Minister Subandrio," January 3, 1963, ACMFA: 105-01792-01.
42. Friedman, *Shadow Cold War*, 43–44.
43. *Mao Zedong Nianpu, 1949–1976*, 4:231–33.
44. *Zhou Enlai Nianpu*, 2:281, 283.
45. Documentary Research Office of the Central Committee of the Chinese Communist Party, *Deng Xiaoping Nianpu, 1904–1974* (Chronology of Deng Xiaoping's life, 1904–1974) (Beijing: Zhongyang Wenxian Chubanshe, 2009), 3:1594–95. In November 1960, Deng told a Vietnamese delegation that Beijing was forced to debate with the Soviets because the latter attacked Mao's five ideas: "east wind," "paper tiger," no fear of a nuclear war, opposition by Indian reactionaries being a good thing, and Mao Zedong Thought.
46. "The Soviet attitude toward the Sino-Indian border issue and the question of Soviet-Indian relations," n.d. (after October 1962), ACMFA: 105-01272-01.
47. *Zhou Enlai Nianpu*, 2:595.
48. "CCP Central Committee's reply to the letter from the Central Committee of the Soviet Communist Party to the Central Committee of our Party on the issue of India-Pakistan relations," October 18, 1965, ACMFA: 109-03980-02. Wang Bingnan and Wu Xiuquan prepared the letter, then Kang Sheng forwarded it to Deng Xiaoping for approval.
49. "TWC's opinion about several important issues of socialist transformation in Tibet (draft plan)," August 1, 1965, ACMFA: 118-01808-01; "Center's directive about the issue of carrying out socialist transformation in Tibet," August 29, 1965, ACMFA: 118-01808-03.
50. Wang Shusheng and Hao Yufeng, *Wulanfu Nianpu* (Chronicle of Ulanhu's life) (Beijing: Zhonggong Dangshi Ziliao Chubanshe, 1989), 574.
51. Qi Zhi, *Neimeng Wenge Shilu: "Minzu Fenlie" yu "Wa Su" Yundong* (Factual record of the cultural revolution in Inner Mongolia: "National splitting" and the campaign of "digging out and purging") (Hong Kong: Tianxingjian Chubanshe, 2010), 145–51.
52. Svetlana Alexievich, *Secondhand Time: The Last of the Soviets*, trans. Bela Shayevich (New York: Random House, 2016), 6.
53. Chen Weiren, "Hu Yaobang and Tibet," accessed May 10, 2009, www.dwnews.com. I also discuss CCP ethnopolitics in the reform era briefly in "Rediscovery of the Frontier in Recent Chinese History," in *The People's Republic of China at 60: An International Assessment*, ed. William C. Kirby (Cambridge, Mass.: Harvard University Press, 2011), 297–318.
54. Li Qun, "Should China's ethnic policy be changed: A debate around Ma Rong," accessed August 26, 2018, http://cnpolitics.org/2014/06/minzu-policies-in-china/; Ma Rong, "Reexamination of China's theories, institutions, and policies about ethnicity," November 5, 2017, accessed August 26, 2018, http://zhanlve.org/?p=3609; Ilham Tohti,

"Does not China's ethnic policies need reexamination?," October 29, 2009, accessed August 26, 2018, http://www.chinesepen.org/blog/archives/101462; Research Office of the State Ethnic Affairs Commission of the PRC, "Face to face with innovative ideas at the Central Ethnic Work Conference," June 1, 2015, accessed August 26, 2018, http://www.seac.gov.cn/art/2015/6/1/art_143_228925.html.

55. Ma Rong, "Reconstructing the ethnic discourse of China," *Zhongyang Shehuizhuyi Xueyuan Xuebao* (Journal of the Central Institute of Socialism), no. 2 (2017), 39–46.

BIBLIOGRAPHY

Archives

Archives of Changchun Municipality, Changchun
Archives of the Chinese Ministry of Foreign Affairs, Beijing
Archives of the Ministry of Foreign Affairs, Taipei
Archives of Fujian Province, Fuzhou
Archives of Gansu Province, Lanzhou
Archives of Garzê Prefecture, Kangding
Archives of Hebei Province, Shijiazhuang
Archives of Jilin Province, Changchun
Archives of Luding County, Luding
Archives of President Chiang Kai-shek, Taipei
Archives of Sichuan Province, Chengdu
Archives of the Supreme National Defense Council, Taipei
Harry S. Truman Library, Independence, Missouri
India Office Records, The British Library, London
John F. Kennedy Library, Boston
National Archives of the United Kingdom, Kew
National Archives of the United States, College Park, Maryland
Second Historical Archives of China, Nanjing

Digital Archives

"Digital Archive: International History Declassified," Woodrow Wilson International Center for Scholars, http://digitalarchive.wilsoncenter.org.

Classified Publications

Diaocha Ziliao (Investigative materials). Research Bureau of the Central Investigation Department of the CCP.
Gongan Gongzuo Jianbao (Brief on public security work). Ministry of Public Security of the PRC.
Gongan Jianshe (Construction of public security). Ministry of Public Security of the PRC.
Ling Xun (Miscellaneous information). United Front Department of the CCP.
Qingbao Jianxun (Intelligence brief). Central Investigation Department of the CCP.
Qingkuang Jianbao (Situation brief). General Office of the CCP Central Committee.
Sixiang Dongtai (Ideological developments). Propaganda Department of the CCP Xinjiang Committee.
Sixiang Dongtai. Propaganda Department of the CCP Yunnan Committee.
Taiwan Qingkuang (Conditions of Taiwan). Research Bureau of the Central Investigation Department of the CCP.
Waishi Dongtai (Developments in foreign affairs). Ministry of Foreign Affairs of the PRC.
Xuanjiao Dongtai (Developments in propaganda and education). Propaganda Department of the CCP.

Personal Collection of Classified Materials

Central Organizational Department of the CCP. *Guanyu Fan Ming tongzhi youpai fandang jituan wenti de fucha baogao (caogao)* (Draft report on the reexamination of the issue of comrade Fan Ming's rightist and anti-party clique), November 13, 1979.
———. *Guanyu Fan Ming tongzhi youpai fandang jiduan wenti de fucha jielun* (Conclusion on the reexamination of the issue of comrade Fan Ming's rightist and anti-party clique), May 7, 1980.
Fan Ming. *Guanyu muqian Xizang diqu tongyi zhanxian gongzuo zhong de jige celue wenti* (Several tactical issues in the current united-front work in Tibet), September 10, 1951.
———. *Liunian bugai, shidang shousuo (Fan Ming huiyilu)* (No reform for six years and contraction to a certain degree [Fan Ming's recollection]).
Fan Ming and Ya Hanzhang. *Guanyu Xizang tongyi fangzhen deng wenti de yijian* (Opinion on the orientation and other issues about the unification of Tibet), October 23, 1951.
Fan Ming tongzhi tan 1957 nian zai Beijing de Xizang gongzuo huiyi (Comrade Fan Ming's talk about the meeting on the Tibet work in Beijing in 1957), October 12–14, 1984.
Guanyu pingpan wenti (On the issue of rebellion pacification), 1959.
Intelligence Department of the [Central] Military Commission. *Xizang gaikuang: Xizang cankao ziliao zhiyi* (Brief survey of Tibet: reference materials on Tibet no. 1), January 1950.
———. *Xizang de neizheng ji zongjiao: Xizang cankao ziliao zhiliu* (Internal contest and religion of Tibet: reference materials on Tibet no. 6), no date.
———. *Xizang jiaotong gaikuang: Xizang cankao ziliao zhiba* (Conditions of transportation in Tibet: Reference materials on Tibet no. 8), February 1950.
Policy Research Office of the Eighteenth Army. *Dui Xizang gezhong zhengce de chubu yijian* (Preliminary opinions on various policies toward Tibet), March 1950.
Sangji Yuexi tongzhi de jianghua (Comrade Sangye Yeshe's speech), no date (1956?).
Tibet Work Committee. *Xizang gongwei dui jingying Xizang zhi jianyi* (Tibet Work Committee's proposal for governing Tibet), May 20, 1950.

Xinanju zhuanbao Xizang gongwei guanyu Changdu diqu chengli zizhi zhengfu deng wenti (Southwest Bureau's communication on issues raised by the Tibet Work Committee in respect to establishing an autonomous government in Chamdo), October 20, 1952.

Zhang Guohua. *Zhongyang lingdao tanhua jilu* (Minutes of a central leader's talk), February 11, 1957.

Zhang Jingwu guanyu dui Fan zhi de tuanjie gongzuo yu Jijinmei suo ti yaoqiu de baogao (Zhang Jingwu's report on unity with the Fan [Ming] detachment and Che Jigmé's demands), December 13, 1951.

Zhang Jingwu guanyu yu Ale Pingwang gaxia deng liuren tanhua qingkuang de baogao (Zhang Jingwu's report on his conversation with Ale Pingwang and other five Kashag officials), October 14, 1951.

Zhang Jingwu guanyu yu Apei huijian suo tan wenti de baogao (Zhang Jingwu's report on issues discussed with Ngabö during their meeting), September 14, 1951.

Zhang Jingwu guanyu shiba ri wan yu Apei tanhua neirong de baogao (Zhang Jingwu's report on his conversation with Ngabö in the evening of the 18th), October 19, 1951.

Zhang Jingwu guanyu yu gaxia daibiao Apei tanhua qingkuang de baogao (Zhang Jingwu's report on his conversation with the Kashag representative Ngabö), October 22, 1951.

Zhonggong Xizang Gongwei kuoda huiyi guanyu kaichu fandang jituan touzi Fan Ming de dangji he junji de jueyi (Resolution of the enlarged CCP Tibet Work Committee meeting on expelling Fan Ming, head of an anti-party clique, from the party and the army), August 3, 1958.

Zhongyang yansu piping Xizang gongwei weijing qingshi shanzi chengli nongmubu de cuowu (Center's serious criticism of the Tibet Work Committee's mistake in establishing an agricultural and pastoral department without asking for permission), January 5, 1953.

Zhou Renshan Riji (Zhou Renshan's diaries).

Chronicles

Aba Zhouzhi (Chronicle of Ngawa prefecture).
Batang Xianzhi (Xubian) (Chronicle of Bathang county [sequel]).
Gansu Shengzhi (Chronicle of Gansu province).
Ganzi Zhouzhi (Chronicle of Garzê prefecture).
Kangding Xianzhi (Chronicle of Kangding county).
Qinghai Shengzhi (Chronicle of Qinghai province).
Sichuan Shengzhi (Chronicle of Sichuan province).
Xizang Zizhiqu Zhi (Chronicle of the Tibetan Autonomous Region).

Unpublished Manuscripts

Chiang Kai-shek Diaries. Hoover Institution, Stanford.
Office of Military Chronicle of the Military Region of Sichuan Province. *Sichuan Shengzhi, Junshi Zhi: Dier Pian: Zhongda Zhanshi (Songshen Gao)* (Chronicle of Sichuan Province: Chronicle of military affairs: Part 2: Important battles [Draft for approval]). September 1996.
——. *Sichuan Shengzhi, Junshi Zhi: Dier Pian: Zhongda Zhanshi (Taolun Gao)* (Chronicle of Sichuan Province: Chronicle of military affairs: Part 2: Important battles [Draft for discussion]). October 1995.

Xu Danlu. *Fengxue Gaoyuan—Kang Zang Diqu Gongzuo Jishi* (Windy and snowy plateau: Account of work in the Xikang-Tibetan region), 1996.

Zhang Xiangming. *Zhang Xiangming 55 nian Xizang Gongzuo Shilu* (Records of Zhang Xiangming's 55-year work in Tibet), 2006.

Zhao Fan. *Zhao Fan Huiyilu* (Zhao Fan's memoirs), 1992.

Published Primary Sources

Central Archives. *Zhonggong Zhongyang Wenjian Xuanji* (Selected documents of the CCP Central Committee). Beijing: Zhonggong Zhongyang Dangxiao Chubanshe, 1989.

———. *Zhonggong Zhongyang Wenjian Xuanji (1949 nian 10 yue—1966 nian 5 yue)* (Selected documents of the CCP Central Committee, October 1949–May 1966). Beijing: Renmin Chubanshe, 2013.

Chai Degeng, ed. *Xinhai Geming Ziliao Congkan* (Collection of materials on the Revolution of 1911). Shanghai: Shanghai Renmin Chubanshe, 2000.

Chiang Kai-shek. *Xian Zongtong Jiang Gong Sixiang Yanlun Zongji* (Complete works of the late president Chiang Kai-shek). Taipei: Guomindang Dangshi Weiyuanhui, 1984.

The Dalai Lama. *Freedom in Exile: The Autobiography of the Dalai Lama.* New York: HarperCollins, 1990.

———. *My Land and My People: The Autobiography of His Holiness the Dalai Lama of Tibet.* London: Weidenfeld and Nicolson, 1962.

Deng Xiaoping. *Deng Xiaoping Xinan Gongzuo Wenji* (Deng Xiaoping's writings on the Southwest work). Beijing and Chongqing: Zhongyang Wenxian Chubanshe and Chongqing Chubanshe, 2006.

Ding Sheng. *Luonan Yingxiong: Ding Sheng Jiangjun Huiyilu* (Ill-fated hero: General Ding Sheng's memoirs). Hong Kong: Thinker, 2009.

Documentary Research Office of the Central Committee of the Chinese Communist Party. *Chen Yun Nianpu* (Chronology of Chen Yun's life). Beijing: Zhongyang Wenxian Chubanshe, 2000.

———. *Deng Xiaoping Nianpu, 1904–1974* (Chronology of Deng Xiaoping's life, 1904–1974). Beijing: Zhongyang Wenxian Chubanshe, 2009.

———. *Liu Shaoqi Nianpu, 1898–1969* (Chronicle of Liu Shaoqi's life, 1898–1969). Beijing: Zhongyang Wenxian Chubanshe, 1996.

———. *Mao Zedong Nianpu, 1893–1949* (Chronicle of Mao Zedong's life, 1893–1949). Beijing: Renmin Chubanshe, 1993.

———. *Mao Zedong Nianpu, 1949–1976* (Chronicle of Mao Zedong's life, 1949–1976). Beijing: Zhongyang Wenxian Chubanshe, 2013.

———. *Zhou Enlai Nianpu, 1898–1949* (Chronicle of Zhou Enlai's life, 1898–1949). Beijing: Zhongyang Wenxian Chubanshe, 1989.

———. *Zhou Enlai Nianpu, 1949–1976* (Chronicle of Zhou Enlai's life, 1949–1976). Beijing: Zhongyang Wenxian Chubanshe, 1997.

He Long. *He Long Junshi Wenxuan* (Selected military writings of He Long). Beijing: Jiefangjun Chubanshe, 1989.

Heping Jiefang Xizang (Peaceful liberation of Tibet). Compiled by Committee of the Tibetan Autonomous Region for Collecting Materials on Party History and Leading Group of the Tibetan Military Region for Collecting Materials on Party History. Lhasa: Xizang Renmin Chubanshe, 1995.

Huang Musong, Wu Zhongxin, Zhao Shouyu, Dai Chuanxian Fengshi Banli Zangshi Baogaoshu (Reports by Huang Musong, Wu Zhongxin, Zhao Shouyu, and Dai Chuanxian about their missions to Tibet). Beijing: Zhongguo Zangxue Chubanshe, 1993.

Huihuang de Ershi Shiji Xin Zhongguo Da Jilu: Xizang Juan (Grand records of the glorious new China in the twentieth century: Volume on Tibet). Beijing: Hongqi Chubanshe, 1999.

Jiushi Banchan Neidi Huodong ji Fan Zang Shouzu Dang'an Xuanbian (Selected archives on the ninth Panchen's activities in the interior and the frustration of his return to Tibet). Beijing: Zhongguo Zangxue Chubanshe, 1992.

Jiushi Banchan Yuanji Zhiji he Shishi Banchan Zhuanshi Zuochuang Dang'an Xuanbian (Selected archives on the condolence mission for the death of the ninth Panchen and the reincarnation and enthronement of the tenth Panchen). Beijing: Zhongguo Zangxue Chubanshe, 1991.

Liangong (Bu), Gongchan Guoji yu Zhongguo Guomin Geming Yundong, 1920–1925 (Soviet Communist Party (Bolshevik), the Comintern, and the Chinese nationalist revolutionary movement, 1920–1925). Beijing: Beijing Tushuguan Chubanshe, 1997.

Lin, Tian. *Jinjun Xizang Riji* (Diaries on the expedition into Tibet). Beijing: Zhongguo Zangxue Chubanshe, 1994.

Liu Shaoqi. *Jianguo Yilai Liu Shaoqi Wengao* (Writings by Liu Shaoqi since the foundation of the state). Beijing: Zhongyang Wenxian Chubanshe, 1998.

Liu Shufa et al. *Chen Yi Nianpu* (Chronicle of Chen Yi's life). Beijing: Renmin Chubanshe, 1995.

Mao Zedong. *Jianguo Yilai Mao Zedong Junshi Wengao* (Mao Zedong's military writings since the establishment of the state). Beijing: Junshi Kexue Chubanshe Zhongyang Wenxian Chubanshe, 2010.

——. *Jianguo Yilai Mao Zedong Wengao* (Writings by Mao Zedong since the foundation of the state). Beijing: Zhongyang Wenxian Chubashe, 1987–1998.

——. *Mao Zedong Ji* (Collected works of Mao Zedong). Tokyo: Suo Suo Sha, 1983.

——. *Mao Zedong Xizang Gongzuo Wenxuan* (Selected writings of Mao Zedong on the Tibet work). Beijing: Zhongyang Wenxian Chubanshe, 2001.

——. *Mao Zedong Zaoqi Wengao* (Early writings of Mao Zedong). Changsha: Hunan Renmin Chubanshe, 1995.

Miao Peiyi. *Miao Peiyi Huiyilu* (Memoirs of Miao Peiyi). Lhasa: Xizang Renmin Chubanshe, 2005.

Ministry of Civil Affairs of the PRC. *Zhonghua Renmin Gongheguo Xianji Yishang Xingzheng Quhua Yange* (Changes of administrative divisions above the county level in the People's Republic of China). Beijing: Cehui Chubanshe, 1986.

Minzu Zhengce Wenjian Huibian (Collected documents on nationality policies). Beijing: Renmin Chubanshe, 1960.

Nehru, Jawaharlal. *Selected Works of Jawaharlal Nehru: Second Series*. New Delhi: Jawaharlal Nehru Memorial Fund, c. 1984–.

Peng Dehuai. *Peng Dehuai Junshi Wenxuan* (Selected military writings of Peng Dehuai). Beijing: Zhongyang Wenxian Chubanshe, 1988.

Pingxi Xizang Panluan (Pacifying the rebellion in Tibet). Compiled by Committee of the Tibetan Autonomous Region for Collecting Materials on Party History and Leading Group of the Tibetan Military Region for Collecting Materials on Party History. Lhasa: Xizang Renmin Chubanshe, 1995.

Shen Zhihua et al. *Eluosi Jiemi Dang'an Xuanbian: Zhong Su Guanxi* (Selected declassified Russian archives: Sino-Soviet relations). Shanghai: Dongfang Chuban Zhongxin, 2014.

Shisanshi Dalai Lama Yuanji Zhiji he Shisishi Dalai Lama Zuochuang Dang'an Xuanbian (Selected archives on the condolence mission for the death of the thirteenth Dalai Lama and the reincarnation and enthronement of the fourteenth Dalai Lama). Compiled by the Chinese Center of Tibetan Studies and the Second Historical Archives of China. Beijing: Zhongguo Zangxue Chubanshe, 1990.

Su Yu Nianpu (Chronicle of Su Yu's life). Beijing: Dangdai Zhongguo Chubanshe, 2006.

Sun Zhongshan. *Sun Zhongshan Quanji* (Complete works of Sun Yat-sen). Beijing: Zhonghua Shuju, 1981.

Thondup, Gyalo, and Anne E. Thurston. *The Noodle Maker of Kalimpong: The Untold Story of My Struggle for Tibet*. New York: PublicAffairs, 2015.

United Front Department of the CCP Central Committee. *Minzu Wenti Wenxian Huibian* (Collection of documents on the national question). Beijing: Zhonggong Zhongyang Dangxiao Chubanshe, 1991.

Waijiaobu Dang'an Congshu: Jiewu Lei: Di Wu Ce: Xizang Juan 1 (Archival series of the Ministry of Foreign Affairs: Border administrations: Book five: Tibet, volume 1). Compiled by the Ministry of Foreign Affairs. Taipei: Waijiaobu, 2005.

Wang Shusheng and Hao Yufeng. *Wulanfu Nianpu* (Chronicle of Ulanhu's life). Beijing: Zhonggong Dangshi Ziliao Chubanshe, 1989.

Wang Yan. *Peng Dehuai Nianpu* (Chronicle of Peng Dehuai's life). Beijing: Renmin Chubanshe, 1998.

Wenshi Ziliao (Literary and historical materials). Published by the Chinese People's Political Consultative Conference.

Xizang Gongzuo Wenxian Xuanbian (Selected documents of the Tibet work). Compiled by the Office of Documentary Research of the CCP Central Committee and the CCP Committee of the Tibetan Autonomous Region. Beijing: Zhongyang Wenxian Chubanshe, 2005.

Xizang Lishi Dang'an Huicui (A collection of historical archives of Tibet). Compiled by the Archives of the Tibetan Autonomous Region. Beijing: Wenwu Chubanshe, 1995.

Xizang Wenshi Ziliao Xuanji (Selected compilation of Tibetan literary and historical materials). Compiled by the Research Committee of Literary and Historical Materials of Tibet, Chinese People's Political Consultative Conference.

Yang Gongsu. *Cangsang Jiushinian: Yige Waijiao Teshi de Huiyi* (My life for ninety years: The recollections of a special diplomatic envoy). Haikou: Hainan Chubanshe, 1999.

Yang Shangkun. *Yang Shangkun Riji* (Yang Shangkun's diaries). Beijing: Zhongyang Wenxian Chubanshe, 2001.

Zhang Yuxin, ed. *Qingchao Zhi Zang Dianzhang Yanjiu* (Study of Qing ordinances and regulations for administering Tibet). Beijing: Zhongguo Zangxue Chubanshe, 2002.

Zhonggong Zhongyang Wenjian Xuanji (Selected documents of the CCP Central Committee). Beijing: Renmin Chubanshe, 1989–1992.

Zhonggong Zhongyang Wenjian Xuanji (1949 nian 10 yue—1966 nian 5 yue) (Selected documents of the CCP Central Committee, October 1949—May 1966). Beijing: Renmin Chubanshe, 2013.

Zhongguo Geming Shi Dang'an Wenxian Guangpan Ku (Collection of archival materials on Chinese revolutionary history, CD-ROM). Compiled and produced by Central Archives and Beijing Chaoxing Company, 1998.

Zhongguo Gongnong Hongjun Disi Fangmianjun Zhanshi Ziliao Xuanbian: Changzheng Shiqi (Selected materials on the combat history of the fourth front army of the Chinese workers' and peasants' red army: The long march period). Beijing: Jiefangjun Chubanshe, 1992.

Zhongguo Renmin Jiefang Zhanzheng Junshi Wenji (Military writings on the Chinese people's war of liberation). Compiled by the Chinese People's Liberation Army Headquarters. N.p.: Zhongguo Renmin Jiefangjun Zongbu, 1951.

Zhou Enlai. *Jianguo Yilai Zhou Enlai Wengao* (Writings by Zhou Enlai since the foundation of the state). Beijing: Zhongyang Wenxian Chubanshe, 2008.

——. *Zhou Enlai Shuxin Xuanji* (Selected communications of Zhou Enlai). Beijing: Zhongyang Wenxian Chubanshe, 1988.

——. *Zhou Enlai Xuanji* (Selected works of Zhou Enlai). Beijing: Renmin Chubanshe, 1984.

Zhou Enlai yu Xizang (Zhou Enlai and Tibet). Compiled by the Office of Party History of the Tibetan Autonomous Region. Beijing: Zhongguo Zangxue Chubanshe, 1998.

Secondary Sources in Chinese

Che Minghuai et al. *Xizang Difang yu Zhongyang Zhengfu Guanxi Shi* (History of the relations between Tibet and the central government. Lhasa: Xizang Renmin Chubanshe, 1995.

Dangdai Zhongguo Minzu Gongzuo Dashiji, 1949–1988 (Chronicle of important events in the nationality work of contemporary China, 1949–1988). Beijing: Minzu Chubanshe, 1989.

Dangdai Zhongguo de Xizang (Tibet of contemporary China). Beijing: Dangdai Zhongguo Chubanshe, 1991.

Duojie Caidan (Dorje Tseten). *Yuan Yilai Xizang Difang yu Zhongyang Zhengfu Guanxi Yanjiu* (Study of the relations between Tibet and the central government since the Yuan). Beijing: Zhongguo Zangxue Chubanshe, 2005.

Fan Ming. *Xizang Neibu Zhizheng: Dalai Lama he Banchan Dashi de Maodun, Zhonggong Gaoceng de Fenqi* (Internal controversies of Tibet: Contradictions between Dalai and Panchen and disagreements among CCP leaders). Carle Place, N.Y.: Mirror Books, 2009.

Feng Mingzhu. *Jindai Zhong Ying Xizang Jiaoshe yu Chuan Zang Bian Qing: Cong Kuoerka zhi Yi dao Huashengdun Huiyi* (Modern Chinese-British diplomacy and the Sichuan-Tibetan frontier: From the battle of Gurkha to the Washington conference). Taipei: Guoli Gugong Bowuyuan, 1996.

Hu Qiaomu. *Hu Qiaomu Huiyi Mao Zedong* (Mao Zedong as remembered by Hu Qiaomu). Beijing: Renmin Chubanshe, 1994.

Huang Yusheng et al. *Xizang Difang yu Zhongyang Zhengfu Guanxi Shi* (History of the relationship between Tibet and the central government). Lhasa: Xizang Renmin Chubanshe, 1995.

Huiyi Sichuan Jiefang (Xubian) (Liberation of Sichuan remembered [sequel]). Chengdu: Sichuan Jiaoyu Chubanshe, 1989.

Ji Youquan. *Baixue: Jiefang Xizang Jishi* (White snow: A factual record of liberation of Tibet). Beijing: Zhongguo Wuzi Chubanshe, 1993.

——. *Xizang Pingpan Jishi* (Account of rebellion pacification in Tibet). Lhasa: Xizang Renmin Chubanshe, 1993.

Jiangbian Jiacuo (Jambey Gyatso). *Li Jue Zhuan* (Biography of Li Jue). Beijing: Zhongguo Zangxue Chubanshe, 2005.

——. *Mao Zedong yu Dalai, Banchan* (Mao Zedong and Dalai and Banchen). Hong Kong: Xindalu Chubanshe, 2008.

——. *Xueshan Mingjiang Tan Guansan* (Renowned snow mountain general Tan Guansan). Beijing: Zhongguo Zangxue Chubanshe, 2001.

Li Jianglin. *Dang Tieniao zai Tiankong Feixiang: 1956–1962 Qingzang Gaoyuan shang de Mimi Zhanzheng* (When iron birds are flying in the sky: The secret war in the Qinghai-Tibetan Plateau from 1956 to 1962). Taipei: Lianjing, 2012.

Liu Xiaoyuan. *Bianjiang Zhongguo* (Frontier China). Hong Kong: Zhongwen Daxue Chubanshe, 2016.

Luo Gangwu. *Xin Zhongguo Minzu Gongzuo Dashi Gailan, 1949–1999* (Survey of important events in the nationality work of the new China, 1949–1999). Beijing: Huawen Chubanshe, 2001.

Meilang Zongzhen (Monlam Tsundrub). *Jindai Xizang Jushang "Bangdachang" zhi Bangda Duojie de Zhengzhi Shengya yu Shangye Licheng* (The political and commercial career of Banda Dorje of the commercial tycoon "Banda Family" in modern Tibet). Lhasa: Xizang Renmin Chubanshe, 2007.

Pang Xianzhi and Jin Chongji. *Mao Zedong Zhuan, 1949–1976* (Biography of Mao Zedong, 1949–1976). Beijing: Zhongyang Wenxian Chubanshe, 2004.

Qi Zhi. *Neimeng Wenge Shilu: "Minzu Fenlie" yu "Wa Su" Yundong* (Factual record of the Cultural Revolution in Inner Mongolia: "national splitting" and the campaign of "digging out and purging"). Hong Kong: Tianxingjian Chubanshe, 2010.

Qiabai Cidanpingcuo et al. *Xizang Tongshi* (Survey of Tibetan history). Lhasa: Xizang Shehui Kexueyuan, Zhongguo Xizang, and Xizang Guji Chubanshe, 1996.

Qinghai Lishi Jiyao (Important events in the history of Qinghai). Compiled by the Qinghai Committee on the Compilation of Provincial Chronicle. Xining: Qinghai Renmin Chubanshe, 1987.

Shen Zhihua. *Zhonghua Renmin Gongheguo Shi Disan Juan: Sikao yu Xuanze: Cong Zhishi Fenzi Huiyi dao Fan Youpai Yundong, 1956–1957* (History of the People's Republic of China, volume 3: Reflection and choice: From intellectual conference to the anti-rightist campaign, 1956–1957). Hong Kong: Chinese University Press, 2008.

Shen Zhihua et al. *Zhong Su Guanxi Shigang, 1917–1991* (Outline history of the Chinese-Soviet relationship, 1917–1991). Beijing: Xinhua Chubanshe, 2007.

Tan Qixiang. *Jianming Zhongguo Lishi Ditu Ji* (Concise atlas of Chinese history). Beijing: Zhongguo Ditu Chubanshe, 1991.

Wang Lixiong. *Tianzang: Xizang de Mingyun* (Sky burial: The fate of Tibet). Brampton, Ontario: Mirror Books, 1998.

Wu Lengxi. *Shinian Lunzhan, 1956–1966: Zhong Su Guanxi Huiyilu* (Ten-year polemics, 1956–1966: A memoir on Sino-Soviet relations). Beijing: Zhongyang Wenxian Chubanshe, 1999.

Wu Zhenhua, ed. *Xizang Diming* (Place names of the Tibetan Autonomous Region). Beijing: Zhongguo Zangxue Chubanshe, 1995.

Xizang Gonglu Jiaotongshi (History of Tibetan highway and transportations). Beijing: Renmin Jiaotong Chubanshe, 1999.

Xu Dashen et al. *Zhonghua Renmin Gongheguo Shilu* (Veritable records of the People's Republic of China). Changchun: Jilin Renmin Chubanshe, 1994.

Zhang Dingyi. *1954 nian Dalai, Banchan Jin Jing Jilue* (Records of Dalai's and Panchen's visit in Beijing in 1954). Beijing: Zhongguo Zangxue Chubanshe, 2005.

Zhang Xiaoming, ed. *Jianzheng Bainian Xizang: Xizang Lishi Jianzhengren Fangtanlu* (Witnessing Tibet in the past century: Interviews with witnesses of Tibetan history). Beijing: Wuzhou Chuanbo Chubanshe, 2004.

Zhao Jialiang and Zhang Xiaoqi. *Banjie Mubei xia de Wangshi: Gao Gang zai Beijing* (Past events underneath a broken tombstone: Gao Gang in Beijing). Hong Kong: Dafeng Chubanshe, 2008.

Zhao Shenying. *Zhang Guohua Jiangjun zai Xizang* (General Zhang Guohua in Tibet). Beijing: Zhongguo Zangxue Chubanshe, 1998.

——. *Zhongyang Zhu Zang Daibiao Zhang Jingwu* (Zhang Jingwu as the Center's representative in Tibet). Beijing: Zhongguo Zangxue Chubanshe, 2001.

Zhao Xinyu et al., eds. *Kangqu Zangzu Shehui Zhenxi Ziliao Jiyao* (Selection of rare and valuable materials on the Tibetan society of the Xikang area). Changdu: Bashu Chubanshe, 2006.

Zhongguo Gongchangdang Xizang Lishi Dashiji, 1949–2004 (Chronology of major historical events of the Chinese Communist Party in Tibet, 1949–2004). Compiled by the Party History Research Office of the Tibetan Autonomous Region Committee of the Chinese Communist Party. Beijing: Zhonggong Dangshi Chubanshe, 2005.

Zhu Lishuang. *Minguo Zhengfu de Xizang Zhuanshi* (Nationalist government's special envoys to Tibet). Hong Kong: Chinese University Press, 2016.

Secondary Sources in English

Andreyev, Alexandre. *Soviet Russia and Tibet: The Debacle of Secret Diplomacy, 1918–1930s*. Leiden: Brill, 2003.

Brophy, David. *Uyghur Nation: Reform and Revolution on the Russia-China Frontier*. Cambridge, Mass.: Harvard University Press, 2016.

Bulag, Uradyn. *Collaborative Nationalism: The Politics of Friendship on China's Mongolian Frontier*. Lanham, Md.: Rowman and Littlefield, 2010.

——. *The Mongols at China's Edge: History and the Politics of National Unity*. Lanham, Md.: Rowman and Littlefield, 2002.

Chan, Victor. *Tibet Handbook: A Pilgrimage Guide*. Chico, Calif.: Moon, 1994.

Chen, Jian. "The Tibetan Rebellion and China's Changing Relations with India and the Soviet Union." *Journal of Cold War Studies* 8, no. 3 (2006): 54–101.

Conboy, Kenneth, and James Morrison. *The CIA's Secret War in Tibet*. Lawrence: University Press of Kansas, 2002.

Crossley, Pamela Kyle. *A Translucent Mirror: History and Identity in Qing Imperial Ideology*. Berkeley: University of California Press, 2000.

Dai, Yingcong. *The Sichuan Frontier and Tibet: Imperial Strategy in the Early Qing*. Seattle: University of Washington Press, 2009.

Diener, Alexander, and Joshua Hagen. *Borders: A Very Short Introduction*. Oxford: Oxford University Press, 2012.

Dunham, Mikel. *Buddha's Warriors: The Story of the CIA-Backed Tibetan Freedom Fighters, the Chinese Invasion, and the Ultimate Fall of Tibet*. New York: Jeremy P. Tarcher, 2004.

Elliott, Mark C. *The Manchu Way: The Eight Banners and Ethnic Identity in Late Imperial China*. Stanford, Calif.: Stanford University Press, 2001.

Fravel, M. Taylor. *Strong Borders, Secure Nation: Cooperation and Conflict in China's Territorial Dispute*. Princeton, N.J.: Princeton University Press, 2008.

Friedman, Jeremy. *Shadow Cold War: The Sino-Soviet Competition for the Third World*. Chapel Hill: University of North Carolina Press, 2015.

Gaddis, John. *The Landscape of History: How Historians Map the Past*. Oxford: Oxford University Press, 2002.

Garver, John W. *Protracted Contest: Sino-Indian Rivalry in the Twentieth Century*. Seattle: University of Washington Press, 2002.

Goldstein, Melvyn C. *A History of Modern Tibet, 1913–1951: The Demise of the Lamaist State*. Berkeley: University of California Press, 1989.

——. *A History of Modern Tibet, Volume Two, 1951–1955: The Calm Before the Storm*. Berkeley: University of California Press, 2007.

——. *A History of Modern Tibet, Volume Three, 1955–1957: The Storm Clouds Descend*. Berkeley: University of California Press, 2014.

Goldstein, Melvyn C., Dawei Sherap, and William R. Siebenschuh. *A Tibetan Revolutionary: The Political Life and Times of Bapa Phüntso Wangye*. Berkeley: University of California Press, 2004.

Grunfeld, A. Tom. *The Making of Modern Tibet*. Armonk, N.Y.: M. E. Sharpe, 1987.

Gup, Ted. *The Book of Honor: The Secret Lives and Deaths of CIA Operatives*. New York: Anchor Books, 2001.

Hilton, Isabel. *The Search for the Panchen Lama*. New York: Norton, 1999.

Hunt, Michael H. *The Genesis of Chinese Communist Foreign Policy*. New York: Columbia University Press, 1996.

Husain, Asad. *British India's Relations with the Kingdom of Nepal, 1857–1947*. London: Allen and Unwin, 1970.

Hyer, Eric. *Pragmatic Dragon: China's Grand Strategy and Boundary Settlements*. Vancouver: University of British Columbia Press, 2015.

Jacobs, Justin. *Xinjiang and the Modern Chinese State*. Seattle: University of Washington Press, 2016.

Khan, Sulmaan W. *Muslim, Trader, Nomad, Spy: China's Cold War and the People of the Tibetan Borderlands*. Chapel Hill: University of North Carolina Press, 2015.

Knaus, John Kenneth. *Orphans of the Cold War: America and the Tibetan Struggle for Survival*. New York: PublicAffairs, 1999.

Kotkin, Stephen, and Bruce A. Elleman, eds. *Mongolia in the Twentieth Century: Landlocked Cosmopolitan*. Armonk, N.Y.: M. E. Sharpe, 1999.

Kux, Dennis. *The United States and Pakistan, 1947–2000: Disenchanted Allies*. Washington, D.C.: Woodrow Wilson Center Press, 2001.

Laird, Thomas. *Into Tibet: The CIA's First Atomic Spy and His Secret Expedition to Lhasa*. New York: Grove Press, 2002.

——. *The Story of Tibet: Conversations with the Dalai Lama*. New York: Grove Press, 2006.

Lattimore, Owen. *Inner Asian Frontiers of China*. Oxford: Oxford University Press, 1988.

Leibold, James. *Reconfiguring Chinese Nationalism: How the Qing Frontier and Its Indigenes Became Chinese*. New York: Palgrave MacMillan, 2007.

Levine, Robert. *A Geography of Time: The Temporal Misadventure of a Social Psychologist, or How Every Culture Keeps Time Just a Little Bit Differently*. New York: Basic Books, 1998.

Li, Jianglin. *Tibet in Agony: Lhasa 1959*. Translated by Susan Wilf. Cambridge, Mass.: Harvard University Press, 2016.

Lin, Hsiao-ting. *Tibet and Nationalist China's Frontier: Intrigues and Ethnopolitics, 1928–49*. Vancouver: University of British Columbia Press, 2006.

Lintner, Bertil. *Great Game East: India, China, and the Struggle for Asia's Most Volatile Frontier*. New Haven, Conn.: Yale University Press, 2015.

Liu, Xiaohong. *Chinese Ambassadors: The Rise of Diplomatic Professionalism Since 1949*. Seattle: University of Washington Press, 2001.

Liu, Xiaoyuan. *Frontier Passages: Ethnopolitics and the Rise of Chinese Communism, 1921–1945*. Washington, D.C.: Woodrow Wilson Center Press, 2004.

——. *A Partnership for Disorder: China, the United States, and Their Policies for the Postwar Disposition of the Japanese Empire, 1941–1945*. Cambridge: Cambridge University Press, 1996.

———. *Recast All Under Heaven: Revolution, War, Diplomacy, and Frontier China in the 20th Century.* New York: Continuum, 2010.
———. *Reins of Liberation: An Entangled History of Mongolian Independence, Chinese Territoriality, and Great Power Hegemony, 1911–1950.* Washington, D.C.: Woodrow Wilson Center Press, 2006.
Mackinder, H. J. "The Geographical Pivot of History." *Geographical Journal* 23, no. 4 (1904): 421–37.
McGranahan, Carole. *Arrested Histories: Tibet, the CIA, and Memories of a Forgotten War.* Durham, N.C.: Duke University Press, 2010.
McKay, Alex. *Tibet and the British Raj: The Frontier Cadre, 1904–1947.* Richmond, Surrey, UK: Curzon, 1997.
Millward, James A. *Eurasian Crossroads: A History of Xinjiang.* New York: Columbia University Press, 2007.
Mosca, Matthew W. *From Frontier Policy to Foreign Policy: The Question of India and the Modern Transformation of Geopolitics in Qing China.* Stanford, Calif.: Stanford University Press, 2013.
Mullaney, Thomas. *Coming to Terms with the Nation: Ethnic Classification in Modern China.* Berkeley: University of California Press, 2010.
Paine, S. C. M. *The Wars for Asia, 1911–1949.* Cambridge: Cambridge University Press, 2012.
Pantsov, Alexander V. *Deng Xiaoping: A Revolutionary Life.* Oxford: Oxford University Press, 2015.
Pantsov, Alexander V., with Steven Levine. *Mao: The Real Story.* New York: Simon & Schuster, 2012.
Perdue, Peter C. *China Marches West: The Qing Conquest of Central Eurasia.* Cambridge, Mass.: Belknap Press, 2005.
Powers, John. *History as Propaganda: Tibetan Exiles Versus the People's Republic of China.* Oxford: Oxford University Press, 2004.
Powers, John, and David Templeman. *Historical Dictionary of Tibet.* Lanham, Md.: Scarecrow Press, 2012.
Radchenko, Sergey. *Two Suns in the Heavens: The Sino-Soviet Struggle for Supremacy, 1962–1967.* Stanford, Calif.: Stanford University Press, 2009.
Reardon-Anderson, James. *Reluctant Pioneers: Chinese Expansion Northward, 1644–1937.* Stanford, Calif.: Stanford University Press, 2005.
Riedel, Bruce. *JFK's Forgotten Crisis: Tibet, the CIA, and the Sino-Indian War.* Washington, D.C.: Brookings Institution Press, 2015.
Rohlf, Gregory. *Building New China, Colonizing Kokonor: Resettlement to Qinghai in the 1950s.* Lanham, Md.: Lexington, 2016.
Rossabi, Morris, ed. *Governing China's Multi-Ethnic Frontiers.* Seattle: University of Washington Press, 2004.
Ryavec, Karl E. *A Historical Atlas of Tibet.* Chicago: University of Chicago Press, 2015.
Schoenhals, Michael. *Spying for the People: Mao's Secret Agents, 1949–1967.* Cambridge: Cambridge University Press, 2013.
Scott, James. *The Art of Not Being Governed: An Anarchist History of Upland Southeast Asia.* New Haven, Conn.: Yale University Press, 2010.
Shakabpa, Tsepon Wangchuck Deden. *One Hundred Thousand Moons: An Advanced Political History of Tibet.* Translated and annotated by Derek F. Maher. Leiden: Brill, 2010.
Shakya, Tsering. *The Dragon in the Land of Snows: A History of Modern Tibet Since 1947.* London: Pimlica, 1999.
Shao Dan. *Remote Homeland, Recovered Borderland: Manchus, Manchukuo, and Manchuria, 1907–1985.* Honolulu: University of Hawaii Press, 2011.

Sheng, Michael M. "Mao, Tibet, and the Korean War." *Journal of Cold War Studies* 8, no. 3 (2006): 15–33.

Singh, Amar Kaur Jasbir. *Himalayan Triangle: A Historical Survey of British India's Relations with Tibet, Sikkim and Bhutan, 1765–1950*. London: British Library, 1988.

Smith, Warren W. *Tibetan Nation: A History of Tibetan Nationalism and Sino-Tibetan Relations*. Boulder, Colo.: Westview Press, 1996.

Tatly, Stephan. *Escape from the Land of Snows: The Young Dalai Lama's Harrowing Flight to Freedom and the Making of a Spiritual Hero*. New York: Crown, 2011.

Tuttle, Gray. *Tibetan Buddhists in the Making of Modern China*. New York: Columbia University Press, 2005.

Vogel, Ezra. *Deng Xiaoping and the Transformation of China*. Cambridge, Mass.: Harvard University Press, 2011.

Wachman, Alan M. *Why Taiwan? Geographic Rationales for China's Territorial Integrity*. Stanford, Calif.: Stanford University Press, 2007.

Wang Lixiong and Tsering Shakya. *The Struggle for Tibet*. New York: Verso, 2009.

Wang Xiuyu. *China's Last Imperial Frontier: Late Qing Expansion in Sichuan's Tibetan Borderlands*. Lanham, Md.: Lexington, 2011.

Westad, Odd Arne. *The Global Cold War: Third World Interventions and the Making of Our Times*. Cambridge: Cambridge University Press, 2007.

Winchakul, Thongchai. *Siam Mapped: A History of the Geo-Body of a Nation*. Honolulu: University of Hawaii Press, 1994.

Zhai, Qiang. "Tibet and Chinese-British-American Relations in the early 1950s." *Journal of Cold War Studies* 8, no. 3 (2006): 34–53.

INDEX

abduction plot, 271, 280–281, 365n115
Acheson, Dean, 36, 90
Alexievich, Svetlana, 309
all under heaven (*tianxia*), 5, 7, 15
amban authority, 16, 18–19, 65
antagonistic gradualism, 225
anti-communism: of Lhasa, 30; politics, 302; of Tibet, 32
anti-imperialism, 70, 306
anti-party activities, 159, 213, 234, 352n60, 355n95
Anti-Rightist Campaign, 233, 256, 260, 341n1
archival information, 3–4
armed forces, 181–182
armed work teams, 116
atomic bombs, 247, 252
autonomous regions, 50; CCP approach to, 292–293; Han cadres in, 366n128; Inner Mongolia as, 47, 77; for minority nationalities, 103; Seventeen-Point Agreement and, 85; of Tibet, 52, 63, 88, 105, 166, 227, 232; Xikang Tibetan, 152–156

Banda Dorje, 172, 197–198, 210
bandit annihilation, 115
"Basic Conclusions on the Democratic Reform in the Garzê Tibetan Autonomous Prefecture," 159
Bator, Osman, 36
Beatty, E. E., 94
Beijing experience, 125–126
Beijing-Lhasa relationship, 158, 176
Beijing operations, 49–50
Bessac, Frank, 92
Bhutto, Zulfikar Ali, 249
big dismount, 216–220, 227, 230
big-nationality chauvinism, 226, 231
blind leap forward, 251
borax mines, 217–218
border demarcation, 16–17
borderlands, 22, 106, 240
border wars, 297–298, 300–301
brand names, 244
Buddhist monasteries, 144
buffer zone, of Tibet, 210–231
bureaucratic bourgeoisie, 46
Burmese Communist Party, 203

capitalism, 12; China and, 235–236; commercial, 238–239; development of, 112; socialism compared to, 236–237, 241, 307; upper-stratum people and, 120; of Western countries, 235–236

Carry the Revolution Through to the End, 12

CCP. *See* Chinese Communist Party

CCP Central Committee: Deng Xiaoping meeting of, 202; historical records of, 276–277; Mao's letter to, 35, 61–62, 321n77; Mao's words clarified by, 61–62; minority socioeconomic reforms forbidden by, 96; political report from, 191–192

CCP leadership, 6; Beijing-Lhasa cooperation and, 176; crisis of, 82; Dalai Lama goal of, 203–204; of Deng Xiaoping, 79–80; dialectic thinking of, 249; directives of, 365n109; dissenting voice within, 123; domestic political problems of, 29; fifty years reform and, 221; geostrategic thinking of, 29; Inner Mongolia model for, 229; leftist and rightist policy options of, 87; Lhasa incident and, 31; Mao conveying opinion to, 275; minority nationalities dealt with by, 46–47, 108; Panchen Lama contacted by, 34; revolutionary policy of, 281; socialist construction elevated by, 247–248; Southwest Bureau setup by, 32–33; Tibetan situation misjudged by, 214; Tibet goals achieved peacefully and, 192–193; TWC organized by, 64–65; Ulanhu as member of, 47

CCP Sichuan Committee, 122, 232; on democratic reform, 139–140, 219; four antis campaign from, 145; mediation measures of, 134–135; Sangye Yeshe in, 136–137

Center (*Zhongyang*), 4, 75, 313n10

Central Delegation: Dalai Lama in positive light and, 178; Lhasa impression of, 170–171; to Tibet, 168–176; Tibetan report by, 171–176

Central Military Commission (CMC), 79

Central Nationality Committee, 152

Central People's Government, 86, 222

central power building, 261

Central Secretariat, 222, 224, 229, 235

Central United Front Department (CUFD), 75, 80, 122, 136, 283; reform schedule adopted by, 170; September 4 directive from, 186–188

Chamdo: battle of, 46, 72, 184, 197; people's liberation committee of, 198; youth arriving in, 263

Chamdo People's Liberation Committee, 197, 350n26

Chamdo Security District of the Tibet Military Region, 210

Che Jigmé, 73

Chengdu Military Region, 141, 257

Chen Geng, 116

Chen Yi, 125, 171, 176–177, 180

Chen Yun, 71, 221, 352n55

Chiang Kai-shek, 23, 253, 299; anticommunist politics of, 302; diary entries of, 302–303; revolutionary stance of, 303; Statement to Tibetan Compatriots from, 302; Taiwan base of, 30; Tibetan-Yi corridor and, 24; U.S attitude disappointing, 303

Chime Gombo, 184, 197

China: as backward country, 165; borderland categories of, 106; capitalism and, 235–236; communism in, 90–91; cooperativization in, 181; economic development of, 246–247; foreign products in, 242; geographic shape of, 26; geopolitical decline of, 24; grand unification of, 22–23; India's border war with, 297–298, 300–301; India's conspiracy against, 301; India's military distance from, 300; India's relations with, 253, 298–299; lost territories of, 7–8; Mao and economic issues of, 208; missionaries in, 94–95; national humiliation maps and, 7–8; Northwest, 39; Republic of, 3, 22; Seventeen-Point Agreement negotiated by, 45, 63–64; smuggling threat to, 240–241; social reforms of, 98–99; Soviet Union's relations with, 304; territorial transformation of, 6–9; Thomas episode and, 38; Tibet and central government of, 95; Tibet's affairs mismanaged by, 66–67; Tibet's geopolitical operations of,

5–6; Tibet's integration with, 166; Tibet's policy of, 85–86; Tibet's relations with, 38–39; Western maps of, 313n19; while there is life, there is hope from, 221; wild domains of, 40. *See also* People's Republic of China
Chinese Civil War (1945–49), 28
Chinese Communist Party (CCP), 1; autonomous region approach of, 292–293; Banda Dorje supporter of, 197–198; bilateral contract of, 56; Center code name for, 4, 75, 313n10; class struggle narrative of, 284–285; Dalai Lama group's suspicions of, 158; Dalai Lama's attitude of, 271; democratic reform meaning to, 335n58; democratic reform preparations by, 209–211; Deng Xiaoping's leadership in, 79–80; Eighth Congress of, 191–192; ethnopolitical accomplishments of, 310; Garzê Prefecture Committee, 141, 143; Garzê Tibetan Autonomous Prefecture Committee, 138; Han Cadres and, 188; Huaihai Campaign of, 110; intelligence, 157; internal unity of, 82–83; international class struggle of, 12; Jinsha River offensive of, 235; Kangding Area Committee, 156, 232; legitimate authority of, 8–9; Liu Geping and policymaking of, 124–125; Long March of, 27–28; Mao and political outlook of, 25–26; mass-oriented politics of, 215–216; mass struggle used by, 113; minority regions practices of, 103; national integration sought by, 48; nationality policy of, 146; nationality work of, 98; policy disagreement in, 131–132; policy grievances against, 196; religion view of, 100; Seventeen-Point Agreement by, 55; Seventeen-Point Agreement violation by, 103; smart class struggle and, 100–101, 104; socialism and, 88; socioeconomic programs of, 252; Stalin's criticism of, 29; Three-Antis campaign of, 78, 329n107; Tibet and agent of change, 92; Tibetan negotiations with, 54–55; Tibetan revolution of, 46; Tibetan society ignorance of, 146; Tibetan support lacking of, 177–178; Tibet's incorporation into, 26–27; under united-front policy, 73; war of liberation of, 29–30; Xichang Prefecture Committee, 116; Zhang Jingwu mediator for, 67
Chinese Communist Revolution, 10–11, 91–93
Chinese Nation (*Zhonghua Minzu*), 22
Chinese Revolution, 9–11, 56
Christian gospel, 94
chronicles of life (*nianpu*), 186, 201, 351n34
Chuan-Zang Highway, 167, 258
Churchill, Winston, 24
Chushi Gangdruk, 258
class-analysis method, 283
class consciousness, 283, 285
class polarization, 99
class struggles: CCP's narrative of, 284–285; from Deng Xiaoping, 305–306; international, 12; lower-class people and, 146; Mao's remarks on, 132; PRC and, 307; in reform war, 129–131; socialist transformation and, 251; Southwest Bureau on spontaneous, 101–102; in Tibet, 118, 229, 304; upper-stratum people and, 288; violent, 137, 140; Xikang Committee on, 108–109. *See also* smart class struggles
CMC. *See* Central Military Commission
coal mines, 217–218
Cold War, 11–13, 91
commercial capitalism, 238–239
Common Program (1949), 27, 95
communism, 12, 248; aggression of, 14; Burmese Communist Party, 203; in China, 90–91; as cruel and inhumane, 194; Great Leap Forward toward, 190; Lhasa's anti-communism and, 30; Tibet's anti-communism and, 32; U.S. imperialism compared to, 30–31
comprehensive rebellion, 256–257, 259, 263, 267
comprehensive struggle, 141
"Conclusions on the Principal Experiences of the Party's Work Among the Minority Nationalities in the Past Few Years" (paper), 98–101
Confucianism, 9
constructive collaboration, 255
consumer goods, 71

388 Index

continuous revolution, 245, 309
cooperative gradualism, 225
cooperativization, 181
counteroffensive, 278
covert plots (*yinmou*), 148–150, 164
cross-border trade, 71
Crossley, Pamela, 18
CUFD. *See* Central United Front Department
Cultural Revolution, 243, 250, 290, 308
culture, of Tibet, 62
Cuola dzong, 253–254
currency, 69, 71, 236

dafazhan. *See* Great Development
Dai Chuanxian, 28
Dajin Monastery, 119, 150, 162
Dalai bridge, 57, 282
Dalai clique approach, 226–227
Dalai Lama: abduction plot of, 271, 280–281, 365n115; CCP leadership winning over, 203–204; CCP's attitude toward, 271; Central Delegation and positive light for, 178; dietary preferences of, 87–88; divine air of, 201–210; fourteenth, 37–38, 42; Indian exile escape of, 280–281, 305, 364n93, 364n98, Indian exile of, 193–194, 279; Kalimpong visit from, 206; as leading reactionary, 270; letter written to, 183; Lhasa departure of, 3–4; Lhasa protests influencing, 271; Lhasa return of, 209, 352n52; Lhasa revolt because of, 267; Mao displeased by, 196; Mao praised by, 158; Mao's attitude toward, 275–276; Mao's letter to, 183–184; McMahon Line crossed by, 280; as military-administrative committee chairman, 64; minority nationalities thoughts of, 154; monastery unity message of, 154–155; Nehru's meeting with, 208–209; Ngabö's warning to, 276; Norbulingka departure of, 277–278; Norbulingka summer palace of, 264; Panchen Lama relations with, 52, 64, 70, 83–84, 86, 174–176, 215; Panchen Lama seeking parity with, 72–74; patriotism of, 92; political goals against, 288–289; power position of, 182; preaching sessions of, 156; reactionaries abduction of, 265–267, 270–271; rebellion conspiracy of, 163–164; rebellion plot suspected of, 281–282; rebellions accusation against, 159–160; rebellions view of, 120; religious and political position of, 54; secret conversations of, 155; Tan Guansan letters from, 272–273; Tibetan Buddhism and, 27, 61–63; Tibetan independence and, 151; Tibetan internal freedom and, 196–197; Tibet as political center for, 171; Tibet's approach centered on, 55–56; Tibet's ruling power of, 70; treason campaign against, 288, 366n133; treatment of, 266–267; TWC report on departure of, 278; TWC welcoming party for, 210; two-pronged travel of, 161; upper-stratum people of, 173–174; winning over, 83–84; Xikang tour of, 160–161; Zhang Guotao compared to, 194–195; Zhang Jingwu's information to, 195–196; Zhou Enlai's conversations with, 351n37; Zhou Enlai's persuasion of, 204
Dalai Lama group: CCP officials suspicious of, 158; incrimination of, 161; influence expanding of, 152–153; religious activities of, 152; Tibetan independence conspiracy of, 344n30; western Sichuan departure of, 162
Dalai line, 184, 266–267, 277
Dayuejin. *See* Great Leap Forward
democracy, people's, 201
democratic reforms, 107; CCP Sichuan Committee on, 139–140, 219; CCP's meaning of, 335n58; CCP's preparations for, 209–211; as dispossession procedure, 119; Fan Zhizhong comments on, 120; in Garzê Prefecture, 138–139; in Lhasa, 176; obstacles to, 142; PCTAR and, 168–169; people's commune with, 261–262; Seventeen-Point Agreement and, 165–166; social engineering in, 169–170; socialist transformation with, 114; in Tibet, 150, 167–168, 185–186, 230–231; TWC's projection of, 177; in western Sichuan, 115, 139
Deng Xiaoping, 11, 35, 39, 226; antagonistic gradualism from, 225; CCP Central Committee meeting of, 202; CCP leadership by, 79–80; class struggles

from, 305–306; Eighth National Congress speech of, 137; ethnic discourse of, 310; Fan Ming's conversation with, 231; feudal aristocrats comment of, 225; Liaoning Province and, 255; local nationalism defined by, 257–258; Mao promoting, 138; Mao's confidence in, 78; monasteries dealt with by, 143; party-state operations of, 80; personnel expansion from, 211–212; policymaking levels of, 273; reforms demanded by, 139–140; Southwest Bureau setup of, 32, 79; ten-point plan of, 76; Tibetan situation from, 77–78, 215–216; Tibetan smuggling warning from, 237; Tibet discussions led by, 210–211; Tibet work conference with, 81; TWC mistakes and, 213–214; unity gesture of, 82–83; war possibility meeting with, 222–223; war situation remarks of, 140; Zhang Guohua advice from, 59–60; Zhang Jingwu message from, 188–189; Zhongnanhai meeting and, 201–202
department of agriculture and pastoral work, 79
dietary preferences, 87–88
diminishing relevance, principle of, 5
Ding Sheng, 277
dispossession procedure, 119
divine air, 201–210
division of labor, 40, 49
double-mistake formula, 179
Drakgo, 118–119
Drungtsi, 272, 363n76
Duan Juxian, 149
Dulles, John F., 247

East Asian scholars, 43
eastern Kham, 93, 115
eastern Turkistan movement, 234
eastern Xikang, 112
ecclesiastical principalities, 44
economic development, 246–247
economic plan, of Tibet, 71
Eighteenth Army, 45–46, 51, 53, 59, 63
Eighth Congress, of CCP, 191–192
Eighth National Congress, 137
Eighth Party Congress, 186
Eisenhower, Dwight D., 205
empty constituency, 18

encirclement without attack, 279
enterprise dismount, 218
ethnicity: borderlands with, 22; conflicts of, 17–18, 115, 166; connections of, 239; discourse on, 310; frontier of, 78–79; minorities of, 229; Tibetan, 187
ethnopolitical zone, 309–310
expenditures, 212

Fan Ming, 33; anti-Party activities of, 213, 234, 352n60, 355n95; background of, 68–69; Dalai clique approach and, 226–227; Deng's conversation with, 231; five doables and four undoables from, 230–231; Goldstein's study on reforms of, 179; Great Development launched by, 179, 213; indirect reform preparations of, 231; as Northwest counterpart, 68; party membership stripped of, 84; separate administration formula rejected, 73–74, 84; Tibetan independence conspiracy and, 344n30; Tibetan political conditions studied by, 50; Tibetan reform preparations from, 179–180; in TWC, 57, 69, 348n83; TWC tabling report by, 71; united-front responsibility of, 41; Zhang Guohua enraging, 81; Zhang Jingwu unity with, 328n71
Fan Zhizhong, 109–110, 120, 137, 335n52, 338n92
Fan Zhongyan (Song poet), 231
Far Eastern Republic, 216
feudalism, 114; aristocrats in, 225; armed forces for, 139; classes in, 143; lords in, 111; monasteries power in, 132
First National People's Congress, 85
Five Principles of Peaceful Coexistence, 298
five-race republic, 21
Ford, Bob, 38, 94
foreign goods, 235–242, 244
foreign relations, 306
foreign trade, 242
four antis campaign, 145
Front Tibet (*qianzang*), 50
Front Tibetan People's Government, 50

Gaddis, John, 5
Galbraith, John, 299

Gannan Tibetan Autonomous Prefecture, 248–250
Gansu officials, 248–249
Gao Feng, 251
Gao Gang, 80, 82, 101, 128
Gao-Rao affair, 101, 330n118
Garzê Committee, 122–123
Garzê Monasteries, 119, 121, 162
Garzê Prefecture, 120; commercial capitalism in, 238–239; democratic reforms in, 138–139; feudal armed forces in, 139; heavy fighting in, 141; Liu Geping understanding issues of, 123; lower classes' grievances in, 143; Mao's reform directives for, 126–131; socialist transformation of, 144–145, 250
Garzê Tibetan Autonomous Prefecture, 108, 112, 153, 162
general showdown (*zong juezhan*), 262–263, 277
geo-ethno-security landscape, 5–7, 295–296, 313n16
geostrategic thinking, 19–20, 23–24, 29
globalization, 15, 19
Goldstein, Melvyn C., 4–5, 312n8; Fan Ming's reforms study of, 179; *A History of Modern Tibet* by, 338n92; Indian visit and, 193–194
Gonpo Tashi, 258
grand unification, 22–23
Great Development, 179, 211; mistakes of, 213–214
great dismount, 217, 233, 300
Great Leap Forward (*Dayuejin*), 251–252, 257; Anti-Rightist Campaign and, 233, 260; toward communist society, 190; Great Development and, 211; people's commune from, 274
ground transportation, 195–196
Grunfeld, A. Tom, 38
guerrilla warfare, 253
Gu Jigang, 291
guns, in Tibetan society, 109–111
Gurkha (*Kuo'erka*), 16
Gyalo Thondup, 204, 253–255, 350n22

Han cadres, 234; in autonomous regions, 366n128; CCP and, 188; minority land reforms by, 97; minority nationalities not trusted by, 119, 129; Tibet with, 183, 211; TWC reduction of, 216–217; Zhang Jingwu numbers of, 352n56
Han Chinese: assimilation of, 232; bad behaviors of, 166; expansion, 14; gifts of nature of, 96; Mao and chauvinism toward, 96–97; PRC and, 227; Zhou Enlai comments on, 95
Hao Keyong. *See* Fan Ming
Harrer, Heinrich, 94
hat metaphor, 88
He Lin, 16, 316nn9–10
He Long, 33, 39, 49, 60
History of Modern Tibet, A (Goldstein), 312n8, 338n92
Hopkinson, A. J., 91
houzang. See Rear Tibet
Huaihai Campaign, 110
Huang Huoqing, 250
Huang Kecheng, 256, 276
Huang Peiqiao, 17
Huang Xinting, 277
Huan Xiang, 247
Hu Hua, 292
human nature, 231–232
Hungary, 195
Hu Yaobang, 309
Hu Zongnan, 36, 40
Hyer, Eric, 296

imperative control, 8
imperialism, 34, 107; anti-imperialist revolution and, 70, 306; communism compared to, 30–31; of Western countries, 201, 301
Important Historical Events of the Chinese Communist Party in Tibet, 1949-2004, 163
inaugurating conference, 106–107
income sources, 174
India, 193–194; anti-Chinese conspiracy of, 301; China's border war with, 297–298, 300–301; China's military distance from, 300; China's relations with, 253, 298–299; Dalai Lama's escape and exile in, 279, 280–281, 305, 364n93, 364n98; Tibet's concerns of, 300; Tibet's territory and, 225
Indian Communist Party, 306

indirect reform preparations, 230–231
inheritance relationship, 15
Inner Mongolia, 28; CCP leadership's model of, 229; emulation model of, 114; ethnic frontier of, 78–79; nationality regional autonomy of, 57; revolutionary seniority of, 73
Inner Mongolian Autonomous Region, 47, 77
institutional dismount, 218
insurmountable difficulties, 42–43
integration, 48
interethnic conflicts: exchanges, 166; in Tibet, 17–18; in western Sichuan, 115
intermediate zones, 15
internal rectification, 234
international class struggle, 12
inter-nationality unity, 177
international politics, 106
intraethnic connections, 229

Jago Topden, 156–158, 161
Jangtsiling, 162
Jian Bozan, 292–293
Jiang Qing, 231
Jiangte radio station, 253
Jikmé Dorji, 254
Jinsha River, 159, 219; CCP offensive near, 235; as sociopolitical divide, 145; two sides of, 222; western side of, 283–284
Ji Youquan, 364n98
juemi. See top secret
junzheng weiyuanhui. See military-administrative committee

Kalimpong, 193, 206
Kalon Surkhang Wangchen Gelek, 163
Kangding Branch Military Region, 143
Kangding Committee, 136–137
Kang Nai'er, 151, 156
Kangxi (emperor), 15–16
Kangzang (Xikang-Tibet) Highway, 58, 63, 166–167
Kang-Zang Highway, 184, 222, 236
Karmapa Lama, 153–154, 161
Kashag: centralized power wanted by, 225; as governing council, 63; ground transportation and, 195–196; officials, 64–66; public security from, 255; rebellions and, 163; reform bureau organized by, 165; Seventeen-Point Agreement accepted by, 88, 165; Tibetan currency and, 71
Kelsang Wangdu, 172
Kennedy, John F., 299
"Key Policies of the People's Republic of China in Implementing Nationality Regional Autonomy," 95
Khampa rebellion, 160
Khenpos Committee, 84
Khrushchev, Nikita, 304–305
Kissinger, Henry, 15
KMT. *See* Kuomintang regime
Kundeling Monastery, 272
Kuo'erka. See Gurkha
Kuomintang bandits, 149
Kuomintang (KMT) regime, 3, 23–25

laboring class, 305
laboring people's liberation, 256, 259
land reforms: Han cadres and minority, 97; Ngabö's proposal on, 173; smart class struggles preconditions for, 99–100; in Tibet, 107
Lan Jixi, 292–293
Lanzhou Military Region, 260
Lao Xizang. See old Tibetans
Latin America, 305
leftist adventurism, 251
leftist policy options, 87
legitimate authority, 8–9
Levine, Robert, 190–191
Lhasa, 18; anti-communist sentiment of, 30; battle of, 278, 279–280; CCP leadership and incident in, 31; Central Delegations impression of, 170–171; Chen Yi arriving in, 180; Chen Yi's mission to, 169; coup failed in, 25; Dalai Lama departing, 3–4; Dalai Lama protests in, 271; Dalai Lama reason for revolt in, 267; Dalai Lama's return to, 209, 352n52; democratic reform in, 176; Mao message on revolt in, 268–270; minority nationalities and, 93; Nehru's discussion about, 209; PLA operations in, 279–280; PRC communications with, 277; PRC's relationship with, 158, 176; rebel

Lhasa (continued)
destruction planned in, 278; reform in, 165; religion in, 199; revolt in, 264–266, 279, 296; right-wing personalities in, 175; situation as treason in, 265–266; six years formula in, 191, 200; social life in, 282; Tibet's autonomy sought by, 197; TMR in, 266; TWC in, 266; TWC message on situation in, 198–200; U.S. reaction to revolt in, 297; Zhang Guohua not in, 264; Zhang Jingwu not in, 264
Liangshan Prefecture, 115, 126–131
Liaoning Province, 255
Liao Zhigao: Beijing experience of, 125–126; Mao's reform directives from, 126–131; reform thoughts of, 133; situation needing correcting and, 142
liberation: of laboring people, 256, 259; Mao's remarks on, 132; peaceful, 51, 70, 132; reform war for, 129–131; war of, 25–34
Liberation Committee of the Chamdo Area, 85
Li Jianglin, 313n11
Li Jingquan, 78, 144, 333n26; meeting remarks of, 126–127; new line of action from, 133; in Sichuan Province, 104–106
Li Jue, 321n77
Li Kenong, 35
Li Ne, 231
Lin, Hsiao-ting, 3
Linxia Hui Autonomous Prefecture, 248–249
Litang Monastery, 121, 172
Liu Bocheng, 32–35, 39, 53, 59
Liu Geping, 76, 137, 151, 159; CCP policymaking according to, 124–125; Garzê Committee denouncing rightist line of, 122–123; Garzê issues understood by, 123; local community responsibilities and, 123–124; as local nationalists, 125, 337n86; reform crisis from, 124; vendettas against, 160
Liu Shaoqi, 46, 48, 54, 181; Beijing operations of, 49–50; campaign targets from, 233–234; minority nationalities policies of, 76, 97; Politburo meeting with, 227–229; political report from, 191–192; principles in mass struggle from, 97–98; socialist transformation from, 113–114; telegram sent by, 76
Liu Wenhui, 29
Li Weihan, 74–76, 79–80, 128–131, 352n55; dismounts suggested by, 218; internal contradictions and, 224; national unity goal of, 220; peaceful reform from, 130–132; reform supported by, 145; Seventeen-Point Agreement from, 63; Tibet remoteness from, 214; Tibet work conference leadership of, 81; united-front approach from, 192
local communities, 123–124
local nationalists, 125, 337n86
lost territories, 7–8
lower-class people, 146
Luo Jialun, 25

Machiavelli, Niccolo, 44–45
machineguns, 116, 267
Mackiernan, Douglas, 36, 92
Mackinder, H. J., 20
Manchu emperors, 5
Mao Zedong: Anti-Rightist Campaign and, 341n1; Carry Revolution Through to End from, 12; CCP Central Committee letter from, 35, 61–62, 321n77; CCP leadership opinion from, 275; CCP's political outlook of, 25–26; China's economic issues from, 208; class struggle remarks of, 132; continuous revolution of, 9, 245, 309; Dalai Lama displeasing, 196; Dalai Lama in India from, 193–194; Dalai Lama praising, 158; Dalai Lama's attitude of, 275–276; Dalai Lama's letter from, 183–184; Dalai Lama's rebellions from, 163–164; daughter's name of, 355n106; Deng Xiaoping and confidence of, 78; Deng Xiaoping promoted by, 138; division of labor from, 40; encirclement without attack from, 279; enemy attack lured by, 270; great Han chauvinism from, 96–97; human nature commentary of, 231–232; information needed by, 283–284; intermediate zones from, 15; liberation remarks of, 132; maxims from, 256; peaceful reform not expected by, 262–263; PLA warnings from, 34; public speeches of, 31–32; rebellion causes

questioned by, 176; reform directives of, 126–131, 134; reform preparations and, 180, 200–201; Sangye Yeshe support by, 135–136; Stalin not trusting, 13; Tan's third letter and, 274; Tibet action called for by, 35, 40–41, 201; Tibetan reactionaries welcomed by, 256–257; Tibetan situation from, 77–78; Tibet reform statement of, 178–179; Tibet's autonomy and, 27; TWC message from, 268–270; TWC telegram from, 58–59; Western world proclamation of, 247; Zhang Guohua's meeting with, 52–53; Zhang Guohua's secret directive from, 57–58; Zhang Jingwu giving information to, 195–196
maps, topographic, 17, 316n11
Marx, Karl, 190
Marxism, 146, 298
massacres, 228
mass-affecting work, 60
mass consciousness (*qunzhong juewu*), 97
mass mobilization, 141, 224, 283
mass struggle, 97–98, 113
mass work, 60, 224
McMahon Line, 206–208; Dalai Lama crossing, 280; legitimizing, 300; U.S. endorsing claim about, 297
Miao Fengshu, 109, 122, 125, 335n52
Mikoyan, Anastas, 13–14, 26
military-administrative committee (*junzheng weiyuanhui*), 63–64
military expeditions, 15
Mindrolling Trichen, 152–153, 155, 161, 343n20
mineral resources, 286
minority nationalities (*shaoshu minzu*), 10, 28, 31, 105, 290; autonomous regions for, 103; CCP Central Committee forbidding reforms for, 96; CCP leadership dealing with, 46–47, 108; Dalai Lama's thoughts about, 154; Han cadres not trusting, 119, 129; land reforms, 97; Lhasa and, 93; Liu Shaoqi policies toward, 76, 97; opinions expressed by, 128–129; oppression of, 102–103; PRC's policymaking regarding, 125; rebellion in areas of, 100; in Seventeen-Point Agreement, 95; Sichuan's bloody conquest of, 121–122; socialist education of, 233; socioeconomic reforms, 96; upper-stratum people of, 99
minority regions, 103, 108
minzu wenti, 46, 324n6
missionaries, 94–95
monasteries: Buddhist, 144; Dajin, 119, 150, 162; Dalai Lama's unity message for, 154–155; Deng Xiaoping dealing with, 143; feudal power of, 132; Garzê, 119, 121, 162; guns at, 111; income sources of, 174; Kundeling, 272; Litang, 121, 172; not touching for now of, 133–134, 137, 144; rebellion joined by, 268; Shouling, 119; Tashilhunpo, 175
Mongolia, 26
Mosca, Matthew W., 8
mosquitoes, 257
multiethnic borderlands, 22
Muslim warlords, 29, 108
mutual assistance groups, 119

National Assembly, 51
national bourgeois, 46, 287, 298–299
national defense (*zui houfang*), 308
national disunity, 256
national humiliation maps, 7–8
nationalism: countries with, 6; local, 257–258; socialism and, 234, 243–244; states with, 12
Nationality Affairs Commission, 75, 95
Nationality Affairs Committee of the People's Congress, 125
nationality autonomy, 31
nationality policy, 146
nationality question. See *minzu wenti*
nationality regional autonomy, 57
nationality work, 98, 181
Nationality Work Committee, 80
National People's Congress, 156
national unity, 220
Nehru, Jawaharlal, 196; Dalai Lama's meeting with, 208–209; Lhasa return discussion of, 209; policy priorities of, 207; Seventeen-Point Agreement and, 197; Tibet concerns of, 206–207; Zhou Enlai's talks with, 205, 207
New Policies, 10, 20, 324n108
New Times, 37

New York Times, 37
Ngabö Ngawang Jigmé, 55, 57, 172; Dalai Lama warned by, 276; Gyalo Thondup accusations against, 350n22; hat metaphor of, 88; land reform proposal of, 173; Seventeen-Point Agreement supported by, 64, 328n71; as trusted Tibetan official, 222–223
nianpu. See chronicles of life
Norbulingka (Dalai Lama's summer palace), 264–265, 268, 272, 277–278
no reform period, 235
Northwest Bureau: division of labor with, 49; Fan Ming from, 68; insurmountable difficulties for, 42–43; Peng Dehuai not included in, 41; Southwest Bureau compared to, 63–74
Northwest China, 39
Northwest Military Political Council, 69

"old Tibetans" (*Lao Xizang*), 11
operational orientation, 58
Opium War, 237
opportunist errors, 28
oppression, of minority nationalities, 102–103
ordained patronage, 17
ordinances (*zhangcheng*), 17, 55
Outer Mongolia, 23, 26
Ouyang Hongzhi, 238
overt stratagems (*yangmou*), 148–150, 164

pacification, of rebellions, 126–127, 250
Panchen Lama: CCP leadership contacting, 34; Dalai Lama and, 64; Dalai Lama parity sought by, 72–74; Dalai Lama's relations with, 52, 70, 83–84, 86, 174–176, 215; He Long view of, 49; in Northwest China, 39; pilot reform projects proposed by, 182; tenth, 33–34; Tibetan enterprise and, 48–49; TWC response by, 364n97; upper-stratum displeased with, 173
Pan Zili, 209
partial rebellions, 259
party narrative, 150–151, 158–164, 344n30
patriotism, of Dalai Lama, 92
PCTAR. See Preparatory Committee for the Tibetan Autonomous Region
peaceful liberation, 51, 70, 132

peaceful negotiations, 363n88
peaceful reform, 110–116, 130–132, 138, 170, 176, 178, 185, 187, 192, 203, 214, 230, 258, 262
peace wave, 307
Peng Dehuai, 32–33, 35, 79, 201; Northwest Bureau not including, 41; Tibet assignment of, 39
Peng Zhen, 214, 219, 224
people-loving practices, 60–61
people's commune, 261–262, 274, 289, 308
people's democracy, 201, 215–216
People's Liberation Army (PLA), 28, 155; good deeds done by, 60; large-scale operations of, 141; Lhasa operations of, 279–280; Mao's warning to, 34; people-loving practices of, 60–61; rebellion with troops of, 262, 267, 364n94; reconnaissance groups of, 277–278; in Sichuan Province, 117; in Tibet, 286, 353n69, 364n94; under Zhang Guohua, 45–46
people's liberation committee, 198
People's Political Consultative Conference (PPCC), 31
people's representatives, 272
People's Republic of China (PRC): 1, 75; anti-imperialist revolution of, 306; class struggle and, 307; Common Program of, 95; Han Chinese and, 227; Lhasa's communications with, 277; Lhasa's relationship with, 158, 176; minority nationalities policymaking of, 125; new society of, 153; reconciliatory orientation from, 133; Second Five-Year Plan of, 186; socialism transition of, 98, 107–108, 119; Soviet Union's relations with, 307–308; Supreme Conference on State Affairs in, 352n51; Tibetan rebel conflicts with, 260; Tibet's incorporation into, 92–93; Tibet's policymaking by, 244–245; triple-twelve message of, 198–199; U.S. adversary of, 296; Western imperialism struggle of, 201, 301; Zhou Enlai to members of, 75–76
People's Revolutionary Commission of Military Affairs, 34–35
personnel expansion, 211–212
Phala Thupten Wöden, 271
Phüntso Wangye, 28, 30, 151, 170

Phurpa Bum Tsering Gyaltsan, 197
pingpan (pacification of rebellions) operations, 115
PLA. *See* People's Liberation Army
Poland, 195
policymaking: CCP and grievances of, 196; CCP disagreement in, 131–132; CCP leadership's leftist and rightist, 87; CCP leadership's revolutionary, 281; Deng Xiaoping's levels of, 273; Liu Geping and, 124–125; nationality, 146; Nehru's priorities in, 207; New Policy in, 10; PRC's, 125, 244–245; purchase-and-sale, 241; revolutionary, 281; Tibetan, 85–86; united-front, 41, 73, 98, 192; waiting game on, 189
Politburo meeting, 227–229
politics: anticommunist, 302; CCP Central Committee report on, 191–192; CCP leadership problems in, 29; CCP's ethnopolitical accomplishments in, 310; CCP's mass-oriented, 215–216; China's geopolitical decline in, 24; Cold War's polarized, 13; Dalai Lama's position in, 54; Dalai Lama to stink in, 288–289; dismount in, 218, 220; ethnopolitical zone in, 309–310; initiatives in, 224; international, 106; landscaping of, 5, 313n16; Liu Shaoqi report on, 191–192; Mao and CCP's outlook on, 25–26; Qing dynasty dialogues in, 21; sociopolitics, 10–12, 26, 43, 145; Tibetan class, 229; Tibetan conditions in, 50; Tibet as center for, 171
Powers, John, 1
PPCC. *See* People's Political Consultative Conference
PRC. *See* People's Republic of China
preaching sessions, 156
"Preliminary Opinion About the Five-Year Plan for the Tibet Region from 1956 to 1960" (paper), 181
"Preliminary Opinion on Various Policies Toward Tibet" (paper), 51
"Preliminary Plan for Implementing Democratic Reform in the Agricultural Tibetan Areas of Sichuan," 111–113
Preparatory Committee for the Tibetan Autonomous Region (PCTAR), 166–169, 183–184, 217, 350n26, 353n70

private importers, 239
profit-pursuing people, 241
"Public Notice on Reforming the Social System of Tibet in Accordance with [the Seventeen-Point] Agreement," 165
public security, 240–241, 255, 360n29
purchase-and-sale policy, 241

Qianlong (emperor), 16–17, 216
qianzang. *See* Front Tibet
Qin Chuanhou, 151
Qing dynasty, 6; amban authority clarity for, 65; empty constituency of, 18; geo-ethno-security landscape of, 7; imperative control and, 8; military force used by, 15; New Policies of, 20, 324n108; political dialogues of, 21; Tibet incorporated by, 16
Qinghai-Gansu situation, 257
Qinghai Province, 108, 114–115, 244
Qingzang (Qinghai-Tibet) Highway, 63, 167, 222
qunzhong juewu. *See* mass consciousness

reactionaries abduction, 265–267, 270–271
Rear Tibet (*houzang*), 50
rebellions: in Chamdo, 46, 72, 184, 197; class consciousness and, 285; comprehensive, 256–257, 259, 263, 267; Dalai Lama's accusations of, 159–160; Dalai Lama's conspiracy for, 163–164; Dalai Lama suspected of, 281–282; Dalai Lama's view of, 120; destruction planned in, 278; Gansu officials and, 248–249; Kashag and, 163; in Lhasa, 264–266, 279, 296; Litang Monastery near, 172; local government suppressing, 273; Mao and causes of, 176; minority nationalities areas with, 100; monasteries joining, 268; neighboring provinces, 260; pacification of, 126–127, 250; partial, 259; *pingpan* operations for, 115; PLA troops in, 262, 267, 364n94; plotters of, 158–164; Sichuan Province with elements for, 138; Tibet pacifying, 191, 286–287; Tibet reactionary cliques causing, 252; training camps for, 250; Ulanhu's pacification of, 125; in western Sichuan, 160; in Xikang Province, 254; youth as soldiers in, 261; Zhou Enlai assertions on, 249–250

rebellious bandit, 250
reconciliatory orientation, 133
reconnaissance groups, 277–278
rectification campaign, 84
Red Army troops, 27–28, 157, 349n12
Red Star Over China (Snow), 13
reformation: of Tibet, 47, 57, 111–113, 167, 182–183, 214; Zhou Enlai's peaceful, 132–133
reforms: CCP leadership and fifty years, 221; China's social, 98–99; CUFD adopting schedule for, 170; Deng Xiaoping demanding, 139–140; Goldstein's study on Fan Ming, 179; Kashag organizing bureau for, 165; land, 97, 99–100, 107, 173; in Lhasa, 165; Liao Zhigao thoughts on, 133; Liu Geping's crisis in, 124; Li Weihan supporting, 145; Mao not expecting peaceful, 262–263; Mao's directives on, 126–131, 134; Mao's preparations for, 180, 200–201; mature conditions for, 228; minority land, 97; minority socioeconomic, 96; Panchen Lama proposing pilot, 182; period of no, 235; Sangye Yeshe opinion on, 141–142; Second Five-Year Plan for, 204–205; Seventeen-Point Agreement and, 107, 214, 220–221; Sichuan Province steps for, 114–115; social, 98–99, 286–287; Tibet's unreadiness for peaceful, 229–230; TWC preparations for, 181; western Sichuan's model of, 218–219; western Sichuan's projects for, 118; Xikang Committee plans for, 108–114; Zhang Jingwu and, 282
reform war: class struggle in, 129–131; for liberation, 129–131; nationality policy in, 146; self-defense militia in, 117; in Sichuan Province, 116, 122; in western Sichuan, 119–120, 142–143, 148–150, 178–179, 203
regional autonomy, 27
regulations, 316n16
religion: ancient ordinances of, 44; CCP's view of, 49, 59–62, 100, 123, 127, 129, 133, 158, 286–287, 291; Dalai Lama group activities in, 152–154, 172–176; Dalai Lama's position in, 54; feudal classes using, 143, 198; in Lhasa, 199; of Tibet, 62, 106, 252

Ren Mingyuan, 109, 335n52
Ren Naiqiang, 60–61
Republic of China (ROC), 3, 22
Resurgence of East Asia, The (East Asian scholars), 43
retreat, 219; Tibet's comprehensive, 220–221; TWC completing steps for, 233
revolutionary mass, 116
revolutionary policy, 281
revolutionary seniority, 73
revolutionary work, 211
Richardson, Hugh E., 37
rightist policy options, 87
right-wing personalities, 175
ROC. *See* Republic of China
Roosevelt, Franklin D., 24
Roshchin, Nikolai, 34–35

Sangdak Lochungtra, 254
Sangye Yeshe, 28; in CCP Sichuan Committee, 136–137; Mao's support of, 135–136; reforms lacking opinion of, 141–142; report from, 136
satellites, 247
Saxe, John Godfrey, 2
Schoenhals, Michael, 360n29
Second Five-Year Plan, 186, 204–205
second-hand shops, 241
Secondhand Time (Alexievich), 309
security measures, 155–156
self-contradictory document, 83–84
self-defense, 116–117
self-sufficiency, 91
separate administration formula, 73–74, 84
September 4 directive, 186–188
serfdom, 99, 126, 215, 282–283
Seventeen-Point Agreement, 55; autonomous region and, 85; CCP's violation of, 103; China and Tibet negotiating, 45, 63–64; collapse of, 164; content of, 57; cooperative gradualism in, 225; democratic reform and, 165–166; Kashag accepting, 88, 165; from Li Weihan, 63; minority nationalities in, 95; Nehru and, 197; Ngabö supporting, 64, 328n71; peaceful reform and, 214; people's democracy from, 201; "Public Notice on Reforming the Social System of Tibet in Accordance with Agreement,"

165; reforms and, 107, 214, 220–221; Tibetan incorporation in, 65; Tibetan reforms and, 107; upper-class figures and, 69–70; Zhang Guohua and, 63
shaoshu minzu. *See* minority nationalities
Shao Xunzheng, 292
Shibaev, P. A., 48
Shouling Monasteries, 119
Sichuan Nationality Work Committee, 144
Sichuan Province: comprehensive struggle in, 141; expansion of, 104; Li Jingquan in, 104–106; minorities bloody conquest in, 121–122; PLA troops in, 117; rebellious elements in, 138; reform steps in, 114–115; reform war in, 116, 122; Su Yu in, 141; Tianbao criticizing leadership of, 135; Tibetan autonomous region in, 105
Sichuan Shengzhi (chronicle), 151
silver drain, 237–238, 241
Sino-Japanese war, 68
six years formula, 191, 200
smart class struggles, 94–98; CCP and, 100–101, 104; disappearance of, 113; land reform preconditions in, 99–100; minority rebellions and, 100; in minority regions, 108; in Tibet, 102
smuggling, 239–241
Snow, Edgar, 13
social engineering, 169–170, 192
socialism: capitalism compared to, 236–237, 241, 307; CCP and, 88; CCP leadership's construction of, 247–248; central power building in, 261; Liu Shaoqi and transformation to, 113–114; minority nationalities education in, 233; nationalism and, 234, 243–244; people's commune in, 289; PRC's transition to, 98, 107–108, 119; in Tibet, 170, 287; waiting game suspending, 236–237
socialist transformation, 238, 335n58; class struggles and, 251; with democratic reforms, 114; of Garzê Prefecture, 144–145, 250; from Liu Shaoqi, 113–114; TWC plan for, 308
social life, in Lhasa, 282
social reforms, 98–99, 286–287
socioeconomics, 95–96, 252
sociopolitics, 10–12, 26, 43, 145
Song poems, 231–232
Song Renqiong, 79, 219, 333n26, 352n55

Southwest Bureau, 33, 42–43; Deng Xiaoping setup of, 32, 79; division of labor with, 49; four points set by, 54; Northwest Bureau compared to, 63–74; on spontaneous class struggles, 101–102; TWC relations with, 77, 326n31; Zhang Guohua forming, 68
Soviet Union, 304, 307–308
Special Economic Zones, 309
Stalin, Joseph, 13, 29
standardization (*zhengguihua*), 212
Standing Committee of the Politburo, 202
Statement to the Tibetan Compatriots, 302
State Nationality Affairs Commission, 192
stone boundary markers, 17, 316n9
strategic dimension, 296
Sun Yat-sen, 7, 9–10, 22, 96
Supreme Conference on State Affairs, 352n51
Surkhang Wangchen Gelek, 151, 271
Su Yu, 141, 339n115

Taipei, 302
Taiwan, 30
Taiwan Strait, 258
Tang dynasty, 41
Tan Guansan, 265, 267, 272–274
Tan Zheng, 201
Tarim Basin, 15
Tashilhunpo Monastery, 175
technology, 247
telecommunications, 289–290
territoriality transformation, 6–9
Third Five-Year Plan, 221
Thomas, Lowell, 36–38, 320n60, 323n91
Three-Antis campaign, 78, 329n107
"Three People's Principles" (Sun Yat-sen), 9–10
three principles of justifiability, 98
Thubten Norbu, 204
Tiananmen case, 238, 357n131
Tianbao, 109–110, 135. *See also* Sangye Yeshe
tianxia. *See* all under heaven
Tibet: amban imperial commissioner of, 16, 18; anthropologist's experience of, 4–5; anti-communism of, 32; anti-imperialism of, 70, 306; backwardness of, 92, 165; big convulsion in, 257; border demarcation of, 16; Buddhist monasteries in, 144; buffer zone of, 210–231; CCP and incorporation of, 26–27; CCP as agent of change in, 92;

Tibet (*continued*)
  CCP leadership goals and peace in, 192–193; CCP leadership misjudging situation in, 214; CCP seeking national integration of, 48; CCP's ignorance of, 146; CCP's negotiations with, 54–55; CCP's revolution in, 46; CCP support lacking for, 177–178; Central Delegation's report on, 171–176; Central Delegation to, 168–176; Chiang Kai-shek and Yi corridor with, 24; China's central government and, 95; China's geopolitical operations in, 5–6; China's integration with, 166; China's mismanaging affairs of, 66–67; China's policy toward, 85–86; China's relations with, 38–39; Chinese Communist Revolution region of, 10–11; citizen's categorized in, 223–224; class politics in, 229; class struggles in, 118, 229, 304; coal and borax mines in, 217–218; Cold War value of, 91; commercial significance of, 242–243; comprehensive changes in, 283; comprehensive retreat from, 220–221; culture and religion of, 62; currency in, 69; Dalai Lama and independence of, 151; Dalai Lama and internal freedom in, 196–197; Dalai Lama as political center of, 171; Dalai Lama-centered approach in, 55–56; Dalai Lama group conspiracy for, 344n30; Dalai Lama's ruling power in, 70; Dalai-Panchen's relations and, 86; democratic reform in, 150, 167–168, 185–186, 230–231; Deng Xiaoping leading discussions on, 210–211; Deng Xiaoping smuggling warning to, 237; Deng Xiaoping's situation in, 77–78, 215–216; ethnicity of, 187; Fan Ming and independence conspiracy in, 344n30; Fan Ming's reform preparations for, 179–180; Fan Ming studying political conditions of, 50; geo-ethno-security landscape of, 295–296; geostrategic significance of, 19–20; great dismount in, 233; guerrilla warfare in, 253; Han Cadres moved into, 183, 211; India and territory of, 225; India's concerns toward, 300; interethnic chains in, 17–18; internal and external borders of, 240; Kashag and currency in, 71; KMT's geostrategic vision of, 23–24; land reforms in, 107; Lhasa seeking autonomy of, 197; Li Weihan and remoteness of, 214; local government of, 273; long-term economic plan for, 71; Mao calling for action on, 35, 40–41, 201; Mao's autonomy for, 27; Mao's statement on reform of, 178–179; Mao Zedong and situation in, 77–78; military expeditions to, 15; National Assembly of, 51; nationality in, 187, 219; Nehru's concerns over, 206–207; neighboring provinces relations with, 167; Ngabö trusted official in, 222–223; ordained patronage in, 17; Panchen Lama and enterprise concerning, 48–49; peaceful reform unreadiness of, 229–230; Peng Dehuai assigned to, 39; people's democracy in, 215–216; PLA's fight against, 286; PLA troops in, 353n69, 364n94; policy waiting game on, 189; PRC rebels conflicts in, 260; PRC's incorporation of, 92–93; PRC's policymaking toward, 244–245; private importers to, 239; public security in, 360n29; Qing dynasty incorporating, 16; reactionaries in, 256–257, 269; reactionary cliques causing rebellions in, 252; rebellions pacified in, 191, 286–287; rebels in, 260; reformation of, 47, 57, 111–113, 167, 182–183, 214; reorganization of, 50; routes entering, 42; Seventeen-Point Agreement and reforms of, 107; Seventeen-Point Agreement incorporation of, 65; Seventeen-Point Agreement negotiated by, 45, 63–64; smart class struggle in, 102; socialism in, 170, 287; socialist systems in, 170; sociopolitical changes in, 10; telecommunications with, 289–290; two-Tibet formula for, 145; unconquerable nationality of, 107–108; unification of, 102–107; upper-stratum reactionaries in, 231; U.S. aid to, 205; U.S. trade interests in, 235; work conference, 80–84; *Xizang Tukao* of, 17; youth moved into, 261; Zhang Jingwu and regions in, 219; Zhou Enlai and new phase for, 88–89; Zhou Enlai and unified, 291–292; Zhou Enlai's two-step change for, 287

Tibetan autonomous region, 52, 63, 88, 105, 166, 227, 232
Tibetan Buddhism, 151; Dalai Lama and, 27, 61–63; Mindrolling Trichen preaching and, 153
Tibetan National Assembly, 363n76
Tibetan National Liberation Army, 55, 72
Tibet Military Region (TMR), 57, 79, 88, 258; in Lhasa, 266; operational orientation in, 58
Tibet Office of Foreign Affairs (TOFA), 242
Tibet Work Committee (TWC): CCP leadership organizing, 64–65; conservative goals of, 224; Dalai Lama's departure report from, 278; Dalai Lama's welcoming party by, 210; democratic reform projection of, 177; Deng Xiaoping and mistakes of, 213–214; department of agriculture and pastoral work from, 79; Fan Ming in, 57, 69, 348n83; Fan Ming's report tabled by, 71; Han Cadre's reduction by, 216–217; infighting of, 67, 74; internal rectification from, 234; in Lhasa, 266; Lhasa situation message from, 198–200; Mao's message to, 268–270; Mao's telegram to, 58–59; mistakes of, 213–214; nationality work of, 181; Panchen Lama response to, 364n97; peaceful negotiations and, 363n88; rectification campaign of, 84; reform preparations of, 181; retreat steps completed by, 233; socialist transformation plan by, 308; Southwest Bureau relations with, 77, 326n31; Zhang Guohua controlling work of, 259–260; Zhang Guohua heading, 53, 179; Zhang Jingwu as leader of, 74; Zhang Jingwu with new policies for, 202
tiger borrows pigs; scholar borrows books, 132, 338n92
TMR. *See* Tibet Military Region
TOFA. *See* Tibet Office of Foreign Affairs
top secret (*juemi*), 159–161
trade, 236
training camps, 250
treason, 265–266, 288, 366n133
Trijang Lobsang Yeshe, 151, 163
Trijang Rinpoche, 152, 175
triple-twelve message, 198–199

Trouillot, Michel-Rolph, 3
Truman, Harry, 36, 90
Tsering Shakya, 2, 4, 193
Tsona Dzong, 254
tunken (agricultural settlement), 261
Tuttle, Gray, 3
TWC. *See* Tibet Work Committee
"Twenty-Nine-Article Ordinance" (1793), 18
two-Tibet formula, 145

Uighur-Kazakh separatist movement, 72
Ulanhu (aka Yun Ze), 28; as CCP member, 47; rebellion pacification in, 125; socioeconomic development of, 95–96
unconquerable nationality, 107–108
unification, of Tibet, 102–107
united-front policy, 98; CCP under, 73; Fan Ming responsibility for, 41; Li Weihan speech and, 192
United States (U.S.): atomic bombs of, 252; Chiang Kai-shek and attitude of, 303; Chinese Communist Revolution empathy of, 91–93; communism compared to imperialism of, 30–31; Lhasa revolt reaction of, 297; McMahon Line endorsed by, 297; PRC adversary of, 296; Tibetan aid from, 205; Tibetan trade interests of, 235
unity-struggle, 245
U Nu (Burmese prime minister), 203, 207
upper-class figures, 69–70
upper-stratum people, 105, 231; capitalism and, 120; class struggle and, 288; of Dalai Lama, 173–174; in Drakgo Province, 118–119; of minority nationalities, 99; Panchen Lama displeasing, 173
U.S. *See* United States

violence, 137, 140, 147

Wachman, Alan M., 5
wages, 212
waiting game: on policymaking, 189; rules of, 190–191; socialism suspended by, 236–237
Wangchen Gelek Surkhang, 64–65
Wang Feng, 82, 169, 234, 243–244
Wang Lixiong, 313n11
Wang Qimei, 48, 51, 85

Wang Weizhou, 137
Wang Yangming, 66
Wang Zhen, 34, 36
war situation, 140
Weber, Max, 8
Wei Huang, 109, 335n52
Wei Yuan, 18–19, 42
Westad, Odd Arne, 11
Western countries: capitalism of, 235–236; globalization from, 19; Mao's proclamation about, 247; peace wave from, 307; PRC struggle against imperialism of, 201, 301
Western maps, of China, 313n19
western Sichuan: Dalai Lama groups leaving, 162; democratic reforms in, 115, 139; interethnic conflicts in, 115; investigation teams in, 125; rebellions in, 160; reform model of, 218–219; reform projects in, 118; reform war in, 119–120, 142–143, 148–150, 178–179, 203; violence spreading in, 147
while there is life, there is hope, 221
White Sect, 153
wild domains, of China, 40
World War II, 24
Wuchang discussions, 274–275

Xiama, 218, 353n68
Xichang Branch Military Region, 141
Xikang Committee, 108–114
Xikang Military Region, 335n52
Xikang Province, 121; Dalai Lama tour of, 160–161; eastern, 112; rebellions in, 254
Xikang Tibetan Association, 254
Xikang Tibetan Autonomous Region, 152–156
Xinhua News Agency, 30–31, 37
Xinjiang, 26
Xizang Tukao (Illustrated examination of Tibet), 17
Xi Zhongxun, 72, 74, 80–83, 226, 352n55
Xuan Zhuang, 209
Xu Danlu, 67–68, 151–152

Ya Hanzhang, 81
Yang Du, 21
Yang Jingren, 81–82
yangmou. See overt stratagems

Yang Shangkun, 364n93
Yarlung Tsangpo River, 292–293
yinmou. See covert plots
Younghusband, Francis, 19–20
youth, arriving in Chamdo, 263
youth, as soldiers, 261
Yuan Shikai, 21–22
Yun Ze. *See* Ulanhu

Zeng Huishan, 279
Zhang Aiping, 140
zhangcheng. See ordinances
Zhang Chengwu, 109–110, 335n52
Zhang Guohua, 43, 192, 234; Deng Xiaoping advice from, 59–60; Fan Ming enraged by, 81; Mao's meeting with, 52–53; Mao's secret directive to, 57–58; not in Lhasa, 264; PLA under, 45–46; Red Army march of, 349n12; Seventeen-Point Agreement and, 63; Southwest Bureau formed around, 68; TWC headed by, 53, 179; TWC's work controlled by, 259–260; Wangchen Gelek Surkhang questioning, 64–65; Zhang Jingwu replacing, 65–66
Zhang Guotao: Dalai Lama compared to, 194–195; opportunist errors of, 28; fallacy, 280–283
Zhang Hang, 149
Zhang Jichun, 333n26
Zhang Jingwu, 169, 234, 349n15; CCP mediating with, 67; class-analysis method and, 283; Dalai Lama information from, 195–196; Deng Xiaoping sending message to, 188–189; Fan Ming unity with, 328n71; Han cadre numbers from, 352n56; *juemi* speech of, 159–161; Mao's information from, 195–196; not in Lhasa, 264; personnel expansion report from, 211–212; reform without war from, 282; Tibetan regions and, 219; TWC and new policies for, 202; as TWC leader, 74; Zhang Guohua replaced by, 65–66
Zhang Xiangming, 74, 179–180
Zhang Xing, 155–156
Zhang Yintang, 19–20
Zhang Zhongliang, 54
Zhao Erfeng, 115
Zhao Fan, 81, 84

zhengguihua. See standardization
Zhengzhi zhudong, 223, 354n87
Zhonghua Minzu. See Chinese Nation
Zhongnanhai meeting, 201–202
Zhongyang. See Center
Zhou Enlai, 29, 31, 40; Dalai Lama's conversations with, 351n37; Dalai Lama's persuasion by, 204; as foreign affairs official, 80; Han Chinese comments of, 95; Lan Jixi's letter to, 292; mass-affecting work coined by, 60; McMahon Line acceptance of, 208; Nehru's talks with, 205, 207; peaceful reform sought by, 132–133; Politburo meeting with, 227–228; to PRC members, 75–76; rebel cases assertions of, 249–250; Roshchin discussions with, 34; Tibetan Autonomous Region from, 166; Tibet's new phase from, 88–89; Tibet's two-step change and, 287; unified Tibet and, 291–292
Zhou Renshan, 268
Zhu De, 80
Zhu Yuanzhang, 316n11
zong juezhan. See general showdown
zui houfang. See national defense